Automating Systems Development

Automating Systems Development

Edited by
David Benyon
The Open University
Milton Keynes, United Kingdom

and
Steve Skidmore
Leicester Polytechnic
Leicester, United Kingdom

Plenum Press • New York and London

Library of Congress Cataloging in Publication Data

International Conference on Computer-Based Tools for Information Systems Analysis,
Design, and Implementation (1987: Leicester, Leicestershire)
   Automating systems development / edited by David Benyon and Steve Skidmore.
     p.   cm.
   "Proceedings of the International Conference on Computer-Based Tools for Infor-
mation Systems Analysis, Design, and Implementation, held April 14–16, 1987, in
Leicester, United Kingdom"—T.p. verso.
   Includes bibliographies and index.
  ISBN-13: 978-1-4612-8302-7   e-ISBN-13: 978-1-4613-1033-4
  DOI: 10.1007/978-1-4613-1033-4
   1. System design—Congresses. 2. System analysis—Congresses. I. Benyon, David. II.
Skidmore, Steve. III. Title.
  QA76.9.S88I565 1987
  004.2′1—dc19   88-17827
                                                            CIP

Proceedings of the International Conference on Computer-Based
Tools for Information Systems Analysis, Design, and Implementation,
held April 14–16, 1987, in Leicester, United Kingdom

© 1988 Plenum Press, New York

Softcover reprint of the hardcover 1st edition 1988

A Division of Plenum Publishing Corporation
233 Spring Street, New York, N.Y. 10013

PREFACE

1 INTRODUCTION

These proceedings are the result of a conference on Automating Systems
Development held at Leicester Polytechnic, England on 14 to 16 April 1987.
The conference was attended by over 170 delegates from industry and academia
and it represents a comprehensive review of the state of the art of the use
of the computer based tools for the analysis, design and construction of
Information Systems (IS).

Two parallel streams ran throughout the conference. The academic, or
research, papers were the fruit of British, European and Canadian research,
with some of the papers reflecting UK Government funded Alvey or European
ESPRIT research projects. Two important touchstones guided the selection
of academic papers. Firstly, they should be primarily concerned with
system, rather than program, development. Secondly, they should be easily
accessible to delegates and readers. We felt that formal mathematical
papers had plenty of other opportunities for airing and publication.

The second stream was the applied programme; a set of formal presentations
given by leading software vendors and consultancies. It is clear that
many advances in systems development are actually applied, rather than research led. Thus it was important for delegates to hear how leading edge
companies view the State of the Art. This was supported by a small exhibi-
tion area where certain vendors demonstrated the software they had introduced in the formal presentation. It was important that companies did not
give "soapbox" marketing presentations, and consequently each vendor was
asked to take a specific theme or application rather than to give an overall view of their product. In general, companies adhered to this spirit
and the conference, and these proceedings, undoubtedly benefitted from
this.

The combination of researchers and practitioners produced a wide-ranging
and thought provoking three days. At its centre was a guest presentation
by Russel Jones, the leading UK writer on automated tools, who discussed
the problems of changing the culture of Data Processing in the light of
new opportunities. A summary of that session is included in these proceedings.

Although the conference was held as two parallel streams, we have decided to amalgamate the presentations into certain themes within an imposed framework, rather than preserve the dichotomy of the actual event. This should help the reader focus on certain parts and issues, and to present the opportunity of seeing that issue from both practical and research perspectives.

Section One   Fourth Generation Languages

Fourth Generation Languages (4GLs) are an important influence on current system development. They have permitted the rapid development of applications and have fuelled the growth of prototyping as a development method. Two of the papers in this section provide a research (Poole) and applied (Alley) view of the development of a Fourth Generation tool. Two further papers present case studies (Radcliffe and Gosling), both concluding with guidelines of good practice. The two remaining papers present 4GLs in the context of a methodology. Wainwright identifies 4GLs as a necessary part of a methodology for a sector that is characterised by fast moving, hard to specify, user developed systems. Haine´s paper places 4GLs in the context of a particular methodology – in this case Martin´s Information Engineering. This continues the theme that these development tools need to be placed into some methodological perspective if they are to be used effectively. This paper introduces an issue that runs through many of the contributions – the central role of the Data Dictionary.

Section Two   Work Bench Tools

The second section of the text looks at research into specific tools to help in different parts of the systems development life-cycle. All of the papers are characterised by addressing certain specific tasks which benefit from computerisation.

Three of the papers are concerned with programming. This is an area which has received a considerable amount of attention and this is reflected in Riha and Rzevski´s comprehensive review of the literature. Two tools for automating code production (MAJIC and SWRPAS) are described in the papers of Sutcliffe and Pardoe respectively.

The other papers in this section concentrate upon specific tasks usually encountered in the development of systems. A good example of this is provided by Helen Sharp´s paper which examines automating the transition of Data Flow Diagrams into Structure Charts. This is a specific tool for an important and time consuming task in Structured Design. The paper by Avison and Chaudhuri also addresses the transformation of models. In this case, from an entity - relationship diagram to physical database designs in a number of implementations.

Section Three   Work Bench Tools within a Methodology

The third and fourth sections of the proceedings are dedicated to automated tools with the division between the sections based upon the generality of the tool. Section Three concentrates upon tools designed to support specific methodologies or techniques. In this respect it can be seen as a natural progression from Section Two.

The papers in this section move from the specific (Jones), discussing the development of a particular tool in a certain environment, to a view of automation in a complete methodology (Macdonald). The papers along the way tackle different issues and problems, concluding with an important review of the difficulties of implementing such workbenches (McCabe).

Most of the major vendors of automated tools are represented in this section. In most instances they are concerned with offering a complete solution to the prospective purchaser by encompassing all aspects of systems development within their product. This is often an extension of a well founded paper-based methodology, although (as Macdonald notes) the methodology is itself likely to change due to automation.

Section Four   Open Tools

In contrast, Section Four examines products specifically defined as "open tools", which may be tailored to accomodate a variety of techniques and methods. These Integrated Project Support Environments (IPSE) are concerned with supporting project development, but do not prescribe how that process should take place.

The six papers of this section provide a good insight into the scope and complexity of providing such an environment and the challenge of developing "open tools". Each focusses on a different aspect of the creation of an IPSE, but all emphasise the need for these tools to be portable and integrated.

Section Five   Environments and Approaches: Other Issues

Section Five picks up three themes that do not fit easily into the adopted framework, yet are fundamental to it. There can be little doubt that an active Data Dictionary is seen to be an essential facility of Fourth Generation Languages and Analyst Workbenches. The first three papers of this section examine the growth, development and implementation of Data Dictionary Systems, from the perspective of two major vendors - MSP and Oracle.

This is followed by an introduction to the concept of the Application Environment. This is an attempt to combine the powerful parts of Fourth Generation Languages and Expert Systems, whilst discarding the parts that make these latter tools either ineffective or esoteric. Frank Jones´ paper examines parys - an application environment that is restrictive in the types of application it can address, but permits applications that are more "fully developed, more quickly and by a less skilled designer than with the use of a 4GL or an expert system shell." The particular application environment addressed by the succeeding paper of Lau and Gough is that of Office Automation.

Section Six   Future Trends

Many of the tools described in the previous four sections are under test or development and so, in this respect, they represent the future. However, the papers we have put together in the final section, Future Trends, are distinguished by their advocacy of radical change in the design and development of information systems.

This section includes the keynote address of the conference given by Russell Jones, the leading British writer in this area, suggesting that the whole culture of systems development must change if automation is to be successful.

3 SUMMARY

These proceedings give a unique insight into the State of the Art of the automation of Information System development from both an applied and a research perspective. The papers range from the exhaustively researched, (e.g. Riha and Rzevski, Dillistone et al, Brown, DeDourek et al) to the considered opinions of experienced individuals (e.g. Russ Jones, Haine, MacDonald). In the middle are the host of practical and technical solutions to many of the problems of IS development. This automation is the most significant event in Information System development since the Structured Revolution of the late 1970´s. It presents new opportunities in Information System development and practice. It will undoubtedly change how many people undertake their jobs and how organisations will plan their IS strategy. All personnel involved in IS development have to be aware of its implications. As Ian Macdonald concludes in his paper to the conference

"The future belongs to automated methodologies"

David Benyon   Steve Skidmore
Open University   Leicester Polytechnic
U.K.   U.K.

October 1987

CONTENTS

SECTION ONE - FOURTH GENERATION LANGUAGES

It is generally recognised that programming languages have passed through three clear-cut generations - machine code, assemblers, and high level procedural languages such as COBOL and FORTRAN. The passage of these generations has been marked by progressive portability, with languages becoming largely independent of the host hardware architecture, and ease of use. The emergence of another generation, Fourth Generation Languages (4GLs) is well documented [MART82], but the variety of software described by such a term has made it difficult to provide an overall definition. The range of software that is either marketed or perceived as a Fourth Generation Language is demonstrated by a survey [LOBE84], which listed about 66 products, ranging from the relatively sophisticated (ORACLE, RAMIS) to the rather simplistic (FMS-80, Autocode).

There is also, clearly, an inextricable relationship between prototyping as a development strategy and the Fourth Generation Languages needed to support that approach. Not all research on prototyping has used 4GLs. For example, one of the most quoted research papers used PASCAL for both Specification and Prototyping teams [BOEH84]. Similarly, 4GLs can (and are) used in a Life Cycle environment, particularly in the search to reduce programming time. However, there is clearly a case for linking the two and this emerges, to varying degrees, in the papers presented in this section.

The section begins by presenting an insight into a development philosophy of a Fourth Generation Environment (TOOL BOX). This Environment was developed by Peat Marwick as an extension of Prime's implementation of the PICK Operating System. The paper suggests that this implementation (INFORMATION) lacked basic facilities and that TOOL BOX was conceived as a complementary product that would move INFORMATION "into the fourth generation". The design philosophy provides an insight into the issues that need to be addressed by a Fourth Generation Environment.

The succeeding four papers describe the use of Fourth Generation Languages in different environments. The first of these (Radcliffe) takes three case studies showing different uses of 4GLs. He concludes by suggesting five fundamental guidelines that should be followed for the successful introduction of a 4GL. The second paper (Gosling) examines the development of a system using the MIMER 4GL, highlighting the problems encountered and how they were solved. This results in four important lessons which should be heeded by application developers.

1

David Wainwight´s paper describes the application of a 4GL approach in the design of flexible manufacturing information systems which are "applicable to the fast moving needs of present day manufacturing industry". A case study is examined within an overall development methodology for this sector. This development methodology aims to be applicable to 4GL environments and will also attempt to be orientated towards ´soft systems concepts´ [CHEC81] as against the "hard systems thinking prevelant in current structured methodologies".

Peter Haine´s contribution attempts to place 4GLs in the context of the Information Engineering principles of Martin and Finkelstein. He argues that if 4GLs are to be effective, then a completely new approach to development must be adopted, "since the hand crafting tools of yesterday´s data processing shop have long since been found wanting".

Finally, Frank Poole examines the development of a Fourth Generation Language based upon a generalised database architecture. He concludes by suggesting that the architecture of DB4GL presents " a stimulating avenue for future research" as it "offers an integrative mechanism for combining both data and process descriptions within the overall application task definition activity".

So, in summary, this section looks at the development of Fourth Generation Languages and their Environments from both a practical (Alley) and research (Poole) point of view. Four case study papers are sandwiched in between, two of which take specific applications (Radcliffe and Gosling), whilst the other two (Wainwright and Haine) comment on issues of methodology.

<u>References</u>

[BOEH84] Boehm B, Gray T. and Seewaldt T. Prototyping Versus Specifying: A Multiproject experiment IEEE Transactions on Software Engineering Vol SE-10, No 3 May 1984 pp290-302.

[CHEC81] Checkland P. Systems Thinking, Systems Practice, John Wiley 1981

[LOBE84] Lobell R. F. Application Program Generators: A State of the Art Survey NCC, 1984

[MART82] Martin J. Application Development without Programmers Prentice-Hall, 1982

TOOL BOX DESIGN PHILOSOPHY

T. Matthews and W. Alley

Peat Marwick Mitchell and Co.

London, UK

1 INTRODUCTION

This paper describes both the design and implementation issues behind
TOOL BOX, our fourth generation environment (4GE) for the PRIME
INFORMATION data management system.

Peat Marwick started developing online systems using Prime's
implementation of the PICK operating system, called INFORMATION, during
1982. Peat Marwick recognised INFORMATION to be a powerful development
environment, but felt it lacked certain facilities which would make it
suitable for rapid systems development in a demanding commercial
environment.

To assist in both its internal systems development and client bespoke
development the Systems Development Group of Peat Marwick decided to
build to build a fourth generation development environment called TOOL
BOX.

The Systems Development Group have enjoyed considerable success with TOOL
BOX, developing systems for Citicorp Investment Bank, Prime Computer,
London Docklands Development Corporation and Kestrel Data Storage. Peat
Marwick's internal Computer Department has also used it to develop
systems for personel management, publication distribution and online
management information retrieval for use by partners and senior managers.

2 PRIME INFORMATION OVERVIEW

INFORMATION provides a relational style database, report generator and a
powerful programming language. INFORMATION offers many significant
technical advantages over standard PICK, which include:

* superior string handling

* superior arithmetic handling

* a "rich" source language offering extra functionality

* record size that can exceed 32k bytes

* user working space that exceeds the normal PICK boundary of 64K Bytes

* support of a larger compiler symbol table

* ability to access routines developed in other programming languages.

Both INFORMATION and PICK have their origins in the third generation of development environments. Standard implementations lack facilities such as a screen handler, field level security, menu builder, roll forward/back recovery, end user orientated query facility and program/version release management capability.

TOOL BOX was designed to overcome these problem areas by complementing INFORMATION, and moving it into the fourth generation.

3 TOOL BOX DESIGN CONSIDERATIONS

When developing any software product, it is necessary to carefully consider not only the functionality to be included, but also the environment in which it will be utilised. With TOOL BOX, we were complementing Prime's excellent INFORMATION data management system, not creating a new and stand alone environment.

The following design concepts were taken into consideration when TOOL BOX was implemented.

i) No loss of procedural flexibility

INFORMATION offers a wide range of procedural and programmer orientated facilities, such as INFO/BASIC the programming language and INFORM its query language. These facilities allow very sophisticated online applications to be developed. To produce a fourth generation environment TOOL BOX needed to offer additional non-procedural utilities.

Peat Marwick did not wish to achieve this requirement by adding a layered product which constrained the host environment. For this reason it was necessary to design TOOL BOX to provide a 4GE which added non-procedural utilities, in a manner that complements INFORMATION rather than removing its flexibility.

ii) Address needs of all Users

TOOL BOX was designed to address the needs of all users of Prime super-mini computers. As well as satisfying the needs of the System Developer, TOOL BOX has also addressed the requirements of both the End User and the System Administration.

The End User needs an environment that is responsive to their ever changing business needs. They need a comprehensive set of tools that are both easy to learn and simple to operate. Prototyping tools should be available to the user, in order to develop screens, report layouts and menus. The tools should also allow the creation of data validation rules and on-line documentation. An ad-hoc enquiry system would allow the End User to create and maintain system reports.

The System Developer needs a set of tools to rapidly generate both simple and sophisticated systems, that will be reliable and easy to

maintain. The tools should be easy to use and allow the System
Developer to be highly productive as soon as possible. The ability
to automatically monitor changes in both programs and routines will
assist the System Developer in maintaining a complete and well
documented edit history for all programs in an application.

The System Administration needs a good security system that is both
easy to implement and maintain. Transaction logging should be
available to allow data recovery in the event of a system failure.
Tools should also be available to allow the System Administrator to
"fine tune" the performance of applications running on the system,
and also to monitor and control both users and system resources.

After acceptance testing the ability to automatically control the
release of system software will help in the successful installation
of a new application.

iii) Easy to Learn

A potential benefit of 4GEs is the reduction in time it should take
to make a new system developer highly productive. With the growth
of data processing and the highly mobile nature of development
staff the time taken to become productive is critical.

It was recognised that all 4GEs require time to learn and TOOL BOX
would be no different. For this reason TOOL BOX commands and
conventions were based on the sound foundations of INFORMATION.
Rather than introduce a new syntax to replace existing INFORMATION
commands in the belief that "we know better´, all existing commands
and facilities were kept and new ones designed to offer the same
conventions and concepts.

iv) Efficient Development and Runtime Operation

Hardware costs may be falling, but they are still a significant
cost to an organisation and so need to be carefully managed.
Therefore, it was necessary to design and implement TOOL BOX to
offer the host environment good development facilities without
compromising the run time performance of the production system.
However, simply offering good run time performance is a compromise
in itself. It is necessary to ensure that the tools employed by
TOOL BOX in the development of an application also perform
efficiently, both in terms of the hardware performance and the
amount of system resources used.

v) TOOL BOX Design Architecture

When designing software products, there is commercial pressure to
bring the solution to the market place as soon as possible.
Experience has shown that if a structured method is not employed,
undue commercial pressure can result in a product being released
which cannot easily be maintained or enhanced.

In the design of TOOL BOX a "bottom up" philosophy was adopted.
Initially all the low level "building blocks" were designed and
implemented, such as a security subsystem, independent terminal and
message handlers etc.

Once the foundations had been laid, the procedural TOOL BOX
utilities, such as the pre-compiler, high speed cross reference and
performance monitoring were implemented. These utilities made use

of the low level building blocks, and offered improved
functionality over standard INFO/BASIC.

On top of these procedural utilities, non-procedural facilities
were implemented, such as the Ad-Hoc Enquiry, Screen Handler and
Menu Builder, to facilitate end user queries and system
prototyping.

This design approach was adopted to ensure that TOOL BOX offers a
set of highly integrated non-procedural software tools for the
development of simple and sophisticated applications.

This provides the System Developer with a powerful range of non-
procedural tools for rapid system development, but also provides
access to the procedural utilities and low level building blocks
when implementing complex applications.

viii) Effective Prototyping Capability

A successful 4GE must allow systems to be rapidly implemented, not
just rapidly developed, the difference being end user acceptance.

The judicious use of prototyping can achieve a much greater end
user input, commitment and acceptance of a system. For TOOL BOX to
be successful, it needed an effective prototyping capability.

TOOL BOX provides this function, by allowing either the end user or
the system developer to design and build online menus, screen
dialogues, validation rules and context sensitive on-line help.
The end user and developer can build an entire prototype online
system and simulate a live running environment by exercising all
possible screen dialogues. During the prototyping phase, the man-
machine interface is evaluated, allowing the optimal screen
dialogue to be rapidly achieved.

Experience has shown that the user's perception of the system they
are going to receive for acceptance testing is greatly enhanced by
employing this technique.

ix)   Development Life Cycle Methodologies

In an increasingly complex and competitive environment, new
developments in technology are making computerisation possible on a
far wider scale than ever before. To ensure the effectiveness of
computer systems, it is imperative that they are designed to meet
the real needs of the organisation and that they are introduced in
a timely and planned manner, with the full co-operation and
commitment of the organisation. A means of ensuring that this is
achieved is by the adoption of an Information Engineering approach
to the development of computer systems.

Peat Marwick have developed and implemented a proven methodology
for the analysis, design, development and implementation of
computer systems, called the System Development Life Cycle (SDLC).
It establishes a consistent framework for the production of
computer systems by:

- providing a documented approach,

- identifying what must be performed to produce a quality system,

- facilitating communication between all members of the project team and client personnel.

SDLC comprises of a series of work programmes divided into phases, tasks and activities, beginning with the point at which a decision has been made to computerise an application and ending with a review of the system in its production environment. The phases of SDLC comprise a requirements definition, conceptual design, detail design, development, implementation and finally a post implementation review to monitor compliance with the initial business requirements.

When designing TOOL BOX we felt that it was necessary for it to be integrated into all phases of Peat Marwick's SDLC methodology. We feel this has been achieved as TOOL BOX has been used successfully during the requirements definition and conceptual design phases to clarify and define the man machine interface, as well as assisting in the rapid production of systems during the development and implementation phases.

4 CONCLUSION

This paper has provided an introduction to the design philosophy of our fourth generation environment, TOOL BOX. It has explained the design objectives behind the extension of a third generation product, INFORMATION, into a facility that makes it suitable for rapid systems development in demanding commercial environments.

THE IMPACT OF FOURTH GENERATION TOOLS IN PRACTICE –

THREE CASE HISTORIES

S. Ratcliffe

INBUCON Management Consultants

Leatherhead, UK

1 INTRODUCTION

Fourth genereation languages (4GL) are being used by software houses, computer departments and end users. Whilst it seems that there are almost as many definitions of the term 4GL as there are products, all those using and selling them would agree that the objective is the same – to improve the speed and ease of development and hence reduce the cost of applications.

The following three case studies examine different ways in which a 4GL can be used:

1.   Developing a system from scratch using a 4GL.

2.   Installing a 4GL packaged system.

3.   Enhancing a COBOL package by ´bolting-on´ a 4GL.

2 CASE STUDY NO1: A BESPOKE SYSTEM FROM A 4GL

Background

A specialist wholesaler with £1 million turnover and business plans for substantial growth over the next five years needed to automate its administrative and accounting systems. The computer system had to reflect the specialist nature of the company and be able to continue to provide the very personal service which was considered a key factor of the firm´s success. Consultants were appointed to investigate and aid the implementation of a suitable computer system.

The Choice of Systems Available

The range of systems reviewed was restricted to single user micro machines with hard disk storage. The throughput of transactions could be handled by such a configuration although the ability to expand to multi-user, multi-tasking was also borne in mind. Following demonstrations and investigations of the available packaged software, it was established that:

i)   None of the packages could cope with all the facilities required.

ii)   Software houses were either not prepared to modify their packages
       or there was little confidence that those dealers who would make
       changes were stable enough to maintain adequate support.

iii)   The cost of employing a programmer to write the system in COBOL or
       BASIC would be too great and the question of future support could
       not easily or cheaply be answered.

The Advantages Expected

The 4GL was selected on the basis of the ease with which the client's
existing senior staff felt they could understand and hence maintain the
programs written in such a language. A professional programmer was
engaged to generate the initial system and it was expected that the 4GL
would result in:

i)   Programs developed at about twice the cost of packaged software,
       but with a saving of 50% on the cost of COBOL programming quotes.

ii)   Program development time being about 50% of the time quoted for
       COBOL programs.

iii)   Maintenance of programs being carried out mainly by the users.

The Advantages Achieved

Prototyping application areas with the programmer and the user working
closely together resulted in very rapid development in the early stages.
The sales and stock control systems became operational in a matter of
weeks and staff confidence in the system was very high. The main reasons
for this seem to be:

i)   The short interval between the user defining his requirement and
       the introduction of the facility on the machine.

ii)   The system having screen and print layouts and terminology with
       which the user was familiar.

iii)   The speed with which bugs were corrected. Because of the user's
       close involvement with prototyping and the ease with which they
       could understand the programs the staff were soon able to point
       out to the programmer exactly where problems and faults were
       occurring.

Twelve months after the equipment was delivered an audit, Figure 1, of
the system revealed that:

(a)   The tasks of developing stock control and sales applications had
       been achieved in about 40% of the time estimated for COBOL
       programs.

(b)   The extra confidence of the staff had pushed progress so that
       further areas had been covered and were operational some 12 months
       ahead of schedule.

(c)   The costs of the sales and stock control systems were more than
       expected, at about three times the package costs, but still showed
       savings of about 40% on the COBOL quotes.

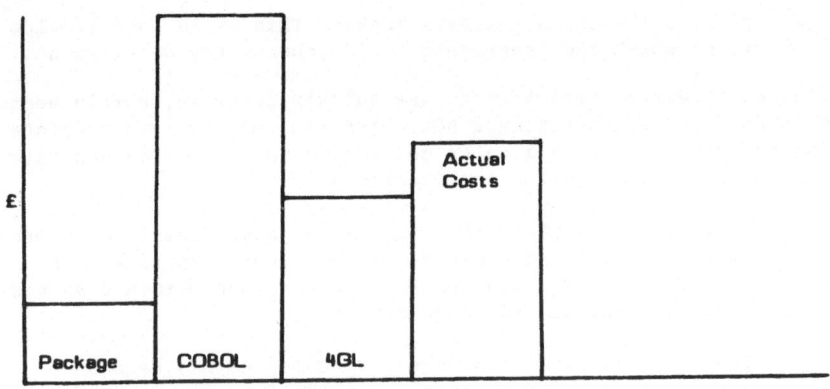

Expected Costs from Suppliers Quotes
v Actual Costs Achieved

IMPLEMENTATION TIMETABLE

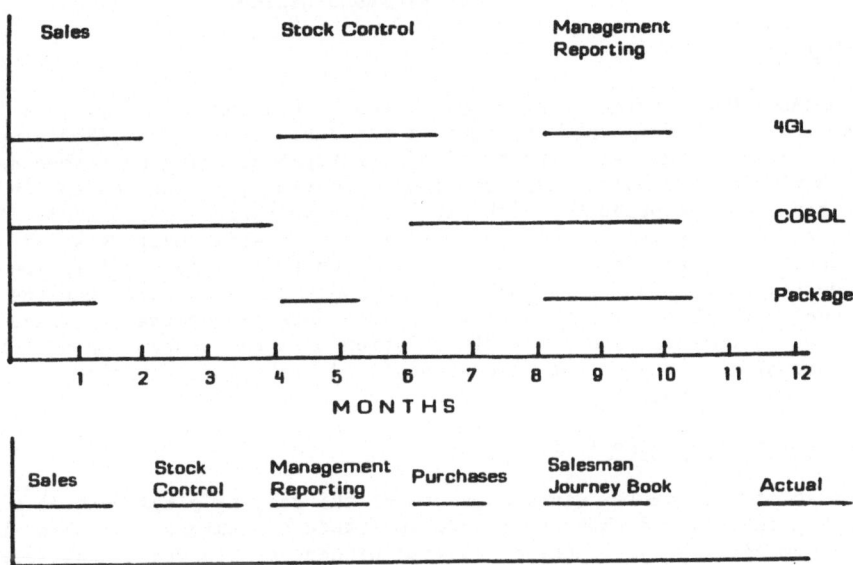

Figure 1 Result of Audit. Case Study 1.

The Pitfalls and Problems Encountered

The initial investment in the consultancy work for specifying the system
as part of the investigation was essential to enable the programmer to
quickly understand the basic requirements of the company. Without this
fundamental knowledge the prototyping phase could not have been so fast
or effective and this was seen as the corner-stone for the rapid acceptance of the system by the user.

Once the user had seen how easily and quickly changes could be made it
became difficult to stop him tinkering with minor modifications. It was
agreed with the senior staff that this was a major factor in the over-
spending of the budget, but this was considered to be worthwhile.

When additional areas (purchases and salesmen's journey book) were considered for development it was realised that to improve cost control, and
maximise the effectiveness of the programmer, it would be necessary to

carry out the normal systems analysis tasks. This would then provide a framework within which the programmer could control the development.

The original hardware specification was quickly outgrown, partly because of the extra needs of operating a 4GL which were not fully appreciated, but also because the user's greater confidence in the system generated more and more additions to the applications.

There were many instances where the programming style resulted in programs which were too slow and these had to be re-written in a more efficient manner. However, this led to programs that were not as easy for the users to understand and hence maintain.

The business was as independent of the programmer as had been anticipated, but the costs of maintenace over the four years the system has been operational has not been as great as the quotes for COBOL systems. Today the system has grown to five users connected to a 75Mb central file server based upon Novell equipment.

3 CASE STUDY NO2. INSTALLING A 4GL PACKAGED SYSTEM

Background

An established manufacturing company with a turnover of £20 million required a computer system to improve its customer service. The company had diverse businesses. About 50% of its turnover being made-to-order items with a high added value and long lead times, whilst the remainder was for standard products which were sold from stock and required a fast response. There was a need for an integrated system covering sales order processing, stock control, manufacturing, shop floor data collection, accounts, payroll and personnel. The company had a computer but the main systems were clerical and there was little data processing expertise. To help with the selection and implementation of a new system consultants were appointed through the governments's Advanced Manufacturing Technology scheme.

The Choice of Systems Available

Because of the complex diverse nature of the company's business it was quickly established that there were no standard packages available which could embody all the features required without considerable modification. The costs and time required, plus the inflexibility of such an approach, did not appeal to the company. The company made some fundamental decisions about its computer strategy:

1. The basic software and hardware should be well proven.

2. There should be only the minimum reliance upon outside software support for running the system.

3. There would not be a large investment in a central computer department, but considerable expertise should be created in each user department.

It was decided at an early stage that the only prospect of satisfying these criteria would be the selection of a package system which had been built using a 4GL. Modifications could be easily and speedily made by the supplier and, in the longer-term, much would be handled by the company itself. A systems administration role was created to oversee the implementation phase and to provide control and a focus for future development and operation. To ensure the system met all the companies needs a project team composed of the senior managers was set up to review all possible suppliers.

At the time (mid 1985) very few software houses could offer a proven, integrated package which covered all the application area and was developed in a 4GL. The project team reviewed the main contenders, and the major factors, with their relative importance in making the selection, are shown in Figure 2.

The successful package was based on the PICK operating system and included a number of tools which the team felt were most suitable and easy to operate.

The Advantages Expected

It was planned that little detailed systems analysis work would be required. The project team was to investigate each application area and with the supplier, develop it to meet the operational needs of each department. This would reduce the cost and time of installation and make the staff feel confident that the system would perform as required.

The Advantages Achieved

The overall cost and time budgets were achieved but not in each application area. The initial approach of prototyping based on the existing software did not work as well as expected and extra costs and time were incurred. Later areas were approaching by beginning with a detailed systems analysis and this resulted in budgets being bettered.

The staff's morale and confidence in the new system was maintained at a very high level throughout the implementation. There were no mysteries for them about the way in which the software performed and they were soon able to appreciate the degree of difficulty in any modifications. The PICK system offered them opportunities to add to the basic software package and they had control over their own system, without the need for a large data processing department. Expertise was to be found in all sections.

The Pitfalls and Problems Encountered

In the early stages delays were caused by very muddled thinking from user were unable to focus on the real issues of the development. To overcome this detailed systems analysis work was performed and the results used asa framework against which development could be undertaken.

Delays were also caused by the lack of good documentation of the software and inadequate support from the supplier. The high degree of flexibility offered by the package and PICK needed a lot of understanding and the integration between application areas required the user to comprehend the consequences of decisions. For the user to produce reports and analysis it is essential that he knows which data files to use, which attributes contain the information and which files are updated by which process.

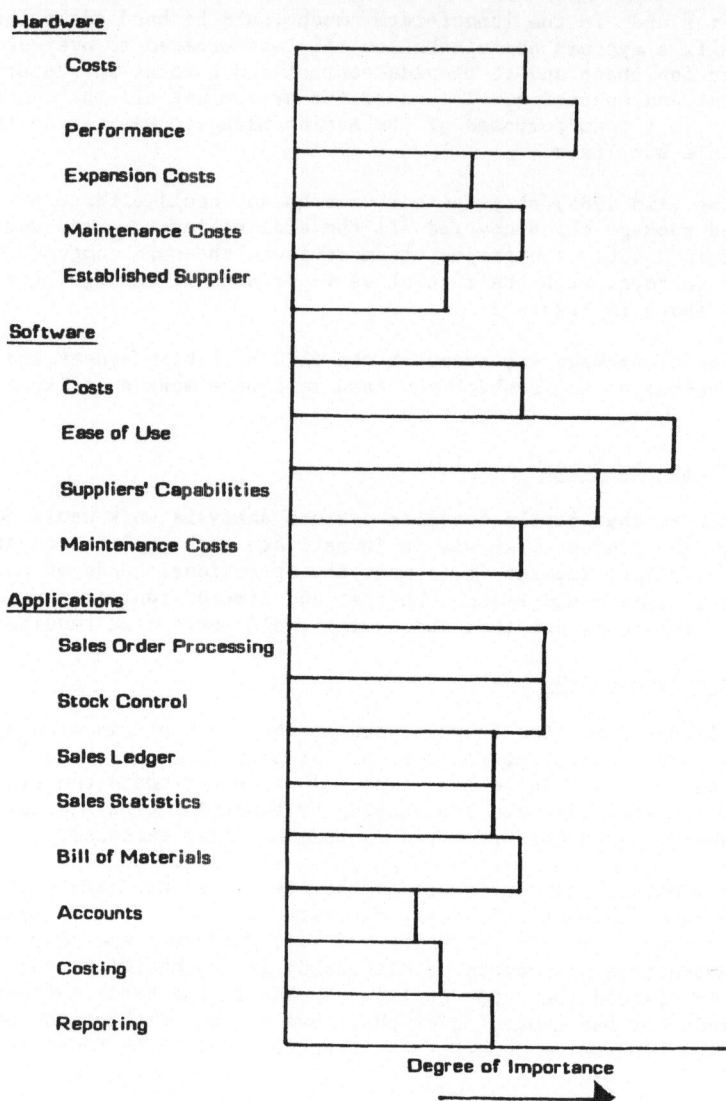

Figure 2. Selection Criteria. Case 2.

The supplier initially failed to provide this information. It all seemed
perfectly obvious and straightforward to supplier's support team!
They had forgotten how elementary concepts can be a complete mystery to
the first time user. However, a support plan was quickly established
which soon overcame these deficiencies.

There has to be some limit to the flexibility of the software. Unless
there is a core of programs which cannot be accessed by the users there
will be difficulty in agreeing the liability of the supplier to debug the
software. Similarly, it is essential that the system administrator can
set up levels of access which he can control and reflects the different
levels of responsibility with the company.

The PICK operating system requires constant attention if response times are to be kept acceptable and disk space used effectively. To bring this about a member of staff must be appointed to the task of system administrator and the appointee must be thoroughly trained in the tasks required.

4 CASE STUDY NO3. ENHANCING A COBOL PACKAGE BY ´BOLTING-ON´ A 4GL

Background

The computer system of a small manufacturing company with a turnover of £ 10 million covered just the sales order processing and accounting functions with only batch operation. Through the government´s Advanced Manufacturing Technology grant scheme consultants were retained to select and implement a new system which would cover all the aspects of administration and production in a real time on-line mode. The company had little in-house data processing expertise and did not feel that it could afford a member of staff devoted full-time to looking after a system.

The choice of Systems Available

A detailed user specification was drawn up by the consultants in conjunction with the company´s own project team of senior managers. From this it was seen that the majority of features required would be available from the major software houses supplying manufacturing system. The only exception being the reporting requirements and additional statistical data the users wanted. The team evaluated a number of leading suppliers, including systems built entirely in 4GLs.

The Advantages Expected

A Unisys XE system was chosen with packaged software (COBOL based) together with a 4GL report generator. The use of packaged software which required only a small number of modifications would mean rapid implementation with good control over costs. The addition of the 4GL would enable the users to add that extra data which was not critical to the day-to-day operation and to interrogate any data in the system without endangering the integrity of it.

The Advantages Achieved

The control of costs was as expected and budget targets were easily achieved. The timetable targets were hit without difficulty. This success can be largely attributed to the thorough systems analysis job performed before implementation began and relied upon the same factors as traditional package projects. The 4GL has been a useful tool, although few users have as yet made extensive use of it.

The Pitfalls and Problems Encountered

Apart from the problems normally found during implementing a computer system, no special difficulties were discovered. Some resistance was offered to the use of the 4GL based system gives considerable long-term benefits which are not so visible in this case. Extra effort has to be made to increase user participation if the flexibility available from the 4GL is to be realised.

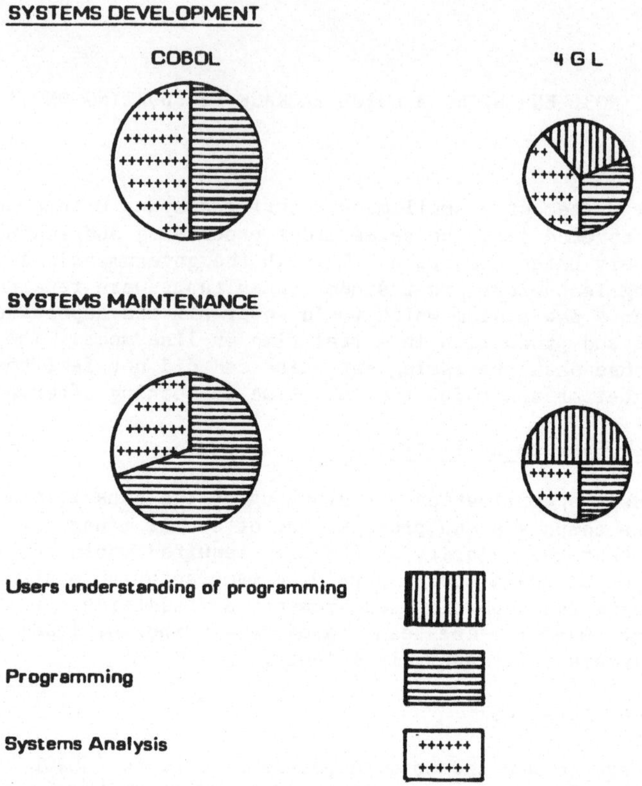

SYSTEMS DEVELOPMENT

COBOL

4 G L

SYSTEMS MAINTENANCE

Users understanding of programming

Programming

Systems Analysis

Figure 3. Effects of 4GL on Analysts and Programmers

5 CONCLUSION

In each of the case studies the use of a 4GL has resulted in:

(a) Faster development.
(b) Cheaper development.
(c) Greater independence for the user.
(e) A close relationship between the computer system and the end user
     which has produced a fuller utilisation of the systems capabilities.

For the successful introduction of a 4GL there are some fundamental
guidelines to be followed:-

(a) A system analysis must be undertaken so that all concerned agree on
     the objectives and have a clear yardstick against which to measure
     and control development. Where a 4GL is being used to develop the
     system (as in studies 1 and 2) the analysis work need not be too
     detailed as much can be achieved by prototyping the programs with
     the user.

(b) There must be good support from the supplier in the early stages to
     explain fully how the 4GL works. This will increase user confidence
     and ensure the highest level of future independence and self-control
     of the system.

(c) The users must have a sufficient level of education and intelligence
     to be able to understand and apply the tools provided by the 4GL.

(d) There must be a core of programs and data files which cannot be
     changed by the end users.

(e) Although expertise should be spread throughout the company, there
     still needs to be a focal point. This will contain a knowledge of
     all parts of the system and can provide a control, a drive for
     further development and fountain of in-depth technical know-how.

The introduction of 4GLs in a business does not mean an end to the data
processing department. The role will change. Figure 3 gives an estimation of the effects of a 4GL on analysts and programmers.

The data processing professional can be more productive but he needs to
replace some traditional programming skills with those for the new tools
and then add new skills to enable him to be more supportive to the end
user. He must remember to give his customers the service they need,
otherwise they just might take it for themselves.

A CASE HISTORY OF THE DEVELOPMENT AND IMPLEMENTATION OF

A SYSTEM USING MIMER AND PROTOTYPING

Mel Gosling

Savant Enterprises

Carnforth, UK

1 INTRODUCTION

From 1983 to 1986 Savant Enterprises held the marketing rights to the MIMER product in the UK. MIMER is a portable relational database management system with a number of associated development tools and fourth generation languages. Savant Enterprises was responsible for the introduction of the MIMER product into the UK.

As part of this introduction, Savant Enterprises contracted to build a number of software and turnkey systems for the new MIMER clients. One of these was a system on Prime for purchase orders. This paper describes the development of that system, highlighting the problems encountered and how they were solved, and contrasts it with a similar development which Savant Enterprises carried out towards the end of 1986 and early 1987.

2 MIMER

Savant Enterprises introduced version 3.1 of MIMER into the UK in 1983. This version consisted, basically, of:

>   DB   –   relational database
>   QL   –   query language (based on tuple calculus)
>   SH   –   screen handler
>   PG   –   program generator

In this version, PG was really a report generator as there was no interface to SH and the main tool for developing interactive applications was either FORTRAN or COBOL, using a low level interface to DB and SH.

During 1985 version 3.2 of MIMER was released, first on DEC VAX and subsequently on Prime. The main difference between 3.1 and 3.2 was that PG was interfaced to SH, and it was possible to develop interactive screen based systems using PG.

PG is a very powerful 4GL, allowing prototyping in a high level interpretive language, which then generates either FORTRAN or COBOL code which can be compiled for use in production. PG was perceived by Savant Enterprises as being an effective tool for applications development.

3 THE PROJECT

As part of the introduction of MIMER, Savant Enterprises offered to develop a purchase order system for one of the initial MIMER clients. This system was to demonstrate the power of PG for development, and also the portability of the product, in that the development would be on Savant's DEC VAX and moved to the client's Prime for production use.

Savant Enterprises propounds a methodology of Information Engineering, based on the recent works by James Martin [MART86 and MART87]. Part of this methodology, which was put forward by James Martin in an earlier work [MART83], is prototyping. Prototyping was an essential part of the analysis, design, and construction of this project.

4 PROTOTYPING

The main part of the system was developed and installed at the client's site during 1984, but unfortunately the prototyping phase did not go as planned. This was caused by the fact that the release 3.2 of MIMER, which enabled PG to be used for screen based applications, was not available until mid way through 1985, over a year late, which meant that the system had to be build in FORTRAN.

Prototyping is not really possible using FORTRAN, despite the fact that most of the screens could be prototyped using SH. The result was that the system as installed was not precisely what the client required, and was in reality, the prototype.

This led to a need for enhancements and modifications to be made, and by late 1985 these had been agreed. By this time PG was available with SH, and the possibility of prototyping the system became a reality. However, by this time, Savant had spent far more on developing the system than had been envisaged and it was not practical to prototype further. Hence a list of changes and enhancements to the existing system was drawn up, which Savant coded using PG.

It turned out that PG was extremely effective in cutting down development time, and in fact many changes were made to the PG code after the new system was shown to the client, before the final production system was handed over. This flexibility did encourage the client to prototype further, but there had to be a cut off point.

5 DATABASE DESIGN

Savant constructed a logical data model for the client using the product Data Designer, and translated this into a physical implementation in MIMER. This part of the project went very smoothly, and all subsequent changes to the database were handled quickly and easily through firstly changing the logical model, where required,and then the database and the application software.

MIMER proved to match up to its claims of providing a high degree of
program and data independence, and no real difficulties were experienced
in maintaining the code through changes in the database design.

6 PORTABILITY

MIMER offered the promise of true portability, being able to develop an
application on machine A and run it on machine B. By and large this was
achieved with a high degree of success, but with two notable exceptions.

Firstly, it had been envisaged that the complete system would be
developed in PG. In reality, a substantial proportion had to be
developed in FORTRAN, and there are crucial differences between FORTRAN
on DEC VAX and FORTRAN on Prime. It was not difficult to amend the code,
but this had not been anticipated at the start.

Secondly, problems were encountered with SH, the screen handler, when
moving from DEC VAX to Prime. Many of these involved special keys, like
arrows, and caused a considerable delay in implementing parts of the
system. However, once these problems had been solved the implementation
went smoothly.

In the later stages of the project though, MIMER lived up to its promise
and all parts of the system were ported smoothly **without the code being
changed.**

7 LESSONS

Several important lessons were learnt from this project, which have been
applied to subsequent projects in which Savant Enterprises has been
involved:

* Do not rely on using development software which has not
  yet been released. Future enhancements are an extra
  benefit, do not plan to use them until they have been
  shown to be fully working.

* Prototyping must be properly controlled, and the control
  mechanism must be in place at the start of the project.

* Use a data modelling tool before designing a database, it
  saves time and money in the long run.

* When using prototyping and a 4GL, use a structured approach to development which involves the users in agreeing
  and helping to develop the prototype. A useful tool for
  doing this was found to be Action Diagrammer.

A recent example of how Savant Enterprises has used these lessons occurred during late 1986 and early 1987 when a bespoke system was
developed for another client who was using MIMER. This system more than
satisfied the user requirements and was provided within the timescale set
and at below the budgeted cost.

References

[MART83] Martin J "An Information Manifesto Systems Vol.1", Savant 1983
[MART86] Martin J "Information Engineering Vol.1", Savant 1986
[MART87] Martin J "Information Engineering Vols. 2-4", Savant 1987

MIMER is a trade marked product of MIMER Information Systems AB of Uppsala, Sweden.

Data Designer is a trademarked product of Knowledge Ware Inc. of USA.

Action Diagrammer is a trademarked product of Knowledge Ware Inc. of USA.

FLEXIBLE DESIGN OF MANUFACTURING INFORMATION

SYSTEMS

D.W. Wainwright

Newcastle Upon Tyne Polytechnic

Newcastle Upon Tyne, UK

1   INTRODUCTION

The aim of the author's research is to produce a methodology for flexible
manufacturing information systems design applicable to the fast moving
needs of present day manufacturing industry.

This paper outlines some of the current views, ideas, and directions
evolving from the research program. This will eventually constitute the
core of the proposed methodology. The research program has examined a
selection of tools and techniques, 4GL environments, prototyping and
analysts workbenches.

The work is being carried out as part of an SERC sponsored Industry and
Academic collaborative project, is being developed within a manufacturing organisation and therefore has a strong practical bias.

This organisation is used as a case example to describe the current use
of new tools and techniques and to assess their suitability for particular application environments. Interesting comparisons can be made
within the case company as to the relative merits of these new approaches
with reference to the more traditional system development tools and
methods which are also in current use.

2   BACKGROUND TO RESEARCH

The introduction of new technologies, specifically manufacturing information systems, into manufacturing organisations is becoming increasingly
important as Companies strive to maintain a competitive edge. Over 65%
of engineering industry is running at least one element of computerised
manufacturing management [WYLE86]. Many companies now regard CIM
(Computer Integrated Manufacture), as an ultimate goal for the efficient
and effective use of resources with fast and flexible response to market
demands.

The current view of management experts [MORT86], is that pure technology
driven solutions are often ineffective from the business point of view
and that clear business objectives and manufacturing strategies [PRAB86]

should be clearly defined before the adoption of a technological
solution.

However, it is often the case that it is difficult to clearly define
objectives and strategies in the light of increasingly strong competition
and fast changing technologies. Therefore it is becoming increasingly
apparent that there is a need for new automated techniques in the field
of systems design and development to enable a quick and flexible response
to systems changes or redesign to stay in accord with 'unclear' objectives or changed strategies.

These new techniques and methods will utilise some of the advanced tools
now available for information systems design such as fourth generation
languages (4GL), relational database technology, distributed database
technology, and analyst workbench tools and environments.

3   MANUFACTURING INFORMATION SYSTEMS

The particular elements of manufacturing information systems that concern
this study are composed of systems covering the areas of materials planning and factory floor monitoring and control. The 1986 Engineering
Computers [ENGI86] survey shows that only 26% of engineering companies
have capacity planning, 37% use MRP, and 54% run stock control.

There are many potential pitfalls in the development and implementation
of manufacturing information systems which are becoming increasingly well
documented, [SHUN86], [MORT86]. Evans [EVAN86], states that the technology cannot be bought off the shelf, and Waterlow [WATE86], in a review of
computer aided production management (CAPM), warns that package solutions
do not represent a panacea, as they can only provide a proportion of the
required functionality relative to an individual organisations needs.

So, it would appear that this particular area of information system
design and development is still best approached via a bespoke software
approach or ideally a flexible modularised package approach. However,
there are always likely to be major constraints in terms of programming
expertise, tools available, and relevant methodologies as is indicated by
the apparent lack of successfully implemented manufacturing information
sub-systems in present manufacturing industry.

Therefore, there is obviously a need to reassess the process of systems
design and development within the field of manufacturing information
systems to provide the building blocks for the ultimate goal of CIM
within manufacturing organisations.

4   CURRENT SYSTEMS DEVELOPMENT

Many current manufacturing information systems have been built using 3GL
languages such as COBOL, and implemented on a multitude of equipment
types using various operating systems. In the past, there has been no
real alternative to this type of craft and labour intensive
implementation. These systems have characteristically very slow development times, are inflexible, are difficult to alter and very expensive to
maintain.

In an attempt to cope with some of these problems, many Companies turned
to structured analysis techniques, first advocated by DeMarco [DEMA78]
and Yourdon [YOUR79] in the 70's as the way forward for improving the
basic design of systems and also productivity in their development. Then
with the proliferation of cheaper computer hardware and packaged
software, including various types of relational database management

systems, there has been an evolution towards fundamental data analysis and design as a pre-requisite to systems design, using various data modelling techniques and third normal form analysis together with functional analysis. Examples of these methodologies are the LSDM (Learmonth and Burchett Management Services Ltd) method, the Information Engineering methodology of James Martin [MART81] and Jackson System Development [JACK83]. They all vary as towards the emphasis placed on data analysis and functional analysis and also as to their relative starting and finishing points within the traditional Systems Development Life Cycle (SDLC).

They generally suffer from the drawbacks of being cumbersome, unintelligible to most users, have long learning curves, are difficult and very labour intensive to manually produce and maintain and difficult to change once the 'specifications' of the system are frozen.

So, current tools and methodologies do not facilitate the ideal systems development environment for a fast moving, hard to specify, user developed manufacturing information system. Therefore it is necessary to examine new tools and more suitable methodologies which are becoming increasingly available with the increased power of hardware and more user oriented types of computer software.

5   NEW TOOLS AND METHODOLOGIES

The tools for fast and flexible development of systems are now available, such as relational database management systems, 4GLs, prototyping and analysts workbenches. However it is the selection of the most suitable tools together with a relevant means of control of the systems design and development in the form of a usable methodology which is difficult. The key issue of a methodology is, is it usable and will it be used. It must also be adaptable and for it to be of any use or value, it must conform to the needs, structure and business mission of the organisation [LEVI84]. Bhabuta [BHAB86], identifies three basic approaches to system development which have some degree of overlap. These are the business analysis approach, the human factors approach, and the software engineering approach. He contends that the approach to systems development must be related to both the types of systems as well as the purpose for which they are developed. Most organisations, due to pressures of 'standardisation', either have or are modelling their application development on the software engineering approach. While this is appropiate for applications which have stable requirements or are designed for long life, it is inappropiate for applications which embody unstable changing requirements or short life or diversity of user interfaces.

6   THE DESIGN AND DEVELOPMENT OF A MANUFACTURING INFORMATION SYSTEM IN
     A PICK BASED 4GL ENVIRONMENT

To illustrate some aspects of the use and suitability of new tools and methods for systems analysis and design, a case company has been used.

The company is a division of the world's leading manufacturer of pressure sensitive materials, operating on a 24hr, 7 day a week basis. Due to the complexities of the manufacturing process, long runs are required to maximise process efficiency. However, this has the counter effect on the important strategic objective of increasing the level of customer service in terms of a very low lead time. Therefore, the company has had to reconsider its manufacturing strategy to support its business objectives and change the former so that a greater emphasis is put on the idea of producing and holding part processed stocks.

To implement this change in business strategy, a large amount of capital investment is being made in new technology.

The manufacturing information systems within this particular case company fall into the category defined by Bhabuta as having changing unstable requirements, short life cycle, diversity of user interfaces, and a large degree of on-line transaction processing complexity. These problems are all generally due to fast changing business requirements as relate to fluctuating manufacturing strategies and operational methods and working procedures.

Pilot Study

The company decided to undertake a pilot study of the new manufacturing strategy, and run a proportion of the business over a 1 yr period to assess it's viability. Therefore, there was an immediate priority for a computerised system to control this aspect of the business and to give it a much greater analytical capability than would be normally required. The present system was not suitable, and in fact was in the process of being translated onto an IBM System 38. Even the proposed enhancements could not cope with the new business strategy, as the system was specified before the new policy was decided, and was being written in the 3GL, COBOL, by an outside software house. So, in effect the new system was out of date even before it had been installed!. There was very little in-house expertise to provide the capability of modification of the system, and the company would have to rely on the expensive option of outside contractors.

This traditional systems development environment has been used as a control to assess the alternative approaches provided by the availability of new tools and techniques. The close proximity of the differing approaches at the reference site enable some interesting comparisons and contrasts to be made and realistically evaluated.

Manufacturing Computer

A manufacturing computer was installed to facilitate the required amount of control over the manufacturing operation. Therefore, the main business administration and large scale capacity planning operations such as accounting, order processing and capacity planning would be performed on the System 38 computer, and the more complex, difficult to specify systems such as shop floor data capture, bar code materials tracking, time and materials recording, various small analytical projects, customer service and stock allocation system for the pilot study, and shop floor scheduling were developed on the manufacturing computer.

To give the possibilty of maximum user ownership and participation in design and development, the chosen system for the manufacturing system was a PICK operating system running on an IBM series -1 minicomputer. The fourth generation applications generator used was System Builder by Atech System Builder Ltd. The computer was not DP controlled but in the charge of a small manufacturing information systems team, really a type of information centre concept but with a manufacturing bias.

7 A 4GL MANUFACTURING INFORMATION SYSTEM

All the modules of the system were designed and developed using all the facilities offered by the PICK environment and the applications generator. The architecture of PICK together with the 4GL enabled several hierarchies to exist which enable different levels of privilege to be provided to different users of the system depending on their level of expertise or needs.

These privileges could be changed very easily to either restrict access for security reasons or provide access for differing business needs. The systems interface with the user via layers of menus which give numerous options for input of transactions, amendments, enquiries and reports. The menu system is quick and easy to learn with users very speedily being able to find their way around the different options to view, add, manipulate, analyse and report data.

Alterations to screen layout, transaction definitions, input or output requirements are readily accomodated by the use of the application generator's tools. The modules having been written using an applications generator, use the same tools and principles as the generator. Therefore they benefit from all the advanced features of a fourth generation system, running on a user oriented PICK operating system.

8   PICK - A FLEXIBLE SYSTEMS ENVIRONMENT

It should be emphasized that PICK is not just an operating system, but an advanced systems development environment with some features of a fourth generation system. The heart of PICK is a semi-relational database which is an inherent part of the operating system not a utility or an add-on. It has many sophisticated features including an English like non procedural query language, Access, an enhanced business oriented form of BASIC, a stored procedure processor PROC, a command processor TCL, a print spooler, and various forms of editor.

These features greatly aid the analyst/programmer, user/developer or naive user. A large proportion of the reporting functions can be made by end users themselves with very little training either by using the query language, Access, or the report generator within the applications generator. This enhances their usage and knowledge of the system to iteratively refine their individual information needs whilst taking a load off the system developers, who are then able to perform more constructive work.

PICK has a hierarchical file structure with one system dictionary and beneath it any number of master dictionaries, one for each account on the system. Each master dictionary can have any number of data dictionaries beneath it, with each one pointing to one or more data files.

A major advantage of this separation of data and dictionary files is that it makes it easy to change relationships without affecting data and this gives the flexibility to change the system to reflect changes in the real world. System builder provides a 'front end' to building and manipulating these dictionaries, enabling users with very little training to specify and mould systems to their actual requirements and not the analysts perceptions.

Another important feature in terms of flexibility and efficient use of the system, is that PICK has variable length records with an item structure capable of sub-division into file, item, attribute, value and subvalue. Attribute values are positionally orientated and expand and contract as needed. This again can help the user actually mould a system to the real world without absolute obedience to the concept of third normal form analysis. The use of multi-valued fields enables extremely easy data entry and storage that is easy to understand.

So, it has been found that these main features facilitate a great degree of flexibility in the design and ongoing development of the manufacturing information system. In the case of design, it means that file design and data dictionaries are rapidly constructed and easily reorganised and expanded to quickly model the world under development. Also, it means that many alternatives can be tried and tested with immediate visibility of the underlying data relationships and any hidden implications.

In the particular case company, it is not uncommon to make changes and enhancements to live systems as regularly as a weekly basis, in fact the approach taken is one of gradual evolution of the modules of the manufacturing information system to reflect changing user requirements.

9   DEVELOPMENT WITH A 4GL

It is the inherent database and data dictionary architecture of the PICK system that make it an ideal base for applications generators, as is demonstrated by the number and variety currently available. In particular, it has been found that the close resemblance of generators such as System Builder to the underlying system actually aid the novice developer to learn and understand the basic functions and operation of the operating system without prior knowledge of the system. This greatly aids productivity, in the sense that the system developer can proceed with a greater degree of non procedural development, ie be concerned with what he wants to do, and not be too concerned with how it is done.

This aspect of non procedural development together with the ability for completely automatic applications documentation greatly enhance development productivity.

Much is currently being written on the power of 4GLs, and their ability to provide short development timescales, easy application maintenance, reduce the applications backlog and enable applications development without programmers. Experience within the case company confirms these claims to varying degrees with productivity increases an order of magnitude greater than COBOL. In this instance it is only necessary to compare the vast amount of new development on the 4GL manufacturing information system within the case company, as opposed to the static development on the administration computer using 3GL COBOL development. When a cost and resources comparison is made there is certainly an order of magnitude difference between the two approaches, with the 4GL approach winning on every front.

However, it is worthwhile to re-iterate the caution expressed by [BUTL86], of the need for good data analysis techniques, database software, data dictionaries and re-organisation.

Data analysis, database design and systems skills become increasingly important as opposed to programming skills which although still very necessary, should be needed in a decreasing proportion of the current 20 to 30 % of the application development that still may need to be written in conventional 3GL.

The flexible systems environment of PICK, together with the 4GL applications generators set of tools has enabled, the majority of the manufacturing information systems development using the technique of prototyping.

Again, much has and is currently being written about prototyping and it has its adherents and its critics as a systems development method or philosophy. Martin, [MART81], differentiates between the various usage of prototyping where the three basic approaches adopted can be to use the prototype to clarify user requirements and tighten up the specification, then write the system using a 3GL or to use the prototype in an iterative manner to define a working system, then rewrite in a 3GL and finally the situation where the prototype can actually evolve into the final system.

Boar, [BOAR86], concentrates on the theme of a prototype as a minature life cycle within the definition step of the classic system development life cycle (SDLC). Boar is of the mind that there is too much missing at the end of the prototype life cycle to directly implement the prototype. These missing features are complete functionality, quality assurance testing, operational run books, performance, training materials and documentation. The technique also has its opponents in the DP community with arguments against that are mainly technical concerning efficiency, machine utilization, slow response times, greater hardware costs, bad systems design and lack of functionality, [PRIZ86].

In the particular case study, these criticisms are probably justified to an extent, but they should be related to the particular type of application in question. It is justified to believe that the aim of fast response, security and maximum machine efficiency should be priorities in complex financial software or military applications, but perhaps different priorities can be assigned to applications relating to fast changing business needs and manufacturing strategies. The priorities operative in these environments are flexibility, extremely quick development times with application developers whose skills lie more in the business analysis areas than programming and finally effectiveness in that the system must solve the business problem it first set out to solve. After all, in today's competitive environment a system that takes years to specify and build may have no business problem left to solve or even no business to go to.

Prototyping has been used extensively in the manufacturing information system's design and development, and is of the type where the prototype becomes the final application. It is the author's view however that the particular method of prototyping approach taken, is a function of the personality and background of the application developer in question. For instance, an experienced programmer may, if faced with a problem such as a difficult validation, immediately search for an exit point out of the 4GL, and write 3GL subroutines as this will be the easiest option in terms of solving the problem quickly. This has implications for later maintenance of the system however, as it presupposes that the person responsible for the maintenance of that application has sufficient programming knowledge, which may not always be the case when a parameter driven 4GL is used in place of a compiled application.

Again the use of parameter driven 4GLs as opposed to pre-generated source code may be open to debate in terms of efficiency and structure of code and flexibility.

In the development of the manufacturing information system it was left to individual developers which route to take, as both options are available within the System Builder application. The authors choice was to sacrifice a degree of functionality of the system and slight inefficiency of speed in favour of easier maintainability non programmer flexibility, standardisation, simplicity and flexibility in terms of the organic nature of the prototyping approach.

Fine tuning of the systems can be attempted at a later stage of the development but only after the system is performing in an effective manner. It has also been found that this technique is of greatest benefit in situations where requirements are extremely difficult to define. Examples of these would include real-time shop floor scheduling, where it is not even certain which type of system is most suitable or what would constitute a good database design for that environment or what the users actually require in terms of operational capabilities. Prototyping in this case greatly enhances the clarification of the potential problems and enables an evolutionary, flexible and iterative theme of design and development.

However, prototyping used with a fourth generation language and development environment is not the complete solution to the flexible design of manufacturing or any type of information systems. There must be some means of control and standardisation of the process in the form of a suitable methodology. Yourdon [YOUR86], believes it is time to restate the case for structured analysis. He states that the importance of structured systems for large and complex systems has been obscured by such recent developments as prototyping, 4GLs, and personal computer facilities. He argues that structured analysis is not obsolete and new tools such as state transition diagrams, and more updated forms of data flow diagramming, together with their automation using pc based workstations and eventually expert systems are enabling structured methodologies to be adapted as a strategy for systems design and development.

Different views abound on the most suitable types of methodology for unstructured problem solving where the objectives might be considered 'soft' as opposed to hard. Veryard [VERY86], favours the use of a 'softened' interpretative form of existing structured techniques. However, Miles [MILE86], concludes that structured analysis is a continuation of 'hard systems thinking' as is the technique of data analysis. Miles advocates a fundamental shift in thinking towards a framework of the soft systems methodology developed by Checkland, [CHEC81].

11   ANALYSTS WORKBENCH

The problems encountered with the design and development of a manufacturing information system are mainly centred around good fundamental data analysis and database design together with a flexible form of readable, clear and professional documentation. System Builder has automatic documentation facilities for all the fundamental parts which comprise the applications development. A notable absentee, however, was a set of diagramming tools, for data flow diagramming, entity attribute relationship diagrams, state transition diagrams etc.. Therefore, initially a DIY approach has been adopted using the Apple Macintosh PC. The high quality graphics, icon and mouse environment, together with the integrated drafting facilities of software such as MacDraw and MacWrite, have enabled very quick, flexible and professional documentation to be produced, which is easily updated and revised.

This documentation facility provides the ability to complement the more formal automatic documentation provided by the applications generator. In the case company, it has been found that this type of tool is most useful in the analysis and design phase of the system development. Very rapid rough cut models of the logical database design can be developed

before being translated into the physical files, dictionaries and screens
which initially drive the embryonic prototype. The diagrams can then be
iteratively refined in step with the evolving prototype and can greatly
enhance visibility and understanding of the system.

Evaluation of a dedicated package, MacCadd developed by Logica, is
currently taking place within the case company, with the aim of it being
the natural development of the DIY approach first adopted. MacCadd is a
knowledge-based set of software design tools, which contains knowledge of
the rules for specific diagram types, and so enforces standards and
structures whilst highlighting inconsistencies.

Within the case example, it has been found that the rapid speed of design
and development using the prototyping concept has outstripped the ability

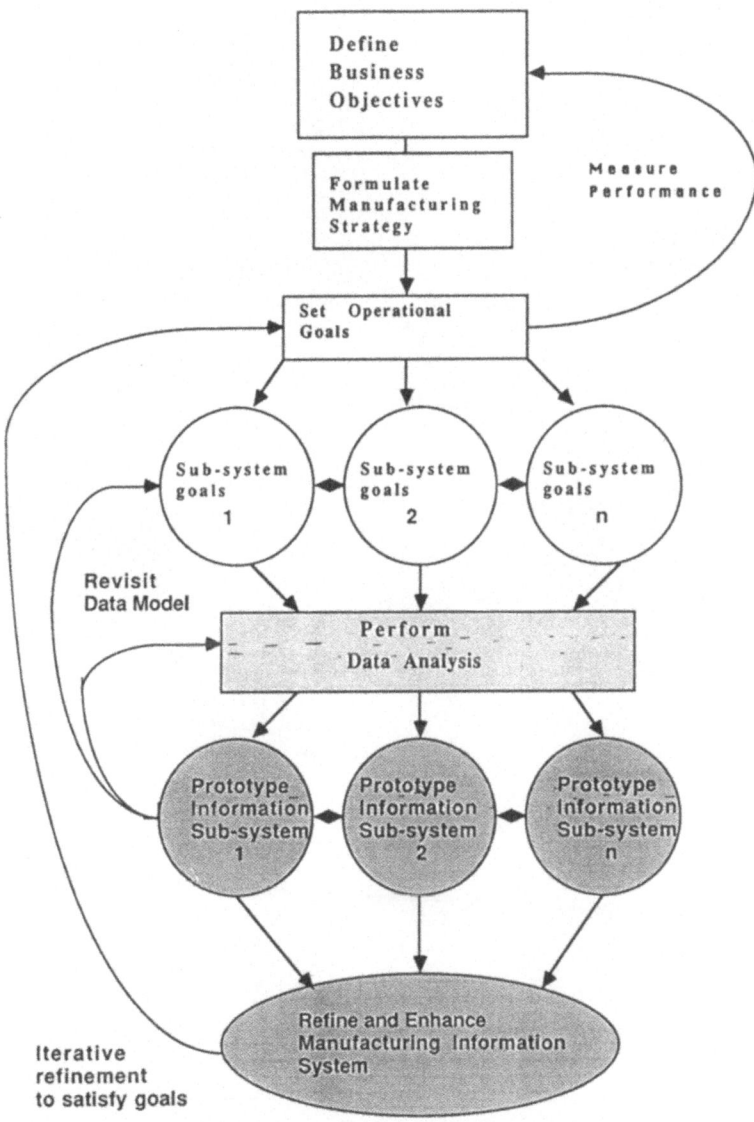

Figure 1   Prototype Model for 4GL Development of a Manufacturing
            Information System

to keep the documentation right up to date. The automated tools provided by the workbench should alleviate this problem to an extent, but there is still a need to comprehensively post document the system.

12 CONCLUSIONS

The idea that there is a need for a new approach to the design and development of manufacturing information systems is now becoming increasingly apparent. This type of system is typically characterised by being extremely difficult to specify, with differing levels of complexity, extremely fast moving and of fundamental importance to an

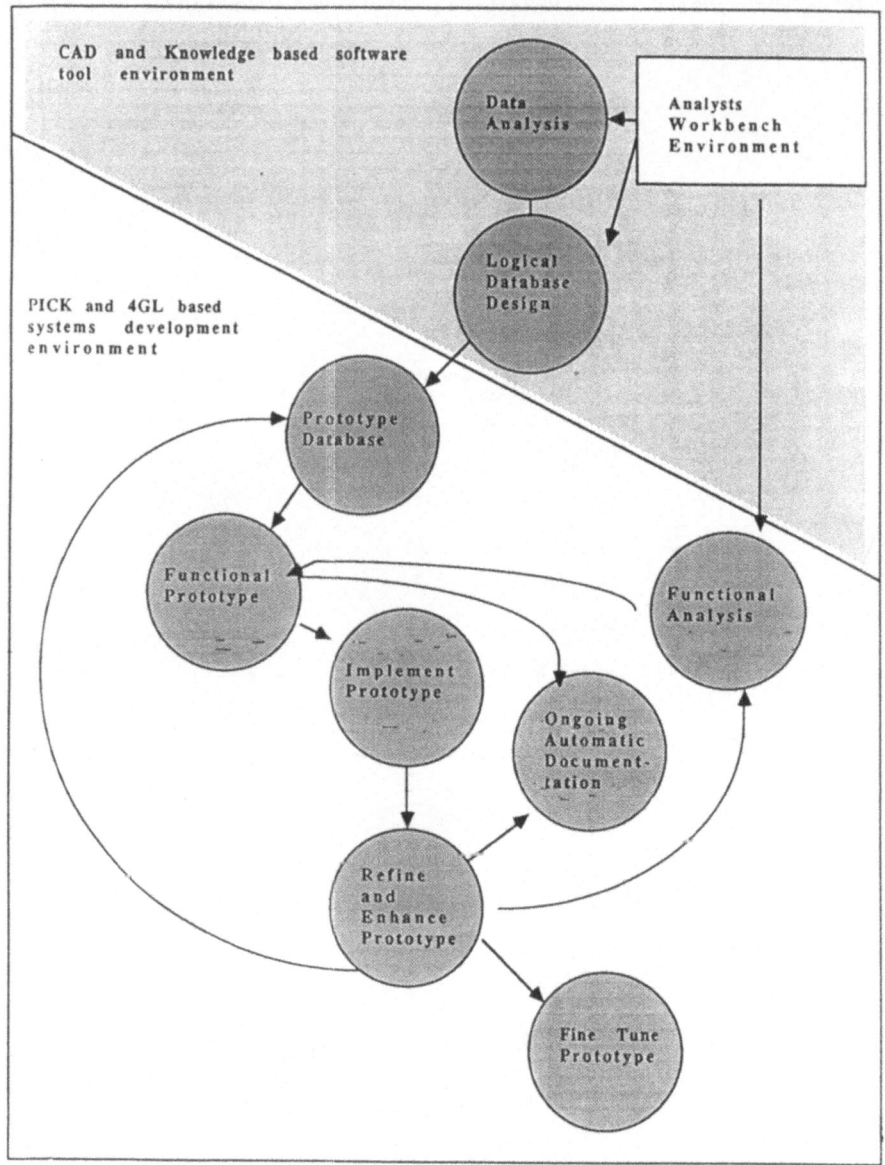

Figure 2   Framework for a PICK based flexible Design of a Manufacturing Information System

organisation in terms of the efficient and effective control of the
manufacturing operation.
Also, the ability to incorporate the fundamental requirement for
flexibility in the system development process, to match the finished
system with changing requirements brought about by revised manufacturing
strategies was a prime objective. The need for flexibility and
evaluation of successful achievement of system objectives is illustrated
in Fig 1.

A system has been designed and developed for a manufacturing
organisation, which takes account of these characteristics, and relies on
the use of a PICK based development environment together with a user
oriented applications developer, System Builder, and also the high
resolution graphics environment of the Macintosh computer for design and
documentation work. A tentative model, Fig 2, can be described for the
main features of this design and development process, which relies
heavily on the iterative theme of prototyping.

It is believed that this particular choice of tools, techniques and
particular environment, greatly facilitate the aims of maximum user
involvement in the design and development process.

Flexibility has been achieved to a great extent with constant
enhancements, necessary changes and an expansion of the total system
taking place on a regular basis. This is accomplished very quickly and
easily, thereby reducing maintenance and increasing development
productivity quite radically.

It is the authors view that these tools and techniques will with further
refinement form the basis for a flexible systems design and development
methodology applicable to 4GL type environments. The methodology will
attempt to be oriented towards the ´soft systems concept´ as opposed to
the traditional ´hard´ systems thinking prevalent in current structured
methodologies. This will enable flexible design and development to be
undertaken and continual evolution of the system to take place in reponse
to changes in the external environment.

13   REFERENCES

[BHAB86] Bhabuta L. "Standards and Systems Development" Data Processing,
Sept 86, vol 28, no 7, pp 345-349

[BOAR86] Boar B. "Application Prototyping A life cycle Perspecti
ve" Journal of Systems Management, vol 37, no 2, Feb 1986.

[BUTL86] Butler M. "Approach the fourth generation with care" DEC Us
er, May 86, pp 63-64

[CHECK81] Checkland P.B "Systems Thinking Systems Practice" Wiley, 1981

[DEMA78] DeMarco T. "Structured Analysis and System Specification"
Yourdon Press 1978.

[ENGI86] Survey - Computers in Manufacturing, "The £ 2.5 billion success
story" Engineering Computers, Nov 86, pp 32-39.

[EVAN86] Evans P. "MAP and CIM" Data Processing, vol 28, no 3, Apr 86, pp
151-155.

[JACK83] Jackson M., "System Development" Prentice-Hall, 1983.

[LEVI86] Levine A. "Systems Development, how to avoid the pitfalls" Canadian Datasystems, Oct 84, vol 16, no 10, pp 92-94.

[MART81] Martin J. and Finklestein C. Information Engineering Vol II, Savant Research Studies, 1981.

[MILE86] Miles R.K. "Author's Response - Soft Appearances Can be Deceptive: A Reply To R. Veryard" Journal of Applied Systems Analysis, vol 13, 1986.

[MORT86] Mortimer J. (Ed.) (Ingersoll Engineers) "Integrated Manufacture" IFS (Pub) Ltd. Bedford, UK. 1985.

[PRAB86] Prabu V. et al "The Role of Manufacturing Strategy in the Introduction of New Technologies" Proceedings of the UK Operations Management Association Conference (5-6 Jan 86), University of Nottingham, Nottingham UK.

[PRIZ86] Prizant A. "Is Prototyping Counterproductive?" Data Processing, vol 28, no 7, Sep 86, p 379.

[SHUN86] Shunk D.L. and Filley R.D. "Systems Integration's Challenges Demand a New Breed of Industrial Engineer" Industrial Engineering, May 86, pp 65-67.

[VERY86] Veryard R. "Computer Systems Analysis, Models and Prototypes: A Reply To R.K. Miles" Journal of Applied Systems Analysis, vol 13, 1986.

[WATE86] Waterlow G. "ACME Initiatives in CAPM Research" ACME Directorate paper presented at the Grantholder's Conference, Sept 86.

[WYLE86] Wyles C. "Survey Manufacturing Management, If you seek that competitive edge" Engineering Computers, Nov 86, pp 32-39.

[YOUR86] Yourdon E. "What ever happened to structured analysis" Datamation, June 1 1986, vol 32, no 11, pp 133-138

[YOUR79] Yourdon E. and Constantine L. "Structured Design" Prentice-Hall 1979

4GL PRODUCTIVITY THROUGH INFORMATION ENGINEERING

Peter Haine

Savant Research Centre

Coventry Lanchester Polytechnic

1   INTRODUCTION

Despite the potential benefits of fourth generation language systems, (4GLs), many users are disillusioned by them and do not believe that they come up to their own expectations, let alone the claims of the software vendor. Are these products not what they are cracked up to be, or are there other reasons why they are not delivering the productivity and flexibility claimed of them?

Certainly we can expect to see some fairly dramatic improvements in such products in the coming years. They really are in their infancy just now, and we should expect to see them mature into more powerful, better integrated systems in the future, with a correspondingly wider range of possible applications. One of the problems is that many of the current products are based on outdated file or data base management systems, or are adapted from early report generators.

Another problem, though, is that users of the products tend to treat them as just another means of implementing systems as in the past. This is to treat the 4GL system very naively, for it has the potential to overcome many of the problems traditionally faced by data processing departments in meeting the needs of their users. It will not be effective if it is used within the context of a traditional system life cycle. This paper addresses the reasons why this is so, and suggests a modified approach to systems development and systems implementation which ensures that 4GL's become fully effective. This approach is based on the Information Engineering principles of Martin and Finkelstein [MART81].

2   PROBLEMS PERCEIVED BY COMPUTER USERS

Customers of the DP department frequently complain that applications can never be built when they are most wanted, that essential changes to them take an inordinate amount of time to implement, and that once delivered the systems do not really match their requirements. What is more, applications generally cost much more to develop and maintain than was originally anticipated.

Why is this? Why are we not able to build flexible systems at realistic costs, and then to maintain them effectively so that they continue

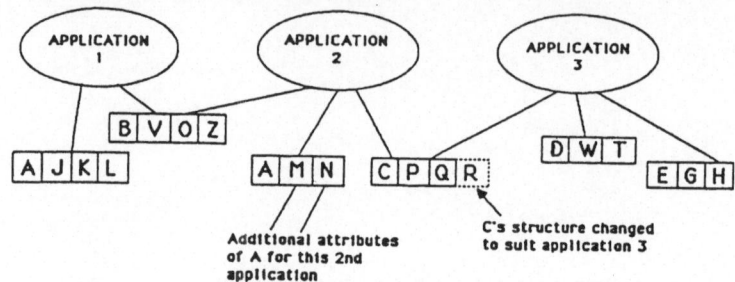

FIGURE 1 Previous applications and file structures often need to be modified at great cost to meet new requirements.

to match the users' needs? The fundamental reason is that systems design is not approached so as to produce flexible systems. Right from the inception of most computer projects, there is an inbuilt rigidity which mitigates against the long term success of the resulting systems. There are a number of aspects to this rigidity. In the first place, the data used by an application is all too frequently coupled tightly to that application (Figure 1). Any other application of the data thus has to use the same file structures, or to maintain an entirely independent set of appropriate files. Secondly, the sheer cost of writing and testing conventional computer programs demands that a complete specification of the program is prepared before development begins. This is simply not realistic, since most users do not begin to fully understand their requirements until they have seen their system emerging. It is particularly difficult for them to agree to specifications which are expressed in the complex structured form of documentation which has become popular in the past few years.

In order to get the best out of 4GL, therefore, we need to adopt quite new approaches to application development. In the first place we need to get our corporate data under control in a way which is quite independent of the applications (the systems and procedures) which use it. Corporate data is a corporate resource and it should be managed as such. A strategic data planning study enables an organisation to obtain a stable view of the data which supports activities in pursuit of goals. The data is modelled to facilitate the definition of the underlying data structures which need to be maintained in order to satisfy the information needs of every part of the organisation.

Such a study is the foundation of the Information Engineering approach. It can be carried out quite independently of present systems and the computer hardware which support them. It views the corporation from the top down, examining the strategies which have been adopted in the various business areas to satisfy corporate goals, and the systems and procedures being effected by the business areas to implement strategies.

This analysis results in a clear view of the many files presently maintained to support systems - and highlights the problem mentioned above of incompatible and inconsistent file structures.

With a comprehensive view of the data used in support of processes, the inter-relationships of data can be explored and an entity chart constructed to document these. The entity chart serves as a reference map when applications are to be built. Within an application area, the data of interest needs to be analysed in much greater detail to provide a

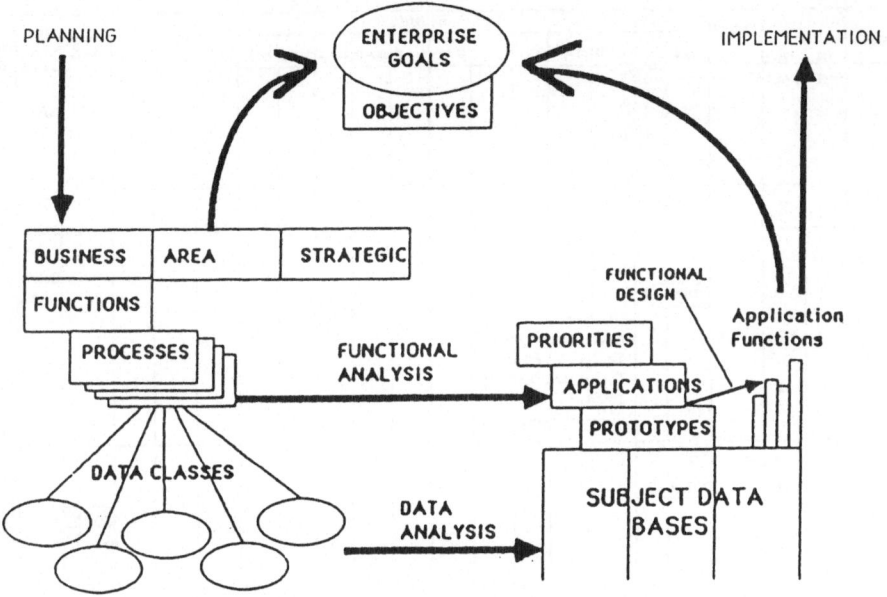

FIGURE 2   The Files and Business Systems in Support of Business
            Objectives.

data base schema and the entity charts focuses attention on the data
of interest, and its relationship with entities which are not directly of
concern. In this way provision can be made in the data base schema for
the future uses of data and relationships which are important in support
of other applications. With the data now managed independently of its
application, the way is open to begin building and converting
applications to run in association with these liberalised data
structures. Bridges to existing applications will need to be created
initially, but in terms of new applications, the full power of 4GL tools
is now available. An important caveat must be put in here, though, for
along with the liberalisation of the access paths to corporate data goes
an important responsibility for the maintenance of integrity and security
of data. It is critically important, therefore, to establish a formal
control framework which manages not only the data elements which are
accessed by various users, but also the interdependency and timing of all
the functions which interact with the data elements.

In the Research Centre at Coventry we have been experimenting with
Application Control Charts (Figure 3) as a vehicle for planning the
operational characteristics of an application. We have implemented a
prototype system under VAX/VMS using the MIMER Data System to support
user access, timing and sequence control for applications running on a
single processor, and using a common data environment, in this case
MIMER. The prototype system leads us to believe that the sort of data
dictionary commonly in use today needs to be significantly enhanced to
handle application control effectively. We believe that in the long term
a Data Dictionary system is required which maintains a control data base
at the heart of corporate operations.

The control Data Base would control exchange of data between machines
operating in a network and for all major applications would handle access
validation, and integrity checking of all data and operations.

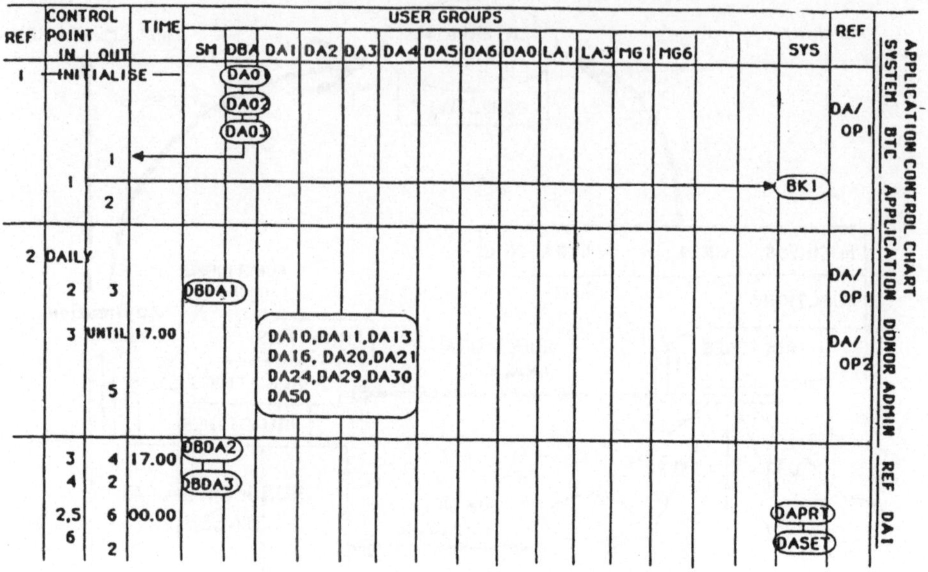

REF	CONTROL POINT IN	CONTROL POINT OUT	TIME	SM	DBA	DA1	DA2	DA3	DA4	DA5	DA6	DA0	LA1	LA3	MG1	MG6	SYS	REF
1	—INITIALISE—				(DA0) (DA02) (DA03)												DA/OP1	
	1	←																
	1	2															→ (BK1)	
2	DAILY																DA/OP1	
	2	3			(DBDA1)												DA/OP1	
	3		UNTIL 17.00			DA10,DA11,DA13 DA16, DA20,DA21 DA24,DA29,DA30 DA50											DA/OP2	
		5																
	3	4	17.00		(DBDA2)													
	4	2			(DBDA3)													
	2,5	6	00.00														(DAPRT)	
	6	2															(DASET)	

Vertical side labels: APPLICATION CONTROL CHART — SYSTEM BTC — APPLICATION — DONOR ADMIN — REF DA1

FIGURE 3   An Application Control Chart

The Application Control Chart is a rather crude (yet effective) manual mechanism for defining the necessary application controls. We believe there is a need for the process to be mechanised, however, and would look to the analyst or designer's workbench to support this activity, along with data and functional design.

With the data under control, many requirements for information can be met using the simple query language and report generation facilities offered by a good 4GL system. Transaction processing and more critical reporting systems will still need to be built as production type systems, but these too may be defined using the prototyping approaches which 4GL products permit. It should be possible with an effective prototyping tool to get an outline of an operational system up and running within a matter of weeks rather than the months which it might take using a conventional programming language. What is more, the user will be fully involved in the development of the prototype, and will have the opportunity to interact with it from an early stage in order to assess its suitability for its purpose. The prototype is then refined until it finally matches the users' requirements as closely as possible. When the requirements change, a return to the final prototype provides a useful starting point for the adaptation of the system.

There has to be control over prototyping, too, otherwise development costs can run well over budget. But these controls can be expressed in the form of application objectives, and a set of prototype evaluation criteria, which assess the nearness of fit of the prototype to the application's objectives.

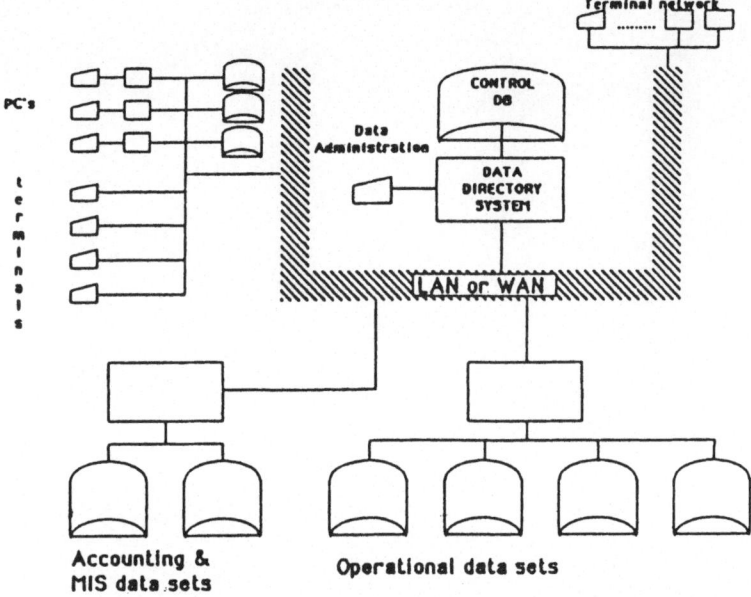

FIGURE 4   A Controlled, Distributed Environment Where an Active Data
Directory Controls Access to all Operational and MIS Data.

3   SUMMARY AND CONCLUSIONS

The Information Engineering methodology sets out to build information
systems on a stable foundation of corporate data. It does not require
that existing data structures are abandoned, but rather it recognises
that a migration must be planned which will ensure that after a period of
initial bridging into these existing structures, the new and more stable
data environment will emerge.

Fourth generation language systems do indeed have the potential to
revolutionise computer application development. But not all of them yet
have a sufficiently well integrated set of application development and
data administration tools to realise this potential. The potential
purchaser will be well advised to consider how well any prospective
product matches up to these requirements. Neither are the 4GL tools in
their own right any panacea. An entirely new approach to development is
called for, but this is long overdue in any case, since the hand crafting
tools of yesterday's data processing shop have long since been found
wanting. The best of the 4GL systems, combined with new approaches to
systems development based on independence of data structures and
prototyping, will be found to improve both the cost effectiveness of the
resulting systems, and the satisfaction of users.

REFERENCE

[MART81]   Information Engineering, James Martin & Clive Finkelstein,
           SAVANT, 1981

DB4GL - AN INTELLIGENT DATABASE SYSTEM

F. Poole

Department of Computer Studies

Sheffield City Polytechnic

ABSTRACT

Current research within the Department of Computer Studies at Sheffield City Polytechnic indicates that it is possible to define a generalised database architecture which results in a worthwhile simplification of the traditional applications programming task. The approach adopted stems from the derivation, from normalisation procedures, of all the association relationships which exist between a set of entities, and then selecting the relevant subset of entities and association relationships for a specific application program. This subset is used to generate a data access schema, which has the important property that multiple data realisations can be performed on linked entities in anticipation of eventual demand. This reduces considerably the need for the programmer to specify explicit file handling operations within an application program. The data access schema is in fact one of four major structural software components in an application program which may be specified and generated. The other components are:-

1. an information description schema, one per entity, which specifies record actions, data item transfers and global integrity rules,

2. a process schema, which contains details of local integrity rules, that is, local to a specific application, and processing requests,

3. a presentation object, which contains details of user presentation in terms of screens, reports and graphical output, as well as error handling and the overall sequencing of the applications task.

In DB4GL it is possible to specify the architectural features of these four software components through the use of special software tools, for example, a normalisation engine, or, a screen painter and also to define integrity rules and simple processing requirements. These specifications are used in the application generation process.

1   INTRODUCTION

The development of relational theory [CODD70], [CODD79] and the resultant query languages [CODD72], [CHAM76], [ZLOO77] provides a framework for much of current data base system research and development. Indeed a draft standard exists [ANSI80] which forms the basis for the development of commercial products [BAT085] which use these relational language constructs as the kernel for high level processing languages. The inclusion of useful software tools to simplify the applications development task in areas such as file definition, screen painting, report generation and spreadsheet modelling results in a fourth generation system (4GS) [WOOD86]. The DB4GL project (Data Base for/forth Generation Languages) [EWIN85a], [EWIN85b] was originally conceived as a software development vehicle to explore mechanisms for specifying integrity rules with pre-condition and post-condition processing rules. The experiments conducted using DB4GL have led to our current approach to 4GS architecture.

2   DATA BASE MODELS

The data base model for DB4GL is based on the entity relationship model [CHEN76], [CHEN80], [CHEN83]. This approach was adopted as it,

1) offers the potential of high logical data independence, inherent in n-ary relational data base models,

2) allows for the definition of suitable relational manipulation languages, and, with suitable extension,

3) yields record at a time data access with a performance potential at least comparable to pointer based systems.

The latter point is crucial to the development of a practical version of DB4GL.

2.1 Data Coupling

In the entity relationship model, a single entity might be thought of in terms of its structure, i.e. as a suitable grouping of attributes to provide an appropriate description of an identifiable unit of information within an application environment. The semantics contained within an application entity are constrained to basic functional dependencies. In order to accommodate more extensive semantics it is possible to enhance the concept of this unit of information to allow extra descriptions to be included which refer both to the entity and also to the individual data attributes which form that entity. Some of these information units describe real world objects and may relate to entity relations, in E-R terminology, with single component entity identifiers. However the fact that multiple attributes may be used in the description of one information unit (denoted by IU) means that normally, multiple views exist for a single IU. For example, a stock item might be characterised by its stock code, description, quantity-on-hand and location. In this context it is reasonable to suggest that a prime view of stock items might be in terms of stock code. Equally, it is quite legitimate for alternative views of stock to be adopted, such as, for example, by location. In this case the alternative view might be adopted, such as, for example, by location. In this case the alternative view might be represented diagramatically as shown in figure 1.

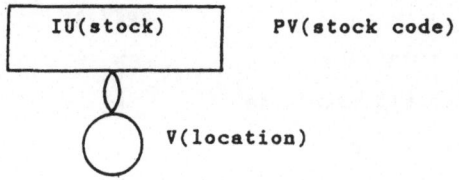

PV represents a prime view, and

V represents a non-prime, or secondary, view.

Figure 1   2 views of an IU

In this case the important properties of a non-prime view are that it includes

1)   the attribute which is central to the view (e.g. location), and

2)   the set of attributes which uniquely identify each occurrence of a prime view, and that it has a pseudo-physical structure represented by,

3)   the sequenced concatenation of (1) and (2) with all attribute types participating as a single identifier.

In the above example, this yields,

V(<u>location</u>, <u>stock code</u>)

This is a strict view formulated according to rules which eliminate potential problems caused by the connection trap [DATE84].   The maintenance of such views must be undertaken in concert with the maintenance of the prime view, unless the non-prime view is either temporary or the consistency of the non-prime view is weak.   If strong consistency is required for a permanent non-prime view then the IU´s representing the non-prime view and prime view are said to be closely coupled.   This is represented diagramatically in figure 2.

Non-prime views may be thought of as view relations, to maintain equivalence with the E-R model.   Moreover depending on whether the prime view is regular or weak then the resultant view relation will be either a regular view relation or a weak view relation.   Hence the major relational components of the extended entity relationship model (EE-R) are shown in figure 3.

Other qualified forms of closely coupled information units exist, where the coupling is subject to integrity constraints.   These are audit logs and replicated IU´s.
2.1.2   Audit logs

There may be several different audit logs within a system and hence

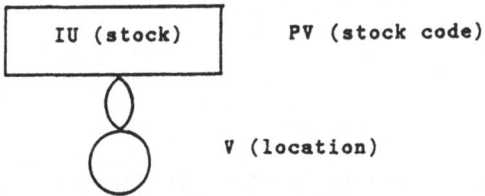

Figure 2 Closely coupled IU´s

	Regular	Weak
entity relations	x	x
relationship relations	x	x
view relations	x	x

Figure 3 types of relations in the EE-R

different related information units. Each of these IU´s represents a
destination for data values acquired from, perhaps, more than one source
IU (see figure 4). The actual log construction task must be governed by
the appropriate integrity and processing rules.

2.1.3 Replication

Normally, replicated IU´s are strongly coupled.

In this example (figure 5) IU_{11}, IU_{12} and IU_{13} represent replicated
information units, which may be stored at different nodes within a
distributed database. The update of any one of these information units
forces the update of the replicas in accordance with the prevailing
consistency environment. For example, such updates might be allowed to
proceed on the basis of the majority voting algorithms with two phase
commit.

2.2 Loosely Coupled Information Units

Two Information Units are said to be loosely coupled if they are not
strongly coupled but possess one or more common attribute types defined
over the same domain of definition.

Such coupling is deducible form the normalisation process [FAGI79],
[BERN76], [SMIT85] where it arises directly from the functional
dependencies between data attributes inherited from the fundamental
problem semantics. Fully automatic detection of loosely coupled

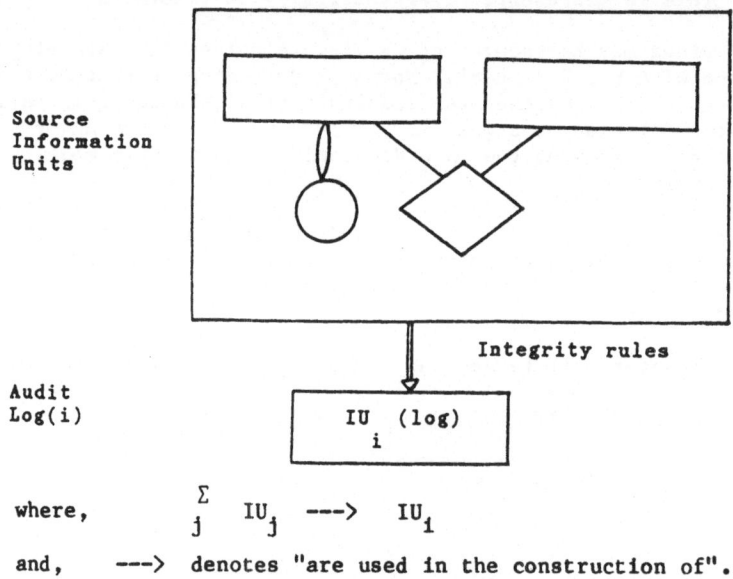

Source
Information
Units

Integrity rules

Audit
Log(i)

IU (log)
i

where, $\sum_j IU_j$ ---> IU_i

and,   ---> denotes "are used in the construction of".

Figure 4 Audit Log

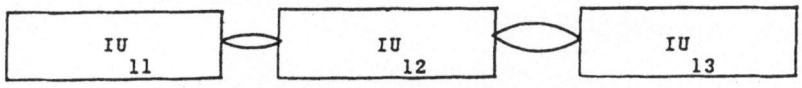

Figure 5 Replicated IUs

relationships requires that the underlying domain of definition is
associated explicity with each attribute type. Furthermore, the
construction of secondary views results in the promulgation of this type
of coupling. Figure 6 illustrates this type of coupling for the loosely
coupled IU's,

IU (Order),   PV (order number, order date, customer number)

IU (Stock Suppliers),   PV (supplier code, stockcode)

IU (Customer),   PV (customer number, customer name, customer
                         address, customer region)

IU (Supplier),   PV (supplier number, supplier name, Supplier
                         address, supplier region)

In this case the data attributes customer region and supplier region are
defined over the same domain, region, which represents a notional
division of the country into different areas.

In figure 6 L(customer number) represents a loose coupling between the
information units IU (Order) and IU(Customer) on the attribute type
customer number.

2.3 Data Access

Consider a situation where customers place orders for stock items. In
this case

-        orders must be defined

-        order details may be listed by customer, where customers are
         identified by name rather than account code.

These problem semantics might be represented diagramatically as shown in
figures 7, 8 and 9. The former identifies the entity relations and
relationship relations. Figures 8 and 9 illustrated how the problem
semantics are incorporated into a structural view by the use of non—prime
views.

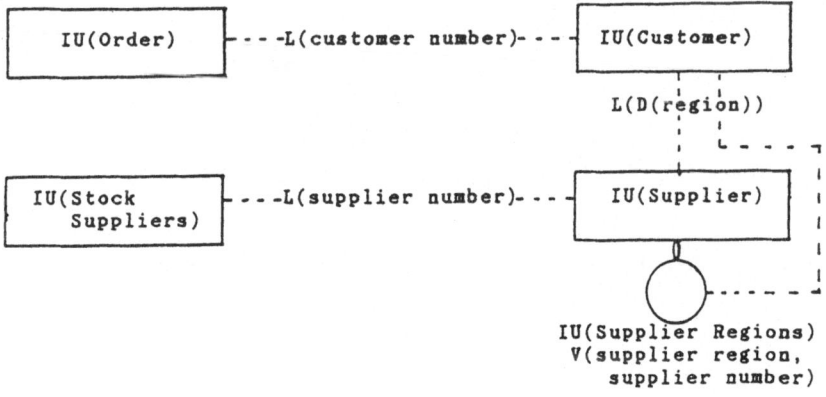

Figure 6 Loose coupling

```
-------------------------------------------------------------------
Regular Entity Relations            Regular Relationship Relations
-------------------------------------------------------------------

IU(Order)
PV(order number)
Attributes (order date
            customer account code)


IU(Customer)
PV(customer account code)           IU(Order Line)
Attributes (customer name           PV(order number
            customer address)           stock code)
                                    Attributes (quantity ordered)


IU(Stock)
PV(stock code)
Attributes (description
            quantity on hand
                    location)
-------------------------------------------------------------------
```

Figure 7 Traditional relations for customers place orders for stock items!

```
----------------------------------
Regular View Relations
----------------------------------

IU   (Customer Names)
  1
 V   (customer name)
     (customer account code)


IU   (Order Details)
  2
 V   (customer account code
              order number)


IU   (Stock Orders)
  3
 V   (stock code
      order number)
----------------------------------
```

Figure 8 Non-prime view structures for customer-order-stock problem

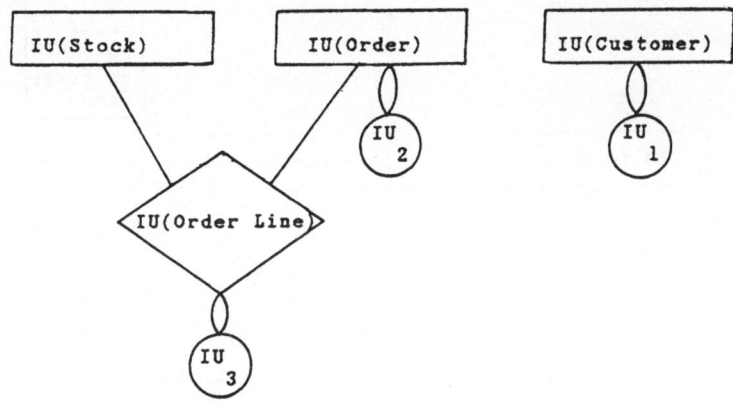

Figure 9 Diagamnatic representation of figure 8

Figure 7 contains details of the traditional E-R model database information units. Figure 8 identifies the non-prime view structures necessary to accommodate the given problem semantics.

In figure 9, IU_1, IU_2 and IU_3 represent the non-prime views as defined in figure 8. To define new orders, starting with an order number, a prime access data diagram (PADD) can be constructed from figure 9 (see figure 10).

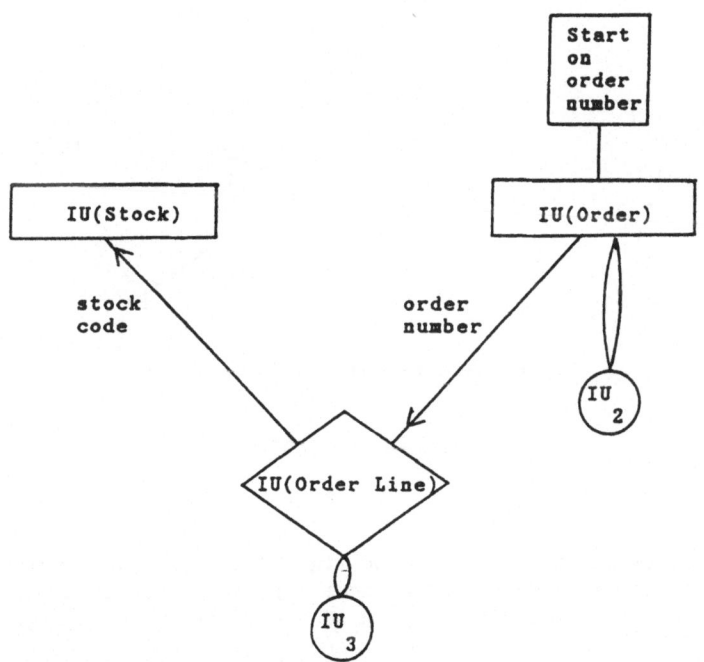

Figure 10 Prime access data diagram (PADD) for customer-order-stock problem

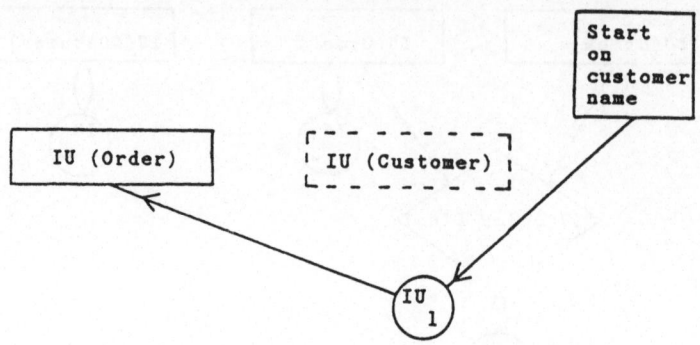

Figure 11 PADD for named customers

Note that the connections between information units must satisfy
referential integrity rules. In this case details of the order are
handled before each order line, and subsequently related stock
information is dealt with.

Figure 11 defines a PADD for the generation of order details which relate
to named customers.
In this case the information unit IU_1 is accessed directly for read only
access without reference to the corresponding information unit for
customers.

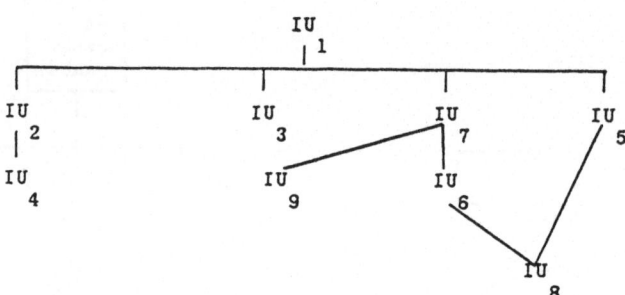

Figure 12 More complex IU structure

The PADD's outlined in figure 10 and figure 11 represent straightforward
hierarchical access. More general access path strategies may be defined,
but first, consider the more complex IU structure shown in figure 12.

For this network of IU's we can state the relationships arising from the couplings shown in the form

$$.IU_1 = M_4(IU_1) . \begin{bmatrix} IU_2 \\ IU_3 \\ IU_7 \\ IU_5 \end{bmatrix}$$

where

- $.IU_1$ defines the rule constrained access to the information unit IU_1.

If successful, the access to IU_1 produces an occurrence of IU_1, OU_1, and

- $M_n(IU_1)$ is an n-dimensional diagonal matrix where n is the number of directly inferior IU's (in PADD terms) coupled to IU_1. $M_n(IU_1)$ represents the transformation which generates an OU_1 and opens up access to the IU's which are coupled to IU_1.

$$M_n(IU_1) = \begin{bmatrix} OU_1 & & & \\ & OU_1 & & \\ & & \ddots & \\ & & & OU_1 \end{bmatrix}$$

Similarly, the lower level network structures of figure 12 give

- $IU_2 = M_1(IU_2) . IU_4$
- $IU_3 = M_1(IU_3) . 1$ (where 1 represents the terminal point)
- $IU_4 = M_1(IU_4) . 1$
- $IU_5 = M_1(IU_5) . (IU_8)$
- $IU_6 = M_1(IU_6) . (IU_8)$
- $IU_7 = M_2(IU_7) . \begin{bmatrix} .IU_6 \\ IU_9 \end{bmatrix}$
- $IU_8 = M_1(IU_8) . 1$
- $IU_9 = M_1(IU_9) . 1$

Hence the access operation into IU_1 with the structure shown in figure 12 yields

$$. IU_1 = \begin{bmatrix} OU_1 & & & \\ & OU_1 & & \\ & & OU_1 & \\ & & & OU_1 \end{bmatrix} . \begin{bmatrix} IU_2 \\ IU_3 \\ IU_7 \\ IU_5 \end{bmatrix}$$

$$= \begin{bmatrix} OU_1 \cdot & IU_2 & & \\ & OU_1 \cdot & IU_3 & \\ & & OU_1 \cdot & IU_7 \\ & & & OU_1 \cdot & IU_5 \end{bmatrix}$$

$$= \begin{bmatrix} OU_1 M_1(IU_2) & \cdot & IU_4 & \\ & OU_1 M_1(IU_3) & \cdot 1 & \\ & & OU_1 M_2(IU_7) \cdot & \begin{bmatrix} IU_6 \\ IU_9 \end{bmatrix} \\ & & & OU_1 M_1(IU_5) \cdot (IU_8) \end{bmatrix}$$

$$= \begin{bmatrix} OU_1 & OU_2 & M_1(IU_4) \cdot 1 & \\ OU_1 & OU_3 & & \\ OU_1 & OU_7 & OU_1 M_1 (IU_6) \cdot IU_8 & \\ OU_1 & OU_7 & OU_1 M_1 (IU_9) \cdot {}^8 1 & \\ OU_1 & OU_5 & M_1 (IU_8) \cdot 1 & \end{bmatrix}$$

$$= \begin{bmatrix} OU_1 & OU_2 & OU_4 & \\ OU_1 & OU_3 & & \\ OU_1 & OU_7 & OU_6 & OU_1 M_1 (IU_8) \cdot 1 \\ OU_1 & OU_7 & OU_9 & \\ OU_1 & OU_5 & OU_8 & \end{bmatrix}$$

$$= \begin{bmatrix} OU_1 & OU_2 & OU_4 & \\ OU_1 & OU_3 & & \\ OU_1 & OU_7 & OU_6 & OU_8 \\ OU_1 & OU_7 & OU_9 & \\ OU_1 & OU_5 & OU_8 & \end{bmatrix}$$

$$= \begin{bmatrix} OU_1 & & & \\ & OU_1 & & \\ & & OU_1 & \\ & & & OU_1 \\ & & & & OU_1 \end{bmatrix} \begin{bmatrix} OU_2 & OU_4 & \\ OU_3 & & \\ OU_7 & OU_6 & OU_9 \\ & OU_5 & \end{bmatrix} \begin{bmatrix} 1 & & & \\ & 1 & & \\ & & OU_8 & \\ & & 1 & \\ & & & OU_8 \end{bmatrix}$$

Note that this formula defines each access path, and also provides the realisation sequence for multi-dependent information units in terms of post-matrix multiplication. In general, if the access point is via information unit IU_j which has "n" directly coupled IU´s and "m" indirect multi-dependent IU´s (for example, in figure 12 access to IU_8 is multi-dependent in that is depends on valves set by IU_5 and IU_6,) then the general access formula, for an information unit IU , is,

$$.IU_j = \underset{(k >= n)}{M_k} (IU_j) \quad \prod_{i=1}^{m+1} \quad M_i \text{ (Ustring)}$$

where

$$\text{Ustring} = \prod_{p = a_p}^{p = b_p} OU_p$$

and a_p and b_p refer to the start and end OU_p in the IU access path, unless Ustring refers to a multi-dependent information unit. In the latter case,

$$\text{Ustring} = 1 \text{ or } OU_i$$

This formula represents general coupling strategies which are in fact a subset of all the possible couplings between IU´s. For one IU,

     - no couplings exist (terminal)
       or
     - IU may be connected to itself (involuted links)

we can represent this as a potential set of couplings

$$1 + C(IU)$$

similarly,

for two IU´s   -   no couplings exist
$(IU_1$ and $IU_2)$ - IU_1 is connected to itself
             -   IU_2 is connected to itself
             -   IU_1 is connected to IU_2

this gives possible couplings

$$1 + C(IU_1) + C(IU_2) + C(IU_1) \, C(IU_2)$$

$$= (1 + C(IU_1)) \quad (1 + C(IU_2))$$

Note that $C(IU_i) \, C(IU_j)$ is interpreted as meaning that the information units IU_i and IU_j have common data attributes.

By induction, assuming that the possible couplings are

$$\prod_{i=1}^{n} (1 + C(IU_i))$$

for n IU´s, then for (n+1) IU´s, the (n+1)the IU may not be coupled to any of the other n IU´s, or, it may be coupled to all the other n IU´s (or any intermediate state). This yields the possible couplings,

$$\prod_{i=1}^{n+1} (1 + C(IU_i))$$

2.3.1   INFORMATION UNIT GROUPS

Consider an attribute cursor which is allowed to point to any attribute A. Any other attribute B is said to be realisable from A if a PADD can be constructed such that the attribute cursor can move from the IY containing A to the IU containing B using loosely coupled relationships. More formally, for attribute $A_i (i=1.....n)$ with attribute cursor $C(A_i)$ then attribute B is said to be realisable if

$$\exists \, T : \quad \prod_{k=i}^{N} T_k \, [\, C(A_k) \,] \implies C(A_j)$$

where
$$T_N \, [\, C(A_N) \,] \quad = \quad C(B)$$

and
$$\implies \text{ denotes "leads to".}$$

and the transformation T moves the cursor between attributes, if they belong to the same IU, or, between IU´s using loosely coupled relationships. In effect, the attribute cursor ranges over both attribute relationships and association relationships.

If we define a set of IU´s such that all attributes within that set of IU´s is realisable then that set of IU´s is called an Information Unit Group (IUG). Furthermore, the major data attributes of those data attributes which identify IU occurrences for each IU within such an IUG are said to represent the natural access points for the IUG. Any other attributes within the IUG represent the unnatural, or unpredicted, access points. These concepts are illustrated in the IUG access diagram in figure 13 (see figure 7 for the corresponding IU definitions). The arrowheads on the loosley coupled relationships in figure 13 represent the direction which gives immediate access either to a specific IU occurrence, or, to the start of a set of relevent IU occurrences.

52

IUG : Customer Orders

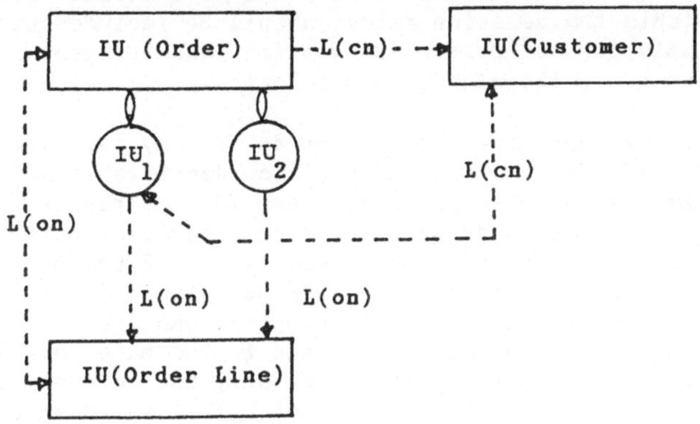
IU (Order)
-L(cn)-
IU(Customer)
IU_1
IU_2
L(cn)
L(on)
L(on)
L(on)
IU(Order Line)

Natural Access Points :-
order number, customer number, order date

Attributes :-

order number	(on)
order date	
customer number	(cn)
stock code	
quantity ordered	
customer name	
customer address	

IU_1 = IU_1 (Customer Orders)

V (customer number
order number)

IU_2 = IU_2 (Date of Orders)

V (order date
order number)

and we observe that

Set (Attributes) = Set (Natural Access Points)

+ Set (Unnatural Access Points)

Figure 13 Information Unit Group (IUG) access diagram

An IUG is a logical grouping of IU's and hence an IU may participate in more than one IUG. The role of IU's within an IUG is critically important and depends on the actions to be performed by the IUG (for example, enquiry, update and deletion). For enquiry, closely coupled IU relationships may be broken across IUG boundaries. For update, closely coupled relationships <u>cannot</u> be broken across IUG boundaries if strong consistency is required. For deletion, problems arise with cascaded IU deletions, in that loosely coupled relationships become important. Typically when orders relate to order lines, which in turn relate to movements of stock against each order line, decisions must be made about the role of the operation of deletion so that finite life histories can be achieved and suitable audit logs generated. Thus the deletion integrity between coupled IU's might be identified as either not specified or integrity rule based. The former places responsibility for consistent deletions within the remit of the applications tasks. Rule based deletion integrity implies that all IU's referred to directly or indirectly within the deletion rules, should be included within the IUG(s) available for use by the application task charged with the responsibility for performing such a deletion.

From a semantic perspective the role of an IUG may parody the concept of entity classes [HAMM81]. Here, a specific identifiable IUG may have associated membership rules for individual IU occurrences. For example, in figure 13, IU (Order) may be limited to future, or call-off, orders if the order date specified is for a future date. If two or more IU's exist with identical data attribute structures but with different semantics, for example, the IU's might refer to supplies who might supply parts, currently supply parts, or, at some stage in the past have supplied parts, then for a given application task only the relevent IU's are included within an IUG. Note the role of $M(IU_i)$ in these circumstances, where appropriate semantic rules are included as part of the transformation.

2.3.2   IUG Binding

Conceptually an IUG may be linked to other IUG's to provide the logical flow and sequencing of data storage and retrieved as it relates to a specific applications task. (see figure 14)

Here, IUG_1 is triggered by the presentation of a value at an access point. Thereafter other IUG's are initiated as appropriate by the transfer of data values into access points (normally, natural access points). An IUG chain, such as shown in figure 14, represents both a localisation of potentially parallel tasks, within an IUG, and a sequentialisation of discrete data handling stages. For instance a specific access might relate to more than one IU. The task of detecting the first IU occurrence within each of the IU's which occurs with the value of the specified access point, is a task that could be performed in parallel. Similarly an IUG could define access point values for subsequent IUG's in the IUG chain. In addition the scope of the data handling activity should be well defined so that only IU occurrences which satisfy the defined criteria for the IUG, will be accepted. Within an applications task IUG's may be used iteratively.

In the DB4GL architecture a <u>data access schema</u> comprises a formal statement of the set of specifications, that define an IUG. Hence each IUG is represented by a different data access schema. An IU is defined through an <u>information unit description schema</u>. Again, the latter comprises a formal statement of the specifications that appertain to a specific IU [BEER86], [SELI79].

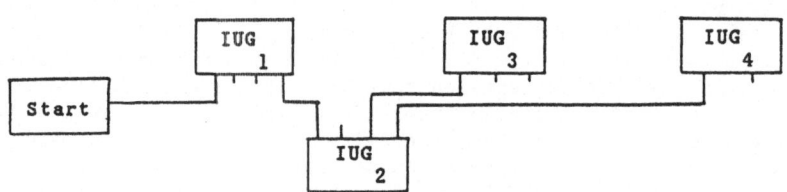

Figure 14 Linking IUGs

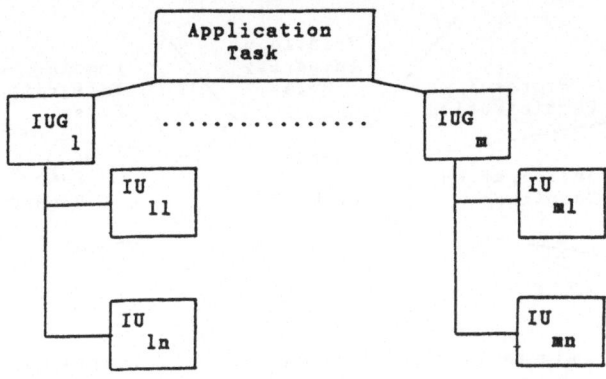

Figure 15 Sumary of extended E-R model (EE-R)

2.4   Summary of the Data Base Model

The model described hitherto possesses the following features

-    the E-R model is extended to include view relations giving the
     extended entity-relationship model (EE-R)

-    an information unit is the generic term applied to the definition of
     a grouping of data attributes which effectively represent one of the
     six relations in the EE-R model

-    an information unit group contains several information units

-    the membership of IU´s in IUG´s raises issued concerning

     - realisability

     - deletion rules.

The structural aspects of the data architecture suggested is summarised
in diagrammatic form in figure 15.
Finally, the database model outlined above does not preclude the
identification and handling of data attributes on an individual basis.
In fact this mechanism is one of the key features of a process model for
DB4GL.

3   A PROCESS MODEL

A single data attribute can play many roles within an applications task,
such as,

-    a data base object
-    the subject of a domain integrity rule
-    part of a predicate in a relational integrity rule
-    a data parameter in an algorithmic manipulation.

This rich multi-dimensional perspective of a data attribute means that it
may be thought of as a multi-faceted object where each facet (F_i) relates
to an n_i-dimensional definition space (see figure 16).

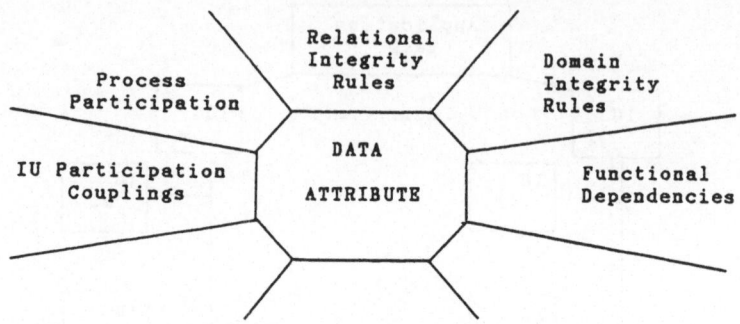

Figure 16 Multi-faceted nature of attributes

Traditionally the request by an applications task to use a specific attribute simplifies this by making assumptions about the context of the request for that attribute. The alternative approach based on the multi-dimensional view of data attributes represents a bottom up approach in which all aspects involving the use of that data attribute are specified. This results in

- generic rules for data attributes and associated IU's

- application task related specifications for data attributes.

In terms this means that another view of the data attribute might be in the terms of specification space (see figure 16) and realisation space, where the traditional task of application program writing is equivalent to the projection of defined IUG specifications into a logical realisation space [WIED86].

3.1 A Data Base Architecture

In section 2.4 we described the features of an architecture which related primarily to a data access and data structuring. In specification space the subspace for functional dependancies, IU participation and couplings relate directly to the existence of access paths, whereas the integrity rules qualify data access and availability as well as providing limited data manipulation, for example, through complex domain integrity rules [DENO86], [EARL85], [MARK86], [MAIE84]. This still does not encompass,

- user presentation objects, screen, report and histogram formats

- more complex processes

and their incorporation into an overall architecture.

User presentation objects raise two immediate issues. Firstly there is the comparatively straightforward task of defining a presentation format and sequence in which data attributes are to be handled. Secondly, for each data attribute involved in the presentation we must specify at the relevant point in the presentation sequence the pre-conditions and post-conditions to which that particular data attribute is subjected. Such a data attribute might be a database object in that it belongs to a database IU, or not. The latter class of objects arise as temporary attributes which exist for the lifetime of the presentation object or the applications task. Such objects might be thought of as belonging to a local IUG which contains IU's which define the current state of an executing presentation objects. These IU's are only known to a particular presentation object and do not belong to the general database. Architecturally, then, there are at least three levels of data. These are,

- the specification data (structured rule based - intension)

- the data base (IU occurrences - extension)

- the local data (the process data states).

A presentation object reflects these different levels of data by identifying

- presentation format and sequencing

- relevant integrity rules which are application specific

- the appropriate database IUG

- the data attributes for the local IUG.

Complex processes may be generic in nature, for example, checking data formats, or application task specific, for example, calculating a bonus contribution to payroll. In both cases these tasks may be represented by suitable routines which are invoked at the appropriate time.

In general, an application task may involve the use of more than one presentation object, and, for complex application requirements,

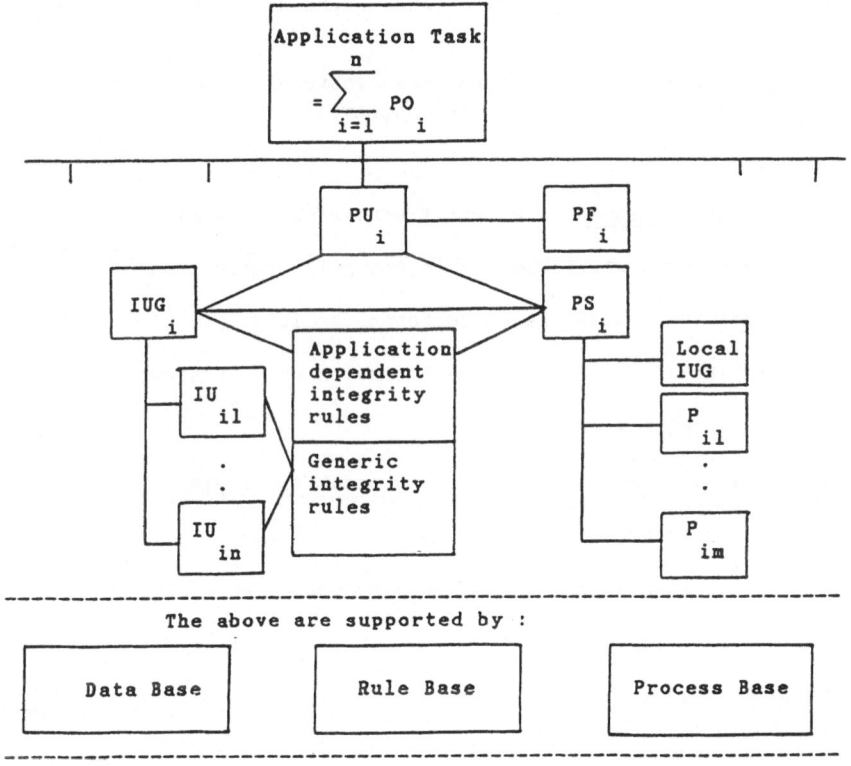

Figure 17 Data Base Architecture

presentation objects may be defined which do not involve user output, for example, intermediate batch file creation. Figure 17 illustrates these concepts.

In figure 17 note that:-

- an applications task may involve several presentation objects PO_i

- one presentation object comprises a presentation unit PU_i which identifies

    - sequencing

    - user actions

    - error handling

  and invokes

    - the presentation format (PF_i)

    - the data access schema (IUG_i)

    - the process schema (PS_i)

- application dependent integrity rules are available to the data access schema, to grant or deny access, and to the process schema

- generic integrity rules are incorporated into appropriate information unit description schemas

- complex processes (P_{ij}) are defined which are invoked by the process schema

- semantic rules relating to the membership of IU's within an IUG are specified within the data access schema.

In summary,

The IU description schema is a formal statement specifying

- individual data attribute domain integrity rules

- the operations which can be performed on IU's

- the operations which can be performed on data attributes

- generic integrity rules.

The data access schema is a formal statement specifying

- the set of relevant IU's

- the IU coupling structures and consequential actions

- relational integrity rules

- semantic rules.

The Presentation Unit is a formal statement specifying

- a data access schema

- a process schema

- a presentation format

- sequencing and flow of control

- error messages

- access points.

The Process Schema is a formal statement specifying

- the actions to be carried out for the creation, modification and enquiry on specific data-attributes

- application dependent integrity rules

- associated processes and invocation rules

- the local information unit group.

The above system components are supported in terms of their specification by

- the process rule base which contains the specifications of all the generic and application dependent rules

- the process base, which comprises the set of executable process which perform

    - generic functions (e.g. encryption)
    - application specific functions (e.g. payroll calculation)
    - rule dependent functions (e.g. summation and averaging).

At execution time the application uses the above if it is fully interpretive, and also the actual data values defined within the database.

3.2 Communication Within Presentation Objects

The apparent complexity of the presentation object structure can only be sustained if the communication architecture does not introduce undue difficulty. In fact the use of the "one-data-attribute-at-a-time" philosophy means that a Basic Communication Unit (BCU) can be defined. The data attributes of a BCU are

- Source indentification
- Destination identification
- IU/Rule identification
- IU data attribute identification
- Type of action
- Operation identification
- Direction of the BCU request
- Value
- Status Code.

More fully,

- <u>Source and destination identification</u> simply identify the components within a presentation object between which the BCU is passed.

- <u>IU/Rule identification</u> defines the specific information unit, or rule, depending on the context of the request.

- <u>IU data attribute identification</u> determines the specific data attribute within an IU which is of interest.

- <u>Type of action</u> identifiers whether an IU operation is required or a simple attribute read or store operation is required, or a rule is required.

- <u>Operating identification</u> species the IU operations which can take place, defined over a set of primitives such as read, store, delete lock and clear IU occurrences.

- <u>Direction of the BCU request</u> applies to the simple attribute actions and therefore, affects

- <u>Value</u>, which may be set before the BCU is transmitted (for output), or, obtained when the BCU is received (for input)

- <u>Status Code</u> indicates the success or otherwise of the BCU request.

This approach allows individual data attributes to be manipulated. However, the individuality of a data attribute is maintained within the specification, the rule base and process base, but not in the actual storage of the data. The importance of the individual data attribute was recognised in DIAM II [SENK76] but the implementation concentrated on the definition of a suitable storage strategy and access language aspects.

3.3 Data Access Schema Realisation

Because the specification rules for an IU define the set of data attributes which identify IU occurrences, the storage of such a data attribute will be handled and noted by the data access schema. Moreover the storage of a data attribute which also exists as a component of another IU identifier, for an IU within the IUG, should result in all instances of that data attribute being similarly updated. If all the identifier components are specified without any interviewing request for a realisation, then this could be done on the basis of, "get the next IU occurrence with identifier components which match those supplied". A successful realisation may then produce new values to enable coupled IU's to be realised. The realisation of an IU occurrence should result in the realisation of associated occurrences for all inferior IU's in a PADD. This arises from the coupling rules using the strategy outlined in section 2.3. If for a given access point for an IUG, all the values are specified for the identifiers of all IU's then the IUG access point is <u>well defined</u>. If an IU exists which does not have values specified for all of its identifier components, then that IU must be scanned such that the first IU occurrence (OU(V)) which conforms with the values of the data attributes specified is actually selected. Such an IU forms a bridge point in the access pattern for DB4GL insofar as all dependent IU's are accessed and then the next match for OU(V) is sought and all dependent IU values detected and so on. Logically this approach normally has consequences in terms of user presentation, and so to that extent it may be more appropriate to redefine the original IUG as two, or more, IUG's. Expressed another way it is often more appropriate to use IUG's

with well defined IUG access points. A well defined IUG access point
effectively represents a point of access to a logical dataset which, in
terms if the application PADD,

-    does not contain repeating groups of data

-    spans one or more IU´s.

This approach allows intelligent data access schemas to be constructed.
The ability to have the correct IU instances available at the correct
time for use by the process schema is a fundamental design feature of
DB4GL.

4   THE DB4GL ARCHITECTURE

The conceptual view of the DB4GL architecture is shown in figure 17. In
practice this means that system specification involves

-    specifying all data attributes in terms of their functional
     dependencies and formats

-    running normalisation software to produce basic IU groupings

-    specifying generic integrity rules

-    specifying generic processes

-    specifying application specific Presentation Objects

-    for each Presentation Object specifying

     - presentation units and data sequencing

     - IU´s and IUG couplings

     - application dependent integrity rules

     - application dependent processes

-    generating the components for all PO´s that make up the application
     task.

Typically one PO may relate to the definition of basic order data.

Figure 18 illustrates a simple screen layout for this PO, where (*)
represents the base co-ordinance for this presentation unit (PO$_1$) on the
screen. This can be varied by the applications task, dynamically, if

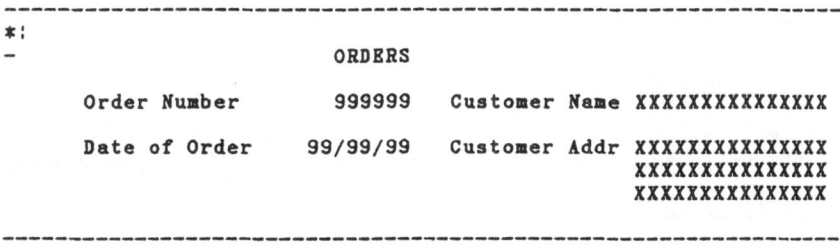

```
       ---------------------------------------------------------------
       *¦
       ⁻                          ORDERS

           Order Number           999999    Customer Name XXXXXXXXXXXXXX

           Date of Order          99/99/99   Customer Addr XXXXXXXXXXXXXX
                                                           XXXXXXXXXXXXXX
                                                           XXXXXXXXXXXXXX

       ---------------------------------------------------------------
```

Figure 18 Screen layout for orders PO

necessary. The data access schema comprises IU(Order) and IU(Customer) with L(customer account code).

Another PO may be defined to describe order lines.
In this case the IUG covers IU (Order Line), IU(Stock) with L(stock code). In figure 19 <u>order number</u> is shown in quotes. The purpose of this is to define order number as an implicit access point to this PO (PO_2). Consequently, order number must be defined by a previous PO before this PO is invoked. Stock code is an explicit access point. There is no need to specify order number as this is checked in the access points for PO_2 which are then checked against the data attributes provided by PO_1.

```
--------------------------------------------------------------------
*:"order number"
 -
      Stock      Stock               Quantity              Total
      Code       Description         Ordered               Price
      XXXXXXX    XXXXXXXXXXXXXXX       999999              9999.99

--------------------------------------------------------------------
```

Figure 19 PO for order lines

The applications task (AT) is definable in terms of these presentation objects as

$$AT = PO_1 (x,y,z,a) = (PO_2(x,y,z,a))$$

x - refers to the start column

y - refers to the start row

z - refers to the number of data occurrences (i.e. repititions of the data component of the PO) before a break, on the presentation media

a - specifies the access point.

This approach impacts on the design of application tasks. Typical examples of hierarchical application tasks are shown in figure 20.

1) $AT_1 = P_1 + (P_2)$

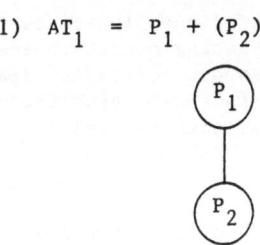

2) $AT_2 = P_1 + (P_2 + (P_3))$

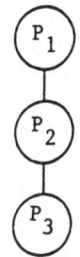

3) $AT_3 = P_1 + (P_2 + P_3)$

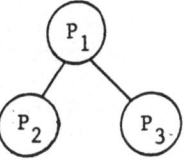

4) $AT_4 = P_1 + (P_2 + (P_3 + (P_4)))$

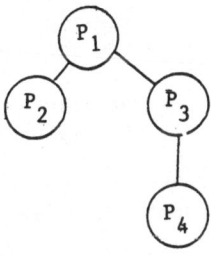

Figure 20 Hierarchical application tasks

In these examples the superior presentation object must provide its
inferior presentation objects with values for the implicit access points
specified by the inferior presentation objects.

4.1 Application Task Implementation

Several application tasks have been specified and developed using a
rudimentary version of DB4GL. Our experience to date indicates that a
more robust product is obtained with less effort on the part of the
applications developer [BLAC86], [BROIY81]. Other benefits include

automatic documentation. In fact our experience indicates that such
documentation is critical when program testing occurs to ensure that the
current specifications are correct and do not contradict specifications
for other application tasks. Finally, the DB4GL architecture does not
preclude the development of ad-hoc query language facilities [LONG78].

5   SUMMARY

The results obtained hitherto indicate that it is possible to integrate
successfully the three levels of data description, for the meta data
base, for the database and for the application specific database within a
generalised data base architecture. This was achieved through a close
examination of the properties of data and the definition and linking
together of presentation objects to parody conventional applications
programming techniques. As a viable applications development vehicle,
then certainly DB4GL does not provide all the answers [RIGS86], [OSBO86].
However the architecture upon which DB4GL is based appears to offer
stimulating avenues for future research investigation in that it offers
an integrative mechanism for combining both data and process description
within the overall application task definition activity.

6   ACKNOWLEDGEMENTS

The author wishes to thank Sheffield City Polytechnic for the support
received during the course of this research, and to B. Hird for his
invaluable comments.

7   REFERENCES

[ANSI80]   "Database language SQL" Draft International Standard
           ISO/DIS9075 available from British Standards Institution.

[BATO85]   Batory D.S. "Modelling the Storage Architecture of Commercial
           Database Systems" ACM TODS Vol 10 (1985) pp 463-528.

[BEER86]   Beeri C. and Kifer M. "An Integrated Approach to Logical Design
           of Relational Database Schemas" ACM TODS Vol II NO 2 (June
           1986).

[BERN76]   Bernstein P.A. "Synthesising Third Normal Form Relations from
           functional Dependencies" ACM TOPS Vol 1 No 1 (1976).

[BLAC86]   Blacklock P. "Standards for programming practices" Data
           Processing Vol 28 No 10 (Dec 1986).

[BROY81]   Broy M. and Pepper P "Program Development as a Formal Activity"
           IEEE Transactions on software (Jan 1981).

[CHAM76]   Chamberlain D.D. et al "Sequel 2: A Unified Approach to Data
           Definition, Manipulation and Control" IBM Journal Research and
           Development Vol 20 No 6 (1976).

[CHEN76]   Chen P.P. "The Entity-Relationship Model - Toward a Unified
           View of Data" ACM TODS Vol 1 No 1 (1976).

[CHEN80]   Chen P.P. (ed.) "The Entity-Relationship approach to Systems
           Analysis and Design" North Holland (1980).

[CHEN83]   Chen P.P. (ed.) "The Entity-Relationship approach to
           Information Modelling and analysis" North Holland (1983).

[CODD70] Codd E.F. "A Relational Model of Data for Large Shared Data Banks" Communications of the ACM Vol 13 No 6 (June 1970).

[CODD79] Codd E.F. "Extending the database relational model to capture more meaning" ACM Transactions on database systems Vol 4 No 4 Dec (1979).

[CODD72] Codd E.F. "Relational Completeness of Data Base Sublanguages" Rustin R. (ed.) Data Base Systems Current Computing 6th Scientific Symposium Prentice-Hall Englewood Cliffs USA (1972).

[DATE84] Date C.J. "An Introduction to Database Systems - Volume II" Addison Wesley (1984).

[DENO86] Denoel E, Roelants D and Vauclair M. "Query translation for coupling PROLOG with a Relational data base management system" 3rd Esprit Conference (project 316) September (1986).

[EARL85] Earl A.N. and Whittington R.P. "Capturing the semantics of an IPSE database" Data Processing Vol 27 No 9 (Nov 1985).

[EWIN85a] Ewin N., Oxley R. and Poole F. "DB4GL :- A Fourth Generation System Prototyping Tool" Sheffield City Polytechnic Report Department of Building R/D/85/2 (1985).

[EWIN85b] Ewin N. "Advanced application software for speculative housing companies" M.Phil thesis (CNAA) Sheffield City Polytechnic, (July 1985),

[FAGI79] Fagin R. "Normal forms and relational database operators" Proc of the ACM SIGMOD (1979) ACM New York.

[HAMM81] Hammer M. and McCleod D. "Database Description with SDM: A Semantic Database Model" ACM TODS Vol 6 No 3 (1981).

[LONG78] Longstaff J., Poole F., Roper J. "The Design of an Alternative Natural Language for Querying a Relational Database" Proc of ACM ICMOD (1978) MILAN

[MAIE84] Maier D, Ullman J.D. and Moshe Y.V., "On the foundations of the Universal Relation Model" ACM TODS Vol 9 (1984) pp 283 - 308.

[MARK86] Mark L. and Roussopoulos N. "Metadata Management" IEEE Computer Vol 19 No 12 (Dec 1986).

[OSBO86] Osborn S.L. and Heaven T.E. "The Design of a Relational Database System with Abstract Data Types for Domains" ACM TODS Vol II No 3 (Sept 1986).

[RIGS86] Van Rigsbergen C.J. "A non-classical logic for information retrieval" The Computer Journal Vol 29 No 6 (1986).

[SELI79] Selinger P.G. et al "Access path selection in a relational database system" Proc ACM SIGMOD (1976) ACM New York pp 23-34.

[SENK76] Senko M.E. and Altman E.B. "DIAM II and levels of Abstraction, The Physical Device Level: A General Model for Access Methods" Systems for Large Data Bases North Holland Publishing Company (1976).

[SMIT85]   Smith H.C. "Database Design: Composing fully Normalised Tables
           from a Rigorous Dependancy Diagram" CACM Vol 28 No 8 (1985).

[WIED86]   Wiederhold G. "Views, Objects and Databases" IEEE Computer Vol
           19 No 12 (Dec 1986).

[WOOD86]   Wood M. (ed.) "Fourth Generation Systems" NCC Software
           Engineering Tools and Methods Issue 4 (Dec 1986).

[ZLOO77]   Zloof M.M. "Query-by-Example: A Database Language" IBM Systems
           Journal Vol 16 No 4 (1977).

SECTION TWO — WORK BENCH TOOLS

In the last few years, the computer-based tools which have become available to the systems analyst and programmer have increased dramatically in their sophistication. The programmer of the 1970s might reasonably expect to be supported by a program editor and perhaps some form of testing tool. In contrast the contemporary analyst and programmer has a range of word processors, diagramming tools, de-buggers, editors and a variety of other computer-based tools to assist in the development task.

This section includes papers which focus on the activities of analysts and programmers and how their functions can be assisted by the use of computer-based tools. The term for these tools is variously; Analyst's Workbench, Workbench tools, Analyst's Tool-kit, etc. All these terms conjure up the idea of an artisans workbench with the craftsman selecting from a variety of specialised tools to help in his task. This image is not far from that of the tool developers. However, some of the tools are very specific whereas others have a more general purpose.

The activities of the analyst and the programmer are varied. However, all systems have to go through a number of stages (if only briefly) before the system can be considered complete. The requirements of the users of the system have to be investigated, analysed and specified. The new system has to be designed in terms of desirable conceptual, logical and physical models. The physical system demands the writing of programs and the specification of files and database schemas. Ultimately the system has to be implemented and monitored and maintained so that it continues to meet the needs of users. Supporting these activities is the need for communication and documentation. It is also important to recognise that these tasks have to be completed with respect to both the static data and the dynamic processes of the system.

The papers in this section represent a variety of views and approaches tackling different aspects of the systems development task. They do not cover all the activities which will be undertaken in the course of developing a computer system, but they do indicate where assistance can be most profitably provided, or where it is lacking in current products. The paper by Parkin, Thornton and Holley is concerned with automating the fact gathering stage of systems analysis. The papers by Sharp and Avison and Chaudhuri are both concerned with specific design issues. Sharp concentrates on the logical design of functions whereas Avison and Chaudhuri are concerned with the logical and physical design of the database.

The next three papers are concerned with programming. Riha and Rzevski provide a detailed and wide-ranging review of how software design can be automated and the different approaches which have been made in the past. They then describe their own system, called LIST, which is a text-based editor providing consistency checking. This tool, they argue, assists greatly in the production of well-designed programs. The paper by Sutcliffe and his colleagues describes a diagram-based editor for generating COBOL code automatically from JSP (Jackson Structured Programming) diagrams. This tool, called MAJIC, is described in detail and illustrated in the paper. The third programming paper is by Pardoe and Wade who have extended the ideas of Knuth to offer a "Literate" programming support environment (LIPSE). They have used these ideas to produce a tool - SWRPAS - for producing Pascal code.

The final paper, by Susan Wright, describes an open-ended tool for producing documentation. It can be configured to suit a variety of environments and is part of a larger project - FORTUNE - which is described in two papers in section Four.

Programming is the area of systems design which has been awarded most attention over the past few years, and this can be seen in the quality of the products which are now available to help this task. Some programming tools are highly specific to a programming methodology and/or programming language (e.g. MAJIC uses the JSP notation). The other areas of system design are now being given more attention. The tool developed by Sharp is highly specific to the use of a methodology (based on data flow diagrams) and concentrates on a particular part of the process (moving from Data Flow Diagrams to Structure Charts). Avison and Chaudhuri's paper is more open ended. Although it requires the use of the Entity-Relationship model as input, it can produce physical database designs in a number of implementations.

The paper by Parkin is unusual in tackling the problems of automating the very early stages of analysis. The authors provide a review of the analyst's activities and the attempts which have been made to automate these tasks. They conclude by outlining the design and prototype of a "fact-finding" tool which takes interview details as input and produces documentation such as flowcharts as output.

CAN FACT-FINDING BE AUTOMATED?

A. Parkin, S.R. Thornton, and P.J. Holley

Leicester Polytechnic
Leicester LE1 9BH

ABSTRACT

Systems analyst activities are discussed. It is suggested that Data Gathering activities are time consuming and difficult activities which are important to successful development of commercial data processing systems. Little help in furthering these activities is given by existing automated tools. A software tool is proposed which could assist the analyst in interviewing, investigation and analysis of the existing system and investigation of new requirements.

1. SYSTEMS ANALYST ACTIVITIES

1.1 Difficulties in analysing analyst activities

Most analyses of analyst activities have been done with a view to assessing personnel training requirements, or personnel selection, but the same analyses could be useful for deciding the scope and nature of automated tools for system development. Unfortunately there are great methodological difficulties in investigating analyst activities.

Three approaches are apparent in computing literature:

(a) Introspection The author has himself been involved in systems analysis and uses his knowledge and insights to decide which behaviours should be the subject of training or automation.

(b) Experiment A problem is given to a sample of analysts under relatively controlled conditions, and their behaviour in solving the problem is recorded, e.g. through verbal protocols where the analyst tries to express his thoughts aloud.

(c) Survey A questionnaire is given to a sample of analysts who are asked to record their behaviour or beliefs.

The main objections to introspection are (a) the author may have unrepresentative experience, and (b) even if the author has representative experience he may be biased or defective in selective behaviours.

The main objections to experiment are (a) practical limitations seriously
curtail the scope and variety of the problems that can be set, with the
result that the behaviours recorded may not be representative, and (b)
"Think-aloud" protocols may change behaviour or fail to reveal important
facets of it.

The main objections to survey are (a) the recorded behaviours may
represent obsolescent practices which are not relevant to the system
development environment of the future, and (b) pre-classifications of
behaviour introduce the researcher's bias.

1.2   Introspections

Systems analysis text books at first sight seem to be a good source of
introspections since topics are presumably included by the authors on
account of their importance to the job. On the other hand, the balance
of a book may have to be modified by the author's knowledge or by the
suitability of the written word as a medium for explaining the topic.

Many authors focus on human communications skills as a very important
part of analyst abilities. Ware [WARE83] for example, having described
the analyst as "an interpreter of the business needs of the user" says
that the most obvious skills a systems analyst should possess are the
ability to read, write, speak and listen. Freeman [FREE 81], complaining
that too many analysts are incapable of producing the results needed,
says that the first reason for this is that the analyst cannot
communicate.

We think it pays to look more deeply at what is meant by communication
skills. It would be a mistake to interpret this as verbal fluency or
"the gift of the gab". For example, one person in our experience had an
extreme stutter which made communication in the ordinary sense very
difficult. Nevertheless, he was a highly valued analyst. We believe
"good communication" occurs between analyst and user when

(a)   the analyst has acquired knowledge which will be deemed by the users
       to be valuable to them, e.g. insights into deficiencies in the
       existing system, proposals for improvements, understanding of the
       operation of the new system; and

(b)   the analyst has an understanding of the user's environment and
       terminology which allows him to ask valuable questions and to
       explain his knowledge in a way which will be readily understood by
       the users.

We would characterise these as the strategic requirements for good
communication. The taught skills of technical writing, making
presentations and interview technique, and communications aids such as
diagramming techniques, are a tactical necessity.

1.3   Experiment

Vitalari and Dickson [VITA 83] and Vitalari [VITA 85] are the only
examples we can find of an experimental approach. Vitalari used
protocol analysis in a quasi-experimental setting to define the types of
knowledge used by 18 experienced systems analysts in solving an accounts
receivable problem. As a result of the experiment, Vitalari proposed
that the knowledge used by systems analysts is best grouped into 6
categories as follows.

1. Core system analysis domain knowledge. Components of systems analyst's knowledge necessary to achieve satisfactory levels of performance.

2. High-rated domain knowledge. Knowledge that distinguishes high-rated analysts from low-rated analysts.

3. Application domain knowledge. Knowledge related to particular information systems applications, such as decision support systems, office automation, transaction processing and end user computing.

4. Functional domain knowledge. Knowledge related to specific management disciplines, such as finance, accounting, production, marketing, public sector computing, information system management, and strategic planning.

5. Organisation specific knowledge. Knowledge specific to the organisation in which the analyst works.

6. Knowledge of methods and techniques. Knowledge related to specific analysis techniques, methodologies and approaches.

Items 1 and 2 above appear to us to overlap the other four, so perhaps these categories should be factored as in Figure 1 below.

Vitalari's work also suggests that the most frequently used knowledge items relate to the functional requirements of the system, the preplanned rules to guide manual or automated tasks, the types of reports the requirements for information and requirements for particular systems functions.

1.4 Surveys

Rosensteel [ROSE 81] conducted a survey for commercial purposes to ascertain the importance of various skills to the job of US systems analysts. The respondents included senior systems analysts, management and representatives of the user community.

The four highest ranked skills overall were writing, listening, speaking and interviewing. Rosensteel says "This proves conclusively that communications ability is perceived to be the most important attribute of the systems analyst. If you can't communicate, the rest is academic". The complete ranking of skills, grouped into general categories, was:

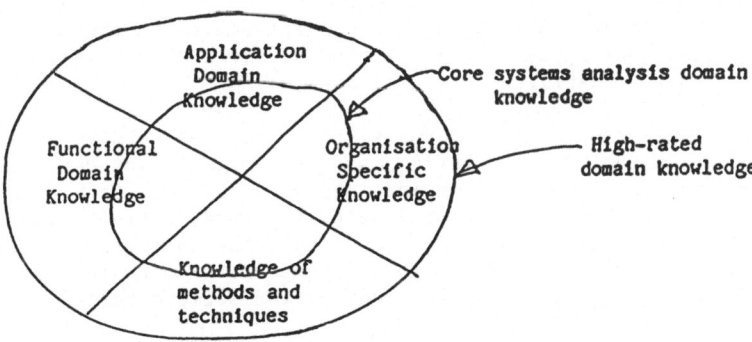

Figure 1 Domains of analyst knowledge

1 Communications
   2 Knowledge of the user area
3 Analysis
4 Project management
5 Systems design
6 Technical knowledge.

Systems analysts rated file/database design abilities more highly than did managers or users.

Crocker [CROC 84] surveyed 256 analysts in 52 UK organisations. Her survey included a requirement for factual information about the length of time spent on individual systems analysis tasks, and an opinion of the skills required to carry out those tasks.

The proportions of time spent by systems analysts for each stage of systems analysis in the period of the survey were as follows.

Feasibility Study	11.9%
Data Gathering	21.6%
Design of Non-computer Procedures	7.5%
Design of Computer System Procedures	18.2%
System Development	32.1%
Implementation	9.2%

System Development included detailed program specifications, user and operating manuals, system trials, implementation planning. Data Gathering included investigating and analysing the existing system, investigating and analysing new requirements, identifying computerised functions, outlining system specifications.

Analysts identified technical skills (file design, file organisation, file access, program suite design, program design, test data design and file creation) as most important to System Development. They identified communication skills (interviewing, fact recording, verbal communication, report writing) as most important to Data Gathering.

1.5 Conclusions on systems analyst activities

Automated tools for systems analysis are likely to be valuable if

(a) they accelerate tasks which otherwise consume a large amount of analyst time

(b) they offer technical assistance for skills important to the tasks, or reduce the likelihood of error when analysts lack important skills.

Even given the methodological caveats, there is overwhelming support for the proposition that Data Gathering is a very significant part of analyst activity, especially when taking into account that Data Gathering tasks also comprise the lion's share of Feasibility Study activities (Crocker, [CROC 84]). It should be stressed here that this conclusion is in the context of business data processing systems; Data Gathering may play a much smaller role in other systems such as real-time embedded systems.

Although it is popular opinion that communication skills are most vital to Data Gathering, we have argued that analyst knowledge is a crucial foundation for the excercise of good communications. This is consistent with Vitalari's verbal protocols, where analysts engaged in a predominantly Data Gathering task mainly mentioned organisation specific knowledge, and made much less allusion to specific communication techniques. The basis of our argument can also be seen in the following hypotheses:

> (a) an analyst who knows what he should find out is likely to get the important facts even if his communications skills are poor

> (b) an analyst who does not know what he should find out is likely to fail to get important facts even if his communication skills are good.

This argument is also consistent with the importance given by users and managers (more than systems analysts) to "knowledge of the user area" in Rosensteel's survey.

This is not to say that communication skills are not important. We see communication skills as having a symbiotic relationship with analyst knowledge such that both are vital to maintaining user confidence in the analyst and his proposals.

2   AUTOMATION OF FACT FINDING

2.1   Definition of fact finding

So far in this paper we have used the term Data Gathering which Crocker identified as a phase of system development. However, because we do not wish our discussion to be associated with any particular view of the development life cycle, we choose for the rest of the paper another term, fact-finding, which in the present context is free from such association.

We assume the main aim of fact finding is to determine the functional requirements of the proposed system. The functional requirements comprise

> (a) the content of any messages passing in the system, i.e. a list of the attributes they contain and their meanings

> (b) the format and medium of each message

> (c) if any attributes result from a computation, the rules for the computation; or if they are conditionally present, the predicate for including the attributes

> (d) the source and destination of each message, whether a human, a department, a process or the database

> (e) the trigger or circumstances which govern the production of the message

> (f) other requirements such as precision, response time etc.

In order to evaluate functional alternatives, the analyst needs to acquire other facts such as

(g)   the purpose and importance of each message

(h)   deficiencies in existing messages

(i)   cost/benefit and planning information or estimates
(j)   organisational policies, personalities and other
      environmental influences.

Investigation and analysis of the existing system is the principal way
in which analysts can aquire these facts. Knowledge of the existing
system is also important to effective communication with users and
management.

2.2   Present automated aids to fact-finding

In his survey of software requirements tools and techniques, Howden
[HOWD 82] mentions HIPO [STAY 76] SAMM [STEV 78] SREM [ALFO 77] PSL/PSA
[TEIC 77] and SADT [ROSS 77]. Automated tools exist for
drawing/redrawing the diagrams used in these techniques (and others),
for some internal consistency checking and to some extent for integrating
the requirements analysis with the data base definition and later
development activities. However, none of the tools give much assistance
to the fact finding process by which the requirements are determined.

The only automated tool related to fact finding we have found is the
Information System Model and Architecture Generator (ISMOD) described by
Hein [HEIN 85]. The main aim of ISMOD is to determine how processes
should be combined into subsystems by reference to the degree of
interaction between processes. To do this the isolation and interaction
of processes are assessed. Isolation of a process is defined as (No. of
data elements created by the process)/(No. of data elements used by the
process). A process with unit isolation therefore is completely
decoupled from other processes - it creates all its own data. As the
isolation measure decreases, so the process is more coupled to other
processes by exchange of data, and it becomes more likely that the
process should be computerised jointly with other processes as a
subsystem. Interaction is measured by the number of data elements passed
from one process to another. If the interaction is high, the two
processes would be considered for combining into a subsystem.

Each process is reviewed against every other process and the percentage
improvement in isolation that could be gained by combining the processes
is measured. The user can experiment with different threshold
improvements in isolation to see the possible subsystems that result;
but, says the author, the user should always be prepared to modify the
system conclusion in the light of human understanding of the processes
and data interaction.

In order to gather the data used as input to ISMOD, interview forms are
completed by interviewees for offline data entry and batch processing.
To a certain extent these forms are parameterised and can be specialised
by the analyst, but it appears that typically each interviewee supplies
information about

    the organisation unit in which he works,
    the processes he undertakes,
    the messages which are input and output to each process,
     the event that triggers the message, whether the message is
     considered satisfactory as regards availability, periodicity,
     delay, content, reliability.

2.3.1. General requirements

In this section we make suggestions for a prototype automated fact-finding tool which could form a basis for assessing the feasibility and usefulness of such tools.

In order to give a reasonably implementable target we propose, unlike ISMOD, that it be assumed that a subsystem for detailed investigation has been identified. We also propose to build minimum functionality into the tool, which can be extended later if experience so dictates.

We propose that the outputs of the tool in the first instance should be consistent with current results of the fact-finding activities of analysts. This would allow the tool to be integrated into existing manual practice or, possibly, to be integrated with other tools which seek to automate design methodologies.

Candidate outputs of the tool include:

1   Interview summaries to be checked by interviewees

2   System flowchart of the existing system which, together with specimens of documents etc used in the system, are an abstraction of items (a), (b) and (d) of section 2.1.

3   Draft entity-relationship model, which is an abstraction of item (a) of section 2.1.

4   Draft dataflow diagrams, which are an abstraction of item (a) of section 2.1 and of item (d) where the sources and destinations are processes, the database or sources/destinations outside the system.

5   Minispecs, which are abstractions of items (c) and (e) of section 2.1.

There are other outputs of factfinding, such as reports to management, proposals for new organisation structures, new methods of working or new technology which we presently consider unsuitable for automation, although human development of these may be assisted by the proposed automated outputs.

We imagine a machine-guided "interview" which elicits the data necessary for the outputs. Since there is knowledge in the list (a) to (j) of section 2.1 which is beyond the scope of the tool, the machine interview cannot supplant the analyst interview. Indeed, as long as the analyst is needed in the development process, it would be a mistake to over-automate fact finding since, as we showed in part 1, the analyst's organisation-specific knowledge is likely to be crucial to successful communication, and this knowledge is most likely obtained by his detailed involvement in the fact finding activity.

The machine could prompt for information and perform some consistency checking in real time. Possibly the analyst could take a portable computer with him to interviews; this may save time, may reduce the need for return visits to check out inconsistencies and loose ends, and may be helpful to inexperienced analysts. Alternatively, the analyst could use a conventional interview guide and enter the results of interview into the machine later.

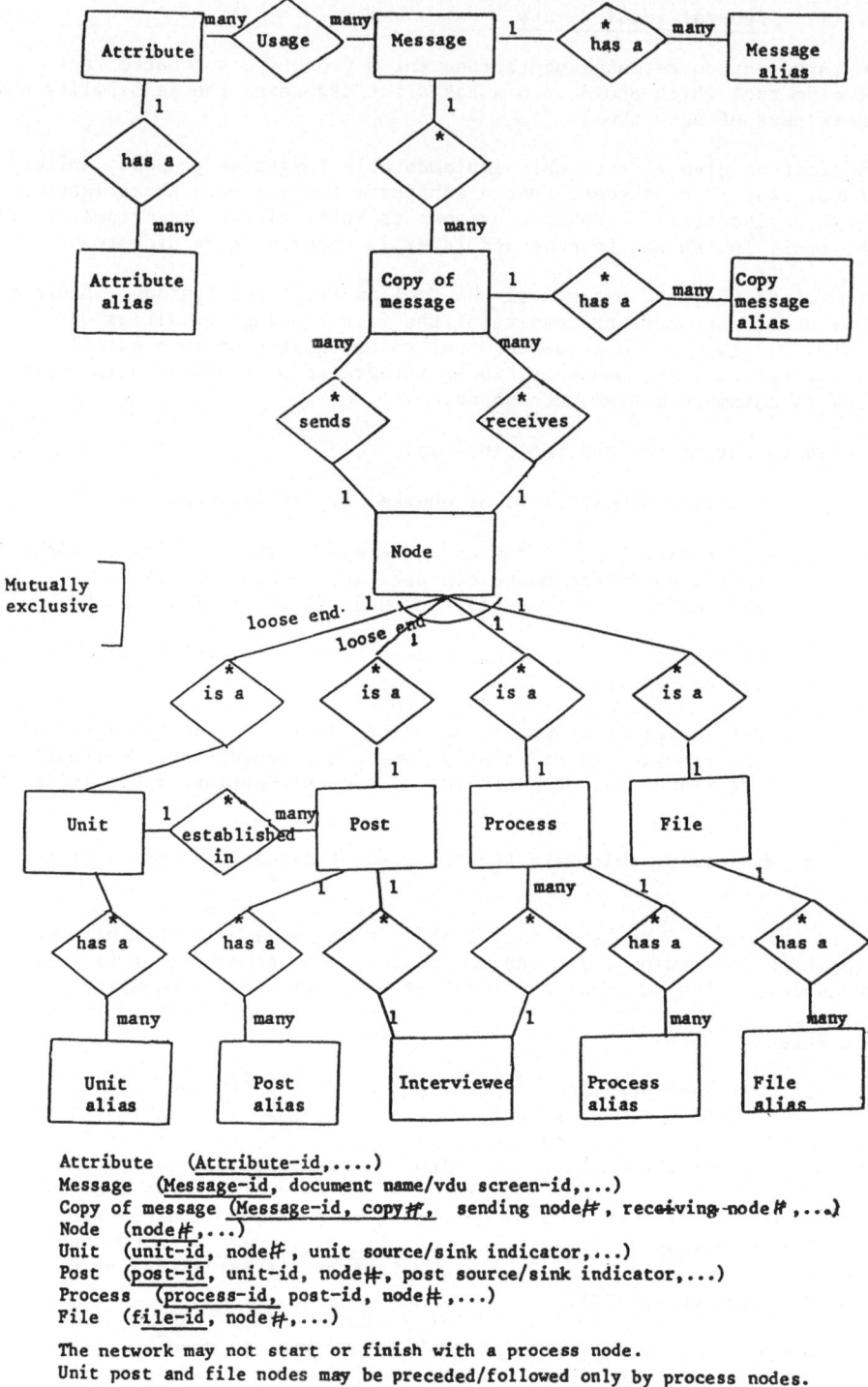

```
Attribute    (Attribute-id,....)
Message    (Message-id, document name/vdu screen-id,...)
Copy of message (Message-id, copy#,  sending node#, receiving node#,...)
Node   (node#,...)
Unit   (unit-id, node#, unit source/sink indicator,...)
Post   (post-id, unit-id, node#, post source/sink indicator,...)
Process  (process-id, post-id, node#,...)
File   (file-id, node#,...)
```

The network may not start or finish with a process node.
Unit post and file nodes may be preceded/followed only by process nodes.

FIGURE 2   Draft E.R Model of system flowcharts

2.3.2   Automated production of the existing system flowchart

We set ourselves the initial target of a tool which prompts for
information to produce an existing system flowchart, and an interview
summary pertaining to it. By an existing system flowchart, we mean a
data flow diagram which shows the existing system, including who does
what.

An existing system flowchart depicts a network of messages passing
between processes which are performed by a process functionary. The
process functionary is usually depicted either as an organisational unit
(e.g. department, section, plant, location) or as a human functionary
identified by titular position (e.g. sales manager, invoice clerk). When
a functionary initiates or terminates a message chain, the process
performed is not recorded; the functionary is considered a source or
sink of messages.

An interviewee represents a functionary. An aim of fact finding is to
discover, in respect of each material process performed by the
interviewee, who are the originators of data used in the process, and
who are the recipients of data produced by the process. Such
originating/receiving functionaries should also have a representative
selected for interview, unless they be sources or sinks in which case an
interview is optional. Any functionary which has not been the subject of
an interview and which is not a source or sink is a loose end in the
analysis.

For the purpose of this exercise a file or data store in the existing
system can also be considered a source or sink, since the file is not
performing any process.

Considering the nodes of the network as being the senders or recipients
of messages, and the arcs of the network as being the messages
connecting the nodes, Figure 2 shows a draft entity-relationship model of
system flowcharts. This assumes that when the same message (collection
of attributes) is sent down more than one arc of the network, then the
occurrence in each arc will be considered a separate copy of that
message.

Figure 2 also assumes that there is only one interviewee per post, i.e. if in fact several persons occupy the post and more than one is interviewed, their information will be treated cumulatively and any contradictions will be resolved viva voce before their information is recorded.

Figure 3 shows a small system flowchart and the tables that result.

2.3.3. Initial Implementation

We envisage implementing a prototype fact finding tool using a relational database. The functions provided will include:-

(a) data entry, query and update of the tables outlined in fig.2

(b) consistency checks at data entry and on request

(c) outputs

The consistency check at data entry will be designed to detect duplicates or aliases. The following consistency checks may be applied on request:-

(a) identification of loose ends i.e. messages with   origination of final destination that is not designated as a source or sink (as with row 1 of Post in figure 3 Node 10)

(b) identification of incomplete table entries

(c) matching of the messages/data items, entered as a result of interviews, to the data resulting from analysis of documents.

The outputs available will include:-

(a) reports on the tables

(b) cross referencing information

(c) a list of data items as the starting point for Entity-Relationship analysis

(d) the data to enable the system flowchart to be drawn

(e) a structured record of the entities relating to a specific interview. This will be returned to the interviewee for confirmation.

At this stage a formatted dialogue is planned using both form based and question/answer approaches.

2.4   CONCLUSION

We have shown that

(a) fact-finding is a worthwhile activity to automate and that there are hardly any tools which do so

(b) it may be feasible to automate the production of an existing system flowchart and corresponding interview summaries.

Obviously there is much research needed on the interface for conducting the interview and exhibiting the results. It may be that an existing system diagram conforming to a widely used standard cannot be produced; but we have shown that in principle it is possible to capture the information that is sufficient to produce such a diagram.

Other outputs can also be derived in principle from the existing system flowchart, i.e.

(a) an (existing system) data flow diagram, being a representation of the existing system flowchart without media/functionary information,

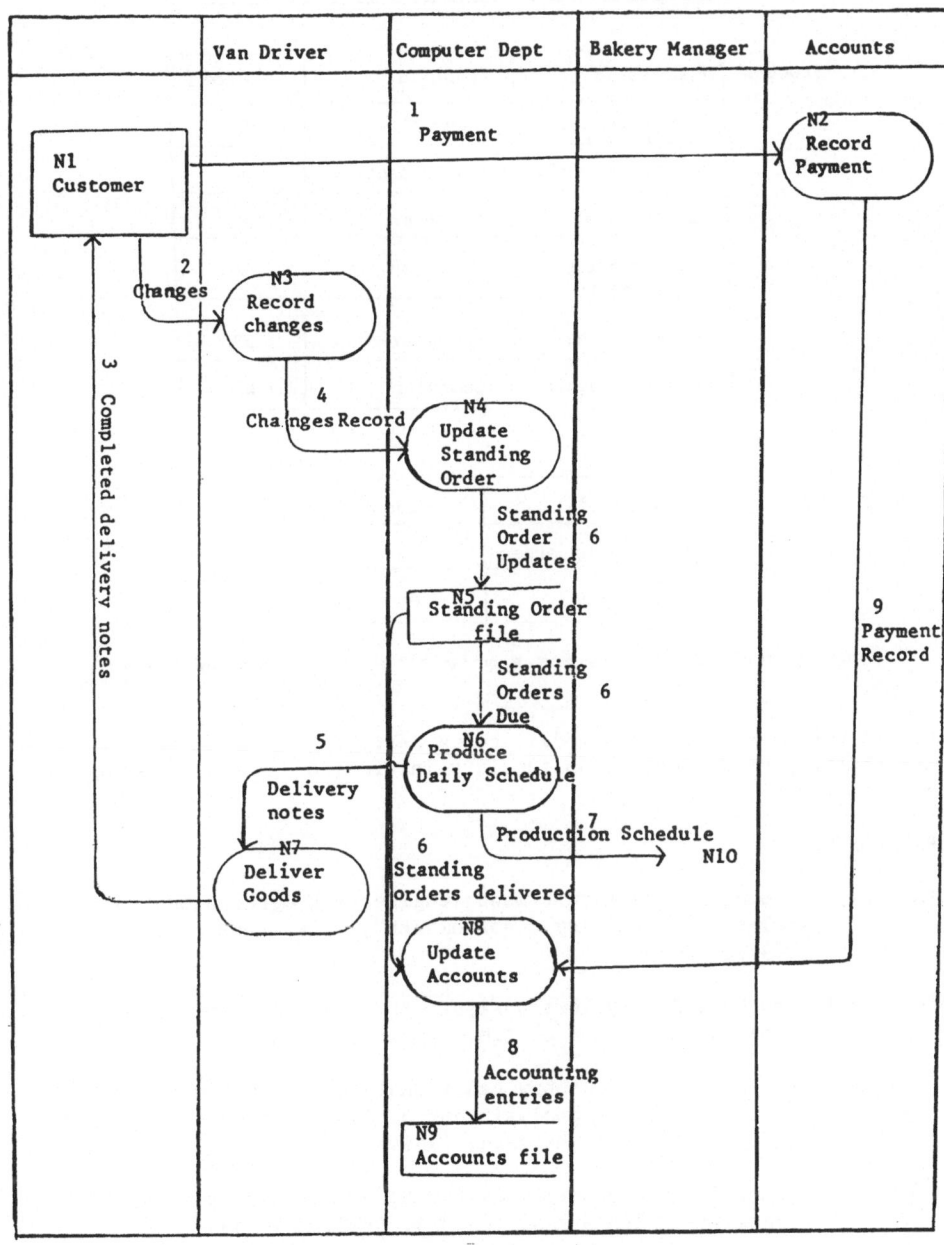

FIGURE 3(a)   Sample system flowchart

Post	Post-id	Unit-id	Node #	Source/Sink Indicator
	Bakery manager	Production	N10	off
	Van driver	Distribution	–	off
	Computer	Comp.dept	–	off
	Accountant#1	Accounts	–	off
	Customer	–	N1	on

Process	Process-id	Post-id	Node #
	Record-changes	Van driver	N3
	Record payments	Accountant # 1	N2
	Update s.o.	Computer	N4
	Produce daily statements	Computer	N6
	Deliver goods	Van driver	N7
	Update accounts	Computer	N8

File	File-id	Node #
	Standing order	N5
	Accounts	N9

FIGURE 3(b)   Relations for sample flowchart (continued overleaf)

(b) an entity-relationship model, being derived from existing system attributes plus degree and optionality information supplied by the analyst.

REFERENCES

[ALFO77]   Alford, M W "A requirements engineering methodology for real-time processing requirements", IEEE Trans Soft Eng, SE-3, 1,1977, 60-68.

[CROCK74] Crocker, P S Systems analysts-training and experience, National Computing Centre, Manchester, 1984.

[FREE81]   Freeman, P "Why Johnny can't analyze", In Cotterman, W et al, Systems analysis and design : a foundation for the 1980's, North Holland, 1981.

[HEIN85]   Hein, K P "Information System Model and Architecture Generator", IBM Sys J, 24, 3/4, 1985, 213-235.

Node

Node #
N1
N2
N3
N4
N5
N6
N7
N8
N9
N10

Message

Message-id	Document name
1	Payment
2	Changes
3	Completed delivery notes
4	Changes record
5	Delivery notes
6	Standing order updates
7	Production schedule
8	Accounting entries
9	Payment record

Copy of message

Message-id	Copy #	Sending node #	Receiving node #
1	1	N1	N2
2	1	N1	N3
3	1	N7	N1
4	1	N3	N4
5	1	N6	N7
6	1	N5	N6
6	2	N5	N8
6	3	N4	N5
7	1	N6	N10
8	1	N8	N9

Fig. 3(b) Relations for sample flowchart continued

REFERENCES

[HOWD82]   Howden, W E "Contemporary software development
             environments", Comm. A.C.M., 25, 5, May 1982, 318-329.

[ROSE81]   Rosensteel, G "Why systems analysis training fails",
             Computer World, Nov 1981.

[ROSS77]   Ross, D T and Schoman, K E "Structured analysis for
             requirements definition", IEEE Trans Soft Eng, SE-3,
             1,1977,6-15.

[TEIC77]   Teichrow, D & Hershey, E "PSL/PSA: a computer-aided
             technique for structured documentation and analysis
             of information processing systems", IEEE Trans Soft Eng
             SE-3, 1, 1977, 41-48.

[VITA83]   Vitalari, N P and Dickson, G W "Problem solving for
             effective systems analysis: an experimental exploration",
             Comm. A.C.M. 26, 11, Nov 1983, 948-56.

[VITA85]   Vitalari, N P "Knowledge as a basis for expertise in
             systems analysis: an empirical study", MIS Quarterly, Sept
             1985 pp 221-241.

[WARE83]   Ware, R "From technician to problem-solver : training
             the systems analyst", Data Management, March 1983,
             pp 20-21.

ACCELERATING THE ANALYSIS/DESIGN TRANSITION WITH THE

TRANSFORM ANALYSER

Helen Sharp

Department of Computer Science, University of London

London, U.K.

ABSTRACT

This paper reports on the development of an automated tool which performs
transform analysis as described in the structured design methodology of
Yourdon and Constantine. It takes as input a set of data flow diagrams
and produces an initial structure chart which can be used as a starting-
point in the design process. The tool's main features are described,
problems encountered in its development are presented, and examples of
its input and output are given. An account of intended future directions
is also included.

1   INTRODUCTION

Many automated tools have been developed for supporting the structured
analysis and structured design techniques of DeMarco [DEMA79] and Yourdon
and Constantine [YOUR79, ISDO, KARI84, TROY81, WILL81, WOOD85]. These
techniques are designed to interface effectively with each other, and to
minimise the risk of losing or distorting information gleaned during
analysis. It is surprising, therefore that the majority of such tools
concentrate either on the analysis stage, or on the design stage, and pay
little or no attention to their interface. When used manually, the
translation or data flow diagrams (DFDs) into structure charts (SCs) can
be performed using a technique known as Transform Analysis. This process
does not produce a polished final design, but merely provides an initial
SC quickly which can then be modified and improved. Unfortunately, for
anything but small systems the process can be quite tedious and time-
consuming if performed manually.

This paper reports on the development of a system which emerged from a
wider research activity aimed at investigating design automation and
support. This system is called the Transform Analyser (TA) and is
intended to shorten the analysis/design transition period by
automatically performing transform analysis on a given levelled set of
DFDs. If used in conjunction with a structured analysis tool and a
structured design tool, the resulting system would provide a very
powerful aid for developing software designs, allowing designers to
produce alternatives quickly and easily.

The next section provides a brief description of transform analysis and
this is followed by details of the TA system itself.

Transform analysis is a major strategy for converting a DFD into a SC. It is intended to produce an initial design which is very modular and well-factored, and although it can result in the generation of many modules which may later be combined, it provides a useful starting-point for the design process. Transform analysis consists of the following steps:

1.   re-state the problem as a DFD consisting of 10-20 process bubbles (Fig. 1a).

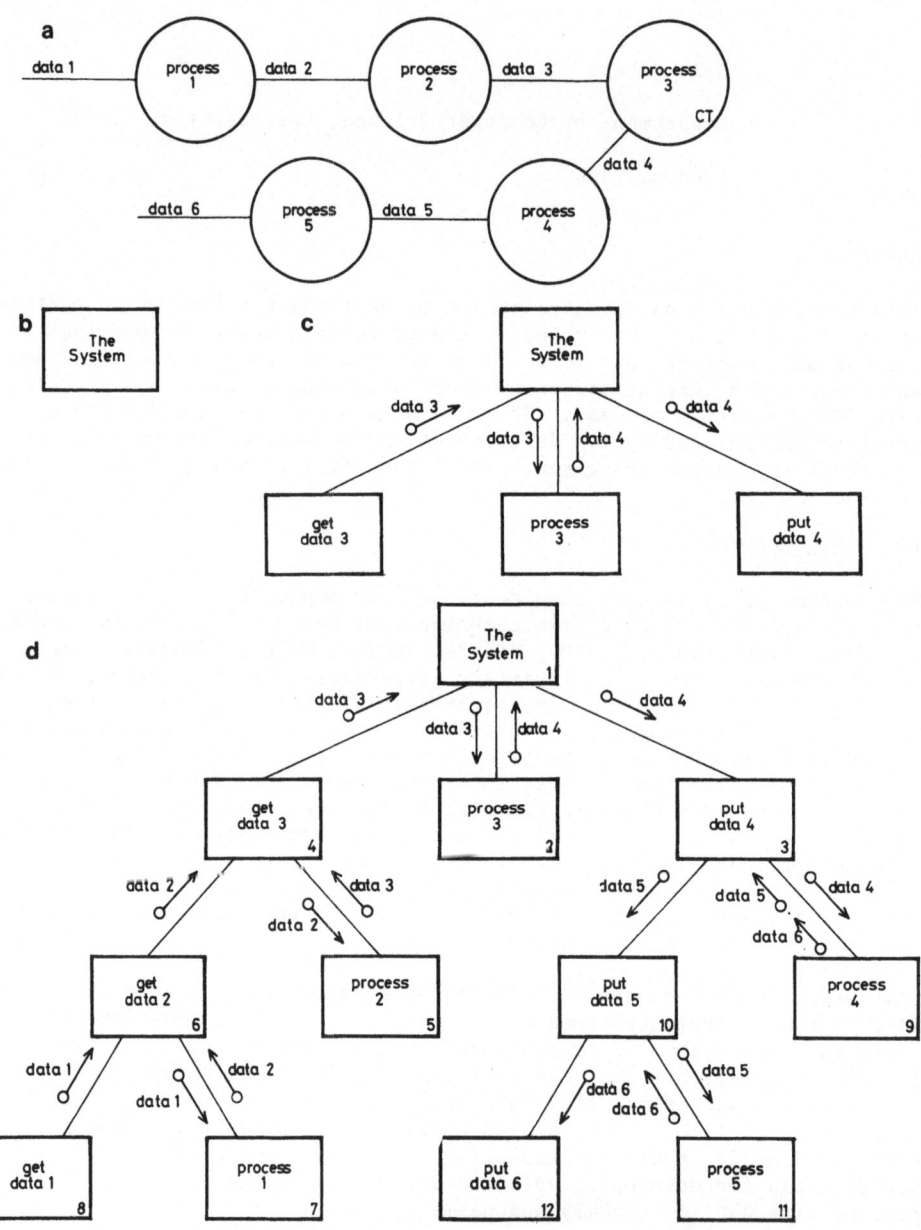

Figure 1 steps in Transform Analysis (TA)

2. identify the main processes or central transforms (CTs) of the system. This is achieved by studying the DFD and locating the main afferent (input) and efferent (output) data flow; those processes left in between the two branches are the central transforms.

3. define the top level module of the system, this is the one which will control the system's overall processing (Fig 1b).

4. define one module for each of the central transforms and each of the main data flows identified in step 2. These are to be situated immediately subordinate to the main module (Fig 1c).

5. factor all processes and data flows in the afferent and efferent branches of the system, until all elements in the DFD are represented in the SC. It does not matter which order the branches are factored in, as long as all children of a particular module have been defined before any of its grandchildren are (Fig 1d).

At the end of transform analysis, an initial SC will have been produced which contains all the information present in the DFD, but no more. Since this will be logical information only, much modification and refinement is required before the design can be considered complete.

In order to automate the above process, it was necessary to decide what the limitations of the system should be. The decisions made are discussed below.

3   DESIGN OF THE TRANSFORM ANALYSER

When considering the automation of transform analysis, the following points were immediately obvious:

1. as indicated above, the TA is intended to use output generated from structured analysis, i.e. a levelled set of DFDs, but it is recommended [PAGE80] that transform analysis should be applied to a fairly high level DFD consisting of 10-20 processes producing one SC for the whole system.

2. identifying CTs requires some knowledge and understanding of the application and if the TA was to perform this task, it would have to be made an intelligent system.

3. steps 3-5 mentioned above are automatable with little or no modification.

Consequently, the TA was designed to process a levelled set of DFDs, and to produce a levelled set of SCs. It assumes that any necessary CTs will be marked on the relevant DFDs, but it can also handle those with no CTs at all. The result of this is that all information captured in the analysis stage of development will be automatically transferred into a form suitable for the design phase, and because it is left to the designer to choose the CTs, it is easy to experiment with alternative initial designs.

4.   TA OUTPUT

The TA system outputs one SC for every DFD in the input set. Consequently, all the examples here show how the system handles the individual diagrams. In order to arrive at a complete system view. it would be necessary to combine all the corresponding diagrams and charts in the set.

Fig 1d shows the output produced when the simple DFD in Fig 1a is input. It is possible to trace the order of module production by looking at the module numbers; the main module is defined first, followed by the central transform modules, afferent/efferent data modules, and finally, elements of the afferent/efferent branches. Note that, as stipulated by the

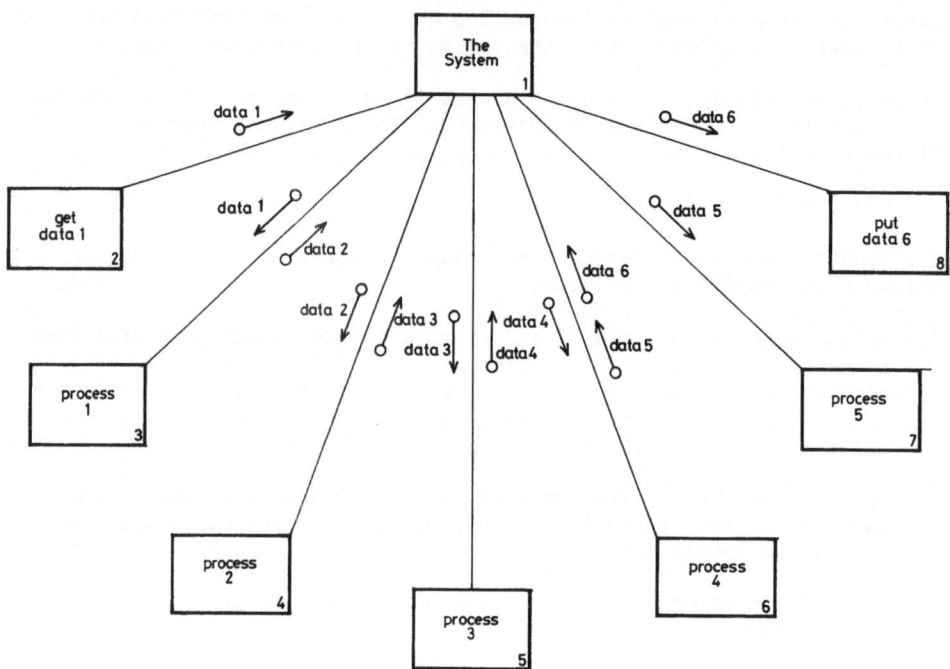

Figure 2   The chart produced if no CTs are marked on the DFD

transform analysis technique, all children of any one module are defined before any of its grandchildren are.

If no CTs were marked on the same DFD, the SC shown in Fig 2 would be generated instead.

5. PROBLEMS AND SOLUTIONS

It was found that the system worked well for simple diagrams like that
shown above, but there were occasions when following transform analysis
exactly resulted in the definition of multiple copies of one module
within a SC. To prevent unnecessary duplication and possible confusion,
the TA therefore had to be programmed to detect such duplications and
ensure that only one instance of the module was retained. If duplicate
definitions occur, the TA will delete all but one of them, and re-route
calls to that one remaining copy (Fig 3). Hence, modules are allowed to
have multiple parents.

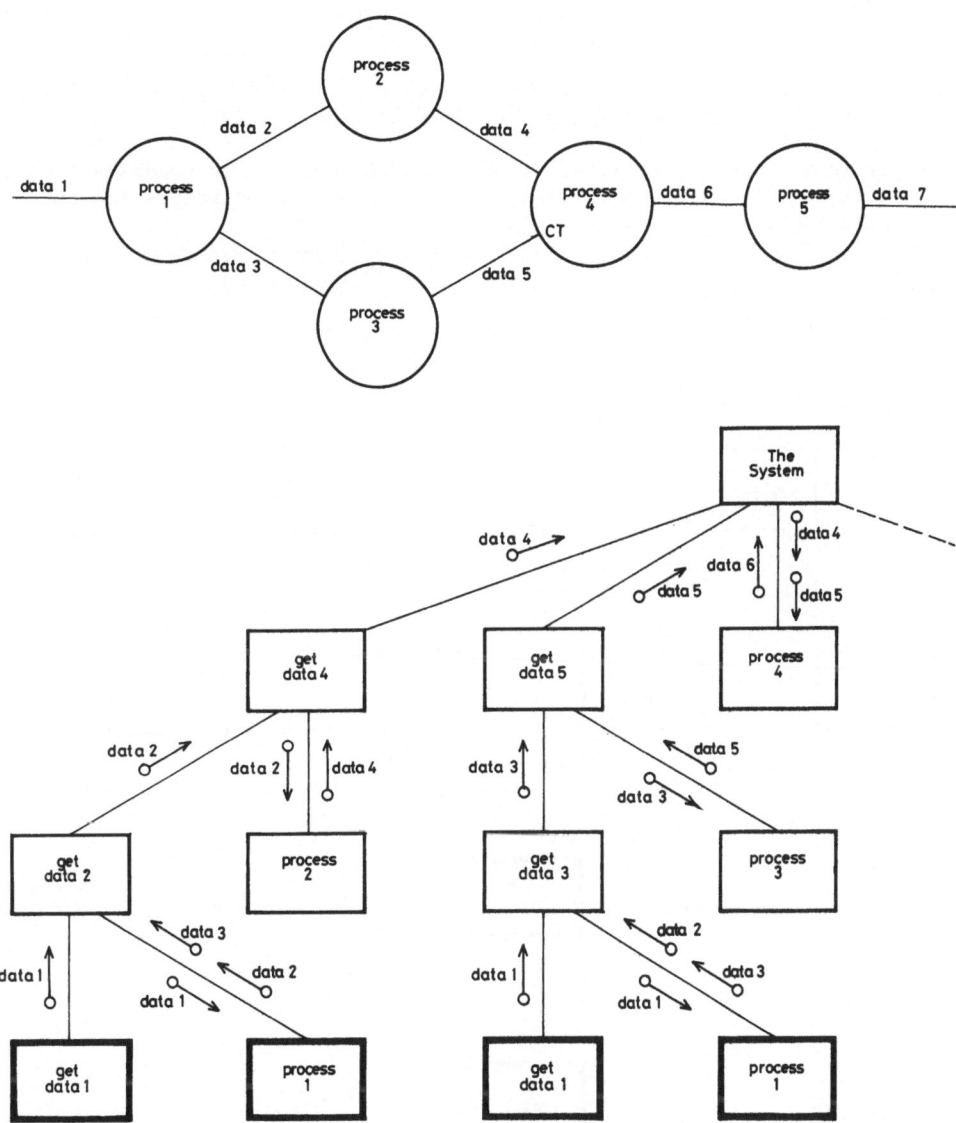

Figure 3 Multiple copies of modules are sometimes generated

It was also found that if a diagram had more than one CT marked on it, the resulting SC had a large fan-out from the main module (i.e. it had many immediate subordinates). To relieve this, the following suggestion taken from Page-Jones [PAGE80] was implemented. If a diagram contains many CTs, insert a dummy intermediate module between the main module and the CT modules (Fig 5). When the design is refined, this dummy module may disappear, but it produces a more balanced initial system.

6. SUMMARY OF FEATURES

The following is a summary of the TA´s features:

1. The TA processes a levelled set of DFDs as output from structured analysis and produces a levelled set of SCs.

2. It assumes that each DFD in the levelled set will have any necessary CTs marked on it by the designer, but it can still process DFDs (and hence, whole systems) with no CTs marked.

3. Any duplicate modules generated during transform analysis will be deleted and the chart structure adjusted accordingly.

4. If many CTs are identified on any one DFD then an intermediate module will be introduced to control the CT modules and to reduce fan-out from the main module.

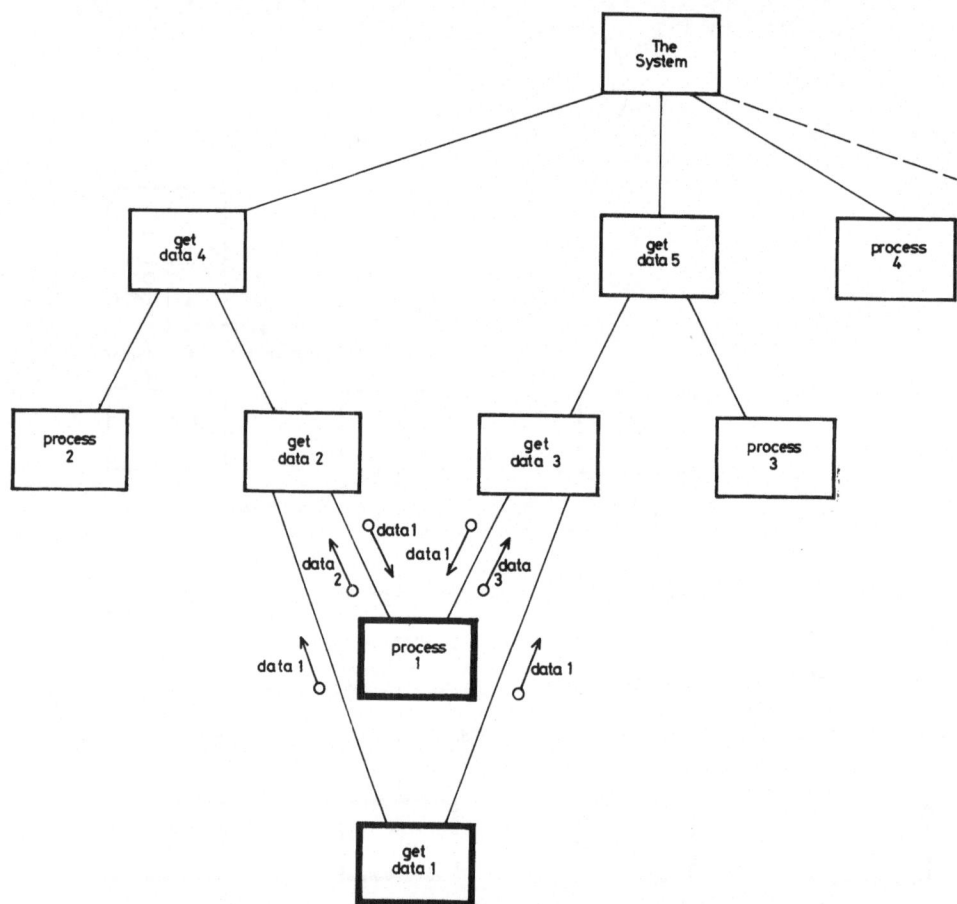

Figure 4   The TA removes duplicate definitions

7 PROBLEMS DURING DEVELOPMENT

The following problems arose during development and have yet to be
solved.

1. the technique for resolving duplicate modules can sometimes result in
    one module having multiple parents at different levels within the
    same branch. The example in Fig 6 is taken from [DEMA79] and
    illustrates the point quite nicely. It may be possible to control
    the structures allowed in the DFDs via a DFD editor hence preventing
    the above situation arising, but the TA should be able to offer a
    sensible structure chart under most circumstances. It is therefore
    necessary to determine where the module should be placed. One
    solution could be to keep only the highest level parent, but this is
    rather simplistic. A better answer would be to analyse the process
    specification for each parent module to determine exactly where the
    data flow or process is required. This, in turn, requires knowledge
    of the modules' function, and is outside the current scope of this
    tool.

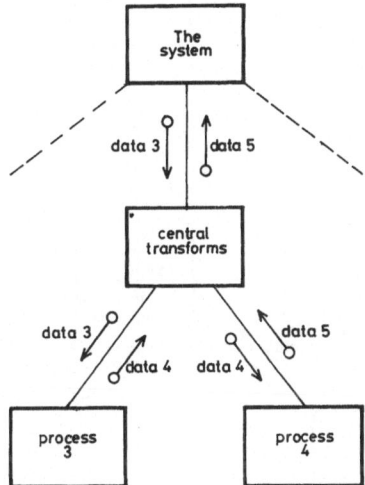

Figure 5   If many CTs are marked, an intermediate dummy is introduced

2. When the set of SCs are combined to form one system, a number of
    superfluous modules will have to be removed. These superfluous
    modules relate to input and output flows from a low level DFD (see
    Fig 2). However, if this DFD is a refinement of a higher level
    process, then those input and output flows will be passed through the
    'main' module for the DFD, and so the modules 'get data 1' and 'put
    data 6' are not required.

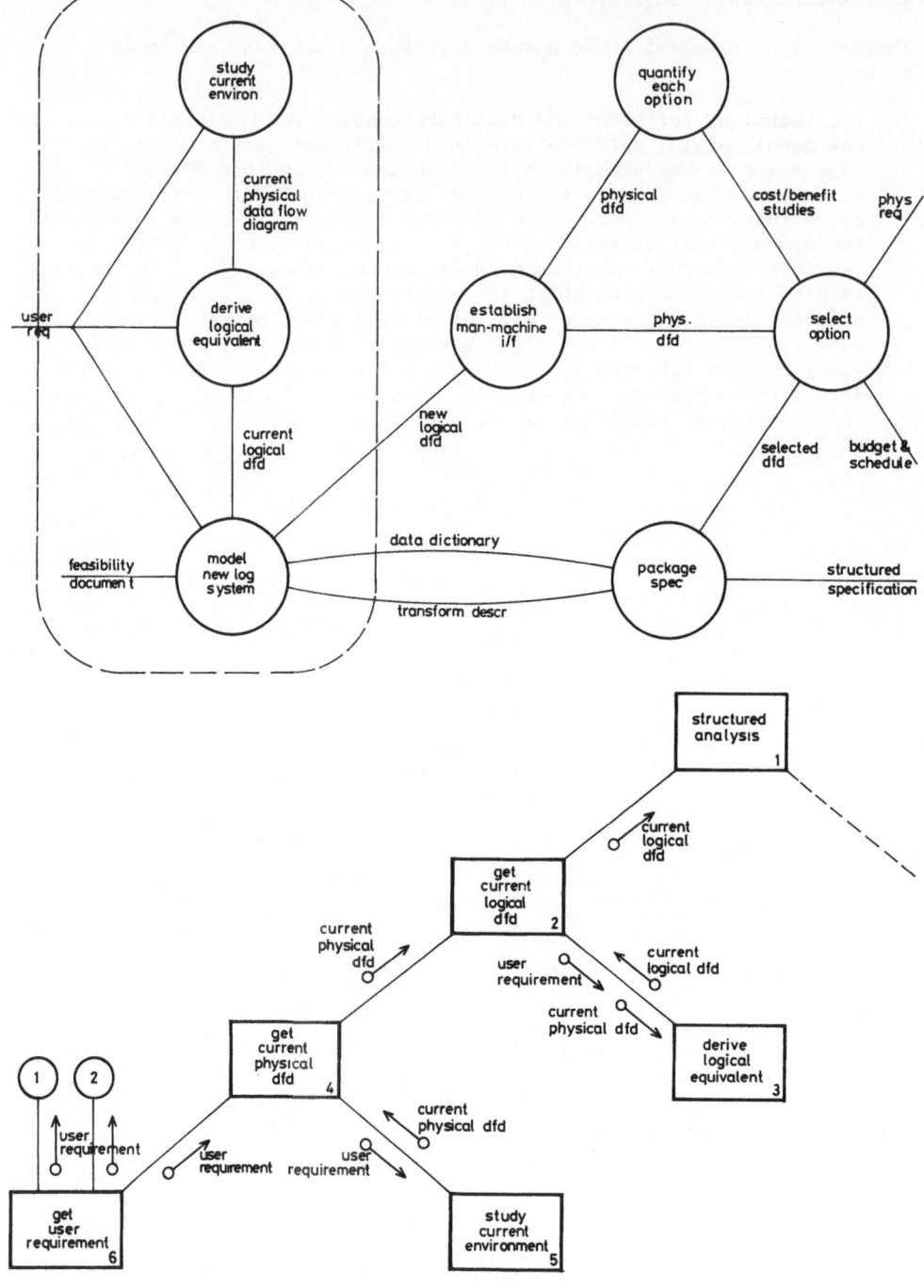

Figure 6   Duplicate modules can appear at different levels

8   FUTURE PROGRESS

The TA system represents only the first stage in the development of a
support environment for the software designer. At present, it can be
linked into a structure chart editor so that its output can be displayed

and modified via a graphics screen, and work is being done on producing a DFD editor.

The next planned extension to the TA system itself involves the addition of some intelligent capacity for refining the designs it produces and for indicating possible central transforms. Much interest is currently focused on the applicability of Artificial Intelligence and Expert Systems techniques to Software Engineering [MOST85] and although work in this area is being done, little evidence of work in the area of design is available. Before any knowledge can be incorporated into the system, however, it is necessary to determine what knowledge is needed. This problem is currently under investigation.

ACKNOWLEDGEMENTS

I would like to thank Mr. C.D. Easteal for his support and encouragement throughout this research and during the preparation of this document. This work is supported by the Science and Engineering Research Council.

REFERENCES

[ISDO]   ISDOS Inc, Structured Architect.

[DEMA79]   DeMarco, Tom, Structured Analysis and System Specification, Prentice-Hall (1979).

[KARI84]   Karimi, Jahangir, "Computer-Aided Approach to Structured Design of Software Systems," pp. 35-47 in Software Engineering : Practice and Experience. Proceedings of the 2nd software engineering conference, ed. E. Girard, North Oxford Academic Publishing Company Ltd. (4-6 June 1984).

[MOST85]   Mostow, Jack, "Foreward: What is AI? And What Does It Have To Do With Software Engineering?," IEEE Transactions On Software Engineering Vol. SE-11(11) (November 1985).

[PAGE80]   Page-Jones, Meilir, The Practical Guide to Structured Systems Design, Yourdon Press (1980).

[TROY81]   Troy, D. and Zweben, S., "Measuring the Quality of Structured Designs," Journal of Systems and Software Vol. 2, pp. 113-120 (1981).

[WILL81]   Willis, R.R., "AIDES: Computer-Aided Design of Software Systems - II," pp. 27-48 in Software Engineering Environments, ed. Horst Hunke, North-Holland (1981).

[WOOD85]   Woodman, M. and Ince, D.C., "A Software Tool for the Construction and Maintenance of Structured Analysis Notation," Software - Practice and Experience Vol. 15(II) (November 1985).

[YOUR79]   Yourdon, Ed and Constantine, Larry L., Structured Design : fundamentals of a discipline of computer program and systems design, Prentice-Hall (1979).

IMPLEMENTING RELATIONAL DATA BASES: AUTOMATING THE MAPPING

PROCESSES

D.E. Avison and J. Chaudhuri

Aston University & Cranfield I.T. Institute

Birmingham and Cranfield, UK

ABSTRACT

The design and implementation of data bases involve four major phases:
deriving the business model, achieved by analysing the structure of an
organisation and its information requirements; the formulation of the
conceptual model, achieved by identifying entities, attributes and
relationships; the logical mapping of the conceptual model onto the data
structure of the target data base management system, and the physical
mapping of this model into the access methods and storage structures used
by that data base management system. The mapping between phases should
be such that there is no loss of information. The accuracy of both the
logical and physical mapping determine the performance of the resulting
system. This paper describes algorithms and software tools which have
been designed to facilitate the implementation of data bases. Some
programs help as documentation aids. Others automate aspects of the
processes. In particular rules for automatically mapping the conceptual
data model to relational data bases are described, and algorithms are
developed for implementing these models on Ingres and Mimer. Copies of
the programs can be obtained directly from the authors.

1   INTRODUCTION

As computers become widely used in organisations, the advantages of
sharing data between different groups of users through the use of data
bases become apparent. Data bases attempt to overcome the problems that
are associated with conventional files: the unnecessary duplication of
data, a lack of consistency of data in those files, and a lack of
flexibility both in updating programs and providing information to
management.

Data bases represent an attempt to model organisations on computer files.
But the real world is so complex that to model any organisation
represents a major problem and early data base experience consisted of
more failures than successes. Avison [AVIS85] proposes a methodology for
implementing data bases with the following phases:

Business model: Business analysis is necessary to gain a background
knowledge of the organisation, such as the goals of the firm, the
management hierarchy, and the various requirements that information

systems may need to fulfill. This is an informal model of the
organisation which lays the foundation for the work that follows.

Conceptual model: This is a formal description of the enterprise in terms
of entities (objects of interest), attributes (facts describing these
objects of interest), and the relationships between entities. This
description, known as the entity-relationship (E-R) model [CHEN76] is
derived from the process of data analysis. It satisfies the criteria of
evolvability (changes in the real world can be reflected in the model),
transformability (the mapping from the conceptual model is not complex),
and stability (changes in the physical model or the logical model need
not change the conceptual model). A process known as functional analysis
is used to verify the E-R model and to provide other information which
aids the success of the data base.

Logical model: This represents a mapping of the conceptual model onto a
computer data base. The form of this model will vary according to the
target data base management system (DBMS). This is the large piece of
software controlling accesses to the data base. The three main forms of
logical model are relations which are tabular representations of data
structures (now adopted by most DBMS), networks which represent complex
many-to-many relationships (the format proposed in Codasyl [CODA71,
CODA87], and hierarchies which are tree structures (now somewhat out-of-
date).

Physical model: This represents a mapping of these data structures onto
computer storage media which will be accessed by the various applications
that require data from the data base. The exact form of the physical
model will depend on the access methods and storage structures available
(a function of the computer hardware and the DBMS), as well as the
application.

The importance of the mapping processes cannot be over-stressed and yet
there is surprisingly little published in this field. Although there are
some rules-of-thumb, mapping has been carried out largely on the basis of
trial-and-error. However they are logical processes where rules can be
formulated if the structures of the target data base are known.
Publications tend to stress the stages rather that the mapping processes
between stages. However, Lusk and Overbeek [LUSK81], Sakai [SAKA80] and
Tsao [TSAO80] have outlined a few steps involved in translating entity-
relationship diagrams into hierarchical (particularly IMS) data bases.
In a separate paper, Avison and Chaudhuri [AVIS87] discuss the mapping
processes onto Codasyl (network) DBMS.

The ability to convert the analysts' data models automatically into a
DBMS will have several affects, in particular it will:

a)   reduce the development time and cost of information systems, and

b)   minimise the possibility of the analysts' model being
     misinterpreted, because they will create the system, not
     programmers.

This paper establishes rules relating to a number of aspects of the
modelling process and describes algorithms for:

1)   Mapping the E-R model onto relational types of DBMS producing
     normalised relations for relational DBMS.

ii) Increasing the performance of the information system by
     organising the data to suit the usage patterns noted in the data
     analysis phase.

iii) Forming the data definition files from the logical model and the physical characteristics of the access paths required.

The rest of this paper is devoted to aspects of the development of data base applications which have been automated. Section 2 describes programs which are used to record the results of data analysis. It also describes a technique to deduce the usage pattern of data and programs which are used to store this information. Section 3 looks at factors which govern the mapping of the E-R model to any target DBMS logical model, and in particular reduce the side effects of updating, and then goes on to describe algorithms for producing relational versions of the model. Section 4 looks at factors which govern the physical implementation of two relational DBMS (Ingres and Mimer), and describes algorithms which facilitate these implementations.

2   DATA ANALYSIS

The E-R approach to represent the conceptual model is widely used in the commercial world. Real world information is represented by entities, attributes and relationships. It is not appropriate here to give a full description of E-R modelling. This can be found in Avison [AVIS85] and elsewhere. Some definitions with examples will suffice.

Objects of interest on the organisation are known as entities and are classified into entity types which have the same properties. Entity types are associated with each other by relationship types. Relationships can be one-to-one, one-to-many and many-to-many. Each uniquely identified entity type is known as an entity occurrence. Attributes define the properties of entities and relationships. The attributes or group of attributes that uniquely identifies an entity occurrence is called the identifier. The identifier of a relationship is formed from the identifiers of the entities participating in the relationship. Where each and every occurrence of an entity type must participate in a relationship type, the membership class of that entity type is classified as obligatory for that relationship type, otherwise it is non-obligatory. In the hospital data base PATIENTS, CONSULTANTS and CLINICAL SESSIONS are entity types. NAME, ADDRESS, HOME DOCTOR can be attributes of the entity type PATIENTS. PATIENTS ´ARE TREATED BY´ CONSULTANTS AND CONSULTANTS ´ARE IN CHARGE OF´ CLINICAL SESSIONS represent the relationship between the entity types PATIENTS and CONSULTANTS and CLINICAL SESSIONS respectively. If the enterprise rules were such that a patient could be treated by more than one consultant and a consultant can treat more than one patient, the the degree of the relationship ´ARE TREATED BY´ is many to many (m:n). If a consultant can be responsible for more than one training session but a clinical session can only be in the charge of a consultant, then the degree of the relationship ´IN CHARGE OF´ is one-to-many (1:n). If any patient must be treated by at least one consultant but not all consultants have to treat patients, then membership of the PATIENT entity type is obligatory and that of the CONSULTANCY entity type non-obligatory in the relationship ´ARE TREATED BY´. A diagrammatic representation of this example is seen as Figure 1. There are commercial software tools available for helping analysts draw these E-R and other diagrams and we are implementing tools which conform to our standards.

Data analysis involves understanding the fundamental nature of organisations and it is not possible to produce rule-of-thumb techniques

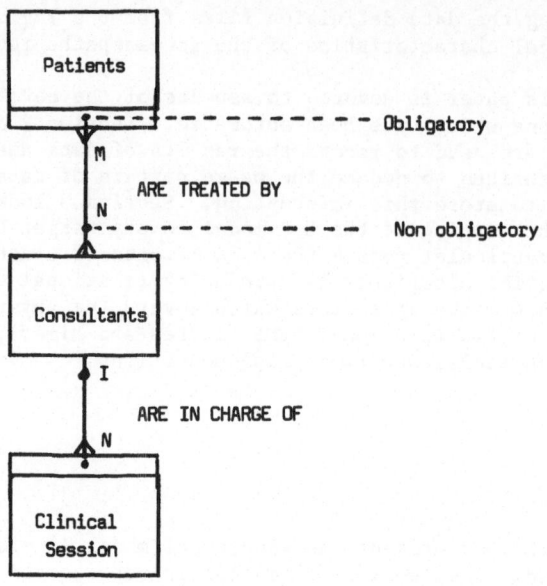

Figure 1   Example E-R diagram

for obtaining the E-R model, much will depend on the analyst's capability
to communicate effectively with members of the organisation. However, we
describe two programs which help to document the results of data
analysis.

An interactive program ENTEST communicates with the data analyst
collecting details about each entity so that all the entities and
attributes are filed. These details include the name of the entity, its
identifying attribute and a description of the attributes. As new
entities are fed in, the program checks whether the entity already exists
and informs the analyst if this is the case. In a later stage of the
project, this dictionary is enhanced with other details such as their
usage pattern. This information will facilitate the implementation of
the model onto the target DBMS. Another interactive program used by the
data analyst, RELTEST, obtains information about the relationships
identified, such as its name (checking for uniqueness), the name of
participating entities (ensuring that these exist by checking the
dictionary obtained from ENTEST), the degree of the relationship, the
membership class of the entities taking part in the relationship and any
attributes of that relationship (ensuring also that these exist in the
dictionary).

Having established an entity model, it is necessary to check the model
against an analysis of the processes and the information requirements
associated with them. This is known as functional analysis. Functions
are concerned with the processing of entities, and the relationships
between the entities identified in data analysis should provide the
necessary access paths between the entities. Information about usage
patterns can also be obtained at this stage.

In our hospital example, one function might be fixing an appointment for
a new patient with a particular consultant. This function is decomposed
into sub-functions such as:

```
select consultant
select her waiting list
select outpatients' session for consultant
book patient for time scheduled for a new patient.
```

A functional entity model shows the entities and access paths necessary
to fulfill this function and the model is compared to the E-R model in
order to check that entities exist and the required access paths exist as
relationships between entities.

The program FUNCTEST stores the information collected in the functional
analysis, finding out interactively the names of the function, their
frequency, the response time required from the system when implemented
and whether the function is to have 'primary' or 'secondary' status.
This information can be displayed in tabular form. A second program
ANALYSIS, analyses this information to produce another table giving a
global view of the usage pattern of the entities, their attributes and
the relationships between them. It denotes which attributes are used
most often to access an entity. It specifies whether an attribute is
used in equality clauses or as a range access. By an equality clause is
meant the value of an attribute provided for searching is compared with
the value of the attribute of the required entity to give an exact match.
For a range access there is no need for an exact match but the value of
the attribute of the required entity should be in the range provided by
the search clause. The analysis also specifies the total frequency of
relationship usage with regard to the access of an entity from another
entity.

The global entity model can be represented graphically where every node
on the graph represents an entity and the edges represent either an
attribute or a relationship or an access path to travel from one entity
to the other. Edges with only a single node on one side represent an
attribute or an access path to access an entity through a particular
value of that attribute. An inward edge, that is an edge marked with an
arrow pointing towards the entity, denotes that the entity towards which
the arrow points is being accessed through that relationship, when the
value of the entity occurrence on the other side is known. The edges
therefore show the navigational paths. The total traversal frequency of
each of these paths is calculated. Details about whether these
attributes or relationships are being used to retrieve a single record or
a subset of records are also noted. Figure 2 shows this type of
graphical representation. We are presently developing software tools to
help draw these diagrams.

3   MAPPING TO LOGICAL MODELS OF TARGET DBMS

Following data analysis, the conceptual model is mapped onto the logical
model. This is the data model of the target DBMS. The accuracy of the
mapping is crucial for the success of the data base implementation: there
should be no loss of information, the original processing specifications
should be satisfied, and it should be independent of any physical
implementation.

Another important factor that governs the logical model design is to
minimise the side effects of updating the logical structure of the data
base. In terms of an E-R conceptual model, there can be three types of
update operation:

    1 inserting or deleting an entity occurrence,

    2 inserting or deleting a relationship occurrence,

3 modifying the values of the attributes of an existing entity or
relationship.

These update operations should not leave the logical structure in an
inconsistent state. To maintain a consistent logical structure, further
update operations are needed. They are the side effects of an update
operation. These side effects should be limited, obvious and
controllable.

Deleting an entity occurrence ´e´ causes:

a) the deletion of an instance of a relationship in which ´e´
    participates, and

b) the deletion of one or more entities in the domain of a
    relationship, with ´e´ in the range where the membership of the
    domain is obligatory.

In figure 3 if the information about PATIENT occurrence Smith is deleted
from the data base, the relationship occurrence Smith IS TREATED BY the
CONSULTANT occurrence Williams should also be deleted. However, if a
CONSULTANT entity occurrence Williams is to be deleted, it is not
sufficient to delete the relationship occurrences in which Williams
participates. It is also necessary to delete information about PATIENT
occurrences being treated by Williams if it is obligatory that all
patients are currently under the care of a consultant.

Deleting a relationship occurrence ´Ex---->Ey´ causes:

a) the deletion of the entity occurrence ´Ey´ if the degree of the
    relationship ´Ex---->Ey´ is 1:1 or 1:n and the membership of
    ´Ey´ is obligatory, or

b) the deletion of the entity occurrence ´Ex´ if the degree of the
    relationship is 1:1 and the membership of ´Ex´ is obligatory, or

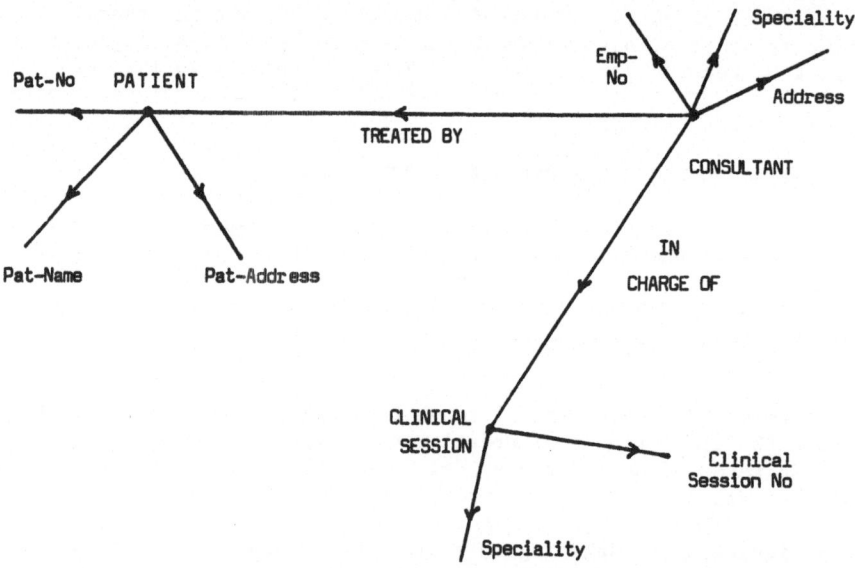

Figure 2 Global entity model

c) the deletion of the entity occurrences ´Ex´ and ´Ey´ if the degree of the relationship is 1:1 and the membership of ´Ex´ and ´Ey´ are obligatory.

Following figure 3, if an occurrence of the relationship ´CONSULTANT----->CLINICAL SESSION´ of degree 1:n is deleted, then it will be necessary to delete the information about the entity CLINICAL SESSION taking part in this relationship occurrence. A particular clinic session only has significance if the consultant is in charge of the clinic.

Inserting an entity ´Ex´ needs:

any entity ´Ey´ in the range of the relationship ´Ex----->Ey´ with ´Ex´ in the domain to exist already if the membership of the domain is obligatory.

For example, before we can introduce an entity occurrence of CLINICAL SESSION in the data base, the information about the CONSULTANT giving it needs to be present in the data base.

Inserting a relationship ´Ex----->Ey´ needs:

that the entity in the domain ´Ex´ and the range ´Ey" to exist already.

Thus, if we wish to specify details about a PATIENT, the information about the patient occurrence and another entity, say DISEASE, should already exist in the data base.

Having established rules which will limit the side-effects of update operations and leave the data model in a consistent state, we look at rules for mapping the E-R conceptual model onto the logical model for a relational DBMS.

In order to use the relational model as a time-varying representation of data, we should be able to insert , delete and modify the tuples. The update operations may sometimes yield uncontrollable side effects. So as to keep these side effects to a minimum, the relations should be in their normalised form.

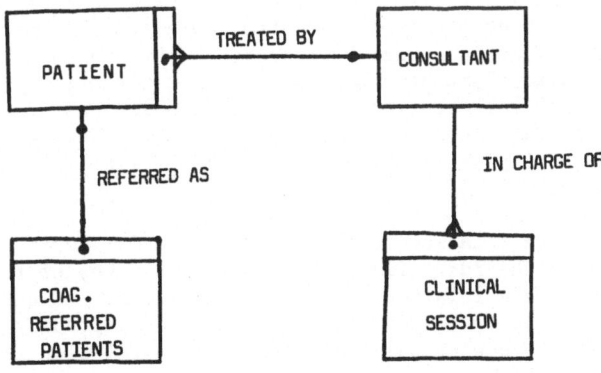

Figure 3   Patients-Consultants example

The crucial concept on which the theory of normalisation is based is that of functional dependence:

An attribute 'Y' of relation 'R' is functionally dependent on attribute 'X' of 'R' if and only if each 'X' value in 'R' has associated with it precisely one 'Y' value in 'R'.

The concept of functional dependence can be extended to cover the case where 'X' or 'Y' may be a combination or attributes. 'Y' is fully functionally dependent on 'X', where 'X' is a combination of attributes, if 'Y' is functionally dependent on 'X' but not on any subset of 'X'.

A relation is said to be in first normal form if and only if all the underlying domains contain non-decomposable values. A relation is in second normal form if it is in first normal form and all the non key attributes are fully dependent on the primary key. A second normal form relation is in third normal form if all the non key attributes are directly on the primary key or any candidate keys.

The concept of multivalued dependency needs to be mentioned before the fourth normal form relations can be defined. An attribute 'B' of 'R' is said to have a multivalued dependence on an attribute 'A' of 'R' if for a given 'A' there is not a single 'B' but a well defined set of 'B'. Functional dependence is just a special case of multivalued dependency. A relation is in fourth normal form if it is in third normal form and if there exists a multivalued dependency (say 'B' of 'R' on 'A' of 'R'), all the other attributes are fully functionally dependent on 'A'. If our objectives is to keep redundancy and side effects of the update operations to the minimum, then it is desirable to keep the relations in a relational model in this fully normalised form.

As we have seen, a major objective in the modelling process is to minimise the uncontrollable side effects that might be caused by any update operations. It should be possible to create or destroy all the properties of an entity or relationship occurrence at the same time as the creation and destruction of the entity or relationship occurrence. This may be achievable through the creation or destruction of a single tuple in the relational model. Moreover, a single relational update should be sufficient to update the property value of an entity or a relationship.

The identifier of an entity set is the property which uniquely identifies and entity occurrence. The identifier of a relationship is the combination of the identifiers of the entities taking part in the relationship. In order to avoid uncontrollable side effects each entity or relationship occurrence must be represented by a unique identifier all through the relational model. Undesirable side effects can also be eliminated if each relation in the relational model only contains information about a single entity or relationship. This ensures that the deletion of an entity or relationship does not delete any other entities or relationships.

There should be one relation in the relational model corresponding to each entity set. The identifier forms the primary key of that relation. The attributes of the relation are the properties of the entity. Each tuple corresponds to each entity occurrence. Corresponding to each relationship in the conceptual model should be a relation in the relational model. The primary key of the relation is the identifier of the relationship. Each tuple in the relation represents an occurrence of the relationship.

There are a few exceptions to these decisions which should improve the efficiency of the relational model without any loss of semantic information.

If two entities ´Ex´ and ´Ey´ take part in a 1:1 or 1:n relation ´Rxy´ where the membership of ´Ey´ is obligatory, it is not necessary to write a relation representing the relationship ´Rxy´. Instead the identifier of the non-obligatory member ´Ex´ can be posted to the relation table for entity ´Ey´ as an attribute. For the entity ´Ey´ to exist it has to take part in this relationship. It can therefore be assumed that taking part in this relationship is a property for this entity type. To delete an instance of the relationship ´Rxy´ it would only be necessary to delete that entity occurrence of ´Ey´. This would automatically delete the relationship and the entity occurrence as required.

In some cases the identifier of an entity type forms a part of the identifier of another closely associated entity type. It is not necessary to have a relation representing the relationship between these two entity types because the information is already available from the primary key of the second entity type. This is a special case of the obligatory membership of an entity discussed in the last paragraph. The membership of the entity with the borrowed identifier will be obligatory in the relationship between this entity and the entity from which it borrowed the identifier.

In a 1:1 or 1:n relation ´Rxy´ between the entities ´Ex´ and ´Ey´ where the membership of ´Ey´ is obligatory, the relationship properties are considered the properties of the entity ´Ey´ is obligatory, for each instance of ´Rxy´ there will be a corresponding occurrence of type ´Ey´. If the membership of ´Ey´ is non-obligatory the relationship might possess attributes. A relationship ´Rxy´ of degree m:n can also have some properties associated with it. It does not matter whether the membership of the entities ´Ex´ and ´Ey´ taking part in it are obligatory or not. These attributes cannot be considered part of the entity attributes because these properties only describe the entities when they are not taking part in that specific relationship. When mapping to a relation in the relational model, m:n relationships with or without properties can be treated alike.

From the above discussions we can formulate the following mapping rules after identifying each entity set by a unique attribute throughout the relational model:

1   For each entity set ´Ex´ form a relation ´R(Ex)´. The primary key of the relation is the key attribute of ´Ex´. The attributes of the relation are (i) the properties of ´Ex´ and (ii) the identifier of entity ´Ey´ if and only if there is a 1:1 or 1:n relationship ´Ey-->Ex´ where the membership of ´Ex´ is obligatory and the identifier of ´Ey´ does not form a part of the identifier of ´Ex´.

2   For each relationship ´Rxy´ between the two entities ´Ex´ and ´Ey´ of degree 1:1 where the membership of both the entities are non-obligatory define a relation ´R(Rxy)´. The attributes of this relation are made up of the identifiers of ´Ex´ and ´Ey´ and the attributes of the relationship. The identifiers of ´Ex´ and ´Ey´ are candidate keys.

3   For each relationship ´Rxy´ between the two entities ´Ex´ and ´Ey´ of degree 1:n where the membership of both the entities are non-

obligatory define a relation ´R(Rxy)´. The attributes of this relation are made up of the identifiers of ´Ex´ and ´Ey´ and the attributes of the relationship. The primary key of ´Rxy´ is the identifier of ´ Ey´.

4   For each relationship ´Rxy´ between the two entities ´Ex´ and ´Ey´ of degree m:n or between more than two entities ´Ex´, ´Ey´,.......´En´ where the membership of the entities are either obligatory or non-obligatory, define a relation ´R9Rxy)´. The attributes of this relation are made up of the identifiers of the participating entities and the properties of the relationship ´Rxy´. The primary key of the relation ´R(Rxy)´ is the combination of the identifiers of the entities taking part.

Program <u>RELMAP</u> examines the list of entities and relationships and applies the mapping rules to obtain the resultant logical model. The output from the program is a list of relations in fourth normal form for the following reasons:

i) The identifiers and properties of the entities and the relationships were defined over atomic (non-decomposable) value sets. The relations derived from them are also defined on atomic domains. Hence the relations are in first normal form.

ii) The relations obtained from any entity set by applying the first mapping rule would contain the identifier ´IDEx´, ´PEx´ the properties of Ex and the identifier of entity ´Ey´, ´IDEy´, if there is a 1:1 or 1:n relationship ´Ex-->Ey´ where the membership of ´Ex´ is obligatory. The functional dependencies in the relations are in the form ´IDEx´-->´PEx´, ´IDEx´-->´IDEy´ and the non key attributes like ´PEx´ and ´IDEy´ are directly fully dependent on the primary key ´IDEx. There is no multivalued dependency. Hence the relations are in fourth normal form.

iii) The form of dependencies in the relations derived by applying the second mapping rule for a 1:1 relationship between ´Ex´ and ´Ey´ where the membership of both the entities are non-obligatory is in the form ´IDEx´-->´IDEy´ and ´IDEx´-->´PRx´. ´IDEx and ´IDEy´ are non-transitively and fully dependent on each other. ´PRx´ is also fully dependent on ´IDEx´ and ´IDEy´ are candidate keys. Hence the relations are in fourth normal form.

iv) The relations obtained by applying the third mapping rule for 1:n relationships between entities ´Ex´ and ´Ey´ where the membership of both the entities are non-obligatory, will have functional dependence in the form ´IDEy´-->´IDEx´ and ´IDEy´-->´PRx´. Hence the relations are in fourth normal form.

v) The relations obtained by applying the fourth mapping rule are defined over the key attributes of the entities taking part and the properties of the relationships. The form of the dependency is ´IDEx´, ´IDEy´,......,´IDEn´-->´PRx´. There is no functional dependency among the identifiers of the entities taking part and ´IDEx´, ´IDEy´,......,´IDEn´ forms the primary key. The relations cannot be decomposed into other third normal form relations because the relationships these represent were non-decomposable. Hence they are also in fourth normal form.

The objective of mapping the E-R conceptual model onto a logical model is to capture all the information and to free the logical model from all update anomolies. The objective of the physical design is to improve the performance of the DBMS. In this section we look first at the factors that govern the physical design process and then describe the physical implementation on the DBMS Ingres and Mimer.

The performance of a DBMS is related to the speed with which the DBMS responds to requests and this is directly dependent on how efficiently the data is stored. This in turn depends on how well the data.base is physically implemented. The performance can be modified by changing the physical structure of the data base to suit the users' needs. The DBMS should be able to offer the data base administrator (DBA) options to structure the data physically so as to enhance the performance. The DBMS should support a number of access methods. The DBA should be able to specify how to store the data on the storage media, the sizes of the memory buffer, etc., but in many DBMS the options open are limited.

The details noted at the functional analysis stage described in section2 are used to help decide on file organisation and access methods. Factors such as how frequently an access path is used, what volume of data is retrieved, what response time is necessary and for what category of function a particular access path is being used, affect the physical organisation of the data.

The characteristics of the access paths decide how data is to be placed and related so as to give fast access. An entity may be accessed either through an attribute or through a relationship. There are three possible ways of organising the elements of an entity to improve access time. We may place the elements of an entity near another associated entity. Alternatively, the elements of the entity which are associated or have a property in common may be clustered. A third option is to invert these entities on an attribute. The first option is desirable though it is not feasible in a relational data base because tuples from different relations cannot be placed near one another. Our objective in physical mapping is therefore to cluster the elements wherever possible, and failing that, to use an inverted file. Clustering on one path will preclude further clustering and inversion will be necessary.

Clustering is achieved either by having an indexed sequential structure or applying some hashing technique. The choice depends on the amount of data retrieved in one particular access (information provided by the functional analysis phase of data analysis). If a small or large subset of a file is retrieved in one particular access then an indexed sequential structure should be chosen. If only a single record is retrieved, then a hashing technique should be applied. Where a particular access path or edge is used to retrieve a single record as well as a subset of records, an indexed sequential structure can be chosen as it will support both types of retrieval successfully. Paths which are used frequently but cannot be supported by the above methods, are supported by secondary indexes. The results obtained by applying the algorithm are consistent with users' experiences.

Severance and Carlis (1977) argue that one measure to improve performance of a data base system is to increase the volume of data transferred with each data access. This can be achieved in a number of ways. One way would be to store contiguously records which are processed sequentially, Severance and Carlis describe how records can be physically positioned according to the speed of response required and the volume of data retrieved. If a fast response is essential, use a hashing technique, otherwise an ISAM structure and access via indexes, unless, if speed is not important, a data base scan will be satisfactory. This is summarised in figure 4. If we are accessing several records and a fast response is needed, then an ISAM structure should be chosen, but where time is not critical, a data base scan will be satisfactory.

Ingres is a full relational system available on machines running under Unix. There are three internal structures available and these are:

1 Heap: which has two main characteristics – duplicate tuples are not removed and the organisation of the tuples is not known. To retrieve a particular tuple, the system has be scan every tuple until it finds one which satisfies the condition. This is not very efficient, particular where it is done on a large amount of data.

2 Hash: In this structure all duplicate tuples are removed and the relations are hashed to a specific domain. The system will provide a fast access for that tuple if the value of the domain is provided because the location of the tuple on the disk will be known to the system.

3 ISAM: In this structure all duplicate tuples are removed and the relations are sorted on one or more domains. Retrievals will be improved by providing the specific value of a domain or the range of values in which the domain lies.

Ingres allows users to specify the storage structures and the system will default to heap structure.

When the logical model is mapped to Ingres, because the relations will be in fully normalised form and have no replication, there will be no problem. However, initially the relations will have a heaped structure and this will not be efficient. We will need to modify the storage structure.

Ingres does not support physical access paths between relations. Instead, the primary key of an entity is added as an attribute or foreign key of another entity. For example there is no physical access path from the relation BLOOD REPORT to the relation that represents the PATIENT. Instead the primary key of the PATIENT entity is added as an attribute of the relation BLOOD REPORT. This means that in the physical design model, the frequency of the identifier must also include the frequencies of all the n:1 and 1:1 relationships with this entity in the range. These adjustments should be performed before we decide on the primary structure of the relations.

The frequency of the identifier should also include the frequencies of all the relationship paths coming into the entity. If the summation of these frequencies and the identifier is greater than the frequency of the path assigned, then the identifier forms the basis of the primary structure of relations. If the chosen path is an attribute then the storage is structured on the basis of this attribute. If the path represents a relationship X-->Y of degree 1:1 or n:1, and the membership of X is obligatory then the identifier of Y forms the basis for the primary storage structure of the relation R(X). If the path represents a relationship X-->Y of degree 1:n or n:1, and the membership of X is not obligatory or a relationship of degree m:n, then there will be another relation in the model that represents this relationship . The primary storage structure of the relation R(X) will then be based of the

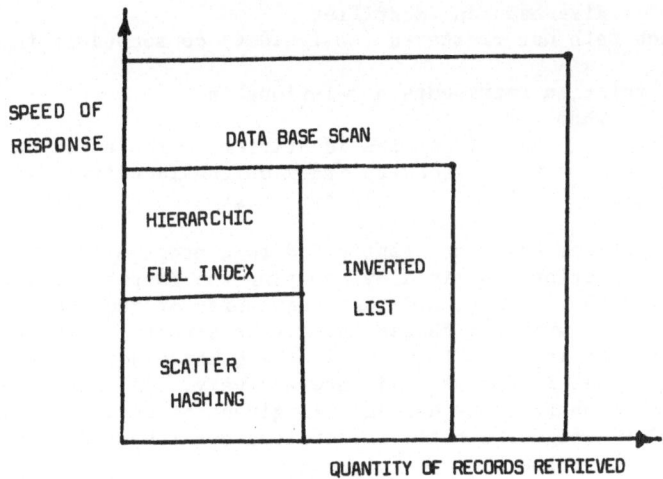

Figure 4   Summary of access methods

identifier of X. The traversal frequency of the path representing the
relationship X-->Y will now have to be added onto the frequency of the
identifier. The primary structure of the relation R (XY) will be based
on the identifier of X or Y, depending on which of the frequencies
between X-->Y or Y--> is greater. The other identifier can be used for
an optional index to the relation.

So far we have discussed the field on which to base the primary structure
of a relation. Whether we choose an ISAM structure which supports a
range access or a hash structure which only supports equality access is
determined from the information on how the access paths are used.
Identifiers are often used in equijoin clauses, that is the particular
field is matched with the appropriate field in a query. The hash
structure is suitable in this situation. An attribute is most often used
in range access, therefore an ISAM structure is appropriate. Of course
there may be cases where the attribute is used frequently for equality
access. In these circumstances a hash structure is suitable. When in
doubt or the particular path supports both equality and range access,
then the ISAM structure is appropriate. The designer should be able to
decide from the frequencies whether a particular path needs to be
supported or not.

From the above discussion we can formulate the following algorithm:

Let   x = identifier path
           y = other path assigned cluster (C)
           Fz = the sum of the frequencies of the
                relationships paths with the particular
                entity in the range

If the relation represents an entity
    Then
           If fx + fz > fy
                Then hash on identifier attribute
           Else If y is an attribute
                Then ISAM on attribute value
           Else is y is a relationship represented
                     by a foreign key
           Then hash on foreign key

```
        Else hash on identifier
For each path not clustered (assigned C) do secondary index
Else
If the relation represents a relationship
        Then
                Hash it on the identifier of the entity A
                Have secondary index on the identifier of
                        the entity B.
```

The above algorithm has been transferred to a program ING which will take as input the relations obtained by applying the mapping rules, the field types from the entity list, and the frequencies of the access paths, and produce relations with the necessary storage structure, ready for implementation of Ingres. As with all the other programs described, it is written to that it can be used interactively. In situations where the decisions are doubtful, the designer is given the change to make a decision. The designer can try the options available and decide on options which give the best performance.

We may conclude that the hash storage structure is advantageous for locating tuples where the exact value is known. ISAM is useful for both range and hash values. In an ISAM structure the directory has to be searched before we can locate the required tuple. Thus it is not as efficient as hash for locating tuples when the exact value is known. When a tuple is inserted, the system first finds the page where the tuple should belong. If the page is not filled then it stores the tuple in that page. Otherwise, it stores in an overflow page. Too many tuples stored in an overflow area affect the performance of the data base. Initially, when we are creating a relation and appending the tuples, it is easier to keep the relations in a heaped structure. Once this is completed we can modify the relations to the structure necessary. We can specify the ´fillfactor´ in the case of ISAM and hash structured relations.

If we have a knowledge of the maximum number of tuples in a relation and the existing number of tuples, we can specify the ´fillfactor´. Let ´y´ be the maximum number and ´x´ be the existing number of tuples, then we assign a ´fillfactor´ of $(x/y)*100$. This is a very rough guide and it assumes that the tuples are evenly distributed.

If we know the number of bytes in each page, the overhead of bytes per page and per tuple, the tuple width and the number of maximum tuples, we can specify the minimum number of pages required for a hash structure.

```
Let the number of bytes per page = x
Let the number of bytes for overhead per each page = y
Let the tuple width = w
Let the tuple overhead = z
Maximum number of tuples = n
Number of tuples per page(t) = (x-y)/(w+z)
Minpage = n/t.
```

This will guarantee that free space is reserved for the relation to grow to its maximum size. When the fillfactor and minpage are both specified, the system computes the number of pages that will be required to store the existing tuples at the specified fillfactor. If this number is less than the minpages, then minpages is used instead. It is not possible to calculate fillfactor and minpages automatically and the interactive programs FILL and MIM which ask the designer for the necessary information and suggest possible values for these factors.

Mimer organises the data base in a number of ´databanks´ each holding relations which are stored on disk according to a B* tree structure and sorted according to the value of the primary key. The B* tree has two sections: data sections, which contains the leaf nodes of the tree and they are the rows of the n-ary relations, and index sections, which contain the non-leaf nodes of the tree and the are the navigational paths to the nodes at the next level. This provides a fast binary search technique to access a particular row of a table. It is quicker to locate a tuple if the primary key is known, though this structure can also be used to process records sequentially. It is also possible to have one or more secondary indices to a table which inverts the table on one or more columns. This will make some data retrieval faster, but will make updating slower. This is one of the few options open to the DBA on organising the storage structure.

The relations defined in the logical model can be directly mapped onto the relations in the Mimer data base, a process similar to the Ingres mapping described earlier.

If the path is an attribute and it is the primary key on the entity, then the relation will automatically have been sorted according to this attribute. If it is not the primary key then the relation can be inverted on this attribute and a secondary index created on this attribute. On the other hand, if it represents a relationship then there are two different situations to consider. The path might represent a relationship XY of degree 1:1 or n:1 where the membership of X is obligatory. In this case the identifier of Y will be a foreign key in the relation R(X). There is no possibility of hashing R(X) on this foreign key. Thus a secondary index should be created for this foreign key.

The path might represent a relationship XY of degree n:1 where the membership of X is not obligatory, or a relationship of degree m:n. In these cases there will be a relation R(XY) in the model representing this relationship. The relation R(XY) will be sorted according to the primary key. For the relationship of degree n:1, the primary key for R(XY) will be the identifier of X. For the relationship m:n, the identifier of R(XY) will be the combination of the identifier of X and Y. In these situations, the relation R(XY) can be inverted on the identifier of Y.

The algorithm for the storage structure will be:

Let x = identifier
     y = other path assigned C

For every entity DO
     If y is an attribute
          Then invert R(X) on this attribute
     Else if y is a relationship XY of
               degree 1:1 or n:1
          Then invert R(X) on the identifier of Y
     Else invert R(XY) on the identifier of Y.

Program MIN (like ING) produces a model suitable for Mimer implementation.

Thus basic guidelines for implementing the relational logical model onto particular relational systems like Ingres and Mimer have been suggested.

The B* tree structure of Mimer expands and shrinks automatically reorganising itself as records are added to or deleted from the data base. Therefore it does not need regular reorganising. In contrast the performance for Ingres will deteriorate with the addition and deletion of tuples and the DBA will need to reorganise the data base from time to time.

5   CONCLUSION

This paper describes research which is:

1   Developing software tools for automatically converting the conceptual model to a relational logical model. No information is lost in the process and there is no redundancy as all the relations are in fourth normal form. The tools save the designer the tedious manual process of going through every entity and relationship in the model and mapping them to relations in the relational model. Parallel research work not described here has produced software for mapping to set and record structures for the Codasyl model. These programs are also available from the authors.

2   Developing software tools for physical design. This analyses the results of functional analysis and suggests ways of structuring the data depending on usage pattern, in other words how frequently entities are being accessed. The tools save the designer from the tedious task of deciding how entities, attributes and relationships are being used by different functions. The software also suggests the access mechanism to be assigned for each of the access paths. This information can be used in deciding the support required in choosing a target DBMS. If the target DBMS is already chosen, it can help in deciding how the physical characteristics of the target DBMS can best be exploited. For example, Ingres supports clustering and indexing, but it is not possible to place tuples from different relations near each other. In Mimer, only secondary indexing can be added to enhance performance.

3   Developing software tools for automatically implementing the data model to a selected DBMS on the basis of the results of a study of the physical and logical characteristics of the DBMS software. This is specific to the particular target DBMS.

A portable microcomputer software package is described in Chaudhuri and Esendal [CHAU86]. Software programs outlined in this paper can be obtained from the authors.

REFERENCES

[AVIS85] Avison, D.E. (1985): Information Systems Development: A Data Base Approach, Blackwell Scientific, Oxford, 1985.

[AVIS87] Avison D.E. and Chaudhuri, J (1987): Implementing Codasyl Data Bases: Automating the Mapping Processors, not yet published.

[CHAU86] Chaudhuri, J and Esendal, H.T. (1986): A Preprocessor Package to Facilitate Data Base Design, Fourth IASTED International Symposium on Applied Mathematics, Innsbruck.

[CHEN76]   Chen, P.P.S (1976): The Entity-Relationship Model – Towards a
           Unified View of Data ACM Transactions on Database Systems, 1,
           1, March 1976.

[CODA71]   Codasyl (1971): Codasyl Data Base Task Group April 1971 Report,
           ACM, New York.

[CODA78]   Codasyl (1978): Codasyl Data Description Language Journal of
           Development, Material Data Management Branch, Department of
           Supply and Services, Ottawa, Ontario.

[LUSK81]   Lusk, E.L. and Overbeek, R.A. (1981): A Practical Design
           Methodology for the Implementation of IMS Database using
           Entity-Relationship Model, ACM-Sigmod International Conference
           on Management of Data, Santa Monica, May 1981.

[SAKA80]   Sakai, H (1980): Entity Relationship Approach to the Conceptual
           Schema Design, ACM-Sigmod International Conference on
           Management of Data, May 1980.

[SEVE77]   Severance, D.G and Carlis, J.V (1977): A Practical Approach to
           Selecting Record Access Paths, ACM Computing Surveys, 9, 4.

[TSAO80]   Tsao, J.H. (1980): Enterprise Schema: An Approach to IMS
           Logical Data Base Design, ACM-Sigmod International Conference
           on Management of Data, May 1980.

PLEX - A STRUCTURED LINE DIAGRAM EDITOR

Susan J. Wright

Software Technology Group, CAP

1   INTRODUCTION

The popularity of the Apple Macintosh and graphical environments such as GEM that run under MS-DOS have resulted in a wave of diagram-based methodology support tools, that take advantage of the facilities offered on low cost personal computers. These tools make the use of a methodology on a project a more attractive prospect, as they automate the time-consuming tasks of producing diagrams, updating diagrams and maintaining links between diagrams. Thus the system design documents can be navigated without leafing through large amounts of paper documentation.

However, for many users of methodologies such tools are too restrictive. It is often necessary to enhance the methodology for a specific system, thus deviating from the published standard, yet a methodology support tool will rarely allow any deviation from the published standard.

A more generalised system is needed that supports a wide range of methodologies and enables users to enhance the base methodology being used to suit their needs. PLEX is such a system, which was developed as CAP's first year work on the Alvey Fortune project, [MCGO87], a research project developing a Documentation Support System for Software Engineers.

PLEX is a line diagram editor which runs on a SUN Workstation and is capable of producing and printing structured diagrams. The diagrams are structured in such a way that they may express relationships between components. PLEX is independent of any particular methodology or type of structured diagram and may be customised to support a variety of structured drawing types.

2   PLEX USER MODEL

PLEX has a simple user model and can be configured for a particular methodology in the following way:

-    Initially the user has available a set of PLEX functions and the basic drawing atoms: line, rectangle, ellipse and text.

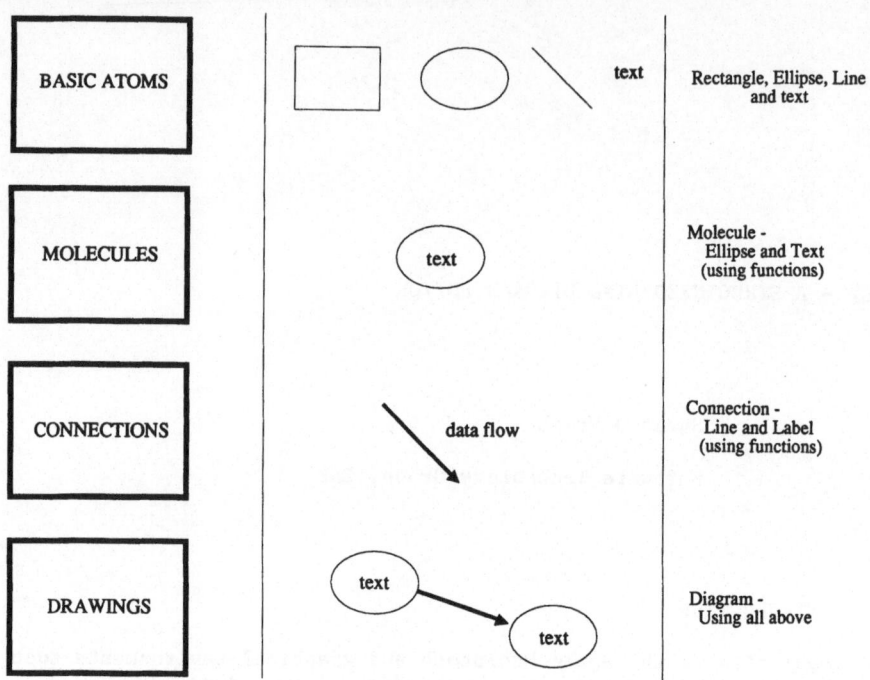

Figure 1 Diagram Editor: Lisa Draw

- These basic atoms, together with the functions provided, are used to create more complex objects which are relevant to the methodology for which PLEX is being configured. These objects, known as molecules, can then be added to the list of drawing objects available to the user. So, for example, a flow charting template could be built up.

- The functions are also used to create Connections (logical links), for example an arrowed line to indicate the direction of flow. Rules governing the connections can then be set up, for example to specify which flow chart objects may be linked by the arrowed line.

Following this, diagrams are created using atoms, molecules and connections in conjunction with PLEX functions (see Figure 1).

Thus PLEX can be simply configured to support a range of diagram based methodologies e.g. MASCOT [ALLW81], Structured Analysis and Design Technique [ROSS77], SSADM [LMBS86].

3   PLEX FEATURES

PLEX provides similar basic functionality to other diagram editors such as Apple's Lisa Draw [BYTE83]. The user-configurability of the system produces diagrams for a wide range of methodologies and the logical linking of objects within the PLEX diagrams (described below) are areas of innovative research.

3.1 Basic Features

The PLEX screen is divided into three sub-windows: the menus, the palette and the drawing area.

The initial palette consists of four basic atoms - text, rectangle, ellipse and line. These can be represented in textual or iconic form on the palette. Palette items can be selected and inserted into the drawing area. Three basic functions are available to the user by the direct use of the mouse buttons - the selection, movement and resizing of individual objects or groups of objects. Fixed box, rubber box, fixed line, and rubber line cursor are provided to give feedback to the user of the action taking place (see Figure 2).

Pull-down menus provide further actions. Objects can be duplicated or deleted and the order of displaying overlapping objects can be changed. Physical attributes of objects can be altered - for example lines may be of varying thicknesses and arrows can be added, rectangles and ellipses may have fill patterns (see Figure 3) and text can be displayed in different fonts, point sizes and styles. Objects can also be aligned in various ways. Various levels of protection can be applied to protect the shape or position of an object. PLEX instructions are specified by a NOUN-VERB method (ie selecting the object then the action) - using this approach the user can be prevented from choosing a command when the selected object(s) is not appropriate to that command. An example of this is a fill pattern action is not being available as a valid option when a line has been selected.

3.2 Molecules and the Creation and Editing of Palette Objects

The basic atoms can be easily combined into more complex single objects, known as molecules (see Figure 4). This is achieved by a menu action which combines all the currently selected objects. Molecules can be nested and may be acted on as a single object or at component level using the functions already described above. A molecule may also be atomised into its components.

The commands in the PLEX pull down menus can also be applied to palette objects. For example the protect shape attribute could be set on the ellipse palette item thus producing a palette item for circles.

The user can create new palette objects in two ways

- duplicating an existing palette object

- placing an object (molecule) created on the drawing area onto the palette

Once a palette object has been created it can be edited using a menu option which produces a special drawing window known as a dialogue (see Figure 5).

The object can be edited in the same way as an object on the drawing area (eg atoms can be added to it, it can be resized and physical attributes can be set). A name and icon for the palette object may also be specified.

PLEX is therefore user-configurable. The creation of user-defined palette objects would usually be performed by a super-user of the PLEX system. In this way PLEX can be customised for a particular methodology or type of diagram.

3.3 Logical Linking

One of the most important areas of PLEX is that of maintaining complex logical links between graphical objects.

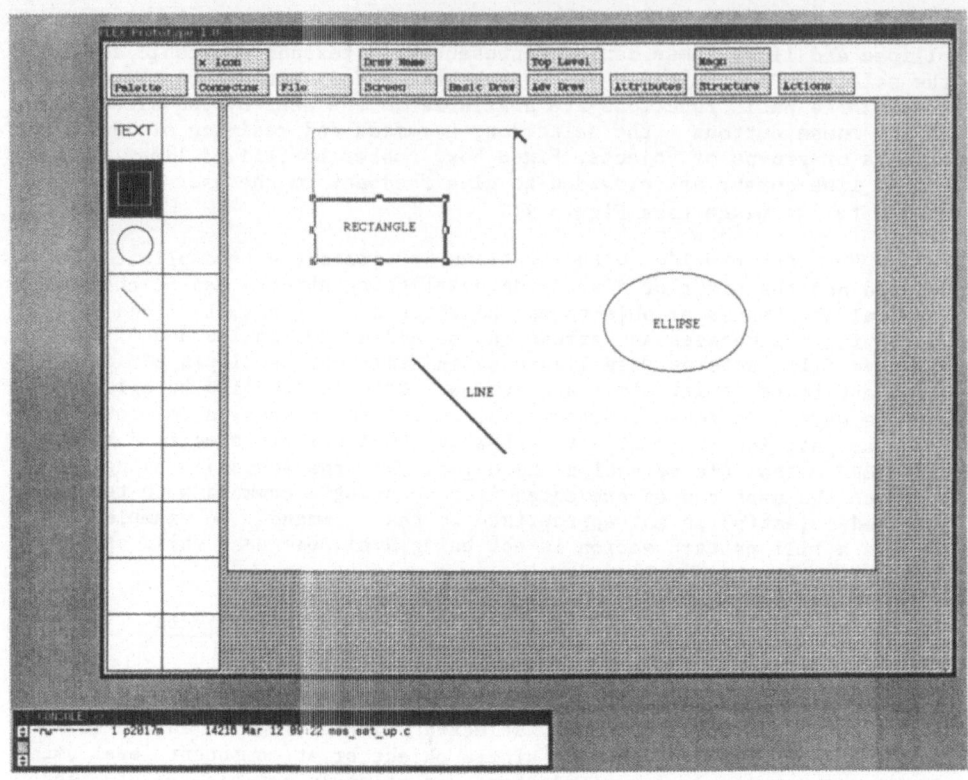

Figure 2   PLEX screen showing rubber box cursor

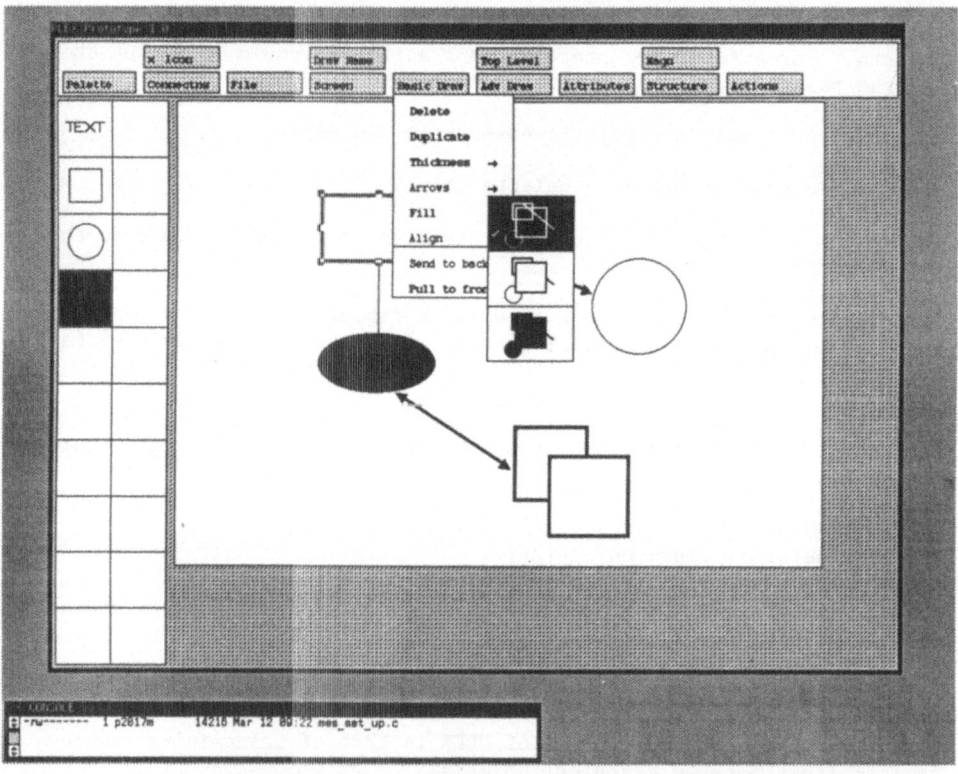

Figure 3   PLEX screen showing physical attributes of objects and iconic walking menu for fill patterns

114

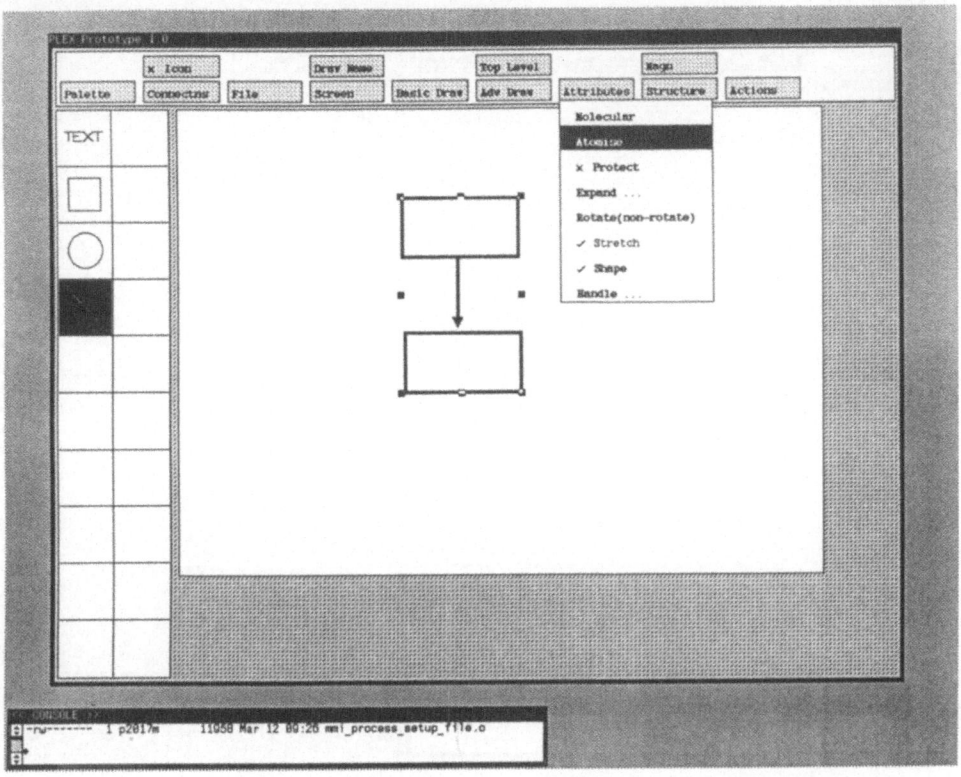

Figure 4   Molecule created from 2 rectangles and an arrowed line

In a diagram (see Figure 6) consisting of logically linked objects, if
one object were to be repositioned the lines representing the logical
links would be automatically repositioned (see Figure 7).

This has been achieved in PLEX by the use of connections and connection
rules, both of which will be set up by the super-user in configuring the
system for a particular use,

>   A Connection is a special type of molecule consisting of connection
>   line and connection items, each of which have several attributes to
>   allow its position to be specified. The connection item could be
>   set to be relative in the middle, start or end of the line, with its
>   angle relative to the line or the horizontal.
>   A Connection Rule consists of an origin, destination, and a
>   connection to be used. The position in which the physical
>   connection is to be drawn can also be specified.

Both connections and connection rules are created and edited by the
super-user and saved in the palette. A user wishing to connect two
objects in the drawing selects an appropriate connection and draws it
between the objects. The validity of the connection would be checked by
the system using the connection rules.

For example in configuring PLEX for data-flow diagrams a data-flow would
be created in the palette as a connection consisting of a line with an
arrow and a textual label.

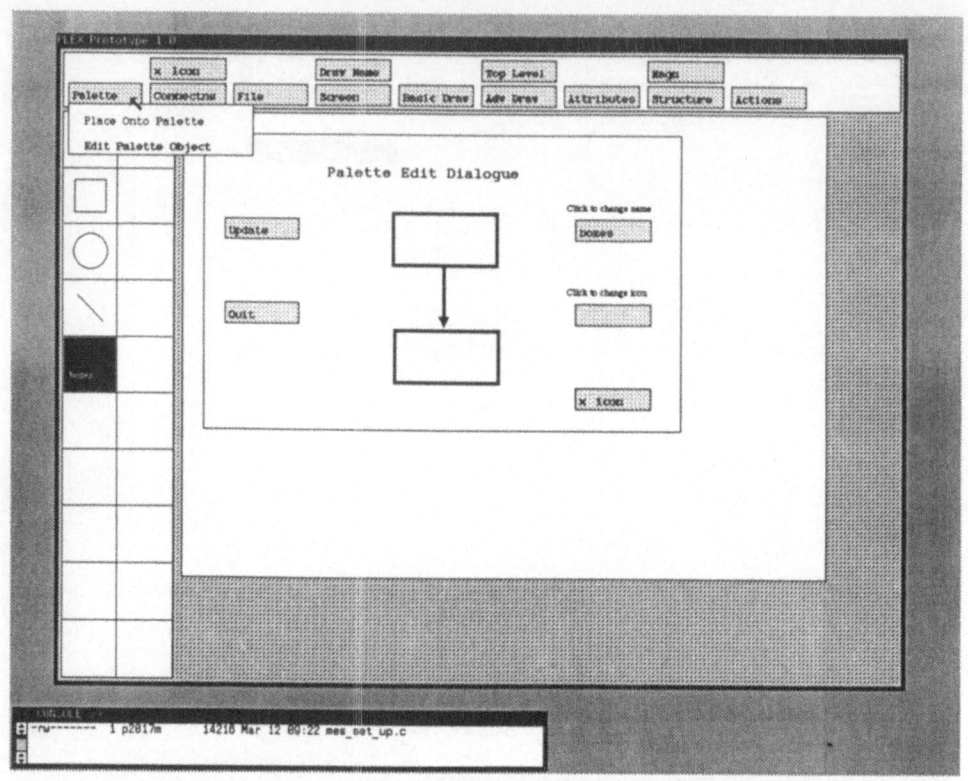

Figure 5 Editing a palette object using a drawing dialogue

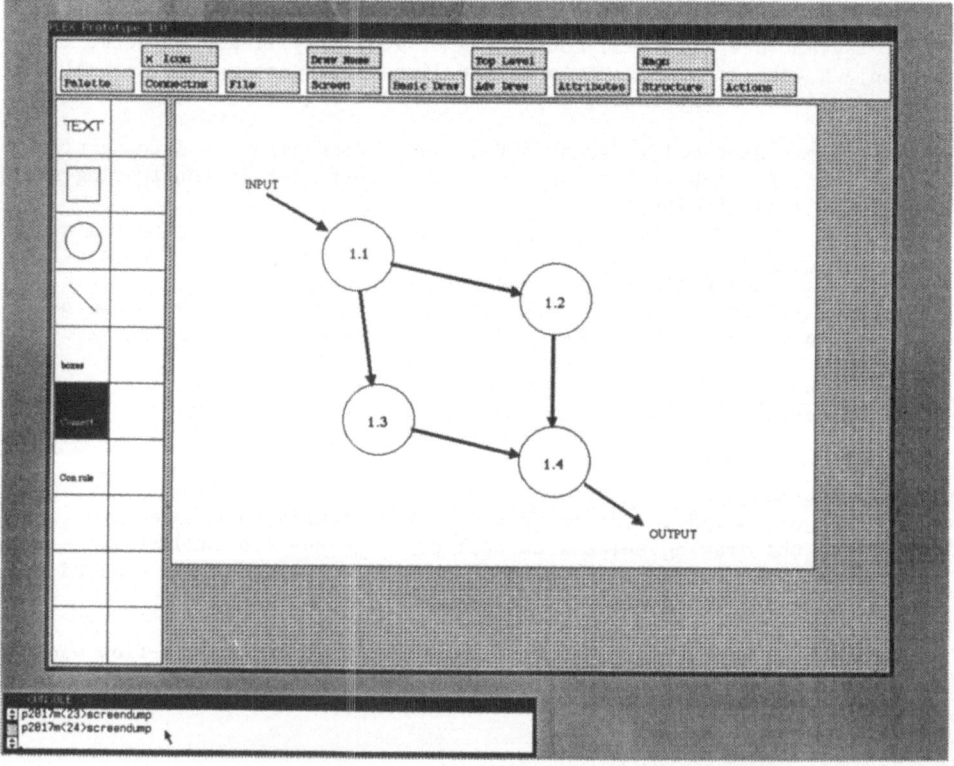

Figure 6 Diagram with connections (logical links)

Various connection rules would be set up to specify the objects between which the data-flow may be drawn. An example of a connection rule therefore would be:

  Origin - Process

  Connection - Data-Flow

  Destination - File

PLEX is therefore in no way tied to any particular methodology but allows the super-user to define his/her own rules and connections for logically linking objects, which may be basic atoms or user-defined palette objects.

3.4 Creation of Drawings

Once the user has set up any palette objects, connections and connection rules which are required to support a particular methodology, diagrams can be created by -

- Inserting the required objects from the palette

- Modifying the inserted objects using the functions provided

- Linking the drawing objects using the connections. The connections drawn would be checked for validity and appropriate positioning against the defined connection rules.

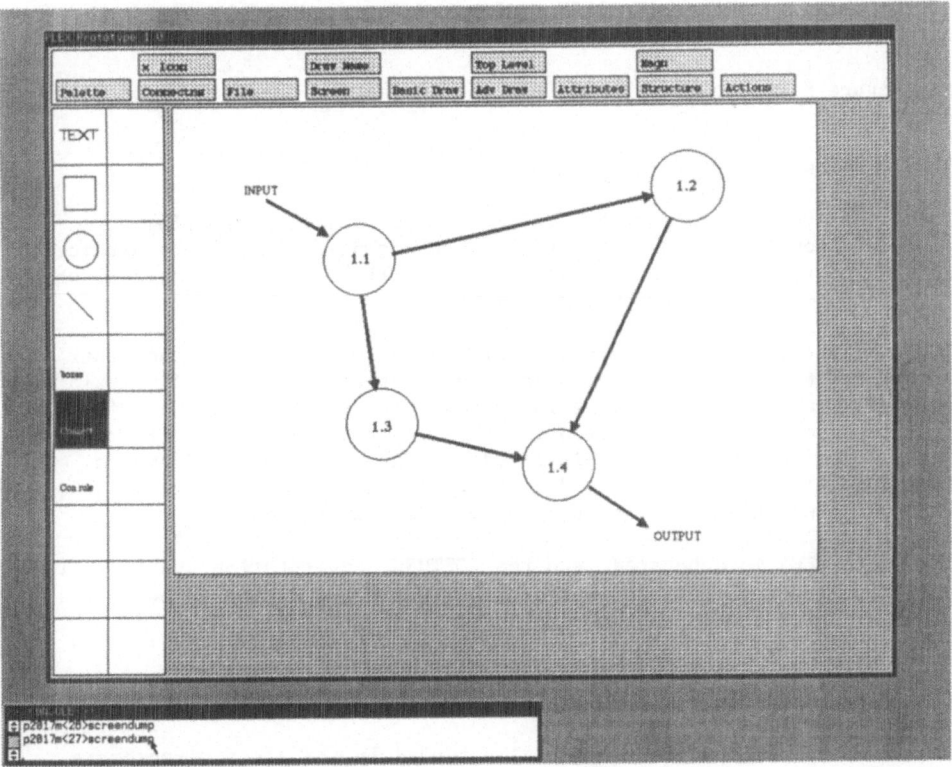

Figure 7   Connections repositioned after the movement of one object

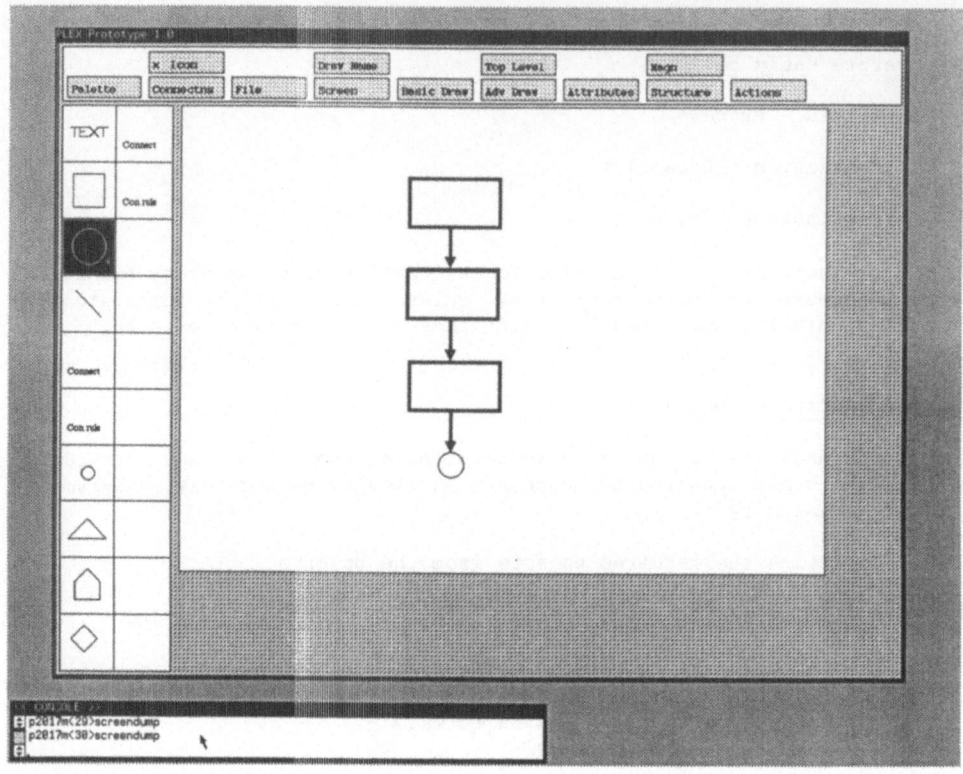

Figure 8   PLEX configured for flow charts

See Figure 8 for an example of PLEX configured for the drawing of flow charts.

3.5   Conclusion - Plex and Fortune

The Alvey FORTUNE project is a collaborative project developing a Documentation Support System for Software Engineers [MCGO87]. Although PLEX is a useful tool in its own right it will be far more powerful when incorporated into the FORTUNE documentation system.

The FORTUNE system will support references between diagrams and other documents stored within the system. Thus the selection of, for example, a process in a diagram could allow access to data dictionary entries for that process, the specification for that process and even the appropriate code. Consistency will be maintained throughout the FORTUNE system. An update applied to a name in a diagram, for example will result in that name being updated in all related occurrences in the system.

Therefore PLEX incorporated into the FORTUNE documentation system will provide a powerful tool for supporting diagram-based methodologies and producing high quality documentation for a system.

4   ACKNOWLEDGEMENTS

The Alvey FORTUNE projet is partially funded by the Alvey Directorate. It is led by CAP Industry, and other collaborators are MARI Advanced

118

Microelectronics Ltd, Baddeley Associates and the University of Kent at Canterbury.

5   REFERENCES

[ALLW81}   Allworth S.T. "Introduction to Real-time Software Design" Macmillan 1981

[BYTE83]   "The Lisa Computer System" Byte Vol 8 No 2 Feb 1983

[LBMS86]   Learmouth and Burchett Management Services. Material available from the vendors 1986

[MCGO87]   McGowan, S. "FORTUNE - An IPSE Documentation Tool" (This volume)

[ROSS77]   Ross D.T. "Structured Analysis for requirements definition" IEEE Trans. on Software Engineering Vol 3, part 2 1977, pp 1-65.

MAJIC - AUTOMATING JSP PROGRAM DESIGN AND DEVELOPMENT

A.F. Sutcliffe, P.J. Layzell, P. Loucopoulos, and
C.G. Davies

The University of Manchester
Institute of Science and Technology
Manchester, UK

1   INTRODUCTION

MAJIC (Michael A. Jackson Integrated Computer program design) is an
integrated program development environment which has been the subject of
research at UMIST for a number of years [EDWA79, TRIA79, SUTC86]. The
principle aim of the project is to assist the program designer with
practical computerised tools and to automate, where practical, the
process of program development. The system supports program development
by the Jackson Structured Programming (JSP) method which bases program
designs on the data structures which the program processes. JSP was
chosen as the method for automated support because it is widely practiced
in industry and it offers a reasonable amount of formality in the program
design process.

The system was envisaged as an integrated set of development tools linked
by a data dictionary which holds all specification details. In addition
to supporting program design activity, MAJIC was designed to
automatically generate code from program specifications; hence giving the
potential for increasing programmer productivity by eliminating the
tedious and error prone coding activity.

This paper describes the functionality and user interface of the MAJIC
system. Before proceeding with a description of the system, a short
description of the JSP method is given. For further details the reader
is referred to Jackson's book [JACK75].

2   THE JSP METHOD

JSP has five main stages:

1   Analyse Data Structures. Data structures which form the program
input and output are analysed to show the time ordering of their
components. In the case of an invoice, this ordering may well be the
invoice number, followed by the customer name and address, then the date
and an iteration of order lines with goods purchased, quantity and cost.
Such ordering is represented in JSP by Data Structure Diagrams which
describe the data structure components and the sequence in which they
occur. There are three component types in the diagram, sequence,
selection and iteration. This step is supported by a Data Structure
Diagrammer in MAJIC.

2   Create Program Structure. Two or more data structures are merged
together to derive the program structure, called correspondence in JSP.
It is effected basically by pattern matching data structure components of
the same type in two data structure diagrams. The idea is to create a
program structure which mirrors the data it is to process, so there is a
part of the program to deal with each part of the input and output data.
This step is supported in MAJIC by a diagram structure pattern matching
facility.

3   Program Structure Design. The program structure may be reorganised
to deal with run time uncertainty, called backtracking in JSP. Further
design may also be necessary if the initial attempt at correspondence
failed. In this case a structure clash is detected and the JSP technique
of inversion is used. The two unreconciled structures are taken and a
common intermediate data structure is designed which matches both
structures. These are then converted from two processes with a common
intermediate file into a main program - subroutine sequence by the
procedure of program inversion.

MAJIC detects structure clashes and supports their resolution with an
inversion sub system for creation of intermediate files and then creating
inverted programs. A backtracking editor allows program restructuring.

4   Detailed Program Design. Design details are called elementary
operations and conditions in JSP. These are the algorithms or processing
detail and the boolean logic necessary for Selections and Iterations.
Elementary operations and conditions are listed and then assigned to
program components. MAJIC supports this step by a list handler for
specification of elementary operations; it then allows allocation of the
operations to the diagram structure, and provides a code editor for entry
of source code level detail.

5   Convert into Schematic Logic and Code. The specification is changed
into text form (i.e. a pseudocode). Schematic logic forms the basis of a
program design from which code can be written. In MAJIC this step is
redundant as code is generated directly from the diagram structure and
elementary operation detail input in step 4.

3   MAJIC USER INTERFACE

3.1   The Majic User-System Interface

JSP uses diagrams to represent data and program structures providing
clear representation of program components and their inter-relationships.
Consequently MAJIC was designed as a diagram driven tool with a user
interface modelling the JSP development process. Graphic representation
is used extensively while the user-system dialogue explicitly guides
users through the steps of the JSP method.

MAJIC employs a high resolution graphics display, which is partitioned
into three areas, for the menu commands, messages and working
operations. Windows are configured as a display on an object, which in
MAJIC can be a structure diagram, a list, or text. If an object is too
large to be fully displayed in a single window then scrolling and scaling
mechanisms are provided as viewports onto the whole object. The MAJIC
display layout is shown in the figure 1.

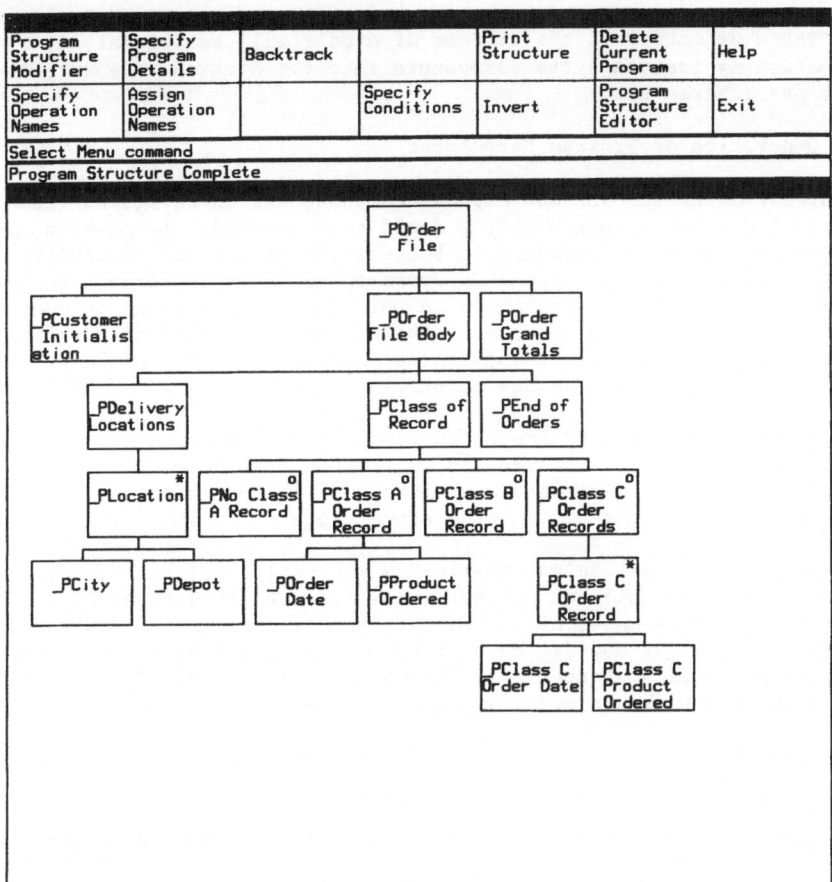

Program Structure Modifier	Specify Program Details	Backtrack		Print Structure	Delete Current Program	Help
Specify Operation Names	Assign Operation Names		Specify Conditions	Invert	Program Structure Editor	Exit

Select Menu command

Program Structure Complete

Figure 1   MAJIC screen display

Three methods of data input are provided. First, text can be input from
the keyboard, although this is restricted to the input of diagram
component and item names. Secondly the user can be presented with items
either in picking lists or in pop up menus. Options and valid components
are selected by pointing. Finally structure components are selected by
pointing to them on a diagram display. Input from pop up menus and
pointing responses is prevalidated while only the data input from the
keyboard is postvalidated. This minimises input of erroneous data.

3.2   The Data Structure Editor

Modelling the data sequences in Data Structure Diagrams is the essence of
JSP. The Data Structure Editor (DSE) provides a powerful tool for the
creation and modification of Data Structures in accordance with the JSP
rules of diagram construction. This facility has the full functionality
of a typical screen editor such as insert, delete, copy, cut and paste
etc., while being specifically tailored to the editing of Jackson
Structure diagrams. The general operation paradigm is for the user to
select the location of an editing operation by pointing to a component
and then to carry out an operation. The DSE editor is shown in figure 2.

Besides providing the full functionality normally expected of a diagram
editor the DSE also maintains integrity of the JSP diagrams by checking

each editing operation to ensure no illegal structures are created. If
the system detects that the outcome of a edit will be illegal, it
automatically inserts extra components into the diagram to ensure the JSP
rules are adhered to.

3.3 Generation of Program Structures

Formalisation of the JSP correspondence phase was investigated [HUGH79]
to see if data structure matching could be automated. Automation,
however, proved to be undesirable because it removed the flexibility of
design choice. Also an automated approach would be inappropriate because
Jackson [JACK75] gives an example in which pattern matching of components
is possible but invalid because of the different conditions pertaining to
the components (Boundary clash). Accordingly a strategy of decision
support for correspondence was adopted.

Program structures in JSP are based upon the data structures which have
already been analysed. Derivation of program structures therefore
entails matching data structures together while remaining faithful to the
ordering of components within each structure.

Correspondence rules are not explicitly stated in JSP; hence, some
extension of the basic set of heuristics provided by Jackson [JACK75] was
necessary. A task model of the correspondence process was derived from
interviews with JSP users. No uniform procedure was apparent so the task
steps represented a synthesis of the various practices. The
correspondence task was modelled as follows:-

(1) Select a data structure to form the basis of the program
     structure.

(2) Pick the first data structure to be corresponded with the
     program structure.

(3) Define the upper boundary of correspondence in a diagram in
     both the program structure diagram (PSD) and the data structure
     diagram (DSD). Initially the root of both diagram trees must
     be chosen. After the first step, components in sub trees in
     both diagrams will be chosen.

(4) Define the lower boundary of correspondence in the DSD. This
     usually delimits a sub tree within the whole DSD.

(5) Match the lowest component for correspondence in the DSD with a
     PSD component. The overall boundary of the sub tree to be
     matched is now defined.

(6) Match components in the sub tree according to their type.

(7) Insert unmatched components of the the DSD into the PSD,
     maintaining their relative time ordering.

(8) Iterate from step 3 until the whole structure is corresponded.

(9) Iterate from step 2 until there are no more data structures to
     be corresponded.

Users select a data structure produced in the structure editor and
declare it as the dominant data structure (DSD) which forms the initial
program structure (see Fig 3). This is merged with successive data
structures until the user is satisfied with the resulting composite

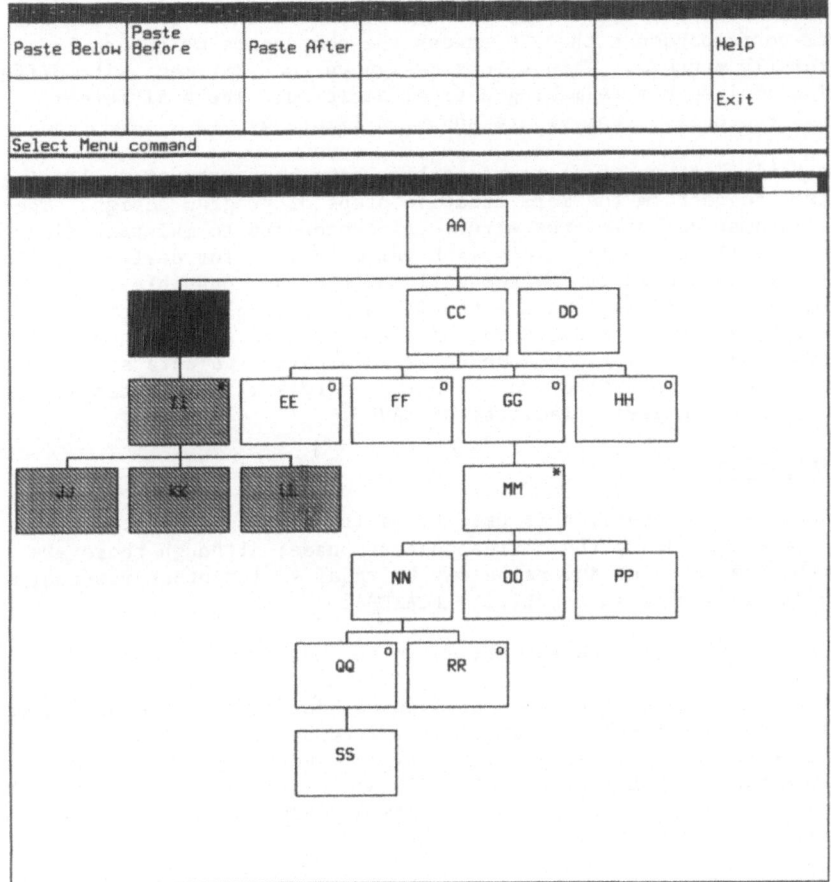

Paste Below	Paste Before	Paste After				Help
						Exit

Select Menu command

Figure 2   Data Structure Editor

	Old Program	Catalogue				Help
						Exit

Select Popup item or Menu command

```
sales file
customer file
new customer file
invoice file
order file
```

Figure 3   Initial Program Structure

program structure. The Progam Structure Generator (PSG) presents the user with both the growing program structure and the data structure being corresponded. By a series of shadings, it shows the user which components are already corresponded and the remaining DSD components which are valid for selection. When another component is picked for further correspondence the PSG shades the components which can be structurally matched. This allows designers to experiment with different matching choices before making a final decision. These different shadings and split displays are shown in Figure 4.

The mechanical steps of pattern matching have been automated, leaving the user free to perform the more creative steps of program design. The system automatically inserts structural components to maintain diagram integrity while prompting users with valid options for design decisions. In some circumstances the system will not find any possible correspondences and detects a potential structure clash. This may be resolved by selecting a different part of the data structure for correspondence; however, in some cases no alternative data structures may be available and the structure clash will persist. This necessitates use of the program inversion facility of MAJIC.

3.4 Inversion

The technique of inversion is used primarily to resolve a structure clash, detected during the correspondence phase; although there are circumstances in which inversion may be required for other reasons, such as scheduling a program's activity [CAME84].

The technique may be summarised in the following steps:

1   Introduce a number of data structures, called intermediate files (ImFs), which can match with previously irreconcilable structures. ImFs will be used for parameter passing between inverted programs. An Imf is created using the DSE facility of MAJIC and can be a totally new data structure, or one of the data structures already available in the system library.

2   Create new program structures using the program fragments and the newly created intermediate file. This is effected using the PSG to correspond ImF data structures into the program structures.

3   A program structure is nominated as the dominant one, and the subordinates are selected from a set of programs shown on pop-up menus. The dominant structure becomes the main program and subordinates will be sub routines called by it. In Jackson's terminology the subordinate is inverted with respect to the dominant.

4   Operations are added to the program structures, using the tools detailed in Section 3.6. The additional operations which have to be allocated to inverted program structures are the conceptual READ and WRITE from/to the ImF. These are translated in COBOL syntax into 'CALL {subroutine-name} USING {ImF-name}' for the program elected as the dominant and EXIT for the program which have been assigned the role of the subroutines.

At this point all the information necessary for inversion has been inserted into the system library, and code for the main program and the subprograms, with their respective calls, can be generated automatically.

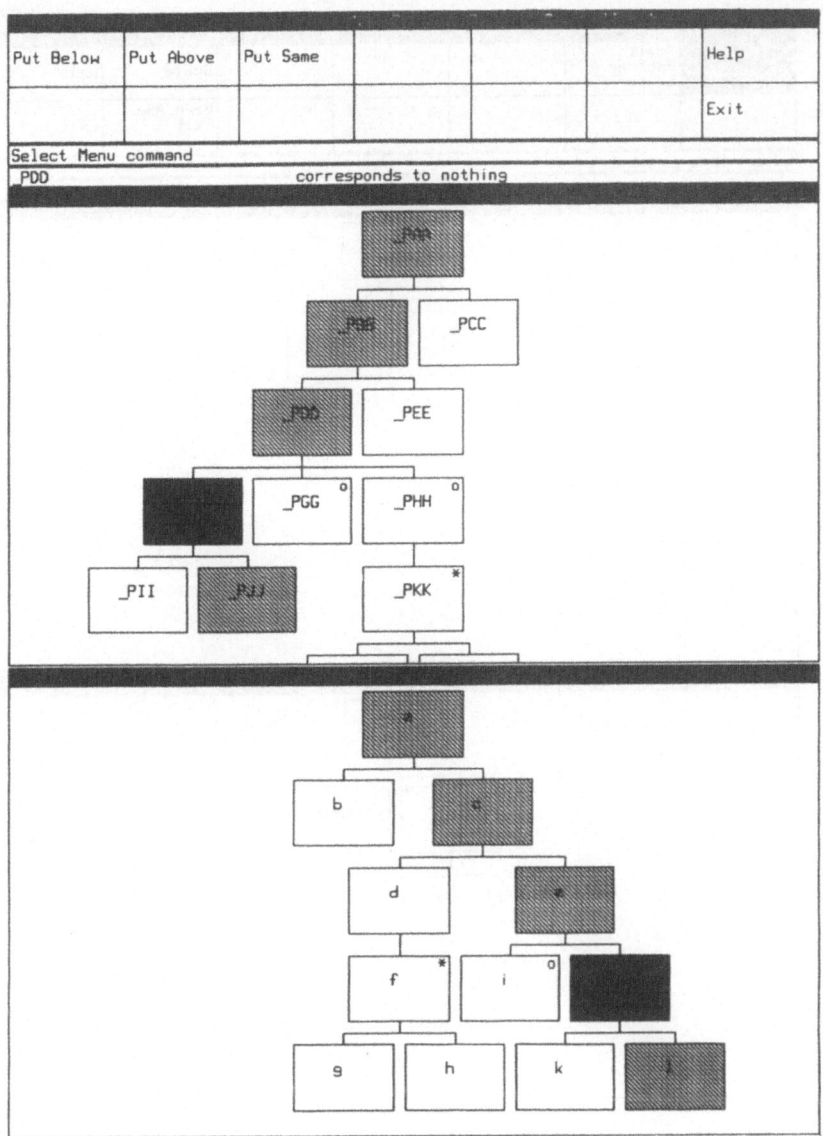

Figure 4   Program structure generator

3.5 Backtracking

In MAJIC, data structures can be designed with the need for backtracking in mind, and then combined to form a program structure. The resulting program structure may then be reorganised using the backtracking facility. Alternatively, this facility can be used directly on program structures which display considerable uncertainty, usually modelled as multiple nested selections in JSP. The program structure is rationalised by separating the normal processing from the exception handling components.

The JSP procedure for backtracking is composed of three steps:

> (1) Assume, or in JSP terms, posit, one path or subtree in a structure to be the correct one.

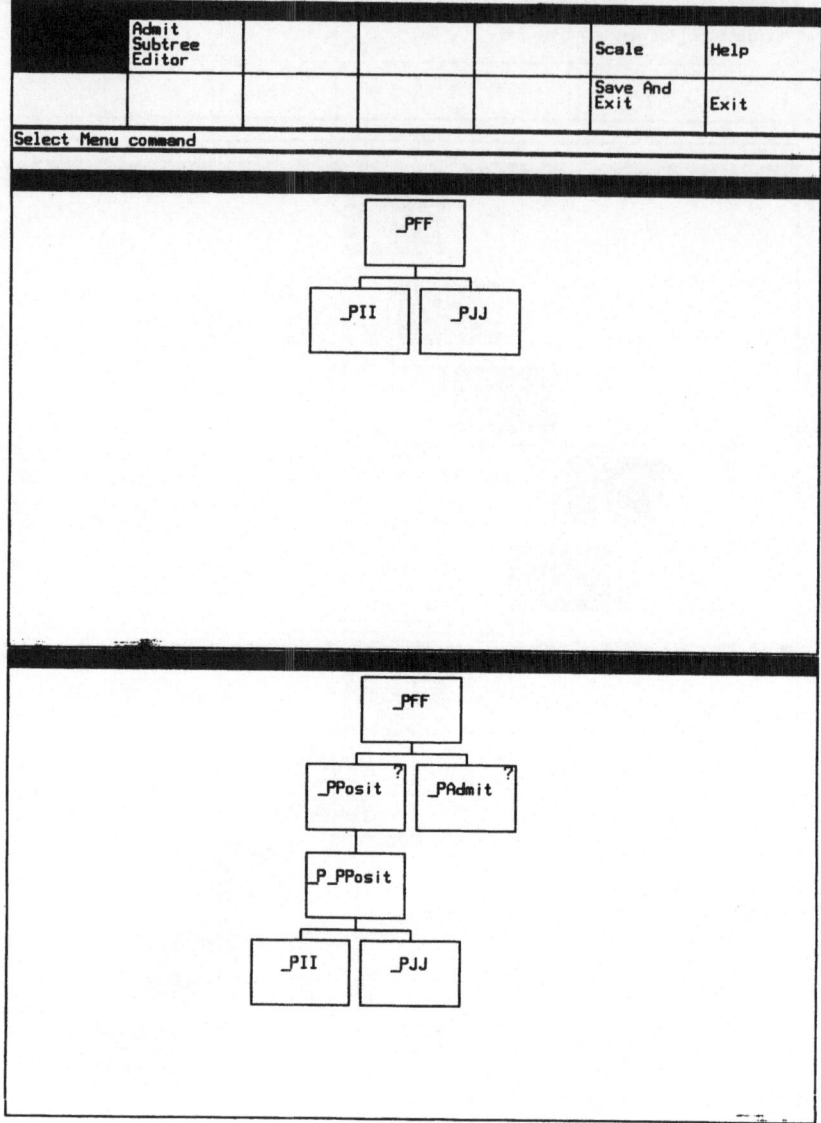

Figure 5   Choosing a sub-tree

(2) Insert test and exit probes, called quits, at points in this
     path where the unexpected may happen and the initial hypothesis
     might be disproved.

(3) Identify and deal with the consequences (called side effects in
     JSP) caused by abandoning the posited path. This becomes the
     admit subtree in the program structure.

In MAJIC the backtracking procedure is supported as follows. The posit-
admit sequence is built in by requesting the user to posit one of the sub
trees in the original structure (Fig. 5). The user may then either build
the admit branch from parts of the structure which are contained within
the posit sub tree or add new components to form the admit branch.

128

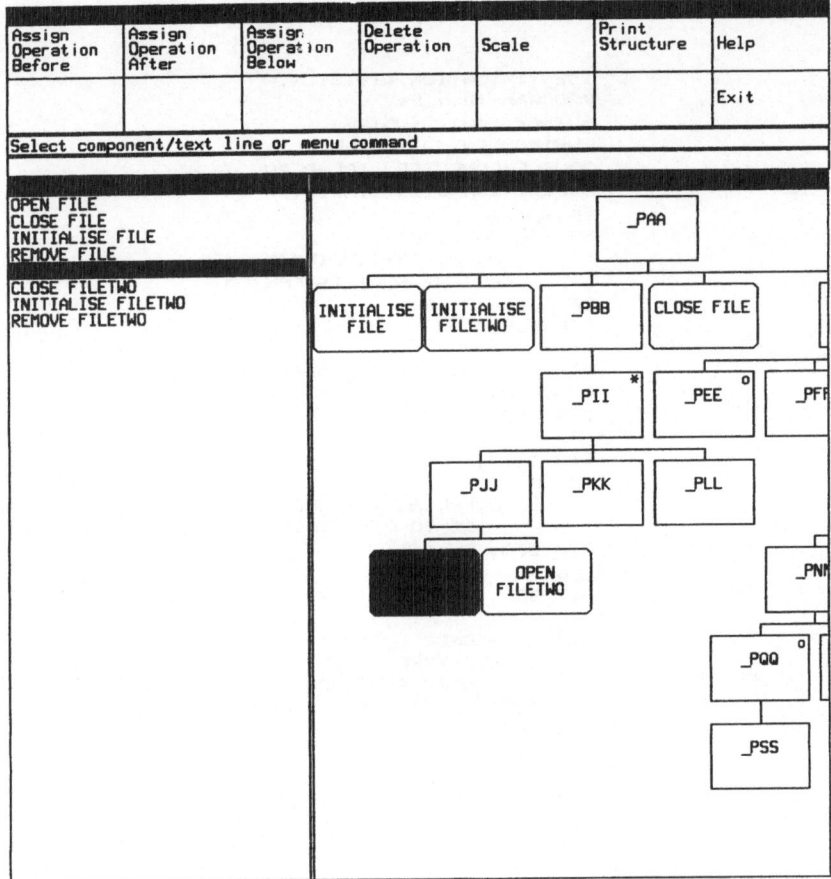

Figure 6   Input of operations during the inversion phase

When the basic structure has been built, the user may select the quit editor or the side effect editor. The quit editor allows the insertion and deletion of quit components into the posit branch. The side effect editor is a complete structure editor for the admit branch. It permits the user to add, change or delete any components in the admit branch so that side effects can be dealt with correctly. Components may be added to handle harmful side effects; alternatively, components may be marked as beneficial or neutral, in which case they are effectively 'comments' and code will not be generated for them.

3.6   Specification of Program Details

On completion of the program structure design, detailed design may proceed. So far only the structure of the program has been displayed, i.e. the procedure or sub routine shells. Detailed processing instructions and logic for control have to be added to the basic program structure.

Addition of program details proceeds in three steps, following the JSP method. First, names are given to each operational detail which must be added to the structure. These are called elementary operations (and conditions for processing logic) in JSP. Elementary operations and conditions are then assigned to components of the program structure.

```
IDENTIFICATION DIVISION.
PROGRAM-ID. _Pa.
AUTHOR. MAJIC-UMIST.
ENVIRONMENT DIVISION.
SOURCE-COMPUTER. ICL-PERQ.
OBJECT-COMPUTER. VAX11.
SELECT a
ASSIGN TO a.DAT
        ORGANIZATION IS INDEXED
        ACCESS MODE IS RANDOM.
DATA DIVISION.
FILE SECTION.
FD a
LABEL RECORD IS STANDARD.
PROCEDURE DIVISION.
G14-SEQ.
*_Pa
G15-ITER.
*_P_Gb
    IF EOF-FLAG = 'TRUE'
        GO TO G15-ITER-END.
G16-SEQ.
*_Pb
G17-SEL.
*_Pc
G18-SEQ-COND.
    IF REC-TYPE = 'C1'
        NEXT SENTENCE
    ELSE GO TO G21-SEQ-COND.
G18-SEQ.
*_Pc1
G19-SEQ.
*_Pe
G23.
*op 1
    elem op one.
G20-SEQ.
*_Pf
G24.
*op 1
    elem op one.
G27.
*op 4
    elem op four.
    GO TO G17-SEL-END.
G21-SEQ-COND.
**IGNORE CONDITION**
*REC-TYPE = 'C2'
G21-SEQ.
*_Pc2
G25.
*op 2
    elem op two.
G17-SEL-END.
G22-SEQ.
*_Pd
G26.
*op 3
    elem op three.
    GO TO G15-ITER.

G15-ITER-END.
PROC-DIV-END.
    STOP RUN.
```

Figure 7 Example code produced

The system supports this step by displaying a list window for the user to enter the elementary operation names. Then the user selects each elementary operation and allocates it to an appropriate position in the program structure. The graphical representation of elementary operations is differentiated from other structure components by rounded corners enabling the user to easily distinguish between the two, see figure 6.

The system then provides for assigning code to elementary operations and conditions which form part of the COBOL Procedure Division. The program structure is displayed with menus of the appropriate program statements for selection in a split screen display. Form filling templates for statements in the target language are presented to guide entry of syntactically correct code. An example of the way that operations are input by the user during the inversion phase is shown if Figure 6. The COBOL Data Division may also be specified using Data structure diagrams and then assigning PIC clauses to the data items. The only omission from a completed specification is the Environment Division details which are currently defaulted to clauses of the user's choice.

The syntax checker ensures that only valid options for the clause being entered are presented in the pop up menu. The menu changes dynamically as the entry progresses adjusting itself to the syntactic rules of COBOL. The whole process is integrated between Data and Procedure divisions so when the user needs to refer to a variable name in a procedure division statement, another pop-up menu displays the data structures currently available within the system.

3.7 Code Generation

In this step the program structure is combined with the design details to generate source code of complete programs in the target language chosen by the user. Currently only COBOL is supported. Code generation is fully automated and once initiated no further user intervention is required. The code generator user supplied data names and design details, while generating dummy names for structural components. The code produced certainly does not look pretty and would not help maintenance (fig 7), however the philosophy behind MAJIC is that programs should only be altered by changing specifications and the generated code need never be inspected.

The MAJIC system is programmed in Pascal and runs under POS on a PERQ workstation.

4   DISCUSSION

The MAJIC system can be regarded as a precursor of the Integrated Project Support Environments which form a central part of the Alvey programme's software engineering strategy [ALVE83]. The Alvey IPSEs aim to provide project management, systems analysis and design tools as well as program development facilities. The more limited ambition of MAJIC reflects the state of the art at the birth of the project is 1979. In spite of its smaller scope, the MAJIC system delivers a set of design tools to support the JSP method which are integrated in an environment to guide the analyst through program development.

Program support environments should provide an integrated set of tools for designers to specify and then construct programs. Furthermore, to really increase programmer productivity these environments should support automatic code generation from designs. As a result program creation and maintenance may be carried out on designs, thus removing one of the time consuming and error prone parts of the development life cycle. MAJIC enables COBOL-74 code to be generated from JSP specifications by providing the designer with a compatible set of tools which perform consistency checking throughout the development life cycle. Furthermore MAJIC actively helps the designers task by prevalidating all input and guiding the user through the JSP method.

The user interface of the MAJIC system makes extensive use of windows and pop up menus to provide concurrent displays (e.g. a diagram structure and a list), and a flexible dialogue structure so user's can choose commands while interacting with a design object. The overall interface, however, has a constrained dialogue which guides the user through the JSP method and prevents mistakes being made in the design process.

MAJIC is not the only JSP support environment. A JSP diagram editor and code generator called PDF (Program Design Facility) is available from the method vendors, Michael Jackson Systems Ltd. PDF, like MAJIC, allows users to build JSP diagrams. However it provides no support for data modelling and correspondence; indeed, its starting point is to directly construct a Program Structure Diagram. PDF is therefore more of a program development tool than an integrated development environment. Other program and system design methods have been automated with diagram tools and text editors to help the construction of specifications and designs, e.g. SADT [ROSS77], ACM/PC1 [BROD82], SSADM [LMBS86]. Although these tools are integrated to the extent that they provide consistency checking and some support for their respectively methods, code generation is not supported. Without automatic code generation the productivity advances which may be anticipated from the introduction of structured methods are unlikely to be realised [MART82].

Many program development environments have been produced varying from the large, but unintegrated set of tools provided in the UNIX programmers' workbench to more specification driven systems such as the Cornell Program Synthesiser [TEIT81]. However, many systems have been restricted in their coverage, because code could only be generated from part of a program specification such as decision tables. Those systems which have provided for code generation from complete program designs have used text based specification methods, based either on method independent pseudocode [TEIT81] or on method specific languages such as PSL/PSA [TEIC77].

Such text based specifications can suffer from problems of tractability because a specification language or pseudocode has to be learned. Diagrams, generally, form a more immediate and comprehensive method of representing information. JSP and MAJIC make extensive use of diagrams which should help the understanding of designs, also the structural nature of the PSD diagrams should make the location of maintenance within systems, easier. Most recent system development methods make extensive use of diagrammatic techniques. In two cases, IE and HOS, [JMA85, MART82] support environments for the methods incorporate automatic code generation. These environments provide functionality which is similar to that of MAJIC.

A limited evaluation of MAJIC was undertaken to establish user opinion on the system. User reaction was generally favourable to the system interface and functionality of the diagram editors, syntax checker etc. The main comment about the correspondence mechanism was that it could be over-complex. Some users confessed that in fact they hardly use correspondence at all instead use the technique of inversion to combine program fragments into a single program with many subroutines. The consensus view was that if correspondence was not obvious from immediate visual inspection of data structures then inversion was used. Whether this practice is a consequence of the lack of automation and could be changed by the MAJIC remains to be seen.

In conclusion, the MAJIC project has demonstrated that automated support of JSP is practical. The system shows many of the features of the Alvey IPSE concept in terms of integration and active support for a design method. The next step in support of the software development task is to provide active heuristic guidance for the designer in terms of an analyst expert system. Such steps are now being taken within advanced the second and third generation of IPSE projects [FLYN86].

5   ACKNOWLEDGEMENTS

The authors are indebted to John Triance and Brian Edwards who started this project and contributed the initial design and much of the implementation. The authors also wish to acknowledge the efforts of many research assistants who have tackled parts of MAJIC over the years, notably Chris Gould, Mike Cave, Ioannis Samaras and Cornelius Harthoorn.

6   REFERENCES

[ALVE83]   Alvey Directorate, Software Engineering Strategy, 1983.

[BROD82]   Brodie, M.L. and Silva, E. Active and Passive Component Modelling. In Automated Tools for Information System Design, eds Schneider H.J. and Wasserman A.I., 1982, pp 41-91.

[CAME84]   Cameron J.R. JSP and JSD: The Jackson approach to software development. IEEE Computer Society press, 1984.

[EDWA79]   Edwards B.J. and Triance J.M. Automation of the Jackson Method of Program Design. Internal Report No 244, Dept of Computation, UMIST, 1979.

[FLYN86]   Flynn D.J., Layzell P.J. and Loucopoulos P. Assisting the Analyst - The aims and approaches of the analyst assist project. In software Engineering 86, eds Barnes D. and Brown P. 1986, pp19-26.

[HUGH79]   Hughes J. A Formalisation and explication of the Michael Jackson Method of program design. Software Practice and Experience Vol 9, 1979, pp 191-202.

[JACK75]   Jackson M.A. Principles of Program Design, Academic press, 1975

[JMA85]   James Martin Associates.
           Information Engineering Factory.
           Descriptive material available from the vendors. 1985.

[LBMS86]   Learmont and Burchet Management Services.
           Data Mate/Auto Mate.
           Material available from the vendors. 1986.

[MART82]   Martin J. Program design which is provably correct. Savant press, 1982.

[ROSS77]   Ross D.T. Structured Analysis for requirements definition. IEEE Trans. on Software Engineering Vol 3 part 2, 1977, pp 1-65.

[SUTC86] Sutcliffe A.G., Layzell P.J., Loucopoulos P., Davies C.G.,
          Samara I., Harthoorn C. MAJIC - an automated program design
          and development aid. In software Engineering 86, eds Barnes D.
          and Brown P., 1986, pp 371-382, Peter Peregrinus.

[TEIC77] Teichrow D. and Hershey E.A. PSL/PSA: A computer aided method
          of systems analysis and specification. IEEE Trans of Software
          Engineering 3(1), 1977, pp 41-48.

[TIEL81] Tieltelbaum, T and Reps, T. The Cornell Program Synthesiser: A
          syntax directed programming environment. Comms of the ACM.
          24(9), 1981, pp 563-573.

[TRIA79] Triance J.M. and Edwards B.J. A computer aided program design
          project. Proc. Euro IFIP-79. 1979.

COMPUTER-AIDED DESIGN OF SOFTWARE: RESEARCH AND EXPERIENCE

Karel Riha and George Rzevski

School of Information Systems

Kingston Polytechnic

ABSTRACT

This paper gives a progress report on a project whose objective is to
investigate how conventional software design methods can best be
computer-aided. The software design method chosen for the initial
investigation is that used in the Evolutionary Design Methodology
[RZEV82].

The main aspect of this research has been an evolutionary development of
a software design tool called LIST (Language Independent Software Tool).
LIST is an interactive software design specification editor with
facilities for checking the software structure for completeness and
consistency. LIST enables the user to display the specified software
structure in a number of ways and to obtain metrics relating to the
complexity of various aspects of the design.

The initial pilot system took about one man-year to design and implement.
Since then LIST has been used for over four years on graduate and
undergraduate courses in software engineering. During this time,
research aimed at investigating what tool features improve the
productivity of the software design process as well as the quality of the
designed software has been carried out. The results of this research
have been used to modify many of the features of LIST and to add new
facilities.

The current version of LIST (4.2/OCT-86) has been implemented in Pascal
in the DEC's UNIX (Ultrix) environment. The user interfaces with LIST
via an ordinary alphanumeric VDU terminal such as TVI 910+ and VT100.

INTRODUCTION

The paper starts by giving a brief background to the project. The next
section summarizes a survey of literature on computer-aided design of
software. In section 3 the approach used in the development of LIST is
outlined. The main features of the current version of LIST are described
in section 4. The paper concludes with a summary of the project's
achievements and a discussion of the relationship between the project and
other work in the same area; possible future enhancements to LIST are

also discussed. The APPENDIX contains extracts from LIST's documentation that was generated by LIST.

1   PROJECT BACKGROUND

The problems experienced by those involved in the development of software have attracted a great deal of attention in the literature. Methods are being proposed almost daily to cope with what is often referred to as the "software crisis" (see Pressman [PRES82] chapter 2), or the "software problem" (see Shooman [SHOO83] chapter 1). Many computer-based tools are being developed to aid one or more software development activities. Some of the methods and tools have achieved success in making the software development process more productive and in improving software quality [MART85].

Methods which were developed initially to be used without computer-based tools will be referred to in this paper as "conventional" methods. Whilst many of the conventional software development methods have gained a wide degree of acceptance (e.g. [WIRT71, JACK75], and [YOUR79]), the introduction of computer-based software development tools has been much slower. There are many reasons for this, the principal one being the lack of off-the-shelf tools that fit well into the potential users' software development environments. Only large software development organizations have the resources to develop their own tools to suit their particular needs [HOWD82]. Even when suitable tools are available, there is the lack of the potential users' awareness of their existence or the mistrust the users have in the claims about the tools benefits (often justified by the first or second hand experience with other tools) [HOUG82].

Thus most software is still being developed using tools that have not changed fundamentally since the advent of interactive text editors and high level programming language interpreters and compilers [HOWD82]. The demand for more software, for larger software systems and for better quality software continues to grow. Only a much greater automation of the software development life-cycle can satisfy this demand [STUC83].

Before the full potential of software development tools can be realized, there is a need for more research into the ways in which software development can be aided by the computer [HABE80, RIDD81]. The research described in this paper has been motivated primarily by the recognition of this need. An ongoing research project at Kingston Polytechnic resulted in the development of the Evolutionary Design Methodology [RZEV80, RZEV82, RZEV84], an information systems design methodology used on postgraduate courses and in industry. The lack of computer-based tool to support the methodology was seen as a serious weakness. A prototype computer-aided design (CAD) of software program developed by an MSc student [WELL80, RZEV81] demonstrated the feasibility of a CAD of software system based on the Evolutionary Design Methodology. The project also identified the need for further research in this area to explore the full potential of CAD techniques in the design of software.

2   LITERATURE SURVEY

In this section the terms of reference for the literature survey are first given. Published descriptions of three categories of software design tools are then surveyed in separate subsections. The section concludes with a brief discussion of possible future developments in this area.

2.1 Terms of reference

For the purpose of the project software design was defined as follows

> SOFTWARE DESIGN is a process of transforming a software requirements definition into a model that specifies how the software is to be implemented. A SOFTWARE DESIGN process results in a progressively less abstract, more detailed and more programming language oriented model of the computer-based part of the system for which the software is being designed. SOFTWARE DESIGN is finished when a blueprint for a machine executable specification is obtained which is correct with respect to the requirements definition and when the implementation of the design becomes a routine application of the knowledge of the target programming language.

Some idea what the state of computer-aided design of software was up to early 1980 can be obtained from the following quote by Martin [MART85]:

> By the early 1970s the term "computer-aided design" (CAD) was common for design engineers. Many CAD packages were sold. Amazingly, ten years later the terms "computer-aided systems analysis" and "computer-aided programming" were still not common. System analysts and programmers, who have done so much to automate everybody else´s jobs, were remarkably reluctant to have their own jobs automated. They sat at their desks with pencils creating designs full of errors, inconsistencies, and omissions that a computerized tool could have detected.

If we define computer-aided design of software as any activity of software design, as defined above, which is aided by a computer, then we find that there is a considerable number of computer-based tools which fall into this category. One could argue, with some justification, that almost any tool which aids the development of software can either directly or indirectly aid the design (including re-design and correction of design errors) of software. For example, a compiler with good error reporting features, such as the Berkeley Pascal compiler [JOY81], can point out several types of design inconsistencies (e.g. variables which are declared but not used or whose values are written but not read) and can thus be an invaluable aid in correcting faulty design.

However, in this paper, the term CAD of software is going to be used only for software design activities which are immediately assisted by a computer-based tool. In other words, only interactive tools which directly support the software design process, are going to be considered in this section. Most of these tools also provide some indirect design-related assistance (e.g. hard-copy design documentation or checking compatibility of design and implementation) and such features will also be examined. The literature search has resulted in an assumption that such tools can be usefully classified as belonging into one of three broad categories:

(1) The tools which concentrate on the detailed or programming language (bottom) end of software design. These tools usually incorporate some type of a syntax-directed editor.

(2) The tools which automate a conventional software design method or technique.

(3) The tools based on novel approaches to software design which would be impossible without a computer-based tool.

Each of these categories will now be looked at in turn, noting the contributions which particular tools have made to the progress of computer-aided design of software and to our understanding of this process.

2.2 Tools for Detailed Software Design

Because of their association with the actual entry of executable code syntax-directed editors are usually thought of as implementation rather then design tools [ALLI83]. The major problem with using syntax-directed editors for designing software is that only one view, a rather low-level programming language oriented view, is available to the designer.
Several systems that have been developed recently attempt to remedy this deficiency. GUIDE [SZAF85], for example, enables the user to display the program hierarchy using Jackson's diagram [JACK75] and to edit this hierarchy using simple commands. PASCAL/HSD system combines program text and graphics in a novel approach to creating and editing programs.

The most promising extension of the syntax-directed approach appears to be PECAN [REIS84]:

> PECAN is a program development system generator for algebraic programming languages. The program development systems it produces support multiple views of the user's program, its semantics and its execution. The program views include a syntax-directed editor, a declaration editor, and a structured flow graph editor. The semantic views include expression trees, data type diagrams, flow graphs, and the symbol table. The execution views shows the program in action and the stack contents as the program executes.

PECAN differs from previous systems by generating complete environments from simple specifications of the target programming language syntax. The generated environments also differ in their use of the power and graphical facilities of a new generation of personal machines and in their support for multiple concurrent views.

2.3 Automated Conventional Software Design Methods

All of the better known and many of the less well known software design methods have had one or more of their techniques automated, with various degrees of success. However, most of the tools which resulted from these attempts at automation would be used only by the designer and his immediate colleagues. Brown [BROW82] puts this proportion as high as 90%. Of the remaining 10% of the tools he asserts that nine out of ten are not used outside the designer's organization. One could similarly argue that for every tool the details of which have been published and are easily available there could be hundreds of tools which are not known to the wider community.

One of the first documented efforts was the TOPD system [SNOW78]. This is a development environment based on a finite-state modelling approach [HEND75]. TOPD allows the development of a program to be done as a series of abstract descriptions, each of which is finite-state model organized as a collection of data abstractions. The TOPD notation allows the description of behaviour in terms of state transitions and the system checks the consistency between a procedure's behavioural and structural descriptions.

The TOPD is only suitable for the development of sequential programs. The DREAM system [RIDD81] is a TOPD-like system for the development of concurrent software systems. The heart of the DREAM system is the DDN language. This language embodies an automata theoretic formalism for modelling parallel systems developed in the period 1973-1975 [RIDD79]. DDN facilitates the conceptualization of concurrent software systems during their architectural design.

Automation of software design methods appears to have been most successful where several different aspects of software development have been automated and integrated. Such a system would normally have a central database where all the project related data is stored. For example, AIDES computer-aided design of software system [WILL81] automates many of the procedures of a variation of the Structured Design methodology [STEV74, JENS75] and is a culmination of six years of practical application of this methodology at Hughes Aircraft Company. Only the guidelines of structured design which have survived the test of time have been retained. Many new software engineering features have been added to make AIDES a unique design methodology.

Stucki [STUC81, STUC83] describes an integrated system for software development called ARGUS, that has been under development at the Boeing Computer Services Company. The ARGUS editor supports the creation and modification of formal data flow diagrams characterizing the software system. These data flow diagrams are complemented by structure charts to support the Structured Design methodology [YOUR79]. The ARGUS programming tools used the design data in the ARGUS database to generate "code documentation template". This template includes relevant design information directly into code so that the consistency between the design and code can be checked.

Jackson's Structured Programming is another widely used software design method for which a number of software tools have been developed. For example, the company founded by Jackson has developed a system called the Program Development Facility (PDF) [MJSL86]. PDF uses interactive graphics to enable the user to construct and edit JSP structures and program designs. PDF generates pseudocode and source code skeleton for several programming languages. MAJIC (M.A. Jackson Interactive Computer-aided program design) [SUTC86, SUTC87] is another program development tool which supports the JSP method. The ultimate objective of MAJIC is that program design and coding should be automated by code generation directly from JSP specifications.

As the cost of interactive high resolution graphics computing decreases so does the need for drawing diagrams by hand. According to Martin [MART85] architects, engineers and circuit designers have been far quicker in exploiting the advantages of "interactive diagramming" which he describes as follows:

> Interactive diagramming on a computer screen has major advantages. It speeds up the process greatly. It enforces standards. The computer may apply many checks to what is being created. It can automate the documentation process. The designers are less likely to do sloppy work.

An example of the state of the art in this area is the MacCadd [LOGI86] package for the Apple Macintosh personal computer. MacCadd is an integrated family of integrated tools for interactive drawing of the following types of system and software representations:

> Data flow diagrams for "Structured Analysis" [GANE79].

> Structure diagrams for "Entity Life Histories", "Jackson Structured Programming" or "Jackson System Development" [JACK75, JACK82].

MASCOT diagrams for real-time software design [ALLW81].

Hierarchical state transition diagrams for modelling of "Finite State Machines" [HEND75].

MacCadd knows the syntax of the diagram type in use and helps the user by enforcing its principal design rules. MacCadd also encourages top down design by allowing any appropriate parts of diagrams to be drawn in more detail on a separate sheet. This process can continue indefinitely. A single MacCadd design is held as a tree of diagram "sheets".

Martin [MART85] is one of several authors who contend that automation of diagramming should lead to automated checking of specifications and automatic generation of program code. This goal has been achieved by the developers of the USE.IT system [MART85]. This system automates the application of the HOS methodology [HAMI76]. HOS (Higher Order Software) is a methodology for creating computable software specifications based on a set of mathematical axioms. The verification with the HOS axioms would be far too tedious for most analysts to carry out by hand. USE.IT enables its user to enter HOS trees using a graphics editor. It then checks that the mathematical rules have been obeyed so that the application logic structure is guaranteed to be correct. USE.IT can then generate program code (e.g. FORTRAN or COBOL) which is guaranteed to be correct with respect to the HOS specification. The main drawback of the USE.IT system is that it is not very high on a scale of user friendliness. The main reason for this appears to be the mathematical nature of the HOS methodology. Martin [MART85] suggests that a suitable "front-end" "end-user" interface could enable more users to benefit from this tool.

2.4 Novel Approaches to CAD of Software

In this subsection two examples of novel approaches to computer-aided design of software will be briefly outlined and discussed.

The first approach belongs to a broad category that has come to be known as "fourth generation" languages (4GL)[MART85a]. However, unlike most 4GL tools it does not suffer from being limited to a narrow area of application. The approach is based on the so called "operational" software development method [ZAVE84]. Using this method an executable specification language is used to develop prototypes in a fraction of the time it would take using ordinary programming languages [BALZ82].

The difference between a language for operational specification and an implementation language is that the specification language is designed for clarity of expression. No account is taken of implementation considerations. However, executable specification languages make much heavier demands on a run-time system than equivalent programs in third generation languages (e.g. COBOL and Ada). Thus the specification has to undergo a process of transformational implementation [SOMM85] which should result in an efficient program without introducing any errors.

It seems likely that today's specification languages will be tomorrow's programming languages. All it requires is that the hardware to support their requirements is designed and built. This is now the topic of much research work. The operational approach to software development is not going to eliminate the need for software design since writing specifications, whether they are executable or not, can be considered an integral part of software design. All that is going to happen, it seems, is that design will be done only at the highest levels with much less need for detailed design. This does not necessarily mean that there will be less design work about as, in keeping with the current trends, the demand for more complex software is bound to grow.

The second novel approach to software design that will be briefly described is a development from systems which exploit pictures in the design and documentation of programs but tend to focus on the graphical representation of individual algorithms and data structures. Pictures in PegaSys (Programming Environment for the Graphical Analysis of SYStems) [MORI85] have a fundamentally different purpose; they are intended to describe the overall design of a program. A program design is described by a hierarchy of pictures related according to precise refinement rules. PegaSys ensures that the pictures denote well-formed logical structures and that the hierarchical refinements adhere to certain rules.

PegaSys presently connects a picture hierarchy to programs written in the Ada programming language in order to determine whether the programs are consistent with the pictures. However, the approach is not based on generating pictures from programs as in PECAN [REIS84], for example. Instead, PegaSys provides a means by which the user can describe and structure the form of a program in terms of the abstractions used in its conceptualization. This approach is based on the belief that it is difficult, if not impossible, to generate these abstractions from the final program.

PegaSys combines a relative ease of user interaction (using icons to compose pictures) with a rigour achieved previously only by using formalisms such as predicate calculus. As such it represents one of the most promising developments in the computer-aided design of software.

2.5 What next?

The best way forward in the field of software development appears to be a greater automation of software design and implementation. Considerable progress has been made in this direction but much more remains to be done. Most software is still being developed using conventional methods. However, an increasing number of software development tools is becoming available and as they get better their acceptance by the software developers is bound to increase. Fourth generation languages already make it possible to eliminate a great deal of detailed software design for many applications [MART85a]. Given the steady advance of artificial intelligence techniques and in the performance of hardware, so called "fifth generation" systems could soon replace most of the current software development practices by computer-aided problem or system analysis.

3   RESEARCH APPROACH

Two distinct research approaches were considered at the start of the present project. These approaches can be briefly summarized as follows:

(1) Investigate existing software design methods and tools and analyse the findings. Formulate comprehensive and detailed requirements for a software design tool and then develop it. Evaluate the effectiveness of the developed tool.

(2) Investigate existing software design methods and tools and analyse the findings. Formulate requirements for a pilot software design tool and then develop the pilot. Evaluate the pilot and then propose and implement modifications. Evaluate the modifications and

then propose and implement further modifications. Repeat the process of evaluating and proposing new modifications until a desired level of effectiveness has been achieved.

The first approach (1) is based on the traditional view of the software life-cycle. Such an approach has been shown to be inappropriate for large systems and when requirements are fuzzy [GLAD82, MCCR82]. The main problem with the traditional approach is in knowing when to stop the requirements analysis so that resources remain to design and implement the system. Another common problem with the traditional approach is the assumption that the user requirements can be ascertained accurately in advance without giving the user an opportunity to try the system out. Unless the system can be easily modified to take into account unforeseen user requirements or reactions it is likely to fail.

The approach (2) is based on the idea of evolutionary refinement based on user feedback [SHNE82] and on the evolutionary view of the software life-cycle [RZEV83]. This type of approach appears to be more appropriate in exploratory projects with limited resources because it carries lower risks of not producing practical results [TRAF85]. There undoubtedly was a need for a tool which only the present project seemed capable of providing. The second approach thus appeared more appropriate.

4   DESCRIPTION OF LIST

LIST adopts an interactive structure editor approach to the specification of the software structures. The user is thus prevented from specifying syntactically illegal structures. The model of software which enables LIST to achieve that is described briefly in the first subsection. The next subsection outlines the user interface for one of the four types of LIST editors, the control flow structure editor. The three other editors, text editor, relations editor and data flow structure editor have a very similar interface and so they are not described in this paper. Subsection 3 discusses the specification and consistency checking of data flow structure. The section concludes with a summary of LIST's capabilities.

4.1   Software structure specification

The structure of the software is specified using a simple entity-relationship [CHEN76] model. The model utilizes three types of entities (modules, data, constructs), various attributes associated with each type of entity (identifier, long identifier, description, date created etc.) and the following relationships between the entity types:

input data of modules (IM)

input data of constructs (IC)

output data of modules (OM)

constituent modules of modules (CM)

constituent data of data (CD)

control relationship (CR)

The user starts the design by specifying the "top" module. Then he has to specify some entities which are directly related to the top module.

Further entities can be specified by relating them to the entities specified previously. In this way a top-down design is encouraged.

For example, the input and output data of the top module could be specified first, followed by the constituent data of some of this data, followed by the constituent modules of the top module, and so on. The design is deemed complete when all the "bottom-level" modules can be either easily coded or have already been coded.

The initial specification of the entities consists of the user-entered "LongId" followed by the "Id" of the entity. The former serves as a brief description of the entity (up to 40 char.) whereas the latter is a unique identifier (up to 12 char.) used to access the entity during the design. The text description of entities (unlimited length) can be entered by the user at any time. All the other attributes of the entities (e.g. date created) are generated automatically.

LIST recognizes several types of software structures based on the above relationships:

> hierarchical structures of modules (based on the CM relationship)
>
> hierarchical structures of data (based on the CD relationship) control flow structures of modules (= algorithms, based on the CR relationship)
>
> data flow structures of modules (based on the IM, OM, IC and CR relationships)

4.2 Control Flow Structure Editor

One unusual aspect of LIST is the entity "construct" and the role this entity plays in the specification of the control flow structure and the data flow structure of modules.

The control flow structure of a module is the specification of the order in which the constituent modules of the module are called. All LIST modules which have a structure (i.e. are not the bottom-level modules) are members of a control relationship (CR) represented by the following table type:

CR(ModuleId, ControlledEntityId, Order)

The controlled entity can be either a module or a construct. This control relationship specifies the order in which the controlled entities are called.

Similarly, all constructs are members of a relationship represented by the table type:

CR(ConstructId, ControlledEntityId, Order)

What this relationship specifies depends on the type of the construct (an attribute of the construct entities):

> a conditional call of one of the controlled entities ("CaseOf" construct; if the condition has to be specified for each "case" then a "When" construct can be "controlled" by the "CaseOf" construct)
>
> a conditional call of all the entities in the order specified by the relationship ("If" and "ElseIf" constructs)

a conditionally repeated call of all the controlled entities in the
order specified by the relationship ("While" and "Until" constructs)

The user specifies the control flow structure of a module by first giving
the entities controlled by the module in the order they are called. If
the entity is a construct the user has to give the entities controlled by
the construct before giving the rest of the entities controlled by the
module. This process is continued recursively until the whole control
flow structure of the module is specified. The interface to do this
resembles entering PDL or pseudocode and having the syntax checked as
soon as each line is entered. The user can also display the control flow
structure as a PDL-like notation (see Figure 1.) which has been annotated
with symbols used in Rothon's Design Structure Diagrams [ROTH79].

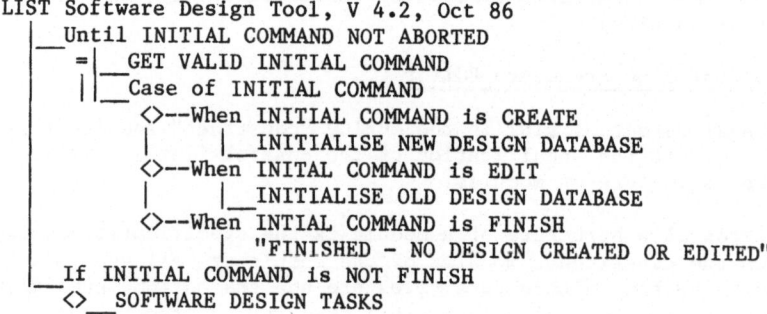

Editing the Control Flow structure of the module: LIST
Requests are: ?,H,D(el),F(in),M(odu),O(ld),R(epl),T(ype);
              C(ase),E(lse),I(f),U(ntil),W(hen),W(hile).

```
LIST Software Design Tool, V 4.2, Oct 86
    |__Until INITIAL COMMAND NOT ABORTED
    |  =|__GET VALID INITIAL COMMAND
    |   |__Case of INITIAL COMMAND
    |        <>--When INITIAL COMMAND is CREATE
    |         |    |__INITIALISE NEW DESIGN DATABASE
    |        <>--When INITAL COMMAND is EDIT
    |         |    |__INITIALISE OLD DESIGN DATABASE
    |        <>--When INTIAL COMMAND is FINISH
    |              |__"FINISHED - NO DESIGN CREATED OR EDITED"
    |__If INITIAL COMMAND is NOT FINISH
       <>__SOFTWARE DESIGN TASKS
```

Figure 1: Screen layout for editing CFS

Figure 1 shows what the user would see on his screen when he has finished
the specification of the control flow structure of LIST (self-
documentation). This can be compared with the content of the "Box -2-"
in the APPENDIX where more LIST's documentation by LIST is given. The
same representation for control flow structure is used there except that
the flow-lines have been extended to obtain a match with data flow
structure of the RHS (LongIds in the PDL belong to the same constructs or
modules as the Ids in the data flow structure on the same line).

The LIST Control Flow Structure (CFS) editor requests:

H   / general Help about this editor
D   / Delete the entity at cursor position from the CFS
F   / Finish editing the CFS
M   / create a new Module and insert below cursor position
O   / insert an Old entity below cursor position
R   / Replace the attributes of entity at cursor position
T   / erase screen, then Type (re-display) the CFS
RETURN or "DOWN arrow" / move closer to or to the module or
          construct on the line below cursor position
"-" or "UP arrow" / move closer to or to the module or
          construct on the line at or above cursor position.

CFS editor "create construct" requests create the following"

C   / "Case of" selection construct
E   / "Else if"/"Else" sequence construct
I   / "If" sequence construct
U   / "Until" loop sequence construct
W   / "When" sequence construct - if nested in a "Case of"
W   / "While" loop sequence construct

Figure 2: Details of the CFS editor requests

The details of the single key request that are used in the control flow
structure editor are given in Figure 2. This is the information that the
user obtains by pressing the "?" key on his keyboard.

The role of the construct entities (e.g. INITIAL COMMAND NOT ABORTED in
Figure 1.) is not only to specifiy the control flow structure but also
the details of the controlling condition. This can be done in the
"LongId" or the "Description" of the constructs and by specifying the
input data relationship of constructs as represented by the following
table type:

IC(ConstructId DatumId Order)

The data specified in this relationship is the "control data" which
determines the flow of the control when the construct is encountered.
One of the consequences of having construct entities is the ability to
treat the control data in the same way as any other data. This
facilitates a more complete design specification which can then be
checked for data flow inconsistencies (see the next subsection).

4.3 Data Flow Structure Specification

The data flow structure of a module specifies which data flows
into/between/out-of which constituent modules. The flow of the control
data can also be fully specified by considering the input to the
constructs. LIST displays data flow structure using a diagram similar to
a Detailed HIPO diagram (see APPENDIX).

LIST provides a complete check on the consistency of the data flow
structure of modules. This is based on the requirement that the input
and output data of a module specify the module´s interface completely.
The data flow structure of the module thus has to be consistent with the
modules´s interface as well as internally.

LIST's data entities can be specified as a hierarchy of other data
entities using the constituent data relationship. In order to encourage
the structuring of data which reflects the structure of the modules (or
the other way round if the data structure-driven design strategy {JACK75}
is used) the following rule is stipulated:

> Input data of a module should either be input by a constituent
> module or have at least one of its constituent data input by a
> constituent module.

Any violation of this rule is reported by LIST as an error. The user is
also warned if there are constituent data not being input where they
could be. An identical rule and error reporting/warning also applies to
the output data of the module.

Some data in a module's data flow structure is internal to the module.
LIST checks that such data is both output by a constituent module and
input by either a constituent module or a construct in the module's data
flow structure. A violation of this rule is reported as an error.

4.4   The capabilities of LIST

Once the user understands the software structure specification concepts
and learns the LIST interface (1-3 hours for most users) he/she has a
simple and yet powerful tool for software design and documentation. The
larger and the more complex the software structure the easier it is to
achieve an elegant, perceivable and modifiable software structure
specification when compared with conventional (manual) methods.

LIST also encourages good design practices such as top-down design,
gotoless algorithm specification, data abstraction, complete module
interface specification, use of meaningful identifiers, keeping a design
log and trying alternative software structures. This makes LIST a useful
tool for teaching software design.

LIST also generates simple design metrics and these have been used in the
guidelines to the users of LIST. The guidelines are based on the
research {KAP082] at Kingston Polytechnic. Part of this research
involved a modified version of LIST which collected data from its users.
The data consisted of various design complexity metrics (e.g. control
flow structure and data flow structure complexity measures) and the
number of "design changes" associated with the modules. On the
assumption that a good design strategy should require the minimum number
of design changes to produce a consistent software structure
specification (see [DUNS77]) optimum design metrics have been identified.
The authors feel that more research is required in this area to obtain
results which are both reliable and generalizable.

5   CONCLUSIONS AND FUTURE RESEARCH

The first subsection summarises what are considered to be the most
significant acheivements on the project. The following subsection
outlines the main influences on the current research and the relationship
to similar type of work that has been carried out elsewhere.

5.1   Achievements of the Project

The main achievement of the project was the formulation and a practical
validation of an approach to computer-aided design of software. A model
for representing the structure of software has been formulated and a tool

(LIST) to manipulate the model developed. LIST has been used to assess a number of ways in which the design of software can be computer-aided.

One of the most useful features of the model is that it enables LIST to check the completeness and consistency of both the data flow and control flow structures across, as well as within, the levels of the software hierarchy. The usefulness of this feature is greatly enhanced by the ability of the model to express both the high-level (architectural) and low-level (detailed) software design specification. By using the LIST data flow structure editor the designer can easily specify the flow of data at all levels of abstraction. This is very difficult to achieve with other data flow representations and thus a proper data flow design is rarely carried out at the low level design of software. The feedback from the users suggests that providing support with checking for a detailed design of the software data flow is one of the most useful features of LIST. This is because LIST helps to ensure that high-level data flows have a complete and consistent refinement at the low-level and because the detailed specification of the data flows assists greatly during the implementation of the software.

The research investigated the effect of different ways of entering and updating the structures. The LIST editors evolved to become highly effective in enabling the users to achieve their objectives. The quality of the user interface was identified as a very significant factor in the effectiveness of LIST. The effectiveness of different ways of displaying the designed software structures has been investigated. Out of many possible types of graphical notations for displaying the hierarchical, control flow and data flow structures those which proved particularly helpful to the designer have been identified. The displays have been redesigned repeatedly to achieve greater clarity in representing the software structures and relationships.

The research also identified a need for a hard copy design documentation whose content and format can be selected by the designer. The feature found particularly helpful was a module's interface specification and graphical display of the control flow and the data flow structures on the same line printer page. A report of any inconsistencies or incomplete design was also included on this page (A3 size approximately), a feature which greatly aided the task of locating and correcting design errors.

Since the development of the first main release of LIST (1.0) data has been collected automatically by LIST on the design activities of the LIST users. The analysis of this data provided an additional feedback during the evolutionary development of LIST. For example, one analysis of this data found a significant correlation between modules' complexity metrics and a number of design changes (creating and deleting relationships between entities) required to eliminate errors. However, the number of such design changes per unit complexity did not show any significant correlation with the modules' complexity. This appeared to contradict some of the previous research into software design complexity control [RZEV80A, KAPO82]. A careful analysis of the results revealed that it would be unwise to generalize the results beyond the circumstances in which they were obtained. It could thus be argued that the effectiveness of LIST and similar tools was unlikely to be improved by imposing a limit on the local complexity of the structures specified by the user but the argument could not be extended to, for example, a manual design technique.

Although the data collected by LIST (unless collected as a part of a carefully controlled experiment) can be open to various interpretations, they have provided an objective measure of the way different versions of

LIST affected the user behaviour. Perhaps the most significant of the collected statistics was the "speed of design changes". This was obtained by dividing the number of "design changes" (creating and deleting relationships between entities) by the time taken to perform these changes. The speed of design changes has seen a mean increase of about three-fold since this statistics was first collected.

An experiment was conducted in March 1986 to assess the effectiveness of LIST. This established that novices could learn to use LIST effectively after only a relatively short practice. Compared with a conventional (manual) design LIST was found to be slightly less productive in sessions lasting two hours. However, this lower productivity was more than made up for by a significantly lower incidence of design errors. Since this experiment further significant enhancements of LIST have been implemented. The statistics collected by LIST have been compared with those collected before the enhancements. In both cases similar groups of users (students) used LIST to design software using the same set of requirements. The results suggest that these latest modifications have increased the mean speed of design changes supported by LIST by about 40 per cent. Although a controlled experiment is needed to ascertain more accurately how this affects the overall effectiveness of LIST, the latest feedback from the users has been very encouraging.

5.2 Relationship to Other Work

The published work to which the results of the research described in this paper are related can be divided into two broad groups. The first group consists of the work which had a direct influence on this research. The second group consists of the work which has been found to be related to the present research but had no obvious influence on its direction.

The Work Which Directly Influenced the Research

A number of publications directly influenced the research described in this paper. The order in which they are given below is approximately chronological as far as the time of their impact on the research is concerned.

The idea for an interactive software design tool came from an MSc project carried out by Wells [WELL80] at Kingston Polytechnic.

The terminology used to describe software structure is based largely on the Evolutionary Design Methodology [RZEV82].

The idea for representing software structure using relations came from a paper by Yau and Grabow [YAU81] in which they showed how to derive relations from a BNF form of Pascal.

The initial user interface of the tool LIST [RZEV83A, RIHA83] was greatly influenced by the TOPS-20 operating system and the SOS editor [DEC80] user interfaces. The latest version of LIST [RIHA86] that has been developed to run in a UNIX operating system environment owes much to that environment [KERN81].

The Program Design Language used for specifying control flow structure is based on the Caine and Gordon's PDL [CAIN75]. The Rothon's paper [ROTH79] greatly influenced the style of the graphical notation for control flow structure and the IBM HIPO technique [IBM74] was the main motivating influence behind the graphical notation for data flow structure. The display of the hierarchical structure of modules and data has been influenced by the Warnier-Orr diagrams [WARN77].

Other Related Work

The literature survey revealed a number of research projects which touched on the topic of computer-aided design of software. There are some which include the development of a software design tool with a graphical representation of the designed software. Those which come closest to the research described in this paper are briefly described below. The description highlights the similarities and points out the differences.

Diaz-Herrera's PhD thesis [DIAZ81] describes the development of an interactive graphical program development system. The main similarity with the current research is the graphical representation of the control flow structure of software using structured flow diagrams and the structure-oriented entry of the specification of control flow structure. The significant difference is that the system has no concept of modular design or data flow structure design and is strongly geared towards a specific programming language (Pascal).

Another approach which has some similarities to the current research is an interactive graphics data flow modelling system STRADA [STUC81] which supports the Structured Design methodology [YOUR79]. The main similarity with the current research is an interactive top-down specification of the flow of data through the system which includes the ability to refine data in terms of constituent data. STRADA also provides consistency and completeness checking as well as cross-referencing in a manner similar to LIST. However, there are many differences between STRADA and the approach adopted in the current research. The most significant is that STRADA has no facilities for representing control flow structure of software and thus limits its scope to systems analysis and database design.

5.3 Possible Future Extensions of LIST

One of the main requirements of the project was that LIST is easily modifiable and portable. None of the major modifications and enhancements have presented any serious problems so far. A move from a TOPS-20 to UNIX was also relatively easily accomplished. The chances for further successful extensions and transportations therefore look good.

An area where the effectiveness of LIST could be improved most drammatically is the medium and the format of the user interface. The availability of relatively cheap high resolution display microcomputers and workstations is beginning to make it feasible to implement a Macintosh-like interface for LIST for enough users to make the effort worthwhile. The ability to display all the information in a documentation box (a line-printer page - see APPENDIX) on one screen with a Windows, Icons, Mouse and Pull-down menus (WIMP) interface should make it significantly easier to design software interactively. Many users of LIST still do some of their design on paper before or while using LIST. The limited amount of information that can be displayed on the VDU screen has been given as a main reason for this.

A decision was made at the start of the project to limit the initial scope of the research to the software design phase of software development. An option of extending the tool to other phases of software development has however been kept open. In particular, LIST has already been used with considerable success for designing the mode of control for human-computer interfaces. Concrete proposals have also been made for generating code from the design specification and it is only a matter of time before these are put into effect.

It has also been decided to keep the model of software design as simple as possible without making the tool too limited in its applicability. The model used by LIST falls into the SEQUENTIAL PROCEDURAL formalism [RIDD80] category (see the Literature Survey). However, there are other important software modelling formalisms, particularly the FUNCTIONAL and CONCURRENT PROCEDURAL formalisms. These have not been addressed in the present project. LIST thus makes a suitable software design tool in the areas where the procedural programming languages which do not have any concurrent programming constructs (e.g. ALGOL, COBOL, FORTRAN, Pascal etc.) are used. LIST would not be suitable for detailed design in the areas where programming languages which include constructs for concurrent processes handling have to be used (e.g. Ada, CORAL, MODULA etc.) or where so called functional or declarative languages are required (e.g. LISP or PROLOG).

In spite of the increasing popularity of the programming languages for which the tool, as it stands, would not be an appropriate design aid, most programming is still carried out using the traditional programming languages. Thus the LIST's model restriction does not appear to limit its applicability unduly and has been more than outweighed by the relative conceptual simplicity of the model. Furthermore, just as some programming languages have been extended to include constructs for handling concurrency [YOUN82], so could LIST be extended if the need arises. For example, a "Concurrent" construct type could be added to the existing construct types to specify concurrent execution. Other features of concurrent software such as "synchronization" would be much more difficult to express with LIST without a significant extension. It could be argued, however, that such details are best left to the implementation phase of software development and that LIST should still be adequate for describing the high level structure of concurrent software in sufficient details for easy implementation. The experience obtained so far tends to support this argument.

References

[ALLE82] Allen, R.B. and Allison, L., and Allworth, S.T., Archer, J., and Conway, R., "COPE: A cooperative programming environment," Cornell TR81-459, vol. 13, no. 3, pp. 453-465, Macmillan Press, 1981.

[ALLI83] Allison, L., "Syntax Directed Program Editing," Software Practice and Experience, vol. 13, pp. 453-465, 1983.

[ALLW81] Allworth, S.T., Introduction to Real-time Software Design, Macmillan Press, 1981.

[BALZ82] Balzer, R.M., Goldman, N.M., and Wile, D.S., "Operational specification as the basis for rapid prototyping," ACM Software Engineering Notes, vol. 7, no. 5, pp. 3-16, 1982.

[BROW82] Brown, P.J., "Tools for Amateurs," in Tools and notions for program construction: An advanced course, ed. Neel, D., pp.377-390, Cambridge University Press, 1982.

[CAIN75] Caine, S.H. and Gordon, E.K., "PDL: A Tool for Software Design," in Proc. National Computer Conference, 44, pp. 271- 276, 1975.

[CHEN76] Chen, P.P.S., "The Entity-Relationship Model - Toward a Unified
          View of Data," ACM Trans. on Database Systems, vol. 1,   March
1976.

[DEC80]   DEC, Getting Started with TOPS-20, Digital Equipment
          Corporation, Marlboro, Mass., 1980.

[DIAZ81] Diaz-Herrera, J.L., "An Interactive Graphical Program
          Development System," PhD Thesis, Lancaster University, March   1981.

[DUNS77] Dunsmore, H.E. and Gannon, J.D., "Experimental Investigation of
          Programming Complexity," in Proc. 16th ACM Technical
          Symposium on Systems Software, vol. 3, ACM, N.Y. and NBS,
          Washington DC, 1977.

[GANE79] Gane, C.P. and Sarson, T., Structured Systems Analysis: tools
          and techniques, Prentice-Hall, Englewood Cliffs, N.J.,   1979.

[GLAD82] Gladden, G.R., "Stop the Life Cycle, I Want to Get Off," ACM
          Software Engineering Notes, vol. 7, no. 2, Apr. 1982.

[HABE80] Haberman, A.N., "Tools for Software System Construction," in
          Software Development Tools, ed. Fairley, R.E., pp. 10- 21,
          Springer-Verlag, 1980.

{HAMI76} Hamilton, M. and Zeldin, S., "Higher Order Software - A
          Methodology for Defining Software," IEEE Trans. on   Software
          Engineering, vol. 2, no. 1, pp. 9-32, Mar.   1976.

[HEND75] Henderson, P., "Finite State Modelling in Program Development,"
          ACM SIGPLAN Notices, vol. 10, no. 6, pp. 221-227, June   1975.

[HOUG82] Houghton, R.C., "Features of Software Development Tools,"
          NBS, Washington D.C., 1982.

[HOWD82] Howden, W.E., "Contemporary Software Development Environments,"
          Communications of the ACM, vol. 25, no. 5, pp. 318-329,   May
1982.

[IBM74]   IBM, "IBM HIPO - A Design Aid and Documentation Technique,"
          GC20-185D, IBM Corporation, White Plains, N.Y., 1974.

[JACK75] Jackson, M.A., Principles of Program Design, Academic   Press,
1975.

[JACK82] Jackson, M.A., System Development, Prentice-Hall, 1982.

[JENS75] Jensen, E.P., 1975 IR&D Structured Design Methodology; Vol I -
          Cost of Modularity, Vol II - Structured Design, Vol III -   The
          Mystique of Structured Design, Hughes Aircraft Company, FR   75-17-691,
          Fullerton, CA., Dec. 1975.

[JOY81]   Joy, W.N., Graham, S.L., and Haley, C.B., Berkeley Pascal
          User's Manual, Version 2.0, University of Califoria,   Berkeley,
1981.

[KAPO82] Kaposi, A.A. and Rzevski, G., "On the Aims and Scope of a
          System Design Methodology," in Progress in Cybernetics and   System
          Research, ed. Trappl, R., Klir, G., Pichler, F., General   Systems
          Methodology, vol. III, pp. 123-129, Hemisphere   Publishing Corporation,
1982.

[KERN81] Kernighan, B.W. and et al., UNIX Programmer's Manual, Seventh Edition, Virtual VAX-11 Version, University of California, Berkeley, CA., June 1981.

[LOGI86] Logica, MacCadd Version 3 Reference Manual, Logica UK, 1986.

[MJSL86] MJSL, "Program Development Facility," Customer Information, Michael Jackson Systems, 1986.

[MART85A] Martin, J., Fourth-Generation Languages, 1, Prentice- Hall, Englewoodd Cliffs, N.J., 1985.

[MART85] Martin, J. and McClure, C., Structured Techniques for Computing, Prentice Hall, 1985.

[MCCR82] McCracken, D.D. and Jackson, M.A., "Life-Cycle Concept Considered Harmful," ACM Software Engineering Notes, vol. 7, no. 2, Apr. 1982.

[MORI85] Moriconi, M. and Hare, D.F., "PegaSys: A System for Graphical Explanation of Program Designs," in Proc. of the ACM SIGPLAN 85 Symposium on Language Issues in Programming Environments, SIG-PLAN Notices, vol. 20, 1985.

[PRES82] Pressman, R.S., Software Engineering (A Practitioner's Approach), McGraw Hill, 1982.

[REIS84] Reiss, P., "Graphical Program Development with PECAN Program Development Systems," in Proc. of the ACM SIGSOFT/SIGPLAN Software Engineering Symposium on Practical Software Development Environments, Software Engineering Notes, vol. 9, May 1984.

[RIDD79] Riddle, W.E., "An Approach to Software System Modelling and Analysis," Computer Languages, vol. 4, pp. 49-66, 1979.

[RIDD80] Riddle, W.E., "Procedural Approaches to Software Design Modelling," in Software Development Tools, ed. Fairley, R.E., pp. 129-141, Springer-Verlag, 1980.

[RIDD81] Riddle, W.E., "An assessment of DREAM," in Software Engineering Environments, ed. Hunke, H., pp. 191-207, North-Holland, 1981.

[RIHA83] Riha, K., LIST User's Manual, Dept. of EECS, Kingston Polytechnic, Kingston upon Thames, 1983.

[RIHA86] Riha, K., LIST User's Manual, Version 4.2, School of Information Systems, Kingston Polytechnic, Kingston upon Thames, 1986.

[ROTH79] Rothon, N.M., "Design Structure Diagrams: A new standard in flow diagrams," Computer Bulletin, Series 2, British Computer Society, March 1979.

[RZEV80] Rzevski, G.R., Woolman, D., and Trafford, D.B., "A Methodology for the Design of CAD Systems and its Implementation in an Industrial Environment, "Proc. 4th Int. Conf. on Computers in Design and Engineering, CAD 80, pp. 22-31, IPC Science and Technology Press, Brighton, March 1980.

[RZEV80A] Rzevski, G., "Systematic Design of Simulation Software," in Proc. Simulation 80, Interlaken, 1980.

[RZEV81] Rzevski, G. and Wells, M.J., "Computer-Aided Design of Engineering Software," in Proc. 2nd intl. conf. on Engineering Software, London, 1981.

[RZEV82] Rzevski, G., Trafford, D.B., and Wells, M.J., "Evolitionary Design Methodology Applied to Information Systems," in Information System Design Mehtodologies - A Comparative Review, ed. Olle, T.W., Sol, H.G., Verrijn, A.A., pp. 427-475, North-Holland, 1982.

[RZEV83] Rzevski, G., "Prototypes Versus Pilot Systems: Strategies for Evolutionary Information System Development," in Proc. Working Conference on Prototyping, ed. Budde, R., Namur, Belgium, 25-28 Oct. 1983.

[RZEV83A] Rzevski, G and Riha, K., "On language-Independant Software Design Tools," in Proc. Workshop on Program Development Tools, Lund, February 1983.

[RZEV84] Rzevski, G., "The Evolutionary Design Methodology," in Proc. IFIP Conf. on Comparison of Design Methodologies, Paris, June 1984.

[SHNE82] Shneiderman, B., "The future of interactive systems and the emergence of direct manipulation," Behaviour and Information Technology, vol. 1, no. 3, pp. 237-256, 1982.

[SHOO83] Shooman, M.L. Software Engineering, McGraw Hill, 1983.

[SNOW78] Snowdon, R.A. and Henderson, P., "The TOPD System for Computer-Aided System Development," in structured Analysis and Design, State of the Art Report, vol. 2. pp. 283-306, Infotech, Maidenhead, England, 1978.

[SOMM85] Sommerville, I, Software Engineering, Addison-Wesley, 1985.

[STEV74] Stevens, W.P., Myers, G.J., and Constantine, L.L., "Structured Design," IBM Systems Journal, vol. 13, no. 1, pp. 114-139, 1974.

[STUC81] Stucki, L.G. and Walker, H.D., "Concepts and Prototypes of ARGUS," in Software Engineering Environments, ed. Hunke, H., pp. 61-79, North-Holland, 1981.

[STUC83] Stucki, L.G., "What about CAD/CAM for Software? The ARGUS Concept," in Proc. Softfair 1983, pp. 129-144, IEEE, 1983.

[SUTC86] Sutcliffe, A.G., "MAJIC - A Computer-Aided Program Design for the Commercial Computer," Alvey News Supplement, no. SE2/18, Alvey, 1986.

[SUTC87] Sutcliffe A.G., Layzell P.J., Loucopoulos P., and Davies C.G. "MAJIC-Automating JSP Program Design and Development, (this volume).

[SZAF85] Szafron, D., Adria, J., and Wilkerson, B., "GUIDE: An environment for software design," INFOR (Canada), vol. 23, no. 1, pp. 31-52, 1985.

[TRAF85]   Trafford, D.B., "An Investigation into Method for the
Evolutionary Development of Computer-Aided Design Systems," PhD
Thesis, CNAA, School of Information Systems, Kingston
Polytechnic, 1985.

[WARN77]   Warnier, J.D., Logical Construction of Programs, Van Nostrand,
New York, 1977.

[WELL80]   Wells, M.J., "Computer Aided Software Design - A Feasibility
Study," MSc. Thesis, CNAA, Kingston Polytechnic, 1980.

[WILL81]   Willis, R.R., "AIDES: Computer Aided Design of Software Systems
- II," in Software Engineering Environments, ed. Hunke, H., pp.
28-48, North-Holland, 1981.

[WIRT71]   Wirth, N., "Program Development by Stepwise Refinement,"
Communications of the ACM, vol. 14, no. 4, pp. 221-227, 1971.

[YAU81]   Yau and Grabow, "Programs using hierarchical graphs," IEEE
Transactions on Software Engineering, vol. 7, p. 6, Nov. 1981.

[YOUN82]   Young, S.J., Real Time Languages: design and development,
Ellis Horwood, 1982.

[YOUR79]   Yourdon, E. and Constantine, L.L., Structured Design -
Fundamentals of a Discipline of Computer Program and System
Design, Prentice-Hall, 1979.

[ZAVE84]   Zave, P., "The operational versus the conventional approach to
software development," Communications of the ACM, vol. 27, pp.
104-118, Feb. 1984.

APPENDIX

```
***********************************************************************
* System: LIST          - Wide Documentation by LIST, version: 4.2/OCT-86*
***********************************************************************


   Box  - 1 -     Levels in the hierarchical structure of system's modules
***********************************************************************
*                                                                     *
* zero: first:  second: third:  fourth: fifth:  sixth:  seventh:eighth: *
* ------------------------------------------------------------------- *
* LIST          (*Ref: S *)                                           *
*  \___| GET-ICMD     (*Ref: SA *)                                    *
*       \____| SET-ICMD-H                                             *
*            | PROMPT-ICMD                                            *
*            | GET-ICMD-CH                                            *
*            | DISPL-ICMDS                                            *
*            | DISPL-ICMD-H                                           *
*            | USER-MANUAL                                            *
*            | SET-ICMD                                               *
*            | INVALID-ICMD                                           *
*       INIT-NEW-DB                                                   *
*       INIT-OLD-DB                                                   *
*       ICMD-F-MSG                                                    *
*       DESIGN-TASKS (*Ref: SB *)                                     *
*        \___| GET-CMD                                                *
*            | CE-TASKS       (*Ref: SBA *)                           *
*            |  \____| GET-CE-OPT                                     *
*            |       | AB-CE-CMD                                      *
*            |       | GET-CE-ID                                      *
*            |       | AB-CE-OPT                                      *
*            |       | CE-RELATION  (*Ref: SBAA *)                    *
*            |       |  \____| INI-REL-EDIT                           *
*            |       |       | GET-REL-REQ                            *
*            |       |       | C-REL-REQ                              *
*            |       |       | D-REL-REQ                              *
*            |       |       | O-REL-REQ                              *
*            |       |       | R-REL-REQ                              *
*            |       |       | T-REL-REQ                              *
*            |       |       | MC-REL-REQ                             *
*            |       |       | F-REL-REQ                              *
*            |       | CE-CFS        (*Ref: SBAB *)                   *
*            |       |  \____| INI-CFS-EDIT                           *
*            |       |       | GET-CF-REQ                             *
*            |       |       | C-CF-REQ                               *
*            |       |       | D-CF-REQ                               *
*            |       |       | O-CF-REQ                               *
*            |       |       | R-CF-REQ                               *
*            |       |       | T-CF-REQ                               *
*            |       |       | MC-CF-REQ                              *
*            |       |       | F-CF-REQ                               *
*            |       | CE-DFS                                         *
*            |       | CE-DESCR                                       *
*            | D-TASKS                                                *
*            | R-TASKS                                                *
*            | S-TASKS                                                *
*            | T-TASKS                                                *
*            | F-TASKS                                                *
***********************************************************************
```

Box - 2 - Module ID/Long ID LIST / LIST Software Design Tool. V 4.2, Oct 86 Date Created: 21 Jan 87 Ref: S
****
* Functional description, last modified: 26 Jan 87   Input data, last modified: 21 Jan 87
* ---   ---
* The program LIST enables the user to enter, update and display   INP-BY-USER / CONTROL AND DESIGN DATA ENTERED BY USER
* software design specification interactively. It displays prompts,   DESIGN-FILE / SOFTWARE DESIGN SPECIFICATION FILE
* error messages and other helpful information (including on-line user
* manual) to enable the user to operate the program without outside   Output data, last modified: 21 Jan 87
* help. It is assumed that the user is familiar with at least one   ---
* procedural programming language and has done the LIST TUTORIAL   OUTP-TO-USER/ DATA DISPLAYED FOR USER AT TERMINAL
* (a guided LIST session with exercises).   DESIGN-FILE / SOFTWARE DESIGN SPECIFICATION FILE
*   DOCUMNT-FILE/ PRINTABLE DESIGN DOCUMENTATION FILE
* LIST can save the design specification (database) in a named file.
* This file can be used in another session to continue the design.   Data Flow structure:
* LIST can also generate a named file containing design documentation -------------------
* in a format suitable for a 132 column alphanumeric printer.
*   ABORT-FLAG   --> ICMD-NOT-AB (*Until*)
*
* Control Flow structure, last modified: 21 Jan 87   INP-BY-USER   --> GET-ICMD   --> OUTP-TO-USER
* ---   SA   --> ICMD
* LIST Software Design Tool, V 4.2, Oct 86
*   ICMD   --> CASE-ICMD   (*Case of*)
* |-- Until INITIAL COMMAND NOT ABORTED
* | |
* | |__ GET VALID INITIAL COMMAND   INP-BY-USER   --> INIT-NEW-DB --> OUTP-TO-USER
* | █   --> DATABASE-ACC
* | |__ Case of INITIAL COMMAND   --> ABORT-FLAG
* | |
* | <>--When INITIAL COMMAND is CREATE   INP-BY-USER   --> INIT-OLD-DB --> OUTP-TO-USER
* | | | DESIGN-FILE   -->   --> DATABASE-ACC
* | | |__ INITIALISE NEW DESIGN DATABASE   --> ABORT-FLAG
* | <>--When INITIAL COMMAND is EDIT
* | | | ICMD   --> ICMD-F-MSG --> OUTP-TO-USER
* | | |__ INITIALISE OLD DESIGN DATABASE
* | <>--When INITIAL COMMAND is FINISH   ICMD   --> ICMD-NE-F   (*If*)
* | | |
* | | |__ "FINISHED - NO DESIGN CREATED OR EDITED"   INP-BY-USER   --> DESIGN-TASKS --> OUTP-TO-USER
* | DATABASE-ACC -->   SB   --> DESIGN-FILE
* |-- If INITIAL COMMAND is NOT FINISH   --> DOCUMNT-FILE
* | <>__ SOFTWARE DESIGN TASKS
* **

156

Box - 3 -   Module ID/Long ID: GET-ICMD   / GET VALID INITIAL COMMAND   Date Created: 21 Jan 87   Ref: SA
****
* Functional description, last modified: 26 Jan 87   Input data, last modified: 21 Jan 87
*   ---
* This module prompts the user to enter the first character of the   INP-BY-USER / CONTROL AND DESIGN DATA ENTERED BY USER
* following initial commands:
*   Output data, last modified: 21 Jan 87
*   ?, HELP, MANUAL, CREATE, EDIT, FINISH.   ---
*   OUTP-TO-USER/ DATA DISPLAYED FOR USER AT TERMINAL
* The first three commands enable the user to obtain required helpful   ICMD   / INITIAL COMMAND
* information. The last three command enable the user to choose
* whether to CREATE new design, EDIT an existing design or FINISH the
* current design session. If the user enters any other character an
* appropriate error message is displayed.
*
*   Data Flow structure:
* ---
* Control Flow structure, last modified: 26 Jan 87
*
* GET VALID INITIAL COMMAND
*   SET-ICMD-H   --> ICMD
* | SET INITIAL COMMAND TO HELP
* | ICMD   -->   ICMD-IN-CEF   (*Until*)
* | Until INITIAL COMMAND in (CREATE, EDIT, FINSH)
* == | PROMPT-ICMD   --> OUTP-TO-USER
* | PROMPT FOR INITIAL COMMAND
* | INP-BY-USER --> GET-ICMD-CH   --> CHARACTER
* | GET INITIAL COMMAND CHARACTER
* | CHARACTER   --> CASE-ICMD-CH (*Case of*)
* | Case of INITIAL COMMAND CHARACTER
* |
*   <>--When CHARACTER is ?
* | |___ DISPLAY DETAILS OF INITIAL COMMANDS   DISPL-ICMDS   --> OUTP-TO-USER
* |
*   <>--When CHARACTER is H
* | |___ DISPLAY INITIAL COMMAND HELP TEXT   DISPL-ICMD-H   --> OUTP-TO-USER
* |
*   <>--When CHARACTER is M
* | |___ LIST USER'S MANUAL   INP-BY-USER --> USER-MANUAL   --> OUTP-TO-USER
* |
*   <>--When CHARACTER in (C, E, F)
* | |___ SET VALID INITIAL COMMAND   CHARACTER   --> SET-ICMD   --> ICMD
* |
*   <>_ "INVALID INITIAL COMMAND"   INVALID-ICMD --> OUTP-TO-USER
*
****

Box — 4 —   Module ID/Long ID DESIGN-TASKS/ SOFTWARE DESIGN TASKS   Date Created: 21 Jan 87   Ref: SB

****

* Functional description, last modified: 26 Jan 87   Input data, last modified: 21 Jan 87
*
* This module supports an interactive software design. The command-   INP-BY-USER / CONTROL AND DESIGN DATA ENTERED BY USER
* driven interface enables the user to choose one of the following   DATABASE-ACC/ DESIGN DATABASE and CURRENT ACCESS INFO
* main tasks:
*   Output data, last modified: 21 Jan 87
*   CREATE new or EDIT existing views in the design database (rela-
*   tions, structures, entities' descriptions).   OUTP-TO-USER/ DATA DISPLAYED FOR USER AT TERMINAL
*   DESIGN-FILE / SOFTWARE DESIGN SPECIFICATION FILE
*   DELETE database entities or REPLACE attributes of entities.   DOCUMNT-FILE/ PRINTABLE DESIGN DOCUMENTATION FILE
*
*   SAVE design database and design documentation in files.
*
*   TYPE (display) the contents of the database and analysis of the
*   design specified there.
*
* The design session is terminated with FINISH command.
*
*   Data Flow structure:
* Control Flow structure, last modified: 21 Jan 87
*
* SOFTWARE DESIGN TASKS   CMD   —> CMD-EQ-F   (*Until1*)
*
*   ┌── Until COMMAND is FINISH   INP-BY-USER —> GET-CMD   —> OUTP-TO-USER
*   ■ ┌─   —> CMD
*   │ │ GET VALID COMMAND
*   │ │   CMD   —> CASE-CMD   (*Case of*)
*   │ └─ Case of COMMAND
*   │ ┌─   INP-BY-USER —> CR-TASKS   —> OUTP-TO-USER
*   │ │ CREATE/EDIT RELATIONS, STRUCTURES, DESCR   DATABASE-ACC —> SBA   —> DATABASE-ACC
*   │◇─│──When COMMAND in (CREATE, EDIT)   CMD   —>
*   │ └─
*   │ ┌─   INP-BY-USER —> D-TASKS   —> OUTP-TO-USER
*   │ │ DELETE ENTITIES FROM DESIGN DATABASE   DATABASE-ACC —>   —> DATABASE-ACC
*   │◇─│──When COMMAND is DELETE
*   │ └─
*   │ ┌─   INP-BY-USER —> R-TASKS   —> OUTP-TO-USER
*   │ │ REPLACE ATTRIBUTES OF ENTITIES   DATABASE-ACC —>   —> DATABASE-ACC
*   │◇─│──When COMMAND is REPLACE
*   │ └─
*   │ ┌─   INP-BY-USER —> S-TASKS   —> OUTP-TO-USER
*   │ │ SAVE DATABASE or DOCUMENTATION   DATABASE-ACC —>   —> DESIGN-FILE
*   │◇─│──When COMMAND is SAVE   —> DOCUMNT-FILE
*   │ └─
*   │ ┌─   INP-BY-USER —> T-TASKS   —> OUTP-TO-USER
*   │ │ TYPE DESIGN SPECIFICATIONS or ANALYSIS   DATABASE-ACC —>
*   │◇─│──When COMMAND is TYPE
*   │ └─
*   │ ┌─   INP-BY-USER —> F-TASKS   —> OUTP-TO-USER
*   │ │ FINISH DESIGN SESSION FORMALITIES   DATABASE-ACC —>   —> DESIGN-FILE
*   └◇─│──When COMMAND is FINISH
*   └─
****

158

SECTION THREE — WORKBENCH TOOLS WITHIN A METHODOLOGY

This section examines "non-generic" Workbench tools which concentrate upon
aspects of workbench products and facilities which are usually specific to a
company or methodology. However, it must be stressed that these papers are
not solely product descriptions. We made the point in the introduction that
applied presentations had to take a particular theme or issue and to look at
this in the context of a product or methodology. As a result, all these
papers present a slightly different angle on the provision of automated
tools for the system developer.

The paper by Jones (LBMS) provides an insight into the design and
development of a data modelling tool for database design. It provides a
practical justification for a personal computer based product (Auto-Mate+)
and discusses the problems of automation in this restricted environment.

The TETRARCH development methodology is outlined in the second paper (Mann)
with specific attention paid to Tetrarch/3 which examines the relatively
neglected issue of software performance and hardware acquisition planning.
This capacity planning facility can be used to evaluate different hardware
and software requirements resulting from different strategies. The paper
concludes with examples of its use.

The INTELLIPSE project (Bader et al) aims to "design and develop knowledge-
based software tools which can support the development of commercial data
processing systems". It is based upon the Structured Systems Development
method developed and promoted by BIS Applied Systems Ltd. The paper
describes the development of an IKBS based "advisor" designed to support the
practitioner by offering both active support and automatic execution of
manual tasks.

The paper by Bruty (Yourdon) concentrates upon the problem of "getting
started" in a project. It rejects functional decomposition on the grounds
that it is implementation dependent and suggests an alternative based around
an understanding of actors, sensors and objects. This will culminate in the
production of an event list identifying events which cause the system to
respond in some way. These concepts are illustrated with the reference to
the definition of a "Lift System".

John Parkinson of Arthur Young Management Consultants examines the
development philosophy and practice behind the Information Engineering

Workbench. He pays particular attention to the integration of IKBS techniques into the product and the hardware structure to support this. The "two stage" nature of the workbench is explained and justified. The paper concludes with a summary of practical experiences and likely future developments.

Ian Macdonald (James Martin Associates) makes the point that systems development methodologies (like 4GLs) must become non-procedural. Systems development must·stress what the business is about. "Methodologies must therefore focus on business modelling". He proceeds to examine the automation of the Information Engineering methodology concentrating on the need for an overall approach to automation rather than the provision of individual tools. He concludes that automation itself will "provide a way of working which is substantially different from manual practice". This is a reflection of how the successful automation of any task usually causes changes in how that task is carried out.

The final paper picks up this theme. The developer of systems has traditionally imposed change on other people and professions; what is likely to happen when the "change agents" are themselves threatened by change?. The paper by McCabe (Price-Waterhouse) looks at this issue. It suggests that "one must exercise the same preparation, caution and effort in automating one´s own working environment as we should, and do, in automating the environments of our customers and clients." Some of the problems and opportunities of implementing such a tool are illustrated with examples from the introduction of EXCELERATOR at Price-Waterhouse.

This section has moved from the specific to the general. It began by examining the development and enhancement of a particular tool (Automate+) in a particular environment (database design). It concludes with a view of automation in an all-encompassing methodology. All views along the spectrum are important and valid and, furthermore, they all raise problems of implementation. A glimpse into these problems is provided by the final paper.

AUTOMATING A SYSTEMS DEVELOPMENT METHODOLOGY:

THE LBMS EXPERIENCE

Nick Jones

LBMS

London, UK

1   INTRODUCTION

LBMS have developed methods and associated software tools to support a variety of IT related tasks including:

*   Systems Analysis and Design

*   Strategic IT Planning

*   Database Design

*   Project Control

This paper considers some of the activities carried out during the database design phase of a project and uses them to illustrate the way in which LBMS have approached the problems of automating a systems development method. The examples discussed are taken from the LBMS Auto-Mate+ product which is a PC tool to support users of the LSDM methodology.

The reader is assumed to be familiar with the basic concepts of databases and relational data analysis.

2   DATABASE DESIGN ACTIVITIES

The database design process involves many activities which are broadly representative of those carried out when using a systems development method such as LSDM and its associated support software. This paper will concentrate on the following specific techniques.

*   Logical Data Modelling

     This technique results in a logical model of the data structures of a business or computer system. The model consists of a pictorial representation of the data structure showing entities and relationships and a set of entity, relationship and data item definitions.

*   Relational Data Analysis

    Data analysis can be used to obtain a more formal model of the
    system data; it generates a set of relations, information on the way
    they were derived and definitions of their constituent data items.

*   Physical Design

    This technique takes logical models produced by (a) or (b) and
    generates a physical database design which is typically represented
    as a text file for input to a DBMS schema compiler.

The activities carried out when using the above techniques can be grouped
into four main classes:

a   Recording Textual Information

    Information is collected by the analyst then recorded, checked and
    cross-referenced in a design database. Examples include recording
    entity and data item definitions. Two classes of text can be
    identified, structured (e.g. object names or volumetric data) which
    can often be validated in some way and unstructured descriptions.

b   Recording Pictorial Information

    Many of the systems views used by LSDM are graphical, examples in
    the area of database design include data structure diagrams and
    database schema diagrams. Support software must provide ways to
    create and maintain such pictures and to associate pictorial and
    textual design information.

c   Utility Functions

    This category includes reporting, picture printing and plotting and
    PC related housekeeping. Auto-Mate handles such functions in a very
    conventional manner and so they will not be considered further in
    this paper.

d   Special Purpose Transformations

    Some method techniques require special purpose support tools that do
    more than just record and check information. These perform method
    specific transformations on the design information and often embed
    method knowledge. Database design examples include relational data
    analysis and transforming an LDS into a physical database schema.

3   THE TARGET ENVIRONMENT

At an early stage in the product design we decided that the target
hardware should be the IBM PC, the main reason for this being user
demand. The PC is a far from ideal environment for many reasons
including:

*   Poor security. Data is vulnerable to misused PCDOS commands, there
    is no way to prevent unauthorised access to, or even deletion of
    files. The only effective security mechanism is a locked room.

*   The hardware and media such as diskettes are easily damaged by
    common office mishaps such as spilt coffee.

162

*   Backups are particularly important but must be carried out by system
     users rather than DP operations staff. They are often forgotten or
     omitted due to the time and effort required to carry them out or the
     user's assumption that nothing will go wrong. (Our experience
     suggests that the users most likely to omit backups are DP
     consultants!)

*   Certain IBM PC graphics controllers have very poor resolution
     (640 x 200 pixels) making it difficult to develop tools which
     maintain graphical system views.

*   Although intended to be a desktop 'personal' tool the PC is in
     practice far from easy to use, hours can be wasted attempting to
     connect peripherals for example. Around 30% of our support calls
     are concerned with PC related problems such as DOS commands or
     setting printer switches.

Despite such disadvantages the PC has many attractions including:

*   Availability - many potential users already posess PCs.

*   Cost - organisations are prepared to pay a few thousand pounds for a
     PC per analyst but are often reluctant to invest £10,000 to £20,000
     for sophisticated Unix workstations although these typically offer
     better graphics and much higher performance.

*   Flexibility - a PC can be used as a stand-alone tool or a mainframe
     terminal as well as an analyst's workbench.

*   Standardisation - the PC architecture is an industry standard,
     machines are easy to obtain and maintain.

We have attempted to hide some of the worst aspects of PCDOS behind the
Auto-Mate menu system, which can detect and intercept some common errors
(such as attempts to re-format the fixed disk). However, the protection
provided by such methods is necessarily limited.

4   PRODUCT ARCHITECTURE

The basic architecture of the Auto-Mate+ product is illustrated in Figure
1, it consists of a set of tools sharing information via a design
database and PCDOS files.

5   MANAGING PICTORIAL INFORMATION

LBMS's experience of IT related methods has shown that pictorial views of
systems are valuable and very popular, the trend in method development
over the past few years has been to make more use of pictures.

In the database design area of LSDM, two main types of diagram are used;
the LDS which illustrates the logical structure of system data, and the
schema diagram which shows the records, sets and indexes of a physical
database design. Figures 2 and 3 show fragments of typical LDS and a
schema diagram.

Both LDS and schema diagrams may be very complex, examples containing
several hundred entities or records are common. Maintaining such large
pictures is seldom practical without software support as the cost of
manually re-drafting a large diagram can be very high. Some Auto-Mate

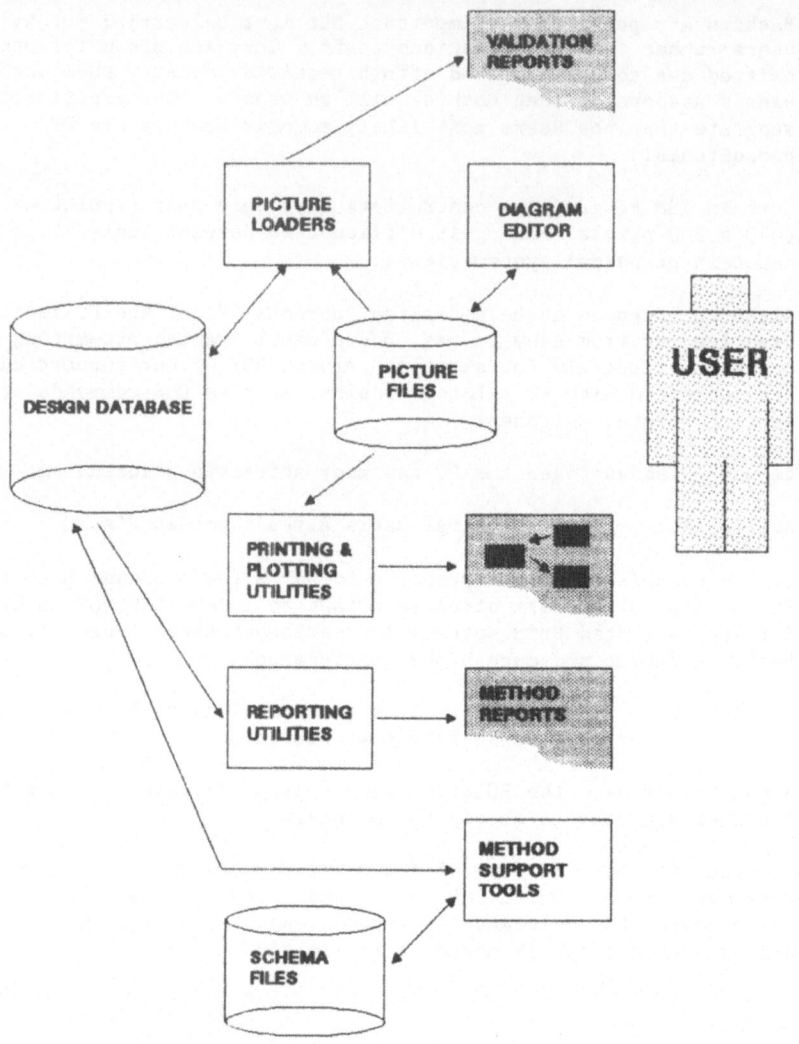

Figure 1   The basic architecture of Automate+

users have stated that the product is cost effective purely as a
pictorial documentation tool for schema diagrams.

6   PICTURE EDITING

The widespread use of pictures in systems development methods means that
a picture editor is a vital component of the support software.
Fortunately the structure of most methodology can be represented as a set
of icons and connecting lines which allowed us to develop a single
parameterised editing tool for many different picture types. Its main
design principles are:

a   It is method related and allows the user to manipulate method
     specific objects such as LDS entities and relationships rather than

just boxes and lines. This is important as experience with CAD packages and PC drawing tools shows that they are too flexible to edit method diagrams effectively.

b   ´Hidden´ functionally is minimised. Commands are explicit and, as far as possible, available at all times. This is unlike some PC based drawing editors which (for example) use click/drag techniques rather than an explicit ´move´ command.

c   The user interface is pictorial (e.g. allowing users to select the object to be added from a menu of pictures rather than a list of object names).

d   The user interface is intended to be easy to learn and re-learn. Once an initial command has been selected prompts lead the user through the editing process. Method support tools are similar to DBMS query languages in that complex interfaces deter the occasional user due to the re-learning effort.

e   The user interface is context sensitive - it provides a set of basic commands such as ADD, DELETE, MOVE etc and takes appropriate action depending on the type of objects(s) the user points to.

f   The same editor is used for all method pictures, this helps to reduce the learning time.

g   Additional facilities are provided for expert users, these include keyboard driven command selection (which is faster then using a mouse) and command repetition.

h   Performance is good, it is fast enough to support a ´sketch pad´ style of working if required.

The editor has now been in use for 18 months and has proved very successful. The changes we have made to it over this period fall into three main categories:

*   Method related enhancements such as adding new classes of object expansion or explosion and new types of picture.

*   Adding new facilities in response to user requests, these were generally suggested by expert users to improve productivity and included:

–   using a ´double click´ mechanism to repeat the last command. This is unfortunately an example of hidden functionality. However, there is a simple and obvious alternative method of command selection for novices.

–   Adding commands to bend lines rather than delete and re-enter them.

–   Panning and zooming the edit window while in the middle of other commands.

*   Extending editor limits.

Before automation, LDS pictures seldom exceeded 300 entities. Once we provided software tools to make picture maintenance easier the size of pictures has increased to the point where our products are now being enhanced to support 1000 entity LDSs.

A picture is only one view of a system design, boxes on an LDS represent entities whose ´contents´ may be recorded on Auto-Mate´s underlying design database. The relationship between a picture and its associated database information may be maintained while the picture is being edited or alternatively, deferred to a convenient moment. We chose to keep the pictures and database strictly separate and provide ´picture loader´ transactions to align the two. The main reasons for this decision were:

* It is difficult to provide good performance in an interactive editor which has to update a complex database during its operation.

* It is easier for the user to create initial sketches or pictures which are incomplete/incorrect as almost no validation needs to be performed while editing.

* The loader provides a convenient site for picture validation, it is only invoked when the user has some confidence in the quality of the picture.

* Operations such as diagram merging can be performed quickly as they are purely pictorial transformations.

* If a database is kept in step with the picture at all times it can be very difficult to provide ´quit´ or ´abort edit´ commands. This implies some form of transaction roll-back in the underlying database. Such facilities are likely to seriously impair performance on a PC.

* Many system views are informal and produced only as a communications aid; these may have no associated database information.

There are some design problems in picture loading transactions - for example matching picture and database objects when re-loading a picture which is already in the database to ensure that no information is lost. Our experience, however, is that solving such problems is far easier than attempting to keep the database in step with a picture at all times.

The main implication of the picture/database separation is that objects do not appear on the database at the moment that they appear on the picture. This makes it impossible to provide facilities to edit the definitions of objects which are selected visually while editing the picture.

8   FORM BASED TRANSACTIONS

Once an LDS picture has been drawn and loaded into the database the analyst can record additional information such as entity descriptions, volumetrics, data item definitions and synonyms.

There is no convenient pictorial representation for such information and so we chose to use conventional form based transactions for entering and maintaining it. A small number of common tasks such as displaying indexes, saving changed objects and abandoning transactions are selected by function keys.

Forms are easy to use and their simplicity is popular (see section 10). However early versions could not always support the style of working of some users who wished to ´jump´ between forms to look at the definition of one object while creating another (e.g. looking at a data item while creating an entity). This requirement has been satisfied in later releases of the product by additional navigational functions.

In some cases forms have side effects determined by the normal working practice of analysts. As an example, data items are often identified while entity or relation definitions are being built up; it is restrictive to insist that the item definitions must exist on the design database before they can be used in an entity. In such cases item skeletons are automatically inserted into the database when they are first referenced.

We have found the form based user interface very suitable for recording and maintaining the definitions of simple objects such as data items, however it is inadequate for more complex structures such as those encountered during data analysis.

9   RELATIONAL DATA ANALYSIS - OVERVIEW

Relational data analysis (TNF) provides an important means of obtaining a view of a system data structure. The approach recommended by LBMS proceeds by taking ´user views´ of the data, such as existing paper forms, and converting these into raw relations (lists of data items). These relations are then normalised and optimised (merging those with common keys) before being converted back to an LDS which gives a clearer view of the resulting data structure. During the process of normalisation data item definitions are also collected and refined in parallel with other tasks.

In practice, TNF involves a certain amount of rework as inconsistencies and errors are identified, so any support tools must allow the user to review and modify normalisation decisions. As a single raw relation can generate a complex tree, deleting the complete tree and re-normalising the relation is not acceptable due to the amount of wasted effort, so a more sophisticated mechanism is needed.

10   RELATIONAL ANALYSIS - THE USER INTERFACE

We took the view that TNF support tools should closely follow the techniques and sequence of operations taught to users in LBMS method training lectures. In this approach the user starts from a single raw relation and carries out a sequence of steps which transform it into a set of third normal form relations.

The main tasks that software has to support are:

*   Entry and maintenance of relations (creating and editing lists of data items) and relation descriptions (text blocks).

*   Selection of single items or groups of items from lists for various operations such as flagging keys, marking inter-data dependencies, composites etc.

*   Extracting groups of data items from relations to form new relations.

*   Maintaining data item definitions (using standard form-based transactions).

*   Producing various reports both during and after normalisation.

*   Maintaining derivation information showing the decisions made while normalising each relation.

A simple form based user interface, such as adopted in Section 8, is unsuitable in this case since most tasks are dealing with lists of objects (e.g. data items, relations etc) and the user needs to be able to ´jump´ to tasks such as reporting and data item maintenance in parallel with normalisation. As a result the normalisation tools use a list-based user interface involving a large number of function keys (up to 30) to select the many available options. The problems of interface complexity are eased (but not totally removed) by ensuring that keys are used consistently. In our experience most users who are prepared to carry out TNF are relatively sophisticated and accept the necessary complexity.

Data item and entity definitions are used both in normalisation and other areas of system design so Auto-Mate provides both form and list based interfaces to maintain them. Interestingly, many users choose the simple but more restricted form interface when they are not performing normalisation and have less need of the extra flexibility.

While it might have been best to use a single style of user interface for all areas of Auto-Mate the tasks of form and list maintenance are so different that providing a simple unified interface would have been very difficult.

11   RELATIONAL ANALYSIS - NORMALISATION

Normalisation is a complex task which is performed in a ´question and answer´ manner following the approach taken on training courses. The user is asked question appropriate to the state of the current relation and provides the information for the software to transform it where necessary. For example given a relation known to be in un-normalised form Auto-Mate would lead the user through the following steps (where S indicates a system action and U a user action):

1   S   Ask if there are any repeating groups in the relation.

2   U   Mark the items in a repeating group.

3   S   Remove the group as a new relation retaining the existing key items.

4   S   Ask the user to mark one or more data items to give the new relation a unique key.

5   U   Mark the new key items.

6   S/U Perform the remaining normalisation steps on the new relation.

7   S   Present the remainder of the relation left after step 3 to allow another repeating group to be identified if required.

Auto-Mate knows the rules of normalisation and so can ask the appropriate questions to lead the user through the task. It also keeps track of all the intermediate relations generated between the raw and third normal form states and presents them for processing when appropriate.

168

At various points in the above process the user may jump to related tasks such as adding a new data item to the relation, browsing the data inventory or printing a normalisation report on the current relation.

The directed interface described above is suitable for most users. However, some do not like being led through all the questions, so an optional 'expert' mode was added which turns off some checks and allows a relation to be promoted directly from one state to another (e.g. first to third normal form in one step).

12   RELATIONAL ANALYSIS – RELATION HISTORY

During normalisation Auto-Mate keeps a record of every intermediate relation created as part of the normalisation tree whose root is a new relation. This allows us to provide the user with normalisation reports showing how relations were derived and makes it possible to return to any intermediate state to correct an error (see 15). This process can result in many hundreds of relations on the database, however this has not proved to be a problem in practice as database sizes seldom exceed 3 Mbytes and this is well within the PC's capabilities.

13   RELATIONAL ANALYSIS – OPTIMISING RELATIONS

Optimisation involves identifying relations with common keys and presenting these to the user who can decide whether or not to allow Auto-Mate to merge them together. This is an easy task to automate and saves a considerable amount of effort when compared with a manual alternative.

14   RELATIONAL ANALYSIS – LDS PICTURE GENERATION

Normalisation can result in hundreds of TNF relations which are not easily understood as a series of reports. They can, however, be converted into an LDS diagram, such as that illustrated in figure 2, which is considerably easier to grasp. The creation of an LDS from an optimised set of relations is a mechanical process which generates entities from relations and creates relationships based on the primary and foreign keys of relations.

The main problems encountered in automating this process arise in the area of picture layout. There is no generally agreed topology for such diagrams and only a few guidelines such as 'place detail entities below their masters'. After some experimentation we adopted the following strategy:

1   Firstly, allocate entities to vertical 'levels' depending on the number of masters above each one. LDSs are generally acyclic but cycles can sometimes occur and have to be handled as a special case.

2   Step (1) may result in a large number of entities on the same vertical level so more levels are introduced by a splitting process which makes the picture roughly square.

3   Entities on the same vertical level are allocated horizontal positions with detail entities located below single masters and between multiple masters where possible. Placement is on a grid which guarantees that there is space to draw the lines in step (4).

4   Finally relationship lines are drawn, directly where possible, otherwise along grid pathways.

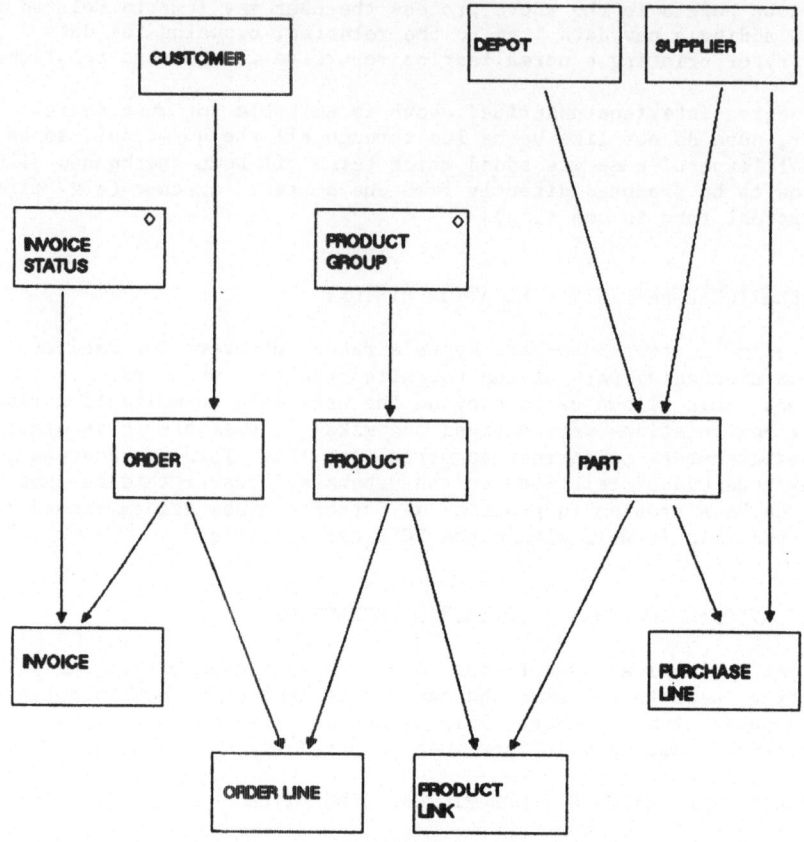

Figure 2   An example LDS diagram

No automatic layout algorithm will suit all users so the resulting picture is generated in diagram editor format and can be edited to alter its topology if required.

Our experience has shown that the picture generation facility is very popular as it makes the results of TNF more usable and is an extremely laborious task if performed manually. One interesting side effect is that it has encouraged users to produce much larger pictures and forced us to increase various diagram editor limits.

15   RELATIONAL ANALYSIS - BACKOUT

As discussed in Section 8, normalisation typically involves a certain amount of re-work. Relations can be complex (150 data items in some cases) so throwing the whole of a normalisation tree away after a mistake is not acceptable. Our solution to this problem was to develop a 'backout' facility which allows a user to navigate the branches of the normalisation tree and can, where necessary, undo all the decisions forward of a specified node. Backout displays the relation at each node of the tree in the format of a normalisation screen with the user's decisions marked.

Backout serves as an interactive review tool in addition to an error correction mechanism, it may be used by staff to view (and if necessary change) the normalisation decisions made by others.

Logical data models such as those produced by relational analysis or manually developed LDSs must be converted into DBMS schemas to produce a usable database. LBMS recommends a two stage approach to this task, a set of 'first cut' rules are applied to transform the LDS into an initial schema which is then modified to achieve the required performance characteristics. The LSDM method includes a library of many sets of such rules and, so far we have automated three of these. Typical rules for the Cullinet IDMS database operate as follows:

a   Make records from selected entities.

b   Deduce physical data item definitions (picture, format etc) from the logical data item definitions collected by the analyst. Set up record element lists.

c   Create indexes on the basis of access requirements which are specified or can be deduced from the LDS

d   Create sets from appropriate relationships and determine set classes and record storage modes from the volumetric information collected by the analyst.

e   Allocate records and indexes to areas depending on the index type and the classes of sets connecting records.

The resulting database design is still represented inside the Auto-Mate design database for the analyst to modify as required.

The knowledge used to perform such design transformations is expressed as a series of rules. We chose to implement these in a Pascal program for reasons of efficiency.

17   PHYSICAL DESIGN - MODIFYING THE SCHEMA

Most DBMS schemas have a visual representation (e.g. figure 3) our experience is that users prefer to view the design as a schema diagram and, where possible, perform design change using the diagram editor rather than the traditional method of editing a schema definition file.

The structure of LDS diagrams and network database schema diagrams is very similar (compare figures 2 and 3) and so the logic use to produce an LDS picture from a set of entities and relationships (see 14) can also be applied to transform a schema design into a a schema picture. Having done this the analyst can amend the design in two ways:

*   Edit the schema picture using the diagram editor and re-load it into the database. Using this approach in the case of a network database the analyst can typically make the following design changes:

        -    Add / delete records.
        -    Add / delete sets.
        -    Change certain set and record properties.
        -    Change area allocations.

*   Use form based transactions to amend non-pictorial aspects of the database design such as the record contents, key definitions and the assignment of areas to physical files.

The same approach may be used for relational databases although less information is generally available on schema diagrams and more changes must be made using form-based transactions.

Once the database design is satisfactory, Auto-Mate can convert it into a schema definition file for transfer to the target machine.

The internal model of the database schema held in Auto-Mate represents only information directly related to the database structure and omits data such as schema compiler directives (e.g. to control listing options). To enable users to add such information, if required, Auto-Mate also includes a integrated text file editor which can be applied to schema files. For ease of use the editor employs the same cursor control conventions as form based transactions.

18   COSMETICS

During the development of Auto-Mate and related products we have been continually improving the cosmetic appearance of screens in response to user requests. It seems that experience of other PC products tends to generate certain user expectations (e.g. for pop-up windows). We have added such features in a number of transactions even though they would sometimes appear to make little difference to the performance or usability of the product.

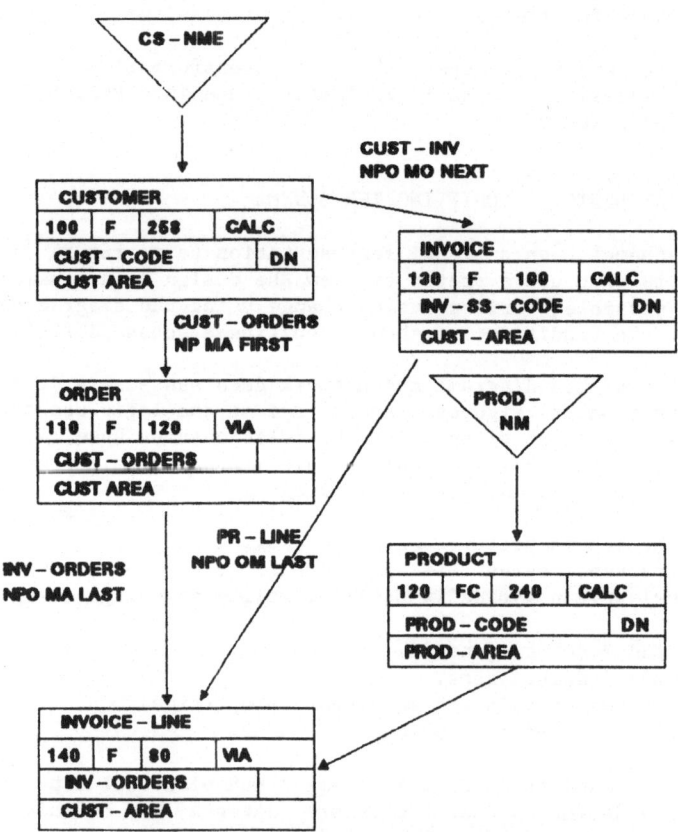

Figure 3   An example DBMS schema

One of our most popular cosmetic enhancements was to replace traditional menus (using a one line textual description of each option) with graphical menus where each option was indicated by a pictorial block and a much briefer description. Such a menu requires the user's eye to scan a two dimensional matrix of option blocks with cryptic descriptions instead of the simple and familiar text lines of the traditional approach and so would seem to be slower to use and less informative despite its popularity.

19   TASK CONTROL

A method such as LSDM provides a framework for the activities of system development and defines the techniques to use and the sequence in which tasks should be carried out. In practice many variations of the method are used for a wide range of projects in addition to conventional systems development (examples include feasibility studies, software maintenance and software product selection.) For this reason we chose not to attempt to enforce any task sequencing on Auto-Mate users, we have provided a set of tools which are integrated via the underlying database and can bed in virtually any order. A minority of users have wanted to enforce sequencing or restrict access to tools but as yet we have not implemented any facilities of this type.

20   SUMMARY

LBMS have developed a variety of software tools to support systems development methods such as LSDM. These tools allow the user to record textual and pictorial information, validate it and assist with a number of complex tasks such as data analysis. This paper has considered the tasks involved in database design and shown how LBMS have approached the problems of automation in the restricted environment of an IBM PC.

TETRARCH - A SYSTEM DEVELOPMENT METHODOLOGY

WITH AUTOMATED TOOLS

R. Mann

PA Computers and Telecommunications

London, UK

1 INTRODUCTION

Today, most companies, serious about Information Technology (IT) can no longer afford the luxury of virtuoso analysis and design, and so use a formal methodology to control computer system development.

The criteria used in selecting the appropriate methodology will differ, however proven structured techniques for analysis and design with well defined deliverables are expected features. Additionally, the methodology should be appropriate for all types of application which may be developed by the user company and should incorporate planning, estimating and project management tools.

Over the last few years significant effort has been made to provide software support, with interactive graphics, as an integral part of the methodology. These tools have the potential of improving the quality, and facilitating the maintenance of analysis and design documentation. Advances have also been made in automating logical and physical database design and providing techniques for application package evaluation.

There are, however, even more exacting requirements for current system design methodology, particularly integration both with Information Systems Planning (ISP) techniques and computer hardware performance modelling tools.

Tetrarch is a fully integrated methodology (Figure 1) comprising three modules:

Tetrarch/1 : Systems Architecture

Tetrarch/2 : Systems and Database Design

Tetrarch/3 : Capacity Planning and Performance Prediction Modelling

This paper focuses attention on Tetrarch/3 and the often neglected issues of software performance and hardware acquisition planning as part of an integrated set of techniques within the total system development methodology.

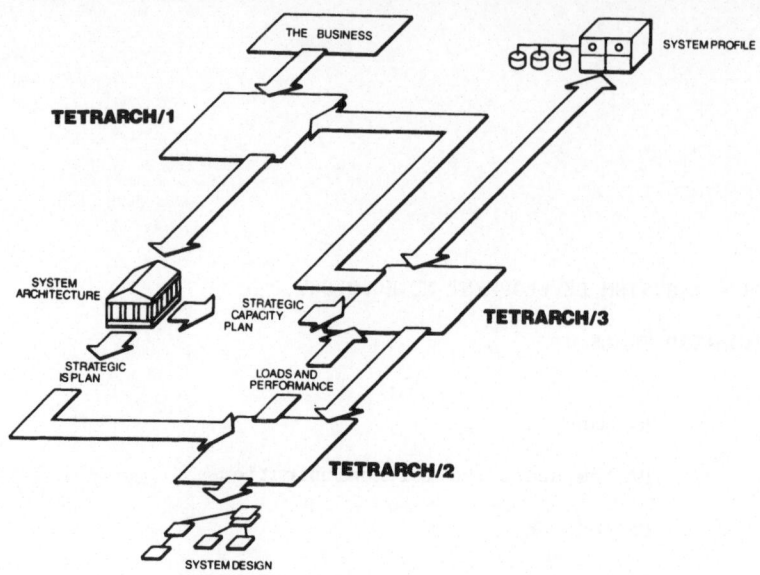

Figure 1   Tetrach Integration

2   THE IMPORTANCE OF HARDWARE PLANNING

There are those who view hardware planning as a fruitless exercise. They
simply state that user demands, development schedules and the complexity
of system internals renders the exercise too imprecise to be useful. The
trouble with this defeatest view is that it doesn't help! Management
still requires 'a view' on hardware acquisition forecasting and system
designers need to know that transactions will be within acceptable
response times constraints.

The fact is that, today, capacity planning is well understood. Models
can be built using proven techniques and the results have been well
validated over more than a decade [BUZE78].

We need capacity planning to:

–   Plan for future growth, taking account of increases in existing
      workload, new system development work and new system operational
      volumes.

–   Avoid discovering performance problems late in the system develop-
      ment life cycle. The initial design will focus on achieving
      expected functionality and manipulation of data. There is, however,
      the need to assess the machine overhead of such a design.

–   Determine appropriate acquisition plans for hardware and software,
      consistent with budget and supplier policy constraints.

–   Influence DBMS and 4GL selection and to access the performance
      implications of database design options.

3   ANALYTICAL MODELLING OF COMPUTER SYSTEMS

Until the early Seventies, the standard technique used for modelling
computer systems was discrete simulation. Specialized languages such as

176

GPSS or Simscript were used to represent different hardware and software components of the system in varying degrees of detail in customised models. These models typically consisted of a thousand small lines of code which had to be debugged before meaningful results could be generated. Thereafter, different scenarios could be evaluated by modifying key parameters and repeatedly rerunning the model.

Because of the need for specialized compilers, programmers, computing time and knowledge of the systems to be modelled, most commercial DP environments could not afford this luxury. As a result, capacity planning management has had no option but to use intuition in estimating required hardware.

Analytical models define sets of mathematical equations to describe the interaction of processes inside any system. These queueing network models, which are based on complex queueing theory, have been found to represent the internal processes of computer systems very accurately. They are easy to formulate and to solve. Typically, they require mere seconds of processing time to determine all utilizations, queue lengths and response times for any given consideration. Once coded, they provided capacity planners with the power to model any computer systems, irrespective of type, even if the modellers are not familiar with the underlying mathematical theory.

Although one would expect that the resultant output is not as accurate as that produced by simulation models, in practice, capacity planners have found that they are accurate enough to evaluate reliably the effects of any hardware changes whether they are in the CPU, memory, or the I/O configuration.

Queueing network models can model any set of interlocking processes. This means that they are not confined to the internals of computer systems. They can also model data communications networks or networks in combination with computer systems. Most important of all, their input parameters can be expressed in user or software terms so that parametric (what if.... ?) analysis can easily be performed.

TETRARCH/3 is a queueing network modelling system which provides sophisticated tools to the capacity planner to perform short-term evaluation of configurations, to predict the performance of systems currently being designed and to plan required hardware in the strategic time frame.

3.1 Tetrarch/3 Network Topology

TETRARCH/3 always assumes that models presented to it are of the form of a set of devices connected together to form a network (see Figure 2). Apart from two special devices called TRAN/JOB and ENTRY, every other device in the network will have a queue of tasks waiting for service.

The CPU task queue is ordered by task priority so that a higher priority task will always be served before a lower priority task. At all other devices, tasks are always served in first come first served (FCFS) order.

3.2 Classes

A computer system usually runs several different types of workload at the same time. Typical examples are batch, timesharing and teleprocessing. These types may be broken down further into classes such as production and test batch, on-line systems development and end-user computing.

Tasks of each class behave differently as they circulate in the network. Batch tasks will move several thousand times between the CPU and internal devices before leaving the computer system, while on-line tasks may only have 5-10 I/O's before leaving. If the model is to be at all realistic, it must be able to represent different classes of workload all operating at the same time. This means that each class must have different parameters defined for it in the model.

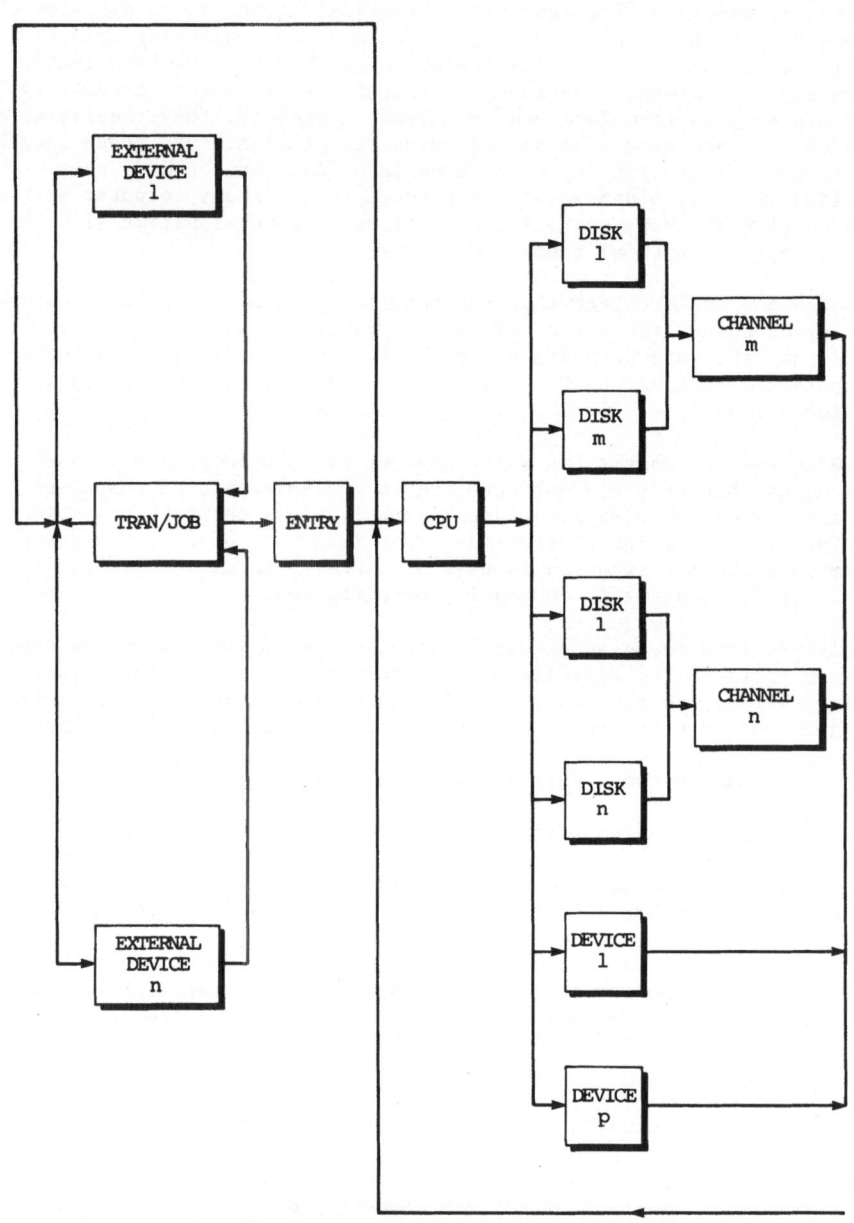

Figure 2   Tetrach/3 Topology

3.3 Queueing and Service Times

When any task arrives at a unit, excluding TRAN/JOB and ENTRY, it must queue for service. In the case of the CPU(s), the queue of tasks waiting for service is sorted by priority of the class (pre-emptive priorities). This ensures that higher priority tasks will always be given service at the CPU before lower priority ones. In the case of all other devices, arriving tasks always queue behind other tasks already at the unit, irrespective of individual class priorities.

When the task eventually reaches the head of the device queue, it is given service by that device. During model-building, a mean or average service time is defined for each unit. In the case of the CPU, a different service time for each class can be defined. This service time is always assumed to be exponentially (randomly) distributed.

In other words, the model does not assume that every task will have exactly the same service time as the tasks served before or after it. The waiting time of a task at any particular unit is defined to be the total time spent in the queue plus the total service time. Similarly, the queue length at a unit is the total number of tasks at the unit including the task actually being served. Both the waiting time and queue length can be specified per class or in total.

3.4 Routing Probabilities (Visit Ratios)

Every task in the network belongs to a particular class. After being served at any device, it can be routed to any other device for service. The probability of being routed to any particular device is closely related to the number of accesses or I/O's that the task makes to that device compared with the number made to other devices.

In other words, if an on-line task makes 10 accesses to disk A and 3 accesses to disk B, the probability that the task will proceed to either disk after service at the CPU is proportional to the relative number of accesses.

To determine the routing probabilities for each class at each unit, the total number of I/O's or accesses which that class makes to the unit must be specified. Channel I/O's need not be specified since they can be derived by totalling the I/O's of devices attached to the channel. Only devices which do not act as channels of other devices need have I/O's specified. Similarly, CPU I/O's or accesses are derived by summing the I/O's of all computer system devices attached to it. It is not necessary to specify any CPU I/O's since they are always calculated automatically by the model.

For each class, the routing probabilities are calculated by taking the ratio of device I/O's to CPU I/O's. The routing probabilities for all classes at the CPU will therefore be 1. The CPU I/O's for each class are the sum of the I/O's of all other devices in the computer system attached to it.

3.5 Some Special System Features Incorporated in the Model

Hardware and software features which are automatically modelled include:

- Virtual Storage and Paging: Facilities are provided to characterise the working set characteristics of the workload. This defines its paging behaviour. During model solution, virtual storage paging is calculated and included in model results. The modeller can then investigate the effect of changing memory size or the number or type of paging devices. If required, working set characteristics of each individual class can be defined.

-    Logical/Physical channel permutations: Disk devices can be attached as flexibly to logical or physical channels as the operating system being modelled permits. This enables Peripheral Processing Units and disk controllers to be modelled in a general way. Logical pathing, used in IBM XA operating systems, can similarly be modelled.

-    Disk Configurations: Disk service time is automatically adjusted for missed rotations dependent on channel utilisation and logical pathing is fully supported. A physical channel can participate in one or more logical channels and can be connected directly to other disks at the same time. Alternative facilities are provided to calculate disk parameters to minimize manual input parameter calculation, irrespective of the source of statistics.

-    Operating System Domain Migration: Queueing by lower priority classes for service within the operating system is automatically modelled. The modeller can define the maximum number of address spaces, virtual machines, regions or partitions by class or combination of classes which may be admitted to the system. This allows integrated systems and networks to be incorporated in the same model.

-    CPU Queueing Discipline: The CPU queueing discipline used is first come first served, pre-emptive priority. This corresponds to conventional operating system practice. Facilities are provided to model both conventional multiprocessors and attached processors.

3.6 Model Output

Model output provides a detailed analysis by system device and workload class. This is expressed in terms of device utilizations, task waiting times and queue lengths. A measurement of workload response times

Class	Tasks	Resp Time	No Trans	Thru/Hour	CPU %
1) TSO	0.568263	0.338700	6040.0	6039.99	7.7
2) DB/DC	0.938536	0.184328	18330.0	18329.98	17.5
3) BATCH	0.338853	406.624023	3.0	3.00	3.6
TOTAL	1.845652				
PAGE RATE = 2.048					

Figure 3   Response times by class

associated with the expected number of transactions in given together with a breakdown of CPU utilization by workload class.

An example of the ´Response Time by Class´ and ´Device Utilization by Class´ is presented as Figures 3 and 4 respectively.

4   PREDICTION MODELLING

The TETRARCH capacity planning methodology is an intrinsic part of the entire TETRARCH methodology. It is the basic technical evaluation tool used in determining technical strategy for the systems architecture and its ability to provide predictions of performance for run units during system design is the key to obtaining the optimum system and database design.

4.1   The System Profile

The system profile is the base model of the existing computer system with its current workload. The term "computer system" is used broadly as it may consist of several computers of different types as well as a communications network. Specific operating system statistics are collected for representative periods of activity. These statistics are analyzed and a TETRARCH/3 source model is created.

Any number of classes of workload (e.g. DB/DC, timesharing, batch) can be defined. Performance statistics will be calculated for each class and the resultant system profile model is usually accurate to within 5%.

Once the model has been built and calibrated, it can be used to evaluate short-term tuning of the system as well as the effect of upgrades. For example, the analyst can interactively evaluate the effects of a multi-threading DBMS instead of single-threading software, enlarging the real memory or upgrading the CPU or disk configuration.

The analyst can then examine each workload class separately to determine expected annual application growth over the planning time frame. For example, a particular workload class may be on-line purchase order management. This may be expected by the user community to grow from the current 1000 transactions per day to 1300, 1800, 2200 and 2600 transactions per day over the next five years. The analyst can then build projected system profile models for each of the next five years.

These extrapolated system profile models are used as the basis for future capacity planning, by interfacing to Tetrarch/1 and Tetrarch/2 as shown in Figure 5.

4.2 Strategic Capacity Planning

During development of the systems architecture, using TETRARCH/1, all computer systems required in the planning time frame, as well as their implementation dates, are defined together with some overall details about volumes and pace of implementation. Strategic capacity planning is a methodology which enables the capacity planning analyst to estimate TETRARCH/3 input parameters for each year of the planning period using a set of given technical reference values. At least one workload class is defined for each such system and this information is superimposed on the model containing the extrapolated system profile.

The resultant model then contains information both about systems currently running on the machine as well as all proposed future systems.

DEVICE	CLASS	0% 10% 20% 30% 40% 50% 60% 70% 80% 90% 100%	%
TRAN/JOB	TOTAL		0.0
ENTRY	TOTAL		0.0
CPU	TOTAL	1 1 1 2 2 2 2 2 2 2 2 3	28.8
CHAN 1	TOTAL		2.0
CHAN 2	TOTAL		2.0
CHAN 3	TOTAL		2.7
CHAN 4	TOTAL		2.7
CPUX	TOTAL	1 1 1 2 2 2 2 2 2 2 2 3	28.8
DISK 1	TOTAL	1 1 1 2 2 2 2 2	17.4
DISK 2	TOTAL	1 1 2 2 2 2 2	16.1
DISK 3	TOTAL	1 1 1 2 2 2 2 2 3 3	22.1
DISK 4	TOTAL	1 1 2 2 2 2 2 2	19.4
TAPES	TOTAL	2 2	5.4
PRINTER	TOTAL	3 3 3 3	9.8
		0% 10% 20% 30% 40% 50% 60% 70% 80% 90% 100%	

Figure 4 - Device utilization by class

These models are then used to evaluate alternative hardware and software strategies and derive a detailed estimate of hardware resource requirements for each year of the planning period.

4.3   Performance Prediction of Run Units/Transactions

During the design phase of each new system, process graphs are created for each envisaged run-unit transaction. A process graph provides details of software logic paths together with database/file and physical device accesses. TETRARCH/2 provides the tools and techniques needs to estimate the TETRARCH/3 input parameters for that system.

Every run-unit is treated as a separate workload in addition to the system profile classes already included in the model. When the model is solved, it produces a prediction of response for that run unit as well as a detailed estimate of its hardware resource usage.

If the performance of any run unit is unacceptable, TETRARCH/2 provides techniques:

-   to redesign the program in question
    or
-   to restructure the physical database design
    or
-   to upgrade the hardware

in order to achieve acceptable performance.

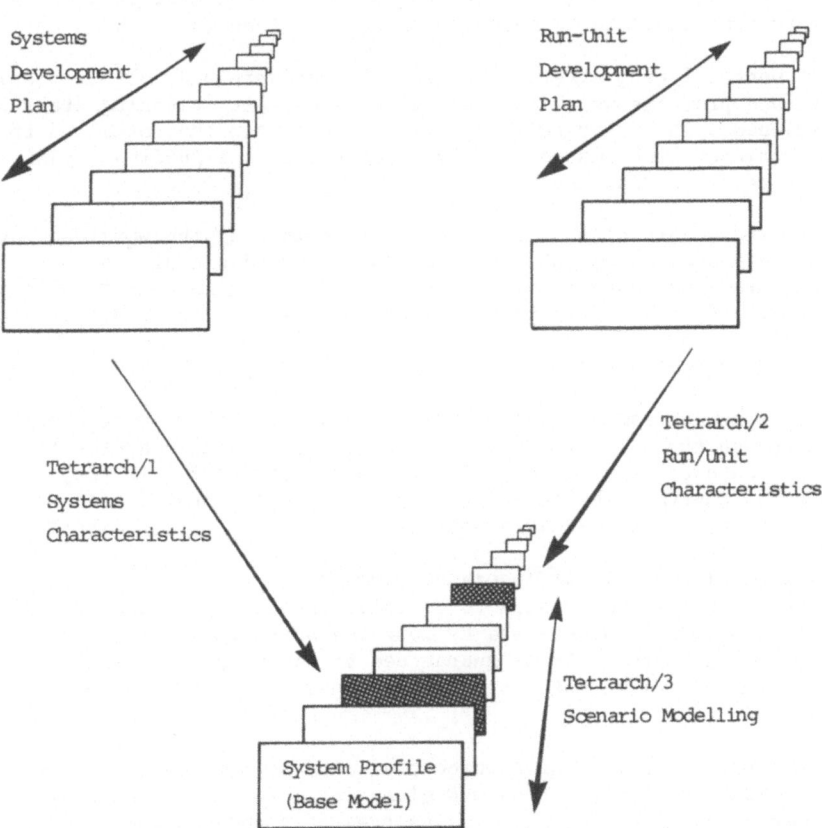

Figure 5   Tetrach/3 Hardware Capacity/Acquisition Planning

Most importantly, the eventual performance prediction in the live environment is predicted before any program is coded. If necessary, the design team can evaluate the use of alternative software such as another DBMS or the use of COBOL instead of a Fourth Generation Language.

These performance prediction results are used by capacity planning staff to refine the estimates of required capacity for that system produced in the strategic capacity planning process.

5   USING CAPACITY PLANNING IN THE REAL WORLD

The primary reason for undertaking any modelling exercise is to understand enough about the present to predict the future, within acceptable levels of accuracy. Computer system modelling provides the opportunity to undertake long term hardware acquisition planning; it also allows system designers to consider performance.

5.1   Acquisition Planning

A major UK company selected a hardware supplier primarily on the basis of two criteria, namely:

-    The software they wanted to install already ran on this equipment.

-    The supplier gave assurances that the machine migration path was more than adequate to support increased volumes.

Some 18 months later, after installing the hardware and software, severe performance problems were experienced and a capacity planning study was commissioned. The study built models of the system and concluded that the performance problems could only be overcome by significant additions of hardware (more Mips and Memory).

However, the models also showed that by distributing the workload more evenly and rescheduling jobs the inevitable upgrades could be phased in over 5 years. The associated budget was infinitely more acceptable to management and the IS director retained important parts of his anatomy.

5.2   A System Design Dilemma

Many insurance companies have to take on new products at very short notice and so the ability to provide a flexible computer system to capture, validate and accept, or reject, new policy details is very important. However, the interrogation of large amounts of data can take significant computer processing time.

A well known international insurance company was faced with a dilemma. They ideally wanted the system to be fully on-line but recognised that the client would be unimpressed by long response times. Acceptable computer performance could be guaranteed by having a partially on-line system with over-night batch but some business might be lost by the delay.

A performance model was built which predicted an acceptable average response time and the go-ahead was given for a fully on-line system to be developed. Actual performance was as predicted and management were assured that they had made the correct decision.

6   CONCLUSION

Tetrarch is a fully integrated systems design methodology which provides automated tools for Strategic Planning, Systems Analysis and Design. The provision of a Performance Prediction and Capacity Planning facility is a unique feature of Tetrarch which extends traditional structured techniques to enable the quantum of technology required to support the application software, to be precisely defined.

References

[BUZE78]   BUZEN J.P.
            "A Queueing Network Model of MVS"
            ACM Computing Surveys, Vol 10, No. 3 1978

INTELLIPSE: A KNOWLEDGE BASED TOOL FOR AN INTEGRATED

PROJECT SUPPORT ENVIRONMENT

Jon Bader, David Hannaford, Alastair Cochran,
and John Edwards

Aston University
and BIS Applied Systems Ltd.
Birmingham, UK

1   INTRODUCTION

This paper describes progress made during the first year of Intellipse, a
project funded under the Alvey Directorate's software engineering
programme. The aim of the three year project, begun in October 1985, is
to design and develop knowledge based software tools which can support
the development of commercial data processing systems. The three project
collaborators are Aston University, BIS Applied Systems Ltd and the Group
Computer Systems Development Team of the British Steel Corporation (Strip
Products Group).

The software tools will exploit IKBS techniques and be based on the
Structured Systems Development (SSD) method developed and promoted by BIS
Applied Systems Ltd. The SSD method will be codified using modular
knowledge bases corresponding to the discrete design phases in the SSD
method. The knowledge bases are a frame-like, meta-knowledge system
implemented in Prolog.

A flexible architecture has been devised which allows the meta-knowledge
base to access lower-level knowledge stored as text or Activity Program
Modules (APMs). The APMs will simulate or actively carry out specific
tasks within the design cycle.

The system will have two modes of operation. Advisor-mode will be a
passive system, offering advice to the designer at various stages in the
development cycle of a DP system. Designer-mode will go further than
current IPSE tools by giving active advice - i.e. it will execute specific design processes and make design decisions based on data supplied by
the designer. The user will access the system in Designer-mode via a
hierarchical menu structure, but in Advisor-mode, the designer will be
able to enter free-form, english-like queries allowing random access to
any point within a knowledge base.

2   THE ALVEY SOFTWARE ENGINEERING STRATEGY

The Alvey committee submitted its report to the government describing an
"Advanced Information Technology Programme" in August 1982. Of the four
enabling technologies identified by the Alvey committee in its report,
software engineering was singled out as of prime importance.

Although the Alvey committee commented that the "...technical leadership ...(of the UK)...software industry is well known..." [ALVE82], their report scorned ad hoc approaches to software development and proposed that:

> "Efficient production, an engineered approach to reliability, conformity with requirements, and economical development and operation must become the UK norm." [ALVE82]

The report went on to propose the development of an <u>Information System Factory</u> (ISF):

> "...An ISF will be a computer system, both hardware and software, which provides an integrated set of tools for producing IT systems using software engineering techniques. It will be developed from successive generations of Integrated Programming Support Environments (IPSEs), starting with a consolidated set of the tools available today." [ALVE82]

The Alvey committee envisaged three generations of IPSEs, with the third generation IPSE being founded on knowledge based tools. The Alvey software engineering strategy published by the Alvey Directorate in November 1983 said that:

> "The 3rd Generation IPSE (or ISF), containing knowledge bases and `intelligent´ tools, requires significant research which must begin now if the 1989 target date for the Information System Factory is to be met." [ALVE83]

In August 1984 the Alvey Software Engineering Directorate published a document which gave a more detailed description of what was envisaged by a third generation IPSE containing knowledge based tools. It suggested that:

> "...intelligent tools may be loosely defined as those which utilise techniques which are normally classified under the general heading IKBS. Such tools may replace conventional tools (e.g. a rule based syntax checker), enhance conventional tools (e.g. intelligent front end to a complex test generator) or provide assistance for tasks which have little, if any, conventional tool support (e.g. expert system advisor for requirements analysis)." [DIGN84]

However, the lack of clarity concerning the role of intelligent tools within the software engineering community, and the need for further research into the applicability of IKBS tools to commercial software engineering, was also acknowledged in the document:

> "IKBS offers a somewhat different paradigm for system development...However, the IKBS paradigm is immature and unproven. It may not deliver as much as it promises when exposed to the commercial and technical constraints of the market place. Indeed it has yet to address, or even recognise, some of the legitimate concerns of the software engineer." [DIGN84]

3   IKBS AND SOFTWARE ENGINEERING

It is clear that the Alvey Directorate believes that some of its objectives for the software engineering industry can be achieved through the development of IKBS tools.

Various claims have been made in the literature for the `intelligent´ problem solving performance which is possible, in different domains, using IKBS techniques. [HAYE83] Wheat Counsellor; Imperial College´s Prolog-based system on the British Nationality Act and Preceptor are three recently developed expert systems in the agricultural, legal and medical domains respectively [POGS85], [CORY84], [McSH85]. We believe that IKBS techniques applied in the DP system development domain can improve productivity and reliability by offering advantages in three distinct areas.

i.   Consistency of design - By codifying a hierarchical development method inside an IKBS tool we can expect designers using the system to be constrained within a general development framework. If the IKBS tool has successfully encompassed the standards demanded by the development method, designs produced using the system should exhibit a high degree of consistency.

ii.   Training of designers - Knowledge based systems can be a powerful training aid. Junior designers could use the system on selected case studies to develop their own designs. Clearly, senior designers would be required to evaluate the trainee´s results but the use of a knowledge based system would reduce the demand on the senior designer´s time, as well as improving the consistency of the training itself.

iii. Spreading of expertise - Currently, there are too few "good" DP system designers in the industry to spread around the many development projects. By encapsulating state-of-the-art design methods and expertise inside an IKBS tool it should be possible to make this expertise available to a much wider range of projects, through the use of the tool by less experienced designers.

We have assumed in this paper that the BIS-SSD method is an appropriate starting point for building a knowledge based support environment. We are not concerned here with a critical appraisal of the SSD method or the various other development methods which are on offer to the UK DP industry. However, in so far as semi-formal methods are being employed, it is fair to say that the BIS method is widely used and has a number of important industrial and government users.

4   ADVISOR/DESIGNER CONCEPT

The definition of intelligent, knowledge based tools that we have adopted for this project is that the tools should go further than existing 1st or 2nd generation tools by being able to perform three basic functions. (By "1st or 2nd generation tools" are meant tools which basically record information and which assume that the designer knows what task should be performed next and how and when that task should be carried out.)

i.   Advise a designer about the SSD method as a whole by answering specific questions about topics which are relevant in the domain.

ii.   Offer active support to the designer in the form of intelligent advice about a specific task within design. This advice should be such that it actively helps the designer make design decisions and perform specific design tasks. An example of such a system would be a tool which supported certain tasks within the data analysis like advising the designer how to choose keys.

iii. Automatically execute tasks or processes within the design phase of SSD which are currently executed manually. An example would be a system which automatically optimised a set of normalised relations.

Following on from this definition, two concrete modes for <u>Intellipse</u> have emerged as important. Advisor-mode is an intelligent thesaurus dealing with the SSD domain. Essentially, it is a knowledge base containing facts, rules, techniques and descriptions relating to all the <u>objects</u> and <u>activities</u> with which the SSD method deals. In this context, examples of <u>objects</u> are `data relations`, `keys` and `transaction profiles`. Examples of activities are `data analysis, `normalisation` and `sizing`.

In Advisor-mode the designer is able to interrogate the knowledge base about any object or activity known to the system. Information can be obtained, for example, about what an object is or why a particular activity is necessary. A description of how to perform an activity is also available. However, in this mode <u>Intellipse</u> is only a <u>passive</u> advisor. It cannot execute, in relation to a real application, any of the design activities it knows about or manipulate any of the objects it describes.

In Designer-mode the user will be able to work on a live project, actively invoking the facts and executing the rules which are passively described in the Advisor-mode knowledge base.

5   KNOWLEDGE BASES AND SYSTEM ARCHITECTURE

The SSD knowledge domain has been divided into six discrete knowledge bases corresponding to the six phases of design defined in the SSD method. The knowledge base hierarchy is illustrated in Figure I.

There are three levels of knowledge in the system. Meta-knowledge about objects and activities (usually referred to as <u>topics</u>) which exist in the domain, intermediate-level knowledge dealing with the types and categories of knowledge available for a particular topic and low-level knowledge corresponding to the facts and rules for a given topic, which is stored in the system as text (for Advisor-mode) or executable code (for Designer-mode).

Knowledge about an individual topic is classified into five distinct categories:

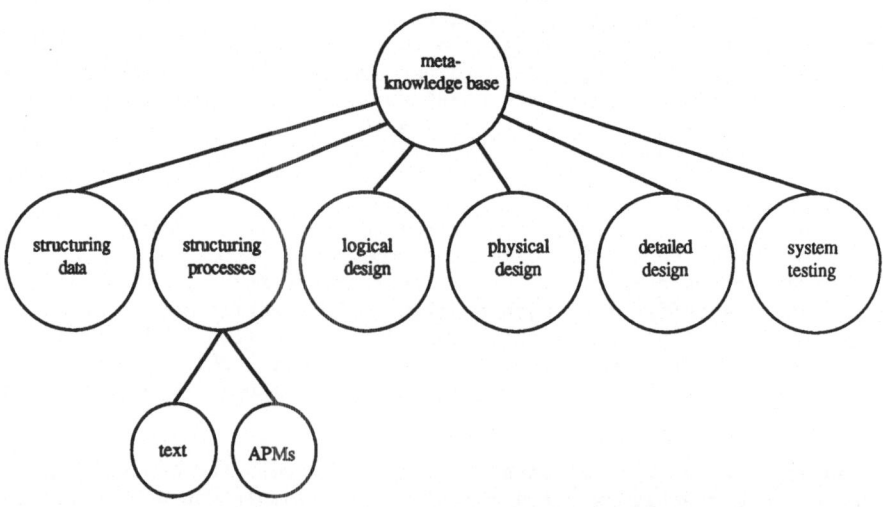

Figure 1   SSD knowledge-base hierarchy

1 descriptive - <u>what</u>
2 procedural - <u>how</u>
3 justificational - <u>why</u>
4 conditional - <u>when</u>
5 illustrative - example

The knowledge representation technique chosen to codify the knowledge bases is a frame-based system which is illustrated in Figure 2. The frame-like knowledge representation scheme uses some, but not all of the features usually associated with frame-based systems proposed by Minsky in 1975 (MINS75). The use of multiple-valued slot categories in the frames enables us to construct a complex, hierarchical structure which can be implemented relatively easily in Prolog. The pattern matching power of the Prolog language can then be exploited to achieve efficient interrogation of the domain.

The use of Prolog to implement the frame-based knowledge bases has also allowed us to build a simple, pattern-matching natural language parser. The user is able to enter free-form, english-like queries to interrogate the knowledge bases allowing the experienced user to by-pass the multiple-level menu system. This capability is desirable since the system will eventually contain knowledge bases covering over one hundred individual topics - each topic having, potentially, several categories of knowledge. The menu structure, which is governed by the frames themselves, will reflect the breadth and complexity of the domain.

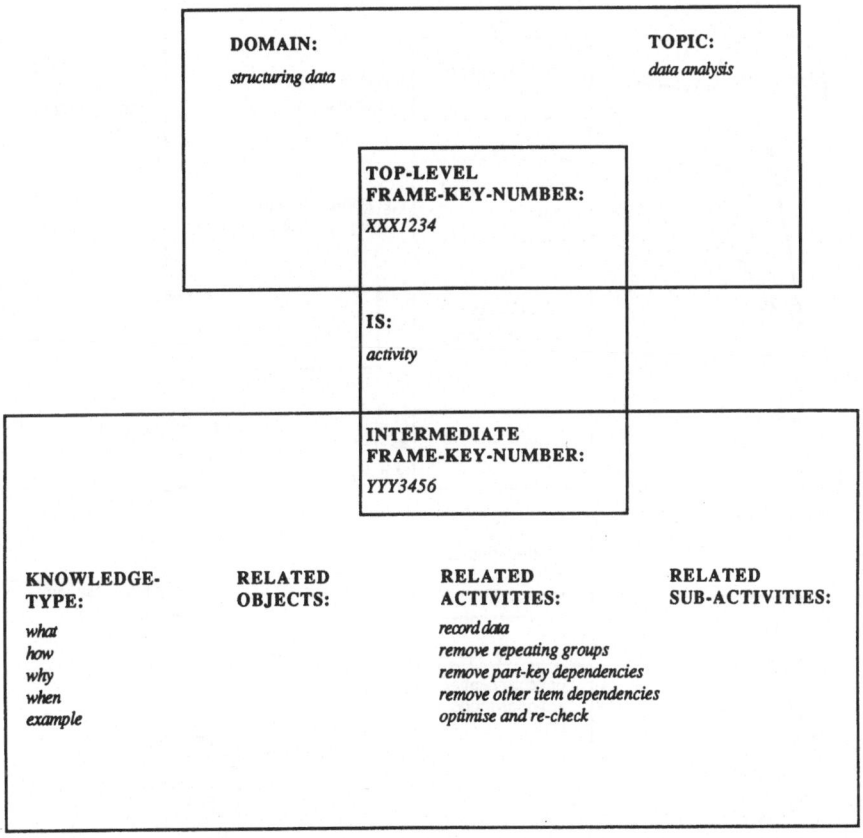

Figure 2 Showing some partially instantiated frames and their inter-relationship

191

Although this is an advantage for the naive user who can be guided
through the domain, step by step, using the interactive menu system, this
could be an inhibiting interface for the experienced user who is already
familiar with the system, or with the SSD method.

Examples of the free-form queries which can be entered into the system
are:

> What is a prime key?
> How do I perform first normal form analysis?
> When do I start the physical design stage?
> Show me an example of a transaction profile

The Activity Program Modules (APMs) will be executable modules which,
together with the meta-level knowledge base, will determine the operation
of Intellipse in Designer-mode. They will be individual, `mini IKBSs´
embodying the facts and rules governing a specific design process, or
non-IKBS, algorithmic-based programs – where the given design process is
being completely automated. An APM could also be an existing tool such
as, for example, an editor or compiler. This architecture will mean that
the Designer-mode system can be built up on an incremental basis.

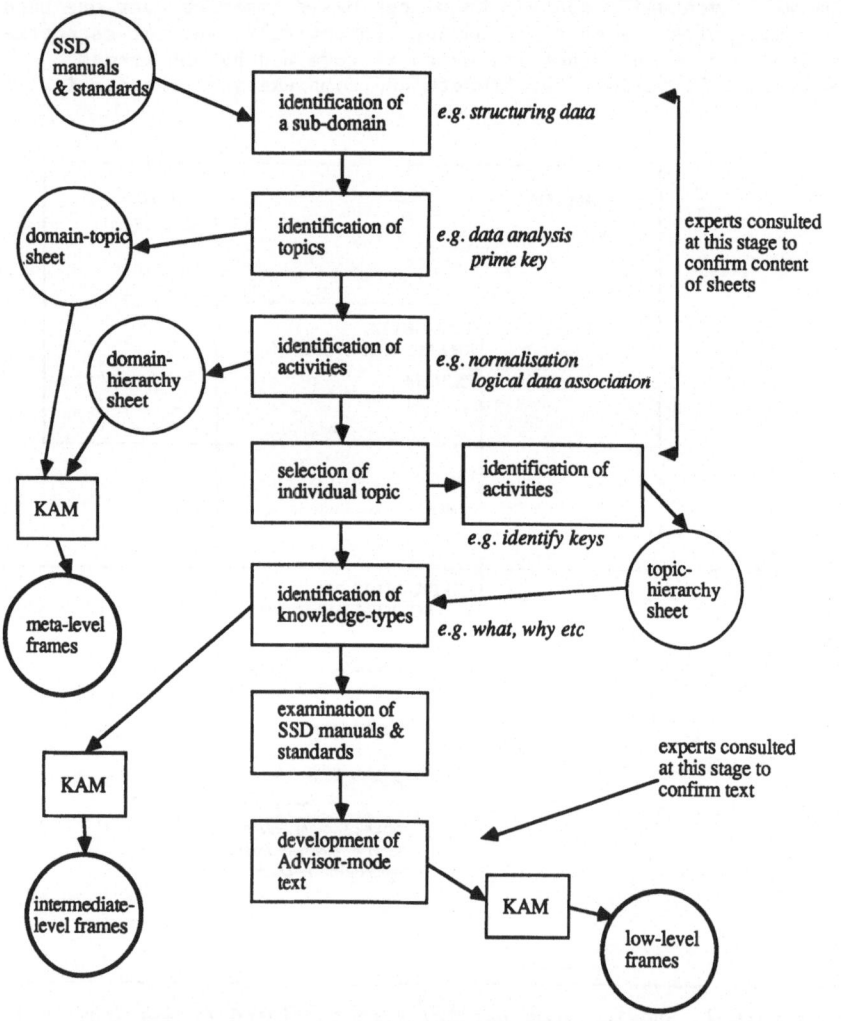

Figure 3   Knowledge Engineering – Stage one procedure

The knowledge engineering inherent in this project has been conceived as a three stage process. Stage one has been concerned with an examination of the SSD manuals and standards documents with a limited involvement of SSD experts. This has provided the basis for the meta-level knowledge base and the low-level text required in the Advisor-mode system.

Stage two will involve a detailed study of the SSD method as it is used by expert practitioners in the real DP environment. This study will examine a live development project as well as conducting extensive knowledge engineering sessions with senior BIS experts and other, industrial users of the SSD method. The aim of stage two is to enrich the knowledge bases developed in stage one and to provide a detailed specification for the APMs which will be at the heart of the Intellipse system.

Stage three will attempt to refine the Advisor-mode knowledge bases in the light of the information obtained during stage two.

A tool for managing the knowledge engineering process has been developed which has also been implemented in Prolog. The Knowledge Acquisition Module (KAM) enables the knowledge engineer to create and edit frames and enter text into the knowledge bases. It also creates and maintains the links between the different levels of frames. The detailed procedure followed during stage one is illustrated in Figure 3.

The creation of the domain-hierarchy-sheets and topic-hierarchy-sheets referred to in Figure III is a crucial step in the knowledge engineering process. These sheets are a diagrammatic representation of the hierarchical set of activities or tasks which are required to complete a specific design process. The domain-hierarchy-sheets deal with high-level activities relevant to a whole sub-domain (like structuring data), whereas the topic-hierarchy-sheets describe the tasks necessary to execute a high-level activity within a sub-domain and already identified on the domain-hierarchy-sheet. The resulting tree-like structure of activities is codified in the knowledge bases and dictates the way a user is guided through the whole design process.

7   MATURITY OF THE DOMAIN

Apart from the assumptions referred to earlier concerning the suitability of the SSD method as a basis for the development of knowledge based tools, a more questionable assumption underlying our work is that the software engineering domain itself is mature enough to be treated in a similar way to, say, the medical or legal domains. The latter domains are, historically, a product of many hundreds of years of development, in which highly sophisticated systems of training, heuristic knowledge and practical methods have been built up.

Software engineering when compared with these more traditional domains has had a very short evolutionary span - measuring a few tens of years. As a result, it has not yet evolved a rigorous system of heuristics or established a widely accepted engineering methodology. Reinforcing this domain immaturity is the lack of a formal, scientific foundation to the software development process.

The other factor which has an important impact on the unstable nature of current software engineering practices is the continuing, rapid advance in hardware technology which fundamentally affects the nature of computer systems. Software engineering principles and techniques established only a few years ago, appropriate to the economic and technical constraints of the technology of that period, are having to be rapidly revised today to take account of, for example, the enormous potential power of the new parallel hardware architectures.

The ultimate long-term aim of the AI community may be to produce black-box systems which accept natural language specifications in at one end and produce executable code at the other. In the meantime, we believe that despite the immaturity of the software engineering process, it can be improved by building knowledge based systems which make available current state-of-the-art techniques to the widest class of projects. Also, the architecture devised for Intellipse will allow its knowledge base to be periodically revised as improvements are made to the SSD method.

8 PROGRESS AND FUTURE PLANS

At the time of writing (December 1986), stage one of the knowledge engineering process is nearly completed and a prototype of the Advisor-mode system is running on an IBM PC-AT. During stage two of the project we will be giving special consideration to the potential users of the Intellipse system when specifying, designing and implementing the Designer-mode system. An evaluation of the Advisor-mode system will also be conducted in an actual DP environment. By the end of the project we hope to be able to draw some initial conclusions about the appropriateness of knowledge based tools to the development of commercial DP systems.

REFERENCES

[ALVE82]   Alvey Committee "The Report of the Alvey Committee", HMSO, 1982.

[ALVE83]   Alvey Directorate "Software Engineering Strategy", November 1983.

[CORY84]   Cory, H.T., Hammond, P., Kowalski, R.A., Kriwaczek, F., Sadri, F., Sergot, M., "The British Nationality Act as a Logic Program" Report, Department of Computing, Imperial College, London, 1984

[DIGN84]   Dignan, Tony "Software Engineering/IKBS Strategy for Knowledge Based IPSE Development", Alvey Directorate, August 1984

[HAYE83]   Hayes-Roth F., Waterman D.A., Lenat, D.B., "Building Expert Systems", Addison-Wesley, 1983.

[McSH85]   McSherry, D., Fullerton, K., "Preceptor: a shell for medical expert systems and its application in a study of prognostic indices in stroke" Expert Systems, Vol 2, no 3, July 1985

[MINS75]   Minsky, M., "A Framework for Representing Knowledge", in "The Psychology of Computer Vision", Ed Winston, P.H. McGraw Hill,1975

[POGS85]   Pogson, J.B., Brown, C.H. "SAVOIR" - Current practical applications of an expert systems package" ISI Ltd, 1985

METHODOLOGIES AND TOOLS FOR REAL-TIME SYSTEMS

A. Bruty

Yourdon International

London, UK

"A beginning is the time for taking most delicate care that the balances are correct..." - from ´Dune´ by Frank Herbert.

1   THE PROBLEM OF "GETTING STARTED"

One of the difficulties with every problem modelling or systems analysis technique is getting started.

As soon as we put pen to paper, or even start to think about a problem, we have begun to make choices; the reverberations of which will be felt throughout the system development life cycle.. Choices to be made include the size and scope of the system, the functionality that shall be included and even the identification of the correct problem to model and solve (in other words choice of the right subject centre). ´Getting started´ is not just how to start but what to start with and where to start from. Just starting can be a major hurdle to begin with.

This appears particularly true where software is involved.

So how can we get started without making too many artificial choices which will affect the system?

In the past, the idea of functional decomposition was considered to be reasonable. However, this method is very subjective and no better than a wet finger in the air when it comes to identifying system behaviour.

Functional decomposition is argued, by Heitmeyer and McLean [PALM84], to be implementation dependant since a more-or-less arbitrary choice among a set of possible decompositions has been made. This may lead to low level functions appearing at unnaturally ´high´ levels of abstraction, leading to disorientation on the reader´s behalf.

Steve Meller and Paul Ward [WARD85] went further to point out that functional decomposition does not guide the developer towards partitioning a system so as to minimise interface complexity.

A basic myth about system decomposition is that there is a natural partitioning for a system. There is not. Partioning of systems is for our own benefit so that we can appreciate the problem. Any partitioning is a distortion of the problem being modelled and we can only hope to minimise this distortion.

Functional decomposition does not achieve this goal consistently.

2   ALTERNATIVES TO FUNCTIONAL DECOMPOSITION

The first problem appears to be, what is ´The System´.

One has to remember that there is no such thing as a system which is not a part of, or sub-set of, another system which is itself a part of, or sub-set of, another system.... So the only way to make the term ´System´ meaningful is to limit the scope or context of it.

A system is an artifact of our observing it to be a system.

In other words any system we care to study will be artificially created by ourselves. We do this by including things of interest to us and omitting those things we find of no interest.

In 1975 Tom De Marco [MARC75] suggested the idea of a System Context Diagram (Figure 1). The Context Diagram is used to limit the domain of study. In other words it limits the scope and therefore the size of the system. The Context Diagram shows sources and sinks of data. "A source or sink is a person or organisation lying outside the context of a system that is a net originator or receiver of system data."

The Context Diagram, therefore, shows the System, the terminators that form part of the system environment and the interactions between the system and its terminators.

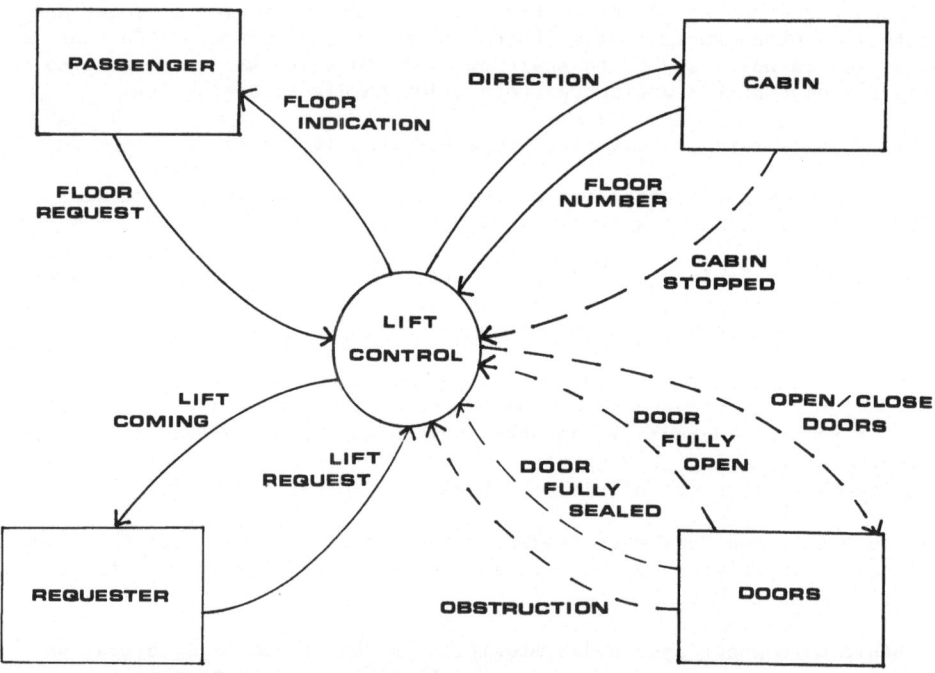

figure 1.   Context diagram for lift system

Taking this idea further we can proceed to identify two different groups
of terminators.

Meller and Ward [WARD85] suggested that a system is surrounded by a
perception space in which the system can perceive entities and an action
space in which the system can act upon these entities. The instruments
of perception are sensors and the instruments of action, actors. As
entities pass through the perception space they can be sensed, then as
they pass through the action space they can be acted upon.

An embedded system cannot perform any useful work without sensors to
sense its environment and actors to act upon its environment. It is not
the entities that pass through the perception/action space that are
important but that the system can ´see´ and ´act´ upon the entities.
Without the correct sensor an entity may pass through the
perception/action space completely unnoticed by the system. Similarly,
without the correct actors no action can take place.

It is these sensors and actors, then, which form one group of
terminators.

Another group of terminators is formed by the general group called
´Objects´.

An object is something which plays a role in the system, can be uniquely
identified by a set of data element values or attributes, can be named,
has state and has effect on, and is affected by, other objects. [FLAV81]
[BOOC86]

Let us consider a Lift. We shall try to identify Objects and
Sensor/Actors that play a role in the system.

First the objects:

PASSENGER someone who travels in the lift. Who gets on a floor and would
like to go to another floor.

REQUESTER someone who resides temporarily at a floor, but wishes to
travel in the lift. Requesters normally have some idea in which direction they wish to travel, either up or down.

LIFT which is travelling up or down, passing floors as it goes, in
response to passengers and requesters.

The lift itself could be classified as a super-type object, and contain
two other sub-objects, namely.

CABIN in which the passengers travel, which is either moving or
stationery.

DOORS which are open or closed.

Now the Sensors and Actors

LIFT BUTTONS the mechanism by which the PASSENGER selects the floor to go
to.
(SENSOR)

FLOOR SENSOR the way in which the LIFT detects the floor it is passing.
(SENSOR)

CABIN MOTOR which drives the CABIN up and down.
(ACTOR)

DOOR MECHANISM which closes and opens the DOORS.
(ACTOR)

FLOOR DISPLAY which informs the PASSENGER of the floor being passed.
(PASSIVE ACTOR)

LIFT COMING DISPLAY which displays to the REQUESTER that the lift is
coming.
(PASSIVE ACTOR)

The last two ACTORS are termed PASSIVE ACTORS because although they
affect the system environment, they are only messages which are intended
for a person! Need I say more.

We need to be able to decide whether to base the model around the problem
(the objects) or how it will be implemented (the sensor/actor
technology). Choosing Objects will lead to an implementation independant
model, but sometimes the Sensor/Actor technology forms part of our basic
understanding of the problem.

3   OBJECTS AND SENSOR/ACTORS: A BASIS FOR CHOICE

Mellor and Ward provided some heuristics to help in choosing between the
Objects and the Sensor/Actor technology in the Perception/Action space.
[WARD85]

Show the objects in the system´s perception/action space when:

*   the sensor/actor technology is not well defined;

*   the sensor/actor technology is not closely related to the subject
     matter of the system;

*   a sensor passively sends through data about the perception space to
     the embedded system;

*   the nature of the data sent to or received from the environment is
     relatively independent of sensor/actor technology;

*   the interface between the system and a human operator is being
     described.

Show the sensor/actor technology when:

*   the sensor/actor technology has been defined in detail;

*   the sensor/actor technology is more closely related to the subject
     matter of the system than to the technology of computer peripheral
     devices;

*   a sensor must be controlled by the embedded system in order to
     perform its function;

*   the nature of the data received from or sent to the environment is
     fundamentally dependent on the choice of sensor or actor.

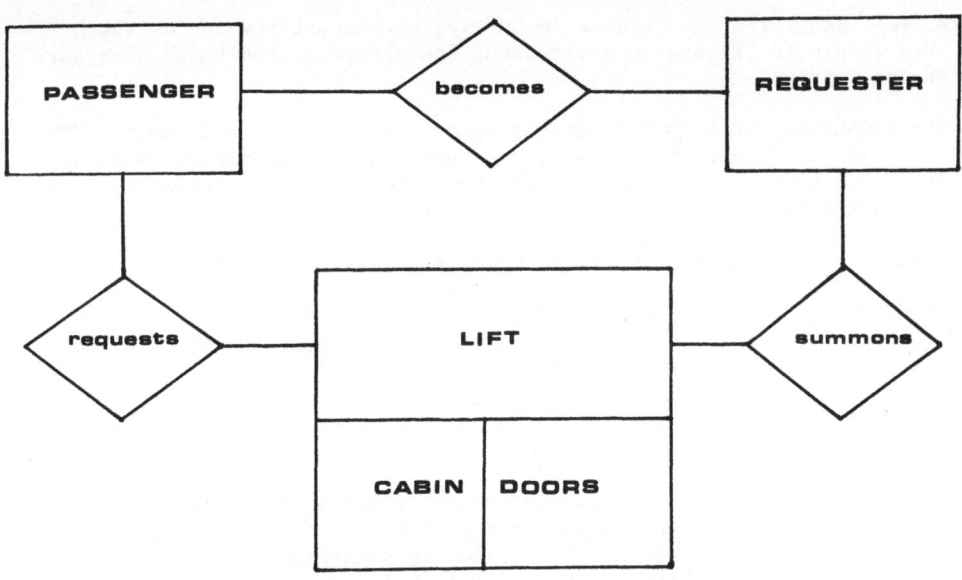

figure 2 Entity-Relationship diagram for lift system

In the case of the Lift the Objects are going to provide us with a model which is driven by the problem. The Sensor/Actor technology will provide a model which is implementation dependant.

Let us look at how the Objects identified relate to each other.

The PASSENGER requests the LIFT to travel to a floor.

The REQUESTER summons the LIFT to his floor.

The REQUESTER (hopefully) becomes a passenger.

The DOORS must not be open until the CABIN is stationary.

The CABIN will not move until the DOORS are closed.

These relationships can be shown in a diagramatic form (Figure 2). Such a diagram shows the objects and relationships between the objects and is thus called an Entity Relationship Diagram!

We can also assign the attributes which uniquely identify the objects which play a role within the lift system:

PASSENGER Desired Floor

REQUESTER Floor
         Current Floor

CABIN   Moving
          Stationary

DOORS   Open
          Closed

Having identified the objects in our system we must now decide which objects are in the system environment (terminators) and which form part of the ´system´.

The PASSENGER and REQUESTER are by observation in the environment. The DOORS and CABIN are physical objects which can be identified as being part of a LIFT system, so we shall place them in the environment. That leaves the LIFT to form the ´Subject Centre´ or ´System´.

Figure 1 shows the Context Diagram for the lift control system.

The flows of data can be derived by associating the sensor/actor technology with the objects. For example, the LIFT BUTTONS and FLOOR DISPLAY are associated with the PASSENGER.

Interactions may be flows of data or material (shown as solid lines) or flows of control (shown as dashed lines).

To summarise - we can construct a Context Diagram from which we can identify external objects which form part of the overall system (terminators), the scope of the system, it´s interactions with the environment and the subject centre - in this case a lift.

4   THE RELATIONSHIP BETWEEN TERMINATORS AND THE SYSTEM

The next problem is to identify the way in which the terminators act upon the system and the way in which the system acts upon its terminators.

The information the terminators send to the system is already shown on the Context Diagram. The Context Diagram does not show what causes that information to be sent, the Event, or how the system will respond to that event.

We can define an event as something that produces a pre-programmed response within the system.

Some of the responses will produce a direct effect on the system environment via the terminators, and other events will produce an indirect response at some later time.

The events can be collected together to form an Event list.

The Event List shows us the events generated in the system environment and how they affect the behaviour of the system. As one can see, most events are associated with specific terminators and with flows into the system. This is not necessarily always true, as an event may be associated with several terminators and/or flows. An event could also be associated with a specific moment in time.

The concept of an external event is that it has a pre-programmed response within the system boundary. Let us examine the lift again in the light of this (Table 1).

The event, ´Passenger selects a floor´ (Event 1), produces a response in the system. This might be, for example, place the floor number in a queue or, simply, move to the floor. Spending a little time thinking about the way in which passengers of lifts behave will tell us that sometimes a floor button is pushed out of sequence and therefore some queueing action is necessary.

TABLE 1
EVENT LIST
FOR THE LIFT SYSTEM

EVENT NUMBER	EVENT	RESPONSE
1	PASSENGER MAKES A FLOOR REQUEST	UPDATE FLOOR QUEUE
2	REQUESTER SUMMONS THE LIFT	UPDATE REQUEST QUEUE
3	FLOOR REACHED	STOP CABIN
4	CABIN STATIONARY	OPEN DOORS
5	DOORS FULLY OPEN	WAIT
6	DOORS FULLY CLOSED	MOVE TO FLOOR
7	TIME TO GO TO GROUND FLOOR	CLOSE DOORS MOVE TO GROUND
8	DOOR OBSTRUCTED	OPEN DOORS CLOSE DOORS
9	TIME TO CLOSE DOORS	CLOSE DOORS
10	REQUESTERS FLOOR REACHED	STOP CABIN OPEN DOORS
11	GROUND FLOOR REACHED	STOP CABIN OPEN DOORS
12	FLOOR PASSED	DISPLAY FLOOR

An event like, "Floor reached´ (Event 3), has an immediately observable effect on the environment; the lift stops moving. Similarly, ´Doors fully closed´ (Event 6), has the effect of moving a lift to a floor.

The temporal events, ´Time to go to ground floor´ (Event 7) causes the doors to close and the cabin to move to the ground floor. ´Time to close doors´ (Event 9) causes the doors to close after a request say.

We are now beginning to identify behaviour within the system, and so far have not had to partition the system unnecessarily into arbitrary units.

5   CONCLUSION

In conclusion, to begin analysis a Context Diagram should be constructed. This forces one to identify the subject centre of the analysis, to choose the appropriate terminators and to identify the interactions between the two. An Event list should also be compiled identifying events which cause a response in the system. This leads to decisions as to what those responses are to be.

One can now proceed to derive system behaviour by projecting the Event List into the ´System´. For the moment, however, it is enough that we have identified a way of starting analysis, while ensuring "...that the balances are correct".

REFERENCES

[MARC78] Tom De Marco "Structured Analysis and Systems Specification"

[PALM84] Stephen M. McMenamin and John F. Palmer "Essential Systems Analysis"

[FLAV81] Matt Flevin "Fundamental Concepts of Information Modelling"

[BOOC86] Grady Booch "Objected Orientated Development" IEEE Transactions on Software Engineering. Volume SE-12, No.2. February 1986.

[WARD85] Paul T. Ward and Stephen J. Mellor "Structured Development for Real-Time Systems."

MAKING STRUCTURED METHODS WORK: USING AN EMBEDDED EXPERT SYSTEM TO
MONITOR THE USE OF METHODOLOGY IN AN ANALYST'S WORKBENCH —
THE INFORMATION ENGINEERING WORKBENCH

John Parkinson

Arthur Young Management Consultants

London, UK

1   INTRODUCTION

The use of rigorous methods for the analysis and design of computerised
information systems is widely seen as essential if the full capabilities
of modern computer technology are to be realised [MART84]. Most methods
are eventually aimed at the automatic generation of executable code from
requirements specifications, as a way of relieving gross resource constraints (commonly called backlogs) and reducing development timescales.
Early attempts, during the 1970´s, to develop rigorous techniques for
software lifecycle management resulted in a number of quite similar
packaged "Methodologies" most of which used diagram based representations
of requirements to replace textual descriptions, in an attempt to increase the effectiveness of the communication between "user" and
"designer" [DECA79], [YOUR75], [ORR77], [WARN81], [GANE77], [CONN85].

Although these techniques were seen as a major advance in improving the
quality of the analysis and design process, they largely failed to deliver their full potential because of the difficulty in actually applying
them in "real world" projects. In particular, diagram drawing and,
especially re-drawing, was slow and tedious, and the results were hard to
validate. Projects using these methods, ran more slowly than those using
conventional methods, and although there were some quality gains, they
were not seen as sufficient to offset the cost of the additional
resources required. In any case, nothing was being done to reduce the
elapsed time in development projects, an equally important objective to
quality and productivity improvements.

One area where some success was achieved was in the design and programming phases of a project. The development of structured programming
techniques allowed program code to be written more logically, and the
results could be debugged faster and changed more easily [JACK75],
[DAHL72].

Although most applications of the techniques generally fell short of
producing error free programs, the basis for the automatic generation of
"provably" correct code seemed to be established [ANDE79].

However without a corresponding improvement in the methods used to
specify requirements, better programming techniques only succeeded in
generating unsatisfactory or unusable applications more rapidly (Garbage

in Garbage out - but faster), and end users remained largely
dissatisfied.

Consequently, in parallel with the development of improved programming
methods, attempts were made to introduce similar methods into the requirements analysis and specification process [TEIC77], [CAIN75],
[CASE81]. Although widely believed to be of value, these attempts still
lacked sufficient rigour to provide the improvements in quality that were
needed for large and complex software development projects.

2   THE DEVELOPMENT OF AUTOMATED SUPPORT TOOLS

By the end of the 1970's, it was clear to many methodologists that a high
degree of automation needed to be applied to requirements analysis and
specification, in the same way that automated project support environments were being developed to assist with the generation and maintenance
of program code. The first generation of products, generally called
Analyst's Workbenches, appeared in about 1983, and were primarily concerned with computerised assistance for the drawing and maintenance of
the diagram types used by structured methodologies [MART85], [ANOR86],
[SMIT86].

These early tools only provided a few simple structure checks on the
diagrams, usually by retrospective review, and considerable manual quality control was still needed. They were, however, soon developed to
provide links to other tools (data dictionaries and Integrated Project
Support Environments (IPSE's)) and made easier to use via WIMP (Windows,
Icons, Mice, Pull Down Menus) and other similar techniques.

Such developments continued to attack the productivity problem, but not
to address the quality issue. Research was now showing that the ratio of
development costs to total lifecycle costs was approaching 1:8 and getting worse, and that the majority of problems in finished systems (over
60%) were caused by errors in analysis and requirements specification
[MART84], [DEMA79]. Clearly the issue of improved quality hinged on
improvements in the analysis process, and, given the essential limits on
unaided human performance, this could only be achieved by extending the
capability of automated support tools.

3   THE INFORMATION ENGINEERING WORKBENCH (IEW)

In 1984, the Information Technology Consulting arm of Arthur Young (AY),
the United States accountancy and consulting services partnership, joined
with KnowledgeWare Incorporated (KWI), then called Database Design Inc.,
and with James Martin, in a project to develop a "second generation" of
structured analysis and design methods and their associated automated
support tools, under the broad heading of Martin's ideas on "Information
Engineering". It was agreed that the project needed to design and build
a set of tools that would not only assist the strategic planner, business
analyst and system designer to be more productive when using structured
techniques, but would also actually "understand" the basic techniques
themselves, and thus be able to monitor how they were being used.

Our own quality assurance work had shown that many errors in specification (abut half of all detected errors) were due to incorrect use of
methodology, and were thus potentially avoidable if compliance was
enforced. A further percentage of errors (35% of the total detected)
resulted from incomplete specification, and although these were difficult
to detect manually, it was felt that they could also be detected by the

tools, using a periodic review of the state of the specification (Checking "Have I finished?" or "is this complete?").

A range of technical options for the required tools was examined, including a review of all currently available products. Because it was intended to make use of the results in our own consulting work, we needed to produce a reasonably low cost solution, and it was decided that the tools should be partly microcomputer based, and that the toolset as a whole should be scalable, to deal with a wide range of development projects. This decision limited the choice of approach to one that could be supported on commercially available microcomputer hardware, essentially on an IBM PC/AT running PC-DOS.

Given these restrictions, the design team felt that a conventional programming approach would be too prone to the same kind of errors that they were trying to eradicate, and too difficult to maintain and extend. KnowledgeWare believed that the best change of success lay within the area of Knowledge Engineering or Expert Systems, and it was decided to base developments on Knowledge Based Systems (KBS) techniques. The designers quickly rejected the idea of building a conventional expert "shell", as being too specialised and "unfriendly", and instead opted to embed the KBS component inside a composite design.

In examining the possible representational approaches, the primary requirement was to match as closely as possible the technique of successive model refinement used by our methodology, and to support the data driven concepts of Information Engineering [MART86], [MART87]. The designers initially rejected a Frame Structure in favour of Production Rules, as the latter appeared to allow for the implementation of usable facilities without a complete representation of the system lifecycle model. It soon became clear, however, that the production rules would need to be underpinned with just such a model, even though it would not initially be complete.

As a result, the IEW is built round three basic concepts:

*   the Meta Model, an abstraction of the system development lifecycle, against which all actual system specifications are compared, implemented as a relational data structure (The Encyclopaedia)

*   the Methodology, implemented as a set of production rules for constructing a specification and comparing the results with the meta model (The Knowledge Coordinator (tm) and Knowledge Analysers (tm))

*   the Diagrammers, implemented as a mouse/window/icon drawing environment for the representation of requirements and the definition of object instances.

For practical reasons it was decided to use existing "environment" software for the developments wherever this was available. This turned out to be both an advantage (rapid initial progress) and a disadvantage (fault correction and edge case management outside of the design team's direct control).

4   STRUCTURE

It soon became clear that the tools would require a more complex structure than had initially been planned. The performance available from the PC-AT and similar machines was insufficient to support both diagram verification and design synthesis for all sizes of development

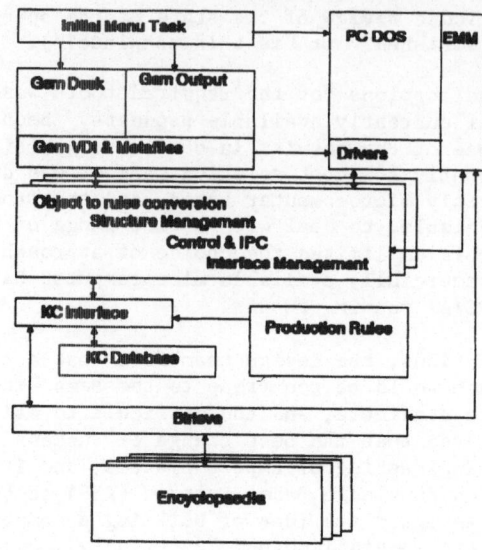

Diagram 1 IEW: Main Components

project. The cost of specialised "AI" hardware was, however, still too high to form the basis for the finished product. The toolset was therefore divided into two components, a PC based set of diagrammers and a mini- or mainframe computer based set of analysers and code generators.

Thus the PC could deal with diagram management and method verification, plus partial completeness checking (local "view" consistency) utilising the available power to handle the user interface and low bandwidth data gathering tasks. The mini- or mainframe component could then provide the high bandwidth and power needed for the consolidation of views, for the synthesis of complete specifications and designs and, eventually, for the generation of program code.

The final structure adopted is shown in diagrams 1 and 2. The PC

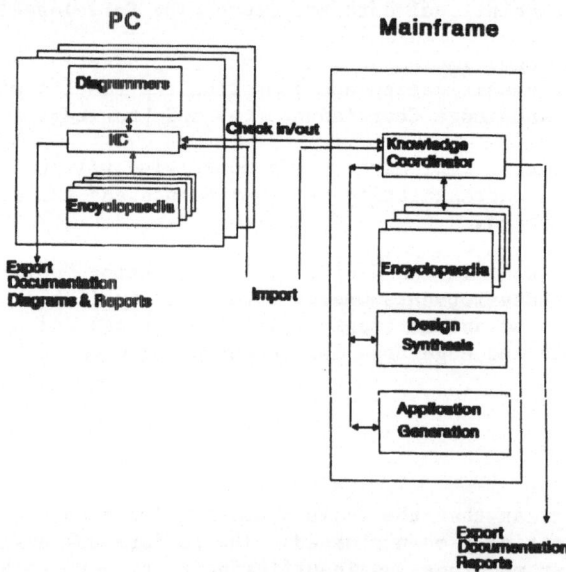

diagram 2. IEW: Overall structure

component consists of an overall management program that checks and initialises the environment, loads the runtime system from disk and presents a conventional menu of options (diagram 3), covering configuration management, housekeeping and output tasks, as well as access to the main workbench functions. Selecting "Run the Workbench" causes the GEM Desktop environment to be loaded and the access task entered. On completion of access control, the command level task is loaded and from this all available tasks can be initiated. Three kinds of tasks (environment and profile management, diagramming and output) are provided. Tasks are selected from "pull down" menus, and only valid choices are enabled.

Once in a diagramming task, the user draws standardised icons for object instances, and provides a "name" (any character string) to identify the instance. Object instances must be unique, although multiple usage (association with a view) is allowed if methodologically valid. Once an instance/usage has been established, it can be added to the existing structure, and the result is then checked for structural correctness and consistency. Valid changes are stored in the Encyclopaedia as object/property/association relations, and as textual descriptions. Checks are implemented via references to the production rules database, which contains some 1400 rules. Current diagrammers support hierarchical decomposition models, dataflow models, entity - relationship - attribute models and procedure specification using Action Diagrams.

On completion of diagramming, the user has available a choice of structure and completeness checks that report on the extent to which some or all of the Encyclopaedia forms a complete and valid set of specifications. Structures can then be transferred to the second component for consolidation (integration with all other local views) and further analysis and/or synthesis.

5   COMPONENT INTEGRATION

PC-DOS is a limited operating system, allowing only a single active task and limiting memory addressing to 1Mb, of which only about 600Kb is available to user programs once DOS and the necessary device drivers are loaded. Since the total object code size for IEW exceeds 1.5Mb, integration of the various functional components is essential. IEW uses the paged memory approach to allow all program code and the production rules database to be loaded into memory. A ramdisk to hold intermediate workfiles, and a facility for update caching are also used to enhance basic PC-AT performance.

Code, written in "C", is provided to convert graphic inputs (changes to diagrams) into goals, and these are evaluated against the production rules and/or the meta model. Results are classified as: failure (you can't do this) in which case the user must try again; partial success (OK, but this has other consequences - are you sure you want to do it?) both requiring the user to provide confirmation before acceptance: and success, in which case the structure change is actioned without further dialogue. For control of integrity, all attempts to delete an object instance are forced to be partial failures, and must be confirmed.

Some operations (e.g. multiple object deletions) cause changes that propagate unpredictably through the model. Rather than investigate unprofitable avenues in assessing the correctness of such operations, and thus requiring extensive interaction with the user, IEW uses backtracking techniques to construct an evaluation hierarchy to automatically process the complete operation, stopping only if a goal fails [CLAR84, GRAY84].

Once again, to preserve integrity, confirmation must be provided before the Encyclopaedia is finally updated.

In many cases, however, single solution evaluation is sufficient (we do not usually want to know all they ways in which a structure change fails, a single explanation is sufficient to guide the user to identify the error) and this is provided for by cuts within the rules. Although this improves evaluation efficiency, it does so at the expense of generality, introducing "procedural" assumptions into the rule set [RADE78]. For this reason, it is an approach that cannot be taken during consolidation (the process of combining multiple local views into a single composite view), where all possible routes for including a new set of views must be evaluated, and during the procedure for data and process structure syntheses. Although it is possible, in some cases, for the synthesis to fail, in the sense that it cannot be completed in finite time, the power of the generalised approach is necessary if we are to have a widely useful set of automated tools [KOR66]. With the current formulation of the meta model and production rules, the synthesis tasks are beyond the capacity of a PC in most real world cases. It is for this reason that the relevant IEW components are implemented on a mini- or mainframe computer.

In documenting the reasons for goal failure, a decision was taken to provide a single explanatory message, couched in terms of the methodology, not the production rules, and not to allow the user to query the result (no "tell me why" facilities). A "help in context" function is provided instead.

6   KNOWLEDGE REPRESENTATION

The "Knowledge" in IEW is in two parts. The meta model and production rules, as described above, form the structure within which a particular requirements specification is developed. This specification itself represents knowledge about a user requirement, and is stored in the Encyclopaedia as an instance of the generalised meta model. It consists of:

*   Object instances and definitions


```
        1  Run the Workbench.

        2  Run the Output program.

        3  Change monitor, mouse, printer or color settings.

        4  Back up an Encyclopedia.

        5  Restore an Encyclopedia.

        6  Repair an Encyclopedia.

        7  Quit.


            Enter your selection :
```

Diagram 3. IEW: Initial Menu

* Object associations, defining usage and relations

* Object properties or attributes, which may be general or usage specific

From this information, a database of facts about the current state of the design is constructed for use in goal evaluation.

The fine structure of the meta model and the details of the production rules are proprietary, and hence not described here. The contents of the Encyclopaedia are likewise not published directly, but are available for external use via an Export facility that restructures the contents as a simple ASCII file.

7   PRACTICAL EXPERIENCE

As with all new and complex software products, practical experience with the early releases of the tools provided some lessons about the approach and the technology chosen. IEW pushes the chosen hardware and software components to the limits of their capability, and in some cases rather beyond it. Faults were discovered in all the third party software components used (including PC-DOS), and these took time to resolve. Testing so complex a structure (there are more than 30 functional components to be integrated on the PC alone) with the relatively crude tools available for the PC proved more difficult than expected. Proving the meta model and production rules was, and is, a major activity, particularly as both continue to be extended to incorporate new functionality [TURN84]. Performance on the PC is acceptable, if not yet always in the sub-second class for all functions, although this is becoming less of a problem as more powerful PC systems become available. Specialist workstation hardware is, however, still too expensive to use as a basis for the tools.

To be positive, however, IEW has achieved practically all of its design goals, particularly in improving the quality of requirements specifications, and in demonstrating the viability of the approach. It has also opened up a whole new series of possible applications for KBS techniques in the management of the software life cycle, which we are beginning to explore.

8   FUTURE DEVELOPMENTS

The major new functions that will be incorporated into toolset over the next 18 months have already been identified, and the design team have a good idea of the profitable areas for longer term investigation. Items to be resolved in the short term primarily concern implementation issues, performance and the management of the user interface, especially the value of cosmetic customisation, allowing the tools to mimic support for other methodologies more closely. Since it has been decided not to allow users to customise the production rules or meta model, appearances may well be of more importance in promoting easy familiarity with the tools than was originally believed.

One clear choice facing the development team concerns the continued use of Prolog to implement the production rules. The performance of a compiled Prolog task in IEW is impressive, but markedly slower than that of compiled C code, thus imposing a bottleneck on throughput and limiting the practical maximum size of PC based models. One solution is to recode the goal evaluation process in C while another is to develop a set of "preliminary" rules that optimises the application of production rules to specific tasks. A third option involves the use of larger database of facts about the current encyclopaedia, but this would impose a demand for more paged memory, itself both a cost and performance constraint. The possible use of a hardware based Prolog system, and the development of a parallel evaluation scheme for goals are also being investigated.

A second choice relates to the use of a multitasking operating system (UNIX is most often mentioned, but virtually everyone has their favourite). The design team can see a need to support concurrently active tasks, particularly diagram output, report generation and communications in parallel with diagramming. What is not clear is the best short term approach, and we are currently waiting to see what release 5 of DOS has to offer.

9   CONCLUSIONS

Knowledge based applications are a relatively new field of development, and there are as yet few products of any type available that use KBS techniques as an integral part of their functioning. The IEW development project has shown that the approach is a practical alternative to conventional design and programming, and that it can be used to build tools that are effective, reliable, fast to learn and easy to use. As microcomputer systems become more powerful, it will be possible to extend the range of functions supported by the PC component of IEW simply by extensions of the meta model and production rules, avoiding constant and costly redesign and redevelopment. When the model and rule set are complete, IEW will support automation of the complete system development lifecycle, from Information Strategy Planning through to application or code generation, with the high level of productivity, reliability and maintainability essential for increasingly complex and costly information systems.

REFERENCES

[ANDE79]   Anderson R. B., Proving Programs Correct, John Wiley & Sons, 1979

[ANDR86]   Andriole S. J. ed., Software Development Tools, Petrocelli Books, 1986

[CAIN75]   Caine S. H. & Gordon E. K., PDL - A tool for Software Design, AFIPS Conference Proceedings, Vol. 44, AFIPS Press, 1975

[CASE81]   Casey B. E. & Taylor B. J., Writing Requirements in English: A Natural Alternative, IEEE Workshop on Software Engineering Standards, August 1981

[CLAR84]   Clark. K. L. & McCabe F. G., micro-PROLOG: Programming in Logic, Prentice-Hall International, 1984

[CONN85]   Connor D., Information System Specification & Design Road Map, Prentice-Hall International, 1985

[DAHL72]   Dahl O. -J., Dijkstra E. W. & Hoare C. A. R., Structured Programming, Academic Press, 1972.

[DEMA79]   Demarco T., Structured Analysis and System Specification, Prentice-Hall, 1979

[GANE77]   Gane C. & Sarson T., Structured Systems Analysis, IST Databooks, Improved System Technologies, 1977

[GRAY84]   Gray P., Logic, Algebra and Databases, Ellis Horwood, 1984

[JACK75]   Jackson M. A., Principles of Program Design, Academic Press, 1975

[KORF66]   Korfhage R.K., Logic and Algorithms, Wiley International, 1966

[MART84]	Martin J., An Information Systems Manifesto, Prentice-Hall, 1984.
[MART85a]	Martin J., System Design from Provably Correct Constructs, Prentice-Hall, 1985
[MART85b]	Martin J. & McClure C., Diagramming Techniques for Analysts and Programmers, Prentice Hall, 1985
[MART86]	Martin J. & Hershey E.A., Information Engineering, A Management White Paper, Arthur Young, 1986
[MART87]	Martin J., Information Engineering, Savant, 1987
[ORR77]	Orr K. T., Structured Systems Development, Yourdon Press, 1977
[RADE78]	Rader R.J., Advanced Software Design Techniques, Petrocelli Books, 1978
[SMIT86]	Smith R. B., Managing Tools for Developing Information Systems, Petrocelli Books 1986
[TEIC77]	Teichroew D. & Hershey E. A. PSL/PSA: A Computer-Aided Technique for Structured Documentation and Analysis. IEEE Transactions on Software Engineering, Jan. 1977
[TURN84]	Turner R., Logics for Artificial Intelligence, Ellis Horwood, 1984
[WARN81]	Warnier J-D., Logical Construction of Systems, Van Nostrand Reinhold, 1981
[YOUR75]	Yourdon E. & Constantine L., Structured Design, Yourdon Press, 1975; Prentice-Hall, 1979

AUTOMATING INFORMATION ENGINEERING

I.G. MacDonald

James Martin Associates

Wimbledon, London UK

1   INTRODUCTION

Much is made of the 'fourth generation' concept and the term is regularly
applied to a multitude of high-level languages and software systems.
However, until recently, development methodologies had little of sub-
stance to offer that reflected the fourth generation and the style of
development implied by the concept.

The key feature of this concept is non-procedurality. The software
encourages you to state <u>what</u> you want to have done. It does not require
you to detail <u>how</u> that is to be achieved. This is a vitally important
feature because it places all of the stress in systems development on
being able to describe what the business is about. Methodologies must
therefore focus on business modelling. Those that focus on how to build
systems are now irrelevant because that can be automated. The
Information Engineering Methodology TM was developed by James Martin
Associates with the intention that it should be automated. This has been
achieved by Texas Instruments in collaboration with JMA in the
Information Engineering Facility TM.

This paper examines the features that made it possible to automate
Information Engineering and looks at some of the effects of automation on
the systems development process, in particular on how systems development
is itself becoming non-procedural. Figure 2 highlights this effect.

2   DEVELOPING INFORMATION SYSTEMS BY INFORMATION ENGINEERING

2.1 Key Requirements

For many years DP practitioners have been supplying automated support
facilities to professionals such as design engineers and architects. At
the same time they have failed to support themselves. The State of the
Art is evidently for other groups.

Tomorrow's information engineer should be looking for a production facility for systems. Ideally the information engineer will be someone
skilled in modelling enterprises and their information needs. He will
have automated support in handling, verifying and prompting for details
of suppositions, facts and generalisations about the enterprise. When a
complete and consistent model is agreed upon, the production facility

will create a prototype and, after trials, will generate the final system.

Today's enterprises are aware of the strategic value of information technology and are aiming to use it to provide automated information support to all of their activities. They recognise that today's technology is fast becoming highly integrated and recognise that this allows them in turn to adopt a highly integrated approach to their development of systems and to deploy it equally in support of a centralised or decentralised organisation. The thrust of information systems development today has therefore moved away from the piecemeal, single-system-at-a-time, problem-driven approach to become planned, broadly-integrated and strategically oriented – providing a full range of information sharing capabilities for the whole enterprise.

This does however impose additional demands on the approach used to develop these systems.

The first is a need for a planned base for all development. A planned information systems strategy is a fundamental requirement for producing enterprise-wide systems, for supporting consistent communication of information within the enterprise, for coordinating development efforts and for achieving the cost savings and productivity that are expected as benefits from today's technology.

The second is a need for comprehensive analysis of all areas of the business where automated support might possibly be provided. This analysis must be driven by the users and should provide means by which they either communicate their requirements to the developers or decide to build their own systems. The analysis provides common understanding, throughout the enterprise, of what the business is all about. It also provides a baseline for coordination of developments and against which progress can be measured.

A third is the need for automated support to the development effort. Fourth generation tools allow systems to be built faster by at least one order of magnitude. There is no excuse for allowing other stages of the life-cycle to become bottlenecks, preventing users from having the information systems service they require.

These demands are met by the concept of 'information engineering'. This refers to the set of inter-related, integrated disciplines which are needed to build a computerised enterprise based on comprehensive data systems. This must be contrasted with software engineering which is the set of disciplines used only for specifying, designing and programming computer software and which becomes implicit in an automated facility.

2.2 Information Engineering Methodology TM

The information engineering concept is one which has been strongly advocated by Martin [MART84], [MART86] and is implemented by James Martin Associates as the Information Engineering Methodology TM [MACD84], [MACD86]. It describes a comprehensive set of stages for the development life cycle, which are modified through automation to give patterns as shown in figures 1 and 2.

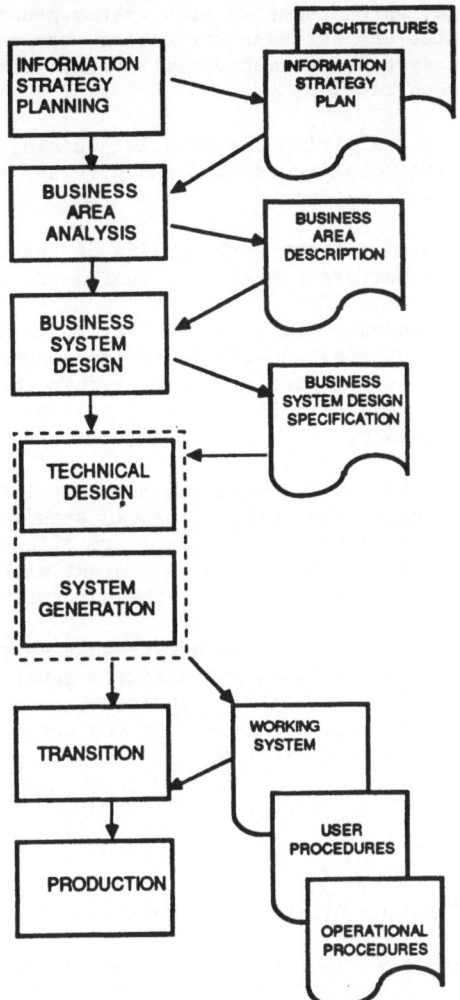

Figure 1   Stages in the Information Engineering Methodology TM

The stages are:

*   Information strategy planning, which develops, from the business
     objectives, an initial information architecture for the enterprise,
     identifies areas where automated support is appropriate and prepares
     a plan to show how these areas should be dealt with.

*   Business area analysis, which takes areas identifed in the plan,
     analyses their components in complete, detailed models which can be
     cross-checked and validated. From these, a selection is made of the
     parts users wish to have supported in their systems.

*   Business system design, which takes those processes which are to be
     supported, works out with the user the best way to handle them as a
     practical set of procedures and dialogues and develops prototypes to
     test ideas.

*   Technical design, which together with system generation tunes the
    design and creates the database structures, the code and the as-
    semblage of the system. Automation is rapidly leading to the merging
    of design and construction.

*   Transition, which deals with the parallel-running, cut-over and fan-
    out periods of the completed system and with any conversion or
    bridging that may be needed.

*   Production, which covers the working life of the system, the
    monitoring of its performance and its tuning and maintenance.

Overlayed on this procedural view is an ability to vary the way things
are done according to circumstance. This forces a concentration on
˝what˝ an enterprise's systems are all about rather than on ˝how˝ they
are to be built. In essence this is the move towards non-procedurality in
our development methodology.

This is illustrated in figure 2. Here the horizontal blocks represent
stages in the methodology. The vertical blocks show when various construction strategies may be employed. These are allowed once enough
information has been gathered to provide a context within which their use
can be properly managed to the benefit of the enterprise as a whole.

The ideal methodology will allow us to define what we want to achieve
with systems and then provide tools (as a fourth generation language
does) which create a solution. Any single system produced in this manner
may not be optimal in its own efficiency but the set of systems will,
since they model the enterprise as a whole.

3   AUTOMATING INFORMATION SYSTEM DEVELOPMENT

Three things have proved essential to achieving success in this area.
They are:

*   Concentration on true automation, not mechanisation.

*   Integrated coverage of all life-cycle stages and all levels of
    development scoping.

*   The presence of a metamodel of the methodology as the central con-
    trolling factor in the automated facility.

3.1 Automation not Mechanisation

Mechanising a process means doing it with machine assistance, in essentially the same manner as before.

Automating the process implies taking advantages of the machine's capabilities to improve upon the original process.

Most of today's workbenches provide mechanised support to systems development, typically by giving machine assistance to the creation and recording of diagrams and documentation. The techniques they support are generally handled in isolation and it is assumed that any linking of techniques will be handled through the intervention of the tool-user, at best by providing interfaces so that outputs from one tool can become inputs to another.

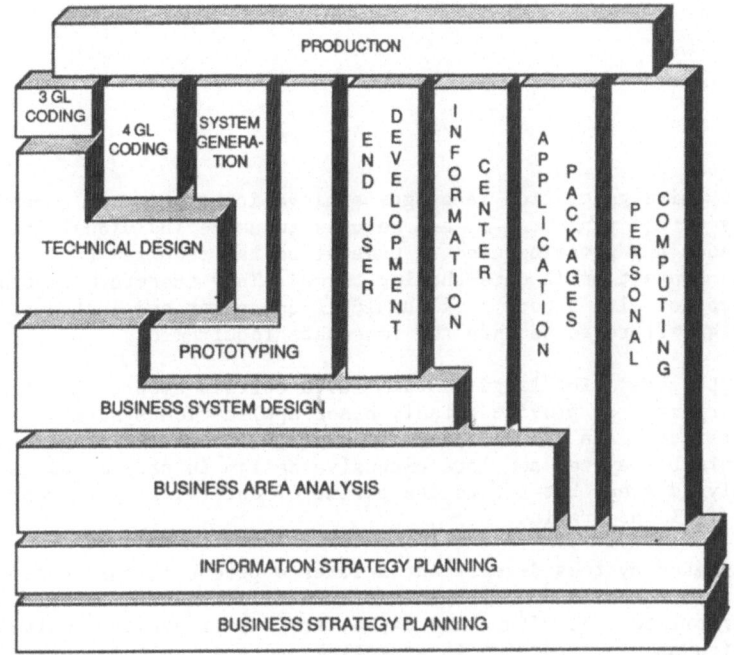

Figure 2   Building Blocks of Information Engineering

To achieve automation it is necessary to view the tasks and techniques as parts of a single coherent development process. Support to them must therefore be designed to provide an integrated whole. When this is achieved, the user finds that the automated methodology can then be used in a very free manner. Almost any feature of the automated support system can be invoked at any time whenever new information is available to be added.

3.2   Integrated Coverage

An integrated view of systems development is essential to automation. This integration must be applied jointly to what is to be developed and what must be done to develop it. If our aim is to produce single automated procedures then our view of the means of achieving it can be limited simply to the technique for building. If programs supporting several procedures are the goal then design effort to ensure proper interworking is needed. Systems containing a collection of programs

require careful analysis of the business since their impact is extensive.
If however our aim is to provide well integrated systems to automate
information systems support to the whole enterprise then thorough
analysis and design prior to construction is essential and must be controlled through the use of strategic planning. To automate the systems
development process for this final aim demands that the automated facility itself provide integrated coverage across the board. Figure 3
illustrates some stages towards full integration in systems development.

In this diagram the three bands on the vertical axis represent aspects of
the development effort and the four bands on the horizontal axis represent levels of intended integration ranging from (non-integrated)
procedure by procedure development to enterprise wide integration.

* Most third generation languages achieve integration of components
  only within programs, so can be used to solve individual problems
  without any pressing need to understand the requirement in a business context or in data-sharing terms. They therefore display a
  footprint with a very small analysis component and just sufficient
  design effort to satisfy the immediate requirement.

* Fourth generation languages aim for a certain amount of integration
  of programs to provide broadly based application systems.
  Significant analysis is needed therefore to ensure integration
  within the system and more extensive design is needed over the
  analysis area, but not to the extent of determing all requirements
  for full integration.

* Automated systems development assumes a potential for enterprise
  wide integration and data-sharing where it is shown to be
  appropriate. To offer this capability, comprehensive analysis,
  design and construction is essential and this must be done within
  the managed context that is provided by strategic planning.

3.3 The Metamodel

The automated systems development methodology requires a high level of
automated support in all stages of the development process. To be
effective, that support must not be too narrowly focussed - it must
include the methods used in the process, management of the process, and
the technical infrastructure.

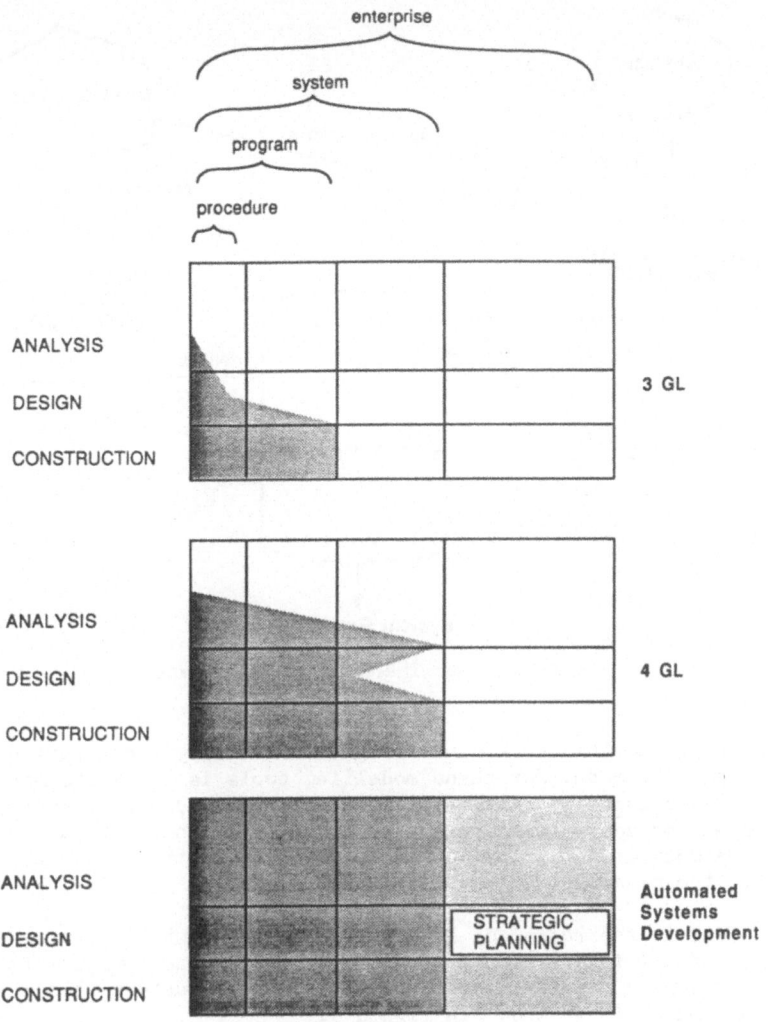

Figure 3   Integration of Systems Development

To know how to support the methods and the specific techniques employed, it is necessary that they be modelled and that the automated facility contain the model, be guided by it and use it to ensure that there is proper adherence to its rules and constraints. If the goal in this is to be able to achieve automated production of systems then the models and techniques must be all of a piece. They must be fully integrated and must deliver all of the information required for systems generation. Likewise the model for them must be a single, coherent model. A collection of sub-models for a loose parcel of techniques (as provided by most of today's workbenches) will never provide the quality and consistency required to achieve systems generation.

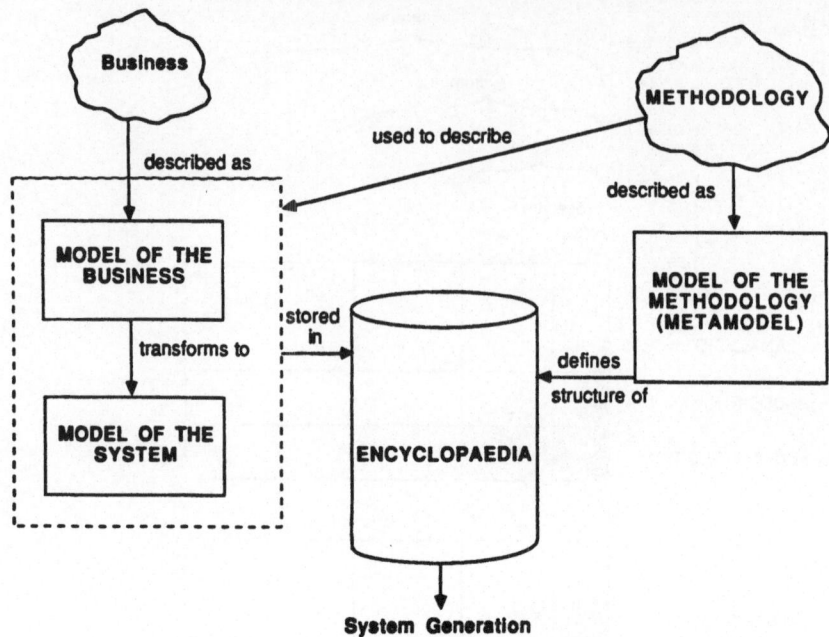

Figure 4   The Metamodel Concept

The methods and techniques are used to model the target enterprise and its systems. The model for these modelling tools is therefore often known as the metamodel. The presence of a single, coherent metamodel within an automated systems production facility is therefore a key feature of the most effective products. Figure 4 illustrates the general concept of the metamodel.

The metamodel is the basis for the encyclopaedia which in turn is the repository of all information about the enterprise and contains the knowledge required to create systems. The basic structure upon which this is all based is as shown in figure 5.

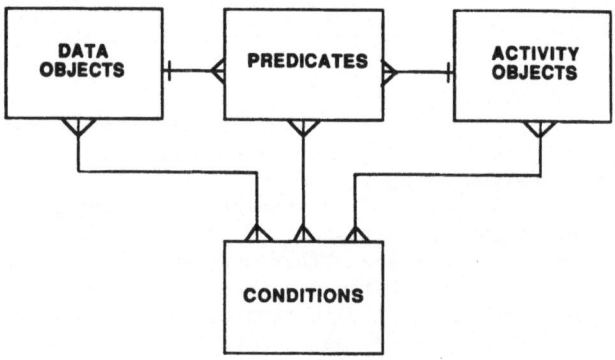

Figure 5   High-Level Modelling Concepts

4   FEATURES FOR AN AUTOMATED SYSTEM

The introduction of automated support to the development process has been pursued for some time [MACD87] through workbenches and IPSEs (integrated project support environments) - sometimes known as CASE tools (computer assisted software engineering). More advanced systems like the Information Engineering Facility TM [GIBS85, SHOR87] are occasionally described by the acronym CADME (computer aided development and maintenance environments [IDC86]). These are beginning to introduce true automation.

To determine whether a system will match up to our requirements for automation and provide capabilities appropriate to the entire life cycle and to varying forms of usage, it is essential that we have some concept of what such a system might include in its architecture.

4.1   Requirements

The key requirements of an architecture and a set of tools can be summarised as follows:

1   The tools must support the capture of all information relating to the business and the technical environment. This information describes data, processes and their interaction and includes the designs for screens, dialogues and reports.

2   The language of representation must be a common syntax across all stages of the methodology. Above all it should be easy to use and, wherever possible, graphic in nature.

3   The internal representation of models must be sufficiently rigorous to allow the mapping of information from each stage of the methodology to the next. The lowest level mapping from design specification to program code must be automatic.

4   The tools must be able to perform complex analyses and queries on the stored information. These should include:

   *   Cluster analysis through algorithms applied to information matrices.
   *   Distribution analysis.
   *   Impact analysis, including 'where used' queries.
   *   Performance simulation for prototype applications.
   *   Abstraction and reverse engineering of summary information from detailed information.
   *   Automatic diagram synthesis from stored models.

5   All the tools should act upon a single repository of information describing the business and its information systems. The information should be stored in a structured and/or relational manner, ie. in a non-graphical form.

6   Adequate access and update authorisation controls should exist.

7   Configuration management should handle versioning at the levels of models, individual diagrams and individual objects and must be able to distinguish between versioning at a local or project level and versioning relevant at enterprise level.

8   Status reports and query facilities should be provided to allow progress monitoring on projects.

9   The tools should, wherever possible, be available on distributed
       workstations, particularly portable equipment, to allow easier user
       participation in the analysis and design.

4.2   Architecture

An architecture for the automated information engineer might therefore
resemble that in figure 6.

The components of this architecture cover:

*   the encyclopaedia, lying at its heart. It supports a metamodel for
       the development life-cycle and the knowledge and rules governing
       good practice throughout the life-cycle. It integrates the informa-
       tion required by all the other components.

*   a database management system and/or a rule-base management system to
       provide all object management within the encyclopaedia and for the
       other components.

*   a layer of fundamental management components which provide basic
       manipulative capabilities for the tools employed by users of the
       systems:

       -        graphics management to deal with all representations of
                objects in graphical terms, their manifestation, their defini-
                tion, their relative positioning.

       -        text management to deal with representations as text and
                with its editing.

       -        configuration management to control versioning and the
                various levels of versioning that are required throughout the
                environment of the facility, together with internal mappings.

       -        encyclopaedia analysis to provide computational capabi-
                lities for the encyclopaedia user in support of analytical tools
                and aspects of project and environment management.

*   a layer of tools for all parts of the life-cycle. These include
       tools for each major stage and incorporate prototyping capabilites
       and generators for systems. Reverse engineering tools allow current
       systems to be modelled and the information captured in the encycl-
       opaedia so that differences between them and newly planned systems
       can be used in determining migration requirements.

*   environment control to support the physical environment of dis-
       tributed workstations, mainframe components and communication,
       access management and messaging between them and all the players in
       every life-cycle role.

*   project management to coordinate projects, schedule project
       resources, monitor project progress and measure productivity.

*   dialogue management for the man-machine interface, providing a
       consistent perception of the system for all of its users but allow-
       ing them to interact with it in a mode matching their role and their
       level of expertise.

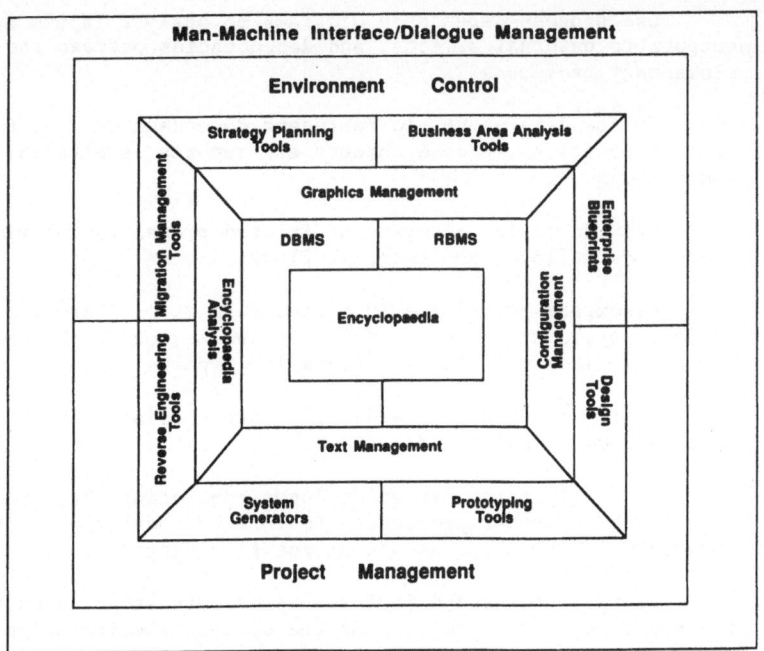

Figure 6   An Architecture for Automated Information Engineering

5   CHANGING NATURE OF THE METHODOLOGY

The fact of automation causes changes to ways of working. When 'first specified, Information Engineering was used manually pending the development of software for automation. To illustrate the effect of automation two examples will be taken [SHOR87]. The first deals with the mapping of business processes to computer system procedures, the second with entity model to database design mapping.

5.1 Process to Procedure Mapping

Elementary business processes are those at a level in the process decomposition that may be executed when the business is in a known, self-consistent state, and finish leaving the business once again self-consistent. Procedures are design objects that provide a mechanism for the implementation of elementary processes.

Guidelines and rules for identifying elementary processes, selecting those for implementation , and choosing the correct design alternative are provided in the Information Engineering Handbooks available from James Martin Associates [JMA86]. For the purposes of this paper, these are simplified in what follows:

5.1.1 Manual approach

Performed clerically, or with non-integrated workbenches and tools, the sequence is:

   1   Using the process decomposition diagram, select elementary
            processes to be supported by procedures. Redraw these as a
            procedure decomposition diagram.

2   Use process dependency diagrams to analyse inputs and
outputs to external objects, and dependencies between the
elementary processes.

3   Choose data stores to represent dependencies from potential alternatives. Choose screens and reports as external inputs
and outputs.

4   Draw data flow diagrams of related procedures showing data
stores, data flows, and external flows.

5   Decompose procedures into procedure steps where a conver-
sational style of interaction during the success unit best suits
the user. Identify likely screens and reports.

6   Verify that data flow diagrams are consistent with the
procedure decomposition diagrams.

7   With the users, design dialogue connections between procedure steps and other procedures to form the best application
interface. Draw these as a dialogue flow diagram.

8   Design screens and implement procedure steps as transactions (or batch programs) using the process specification from
analysis.

Steps 3 to 8 would typically be iterative, creating a significant
documentation and diagram maintenance problem since each diagram relies
on information documented in a diagram at an earlier step. Changes made
at earlier steps would usually be proliferated to diagrams used later.

5.1.2 Automated approach

The Information Engineering Facility TM dramatically simplifies this task
and thereby enhances the power of the methodology. Since each diagramming tool in the analysis and design toolsets operates within the
knowledge of the same encyclopaedia, all the required analysis information is available to the mapping tools. Here is the sequence of steps
for the same example using this product:

1   Select elementary processes to be implemented by pointing
at their representations on the process decomposition diagram.

2   Using the transformation facility of the dialogue flow
diagram, create a procedure and choose from a list of selected
elementary processes to be implemented by that procedure.

3   Repeat step 2 for all procedures in the application.

4   Use the dialogue flow diagram facilities to specify
dialogue connections, and create procedure steps.

5   Use the screen designer diagram and the procedure step
action diagram to complete the specifications.

It is not just the description of these approaches that changes. There
are fundamental underlying differences such as the following:

*   Steps 2 and 3 of the manual approach appear to have gone. This is
not so, they are simply performed by the transformation software.

Objects in the encyclopaedia representing the elementary processes
and their dependencies have been analysed and mapped into objects
representing data flows, data stores and procedures. Consistency
between these is now guaranteed.

* The use of the data flow diagram and the procedure decomposition
  diagram to document intermediate design decisions and provide a
  check on consistency of the design tasks is no longer necessary.
  Software now ensures this.

* Step 8 from the manual approach becomes straightforward. The
  procedure action diagrams for each procedure step are created
  automatically by the mapping software, and the input and output data
  flows are calculated and made ready for placement on the screen
  design diagram. The application generation facilities can then
  generate the appropriate programs from the action diagrams.

* Documentation is minimised and always self-consistent. For example,
  dialogue flow conditions are kept in line with conditions in action
  diagrams. All dialogue links are built into the generated programs
  with no further programming required.

5.2 Entity Model to Data Model Transformation

The problem here is to take the conceptual data model represented by an
entity relationship diagram, analyse and aggregate its usage, as indicated by the interaction of business processes with its elements
(entities, relationships, attributes), and produce an efficient external
schema or data structure in terms of a particular DBMS.

Again this mapping is generically one-to-many since the same parts (and
overlapping parts) of the design models could be implemented by different
DBMS products.

5.2.1 Manual approach

Done clerically, this is a complex activity involving the collating of
many behavioural summaries containing frequencies, probabilities and
access directions. This aggregation is followed by addressing structural
aspects of the entity model with the data structuring constraints of the
DBMS. For this reason Information Engineering breaks the process into
two parts: one, to produce a preliminary data structure purely from
knowledge gathered during analysis, a second to consider all factors
needed to produce an optimal data structure meeting the needs of all
known (and planned) uses of the database.

5.2.2. Automated approach

In the Information Engineering Facility TM the database design task will
be handled by one tool - the data structure diagrammer, which executes
transformation rules and graphically maintains DBMS-specific data models.
Again, it is the integration of all toolsets through the encyclopaedia
which enables this to happen.

Once the area of the entity model for implementation is defined and
aggregated, the designer enters the design cycle, not with an empty model
but with a first- cut data structure, designed through the application of
design rules, by the software itself. The designer may now choose to
edit this design (provided no DBMS constraints or analysis results are
violated), using the diagrammer.

Some time after the design cycle or perhaps after prototyping, the designer may re-run these transformation rules and expect better design as more information becomes available. For example, expected frequencies may be replaced by observed frequencies.

5.3 Consequences of Automation

In both illustrations the advent of automation provides a way of working which is substantially different from manual practice. This, of course, is a normal consequence of automation. Those areas affected first are the clerical components of documenting and diagramming. The first major technical impact is on the management of mappings between design and construction and between analysis and design. These have real effects on ways of working brought about by an extension of the concept of information hiding. This protects work done at a high level of abstraction from the consequences of lower level implementation. The practical consequence of this is to move the emphasis within the methodology even more strongly towards adequate modelling of the business. Automatic generation of (prototype) systems based on the business model is now a realisable goal and may be expected to have a major impact on current notions of the nature of information systems development.

6   FUTURE DIRECTIONS

The immediate future for automated systems development products must depend on their success at demonstrating, in a robust manner, their ability to generate substantial collections of application systems. Once over this hurdle the next major target must be to add intelligent or expert capabilities.

This is likely to happen in selected areas to begin with, eg. in handling rules for mapping from entity relationship models to database structures. Later it could incorporate intelligent interaction with the analyst or the business user in the process of modelling enterprises.

There is no reason why systems of this sort should not be used for generating generalised application packages or to drive 4GLs or a wide variety of system generators. They could therefore become major tools in both the development centre and the information centre.

It is also reasonable to expect that many of today's 4GL, generator or DBMS vendors will enter this market by building CASE/CADME products which further automate the development cycle for their existing products. Whether these will be sufficiently general, in terms of the range of uses they aspire to, remains to be seen. As yet there have been no significant announcements.

The only immediately visible glimpse into the future is provided by projects in the Alvey, ESPRIT and EUREKA prgrammes . The largest and most relevant of these is the ESPRIT RUBRIC project led by James Martin Associates [VANA86] RUBRIC aims to provide a rule-based approach to information systems development which will prototype an intelligent CADME system. The architecture for such a system is illustrated in figure 7.

In this architecture the Unified Rule Base contains the data model, the rules governing the business application and the mapping of the data

model to man- machine interface definitions, while the URB Manager updates and retrieves the rule base contents.

The Fact and Rule Acquisition module handles the capture, updating and
presentation to the user of the data model, rules and mapping to the man-
machine interface. It allows a variety of forms of input and output
including graphics and tabular reports.

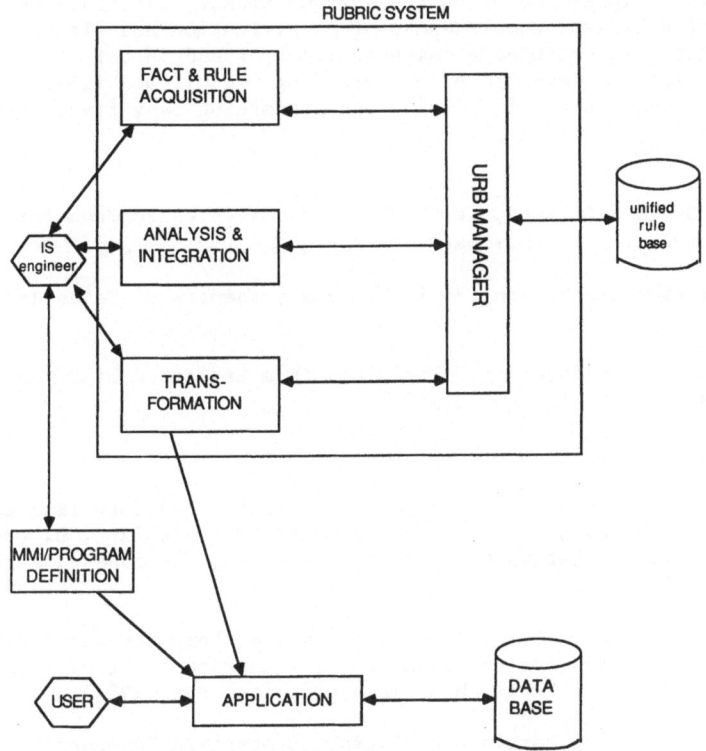

Figure 7   The RUBRIC Architecture

The Analysis and Integration module integrates the different user views
of the same business area and checks the compatibility of these user
views.

Finally, the Transformation module is used when the URB is specified,
analysed and integrated. It translates it into a form that can be used
at run time by an application capable of exploiting the rules and handling the database through a sophisticated user interface.

We anticipate systems of this sort emerging onto the market within the
next three years and becoming almost commonplace within five - but by
then the focus will have shifted.

7   CONCLUSION

The future belongs to automated methodologies.

Second-generation documentation standards and third-generation manual methodologies are rapidly giving way to the integrated combination of workbenches, encyclopaedia and system generators which provide the automated support today's developer requires.

The first successful example of this is the Information Engineering Methodology TM and its automation within the Information Engineering Facility TM. Experience with these has already demonstrated major gains in clarity of expression of business requirements, adherence to standards, speed of progress, completeness of specification and flexibility in work paterns. The knowledge database incorporated in this tool ensures quality in systems development by demanding rigour, and improves the speed of production by simplifying and automating many traditional tasks.

ACKNOWLEDGEMENTS

Thanks to David Fairbairn, Keith Short and Steve Wassermann for contributing material to this paper.

The Information Engineering Facility is a trademark of Texas Instruments Inc.

The Information Engineering Methodology is a trademark of James Martin Associates.

REFERENCES

[GIBS85]   Gibson, W.E. and Macdonald, I.G., The Corporate Database – automating the development process, in: Iggulden, D. (ed), The Corporate Database, (Pergamon Infotech, Maidenhead, England, 1985).

[IDC86]   International Data Corporation, Computer-aided Development and Maintenance Environments: a blueprint for the fifth generation (IDC, Framingham, Massachusetts, USA, 1986).

[JMA86]   James Martin Associates, Information Engineering Handbooks (JMA, Wimbledon, England, 1986).

[MACD84]   Macdonald, I.G., Information Engineering – a methodology to match fourth generation tools, in: Tozer, E.E. (ed), Application Development Tools (Pergamon Infotech, Maidenhead, England, 1984).

[MACD86]   Macdonald, I.G., Information Engineering, in: Olle T.W., Sol, H. and Verijn-Stuart, A. (eds), CRIS '86 – improving the practice (North-Holland, Amsterdam, 1986)

[MACD87]   Macdonald, I.G., Automating the Information Engineer: IPSEs and Workbenches in Context, in: Rock-Evans, R. (ed) Analyst Workbenches, (Pergamon Infotech, Maidenhead, England, 1987).

[MART84]   Martin, J., An Information Systems Manifesto (Prentice-Hall Inc., Englewood Cliffs, New Jersey, USA, 1984).

[MART86]   Martin, J., Information Engineering (vols 1 & 2) (Savant, Lancaster, England, 1986).

[SHOR87]   Short, K.W., Analyst's Workbenches: Design and Other
Mapping Issues, in: Rock-Evans, R. (ed), Analyst Workbenches,
(Pergamon Infotech, Maidenhead, England, 1987).

[VANA86]   Van Assche, F. and Venken, R., RUBRIC - Project 928
Progress Report (ESPRIT, 1986). See also Venken et al in this
volume.

INTRODUCING WORKBENCH TOOLS INTO A DEVELOPMENT

ENVIRONMENT

Tom McCabe

Price-Waterhouse

London, UK

1   INTRODUCTION

The purpose of this paper is to consider the issues involved in introducing workbench tools into a development environment. Although this is, in
itself, only one of a number of factors which need to be considered in
the selection and implementation process it is important in ensuring that
the use of workbench tools is a cost-effective approach to developing
computer systems. In this paper we will consider why the method of
introduction is important and illustrate this by describing how Price
Waterhouse has introduced a specific tool into its own systems consultancy work.

2   WHAT ARE THE BENEFITS OF WORKBENCH TOOLS?

It is clear that introducing workbench tools into a development environment provides benefits to the departments in which they are to be used.
The benefits which can immediately be seen are:

(1)   Documentation can be created and amended more quickly.

(2)   The documentation produced is of a consistent and high
quality.

(3)   As a spin off, the analyst's time is freed to allow more
effort to be put into fact-finding and thinking. This
should result in a higher quality of product from the
analysis.

For these reasons a lot of enthusiasm was generated when workbench tools
were first introduced to the IT world and users have consistently
reported success in the use of such tools. Our research indicates
productivity improvements **in** development **alone** of 6-10% of analysts'
time.

In this paper we will not review benefits in any more detail, as we
believe they are self-evident. However, if one is to consider using such
tools, there are still other issues to be addressed.

3   WHAT ARE THE ISSUES IN IMPLEMENTING WORKBENCH TOOLS?

It is simply not enough to claim that a workbench should be purchased because it will be beneficial. The benefits must be maximised by paying careful attention to:

(1)   The SELECTION of individual tools for purchase.

(2)   The way in which they are INTRODUCED into the development environment.

(3)   The way in which they are USED.

The first of these issues will not be discussed here. The question of which tool or tools to SELECT, given the increasing number available, is obviously crucial to maximising the benefits of the tools and needs to take careful account of the type of development work which they are used to automate. However, it merits at least a paper, if not a seminar, to itself.

Similarly, the question of how and at what times to USE the tools suggests a large number of corollary questions, which form an issue by themselves and should be addressed in a separate paper.

4   HOW SHOULD WE INTRODUCE WORKBENCH TOOLS?

The question which we do wish to address is that of how to introduce the tools most effectively into the IT environment. This question is concerned with the preparation work which must be done "up front" by those responsible for purchasing the tools and distributing them within an organisation. It is a practical question of management and planning, rather than a technical or theoretical issue.

We will approach this subject as follows:

1   We will show why the introduction process is particularly important.

2   We will discuss some of the issues which are relevant to the introduction of such tools.

3   We will look at the ways in which these issues can be addressed, and discuss the work which we undertook at Price Waterhouse to introduce a specific tool into our consultancy.

4   Finally, we will look at the experience to be gained in doing this work and the conclusions which can be drawn, both for our own case and for other IT environments. It should be stated now that we would certainly recommend anybody introducing workbench tools to undertake preparatory work in doing so, rather than simply "letting them loose".

4.1   WHY IS INTRODUCTION AN ISSUE?

The emergence of workbench tools has been referred to by James Martin as a process of "automating the automaters". This simple phase, provides an insight into the sorts of questions that should be considered when introducing these tools. It shows that the same preparation, caution and effort should be exercised in automating our own working environment as we should, and do, exercise in automating the working environments of our clients or customers.

For instance, if we develop a financial reporting system we do not assume that the work has been completed when the system has been written and tested. It is also part of the IT department's function to ensure that user manuals are written clearly, that training for the users is provided, that the new organisational structure of the accounts department is considered carefully and that the transition between the manual or previous computer system and the new system is achieved as smoothly as possible. Even if the new financial reporting system is well designed, and sure to increase the effectiveness of the accounts department no matter how it is introduced, the manner of the introduction should make as much difference as the system itself.

Since the management of the introduction of software is an important consideration when introducing the software into an accounts department, the same must be true when introducing it into any other department or area of work.

BUT ..... A WORKBENCH TOOL IS VERY DIFFERENT FROM A FINANCIAL REPORTING
SYSTEM

However, there are some, who would argue that this is not an acceptable analogy for the introduction of workbench tools to IT professionals.

A number of reasons are advanced to support this argument.

(1) Expense

These tools are largely not of the same scale as financial reporting systems, or other large scale applications which are developed for clients. They are PC-based, usually used in standalone mode, and relatively inexpensive when compared to the sort of systems usually developed by IT professionals for their users. Extra expense incurred in introducing the tools could be seen to be disproportionate to the initial cost of the tool.

(2) User-friendliness

Workbench tools are designed to be, and indeed are, extremely user-friendly. The use of icons, mice and other features made available on Pcs should mean that the tools need no introduction to the user. They should be self-explanatory, as should their usage.

(3) Does the physician really need healing?

It may seem to insult the technical competence of an IT professional to suggest that he needs to be introduced to technology as carefully as he needs to introduce it to others. Systems designer's and analyst's work revolves around the use of technology, and so it should be in their nature to use technology themselves.

4.2 HOW ARE THESE POINTS ANSWERED?

The first point, that the tools are INEXPENSIVE AND SMALL IN SCALE, can be dealt with by pointing to the assumption that simply because a package is cheap, little attention need be paid to it. This is obviously an invalid deduction. It is not the price of a package which is important, it is the effect on the working environment. Workbench tools are currently affecting DP professional's work significantly and are likely to do so even more as they become more advanced.

Secondly, the point about USER-FRIENDLINESS is very deceptive. The fact that a product looks attractive and easily produces high-quality output does not mean that the use to which it is being put is as effective as it could be. Indeed, many of these packages have a large range of features and can be taken to various levels of detail. Consideration must be made about which features to use and how to use them, even if any one feature or mode of use is simple enough in itself.

Finally, the argument that IT staff, should necessarily be able to assimilate the use of technology in their own environment is optimistic, to say the least. They are still very likely to be set in their own working habits. Even if they find it easy to appreciate the use of technology, and are not apprehensive about using technical equipment, the "automation of the automaters" is still a change in working habits and a change cannot be made effectively without being managed. Moreover, many users of workbench tools will not necessarily always have "hands-on" experience of technology; the analysts who specify a financial reporting system may be accountants, for instance.

Given, then, that we must accept the importance of paying careful consideration to the introduction of workbench tools, there are a number of issues that need to be addressed in this particular area of automation.

5   WHAT ARE THE ISSUES AFFECTING INTRODUCTION?

The issues to be addressed include:

    (1) The integration with existing methodologies.

    (2) Standardising the usage of the tool.

    (3) Shortening the learning curve of users.

    (4) Exploiting the full potential of the tool.

5.1 Integrating with existing methodologies

This issue is critical, and in order to explain it we should briefly define the terms involved. These terms will also be used later in the paper.

It is usual, and certainly desirable, for an IT department to have standards; these are the rules which state which tasks need to be performed when undertaking assignments. Within these, there may exist various techniques to be used when implementing the standard tasks (e.g. the drawing of Gane and Sarson Data Flow Diagrams). If these standards and techniques are inter-related and comprehensive (i.e. they cover all of the work done by the department) then they are said to form a methodology. A methodology will also cover the use of tools which help in the execution of the standard tasks, and project management guidelines, to ensure the planning and monitoring of the tasks.

There are a number of methodologies available to IT departments as a package. Alternatively, IT departments can develop their own. In either case, if new workbench tools are introduced into the environment it is essential that they are integrated into the methodology - otherwise either the methodology or the tools will cease to be effective.

5.2 Standardising the usage of the tool

There is also a need to create standards for the usage of the product itself. Many tools are complex in that they support a range of different activities and even provide several different means of supporting each of them. Standardising on the use of these will:

- Assist in the consistency of presentation of the material prepared.

- Help the development staff work more quickly as their choice of facilities becomes automatic.

- Avoid the conflict that may arise if development staff, that have been using the tool in different ways within different projects, come together to work on the same project.

5.3 Shortening the learning curve

It is obviously desirable to shorten the learning curve of those who are going to use the tool. The more quickly users can learn how to use it the more productive they will be. The extent to which the software is user-friendly is clearly important here; however, one should consider whether there are preparations which those responsible for the introduction can make in order to shorten the learning curve even more. Common means of doing this include running briefing sessions and sending staff on training courses.

5.4 Exploiting the full potential

Finally, it is necessary to consider if there are any other features of the tools providing benefits which can be capitalised upon. This may seem a rather open-ended suggestion. However, if the tools are going to change the way in which work takes place, potential benefits or possible means of maximising the benefits, may not be immediately obvious. The product may, for instance, assist in unexpected areas of systems development.

Having established that the manner of the introduction of such tools is clearly an important issue to be addressed, and raised some of the questions to be answered in addressing these issues, we now examine some of the solutions to these problems. In doing so, we shall discuss some of the work which we have undertaken in Price Waterhouse in introducing one of these workbench tools into our management consultancy practice.

6   SOME SOLUTIONS TO PROBLEMS RAISED

It is a truism to state that the solutions to the problems raised and indeed the relative significance of the problems themselves, depend on the individual development environment and the tools chosen or being introduced to that environment. In some IT departments, for instance, there is a rule that a stated external methodology must always be used. If there is a tool which is specifically designed for that methodology, then the problem about integrating the tool with the methodology is already solved.

An example of this tool AUTOMATE, which is specifically designed for SSADM. This product could therefore be introduced relatively easily into government DP departments, since SSADM is the methodology selected for use within those departments.

However, not all of these problems are usually so easily solved or bypassed. To consider a more complex case, and also to show an example of how some of the other problems may be addressed, it is appropriate to discuss a particular case study. Since our own case is quite relevant, we shall actually be discussing "The case of Price Waterhouse", and in particular our introduction of the tool EXCELERATOR.

First, a brief piece of background information about the firm, the IT environment and the tool itself.

6.1 Background to our own case

Price Waterhouse is an international management consultancy with a substantial part of our work being in IT. The IT work we undertake for clients covers the whole spectrum of the industry, from IT strategy studies through to programming and beyond. Moreover, this work is undertaken for a very diverse range and size of clients in the public and private sector.

To support this work we have developed a System Management Methodology (SMM), laying down the phases and activities to be undertaken and the deliverables expected within all types of system-related assignments. Since we sometimes have to work within the framework of standards or methodologies imposed by our clients, this methodology is flexible and modular so that it can, if necessary, interleave with other methodologies.

Various modules within this methodology, such as project estimating and package evaluation, have been automated by tools which were developed in-house. However, for the specific area of systems analysis and design, we elected to choose an external package. The package we chose was EXCELERATOR, supplied by the American company Index Technology Corporation (InTech).

In broad terms, EXCELERATOR is a tool which allows the designing of various types of diagrams such as DFDs and Entity Relationship models and the relating of these diagrams both to each other and to a data dictionary, which is the "core" of the system. Validation is available to check the consistency and integrity of the diagrams used the dictionary and there are also facilities for creating mock-up screens and reports, again based on the dictionary. A particular feature of the product which made it very useful to us is that it is _not_ geared to any specific methodology: for instance, it allows many different types of diagram to be created and does not impose a rigid sequence of tasks when setting up a model. Thus we could use it in working for a variety of different clients with different methodological approaches.

In order to introduce this product into our practice, we needed to find a way of integrating its use into our own methodology, as well as looking for other ways in which its potential could be exploited.

To these ends, we conceived two projects which were to be undertaken as part of the introduction of the tool. These were:

(1) To customise EXCELERATOR to fit our own methodology.

(2) To develop a generic, or "template" specification of requirements for a general ledger system.

In order to illustrate the aims of these projects and to show how they met the problems raised earlier in this paper it is worth discussing them a little further.

6.2 Customisation of EXCELERATOR

The principal aim of customising EXCELERATOR was to provide a means of
automating our methodology in areas served by EXCELERATOR, i.e. systems
analysis and design. This required the creation of new types of diagram
and of new entites to reside in the data dictionary.

In order to achieve this customisation we were able to obtain pre-release
("beta-test") copies of a product called CUSTOMISER, which was due to be
released in January 1987. This product specifically allows the user to
be able to create additional diagrams and objects, to populate them
together with corresponding types of element or entity, and to add to the
data dictionary.

The customisation brought the product into the domain of our own practice, and our own methodology. By achieving this with a flexible product
such as EXCELERATOR, we have a doubly powerful tool, since the same tool
services both assignments where we use our own methodology and assignments which require the use of some other form of diagram which
EXCELERATOR supports.

6.3 Development of a template

The other project which we undertook was to produce an example (or
"template", as we called it) specification of requirements for a general
ledger system, using the EXCELERATOR product. This was to be created as
a generic specification; it was a project in itself, not a by-product of
any other work we happened to be doing at the time, although a lot of the
input to the project obviously came from consultants who had specified
general ledger systems on previous occasions.

This project was not an answer to a specific problem, in the sense that
the customisation addressed the issue of integrating the tool within our
own methodology. It was rather aimed at adding value to the use of the
product. This is reflected in the aims of the project. To

(1) Speed up the production of requirement specifications for
     general ledger systems.

(2) Set a standard for the usage of EXCELERATOR.

(3) Provide a vehicle which would be useful for demonstrating
     EXCELERATOR.

Speeding up production of specifications

The most obvious aim was the speeding up of the specification of requirements for general ledger systems in the future. This benefit is clearly
a special advantage to a consultancy such as ourselves and, of course, to
our clients, since we undertake many requirements specifications of a
similar nature. For any particular type of general ledger system that we
specify, as much as 80% of the requirements are common to all of the
specifications produced. In future, a consultant doing such work will be
able to use the template as a basis for the specification and add to, or
subtract from it, in order to tailor it to a specific client's needs,
instead of starting from scratch. In fact we intend the general ledger
template to be the first of several that we produce.

Setting standards for usage

A common problem in the implementation of any new product and indeed in developing a set of standards, is that there is not a coherent example of the correct use of them. When this happens, users are liable (at best) to use the product in a variety of different ways, causing problems if they ever work together on the same project. At worst, the product may be misused or fall into disrepute simply because an example of good use has not been clearly demonstrated.

In order to use the template to avoid this pitfall we were therefore very careful to use all the relevant facilities correctly, consistently and comprehensively when establishing the template system.

The template as a demonstration tool

Finally, the template could be used as a demonstration tool for both our own consultants and clients alike. A general ledger system is a system that most IT staff are likely to be familiar with, and hence is an excellent vehicle for showing the facilities available in a workbench tool. An added advantage of the template is that being generic, it does not contain any confidential areas to inhibit us from showing it to clients.

In an earlier section we started that the major problems to address in introducing a workbench tool lay in integrating the tool with existing methodologies, in standardising the use of the product, in shortening the learning curve of users, and in seeking further ways in which value can be added to the use of the product. It should be clear that the projects which we undertook did indeed address these problems. We should now consider the experience we have gained, and seek to draw some general conclusions from that experience.

7   EXPERIENCE GAINED

There are two ways in which one may derive useful experience from undertaking such projects: first, from <u>doing</u> such projects; secondly from using the products which result from the projects.

7.1   Experience from doing the Products

The experience gained from doing the introductory projects themselves consisted principally in gaining a greater understanding of the way in which the tool should be used and a perception of its strengths and limitations. Such experience highlights issues which are being generally debated about workbench tools, in particular:

(1)   The need for more comprehensive automation of methodologies.

(2)   The reinforcement of the benefits of a template.

(3)   The cost-effectiveness of introductory work.

The need for a Comprehensive Workbench Tool

This need was highlighted during the development of our customised version of EXCELERATOR. The point to be noted lies in the fact that it was clear that the product was only relevant for automating certain phases of the development cycle, namely those of analysis and design. Certain other phases which required more complex calculations than EXCELERATOR provided, has already been automated by separate in-house software packages. At the other extreme, it was felt that some forms required by our standards were best left to being drawn up simply on a word processor.

This point is not altogether surprising, since EXCELERATOR itself is marketed solely as an analysis and design aid. However, putting it in the context of a methodology suggests the requirement for a more comprehensive and unified tool, taking the user through all the steps of the systems development process. Such a product should:

- Ensure a greater degree of consistency and logical flow between the work done in all phases.

- Enforce the methodology itself more fully (by virtue of the fact that PC-based tools help to discipline the users of them into using structured techniques)

- Speed up development further by requiring the users to learn only one tool, instead of several.

The template - the benefits reinforced

As far as the template was concerned, some of the issues encountered in producing it reinforced our view that templates are a very useful aid. One of these was the decision regarding the depth to which we should go in the use of EXCELERATOR facilities when producing the template.

There are a very large number of forms, diagrams and relationships that EXCELERATOR enables the user to construct in producing a requirements specification, and it was necessary to decide which of them to include or exclude. By steering a middle course, we were able to ensure that the template would be more likely to be close to the specific level of depth required on any particular assignment.

This shows how constructing a generic template is much more effective than relying on a "copyability factor" between assignments of a similar nature. Experience has shown that similar assignments may often require very different levels of depth in the specifications produced.

The cost-effectiveness of introductory projects

The fact that workbench tools are easy to use means that introductory projects themselves are quickly achieved.

Using CUSTOMISER, for instance, we were able to create the customised product PWEXCEL in just 6 man-weeks. Although this figure includes the learning curve, and some delays due to bugs in the beta-test version of CUSTOMISER, we were able in that time to automate the creation of some 30 different forms contained within the system development methodology of SMM, together with all the corresponding objects which they require.

When one compares the relatively small time spent on the project with the investment required to develop a methodology or to purchase sufficient numbers of such products as EXCELERATOR, it seems as if a cost justification would be simply a formality.

7.2 Experience from using the Output of the Projects

It is too early to draw any strong conclusions at the time of writing this paper. The main reason for this is that the customised product, PWEXCEL, requires a version of EXCELERATOR which has not yet been released in the UK.

However, the template has been useful on a large number of assignments. For instance, the documentation from the template has been a very good illustration when we have wished to discuss the use and potential of workbench tools within a clients' environments. We are also issuing an "information pack" on EXCELERATOR to consultants, consisting of a concise, simplified overview and guide to using the product, together with documentation from the template as an example.

In short, the experience we have gained since undertaking the projects does not conflict at all with our expectations or intentions.

Various consultants have already undertaken assignments on which they have used the native EXCELERATOR, or indeed certain other tools, without the benefit of the products from such introductory projects. This was of course inevitable and totally justifiable - as stated earlier, these tools are beneficial to development work even without emphasis being placed on their introduction. The point we would make, however, is that doing such projects <u>adds</u> to the value of the tool within the context of one's practice.

8   GENERAL CONCLUSIONS

As will have been apparent throughout, the discussion in this paper, the main conclusion that we would draw from our own experience in introducing workbench tools is that the introduction must itself be <u>managed</u>. By this we mean that it is not sufficient to simply decide to purchase and use such tools. Plans for introducing the tools must be made in order to ensure maximum benefit.

In our own case, we have highlighted two particular areas in which attention paid to the manner of introduction is particularly important. These are in the integration of the product with existing or proposed methodologies and in the establishment of examples of, or aids to, the effective use of the tools.

<u>The Way Ahead</u>

Having argued that projects such as our own should be given careful consideration in introducing workbench tools, it remains to look ahead to the future of workbench tools in general and the extent to which our arguments will continue to be applicable. Indeed, some would say that the arguments have come too late, since such tools have already been introduced to working environments. We are now waiting for the next generation of tools to emerge - tools which will not only assist with the analysis or design of computer systems, but which will also automate the generation of the systems themselves based on information provided by the analysts.

In response to this, it must be said that the arguments we have propounded are generic, and will remain true. New, more powerful tools may take over, or even remove, many of the IT functions. However, given that they will do so, there is even more reason to manage their introduction carefully; it will always be necessary to ensure that they are integrated smoothly into the existing procedures and methodologies; and it will obviously be necessary to ensure that the benefit to be obtained can be maximised. Indeed, the greater the impact that new tools will have, the greater the need to <u>manage them effectively</u>.

Our emphasis on introducing effective working practices will not need to change even when the technology does. We believe that it provides considerable comfort to potential users who are concerned that the technology will overtake them, to realize that there are still many long-term benefits that can be gained by starting to use automated tools NOW.

SECTION FOUR - OPEN TOOLS

This section is concerned with systems which provide an environment in which information systems can be developed. The term "Integrated Project Support Environments" (IPSE) is usually used in the United Kingdom to describe a collection of integrated tools aimed at supporting the development of information systems from analysis through to implementation and maintenance. Unlike the tools described in Section Three, there is no requirement to follow a methodology. IPSEs are concerned with supporting project development, but do not prescribe how that process should take place.

An important feature of IPSEs is their ability to share data and accomodate a variety of tools. Lyon [LYON86] also emphasizes that an IPSE should be "extensible", i.e. the tools and methods which it supports must be able to grow as the organisation develops, and it should be based on a centralised database of system and project related objects such as programming modules, diagrams, files, etc.. The European "Esprit" initiative has focussed on this need to share data and accomodate new tools and has developed a standard for tool developers known as the Portable Common Tools Environment (PCTE). An alternative standard (CAIS) is under development in the USA.

PCTE is an example of a "Public Tool Interface" (PTI). The objective of a public tool interface is to allow tools to be transported from one implementation to another. Provided the PTI is the same in two environments, the tools will be portable. PCTE has been designed so that most Unix tools will operate in that environment.

The papers in this section all stress different aspects of IPSEs. For example, McGowan emphasises documentation, Dillistone and his colleagues discuss database design and Rumph highlights version control. Consequently we prefer to call this section "Open Tools" rather than "Integrated Project Support Environments" to emphasise the portability of the tools and the architecture of the environments.

In the first paper, Sellars describes the BIS/IPSE and focusses on the difference between analyst workbenches and IPSEs. His title "IPSEs in support of teams" captures this difference succinctly. The paper highlights the major components of the IPSE and discusses the tools which are supported. Rumph's paper emphasises the PTI feature of IPSEs in a description of the "Perspective Kernel" which is defined as "a general purpose framework for building IPSEs". He draws attention to the variety of users of IPSEs and the roles which such a system must support.

The two papers from CAP (McGowan and Verral) describe two aspects of the FORTUNE project. This is a "software engineer's documentation support tool" which is designed to interface with other tools and to be incorporated into IPSEs. It is clearly important, therefore, that FORTUNE is compatible with other tools. This is accomplished by adhering to the standards of PCTE. McGowan gives a review of the problems of documentation in large projects, arguing that "the system is its documentation", before going on to describe the FORTUNE project. Verral devotes his paper to an examination of the problems of translating one representation (e.g. diagrammatic) into another (e.g. Prolog source code). He describes a tool based on augmented transition networks (ATNs) which will automate the integration of data from different systems "by seeking the existence of a general purpose piece of software which could be parameterised to perform the specific integration sought".

The final two papers are concerned with the development of the ASPECT IPSE. Brown gives a thorough discussion of IPSEs and tools, arguing that an IPSE is "...a mechanism for providing the infrastructure to support the complex decision-making process of software development". He then concentrates on the desirability of a "view mechanism" to provide appropriate access to the PTI for the "large and diverse group of users and applications which will wish to make use of the data". Dillistone et al. discuss the database design of the ASPECT IPSE which is based on the extended relational model (RM/T) proposed by Codd in the late 1970s [CODD79]. The paper provides a detailed examination of RM/T before looking at how it can be used within an IPSE.

Taken together, these six papers provide a good insight into the scope and complexity of providing an Integrated Project Support Environment. Each focusses on a different aspect of the design and development of an IPSE, but all emphasise the need for these tools to be portable and integrated.

References

[CODD79]   Codd E.F. "Extending the Database Relational Model to Capture More Meaning" ACM TODS 4(4) Dec 1979 pp 397-434

[LYON86]   Lyons T.G.L. "The Public Tool Interface in Software Engineering Environments" in Software Engineering Journal 1(5) Nov 1986 pp 254-258

IPSES IN SUPPORT OF TEAMS

P. Sellars

BIS Applied Systems Ltd

London, UK

1 INTRODUCTION

Much of the current debate on the relative merits of IPSEs and
Workbenches obscures the most important difference between these classes
of software development aid: an IPSE provides support to project teams; a
Workbench provides support to an individual.

Both types of product include tools for use during the development life-
cycle but an IPSE can be expected to additionally provide an
infrastructure which enables the users of the tools to act in a co-
operative yet controlled fashion and a documentation management system
which organises the objects produced.

It is now well-established that, for large project teams, much of the
available resource is consumed by the sheer effort of maintaining
communication and control. Potential benefits to be obtained from a
large number of individuals working in co-operation are rarely realised.
If significant gains are to be made in the productivity of software
developers then it is these synergistic properties of teams which must be
tapped. The current generation of IPSEs are a step along this road.

This paper looks at the characteristics of IPSEs which attempt to exploit
the latent capacity of teams and at some of the problems that need to be
overcome.

Many of the problems arise from the very fact of trying to shift the
burden of communication and control from people to the machine. These
problems have to solved by recognising how people carry out their work
and by providing an environment which facilitates the process.

2   CHARACTERISTICS

2.1 Re-usable Components

The potential benefits to be achieved from the re-use of software
components are widely recognised. In the context of an IPSE, the notion
of re-usability is extended to all of the documentation produced during

the development life-cycle. As is the case with software components, re-use can be of well-defined document modules produced for the purpose, or of fragments of documentation requiring modification before use.

The implication for an IPSE is that mechanisms are needed to allow browsing through documents produced by other people or projects and to allow selected items to be copied and re-used. Hence, it must be apparent where any particular document is to be found and how it can be retrieved. Libraries must be capable of being designated separately for documents pertaining to projects, common utilities and various functional domains.

2.2 Control Mechanisms

An important feature of an IPSE is the degree to which the facilities for the conduct of the project are integrated with the facilities for managing the project. Control mechanisms are required for the conduct of tasks, monitoring of resource consumption and authorisation of changes, as well as for evaluating the consistency of the objects produced.

At the heart of this is the notion that every item of documentation produced or changed should be capable of being associated directly with a specific authorisation arising from the control of the project. In turn it should be possible to track the products associated with a nominated authorisation and to determine their status.

Similarly, mechanisms are required to capture data on the resource consumption of tasks. It is tempting to consider capturing this information directly from individuals' usage of the IPSE, but because of the nature of system development tasks it is generally necessary for time spent to be input explicitly.

In the situation where the many members of a project team are each producing inter-related documents, the IPSE must provide the mechanism for allowing the results to be co-ordinated and organised. Consistency control in a multi-user environment needs to operate at two levels: consistency control across the set of objects produced by an individual; and project-wide consistency checking when the objects are submitted to the project library.

2.3 Access Control

Access control in a multi-user environment requires recognition of the life-cycle of documents produced during system development.

Documents begin their life as the property of the author and during this stage are likely to be changed frequently as the author's ideas are developed. At some point, however, the document is regarded as complete and becomes the property of the project. Further change to the document must then be strictly controlled. The mechanism for change involves the generation of a new version of the document which initially becomes the property of an individual once more.

Hence the IPSE must provide personal work areas owned individually by members of the project team and secure areas where documents are protected from unauthorised change.

By default one would expect all documents to be viewable and copyable by all users of the IPSE but there need to be private locations available where such access is prevented unless authorised. A project may produce documents only some of which are private; alternatively, a project may be entirely private but worked on by people who simultaneously are working on public documents associated with other projects.

3   BIS/IPSE

BIS/IPSE is here described in terms of its architecture, its method of implementation, the user interface and the tools provided.

3.1 Architecture

BIS/IPSE is a project support environment whose principal elements are:

- a well-defined methodology whose principles and application guide the operations of the environment.

- a congenial software framework providing facilities for the conduct of tasks and the control; sharing and re-use of the various objects produced.

- software tools capable of supporting an encouraging use of the techniques prescribed by the methodology.

BIS/IPSE has been designed to provide an environment within which software tools can be used in co-operation with one another and where the operation of the tools can be governed by the preferred working practices of the particular installation.

The principal features of the architecture are:

- the concept of a Methods and Standards Library used to drive software tools. For any particular installation, the library determines the conventions to be employed and the styles of document to be produced. A variety of system development methodologies can be supported

- Provision of user work areas within which individual members of a project team can work on their specific tasks, together with shared areas (eg documentation libraries) to which each person can contribute in a controlled fashion

- a document storage system based on installation-defined categorisation of documents. Once defined for an installation, the structure is replicated for each document location required.

3.2 Implementation

The implementation of BIS/IPSE has been designed to take advantage of low-cost hardware configurations so that computer resources can realistically be dedicated to the support of even small project teams. Communications between the dedicated support machine and the ´target´ machines enable BIS/IPSE to be readily implemented within existing environments. In addition, the support machines can themselves be networked together.

The distinctive features of the implementation are:

- Multi-user implementation providing support for small and large project teams and enabling both co-operative working and re-useability of components.

- Definition of graphics primitives to enable high-quality diagramming on low-cost workstations and printers.

- Portability across a range of machines from PCs through departmental computers to mainframes.

3.3 User Interface

BIS/IPSE is intended for use by a broad community of users: a project team may include business practitioners as well as systems analysts and programmers. Some users will employ the facilities as an integral part of their work; others will require access on a less regular basis. Hence the user interface has been designed to take account of both ´novice´ and ´expert´ users.

The characteristics of the user interface are:

- Recognition of the various roles which contributors to a system development project may have. Ease of use, as well as security and control, is aided by providing sub-sets of facilities appropriate to each role.

- Uniform style of access across a range of special purpose tools.

- Use of scrollable picking lists to allow easy browsing and selection of objects and avoiding the traditional requirement for terse naming of the objects produced during system development.

- Definition of flexible structures for document storage enabling the user to be shielded from decisions on physical use of the file store.

- An extensive set of engraved function keys covering most commonly used primitive functions.

- Context dependent Help facilities throughout the system.

3.4 Tools

The tools provided in the BIS/IPSE support system development techniques commonly used in the commercial data processing industry.

In addition to conventional types of tool such as text editors, diagram editors and project control facilities, BIS/IPSE includes tools for producing and cross-referencing free-format documents. Typically such documents are those specifying individual components of an application system.

The intention here is to provide the type of facilities normally associated with a data dictionary but to enable them to operate on documents with no imposed format constraints. The tools are used when it is desired to monitor the consistency of the cross-references between one document and another and the completeness of an inter-related set of documentation.

During the life of an application system, the tools enable the impact of a proposed change to be assessed: queries can be made on where any particular system component is used so that the effect of changing it can be gauged. Such tools provide a very powerful means of managing and manipulating specifications of complex application systems.

It is the use of these tools which has enabled BIS Applied Systems to use BIS/IPSE as a vehicle for the development of Automated Business Models: logical representations of the business systems required to support particular application areas. Such models provide a convenient level of system packaging, avoiding the constraints of ´hard-coded´ packages while reducing the expense of entirely bespoke systems. The logical representation of a particular application can be manipulated in a controlled manner in response to the requirements of a specific physical implementation.

PERSPECTIVE KERNEL - THE BASIS FOR A GENERAL PURPOSE IPSE

P. Rumph and P. Rusling

Systems Designers Ltd

Camberley, UK

1   INTRODUCTION

The Perspective Kernel (PK) provides a well-engineered base on which to construct Integrated Project Support Environments. It does this by tackling the underlying problems which made IPSE's necessary:-

* the need to support the whole project life cycle

* the need to help technical management control medium to large project teams of technical staff

* the need for configuration management and version control across the whole project

However, the Perspective Kernel does not dictate the tools or methods the team must use. The project manager can choose the appropriate tools, the appropriate controls, and embed these within his own project-specific, company-specific (or even product-specific) environment.

A major benefit of this approach is that the introduction of an environment into a project can naturally evolve from a simple system (perhaps supporting the programming phase only) into a full IPSE as and when new tools become available

Equally the Perspective Kernel facilities can be retro-fitted to existing tools for projects already well under way, or to help tackle the maintenance problems of existing systems.

PK based IPSEs are primarily intended for use on major real-time projects, which typically require development teams, often geographically distributed, to produce reliable high-quality systems to strict budgets and timescales.

2   FACILITIES

On major software development projects, the team members need to work together, concurrently and co-operatively. Control needs to be exercised on what each member should do, what each member has done, and what overall progress has been achieved. Throughout the development, quality can only be ensured by correct development, acceptance, and change control procedures.

PK provides a set of facilities to allow such control to be achieved; these are described in the following sections.

2.1   Project Teams

All project data resides or is accessed through the multi-user multi-access PK database.

The PK database is divided into domains which each represent a user role. A project member may have many roles on a project, but will use a different domain for each role. An individual may have one domain for his main task as Designer, say, and a separate domain when he acts as reviewer for project documentation. Thus domains provide a means for controlling concurrency of access and isolate users from multi-access conflicts.

Each domain has associated with it a set of privileges which define the rights which the corresponding user role has for the operation of project control functions and tools. For example, a domain used by a Designer of a sub-system might have privileges allowing read access to specification data, and for use of a design tool; an equivalent programmer domain would have read access both to specification and design data, but no access to the design tool.

2.2   Items, Versions, and Variants

Database objects are visible to users as items which have a unique name within a domain, and are of one of a set of pre-defined item types. These items may actually be the root nodes of more complex data structures containing attributes, entities, and relationships with other items or entities.

In order to support progressive development and the sharing of stable issues of items, PK provides for versions of items to be established and maintained. The chosen version scheme allows for each version to be accorded a level of importance and formality. This is achieved by identifying each version by a Dewey-decimal-like code where the number of levels indicate the degree of (in)formality, as in the following example:-

1	top-level formal version
1.1	second-level less formal version
1.2	development of 1.1
1.2.1	sub-development of 1.2
1.2.2	development of 1.2.1
1.3	completed sub-development
2	formal version of 1.3

Within a version level, a source item may be modified using the standard host editor to produce the next version at that level.

PK also supports the parallel development of variants of an item by the establishment of baselines. This is useful where special variants are required for example for performance optimisation or bug fixing.

2.3 Quality Control

The version numbering scheme described above operates in conjunction with the PK privilege mechanism for any change of version level. In order to move an item version up or down a level it is necessary to use a promote or demote function which can have a degree of privilege and formality associated with it according to the version level.

For example, to promote item version 1.3 to formal version 2 could require a special privilege which might only be granted to the QA Manager. Similarly, to demote a version for further development could require the authority of a change control role who would formally declare the purpose of the proposed work.

Thus a project may associate particular QA states with different levels and control the degree of authorisation required to change version level. As a consequence, the status of an item is always known from its version number. Thus version 3.5.2.11 might be an untested item (in common with all items having four levels), and item 3.5.3 would be known to have been approved as a tested item by an independent reviewer (someone with authority to change items of this type form level four to level three). In a similar way an item with version number 8 would be known to be fully approved and certified as complete.

These controls can be tailored to meet the needs of a particular business or project, and may be modified (by special privilege) during the lifetime of a project.

Other support for Quality Control is provided by the maintenance of history records for all significant PK operations. This provides traceability and gives an audit trail for these operations.

By the appropriate instrumentation of PK operations, it is possible to gather metrics which can be used to improve future planning and estimating.

2.4 Data Sharing

The use of version control ensures that each version of an item is distinct and cannot later be modified. If changes are necessary, a new version must be created.

This regime enables stable versions of items to be shared within a project. PK provides a set of facilities in the form of a double-handshake to control such item sharing.

When an item has been developed to the level necessary for release within the project, the developer may publish that particular version of the item to the desired recipient domains. The users of these domains may then choose whether and when they should formally acquire that item version. That action provides them with read-only access, which might be required, for example, for integration purposes.

The developer of that item version can at some stage decide that it should be withdrawn, for example, when it becomes obsolete or a bug has been fixed. However, the access to that item version cannot be deleted by a developer until all ´acquirers´ have disposed of it.

These facilities ensure dependable access to stable data.

2.5 Work Allocation

To enable and control the allocation of development work, PK provides a similar set of double-handshake facilities to offer read-write access to item version sets.

A team leader (say) can allocate an item (at a version level) with suitable development privileges to a particular development domain. The user responsible for that domain can then formally receive that work, and proceed to perform the necessary development work (which might involve onward allocation).

When development has been completed, the domain user returns the item to the original allocator who formally accepts it when he is satisfied of its quality. Alternatively the return may be under the control of an independent reviewer.

2.6 Configurations

As well as facilities operating on individual items and their versions, PK also supports user-specified sets (configurations) of such item versions, which have a collective purpose and a collective status.

These configurations, apart from defining the set of item versions from which they are constituted, are also items in their own right, and can therefore be versioned, shared, and allocated for development. Such operations on a configuration automatically apply the corresponding action to all their constituent item versions. For example, the publication of a configuration, publishes all of the item versions which it contains.

An item version may be used in many different configurations, and any dependencies which are derived through each usage of it are held within the relevant configurations.

Configurations also provide a simplified context in which development tools can operate, in that only one version of any item may exist within the configuration, therefore the tools need not be aware of the versioning system.

3   DEVELOPMENT BACKGROUND

Since 1973 Systems Designers has had a major involvement in the design, development and supply of compilers, tools, and environments in support of projects developing real time systems.

3.1   Context

The Groups´ CONTEXT System was the first in the world which offered host/target debugging capability to projects developing systems for embedded micro-computers. CONTEXT was also the first system to provide programming support for a major design methodology - in this case the MASCOT real-time design method. The database for CONTEXT supported a single user, but as more powerful microprocessors became available development teams became larger and the problems of interaction between team members needed to be addressed.

3.2 Perspective

In 1982 Systems Designers introduced the Perspective system to support these larger project teams. With Perspective, team members are able to undertake their individual activities in their own private area of the database, whilst activities requiring collaboration with other team members are controlled at a team level. Other features offered by Perspective included a design language to control the development process, and configuration and version control features to support the development needs of teams as well as individuals. In total these innovations provide for the management and design control essential to the success of such projects, while still giving strong support to the individual team member performing a particular task. Perspective is currently in use on major multi-national aerospace projects.

3.3 Perspective Kernel

Incorporating research work from the Alvey ASPECT project (which had indicated the need for an IPSE to be open) and earlier work on a database management kernel, the development of a general purpose IPSE framework (PK) began in mid 1985. The first delivery of a PK-based IPSE, known as Horizon, was made to British Aerospace in October 1986. Horizon supports embedded systems development using Mascot-3 and Coral.

Central to PK is a set of facilities which provide low-level services to the project control functions and to the tools which will operate within the PK framework.

These facilities provide such services as:

*   data modelling – employing the ERA style of data modelling,

*   data management – providing resilience and recovery from catastrophic events,

*   file management,

*   terminal handling – employing split-screen techniques on VT100 compatible terminals, and

*   tool management – initiation, termination, and communication.

All of these facilities are made available through a formal interface which is known as the **Public Tool Interface** (PTI). Tools may be developed to use this interface, and may be integrated together to provide cohesive support to the software development process.

A special part of this PTI enables the use of tools which have no knowledge of PK; this is known as the **Open Tool Interface**. Use of this capability allows existing tools to be installed in PK, and permits PK to be introduced to control projects which are already underway.

4 CONCLUSION

From this paper it can be seen that PK incorporates the knowledge gained from developing Perspective and from Perspective users´ feedback. PK exploits state-of-the-art technology to provide a framework for a general purpose IPSE which permits both use on current projects and evolution to suit projects of the future.

FORTUNE-AN IPSE DOCUMENTATION TOOL

Stuart McGowan

CAP - Software Technology Group

ABSTRACT

The key to further automating the development of computer-based systems
is a software development environment that supports all the stages of the
software development life cycle. With the introduction in recent years
of Integrated Project Support Environments (IPSE´s) and other Software
Engineering Environments based on databases, it is clear that advances
are being made in software development support. Over the next decade we
can expect the use of IPSE´s and other advanced environments to become
common in the software industry.

The production and maintenance of documentation is a major activity in
software development, so an essential element of any software development
environment is a documentation tool aimed specifically at meeting the
needs of software engineers and others involved in the process of
producing software. Without such a tool no environment can claim to
fully support a project throughout its life cycle.

This paper describes FORTUNE - a software engineers documentation support
tool that has been designed specifically to be incorporated into IPSE´s
and to interface with other software tools. FORTUNE is being developed
by a collaboration as part of the Alvey Software Engineering program and
is aimed at intercepting the technology that will be available to
software developers by the end of the 1980´s - workstations and laser
printers, as well as IPSE´s.

1   INTRODUCTION - SOFTWARE DEVELOPMENT AND DOCUMENTATION

The traditional model used for describing the development of software-
based systems is the life-cycle model (see fig. 1). The system starts
with an idea; the idea is transformed into a more concrete form (for
example, a requirements specification); this in turn forms the basis for
the system design, form which the code is produced. The current efforts
aimed at automating software development are concentrating on three
approaches:

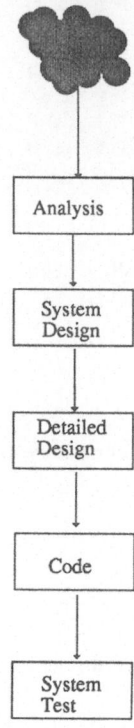

figure 1. Traditional life cycle model

Automating individual stages in the life cycle. Software tools are
becoming increasingly widely used in software development. For many
years this effort has been focused primarily on increasing the
productivity of programmers. Fourth generation languages, often
associated with databases, can lead to dramatic increases in programmer
productivity. However, more recently the emphasis has shifted to
providing the analyst and the designer with methodologies such as Yourdon
[WARD85], Jackson System Development [JACK83], etc. that can be used to
ensure that the design of a system is consistent within itself and also
with the functional analysis. Such methodologies are useful on their own
but their potential can only be fully exploited when they are supported
by a tool or a toolset.

Automating the complete life-cycle. Although individual stand-alone
tools that tackle single aspects of software development are undoubtedly
making a major contribution to improvements in software productivity at
present, over the next few years the Integrated Project Support
Environment (IPSE) will become more widely used and is likely to have a
far greater impact on productivity.

The current generation of IPSE's provide a toolset capable of supporting
all the stages of software development. The IPSE kernel, or core,
provides the toolset with a common user interface that interacts in a
unified and consistent manner with the user, and a database which all
tools can use, thus keeping all of a project's information in a single
information base.

Eliminating stages from the life cycle model. Perhaps the ultimate
target of automating software development is executable functional

specifications - in other words to dispense with as many stages from the traditional life cycle model as possible. Some progress has been made towards this, notably with the development and use in recent years of formal methods such as VDM [JONE80] and Z [NORR86]. The possibility of animating a formal functional specification is being investigated further in the work on the me too [MINK81] method and language. Even if this approach is taken to its logical conclusion the need for an IPSE will still remain because of the necessity of supporting, in a unified and integrated manner, the formal method toolset together with, for example, project management tools, version and configuration management tools, and a documentation tool.

At any stage in the development of software the system can be regarded as a set of documents. So at the completion of the systems analysis stage the system may consist of the functional requirements document; at the completion of the design stage the system may consist of the functional requirements document and the design documents. The exceptions to this follow the completion of the system testing. At this stage, as well as the documentation (i.e. design documents, source code and user documentation, etc.) the system also comprises executable code - i.e. the software itself. However, even at this and subsequent stages (e.g. during system maintenance) a change to the system will be effected by a change to its documentation. In other words for most of the stages in the project life cycle, the system is its documentation. This is illustrated in fig. 2.

Currently, documentation is a major activity on all large projects. On many projects it has been identified as the single largest expense element [JONE86]. Documentation affects every stage in a project - not just single life cycle stages. It is clear, then, that the documentation activities should be automated as far as possible and that a documentation tool should be provided as an essential component of any IPSE that claims to provide full support for software development throughout all its stages. This will remain true even if we succeed in eliminating the majority of these stages, because we will still need a documentation tool that is capable of maintaining the relationships between, say, the functional specification and the user documentation, so that a change made to the former will result in an automatic indication that the corresponding section(s) of the latter will need to be updated.

A need for a specialised documentation tool aimed specifically at the requirements of software engineers has therefore been identified. The remaining sections of this paper describe the documentation tools likely to be found in use at present on software projects, the technology that we believe will become available to software engineers by the end of the decade, and the advanced documentation tools that are already making use of this technology. Lastly, the paper describes FORTUNE, a documentation tool aimed specifically at meeting the needs of software engineers by intercepting the technology that will be widely available to software engineers at the end of the decade.

2   SOFTWARE DOCUMENTATION TODAY

Typically, a project's documentation is produced on a wide variety of machines using a large number of different systems. For example, the target machine may be used for producing the source code, a stand-alone word processor for the functional requirements document, a drawing editor on a Personal Computer for the design diagrams, and the user documentation may be produced using typesetter output from a batch mark up system such as troff [KERN82].

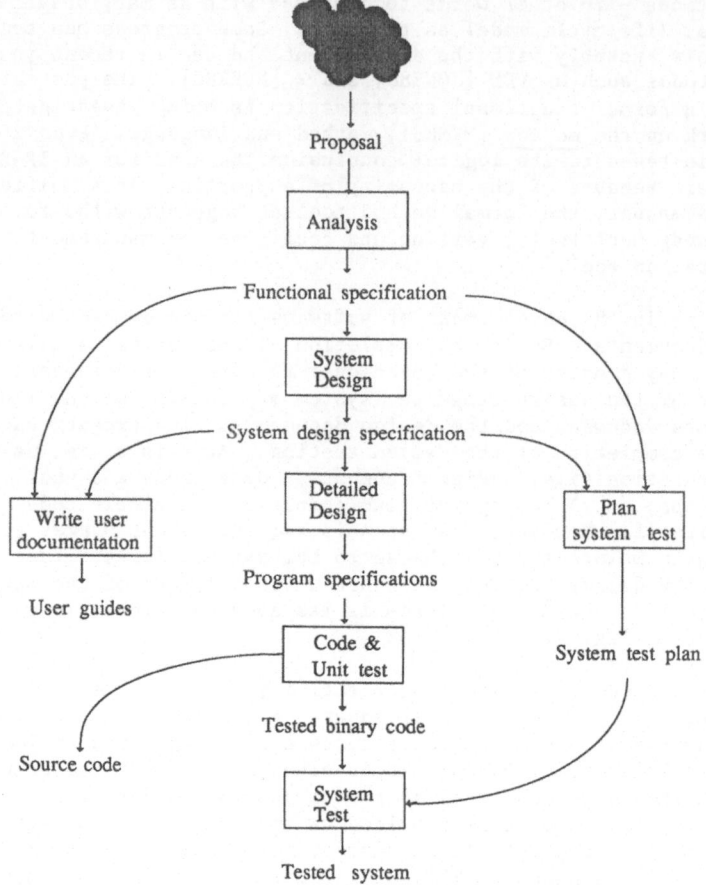

Proposal

Analysis

Functional specification

System
Design

System design specification

Write user
documentation

Detailed
Design

Plan
system test

User guides

Program specifications

Code &
Unit test

System test plan

Source code

Tested binary code

System
Test

Tested system

figure 2. Life cycle model showing inputs and outputs

This approach to documentation is clearly not satisfactory, and in the
light of the statement that we have made above, that for much of the
system development process the system is its documentation, we can see
that it would be of enormous benefit to keep all of a project's
documentation in a single logical information base and use just one tool
to create, access and update it.

Batch vs interactive systems

With the increase in popularity in recent years of Unix, there has been a
simultaneous increase in the use by software engineers of batch systems
using mark up languages. The most widely used of these is troff which,
with its standard preprocessors, provide a powerful set of features for
producing high quality typeset output for text documents. Until recently
this output quality could not be matched by systems that offered what-
you-see-is-what-you-get (WYSIWYG) in terms of hyphenation and line-
breaks. Very few word processors, even now, are capable of taking full
advantage of anything more sophisticated than a daisy wheel printer with
one font. On the other hand, batch systems are unsuitable for use by
secretaries and typists, and for documents that include diagrams, tables
and equations as well as text. In other words they are unsuitable for
use for the type of document typically produced by software engineers.

For these documents an accurate representation of the final printed document should be available on screen to allow the user easy navigation of the document and editing of textual and graphical information.

Current technology and its implications for documentation

The technology to support a documentation system capable of producing high quality output and offering the user WYSIWYG representation of documents containing graphical elements as well as text is now becoming more widely available in the form of workstations with high-resolution bit-mapped screens, and low-cost laser printers that offer high quality output.

We can expect the next generation of Personal Computers to have the same functionality as the current generation of high performance workstations. As the software industry changes from being a labour extensive one at present to being capital-intensive, we can expect to see workstations brought to the desks of software engineers. At the same time, laser printers will continue to fall in price and 'desktop publishing' capability will spread to the desks of software developers.

There is a growing consciousness of the need for standards both for workstations and for laser printers. For workstations Unix has already been adopted as the de facto standard operating system, and standards such as NeWS and X-Windows are being proposed for windowing environments. For laser printers, Page Description Languages (PDL's) such as Postscript have already gained widespread acceptance. Complying with standards such as these is the route to achieving maximum portability.

Current advanced documentation tools

The most technically advanced documentation tools are already beginning to make use of workstation and laser printer technology.

Interestingly, these systems have their origins in a variety of different sources. Word processor manufacturers are now beginning to develop word processing software on bit-mapped screens and are including the support of graphics. Developers of CAD/CAM support tools on workstations are adding text handling to their systems. Page composition systems, over which the user has total control of the layout of a document, are also being enhanced with graphics handling and more sophisticated text handling.

The result of this is that advanced documentation systems with very similar functionality but with different emphases are now becoming available.

Typical features of these systems are:

-   interactive WYSIWYG editing of text giving an accurate view of the font and type face as well as the line breaks and pagination

-   interactive WYSIWYG editing of diagrams

-   support of both text and diagrams within the same document

-   high quality output by the use of PDL's and a laser printer

-   an advanced MMI making use of windows, icons, menus and pointing devices

As the hardware to support such systems becomes more and more widely available we can expect to see these advanced systems being more widely used and a corresponding decline in the use of the harder to use batch documentation systems.

3   DOCUMENTATION FOR SOFTWARE ENGINEERS

Advanced systems with features such as those listed above are now just starting to be used for software documentation. However, it is unlikely that any of the current generation of documentation tools could be used by a project for all its documentation. For example, analysts and designers would continue to use methodology support tools, and project managers would continue to use project planning and monitoring tools to produce a significant amount of a project's documentation. Also, software engineers have additional requirements over and above those of other users.

FORTUNE is a documentation tool that has been designed to meet these requirements. It is currently being implemented by a collaborative project as part of the Alvey Software Engineering program. In this section we discuss the features that are included in FORTUNE that enable it to support software development through all the life cycle stages.

Cross referencing – modelling relationships

Cross referencing within a document is needed by all users of documentation systems for quick and easy navigation of the document. Indexes, lists for references, contents lists and footnotes are all examples of this type of cross referencing and there are others of the sort 'see page 7' or 'refer to section 3.2'. Some documentation tools already support this level of cross referencing.

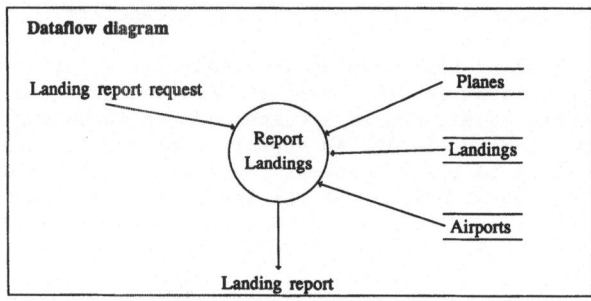

figure 3. Relationships between documents

However, software engineers need to be able to model relationships not just between elements within the same document, but between objects within a project — and in particular between different representations in a project's life cycle. In other words there is a need for cross referencing between documents as well as within documents. FORTUNE will allow relationships to be established between documents. This will allow, for example, a requirement specified in the functional requirement document to be traced through the design document and code to the user documentation and to any change requests that affect it during the maintenance phase.

This degree of cross referencing will enable, for example, elements in a dataflow diagram to refer to further dataflow diagrams, a data dictionary, code, and a program specification; all of these are different documents and most are different types of document. (see fig. 3).

Methodology support

There is no methodology which has been proved to be better than all other methodologies. The choice of a particular methodology for use on a particular project depends on a variety of factors including the type of application, the support tools available, the personal preference (for example, because of familiarity) of the designer for a particular methodology, the need to meet a company's standards, etc. Therefore, for a documentation tool to be able to offer full support to a user it must fit in with the user's methods and languages rather than force him to use a specific methodology.

FORTUNE will therefore be independent of any one fixed methodology and will offer support for as wide a range of methodologies as possible by allowing a user to configure FORTUNE to support the methodology being used. In particular, FORTUNE incorporates a structured line diagram editor, known as PLEX [WRIG87] which can be configured to support a range of diagram-based methodologies.

The user-configurability of PLEX will be extended within FORTUNE to cover not just diagrams but whole documents. So a generic document class can be defined and all specific instances of that class of document will conform to the generic standards specified. Hence at the start of a project a project manager may define exactly what documents are to be produced and the format (logical structure) of each of the documents.

The concept of methodology support by user configurability could be extended further in the future to include mathematics-based methods as well diagram-based methodologies. So FORTUNE could be configured with the rules for supporting, say, a specific formal notation so that syntactically correct documents using that notation could easily be written.

Another aspect of user-configurability is closely connected with the area of cross referencing already mentioned above. It is left to the user to define which relationships within a project's documentation are valid. This will restrict cross references that may be established to those of a valid type. For example, if the user configures FORTUNE at the outset of a project in such a way that a dataflow diagram may not directly refer to a module of source code, but may only do so indirectly via a program specification, then direct cross references from a diagram to code will be invalid and FORTUNE will not allow them to be set up.

Integration with IPSE's

As we have already stated in the introduction, FORTUNE has been designed to interface at the database and user interface level.

Just as PLEX, FORTUNE's diagram editor, is a useful stand-alone tool but is far more powerful when incorporated into a documentation tool, so FORTUNE's capability will be greatly enhanced when used as a tool within an IPSE.

The advantages of FORTUNE being used as part of an IPSE are apparent when we consider the different users of FORTUNE. We have already stated above that at any stage in the development of software, a system can be regarded as its own documentation. Similarly, we can regard all the people who work on a particular representation and transform it into another representation, as 'documenters'. For example, an analyst will use FORTUNE to produce a functional specification, a designer will use it to produce the design documents, etc. It is at these 'documenters' (i.e. software engineers) that FORTUNE is primarily aimed.

However, as a stand-alone tool FORTUNE may be less useful than others for meeting some of the documentation requirements of the users. For example, a designer would not use FORTUNE for creating and editing diagrams that conform to a specific methodology if a methodology support tool available on a PC gave him/her facilities not only for drawing diagrams but for analysing them, validating them for consistency, producing data dictionaries automatically, etc. In this case we would still be in the position where the project's documentation is produced on a variety of different systems on a potentially large number of machines.

As mentioned above software tools can achieve maximum portability by adhering to existing standards whenever they exist. This is as true in the area of IPSE interfaces as it is for areas such as windowing systems and PDL's. FORTUNE will therefore be compatible with the interfaces defined by the Esprit Portable Common Tool Environment (PCTE) definition [BULL84].

PCTE includes definitions for communication mechanisms, inter process communication and distribution mechanisms as well as for a database and user interface. It has been adopted by the Esprit initiative as an environment for all the software tools being developed under the Esprit Software Technology program. Currently a full implementation of PCTE is being ported to a variety of workstations, further research and commercial prototypes are being developed, and existing IPSE manufacturers are adopting the PCTE interfaces for their own IPSE's. For a complete description of PCTE see [BULL84].

We regard it as essential, therefore, that FORTUNE can make use of PCTE and thus be able to share data with the wide variety of other software tools currently being developed to exploit PCTE's potential.

We can see then that since FORTUNE can share data with, for example, analysis and design tools, and with project management tools integration with PCTE-based IPSE's will enable all of a project's documentation to be stored in a single logical information base, and that it will be easily accessible to anyone working on the project.

Integration with other tools

Although the advantages offered by IPSE's of sharing data are considerable and greatly increase the potential of any tool incorporated into an IPSE toolset, there is a further level of integration which is being investigated by the FORTUNE project. This is direct integration with other software tools.

Tools such as spelling checkers and encryption programs will need to be invoked directly from FORTUNE rather than run as separate stand alone tools. Other tools directly related to documentation include version control and configuration management tools which, in conjunction with FORTUNE, will constitute a complete documentation support and management system. The degree of integration that is possible, and the methods of integrating FORTUNE with these and other tools will form a major part of the research of the FORTUNE project.

4   CONCLUSION

The major aims of software engineering are to improve both the productivity of the software development process and the quality of the software produced.

Producing documentation is a major activity in software development. This is particularly true on large projects where it is frequently the single most expensive element. Documentation is also an essential part of the final system. This applies not just to the user documentation but also to the documentation produced during software development which is essential to the system maintenance phase.

The quality, in terms of both content and presentation of all this documentation is just as important as the quality of the software itself.

Despite this, documentation is frequently neglected by software engineers, and little effort has been spent on providing tools to assist software engineers in this activity.

The aims of the FORTUNE project are to make software developers aware of the importance of documentation and to develop a tool to support the documentation activities throughout the whole project life cycle. FORTUNE will make a significant impact on a project's productivity, and on the quality of its end result.

5   CURRENT STATUS OF THE FORTUNE PROJECT

The FORTUNE project is a 3 year project scheduled for completion in October 1988. the first phase of the project, in which each of the collaborators worked on separate aspects of the final system and produced exemplar prototypes to demonstrate the results of this work, is now complete.

In the second phase, which started at the end of 1986, the results from the first phase are being brought together and the FORTUNE system itself is being developed.

6   ACKNOWLEDGEMENTS

The FORTUNE project is partly funded by the Department of Trade and Industry through the Alvey initiative's Software Engineering program. The collaboration carrying out the work is led by CAP; the other collaborators are MARI Advanced Microelectrics Limited, Baddeley Associates Limited, and the University of Kent.

7   REFERENCES

[BULL84] Bull, GEC, ICL, Nixdorf, Olivetti, Siemens, ´PCTE - A basis for
          a portable common tool environment; functional specification´,
          1986.

[JACK83] Jackson, M.A., ´System development´, Prentice-Hall
          International, 1983.

[JONE80] Jones, C.B., ´Software development: a rigorous approach´,
          Prentice-Hall, 1980.

[JONE86] Jones, C., ´Programming Productivity´, McGraw Hill, 1986.

[KERN82] Kernighan, B.W., ´A typesetter-independent troff´, Computer
          Science Technical Report, 97, Bell Laboratories, 1982.

[MINK81] Minkowitz, C.J., ´Specification to prototype - a comparison of
          two formal methods of software design´, Department of Computing
          Science, University of Stirling, 1981.

[NORR86] Norris, M., ´Z (a formal specification method)´, Starts debrief
          report, 1986.

[WARD85] Ward, P.T. and Mellor, S.J., ´Structured development for real-
          time systems´, Yourdon Press, 1985.

[WRIG87] Wright, S.J., ´PLEX - a structured line diagram editor´, in
          this volume.

AN INVESTIGATION INTO A SYSTEMS DEVELOPMENT TECHNIQUE

M. S. Verrall

CAP Industry Ltd.

London, UK

1   INTRODUCTION

The subject of this paper is a case study of an exploration of a technique for automating systems development. It gives the objectives and course of the exploration and the conclusions arrived at. A subsidary aim for the presentation is to publicise the technique explored.

With the ever widening spread of application of computing techniques the world contains an increasing number of software systems. As this happens the question "how does this system solve our problem?" contains in larger and larger measure the question "how will our system fit in with other ones?". The issue of integration is thus a fundamental issue and will grow in importance as we seek both to retain the investment already made in existing software and to enhance the value of the investments we will make.

The aspect of systems development under study was that of developing software for the integration of the data of different systems. The aim was to automate this by seeking the existence of a general purpose piece of software which could be parameterised to perform the specific integration sought.

The paper is tripartite. The first part lays out the objectives of the study carried out. The second part describes the way in which the intentions of the study were satisfied; it gives an exposition of the technique investigated, a specification of how that technique was made manifest and a description of the experiment carried out. The third part lists the conclusions reached.

2   OBJECTIVES

The objectives of the study were as follows.

1.   To determine whether such a translation as those exemplified below is possible.

2.   To see if there is in existence a likely technique for achieving this translation and to investigate its suitability.

3.   To find the practical difficulties which arise when an attempt is
     made to implement this technique.

The objectives were achieved in two stages. Firstly, by the implementation of a piece of software, the ATN Interpreter described in section 4,
capable of performing translations by means of the sought technique and
in which the main drive was to obtain a minimal but representative
prototype and leave out aspects of creating a production quality piece of
software. Secondly, by carrying through a particular translation – the
first of the illustrative examples below – with the aim of discovering
the advantages and drawbacks of the technique. The example is discussed
in section 5.

2.1   Exemplifying Translations

There is being developed by CAP Industry Ltd under the aegis of Alvey a
software engineers' documentation support system, FORTUNE [MCGO87]. This
tool will be able to be run by itself or as part of a software engineering environment, for example the ESPRIT sponsored development PACT (PCTE
Added Common Tools) [PACT85]. The requirement for two translations
between elements of FORTUNE and other components of a software engineering environment has been envisioned.

The first translation is between a diagrammatic representation of a
process control logic network as created by the diagram drawer, Plex
[WRIG87], in Fortune and the source file for a Prolog interpreter; the
second translation is between a specification written in structured
English, whose vocabulary is limited to the specific application domain
of process control, and the source for a Lisp interpreter.

These examples were sufficiently representative to enable the work done
in this study to be built around them.

3   TECHNIQUE

The path followed in seeking a solution to the problem defined in section
2 has been to discover a candidate technique, modify it as necessary and
implement and evaluate a prototype.

The technique identified in Augmented Transition Networks, ATNs, which
are widely used in the field of natural language analysis. They first
made their appearance with reference [WOOD70], the standard exposition is
reference [BATE78] and the principal reference for this work is reference
[CHRI83] and other papers in reference [BOLC83]. Greater detail on this
study can be found in reference [VERR86].

3.1   Reasons for Choice of This Technique

As there was no known restriction on the data which was to be translated
and as the data had been constructed without regard to the ability to be
translated, a technique was needed which had the power to compute any
computable function and did not place any theoretical limits on the
translation.

ATNs were chosen for their power and generality and because they are an
established technique. ATNs also have a high level diagrammatic representation which seemed to be helpful.

Their power is reflected in the statement that they are as powerful as Turing machines; but of course this says nothing about their utility for the problem in hand, the evaluation of which is the objective of this study.

3.2 Description of Augmented Transition Networks

This section contains the description of ATNs in the form of a tutorial in which their functionality is expanded incrementally.

This description starts with the concept of finite-state automation and builds upon it; the discussion is couched in terms of the materialisation of finite-state automata as state-transition diagrams. The terminology for a state-transition diagram is that it is a directed graph made up of states joined by arcs.

The following example is developed. Consider a finite-state automaton which accepts sentences about what the speaker eats and build upon it to get an ATN which makes a statement about the speaker's morals. The finite-state automaton accepts sentences like "I eat meat and eggs and fish."; it looks like this:

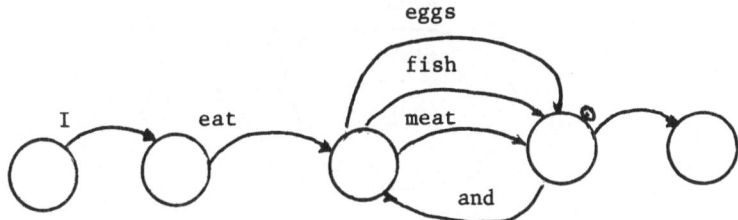

To the concept of a deterministic finite-state automation are added the following concepts: backtracking, nesting, tests, actions and data structures. These are explained incrementally in what follows.

3.2.1 Backtracking

The first concept to be added is that of backtracking. If it is not possible to take any of the arcs leading from a state (they are each said to fail) then the automaton backtracks along the arc leading to that state (which is thereby said to fail), rewinds the input and tries another arc leading from the state from which the backtracked arc lead.

The example is extended to accept sentences which include vegetables among the things I eat to accept sentences saying that I eat vegetables but not other things (the rather artificial example lets a lot of other sentences slip through). Backtracking will occur if the wrong "vegetables" arc is taken; the "but" or "and" will fail, there are no more arcs leading from that state, the state will fail, the "vegetables" arc leading to that state will fail, and the other "vegetables" arc will be discovered and taken.

Typical accepted sentences are "I eat eggs and veg and fish and meat." and "I eat veg but not fish.". The automaton looks like this:

3.2.2. Nesting

The second concept to be added is that of nesting. The graph may be considered as made up of several sub-graphs (which may be disjoint, but which need not be so) having one or more entry and exit states. In traversing the graph the automaton encounters an arc marked not with an input signal but with the name of a sub-graph (the name of the sub-graph's entry state); at that point traversal of the arc is suspended and the automaton proceeds to the entry state of the sub-graph. The sub-graph is then traversed until an arc is encountered which is marked not with an input signal but with the instruction to return to the suspended arc and carry on from there; this then takes place.

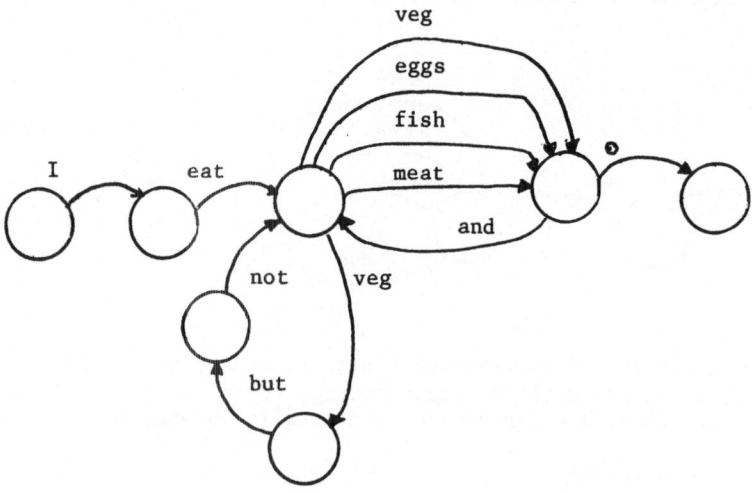

Nesting may continue to any depth as sub-graphs may enter other sub-graphs. Traditionally the respective arcs are called seek and send arcs. In terms of grammar theory the seek arc is marked with a non-terminal rather than a terminal symbol. It should be observed that the graph we now have is rather improper as the send arcs do not lead to states but just dangle in mid-air. Backtracking is accomplished easily as neither seek nor send arc consume input.

The example is extended so that it accepts only those sentences in which any notion of vegetables comes first, if at all, for instance: "I eat veg but not meat." or "I eat veg and meat.". Observe that the notion of eating animals has been separated into a sub-graph and that the top level is also a sub-graph.

3.2.3. Tests

The third concept to be added is that of generating the tests on arcs.
The only tests that we have so far are these: "is the input this signal?"
and, by nesting, "are the next inputs a member of this set of sequences
of signals?". To these are added the idea that the network writer can
specify a test that is performed by the automaton to see whether it
should traverse the arc. The simplest example of this, which is really
just a matter of notational convenience in combining several arcs between
the same pair of states, is a test to see if the input is a member of a
set of signals. Backtracking is not explicitly catered for as the tests
are assumed to be side-effect free and hence no ´untesting´ is done when
backtracking along an arc. Nesting is catered for thus: no generalised
testing is permitted on seek or send arcs, but a send arc tests to see if
the state the sub-graph was entered at was one of a list that are recognized by reaching this exiting state.

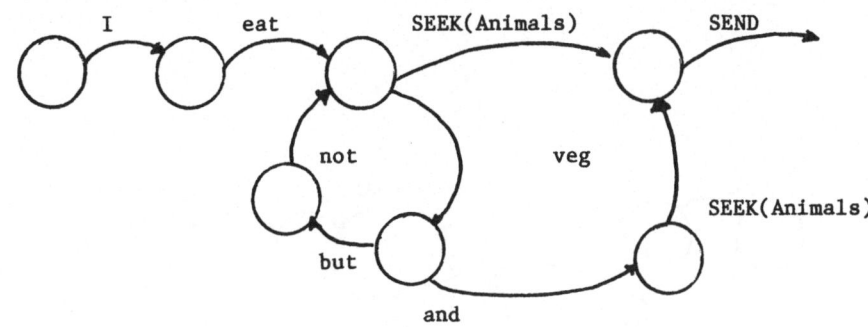

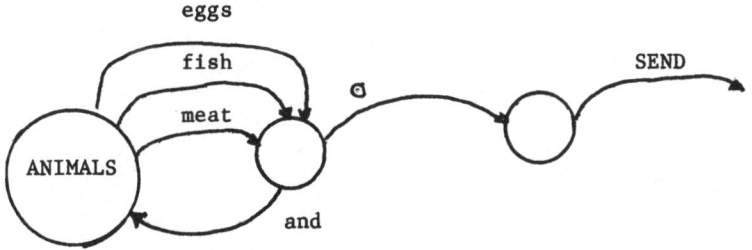

In the example two tests are illustrated, WORD tests whether the input
word is one of a list of a list of words; TEST is a general caller of
test routines, in this case a routine to look ahead and see if the next
word of input is one of a list of words (in the example the list just
consists of the full stop). The sentences accepted are the same as those
accepted by the preceding example.

3.2.4. Actions

The fourth concept to be added is that of allowing action to take place upon traversal of arcs. The actions do two things: they cause some activity to be performed (e.g. access to internal data structures, see below) and they affect the walking of the graph. The manner in which they affect the walking of the graph is by causing a more extensive form of backtracking to take place. This backtracking can be of four sorts: back along the arc on which action is (this is equivalent to a test), back to a named state, back to the entry of the current sub-graph or back to the start of the whole graph.

The effect of backtracking along an arc on which an action is placed is not catered for as actions are not undone - this could be improved in future developments. Nesting is catered for thus: seek arcs have two actions, one performed before entering the sub-network and one performed after returning therefrom, send arcs have two actions, one to modify the current input, the other a usual action.

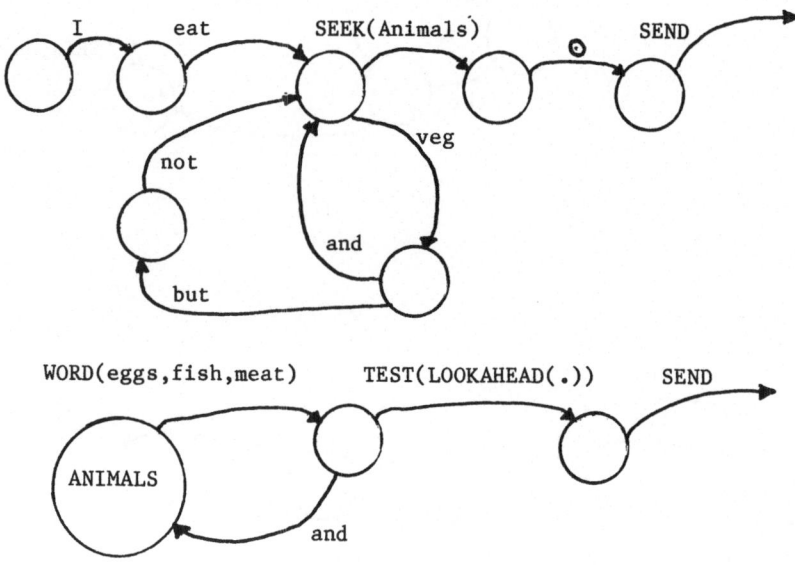

The example is extended to show actions which cause writing of output. The automation accepts, among others, these sentences: "I eat veg and meat." and "I eat veg but not eggs and fish." to produce, correspondingly, these outputs: "I am an omnivore" and "I am a vegetarian".

272

3.2.5.   Internal data structures

The fifth concept to be added is that of internal data structures which
are available to the network writer. This enables the walk through the
graph to be remembered thus delaying bifurcation and output to the point
where they are wanted. The internal data structures supplied are the
current input signal and those traditionally known as ´registers´.
Register identification is two part: by nesting level and then by name.
The structure of each register is that of a double-ended queue.
Registers are created when first written to and deleted when taking the
send arc at that nesting level.

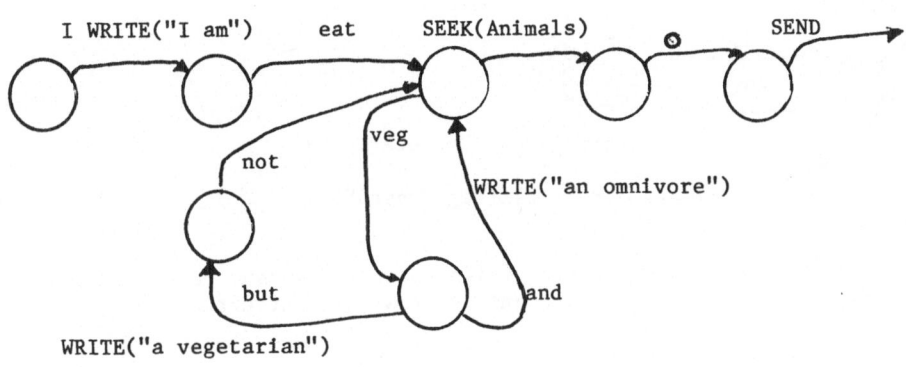

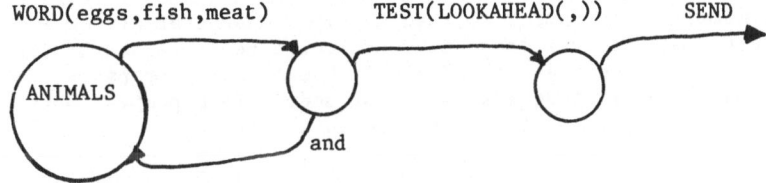

In the extended example the following actions will be seen in somewhat
abbreviated form:

SETL(register,value) to set the left-hand end of a register,

SEEL(register) to get the value of the left-hand end of a register,

EQ(string,string) to test the equality of two strings and fail the
arc if unequal.

Sentences accepted include these: "I eat veg and beef.", "I eat veg but
not fish." and "I eat veg but not eggs.". They produce the following
outputs: "I am an omnivore", "I am a vegetarian" and "I am a vegan".

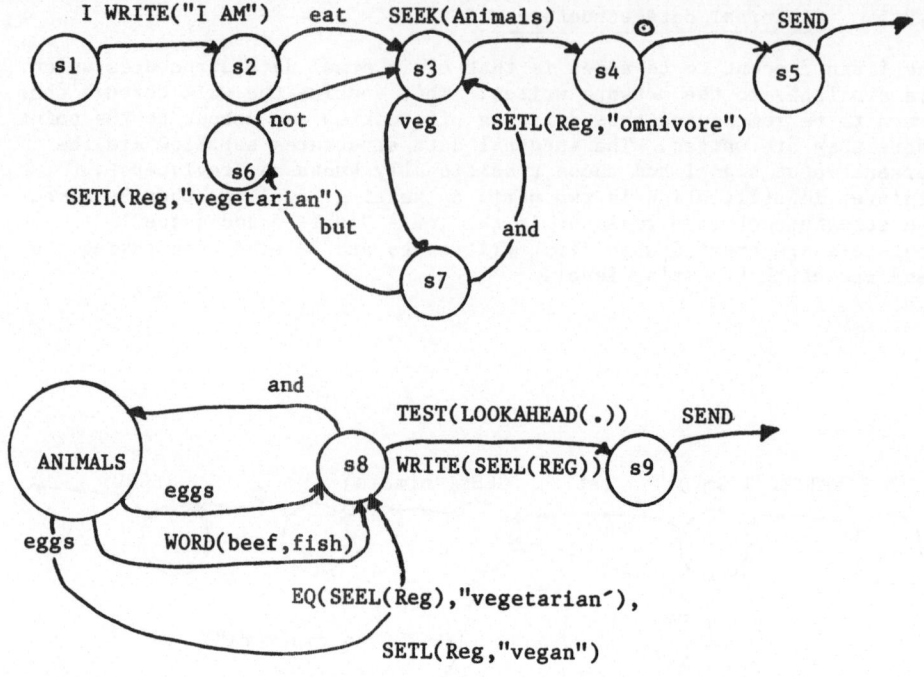

Thus an ATN automaton comprises finite-state automaton, backtracking, nesting, arc-tests, arc-actions and internal data structures.

3.2.6.   Other features

It is worth at this point discussing the input and output models supported. Input is supplied to the automaton as a linear stream or words by routines which expect to read a simple character stream - though a more complicated external data structure could be traversed by the input routines provided that it had a suitable ordering property. There is only a simple linear word stream output model, more complex output is accomplished by actions written by the network writer.

There are two features in ATNs in the realm of natural language analysis which do not appear herein, the lexicon and alternate parsing strategies. The lexicon is a dictionary, giving for each word in the accepted vocabulary its implicit attributes (e.g. part of speech, root), which can be read by actions; as the specific problem studied did not exhibit such features the lexicon was dropped.

Alternate parsing facilities allow (i) arcs to be grouped together such that if one fails all in that group fail, (ii) the automaton to switch between depth-first and breadth-first exploration of the graph; the illustrative examples only required straightforward depth-first searching and thus alternate parsing facilities were not supplied.

3.3 Usage of Augmented Transaction Networks

Using the technique of ATNs means that work proceeds by two stages:
firstly a network (annotated graph) is written and secondly the automaton
acts upon input guided by the network to produce output.

The network writer proceeds by these steps:

- describe the topology of the network, i.e. give all the sub-graphs
  of which it is composed identifying their entry and exit states and
  nominate one of these entry states as the state at which the whole
  network is entered.

- for each arc give the test and action it is to perform.

- if there are tests and actions used which are not supplied with the
  automaton, implement them.

4   IMPLEMENTATION

The first stage in the realisation of the solution path was to implement
the Augmented Transition Network system which this section describes.

It gives an overview of the components of the ATN System implemented,
describes how it is realised in software and how this software should be
used and behaves.

4.1 Architecture

The end user, who is just interested in converting information, runs the
ATN Automaton on the Input File produce the Output File.

The network writer writes a Network Description and passes it through the
Network Generator to produce a Network which is incorporated into the ATN
Automaton, this is shown below. The Automaton is then run in development
mode using Debug Interaction.

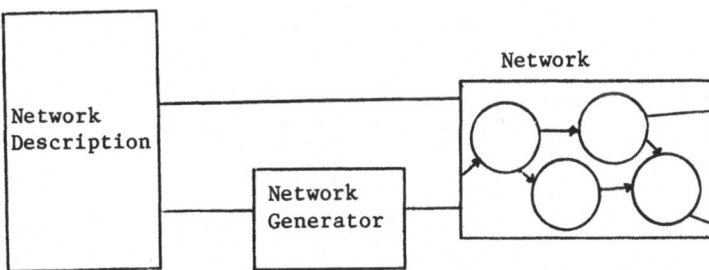

The ATN Automaton is composed of three parts: Network, Executor and
Internal Data Structures. The Executor drives the ATN Automation.

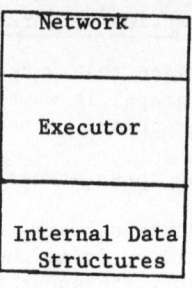

The Network Generator and Executor are collectively known as the Interpreter, for historical reasons.

A figure illustrating the whole architecture of the ATN Automaton follows (figure 1); in drawing the figure conventions have been applied concerning single and double lines, shading and dashed lines. A single line between two components or between a component and another part of the Automaton indicates an interaction; a double line indicates no interaction. A shaded area indicates that (part of a) component is supplied by the network writer. There is no significance in the fact that the String Functions component is shown in two parts - this is caused by the limitations of diagramming and the two parts should be

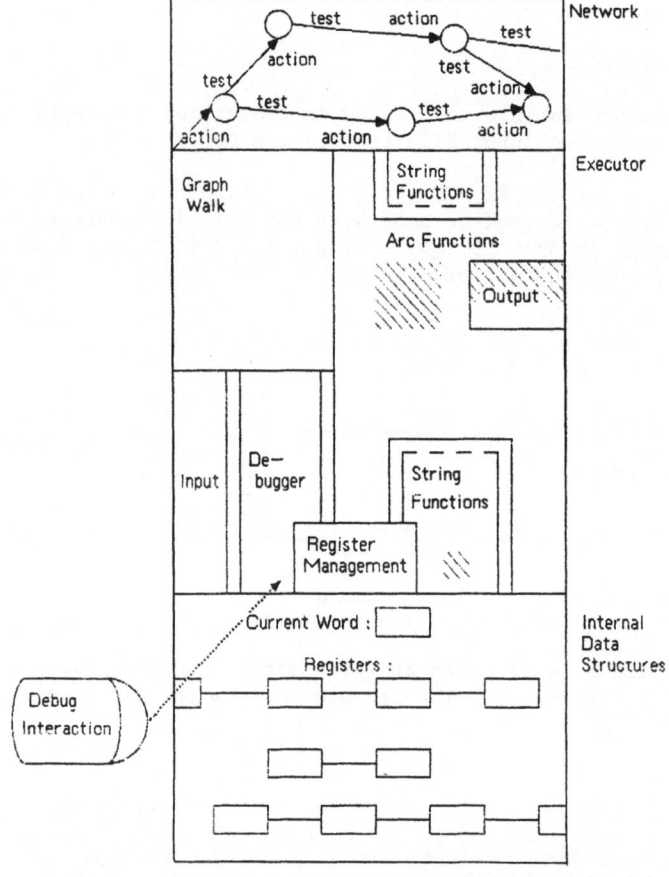

Figure 1   Augmented Transition Network Automaton architecture

considered as one joined along the dashed edge.

The components of the Executor are:

Graph Walk, which is concerned with moving through states and arcs and also with entering and exiting sub-networks,

Arc Functions, which are called to test or action an arc,

Input, which presents the input file to the rest of the Executor as a stream of words by setting the value of Current Word,

Output, which produces the Output File the user wants,

String Functions, which manipulate strings (the data type handled by the automaton),

Debugger, a built-in debugging aid for controlling the Executor and overseeing Internal Data Structures,

Register Management, which is concerned with the location of Registers not with the manipulation of their contents (which is done by Arc and String Functions),

There are two internal Data Structures available to the Executor:

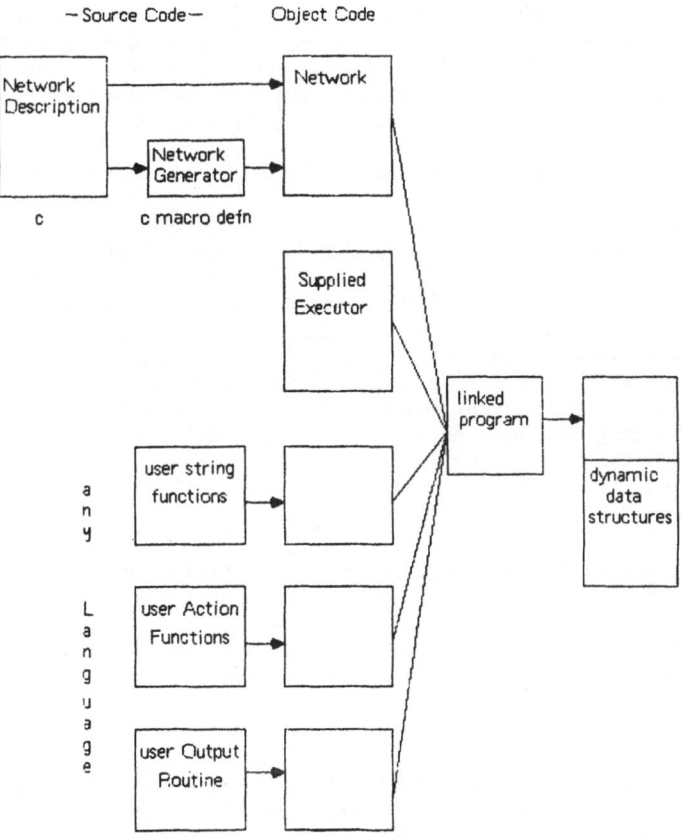

Figure 2 "Building the ATN Automation Process"

Current Word, which holds a string being the word from the Input
File currently being processed (Input decides what a word is)

Registers, which are a collection of double-ended queues, the elements of the queues being strings; registers have a two-part name –
the first being the number of the network nesting level for which
they were created, the second being purely mnemonic.

4.2 Physical Manifestation

The entire ATN System is realised as a single process created from a
program written in C [KERN78], as illustrated in figure 2.

The Network Description is composed of C data definitions (which directly
become part of the Network) and C macro calls. The Network Generator is
a set of C macro definitions, which may include some supplied by the

Network Writer. Thus the Network Description and Network Generator are
compiled together to create the Network.

The parts of the Executor supplied by the network writer, Output and
optional String and Arc Functions, are written in whatever language the
network writer wishes (though, of course, they must conform to C calling
conventions) and compiled by him. The rest of the Executor is composed
of compiled C functions.

As for Internal Data Structures, the static data structures (Current Word
and the pointer to Registers, are supplied as compiled data definitions
and the dynamic data structures (Registers) created during execution of
the ATN Automaton process. Thus the ATN Automaton is created by linking
together the Network, network writer's part of the Executor, the supplied
part of the Executor and the Internal Data Structures.

The ATN Automaton program then runs as a single process which may operate
in one of the two modes:

normal, when it reads the Input File and writes the Output File,

debug, when it also has Debug Interaction with the user.

The ATN System is written in C as this is the standard for the FORTUNE
project; it was developed on a Sun/3 workstation as this supplied the
best development environment – principally, it has an interactive C
program debugging aid and the offering of the other systems available to
the author in the way of such aids were negligible.

5 EXPERIMENTATION

Having implemented the ATN Interpreter and verified the design for its
basic soundness with a large number of fragmentary Network Descriptions,
an experimental trial was held to validate the Interpreter as being an
effective piece of software. For this purpose the first of the illustrative examples given in section 2, Plex diagram to Prolog code, was used.

5.1 Diagram

The type of diagram to be considered is a process control logic diagram.
This type of diagram shows the functioning of an activity in terms of
the combination of subsidiary activities and finally components (e.g.

278

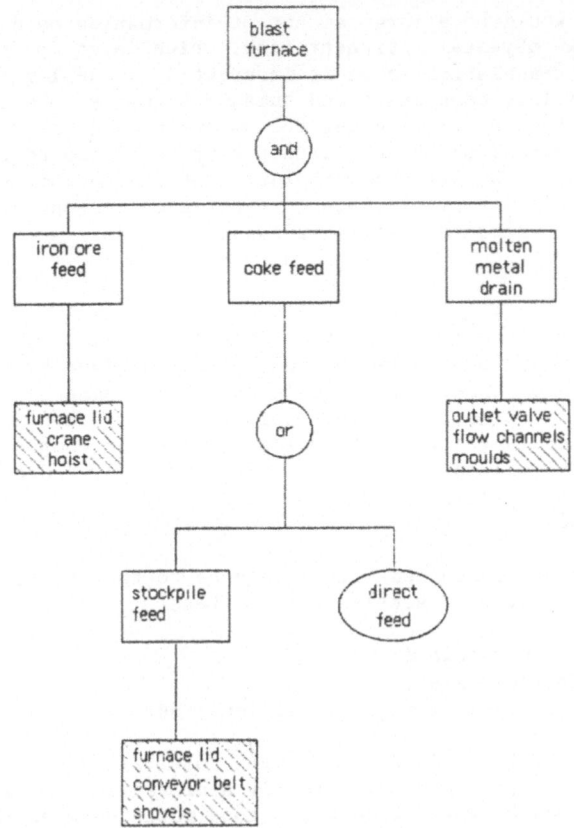

Figure 3. Operation of Blast Furnace

valves, meters and pumps) and human actions. The following example
(figure 3) illustrates a typical diagram; in it activities are shown by
plain rectangles, lists of components by shaded rectangles, human action
by ellipses and logical conjunction and disjunction by circles annotated
by ´and´ and ´or´.

It states that the operation of an imaginary blast furnace requires that
the activities of iron-ore feed, coke feed and molten metal drain are in
operation. The iron-ore feed requires that these components: furnace
lid, crane, hoist are working. The coke feed requires that either the
stock pile feed is in operation or that human action for direct feed
takes place. Similarily the molten metal drain and stock pile feed each
require that three components are working.

5.2 Plex

In its present stage of development Plex can manipulate drawings on-line
but cannot yet permanently store them away. Thus, rather than use Plex
directly it is necessary to hand translate drawings into their anticipated stored form. This stored form is made up of three parts:
palette, drawing objects list and connections list and is held as a UNIX
text file. The palette specifies the repertoire of shapes available for
the construction of a drawing; the list of drawing objects specifies what
shapes occur and gives the text associated with each; the list of connections specifies the connections between the shapes (which are in terms of
the identifications of the shapes and of which the lines on the diagram
are only a physical representation).

Normally there would be a large amount of information held in this stored form (e.g. drawn physical representation) which is not pertinent to performing the translation which is interested in the logical relation-ships of activities, components and human actions; so the contents of the file are simplified by leaving out the uninteresting information as it would have to be read by the ATN Interpreter merely to be thrown away, thereby increasing the size and complexity of the network to no purpose. This simplification is permissible as extra arcs can easily be introduced merely to absorb extraneous words of input.

5.3 Prolog

The target of the translation is the language Prolog [CLOC84]. The Prolog produced only expresses the relationships given by the diagram, as it stands it is not executable. To be executable some semantics must be attached to the terminating shapes: components and human actions. This would be supplied in the form of Prolog clauses for components and human action by whoever wished to make use of the translated diagrams.

6 CONCLUSIONS

The conclusions are discussed with reference to the objectives of the study which were given in section 2.1 as these:

> is translation possible,
> does a technique exist,
> and what are the implemention difficulties?

The most important fact to note under the possibility of a translation being performed is that one was actually achieved in the case of the example. This was because there was a good match between the underlying abstract syntax of the Plex and Prolog representations of the information; with a poorer match the translation will become difficult, whether this then leaves the realm of the possible is not known. A second fact is that there are bounds on the problem beyond which transla-tion would differ qualitatively; the bounds are input from or output to other than files and multiple input and output streams.

The technique, ATN´s, exists and is judged with respect to the attributes of effectiveness, ease of use and convenience of use.

The technique demonstrated its effectiveness by performing the example translation sought.

The example is believed to be representative of the scope of the technique; from this it may be inferred that the technique is applicable throughout its scope. The size of the example shows that the technique is applicable to small problems, where smallness is measured both in terms of size of network and size of input. Large networks, provided that they are partitioned into comprehensible sub-networks, present no additional problems.

There was a certain amount of difficulty found in arriving at an ap-propriate and correct ATN for performing the example translation. This difficulty was not too great and the technique would not be too difficult for a reasonably adept software engineer to use.

The convenience of the technique can be weighed in several balances. On the one hand it would seem that the style of use is that of an inferior flowcharting method combined with an assembly language control structure; on the other hand a straw poll of my colleagues showed that reading the diagrammatic form of a network was preferred to reading C code (which in turn was preferred to the textual form). The introduction of registers reduces the complexity of a finite state automaton, but they are dynamic data structures and therefore more difficult to think about. In working out the network for the example it was necessary to draw a series of sketches of the registers at various times during the execution of the network to be sure of what was happening. Syntax errors in the input stream cause total failure of the translation. This is a good thing because recovery mechanisms must therefore be explicitly thought out for inclusion in the network – though their sheer volume will obscure the true purpose of the network. Failure is a nuisance, though, as it is extremely tedious to have the translation fail completely because of one unthought of input error. Thus, the technique is neither particularly convenient nor inconvenient to use.

The implementation difficulties are discussed at length in the detailed report [VERR86], it is sufficient to observe that they were not insurmountable as an ATN Automaton was successfully implemented.

To sum up – Augmented Transition Networks accomplished the example translation but did not expedite it.

7   ACKNOWLEDGEMENTS

This work was part of the FORTUNE project which is partially funded by the Software Engineering panel of the Alvey IT programme of the U.K. Department of Trade and Industry. The FORTUNE consortium is led by CAP Industry Ltd and includes MARI Advanced Microelectronics Ltd, Baddeley Associates Ltd and the University of Kent at Canterbury. The author wishes to thank J.J. Florentin and I.M. Richmond for their encouragement and interest.

8   REFERENCES

[BATE78] Bates, M. The Theory and Practice of Augmented Transition Network Grammers, in Bolc, L. (ed), Natural Language Communication with Computers, Springer-Verlag (1978)

[BOLC83] Bolc, L. (ed.). The Design of Interpreters, Compilers and Editors for Augmented Transition Networks, Springer-Verlag (1983)

[CLOC84] Clocksin, W.F. and Mellish, C.S. Programming in Prolog, Springer-Verlag (1984)

[CHRI83] Christaller, T. An ATN Programming Environment, in [BOLC83]

[PACT85] PACT, ESPRIT Project 951, PCTE Added Common Tools, Technical annex to contract (1985)

[KERN78] Kernighan, B.W. and Ritchie, D.M. The C Programming Language, Prentice-Hall (1978)

[MCGO87] McGowan, S.M. FORTUNE – An IPSE Documentation Tool, in this volume

[VERR86] Verrall. M.S. An Investigation into the Use of Augmented Transition Networks for Information Transfer, Alvey FORTUNE project, deliverable number 5 (1986)

[WOOD70]   Wood, W.A. Transition Network Grammars for Natural Language
           Analysis in Communications of the ACM Vol.13 No.10 591-606
           (1970)

[WRIG87]   Wright, S.J. Plex - A structured Line Diagram Editor in this
           volume.

A VIEW MECHANISM FOR AN INTEGRATED PROJECT SUPPORT

ENVIRONMENT

Alan W. Brown

Computing Laboratory

University of Newcastle upon Tyne, UK

ABSTRACT

In an attempt to increase efficiency and improve quality of large-scale
software production. Integrated Project Support Environments (IPSEs) are
being built which integrate a set of tools, methods, and techniques to
support the complete software development life cycle. Many IPSE's
provide integration with the environment by maintaining all project data
in a central database.

This paper proposes extending the traditional database notion of views to
provide a mechanism with an IPSE database that allows abstract interfaces
to the project data to be defined. All IPSE users and tools access the
project data through an abstract interface suited to their particular
needs. The design of an IPSE view mechanism is discussed in some detail,
followed by a description of an implementation of a view mechanism with
the Alvey-funded ASPECT project.

1   INTRODUCTION

In implementing a software system, a number of tasks must be carried out
to convert the initial system requirements into a complete running system
which meets those constraints. For a large system, the process of
software development can take many months (or years) to complete,
involve a large group of people, and cost thousands of pounds, so it is
not surprising that this is receiving a great deal of attention. In the
past the main thrust of attempts to improve the efficiency and quality of
software has been in the development of individual techniques and
automated tools to help with one or more of the development activities,
speeding up that task, and ensuring its correctness. Although many of
these are widely in use and have been of great benefit, the problems of
software production persist, many systems being known to be inefficient,
poorly maintained, and difficult to use. From this we can draw the
conclusion that even though there has been a great improvement in the
number and quality to tools available there is still some way to go
before we see a way through the problems.

Coupled with the existing inadequacies in software development is the
equally important trend for the increased use of software in ever more
diverse applications. This has led to the development of larger and more
complex software systems, particularly embedded real-time applications,

on which a large amount of effort needs to be spent on organisation and administration of the development system [ROWL83, CRON86].

One of the important areas in which it is expected that improvements can be made in productivity and quality of software products is in providing development environments in which integration and co-operation between tools, users, and techniques is actively encouraged through automated support. Without this support, at least the following problems may be experienced:

- different development tools often overlap in their roles and duplicate effort;

- tools designed to fit different development methods can often interfere with each other, produce inconsistent results, or are totally incompatible;

- no overall control is provided to keep track of all the system pieces which are developed during a project. This leads to configuration difficulties when building derived components, and makes it impossible for management to assess the progress of the project;

- current practice relies heavily on manual co-operation and communication to ensure that group members can work independently and yet as a team. Such problems are compounded in large, distributed projects.

Of the different approaches which are currently being tried to solve the above problems, the development of Integrated Project Support Environments (IPSEs) is receiving most attention.

2   INTEGRATED PROJECT SUPPORT ENVIRONMENTS (IPSES)

The traditional environments in which software is developed consist of a machine operating system and filing system, together with an ad hoc collection of development tools which cover some part of the development life-cycle. A software product is progressed by applying the development tools in some sequence. However, as the tools are often written without knowledge of the other tools with which they interact, each tool may expect input in some local format, and produce results which other tools cannot directly access. This leads to automated or manual filters being used to convert data from one format to another. The connection of tools in this environment is typified in figure 1.

The notion of an IPSE differs from the traditional development environment in that the integration and co-operation of development tools is seen as a key area in improving software production. One of the most fundamental ways to view an IPSE is as a mechanism for providing the infrastructure to support the complex decision-making process which is the basis of a developing software product. From this perspective, the

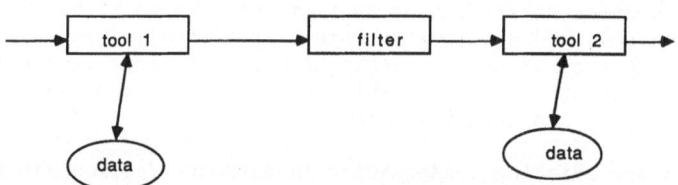

FIGURE 1:   Connection of Tools in a Traditional Development Environment

development of a software project is seen as the manipulation of a set of complex objects where all actions taken are governed by past experience, and directed by a plan for the future. The aim is to ensure that at any point in the development of a project the present state of the system is consistent with past experience, and that a complete, integrated plan exists for future development. This must be achieved within the context of changing project requirements, the existence of errors and inconsistencies, and a myriad of organisational constraints, all of which are inherent in any large project.

Seen in this way, software development is a complicated exercise in information control and manipulation. Any environment designed to support this process must be fundamentally based on mechanisms for data capture, analysis, manipulation, and control. It is not surprising, then, to see that many IPSE's currently being developed are based on a central repository of structured development data together with an interface to this information that allows controlled access by all users and tools [ALDE85, USDO85].

Communication between users and tools is through this interface, accessing the common data structures in which all information is stored. The connection of tools in such an environment is given in figure 2.

The use of a centrally controlled repository, or database, can provide at least the following advantages:

- The amount of redundantly stored data is greatly reduced. This helps reduce the number of inconsistencies in the data

- A consistent format is used for all data. This enhances communication between applications making use of the data, and provides a basis for tool writers to construct new applications;

- A controlled interface to all project data increases the amount of data validation that is possible. In this way, the checks necessary to maintain data integrity are no longer embedded in each of the tools, but centrally maintained, and uniformly applied.

- A central point is provided at which project standards can be enforced. This is important in large, distributed projects.

- Management visibility is increased, as we now have a consistent method of development over which they have some direct control.

In summary, we can say that use of a database provides central control of

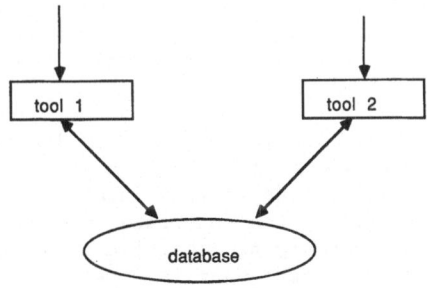

FIGURE 2:   Connection of Tools in an IPSE Built on a Central Database

all operational data, [DATE86] and is the basis of integration between
tools in a development environment.

3   THE NEED FOR A VIEW MECHANISM

One of the consequences of maintaining data in a shared database is that
all applications which access the data must work with a single,
predefined set of data structures and operators. However, in some
database applications, and particularly software engineering, a large and
diverse group of users and applications will wish to make use of the
data. For example, it is expected that a complete IPSE would be used by
project managers, quality assurance groups, clerical and administrative
staff, as well as software engineers and programmers. Also, if we wish
to use existing development tools in our IPSE, then it would be necessary
to re-write some or all of the tools to interact with the database
interface that the tool provides. The interface to which the tools are
written, often known as Public Tool Interface (PTI), needs to be stable,
but if it is also fixed and inextensible, then the following observations
can be made:

-   data structures and operators suited to one application, or class of
    user, may be inefficient, unnatural, and time-consuming to other
    users;

-   the level at which database interaction occurs through the PTI may
    be too abstract for some users (e.g. programmers), while too low-
    level for others (eg. project managers). The working requirements
    of these users are very different;

-   there will be some data which is of relevance to only a subset of
    users, and we may want to restrict access to such data to other
    users so that they are not confused by this unnecessary information;

-   often databases contain sensitive information which we may not wish
    to be generally available. Many different levels of security may
    exist, and we need a mechanism to control access to data at
    different levels. For example, if an IPSE is used in the
    development of a large, real-time application, we would need to
    record data about project costings, security procedures used by the
    application, and intimate details of working practices. It would
    not be desirable to allow all IPSE users to access to this
    information;

-   for similar reasons, we may want to restrict the operations
    different classes of user are allowed to perform on data. For
    example, at the lowest level, a user may be given read-only access
    to certain information.

Early in the development of conventional database systems the need for
such functions was apparent, and a mechanism often used to tackle some or
all of these problems is the creation of **external views** of the underlying
database.

A view mechanism allows the creation of abstract interfaces to a
database. Each interface can be tailored to a particular class of users
needs, at an abstract level suited to those users' style of interaction.
The view mapping, which defines the interface in terms of the underlying
database, filters out unnecessary or sensitive data, and may derive new
abstract data and operators. Each user is working at an abstract level
suited to their particular role, and as a result, may make quicker

progress with their task, interfere less with other users, and consequently produce more accurate results.

In a Software Engineering application, the ability to provide abstract tool interfaces to the PTI, and in this way extend the PTI, is particularly useful. Clearly tools which access the data will interact with the database at different abstract levels, which a view mechanism can support. More importantly, it is expected that existing tools will be ported to new IPSE´s, potentially requiring a great deal of rewriting. A view mechanism, however, could be used to define abstract interfaces to the database which require a minimum amount of change to the tool itself to allow it to run in the new environment.

A first attempt at designing and implementing such a view mechanism is discussed below with in the context of a particular IPSE. It is expected, however, that many of the ideas described here are independent of the IPSE used.

4   THE BASIS OF A VIEW MECHANISM FOR AN IPSE

Having discussed the need for a view mechanism, it is necessary to examine existing mechanisms which have been used in similar situations in order to provide the kind of functionality we are seeking. In particular, we can look at the traditional database notion of a view to see how it can be adapted to an IPSE. In fact, we will see that the extension of a view mechanism towards abstract data types is required.

4.1 Traditional Database Views

In existing database systems, views are used in a very simple way to provide abstractions of the data [STON86, ASTR76]. Through the definition of a view, a new abstract data object can be created which is some combination of existing data objects. In this way, a view is synonymous with a stored query, defined (for relational data-bases) using the relational algebra or calculus provided by the database system, Whenever access to a view is required, the stored query is evaluated within the context of the current state of the database. Hence, a database view can be thought of as a "window" on the database.

Nesting of views to any level is also possible, by using one view object in the definition of another view. When a nested view is evaluated, we can envisage a tree of stored queries being evaluated in an interpretive fashion (as an optimisation this interpretive process is often pre-compiled).

Though the simplicity and elegance of this approach are attractive, there are a number of drawbacks to this when we wish to design a view mechanism for an IPSE that provides environments in which tools and users access data.

1.   Providing a Closed Environment

We would like tools and users to operate in an environment which is closed in the sense that the only access to data is through the objects provided in that environment. We do not want users to be able to access lower-level objects, by-passing the interface that has been provided. In existing database view mechanisms, however, the view objects that are defined are used to extend the set of data objects available to users, and access to all objects is possible.

2. Defining Abstract Operators

Existing database view mechanisms only allow abstraction of data via stored queries, not the ability to define new abstract operators on the data. For an IPSE view mechanism, we need to be able to create environments in which the users work that include abstract operators to manipulate the available data objects. Such operators are an essential component of an environment.

3. Updating View Objects

A well-documented problem with database view mechanisms is the issue of updating view objects [KELL85, BANC79]. The usual approach is to devise an algorithm which decides by examining the definition of the object, whether it is possible to insert, update or delete elements of that object. When is is not possible to uniquely determine the inverse of the object mapping, then updates to the object are not allowed.

For an IPSE view mechanism, this approach is unsatisfactory as we wish to have the choice whether or not to allow updates to all view objects, irrespective of their definition. Only in this way will we have the necessary generality to allow the possibility of creating interfaces to the data. In the traditional data-base approach, the decision as to whether update of a view object is allowed is made as a consequence of the way the object was defined. In IPSE databases a more flexible approach is required, so that the view definer can have greater control over which objects are updatable. For example, we may want a restricted "read-only" environment for some users, even though update of the data objects is possible for others.

4.2 Views and Abstract Data Types

The approach we have taken to designing the IPSE view mechanism is to extend the traditional database notion of a view by incorporating ideas used in programming languages in creating abstract data types (adt's) [SHAW84].

Following the "package" concept of Ada (and similar constructs in other languages), an adt allows us to create abstractions of the basic data structures and operators available in the language, and provides strict support for enforcing those abstractions [BOOC83]. An adt basically consists of two parts: a set of data structures, and a set of operators which manipulate those structures.

The data structures provided are derived from existing lower-level data objects by a re-definition using the constructs available in the programming language. This is analogous to defining a view object from lower-level objects using the relational algebra or calculus as the host language. However, with adt's, a hierarchy of data structures is enforced. The new structures are derived from a set of parent structures, without any knowledge of other lower-level structures. Hence, a strict hierarchy of abstract data objects is constructed.

The other component of an adt is a set of operators which manipulate the defined data structures. These operators are expressed in a host programming language, and make calls to the defined parent operators, which manipulate the parent data structures. A strict abstract operator hierarchy is constructed, similar to the data.

An advantage of this approach is that manipulative and update operators are both similarly defined. This means that all the update operators required for an adt have predefined effects on the data structures. No changes to the data structures are possible other than through these operators.

Therefore, we can view the definition of an adt in a program as the creation of an abstract interface to the data structures of the program, with both data and operators tailored to the needs of a particular application. The view mechanism needed for an IPSE can be seen as the use of an adt mechanism on top of the IPSE database. The first steps toward this have already been taken in existing database systems, using a simple view mechanism to allow abstract data objects to be defined and accessed, while what is proposed here is to extend that mechanism to more closely resemble the adt approach.

However, an important distinction between the programming language approach to adt's and the view mechanism needed for an IPSE concerns the support given at a project level, as opposed to a programming level. In most programming languages, data is not persistent between program invocations other than through very simple file-based mechanisms. The adt mechanisms are provided for use of transitory data in the execution of a single program. Clearly, in an IPSE application it is necessary to provide a project level view mechanism which acts on data that is both structured and persistent. The data should be available for many different programs, users and tools to operate on, similar to the use of data in traditional database applications, where many diverse groups within a large enterprise may require access to the same set of data.

We now describe how an IPSE view mechanism based on these principles has been specified within a particular IPSE called ASPECT, and discuss the progress of the prototype implementation that is currently under development.

5   AN IMPLEMENTATION OF A VIEWS MECHANISM

5.1 The Aspect Project

The ASPECT project is an Alvey-funded research project aimed at the development of an IPSE called ASPECT [HALL85, DILL87]. The approach taken is to provide an infrastructure into which tools can be embedded, and to provide integration through a central structured repository in which all data created during the life time of a software project is recorded. The services provided by an ASPECT system can be divided into a number of areas:

-    distribution;

-    human-computer interface;

-    host-target facilities;

-    Information Base.

Details of the first three areas can be found elsewhere, [HALL85] while below we briefly describe the ASPECT Information Base.

5.2 The Aspect Information Base

At the heart of an ASPECT system is an Information Base which is the structured repository for all data created in the development of a software project [BROW86a]. The Information Base is a database, but contains in addition

- its own definition; structural information about the database itself is stored and can be accessed in an identical way to all other data;

- a rules mechanism to support the definition and application of user-defined constraints on the database;

- built-in software engineering functions, particularly for identification of versions, and building configurations of data items.

Access to these, and all other functions of ASPECT, is via the ASPECT Public Tool Interface (PTI), which provides a formal tool writer's interface through which the services of the Information Base are available [ROBI86, BROW86b].

5.3 The Aspect View Mechanism

Recognising the arguments presented earlier, an important feature of the ASPECT PTI is that it includes facilities for its own extension through a view mechanism. This means that a set of primitive functions are available at the PTI to enable users and tools to define and make use of abstract data and operators in a structured and controlled way.

The approach taken in ASPECT is to insist that all users of an ASPECT system work within an **abstract environment (AE)** which provides an abstract interface to the ASPECT system built upon the facilities available at the PTI. The AE provides a set of data objects and operators tailored to that particular class of user's needs. The user cannot access the Information Base other than through the facilities offered in their AE. Then, when a user is assigned an activity to be carried out in the ASPECT system, that user is also given an AE in which to execute the activity. This will provide the data and operators necessary to perform the activity at an abstract level which is appropriate to the task.

Similarly, a tool that runs within ASPECT which has not been written to the primitives specified at the PTI, known to ASPECT as a 'foreign' tool, will run within an AE which has been defined to emulate the tool's native operating environment. The data and operators seen by this tool will be mapped to underlying ASPECT PTI operations, which make controlled calls to the Information Base.

By way of an example, we can examine the approach to be used in ASPECT to allow the UNIX tool set to operate within an ASPECT IPSE. The tools provided by UNIX are written to a set of primitives which allow access to the UNIX operating system and filing system facilities. For example, data is presented as a collection of files related in a tree structure, and operators exist to open files, read data from a file, and close files. If UNIX tools are to be made available in an ASPECT system, then there are three possible ways in which they could be integrated:

1   As ASPECT is hosted on a UNIX system, these tools could be allowed to bypass the ASPECT PTI and directly interact with the operating system;

2   The tools could be partially re-written to make ASPECT PTI calls instead of UNIX system calls;

3   A view of the ASPECT PTI could be defined which closely resembles the UNIX system call interface. With minimum modification, the

tools can then run within this view, and still access the ASPECT services through the PTI.

The first of these alternatives was rejected as it destroys the desired uniformity of approach to tool integration that ASPECT intends to provide, it side-steps the semantically-rich interface offered at the PTI, and it binds ASPECT to the UNIX operating system as its host. The second possibility is unattractive as it requires a great deal of redundant work re-writing tools that already exist. The third alternative, which has been adopted by ASPECT, means that all tools, written to any interface, can be uniformly integrated into an ASPECT system by defining a suitable view of the ASPECT PTI. By insisting that all data access and manipulation is ultimately performed through the PTI, the integrity constraints enforced there are consistently applied. This special UNIX view of the PTI is known as the ASPECT Open Tool Interface (OTI). Currently being investigated by the project is the extent to which ASPECT OTI can be implemented using the view mechanism, without regard for the semantics of the tools themselves.

5.3.1   Hierarchies of AE's

It is intended that the ASPECT view mechanism will be used at a project level, with the definition of AE's taking place in hierarchical fashion mirroring the traditional project structure. Hence, all the objects available in one AE will be defined purely in terms of those in its parent AE in the hierarchy. The lowest level AE at the root of this hierarchy, known as the Base Environment (BE), is the complete ASPECT PTI itself, available to manipulate all the data maintained in the Information Base with the operators provided at the PTI. As each AE is created, and the AE hierarchy is extended, interfaces to the Information Base will be provided at increasingly higher abstract levels.

Operating within a particular AE in this hierarchy, evaluation of a data object, or execution of an operation, will result in this call being interpreted at successively lower levels, until a sequence of calls to ASPECT PTI functions is made on the lowest data items. These operations will then be executed to create the effect requested by the single high level operation.

5.3.2   An example

To illustrate the ASPECT view mechanism in use, consider the simple example given below.

Suppose we held data in our Information Base concerning programmers, change requests for software components, and assignments of programmers to carry out these change requests. Represented in simple relational terms, the Information Base may contain the following data:

PROGRAMMERS		
PROG ID	NAME	AGE
p1	fred	32
p2	joe	21
p3	jane	26

CHANGE REQUESTS			
CR ID	DESCRIPTION	REPORT DATE	STATUS
cr1	fault in output	12-10-85	outstanding
cr2	crashes on output	8-11-85	completed
cr3	update documentation	23-6-86	outstanding
cr4	add new option	15-7-86	outstanding

ASSIGNMENTS		
PROG ID	CR ID	DEADLINE
p1	cr1	18-3-86
p2	cr2	20-8-86
p2	cr4	7-10-86

Coupled with this data will be a set of operators to insert, delete, and update individual tuples of each relation.

This lowest level view, or Base Environment (BE), will be used by the project controller who is responsible for all project data, and for initially setting up the AE hierarchy. For example, the project controller may wish to define the AE for the chief programmer which shows all assigned change requests with the programmers assigned to them, and also an operator to change the status of a change request to "completed" when the change has been carried out by junior programmers.

To do this, the project controller, who is working with in the Base Environment , will define the data objects and operators necessary for the chief programmers in terms of the data and operators available in the Base Environment. When the chief programmer works in this AE, it may contain the following data:

CR ID	DESCRIPTION	REPORT DATE	STATUS	NAME	DEADLINE
cr1	fault in output	12-10-85	outstanding	fred	18-3-86
cr2	crashes on output	8-11-85	completed	joe	20-8-86
cr4	add new option	15-7-86	outstanding	joe	7-10-86

Also, an operator "change-status" will be available, which, given the identifier of a change request in the data object, will change the status of that request from "outstanding" to "completed". This operator will have been defined by the project controller as a sequence of lower level operations to insert, delete, and update individual tuples of relations using the operators provided in the BE.

Now suppose the chief programmer wishes to define an AE in which a junior programmer can work that only allows that programmer to see his/her own outstanding change requests, and not be given any operators to amend them. The chief programmer would do this by defining the AE in terms of the data and operators he/she has available in his/her own AE. In effect, the newly defined AE would be a further abstraction on what he/she has available. For example, this may result in the data shown below, with no operators being defined to manipulate or update this data:

CR ID	DESCRIPTION	DEADLINE
CR4	ADD NEW OPTION	7-10-86

The final result, then, will be a simple hierarchy of AE's with the Base
Environment at the root, and the chief programmer and junior programmer
AE's at subsequent levels, as shown in figure 3.

Clearly, this is an over-simplified example to give a flavour of the
ASPECT view mechanism in operation. Without much difficulty, it is
possible to envisage how this example could be extended to support a much
larger project.

5.4 Current Status of Implementation

Implementation of the ASPECT view mechanism, as with all ASPECT
facilities, has been carried out by the specification and implementation
of two separate prototypes. The facilities provided by the first of
these have been fully specified using the normal notation Z [SUFR85], and
have been implemented and demonstrated within the project.

The purpose of the first prototype was to demonstrate the feasibility of
the approach that had been discussed, and to provide feedback for further
development.

To do this, the functionality of the view mechanism was reduced so that
only data in relational form could be defined within an AE, and a single
set of relational operators to manipulate these objects was inherited in
each AE. This still provided a mechanism at least as powerful as those
available in many existing relational database management systems.

The view mechanism was implemented as a series of C language functions
written on top of an ASPECT PTI which itself was implemented as a set C
language functions. These primitives interact with the ASPECT
Information Base, which is an implementation of Codd's Extended
Relational Model (RM/T) [CODD79, DATE83] on top of the commercially
available relational database management system, DB++.

Users of the view mechanism invoked the view primitives through writing a
C program, including the library of view functions provided, and making
calls to the individual view primitives. Information concerning which
AE's had been defined, the objects contained in an AE, and the mappings
between AE objects, were all held as entities in the ASPECT Information
Base, and hence were accessible to the primitives when validation was
required. This was a uniform, integrated approach to implementation, as
all the data created by the view mechanism was maintained within the
Information Base, controlled by the integrity constraints imposed on it,

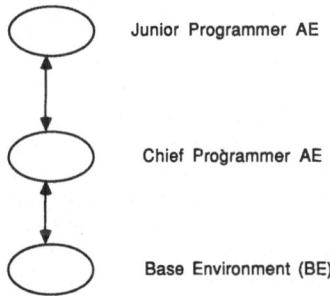

FIGURE 3 The Hierarchy of AE's created in this example

and available to users and tools in the same way that all other ASPECT data is accessed.

The second prototype view mechanism is currently being specified as an extension of the earlier work, and follows analysis and evaluation of the initial implementation. In particular, the initial prototype is to be extended in two ways:

- by the ability to define abstract operators within an AE allowing the full functionality of the view mechanism described earlier;

- using a more expressive language to define data abstractions to allow arbitrary data transformations between AE's.

In addition to this work, it is planned that the ASPECT view mechanism will be demonstrated in two ways. Firstly, a tool will be built on top of the view mechanism to allow AE's to be created interactively. In the first prototype, a C programming language interface was the only way to access the view primitives. For the second prototype, an interactive view definition tool will be developed to remove much of the burden of defining an AE. Secondly, at least some part of the ASPECT Open Tool Interface (OTI), will be supported as an AE. This will enable a number of UNIX tools to run within ASPECT by providing those tools with a view of the PTI resembling their native environment.

Specification in Z of this second phase of work is almost complete, with the implementation to be completed in early Summer 1987.

6   OVERVIEW OF RELATED WORK

The background and influences of the work reported here have come from a number of different areas of computing. A brief summary of these is given below.

6.1 Databases

From the early implementations of database systems, the usefulness of being able to present a number of external representations of the same logical information was apparent. This is perhaps best described in the reports of the ANSI/SPARC Study Group [TSIC78]. As a result, many database systems provide facilities for selection and abstraction of data through a views mechanism. As described earlier, however, the majority of systems use a view mechanism only to allow new data objects to be available to the user; there is no attempt to define operators specifically for this new view, so that it is not possible to create an abstract data type in a database system.

6.1.1. Adding abstract data types to a database

The trend in the last few years has been to use databases for an increasingly varied range of applications. This has greatly influenced current work in the area, with many researchers proposing new database architectures and mechanisms better suited to a particular application [LORI81, BUCH84]. One of the proposals of interest is the adding of abstract data type (adt) facilities to a relational database [OSBO86, ONG79]. This mechanism allows users to create their own domains, and operators on the domains, from which data values in the database can be drawn. In this way, the complex data objects which are commonly found in design applications can be more closely modelled. Unfortunately, in this work there has been no attempt to couple the use of adt's with a hierarchical view mechanism that collects the abstract objects to form

294

environments in which users work. This use of the view mechanism as a project-level device has been ignored.

6.2 Programming Languages

6.2.1   Abstract data types and objects

A constant theme within the development of programming languages has been increasing the support provided for data abstraction [SHAW84]. Ultimately, this has led to the development of abstract data typing facilities within programming languages, exemplified by the "package" concept of Ada [BOOC83], and the concept of objects in object-oriented programming languages such as C++ [STRO86]. The overriding need for these concepts has been to control the complexity inherent in the large applications now being addressed by computer systems. In most of these system, however, there is no attempt to tie the languages to a repository for structured data such as a database.

6.2.2   Adding a persistent data store

One of the problems with many programming languages which deal with data at an object level, is that there are no facilities in the language to record the objects in a data store that persists between program invocations [ATKI78]. Attempts to address this have progressed in three ways:

-    the addition of ad hoc constructs in a programming language in order to support a database model. For example, the addition of relational constructs in to an existing programming language [SCHM77].

-    design of programming languages specifically to interact with data in a persistent store. For example, the languages PLAIN [WASS79] and RIGEL [ROWE79] are specifically designed for the construction of database applications.

-    developing techniques to support persistent data which use the constructs already available in a programming language. PS-Algol is an example of such an approach [ATKI81].

Very little use is made of views in any of these languages, though RIGEL does have facilities for creating view modules without enforcing a view hierarchy.

In a recent paper by Wiederhold [WIED86] proposals are made to add persistent objects to an object oriented system for Computer-Aided Design applications through the use of database views. The resultant "view-objects" appear very similar to the objects defined within an ASPECT AE, though at a programmer-level as opposed to a project level. It will be interesting to see how his work develops.

6.3 Programming Support Environments

Perhaps the work that is most closely related to the ideas presented here have been carried out in the context of developing structure editing environments [KAIS85, GARL83].

A number of programming environments are based on the notion of a set of tools which manipulate a program that is stored in the form of an abstract syntax tree. The single representation of often inappropriate for many tools, so by providing a view mechanism, the individual tools can work within a view of the program suited to their needs. Although in a different domain, this work has very similar aims to that presented here.

7 CONCLUSIONS

Arising from the need to produce well-engineered software for increasingly complex applications at an economical cost, the current trend is to integrate automated development tools within an environment that provides the infrastructure necessary to ensure that individual tools are used consistently and effectively within a large software project. The tools interact with the support environment through a well-defined interface, known as a Public Tool Interface (PTI), that provides the primitives necessary to access and manipulate the development data [LYON86].

This paper has discussed the need for an extended view mechanism within an environment to allow the tools to interface with the environment at abstract levels suited to their individual needs. The view mechanism allows abstractions of the PTI to be created which permit the tools to access data in the format each tool expects, and using operators that are meaningful at that level, while preserving at a lower-level the consistent semantic interface provided by the PTI.

An equally important use for the view mechanism is as a project-level mechanism for providing abstract environments in which users can access project data and perform development activities. The view mechanism provides the ability to maintain control of data interactions at a project-level, and to restrict the data and operations each class of user is allowed to perform.

A particular implementation of such a view mechanism, within the ASPECT project, allows the creation of abstract environments (AE's) in a hierarchy, mirroring the hierarchical composition of many development projects. Through this implementation the practical feasibility of many of the ideas discussed here will be evaluated.

8 ACKNOWLEDGEMENTS

ASPECT is funded by SERC through the Alvey Software Engineering Directorate, and involves a consortium comprising Systems Designers, the Universities of York and Newcastle upon Tyne, MARI and ICL.

The work reported here has benefited greatly from the ideas and enthusiasm of many of the ASPECT team, in particular Peter Hitchcox, Ray Weedon, Dave Robinson, Ant Earl, Dick Whittington and Ben Dillistone - not forgetting the work of Anthony Hall in the early days of the project. Thanks also to Brian Randell for commenting on earlier drafts of this paper.

9 REFERENCES

[ALDE85] Alderson, A., Bott, M.F., "An Overview of the Eclipse Project", pp. 100-113 in Integrated Project Support Environments, ed. J. McDermid, Peter Peregrinus (1985).

[ASTR76] Astrahan, M.M. and others. "System R: Relational Approach to Database Management," ACM TODS 1(2) (June 1976).

[ATKI78]   Atkinson, M.P., "Database Systems and Programming Languages," Proceedings of 4th VLDB Conference, pp. 408-419 (September 1978).

[ATKI81]   Atkinson, M.P., Chisolm, K., and Cockshott, P., "PS-Algol: an Algol with a Persistent Heap," CSR-94-81, University of Edinburgh (December 1981).

[BANC79]   Bancilhon, F., "Supporting View Updates in Relational Databases," in Database Architectures, ed. Bracci, North Holland (1979).

[BOOC83]   Booch, G., Software Engineering with Ada, Benjamin/Cummings Pub. Co (1983).

[BROW86a] Brown, A.W., Earl, A.N., Hitchcock, P., Weedon, R., and Whittington, R.P., "The Use of Databases for Software Engineering," pp. 55-70 in Proceedings of the Fifth British National Conference on Databases (BNCOD5). ed. E.A. Oxborrow (14th - 16th July 1986).

[BROW86b] Brown, A.W., Robinson, D.S., and Weedon, R.A., "Managing Software Development," pp. 197-235 in Software Engineering '86, ed. P. Brown, Peter Peregrinus (1986).

[BUCH84]   Buchmann, A.P., "Current Trends in CAD Databases," Computer-Aided Design 16 (May 1984).

[CODD79]   Codd, E.F., "Extending the Database Relational Model to Capture More Meaning," ACM Transactions on Database Systems, IBM Research Laboratory 4(4), pp. 397-434 (December 1979).

[CRON86]   Cronshaw, P., "The Experimental Aircraft Programme software toolset," Software Engineering Journal, pp. 236-247 (November 1986).

[DATE83]   Date, C.J., An Introduction to Database Systems Volume II, Addison-Wesley (1983).

[DATE86]   Date, C.J., An Introduction to Database Systems Vol 1, Addison-Wesley (1986).

[DILL87]   Dillistone, B.R., Earl, A.N. and Whittington, R.P., "Using Databases to Automate System Development," This Volume.

[GARL83]   Garlan, D.B., "Views for Tools in Software Development Environments," Ph.D Thesis Proposal, Carnegie-Mellon University (May 1983).

[HALL85]   Hall, J.A., Hitchcock, P., and Took, R., "An overview of the ASPECT Architecture," pp. 86-99 in Integrated Project Support Environments, ed. J. McDermid, Peter Peregrinus Ltd. (1985).

[KAIS85]   Kaiser, G.E., "Semantics for Structure Editing Environments," CMU-C5-85-131, Carnegie-Mellon University (May 1985).

[KELL85]   Keller, A.M., "Updating Relational Databases Through Views," Ph.D Thesis, Stanford University (Feb 1985).

[LORI81]   Lorie, R.A. Issues in Databases for Design Applications., IBM Research Report (1981).

[LYON86]   Lyons, T.G.L., "The Public Tool Interface in Software Engineering Environments," Software Journal 1(6), pp. 254-258 (November 1986).

[ONG79]   Ong, J., Fogg, D., and Stonebraker, M., "Implementation of Abstraction in the Relational Database INGRES." ACM SIGMOD 14(1). pp. 1-14 (1979).

[OSBO86]   Osborn, S.L. and Heaven, T.E., "The Design of a Relational Database System with Abstract Data Types for Domains," ACM TODS 11(3), pp. 357-373 (September 1986).

[ROBI86]   Robinson, D.S., "ASPECT - Specification of the Public Tool Interface," aspect/wb/pub/pti/Zspec2.1, Systems Designers PLC. (July 1986).

[ROWE79]   Rowe, L.A. and Shoens, K.A., "Data Abstraction, Views and Updates in RIEGEL," ACM.SIGMOD (1979).

[ROWL83]   Rowland, B.R. and Welsch, R.J., "Software Development System," Bell Systems Technical Journal 62(1) (January 1983).

[SCHM77]   Schmidt, J.W., "Some High-Level Language Constructs for Data of Type Relation," ACM TODS 2(3), pp. 247-261 (September 1977).

[SHAW84]   Shaw, M., "Abstraction Techniques in Modern Programming Languages," IEEE Software pp. 10-26 (October 1984).

[STON86]   Stonebraker, M., The INGRES Papers, Addison-Wesley (1986).

[STRO86]   Stroustrup, B., The C++ Programming Language, Addison-Wesley (1986).

[SUFR85]   Sufrin, B., Morgan, C., Sorensen, I., and Hayes, I., Notes for a Z Handbook Part 1 - Mathematical Language, Oxford University Computing Laboratory, PRG, July 1985.

[TSIC78]   Tsichritzis, D.C. and Klug, A., "The ANSI/X3/SPARC DBMS framework report of the study group on database management systems," Inf. Syst. 3 pp. 173-191 (1978).

[USDA85]   US.DOD., "Common APSE Interface Set (CAIS)." Proposed MIL-STD-CAIS (January 1985).

[WASS79]   Wasserman, A.I., "The Data Management Facilities of PLAIN," Proceedings of ACM SIGMOD International Conference on the Management of Data (1979).

[WIED86]   Wiederhold, G., "Views, Objects, and Databases," IEEE Computer, pp. 37-44 (December 1986).

USING DATABASES TO AUTOMATE SYSTEM DEVELOPMENT

B.R. Dillistone, A.N. Earl and R.P. Whittington

Department of Computer Science, University of York

England.

ABSTRACT

This paper derives from work carried out as part of the Alvey supported
Aspect project. The project brings together a number of organisations
with a common interest in integrated project support environments
(IPSEs), and allows research and development into various realms of IPSE
development and use. One of these realms involves the application of
databases to the problems of software development: managing the large and
complex collection of data objects that arise during the development of
large and complex software systems.

We describe an abstract formalism that we have adopted as a means of
absorbing the complexity of data modelling in an IPSE, illustrate the
application of the formalism by means of a simple example and summarise
the software support that is necessary.

ACKNOWLEDGEMENTS

Aspect is funded by SERC through the Alvey Software Engineering
Directorate, and involves a consortium comprising Systems Designers, the
Universities of Newcastle upon Tyne and York, MARI, and ICL.

Credit is due to many members of the project for their ideas and contributions to this work, especially Dave Robinson, Peter Hitchcock, Alan
Brown, Ray Weedon, and Anthony Hall (no longer on the project).

1   INTRODUCTION

The Aspect project is funded through the Alvey Software Engineering
Directorate. It involves a consortium comprising Systems Designers, ICL,
MARI, and the Universities of York and Newcastle-upon-Tyne; and provides
a framework for collaborative research into and development of integrated
project support environments (IPSE's).

For flexibility, the project team decided not to build a single, all-
embracing IPSE, but to concentrate on an 'IPSE kit': a library of parts
which can be configured to produce an IPSE that meets the requirements of
a development project. This library will include human-computer interface components, target system interface components (to assist in the

development of real-time distributed target software) and information base interface components. This paper reports on the _Aspect_ approach to the last of these.

It has been appreciated for some time that database techniques can bring to the development and management of information systems the same benefits that they bring to the class of commercial applications that spawned them (see [VERN84] for a survey of the relevant literature); essentially, these result from high-level manipulation interfaces, automatic integrity control, and the support of transactions. The differences in requirement of design-orientated database management systems have been addressed elsewhere (for example [BOER85, GUTT82]), and, although it is not useful to repeat the details here, the following points are worth making.

*   In a typical commercial application the number of instances per type is very large, whereas in a typical design system this is less so (clearly this depends on the way in which the design process is formulated, but it is, nevertheless, a useful observation).

*   In a design system the number of types of relationship between data objects is large, as compared to the number found in typical commercial applications, and moreover, new types of relationship are occasionally required to be created dynamically. This means that it is more difficult (and more important) to maintain the integrity of a design database.

*   A design system typically manages the configuration of a design using recursive structures - such types of structure are less common in commercial applications.

The above points indicate that design systems in general (including IPSE's) require not only database techniques typically found in commercial applications, but also enhanced techniques for managing the increased complexity of design applications, and for meeting the requirements for new functionalities. It is also worth noting that, although design applications are not equal in magnitude to very large commercial application databases, it is not unusual for a software engineering database to exceed 1000 Megabytes.

In an _Aspect_ IPSE, all data objects are held in a shareable repository called an information base (the term is taken from [GRIE82] and has the sense of a self-describing, heterogeneous collection of data). Tools, sources, symbol tables, process histories, budgets, assignments of staff to activities, etc, are all captured by a common formalism, and it is the nature of this formalism and the effect which this approach has that we address in this paper.

Software engineering is a complex discipline. A good development environment is one that absorbs much of this complexity, thus freeing the developer (including the project manager, the tool writer and the developer of the the target software) to concentrate on the skilled tasks for which they are trained. It is our thesis that the key to absorbing this complexity is the abstract modelling formalism; the more abstract the formalism, the more complexity that is absorbed, and the more the developer is freed.

Other projects have based their work on a similar thesis, [UDAG84, BULL84] but none of these use such high-level concepts as we have chosen to base our work on. In addition, no project of similar size that we know of has formally defined the semantics of their formalism . Such an

300

activity is necessary prior to adopting a formalism that we will have such crucial consequences on all environments that are built upon it. We have applied a formal specification language, Z, [SUFR85] to define our formalism, and this definition activity uncovered several interesting shortcomings with the formalism that we adopted.

This paper first describes the data modelling formalism that we are using and then gives an example of its application to the problem of version management in a development environment. This example is not intended to be an ideal solution to this problem (indeed, the Aspect project aims to provide no single solution to such problems, but a framework in which any solution can be expressed), but rather an illustration of the effectiveness of the formalism, and a demonstration of the degree to which complexity can be absorbed by the use of the approach taken, to underline our claim that for a development environment to be practical it must be based on a well-defined abstract database modelling formalism.

2   THE MODELLING FORMALISM

Having decided that it was only through using an abstract modelling formalism as its foundation that the information base of our IPSEs could manage the complexity of data and their relationships, we chose the Extended Relational Model (RM/T) as the most appropriate existing model.

RM/T was first proposed by Codd [CODD79] and was then revised and clarified by Date [DATE83]. Those publications formed the entire description and discussion of RM/T until we initiated an investigation as to its applicability in supporting software engineering. Since then we have published a complete formal specification of RM/T [WALK86] and other papers describing its use [EARL85] and specification [EARL86].

Later in this section we shall describe some of the features of RM/T which are of particular importance in supporting an IPSE. But firstly, we wish to outline our approach of using the existing, informal descriptions of RM/T as the basis for developing a formal specification of RM/T, through which toolwriters and the other members of the Aspect project could examine the exact functionality of the database even before implementation had begun.

LEVELS OF FORMALISM

We have been dealing with a number of levels of formalism and the example in the next section of this paper will introduce even more levels. It is important to distinguish clearly between these levels.

There is RM/T itself, which is a semantic data modelling formalism. We can use this formalism (in whatever notation seems appropriate) to model real-world systems or systems we wish to build and/or study. Then there are descriptions of RM/T. Codd's and Date's descriptions use the formalism of English (with some additional mathematical and diagrammatic formalism). Our Z description uses the formalisms of mathematical set theory and predicate calculus with an accompanying description of the mathematics in English. We have used the existing, informal English descriptions to create a formal, Z description of RM/T so that we know exactly what is meant by any description of a system in terms of RM/T. It also means that our final level of formalism, an implementation of RM/T in some programming language, can be verified against the formal specification.

One of the main benefits from developing a formal specification of RM/T was the discovery of omissions, errors, and areas of uncertainty in the existing descriptions of RM/T. We can categorise these problems into three areas. Firstly, there are discrepancies of a theoretical nature. For example, neither of their different catalog structures effectively cover the self-referential requirements implied by the model. Another example is where they say that subtypes of kernel entity-types must also be kernel. This is not true. Secondly, there are many additional operators required to update the database, and these should be expressed at the level of Create entity-type rather than Create relation. Thirdly, their descriptions mix the two levels of formalism within RM/T itself. They are the level which contains entity-types and attributes, and the level of database relations (i.e. e-relations and p-relations). We have not only clearly separated those two levels within our formal specification but also defined a mapping between those two levels.

THE SPECIFICATION OF RM/T

We now describe in more detail some of the concepts within RM/T. It is not our intention to present a complete formal specification here. The concepts are chosen because they are concepts which give particularly good support for an IPSE, or because they are used in the example in the next section.

There are three parts to any data model. Firstly, there are the objects and their structure. Secondly, there are operations which can be performed on the data structures. And thirdly, there are rules concerning both the state of the data structures and the operations which may be applied to change their state.

The basic objects within an RM/T database are called **entities** and are uniquely identified by system-generated **surrogates**. These allow us to provide a flexible approach to naming and to overcome some of the problems traditionally associated with naming [KENT79]. Structure is imposed upon the collection of entities by insisting that each is of at least a single **entity-type**. Associated with each entity-type is a set of **attributes** within which single-valued pieces of information about entities of that type can be held. There is a subtype hierarchy allowing inheritance of attributes and overcoming of the property applicable problem.

The classification of entity-types into kernel, associative, characteristic, and designative enables the set of integrity rules to be imposed on the relevant entities. For example, if an entity-type is associative, then any entity of that type must associate two or more existing entities of the relevant types.

Let us now look at how these ideas can be formally expressed in Z. Z uses the notation of set theory slightly extended to enable pieces of mathematical text to be named and thus manipulated. We will explain those extensions as they are introduced.

Suppose then, that we have the set of all possible entity types, ET. The set of entity types in our database will be called "entity_types". We assume that this set can be partitioned into sets of entity types of different classes.

We say this in Z by means of a schema called ETYPES. This is simply a box, the top half of which is known as the signature and contains declarations of variable along with their types, and the bottom half is called the predicate part and contains predicates relating to the variables.

```
ETYPES

     entity_types,
     kernel,
     associative,
     characteristic,
     designative          :|F ET
   _____

                          ETYPES.1
   <kernel, associative, characteristic>
                          partitions entity_types

                          ETYPES.2
     designative ⊆ entity_types
```

ETYPES.1: The set entity_types is partitioned by the sets kernel, associative, and characteristic.

ETYPES.2: The set designative is a subset of entity_types so that any entity-type can be designative.

Entities

Suppose we have a set of all the possible entities, E. We call the set of entities in the database, <u>entities</u>.

We know that single entities can be of several types and so the database must allow us to express some relationship between entities and entity-types. To do this, we incorporate a function called, <u>type of entity</u>.
[E]

```
ENTS

     ETYPES
     entities      :  |FE
     type_of_entity : E --|➔ |F ET
   _____

                     ENTS.1
   ∪rng type_of_entity ⊆ entity_types

                     ENTS.2
   ∀e:entities . #type_of_entity(e)≥1
```

This is our first example of schema <u>inclusion</u> which means that all the declarations in ETYPES are considered present in the signature of ENTS, and all the predicates of ETYPES are present within the predicate part of ENTS.

ENTS.1: The types of an entity are always entity-types which exist in the database.

ENTS.2: All entities in the database are of at least one type. We will further constrain this in our description of subtypes so that an entity can be of only one type other than all its supertypes.

In our complete specification, we continue by describing a subtype hierarchy of entity types, having introduced attributes and values. We skip those definitions here and go on to present the schema that relates attributes to their types and values.

```
AT_VALUES

    ATTRIBUTES
    VALUES
    type_of_attribute          : AT --|--> VTYPE
    attribute_value            : E --> AT --|--> V
    _____

    dom attribute_value=entities

                          AT_VALUES.1
    rng type_of_attribute ⊆ value_types ∧

    dom type_of_attribute = attributes


                                        AT_VALUES.2
    ∀ et:entity types; e:entities; a:attributes⌐
              et ∈ type_of_entity(e)
              a ∈ attributes_of(et)
          attribute_value(e)(a) ∈
              domain_of(type_of_attribute(a))
```

AT_VALUES.1: ensures that every attribute in the database has a value type which exists in the database.

AT_VALUES.2: says that all values of attributes come from the correct domain.
Let us also look at how we define associative entity-types.

ASSOCIATIONS

```
┌─────────────────────────────────────────────────────────────────┐
│   ENTS                                                           │
│   AT_VALUES                                                      │
│   associates        : ET --|─→ AT --|─→ ET                      │
├──────────────────────────┘                                      │
│                                                                 │
│      dom associates = associative                               │
│      dom rng associates ⊆ attributes                            │
│                                                                 │
│      rng rng associates ⊆ entity_types                          │
│                                                                 │
│                         ASSOCIATIONS.1                          │
│      ∀ aet : dom associates; a:attributes|                      │
│               a ∈ dom associates(aet).                          │
│            a ∈ attributes_of(aet) ∧                             │
│            type_of_attribute(a) = e_type                        │
│                                                                 │
│                            ASSOCIATIONS.2                       │
│                                                                 │
│      ∀ aet : associative                                        │
│      ∃≥2 aa : attributes |                                      │
│                     aa ∈ attributes_of(aet).                    │
│         aa    dom associates(aet)                               │
│                                                                 │
│                            ASSOCIATIONS.3                       │
│      ∀ aet:associative; ae:entities; aa:attributes |            │
│            aet ∈ type_of_entity(ae) ∧                           │
│            aa ∈ dom associates(aet)                             │
│      ∃ et:entity_types; e:entities |                            │
│               et ∈ type_of_entity(e) ∧                          │
│               (aa |─→ et) ∈ associates(aet).                    │
│         attribute_value(ae)(aa) = e                             │
│                                                                 │
└─────────────────────────────────────────────────────────────────┘
```

ASSOCIATIONS.1: says that attributes which hold the associative
references are of type e_type. That is the value type of surrogates.

ASSOCIATIONS.2: says that there must be at least two participants in an
association.

ASSOCIATIONS.3: says that an associative entity can only exist if all the
participants in the association also exist, i.e. Integrity Rule 6
(Association Integrity).

In our complete specification we define designative and characteristic
entity-types in a similar fashion. We then introduce a mapping from the
abstract ideas of entities and entity-types to their more concrete representation in terms of Codd's relations. In brief, an entity-type maps to
an E-relation which contains all the surrogates of entities of that type,
and a set of P-relations which hold the values of attributes of entities
of that type. Out definition of a relation is very straightforward.

REL _____

> attributes : $\mathbb{F}$ AT
> tuples : $\mathbb{P}$ TUP
>
> _____
>
> REL.1
> $\forall$ t : tuples . dom t = attributes

That is, a relation is a set of attributes, and a set of tuples

REL.1: the domain of each tuple is exactly the set of attributes.

We present here, some of our definitions of operations upon relations.

Firstly, we give an example of an operation from the basic relational model. There are a multitude of operations that can be defined to cover the functionality of the basic relational model. We chose to follow the operators in [HALL75]. Generalised Intersection (join) is probably the most useful of our relational operators. Informally, it is set intersection when the relations are union compatible (i.e. have identical attributes). It is cartesian product when there are no attributes in common. All other cases are equivalent to natural-join.

We have defined it here as a Z <u>function</u>. This is indicated by the double lines across the top of the box. The $\lhd$ symbol is <u>domain restriction.</u>

> join : REL REL $\longrightarrow\!\!\!\!\rightarrow$ REL
> ==
>
> $\forall$ r1,r2:REL .
>
> INTERSECT.1
> join(r1,r2).attributes = r1.attributes $\cup$ r2.attributes
>
> INTERSECT.2
> join(r1,r2).tuples =
>   {t:TUP |
>   dom t $\in$ (r1.attributes $\cup$ r2.attributes) $\wedge$
>   r1.attributes $\lhd$ t $\in$ r1.tuples $\wedge$
>   r2.attributes $\lhd$ t $\in$ r2.tuples
>   }

INTERSECT.1: The attributes of the result is the union of the attributes of the operands.

INTERSECT.2: The tuples of the result are those from either relation whose values do not differ wherever the attributes overlap.

Another example is Generalised Project (project) which also allows attributes to be renamed.

$$\text{project : REL} \times (\text{AT} \dashmapsto \text{AT}) \dashrightarrow \text{REL}$$

GPROJECT.1
$$\forall \text{r:REL; q:AT} \dashmapsto \text{AT} \mid$$
$$\forall \text{a:AT} \mid \text{a} \in (\text{rng q} \cap \text{r.attributes}),$$
$$\text{Type\_of a} = \text{Type\_of } (q^{-1}(a)).$$

GPROJECT.2
$$\text{project(r,q).attributes} = q^{-1}(\text{r.attributes} \cap \text{rng q})$$

GPROJECT.3
$$\text{project(r,q).tuples} = \{\text{t:TUP} \mid \text{t} \in \text{r.tuples} \bullet \text{q; t}\}$$

GPROJECT.1: q is a function from NEW attributes to OLD attributes. And we have to include the constraint on q that the new attributes are of the same types as the old attributes.

GPROJECT.2: The attributes of the result are the ones mapped from in q which are also in the given relation.

GPROJECT.3: The tuples of the result are the tuples of the original relation except that some attributes may be missing or renamed as specified in q.

We also give an example of one of the similar RM/T operators. Informally, PTUPLE(r) promotes each tuple of a relation into an individual relation.

$$\text{PTUPLE : REL} \rightarrowtail \text{P REL}$$

PTUPLE.1
$$\text{PTUPLE(r)} = \{\text{rel:REL} \mid \text{rel.attributes} = \text{R.attributes} \wedge$$
$$\text{rel.tuples} \subseteq \text{r.tuples} \wedge$$
$$\#\text{rel.tuples} = 1$$
$$\}$$

PTUPLE.1: Returns the set of relations with the same attributes as the one given and with just one tuple from the one given.

One of the most important concepts within RM/T is the **Catalog** (or data dictionary). This holds all the information concerning the structure of the database itself. Its importance within an integrated environment is twofold. Its contents are exactly specified and can thus be kept up-to-date automatically. And it can be queried in just the same way as any of the other entity-types in the database. We feel that one of the strengths of our specification is that we have specified the catalog entities just as entities whose existence and values can be expressed in terms of the current database state. We have avoided confusion by not specifying the catalog in terms of relations.

RM/T is an extension of the basic relational model [CODD70]. This offers the advantage of a strong foundation of previous work and theory upon

which to build. For example, the study of query languages, or the study
of distribution of relational databases. Within RM/T there is a representation of entity-types and entities defined in terms of relations.
The operations of RM/T are a superset of the relational algebra. The
additional operators are of particular use to the database designer and
view-definer.

3   AN EXAMPLE

We now present a simple example of the use of RM/T. The aim is to show
how and why RM/T might be used to construct part of software development
environment. The example chosen is of a very simple version control
system. Note that the purpose of the example is to illustrate the use of
RM/T as a data engineering formalism and not to present a version control
system. Part of the Aspect project is concerned with configuration and
version control and this work is described in [DILL86].

This version control system simply allows releases and variants.
Releases are numbered (arbitrarily) and variants will be given file names
which will allow access to corresponding text. So, diagrammatically, an
example of the system might be:

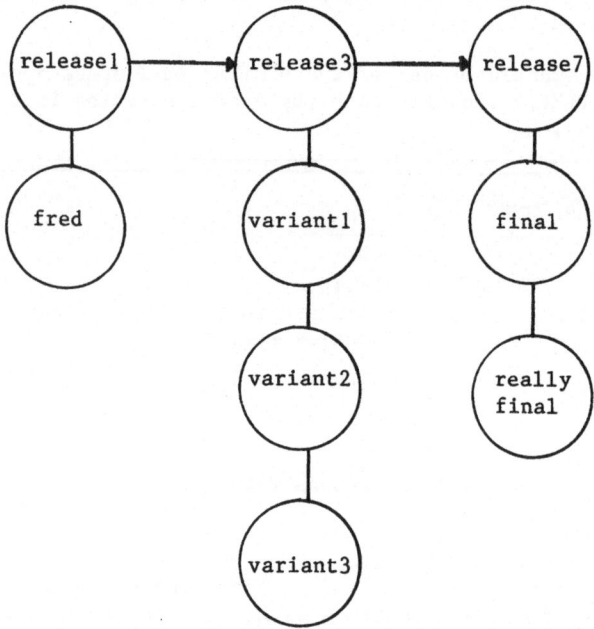

We now describe the RM/T relations that are used to define this system.
In the interests of brevity and clarity the issue of naming has been
omitted and so names, rather than surrogates, are used directly.

308

Five entity types are needed:

1   The fist defines the structure of the system by defining allowable
    associations between objects (variants and releases). This
    entity type is:

    assoc_type (assoc¢, assoc_name)

    The entity is represented with a p-relation, which , in this case,
    is constant and so may be given. Note that we assume that only one
    p-relation is being used for each entity type. For a full explana-
    tion of the relationship between p-relations and entity types see
    [16].

assoc¢	assoc_name
A	variant
B	release

Note that for all these examples surrogates will be single capital
letters.

2   The second entity type is "associations" which records the actual
    links between objects in the system.

    associations (obj1¢, obj2¢, assoc¢)

3   The third is the list of all of the objects in the system.

    objects (obj¢)

4/5 There are two subtypes of this entity type. The first contains
    those objects that are variants and the second those that are
    releases (all objects are either variants or releases.

    object_variant (obj¢, variant_name)

    object_release (obj¢, release_name)

There is in fact an additional relation, the "root" entity type, which
must exist as the supertype of all the other entity types. Since this
simply lists all the current surrogates it will be ignored for the sake
of simplicity and clarity.

To illustrate the above, we now create example entities to illustrate the
p-relations that would exist if the system were in use, followed by
illustrations of the use of the RM/T operators to use and examine the
system.

Given the example described above, we generate the following tuples in
the p-relations "objects", "object_variant", "object_release" and
"associations".

objects

obj¢
C
D
E
F
G
H
I
J
K

object_release

obj¢	release_number
C	1
D	3
E	7

Object_variant

obj¢	variant_name
F	fred
G	variant1
H	variant2
I	variant3
J	final
K	reallyfinal

associations

obj1¢	obj2¢	assoc¢
C	F	A
C	D	B
D	G	A
G	H	A
H	I	A
D	E	B
E	J	A
J	K	A

These entities now define the version control system in use. The standard RM/T operators may be used on their associated p-relations to
perform simple queries. So, for example, if we required a list of all
variants then a projection of object_variant over variant_name will give
this. Also tools may be written as arbitrarily complex RM/T queries.
Two examples are now given to illustrate this.

1   Give all variant names for release number 3.

In addition to the standard relational operators, project, select and
join, we use the RM/T operators close and bar. Bar is the complement of
project and so returns the relation with attributes not given in the call
of bar. Close returns the transitive closure of the relation supplied.
Rename changes the name of an attribute in a relation (in strict RM/T
this is done by a generalised project).

We build up this operation incrementally. Firstly we need a mapping from
each version to each of its variants. This is the closure of the associations relation restricted to variants. So we have:

stage1 = close (bar (select (associations , assoc = variant) ,
                    assoc¢))

We must now pick out from this relation those that correspond to release 3. For this we need the surrogate for release 3 and we must rename this attribute so that we can join it with the first attribute of stage1.

stage2 = rename (select (object_release , release_number = 3) ,
                                    obj = obj1)

Joining stage1 and stage2 gives a relation which includes a mapping from release 3 to each associated variant. We then join this with object_variant over the field obj2 (by renaming obj from object_variant), which adds the names of the variants of release 3.

stage3 = join (join (stage1 , stage2) ,
                    rename (object_variant , obj = obj2))

To obtain the required list of variant names we project stage3 over variant_name.

operation = project (stage3 , variant_name)

2   Create a new variant called extra_changes to release 3.

The new operation here is create entity. This creates a new (unique) surrogate which is inserted into the appropriate E-relation and then makes the appropriate entries into the P-relation.

create_entity (object_variant , variant_name = extra_changes)

create_entity (associations , obj = variant3 ,
                    obj = extra_changes , assoc = variant)

To create a new version we create a new entity to represent the new version and then a new association to link this version into the model.

4   SOFTWARE SUPPORT

Having developed the database modelling formalism described above we now describe the superstructure above this engine that is necessary for system development. All of the superstructure is written in terms of the interface and facilities provided by the engine but it is all considered necessary for an ASPECT information base. There are four areas: rules, views, activities and configuration management.

Activities form the transaction model of an ASPECT IPSE and therefore the recovery model. The nesting of activities allows a project to be controlled in a hierarchical manner. Rules may then be used to require that certain conditions in the information base are satisfied before, during and after an activity executes.

Views allow the concept of abstraction to be applied at the project wide level by allowing the abstraction of data, operations and rules. This allows the creation of abstract environments appropriate to the task to be performed [BROW87].

Configuration management could be handled in the simplistic way described above but within ASPECT a modelling formalism has been developed which allows the modelling of information relevant to CM. In particular we can allow the description of the structure of a system at a logical level together with instantiations that may actually exist. In addition we may model many such systems within the model allowing the natural description of system variants and releases.

This superstructure is described in more detail in [WALK86].

5   SUMMARY AND CONCLUSIONS

We have presented the ASPECT approach to the use of databases within system development. This consists of a data modelling formalism, which was illustrated by a example, and a superstructure which together forms the ASPECT Information Base.

The example itself illustrates an advantage of this approach; the high level of data manipulation allows rapid tool development, but a further benefit: the integrity provided, is also apparent. Since the entity type that we have called 'associations' is itself associative, no component association can inadvertently be deleted (associative integrity requires that for an associative entity to exist, the entities that it associates must also exist, sensibly enough); this means that no object that has been created as a variant or release can be removed unless it has first been 'unlinked' from its associated variants and releases. This and other integrity rules are provided as immediate consequences of the formalism, and go a long way toward simplifying the applications (i.e. tools) that manipulate an information base, in addition to guaranteeing a greater degree of data consistency.

The example therefore demonstrates two senses in which an abstract for-malism can support data engineering in an IPSE.

The Aspect Information Base has been prototyped, the experience of which is currently being used to specify and implement a further prototype which will be industrially evaluated during 87/88. This evaluation will allow us to determine whether the level of data abstraction chosen is correct.

6   REFERENCES

[BOER85]   Boerstra(ed.), M.L., Engineering Databases, Elsevier, Association for Applications in Engineering, Zoetermeer, The Netherlands (1985).

[BROW87]   Brown, A.W. "A View Mechanism for an integrated Project Support Environment" This volume.

[BULL84]   Bull, ICL, Nixdorf, Olivetti, and Siemens, PCTE: A basis for a Portable Common Tool Environment - Functional Specifications, 1984.

[CODD70]   Codd, E.F., "A Relational Model of Data for Large Shared Data Banks," Communications of ACM 13(6), pp.377-387 (June 1970).

[CODD79]   Codd, E.F. "Extending the Database Relational Model to Capture More Meaning" ACM Transactions on Database Systems, IBM Research Laboratory 4(4), pp. 397-434 (December 1979).

[DATE83]   Date, C.J., An Introduction to Database Systems Volume II, Addison Wesley (1983).

[DILL86]   Dillistone, B.R., "VCMF - A Version and Configuration Modelling Formalism", pp. 145-163 in Proceedings of Software Engineering

´86, ed. D. Barnes and P. Brown, Peter Peregrinus, Southampton (September 1986).

[EARL85] Earl, A.N. and Whittington, R.P., "Capturing the Semantics of an IPSE Database - Problems, Solutions and an Example," Data Processing 27(9), Butterworth (November 1985).

[EARL86] Earl, A.N., Whittington, R.P., Hitchcock, P., and Hall, J.A., "Specifying a Semantic Model for use in an Integrated Project Support Environment," in Proceedings of Software Engineering Environments, Peter Peregrinus Ltd., Lancaster University (2nd-4th April 1986),

[GRIE82] Griethuysen, J.J. Van, "Concepts and Terminology for Conceptual Schema and the Information base," Report of ISO TC97/SC5/WG3 (1982).

[GUTT82] Guttman, A. and Stonebraker, M., "Using a Relational Database System for Computer Aided Design Data," Database Eng. 5(2), pp. 21-28 (1982).

[HALL75] Hall, P.A., Hitchcock, P., and Todd, S.J., "An Algebra of Relations for Machine Computation," pp. 225-232 in Proceedings of 23rd ACM Symposium on Principles of Programming Languages (1975).

[KENT79] Kent, W., "The Entity Join," Proc. 5th International Conf. on Very Large Data Bases (October 1979).

[SUFR85] Sufrin, B., Morgan, C., Sorensen, I., and Hayes, I., Notes for a Z Handbook Part 1 - Mathematical Language, Oxford University Computing Laboratory, PRG, July 1985.

[UDAG84] Udagawa, Y. and Mizoguchi, T, "An Extended Relational Database System for Engineering Data Management," IEEE Data Base Engineering, Mitsubishi Electric Corporation, Kamakura City, Japan 7(2), pp. 119-127 (June 1984).

KNUTH WITH KNOBS ON - LITERATE PROGRAM DEVELOPMENT

J.P. Pardoe and S.J. Wade

Software Development Group, Liverpool Polytechnic

Liverpool, UK.

1   INTRODUCTION

Two years ago the authors read Knuth's "Literate Programming" [KNUT84]
with great excitement feeling that a door had been opened to superior
programming techniques and methodologies. This immediate rapture was
somewhat abated when they realised just how limited was the potential
user community; the idea was too good to be restricted to the computer
scientists and systems programmers of this world. Knuth himself describes
his program WEB as:

'specifically for the peculiar breed of people who are called computer
scientists'.

The authors felt that it should be possible to bring it to a wider
audience. They wished to produce a similar but more extensive tool which
would be usable by both the novice and professional applications
programmer.

The first tentative steps in this direction were taken envisaging an
interactive design system, but it was soon realised that this might
encourage a 'design at the terminal' approach which would be counterproductive to the authors' perception of effective software production.
The idea was rapidly shelved.

The seminal concept, however, was still firmly implanted and simply would
not go away; so the authors rethought their position and the concepts of
LIPSE (LIterate Programming Support Environment) were born.

A pre-processor system was envisaged which would be seen by the user as a
minor extension of the target programming language but would address as
many as possible of the major principles of quality software production
(Boehm's 'intermediate constructs' [BOEH78]).

Reliability -   by facilitating the program design process.

Understandability - by enhancing the presentation of source code,
                    - automating the documentation process.

Testability -   by providing testing and debugging aids.

Human Engineering - by the provision of a system for examining the
types and frequency of programming errors.

Modifiability -   by facilitating program maintenance with the
production of summaries and indexes.

Any lingering doubts the authors might have had about the desirability of
this project were disabused when it became increasingly obvious that a
tool of this kind was virtually a prerequisite for the production of such
a piece of software. Throughout the design and implementation phases of
its construction the previous version of itself was used as the
development tool and it is felt that had this not been done no
significant progress would have been made in the available time scale.

In producing this pre-processor a number of well established techniques
were brought together:

* the idea of pre-processing a High Level Language (H.L.L.) to
  enhance its facilities; [KERN76]

* the use of a program design language; [CAIN75]

* the use of "structured programming" by stepwise refinement using
  an informal program design language; [WIRT71]

* the extraction from design statements and source code of a summary
  of each procedure/subprogram within a program; [KNUT84]

* program formatting to enhance code readability; [PETE77]

* the use of traces and software instrumentors (test coverage
  analyzers). [FAIR85]

The result is a software tool (SWRPAS - Step-Wise Refinement for PAScal)
which has proved useful both for serious software production and as a
training tool for the novice.

The aim of this paper is to promote the concepts which have been brought
together by this tool. They form an integrated whole which has achieved
the objectives set out above.

2   THE AUGMENTED LANGUAGE

The initial concept was to include design information within the comment
structure of the chosen object language, in this case Pascal. However,
the authors soon realised that this implied an unwarranted restriction as
well as causing undue backtracking problems in the parsing stage. In the
current implementation the notation :

<* natural language design statement *>_____<reference>

is used to stand for a section of sequential code. Similarly, structural
design statements are of the form :

<* KEYWORD natural language statement *>_____<reference>

the parser is case sensitive to the keyword so as to impose the minimum
of restrictions upon the construction of the natural language design
statements. Thus a simple data processing application program can be
rendered in top level design as in figure 1

```
BEGIN
    (* Initialise for process *)_____<M1.1>
    (* Read ahead *)_____<M1.3>
    (* WHILE not at the end of transaction file DO *)__<M1.5>
        BEGIN
            (* Process an individual data item *)_____<M1.7>
            (* Read the next transaction record *)_____<M1.9>
        END ;
    (* Finalisation for process *)_____<M1.11>
END.
```

Figure 1 top Level Design

The individual design statements can now be instantiated using a very
similar syntactic arrangement. The designed blocks are introduced by
their reference contained in double angle brackets and may themselves be
either further refined by design statements or given as pure code in the
target language. For example, from the top level design above two
instantiations might be as in figure 2

In the second of the examples of Figure 2 it will be seen that the title
has been inherited from the parent design statement. This is an
automatic feature of the pre-processor, the programmer need only supply
the reference as seen in the first example.

In this way a complete program can be built up in a fashion which the
authors believe to be natural, logical and to a certain extent prescribed
by the design methodology being used. The last of these is reinforced by
the pre-processor flagging as errors various activities the use of which
although in itself not wrong, may give rise to poorly designed code
leading to difficulties of maintenance.

In a professional environment partially designed programs can be used to
good effect by the program designer/systems analyst. The top level
design can be passed to the programming team, each member of which can be
made responsible for the further design and final instantiation of the
various components. Further, a partially designed program can be tested
if given the appropriate facilities. For the novice programmer,
completing a partially designed program makes an ideal exercise while at
the same time introducing the concepts of sound program design.

3   PROGRAM FEATURES

3.1 The Conceptual Context

A software system must be designed initially with a view towards life-
cycle costs. This is especially important since present estimates are
that from 50 to 90 per cent. of the cost of soft ware is spent in the
maintenance phase [SHOO83]. Every phase of the life-cycle must be well
documented; and all corrections and modifications should be referred back
to the initial design stage. The importance of the latter has only been
realised since the introduction of formal design methodologies and
although the former has always been recognised it is its lack in practice

```
<<M1.1>>
    (* Open and initialise files *)_____<M1.1.1>
    (* Initialise program variables *)_____<M1.1.3>


<<M1.5>>_____(* WHILE not at the end of transaction ~
                            file DO *)
    WHILE NOT Eof (trans) DO
```

Figure 2 Instantiations of <MI-1> and <MI-5>

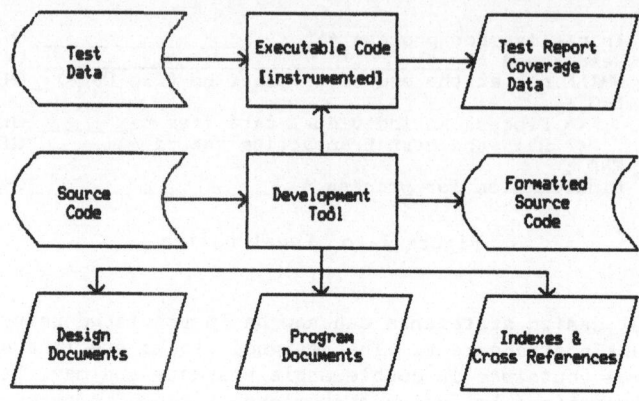

Figure 3 A Modern Development Tool

which is the prime cause of software ´aging´. A modern software
development tool should, therefore, facilitate maintenance and contribute
towards the control of life-cycle costs as well as addressing directly,
at all stages, the effective production of documentation and the use of
formal design methods. The tool developed adheres to the diagrammatic
structure shown in figure 3

3.2 A Single Source Document

There is only a single source document from which both the documentation
and executable code are derived; the code and documentation are
inextricably linked and updated together. The nature of that single
source document addresses the problem of always returning to the original
design phase since any addit ional code can only be interfaced to the
existing program at design level.

3.3 The Documentation

The primary document consists of a summary for each procedure of the
program. This contains the context in which the procedure is used and a
textual summary of its operation taken from its design statements. The
example given in figure 4 is the procedure which is primarily involved in
producing this level of documentation.

An example of the indexes produced by the tool is the procedure index.
This gives the formatted source document page references for both the
start of each procedure definition and the scope of the corresponding
design blocks. The example given in figure 5 is a partial index for the
tool itself. The design block index and the forward reference index are
the other currently available indexes.

Diagrammatic output is currently confined to the production of structure
diagrams on a graph plotter for each procedure. A small example is given
in figure 6 the procedure chosen being from the tool itself.

3.4 Source Document Formatting

A major part of the pre-processor is the language formatter. The
aesthetics of formatting are very subjective, but for Pascal the authors
have largely adhered to the standards used by the Stanford University
Pascal formatter PFORM (widely available in the academic community).
This is naturally extended to cover the augmented language and includes

options to allow variation in presentation and renumbering of the design references, which is frequently required after modifications have been made to the source code.

Since the compiler has no access to the original source code and its error messages refer to the generated executable code, the formatter must perform syntactical analysis. This is an essential aid to primary error correction. Further, as the generated executable code is not intended to be human readable, this removes the temptation to patch directly the target language code. This is, in effect, an incentive towards design level maintenance.

3.5 Testing facilities

Aids to the testing of the source code are provided by options which allow tracing in whole or in part of the execution of the code and an

```
PROCEDURE Makerno (start,
                   finish            : progpointer) ;
```

Write .RNO statements from fragmented design

Declared in: Builddoc   Uses: Used by:
                              Makerno   Builddoc
                              Testblock   Makerno

Global Identifiers used:
    CONST
        blank   = ' ' ;
    VAR
        desindent   : posint ;   (* 'Own variable' for Makerno *)

External Identifiers used: none.

Local Identifiers used:
    VAR
        progptr   : progpointer ; (* Statement list pointer *)
        nextwrapped,.   (* If next line is wrapped *)
        finishedblock   : boolean ;   (* If current block at end *)
        elabindent   : integer ;   (* Current refinement indentation *)
        cntr   : posint ;   (* General purpose counter *)

```
BEGIN (* Makerno *)
    Obtain start position of block being processed {P591.1}
    REPEAT
        Skip over any design block headings {P591.3}
        Write as necessary the current line and extensions to .RNO file {P591.5}
        <<<<P591.5.......
            IF current line qualifies for inclusion in .RNO file THEN {P591.5.1}
                Point backwards to beginning if wrapped {P591.5.3}
                IF a design statement THEN {P591.5.5}
                    Write left margin (indentation) {P591.5.7}
                    Skip blanks and ref initiating symbol(s) {P591.5.9}
                    WHILE not the end of the design statement DO {P591.5.11}
                        WHILE not at the end of the current line DO {P591.5.13}
                            Write a character (except tilde) to output {P591.5.15}
                        Advance to next line in list {P591.5.17}
                        Skip any leading blanks {P591.5.19}
                    WITH the last line of the design statement DO {P591.5.21}
                        Write characters upto design comment end {P591.5.23}
                        Skip upto design reference {P591.5.25}
                        Write design reference in Braces {P591.5.27}
                ELSE
                    Write the line(s) to .RNO {P591.5.29}
        <<<<P591.5
        Determine if last line of block {P591.7}
        IF a designed block to be processed THEN {P591.9}
            Process designed block (includes recursive call ) {P591.11}
        Advance source line list pointer {P591.13}
    UNTIL finishedblock ;
END (* Makerno *) ;
```

Figure 4 Details of procedure

```
PROCEDURE INDEX
      * Main *             .. .. .. .. page :  1  ref : 1          on pp 123 .. 128
      Builddoc             .. .. .. .. page : 94  ref : P590       on pp 100 .. 103
         Makerno              .. .. .. page : 94  ref : P591       on pp 95 .. 98
            Testblock            .. .. page : 95  ref : F593       on p  95
         Scanlist             .. .. .. page : 98  ref : P595       on pp 98 .. 99
      Buildreslist         .. .. .. .. page :116  ref : P650       on pp 117 .. 121
      Crossref             .. .. .. .. page : 84  ref : P550       on p  85
      Diagnostics          .. .. .. .. page :  7  ref : P10        on pp  7 .. 9
      Disablectrly         .. .. .. .. page :  7  ref : EXTERNAL
      Docomment            .. .. .. .. page : 37  ref : P350       on pp 42 .. 45
         Options              .. .. .. page : 37  ref : P351       on p  38
         Renumberprocess .. .. .. .. page : 38  ref : P353       on pp 39 .. 41
            Append               .. .. page : 39  ref : P355       on p  39
```

Figure 5 Procedure Index for SWRPAS

automated coverage option which assesses the extent to which test data exercises the code. Both of these facilities are based upon the designed block unit, thus allowing finer control than is often offered by other such tools.

Even a partially designed program can be tested. The tool automatically inserts suitable tracing statements to indicate the intended execution of as yet uncoded refinements.

3.6 Design Method Encouragement

The source language processed by the tool is a superset of Pascal, hence it is possible to use it simply as a formatter without giving any consideration to the use of design statements. However, encouragement to use design statements is given in two ways. Firstly, a programmable switch may be set in order to flag any section of coding which is deemed to be too long or too complex to be used directly without intervening design statements. This has been implemented by counting the statements within a compound statement and when a prescribed limit is exceeded an error message is displayed and written into the formatted source document. Secondly, the mixing of target language code and design language statements in the same designed block may be similarly flagged.

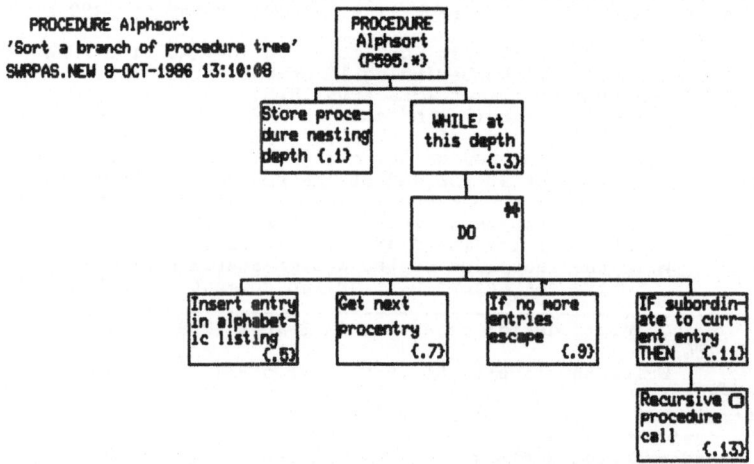

Figure 6 Structure Diagram for SWRPAS

3.7 Performance Monitoring

To achieve sound software project management it is necessary to remember that the conclusions of the Sackman study [SACK67] are still relevent today. There are large disparities between the performances of individual programmers and as Shooman states: 'Thus, we are still concerned with methods of promoting a poor programmer to an average one, and an average performer to a good performer.' [SHOO83]

In order to achieve its objectives, this tool must analyse the syntax of design statements and target code. It is relatively easy, therefore, to log the errors found in the source document and hence provide a facility for analysis. There are obvious benefits to be gained in the training environment from the appraisal of novice performance in programming design and coding exercises. Equally, Software Project Management could take advantage of this facility to establish constructively common error profiles for both staff and application groups in order to improve quality and efficiency of the individual and the product.

4   AN EXAMPLE

As the chosen design methodology for this prototype implementation is stepwise refinement it seems appropriate to use as an example that given by Wirth in his original paper on this methodology [WIRT71] - The Eight Queen Problem. Given as figure 7 is the formatted source code for this example. The output is normally paged and carries a page header on each page. For the current purpose these have been omitted after the first.

5   CONCLUSION

The main aim of LIPSE is to enable the production of high quality software and improve programmer productivity in a high level language environment. This, the authors believe, is achievable by the construction of software tools which take as their basis a design methodology and the programming language.

The authors have now produced a prototype version using top-down design with stepwise refinement and Pascal, which is currently being field tested with good results by their B.Sc. Computer Studies students.

The power of the tool has been seen by its users to lie in its ease of use and the automatic production of design and program documentation suitably indexed and cross-referenced. While the authors in their pedagogical roles have found the human performance monitoring features extremely valuable.

A colaborative research program has been planned in order to refine and extend the existing prototype and to develop versions with different design methodology/language bases. The development of a version based on COBOL while keeping the existing design methodology is an initial objective. In the longer term, it is envisaged that the basic philosophy of LIPSE will lead to extensive further developments.

```
PROGRAM Eightqueensl (output) ;
(*
     A realisation of the example used in Wirth's original Stepwise
     Refinement paper (Comm.ACM April '71, Volume 14, Number 4) using
     SWRPAS as the design tool.
  -
     Given are an 8x8 chessboard and 8 queens which are hostile to
     each other.  Find a position for each queen (a configuration)
     such that no queen may be taken by any other queen (i.e. such
     that every row, column, and diagonal contains at most one queen).
*)

CONST
     columnmax          = 8 ;              (* No. of columns on board *)
     columnmaxplusl     = 9 ;
     rowmax             = 8 ;              (* No. of rows on board *)
     blboundl           = 2 ;
     blbound2           = 16 ;            (* columnmax + rowmax *)
     brboundl           = - 7 ;           (* 1 - columnmax *)
     brbound2           = 7 ;             (* rowmax - 1 *)

TYPE
     columnindex        = 1 .. columnmax ;
     rowindex           = 0 .. rowmax ;
     board              = ARRAY [columnindex] OF rowindex ;

VAR
     currentcolumn      : 0 .. columnmaxplusl ;
     currentrow         : rowindex ;
     currentboard       : board ;
     rowok              : ARRAY [columnindex] OF boolean ;
                                            (* Check arrays for rows *)
     bltrok             : ARRAY [blboundl .. blbound2] OF boolean ;
                                            (* Check array for / diagonals *)
     brtlok             : ARRAY [brboundl .. brbound2] OF boolean ;
                                            (* Check array for \ diagonals *)
     safe               : boolean ;
     cntr,
     cnt                : integer ;

BEGIN (* Main Program *)
     (* Consider the first column *)_____(1.1)
     REPEAT
        (* Try the current column *)_____(1.3)
        (* IF a 'safe' position can be found THEN *)_____(1.5)
           BEGIN
           (* Establish a queen in this 'safe' position *)____(1.7)
           (* Consider the next column *)_____(1.9)
           END
        ELSE
           BEGIN
           (* Regress to a previous column *)_____(1.11)
           END ;
     (* UNTIL the last column is done OR regression leaves the first ~
     column *)_____(1.13)
     (* IF solution found THEN *)_____(1.15)
        BEGIN
        (* Output solution *)_____(1.17)
        END ;
END.

DBEGIN
```

Figure 7 code for queen problem

```
<<1.1>>_____(* Consider the first column *)
(*
     The problem essentially consists of inspecting the safety of
     squares.  A pointer variable designates the currently inspected
     square.  The column in which this square lies is called the
     currently inspected column.  This procedure initialises the
     pointer to denote the first column.  It also initialises the
     arrays used for inspection.
*)
     <* Initialise inspection arrays *>_____<1.1.1>
     <* Set to start of first column *>_____<1.1.3>

<<1.1.1>>_____(* Initialise inspection arrays *)
     FOR cntr := 1 TO columnmax DO
        rowok [cntr] := true ;
     FOR cntr := blbound1 TO blbound2 DO
        bltrok [cntr] := true ;
     FOR cntr := brbound1 TO brbound2 DO
        brtlok [cntr] := true ;

<<1.1.3>>_____(* Set to start of first column *)
     currentcolumn := 1 ;
     currentrow := 0 ;

<<1.3>>_____(* Try the current column *)
(*
     Starting at the current square of inspection in the currently
     considered column, move down the column either until a safe
     square is found, or until the last square is reached and that
     is also unsafe.
*)
     REPEAT
        <* Advance the pointer in this column *>_____<1.3.1>
        <* Test if this square is safe *>_____<1.3.3>
     <* UNTIL the square is safe OR last square reached *>____<1.3.5>

<<1.3.1>>_____(* Advance the pointer in this column *)
     currentrow := Succ (currentrow) ;

<<1.3.3>>_____(* Test if this square is safe *)
     safe := rowok [currentrow] AND bltrok [currentrow + currentcolumn] AND
        brtlok [currentrow - currentcolumn] ;

<<1.3.5>>_____(* UNTIL the square is safe OR last square reached *)
     UNTIL safe OR (currentrow = rowmax) ;

<<1.5>>_____(* IF a 'safe' position can be found THEN *)
     IF safe THEN

<<1.7>>_____(* Establish a queen in this 'safe' position *)
(*
     A queen is positioned on the last inspected square.
*)
     rowok [currentrow] := false ;
     bltrok [currentrow + currentcolumn] := false ;
     brtlok [currentrow - currentcolumn] := false ;

<<1.9>>_____(* Consider the next column *)
     currentboard [currentcolumn] := currentrow ;
     currentcolumn := Succ (currentcolumn) ;
     currentrow := 0 ;

<<1.11>>_____(* Regress to a previous column *)
(*
     Regress to a column where it is possible to move the positioned
     queen further down, and remove the queens positioned in the
     columns over which regression takes place.  Note that we may
     have to regress over at most two columns.
*)
```

                                                              (continued)

                                                                      323

```
            <* Reconsider the prior column *>_____<1.11.1>
            <* IF NOT regressed out of first column THEN *>_____<1.11.3>
               BEGIN
               <* Remove the queen from the current column *>_____<1.11.5>
               <* IF the queen is on the last square THEN *>_____<1.11.7>
                  BEGIN
                  <* Reconsider the prior column *>_____<1.11.1>
                  <* IF NOT regressed out of first column THEN *>____<1.11.3>
                     BEGIN
                     <* Remove the queen from the current column *>__<1.11.5>
                     END ;
                  END ;
               END ;
            END ;

   <<1.11.1>>_____<* Reconsider the prior column *>
      currentcolumn := Pred (currentcolumn) ;

   <<1.11.3>>_____<* IF NOT regressed out of first column THEN *>
      IF NOT (currentcolumn < 1) THEN

   <<1.11.5>>_____<* Remove the queen from the current column *>
      currentrow := currentboard [currentcolumn] ;
      rowok [currentrow] := true ;
      bltrok [currentrow + currentcolumn] := true ;
      brtlok [currentrow - currentcolumn] := true ;

   <<1.11.7>>_____<* IF the queen is on the last square THEN *>
      IF currentrow = rowmax THEN

   <<1.13>>_____<* UNTIL the last column is done OR regression ~
                             leaves the first column *>
      UNTIL (currentcolumn > columnmax) OR (currentcolumn < 1) ;

   <<1.15>>_____<* IF solution found THEN *>
      IF currentcolumn > columnmax THEN

   <<1.17>>_____<* Output solution *>
      FOR cntr := 1 TO columnmax DO
         BEGIN
         FOR cnt := 1 TO Pred (currentboard [cntr] ) DO
            Write ('[ ]') ;
         Write ('[Q]') ;
         FOR cnt := Succ (currentboard [cntr] ) TO rowmax DO
            Write ('[ ]') ;
         Writeln ;
         END ;
      Writeln ;

DEND
```

Fig. 7 (continued)

REFERENCES

[BOEH78]   Characteristics of Software Quality; B.Boehm et al; North
           Holland Publishing Company, 1978.

[CAIN75]   PDL – A Tool for Software Design; S.Caine & K.Gordon; Proc.
           Nat. Comp. Conf.; AFIPS Press, 1975.

[FAIR85]   Software Engineering Concepts; McGraw Hill; 1985.

[KERN76]   Software Tools; B.W.Kernighan & P.J.Plauger; Addison–Wesley,
           Reading, Mass., 1976.

[KNUT84]   Literate Programming; D.E.Knuth; Computer Journal, May, 1984.

[PETE77]   On the Formatting of Pascal Programs; J.L.Peterson; SIGPLAN
           Notices 12:12, December, 1977.

[SACK67]   Computers, System Science, and Evolving Society; H.Sackman;
           Wiley, New York, 1967.

[SHOO83]   Software Engineering; M.L.Shooman; McGraw Hill; 1983.

[WIRT71]   Program Development by Stepwise Refinement; N.Wirth; Comm.ACM,
           Volume 14, Number 4, April, 1971.

Appendix A

Block:

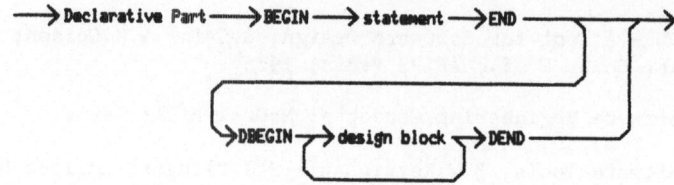

Design Block:

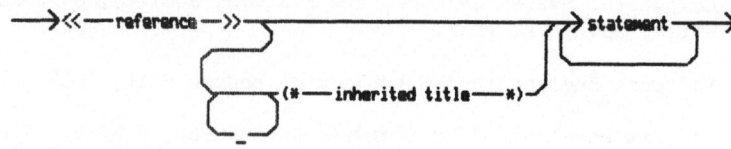

Statement:

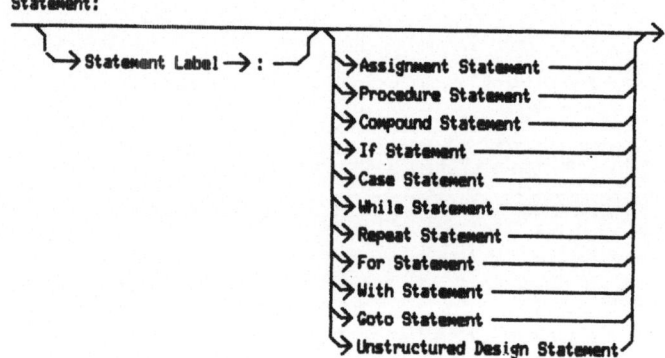

KEYWORD Design Statement:

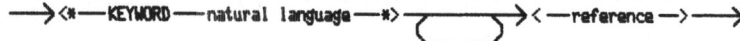

Unstructured Design Statement:

Case Statement:

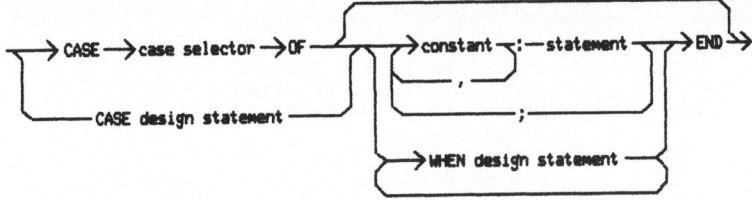

For Statement:

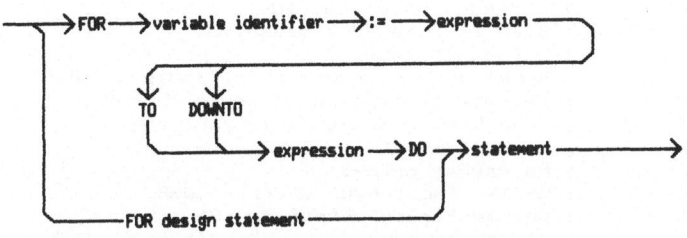

If Statement:

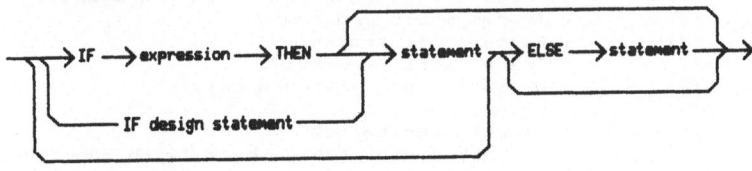

Repeat Statement:

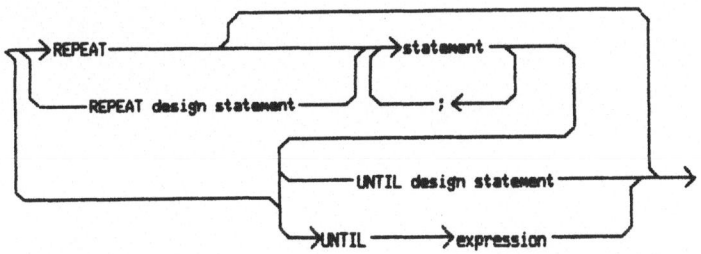

With Statement:

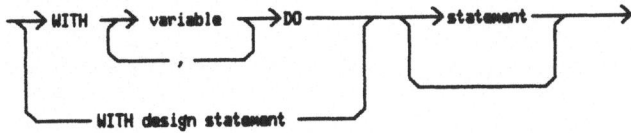

While Statement:

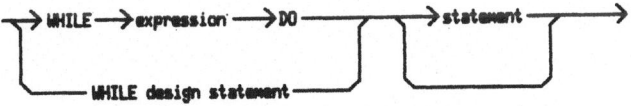

Appendix B   Program Options.

```
/B      : Indent set after begin
/C      : No automatic compilation
/D:n    : Design level warnings
/D      : Diagnostics
/DBC    : Inhibit destruct for DBC's input
/DI     : Design block integrity inhibited
/E      : Error messages in printed output
/F      : Forms output (i.e. headings at every page head)
          - automatically set for Xperts.
/G      : Graphical documentation
/I      : Indices output to .IND
/L      : Else_if construct disabled
/N      : Output to .NEW
/NP     : Renumbers procedures etc. (output .NEW)
/NR     : Renumbers refinements (output .NEW)
/NT     : Renumbers completely (output .NEW)
/O      : No SWR output
/P      : No Pascal output
/Q      : No SWR input back up file .QWR
/R      : Documentation output to .RNO
/SP     : Renumbers procedures etc. (output .SWR)
/SR     : Renumbers refinements (output .SWR)
/ST     : Renumbers completely (output .SWR)
/TP     : Trace probes inserted (with Xpert only)
/TT     : Traces whole program
/TX     : Removes all traces
/T      : Trace facility enabled
/U      : Unusual input (Authors only)
/W      : Wide output (132)
/X      : Expert user switch
/Z      : Inhibit symbol table check (with Xpert only)
```

SECTION FIVE — ENVIRONMENTS AND APPROACHES: OTHER ISSUES

DATA DICTIONARIES

This section looks at three aspects which do not easily fit into the other
parts of our adopted framework. The first of these is Data Dictionaries.
In some respects dictionaries fit into most sections. They are fundamental
to Analyst Workbenches, Fourth Generation Languages and IPSEs. One of
Martin's [MART82] requirements of a Fourth Generation Language was that it
should have an integrated and active Data Dictionary. Similarly, most
Analyst Workbenches are supported by a resource that contains information
about the enterprise and contains the knowledge required to create systems.
The term "encyclopaedia" is often used to describe this resource to
distinguish it from the historically passive nature of the "Dictionary".

The paper by Phil Redfearn of MSP provides an introduction to the role of
Data Dictionaries and reflects upon their past and future development. The
implementation of MSP's Data Dictionary DATAMANGER at a major international
bank is then examined by Simon Tyrrell-Lewis. This latter paper includes an
important word of warning "about the problems of selling the need for
methodologies and tools to management and development staff". Sandwiched
between these two papers is a contribution from ORACLE UK which examines how
an intelligent dictionary can support all aspects of the development life
cycle.

APPLICATION ENVIRONMENTS

Application Environments is the sub-heading we have given to the paper 5
presented by Jones (from BIT) and Lau. The former paper defines the concept
of an Application Environment bringing together two important approaches
(4GLs and expert systems) to software development and productivity. It
argues that the very flexibility of 4GLs make them unusable to end users
whilst expert systems lack very basic functions and utilities. BIT have
attempted to produce an approach and a tool (PARYS) that combines
the strengths of these two approaches. Example systems are used to
demonstrate the concept of the Application Environment.

The paper by Lau and Gough presents a high level design methodology for the
Application Environment of Office Automation. It suggests a three level
approach including an "Automatability-Index" designed to provide an early
indication of the desirability of automation. The methodology places stress
on visual presentations supported by automated graphing tools.

ALTERNATIVE PARADIGMS

The two papers examined here make certain references to issues addressed in other parts of the framework, but they are sufficiently distinct and individual to be accorded their own sub-section. The introduction to these proceedings made reference to the process and data driven models and these have been commented on in several individual papers (see, for example, Tyrrell-Lewis in this section). Topping's paper is directly relevant to the debate about these two approaches to development. His purpose is "to advocate a more process orientated view of system development" and supports this with Industrial Real-Time Basic (IRTB) - a systems development environment within which process orientated design methods can be expressed directly and simply. In some respects Potts' paper is a rejection of both of these approaches in the context of the development of prototype systems. He favours the concepts of frames and messages to provide a consistent and coherent architecture for the prototyping environment. Furthermore, he feels that such an architecture can readily be extended to support knowledge based expert systems.

SUMMARY

This section examines three areas which are fundamental to system development but do not fit easily into our adopted framework. All the papers in this section have something to say about one or more of the following fundamental themes:

    Data Dictionaries
    Fourth Generation Languages
    Expert Systems
    Data and Process driven models.

In a sense, they encompass the framework, rather than lie outside it.

REFERENCES

[MART82] Application Development without Programmers, Prentice-Hall, 1982

THE ROLE OF THE CORPORATE DICTIONARY

P. Redfearn

Manager Software Products Ltd

Leicester, UK

1   INTRODUCTION

Over a period of some fifteen years data dictionary systems have evolved
from simple cross-referencing mechanisms to sophisticated systems
development productivity tools.

This paper looks back at the progress made over this period, identifies
today's state-of-the-art position and suggests how this area will further
evolve in the years to come.

The term "data dictionary" has come to be used for describing a variety
of products. In this paper we examine the broad range of facilities that
this all-embracing term has been used to cover.

More recently, terms such as encyclopedia and knowledgebase have emerged.
These terms are also considered and some suggestions made as to the
differences that may exist between these and the traditional dictionary.

2   MSP BACKGROUND

MANAGER SOFTWARE PRODUCTS has for many years been the leading vendor in
the area of dictionary-driven software.

DATAMANAGER, the heart of MSP'S product range, is the best-known
dictionary system in the world. Some 1500 organisations across the globe
make use of DATAMANAGER. In the UK alone there are approximately 160
user sites.

3   THE EVOLUTION OF DICTIONARY SYSTEMS

The first type of dictionary system was very much a manually-held card
index system. Many organisations identified a need to keep track of
which files and records were used in which programs. This made it easier
to identify those programs which needed recompiling in the event of a
change to a record or file structure. Organisations began to see the
benefit of using standard names for data items although it was fairly

common for data items to be prefixed with some kind of file or record identifier.

The advent of the DBMS provided additional reasons to pursue this approach. DBMS products such as DL/I tended to have restrictions on the length of data names (this is still the case today with a number of products).

At that time the move towards database technology was occurring with the belief that it was possible for all of an organisation's data to be stored in a single database. It was, therefore, a fundamental requirement that each item of data would need to be identified by a unique field name. The original database dream later proved to be just a dream and organisations found that they were forced to hold multiple databases, but the dictionary was here to stay. IBM released a dictionary system to support the IMS environment.

The subsequent unbundling of IBM software saw the third-party software vendors enter the marketplace. A number of independent dictionary systems were developed. UCC10, Data Catalog and DATAMANAGER were all early contenders in this market.

Some products, such as UCC10, operated specifically in the IMS environment. Others, such as DATAMANAGER, provided support for several different database environments whilst not requiring a DBMS for their own operations. The significance of the "independent" (i.e. not DBMS dependent) dictionary system was perhaps not fully realised at this time but became apparent at a later date.

Dictionary systems at this time were very oriented towards documenting and cross-referencing the physical aspects of data processing - systems, programs, files, databases, items etc. DDS from ICL with its four-quadrant (logical/physical and data/process) approach was one of the first dictionary systems of offer the ability to document the logical as well as the physical side of data processing.

So the dictionary system had moved on from being a dba and programmer tool. It was beginning to provide assistance to the analyst and designer too. In the late 70s most of the leading dictionary systems were enhanced to provide a facility which is probably best known as extensibility. This allowed the dictionary user to utilise a wider range of dictionary object types such that the dictionary system could provide support for all stages of the system life cycle - from feasibility study to implementation.

Subsequent enhancements in some products were sufficient to allow the user to select any object type whatsoever and to specify any associated attribute clauses. Suddenly it was possible to use a dictionary system as a miniature dbms. Dictionary users began to use separate dictionaries to record, for example, their technical reference library, their communications network and, would you believe it, even their oil wells!

The other development occurring at this time was the move, by some vendors, towards an environment whereby the dbms and a range of development tools (application generator, report writer etc) were centred round an integral dictionary. Cullinet (then Cullinane) with IDMS and IDD was amongst the first companies to adopt this approach. The dictionary system was at this point evolving from being predominantly "passive" to being "active". Instead of a tool which was oriented towards effective systems documentation, the dictionary system became much more of a productivity tool.

These two trends;
- more integration with other tools
- a more active dictionary role

were to continue, and together with a third trend - the move by large
organisations towards more emphasis on data administration - were to
bring us to today's sophisticated products.

4   DICTIONARY SYSTEMS TODAY

Today, almost every software product whether it is a dbms, a 4GL, an end
user query language or an application package, has some form of integral
directory facility.

These directory facilities are often specific to the environment in
which they operate, have limited functionality, and cannot really be
described as true dictionary systems. They are in place to ensure the
smooth running of the "driver" product rather than provide a means of
defining and cross-referencing corporate data definitions. Popular
products such as FOCUS from Information Builders and MANTIS from Cincom
contain this type of directory.

All of the major independent dbms vendors - Cullinet, ADR, Cincom and
Software AG - have dictionary systems integrated with their dbms
offerings. It is rather surprising, therefore, to discover that IBM has
yet to provide any dictionary support in the DB2 environment.

The growth in the number of products containing some form of dictionary
or directory capability has, at least in part, led to the concept of the
corporate dictionary. This is a high-level, free-standing dictionary
system with a range of user friendly facilities and serves and as a
centralised data management tool. In order for this to work in practice
there must be "bridges" in place to transport dictionary definitions
between the corporate dictionary and the various "slave" dictionaries and
directories. One dictionary vendor, MSP, is soon to release an automated
dictionary-to-dictionary mechanism which will allow the user to develop
sets of translation rules for interfacing to slave dictionaries of the
user's choice.

Dictionary systems today are much more active than they have been in the
past. In a number of cases dictionary systems now drive data analysis
and database design tools, application generators, report writers etc.
In many installations the dictionary is now an integral part of the
systems development process with the dictionary being utilised to coordinate the various phases of systems development.

Dictionary systems can also be used to provide a suitable harness for the
introduction of new technology. Here are three examples;

- 4GL products; particularly where these are used in end-user
  departments. It can be all too easy to neglect the issues of naming
  standards, standardised data formats etc which are so vital to
  effective data management. Some of the most successful users of 4GL
  products are those organisations where a corporate dictionary has been
  used to drive the 4GL.

- Relational database; although some installations have been able to move
  directly into a relational database environment, the majority of
  organisations utilising, or about to utilise, relational database
  products have existing hierarchical or network database applications

already in production. Co-ordinating this multiple database environment is ideally suited to a dictionary system which can be interfaced with each type of DBMS.

- Analyst workbenches; one of the most exciting new technology directions has seen the introduction, over the last few years, of analyst workbench products. These products utilise the advanced graphics capabilities which are available on IBM and compatible micro systems in order to provide the analyst with the ability to create dataflow diagrams, entity models etc directly on the screen. Whilst this type of product can increase the analyst's productivity almost overnight, there is a danger that development will continue in an unco-ordinated fashion particularly as the majority of analyst workbench products have yet to be networked. Where the workbench tool can be connected to a corporate dictionary on the mainframe, it is more likely that the benefits of productivity at the workstation will not be neglected by the problems of unco-ordinated, uncontrolled development.

5. FUTURE DIRECTIONS

A small but influential number of vendors have already started on a new path which is likely to be more strategic than anything we have seen to date.

This involves the use of dictionary-based technology to provide support for the new IPSE (Integrated Project Support Environment) developments.

IPSE products now beginning to appear on the market will need to utilise an advanced form of dictionary - sometimes referred to as an encyclopaedia or (and this is perhaps the more suitable term) a knowledgebase.

The knowledgebase will not only need to provide a dictionary capability but will also need to contain a "rulebase", and a very flexible "human interface".

IPSE's are really a combination of a methodology (rulebase), software to automate the phases/tasks/activities etc within the methodology and a user friendly front end (human interface) to navigate the user through the systems development process.

A number of the leading methodology vendors (e.g. LBMS, JMA, BIS) have already started to introduce software support for their methodologies. A slightly different approach is being taken by MSP where existing dictionary software is being enhanced and integrated with a methodology. It can be argued that the most successful IPSE products will be those that incorporate a sophisticated and flexible knowledgebase.

In addition to the IPSE development, it is likely that corporate dictionaries will become more prevalent and integration between the corporate dictionary and other dictionaries may be a critical issue. There will be more direct access to the corporate dictionary from end-user departments.

6 SUMMARY

The dictionary system, albeit with increasingly sophisticated facilities,is, without doubt, here to stay. Progress since the early days of primitive cross-reference systems has been rapid.

Dictionary systems have become more active and will continue to move in the direction of driving the systems development process.

Dictionary vendors will continue to address and utilise new technologies. The principles of expert systems and artificial intelligence are a natural progression in dictionary technology. IPSE products will be dictionary driven.

7 CONCLUSION

As any data administrator will tell you, a dictionary system is a vital tool to support data management. It is difficult to encourage and enforce the use of the dictionary in the development environment as many dictionary benefits are seen to be intangible. Much effort goes into ensuring that the dictionary is up-to-date, standardised and widely used.

In the future, data administrators will be less subject to tearing their hair out. The knowledge base will automatically be built and maintained as an integral, transparent part of the systems development process. The data dictionary will have come of age.

ENTITY MODELLING AND INTELLIGENT DICTIONARIES

Richard Barker

Oracle Corporation (UK) Ltd.

1   INTRODUCTION

Intelligent computerised dictionary systems are now actively supporting
the implementation process for computer systems and fulfilling their
promise of a few years ago. This document describes , in brief the
development life cycle, what a dictionary is and how an intelligent one
may help that process.

2   THE DEVELOPMENT LIFE CYCLE

The success of any important development is highly dependant on the
method and techniques used during its construction. The following
description is of a classic development life cycle, as used by ORACLE
Corporation in the form of the SQL* Development Method. Similar
Structured approaches are available from other vendors, such as James
Martin, CACI and LBMS.

The SQL* Development Method is an integrated set of tools and techniques
which enables commercial, financial, government and other organisations
to develop integrated systems to meet their business needs. These needs
fall broadly into two major areas; those to support operational
requirements and those to support the ever growing needs of Management.

The method utilises a step by step structured approach to building a
system to which one would see strong parallels in any thriving
manufacturing industry. It incorporates powerful modelling tools,
communication techniques, clearly defined tasks and deliverables, quality
and completeness checks and other activities to help build a high
quality, well documented system to meet the business needs.

In general, the method is being employed to develop high performance
multi-user relational database management systems to meet the current and
future needs of business.

A standard method is adopted for addressing any requirement:-

- determine the scope
- determine the need
- confirm the understanding
- produce a framework within which one can develop systems with confidence
- devise a development plan and strategy for use of technology
- determine and state the requirement in detail design
- build, test and document
- train and educate
- convert
- operate the system
- review and maintain

A large number of tasks have to be carried out in a methodical manner to assure the success of any major development. This method groups the taks into major stages, (see figure 1), which together constitute the development life cycle.

3   DATA DICTIONARIES

Data Dictionaries are normally computerised systems which envoled from the need to have common standard definitions for computer files. These days, they are very comprehensive databases which provide computer assistance to analysts, designers and programmers.

Some dictionaries only support the designer and implementor in a passive manner, where the dictionary acts as a documentation tool for recording the results of database design. On-line dictionaries as used by the kernel of the ORACLE RDBMS, are used to control the second by second access to the user database and its data definition. Some systems have gone further to record some of the program documentation and cross-referenced it to the data definition.

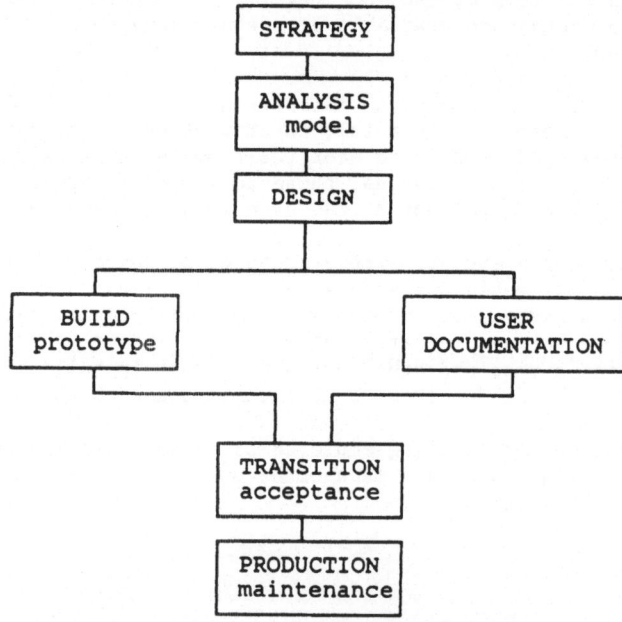

Figure 1   Development Life Cycle

Dictionaries which live up to their true potential have added a business level, which enables analysts to record the details about the business in terms of:-

-   information needs
-   functions
-   events
-   objectives and priorities

This level of passive dictionary is extremely useful as it can provide full system documentation, cross references, paper documentation and interrogation facilities to help the developers and maintenance staff. To be really useful the dictionaries are usually implemented using a database management system, which can be used to provide access control, security, integrity and recovery of the dictionary data. The reporting and query facilities can then often be used to good advantage to help the developer.

Dictionaries are accessed by one of two different means. Initially, many were only accessible by special language constraints which had to be learnt like any other computer language. These days the friendly user interfaces which are made available to end-users have been made equally available to development staff. Thus interfaces via form-filling screens and graphics are now the order of the day.

Most dictionaries are limited to the enviroment of their host DBMS or are only available in single user mode on personal computers. Those which offer multi-user capability with a choice of user interface tend to provide higher levels of productivity and control.

But what is an ACTIVE dictionary?

"Active" implies some form of built in intelligence or some other capability which actually speeds up the developer in some way by automating some of the tasks, improving the quality or otherwise, encouraging improved deliverables.

Each stage and task has a description, a set of guidelines and clearly laid out set of things which have to be produced - the deliverables. These deliverables are classified into those which are essential, useful and those which may apply dependent on the exact terms of reference for the stage.

The SQL* Development Method contains many activities, within each stage, which iterate between looking at the business first from a functional basis then from a data orientated basis. Neither is sufficient on its own right, but each provides a completeness and quality check on the other (see figure 2).

4   INTELLIGENT DICTIONARIES

What do we mean by intelligence, when used in a data dictionary context?

Intelligence can mean many things. Intelligence can take the form of memory, recall, association, understanding and prediction or synthesis based on known fact. This may not be a complete or academically accurate list, but does give us the opportunity of assessing a data dictionary's potential for exhibiting intelligence.

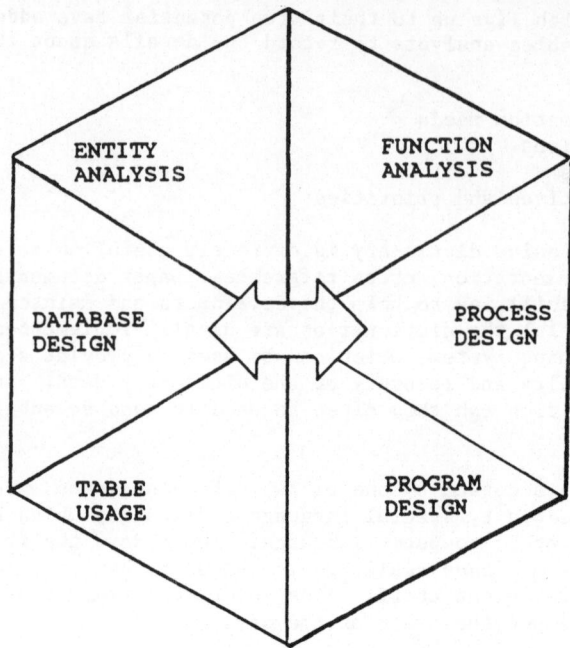

Figure 2   Cross check at all stages

Most data dictionaries provide capability to store data, recall it in various forms and associate related elements eg, which programs process what data. There are, however, other aspects which have been brought together under the headings of passive intelligence and active.

4.1   Passive Intelligence

Passive Intelligence of a dictionary is when a set of rules, conditions, checklists, etc can be programed into the system to help and guide the developer. Often people made terrible mistakes by forgetting to do that which they know they should and can benefit from a quality assurance robot looking over their shoulder.

Examples of passive intelligence are:-

- <u>Online validation</u>

   Checking for valid keys, allowable combinations, synonym usage, decoding and standardisation of instructions are an obvious, but important, starting point. Terminology is of vital importance in any development as rarely does one ever get a company where

   "a word always has the same meaning" and

   "different words are never used for the same thing".

   To meet this problem some dictionaries now support on an interactive basis both synonyms and homynyms, along with a full glossary of terms, thesaurus and dictionary capability.

- Prompts

    A good dictionary system will encourage or even insist that the developer thinks about the full needs of any dictionary element, even if they are not used all the time, by means of prompts, reminders and back-up help messages.

    A five year projected growth of data may not be useful in all cases, but when it is it can be vital. A second aspect is the use of sensible defaults, such as the average length of character fields is 60% of the maximum.

- Quality Checks

    Completeness and consistency is always a problem when doing both analysis and design. A dictionary which can re-examine its contents from many directions is very useful.

    eg. Does each item of data have a function for creation, change, removal and even to use it for some useful purpose.

- Catalytic

    Many dictionary elements, such as a program definition, may be thought of in several ways. The way of recording the detail may be graphical (eg dataflow diagram) but textual representation, pure English or an alternative diagrammatic form can catalytically promote further thought and improvements.

    One of the most powerful techniques found has been the layout of diagrams against pre-determined precedence rules which tends to group similar things together and beg the question "Are they really the same?"

Passive Intelligence is the triggering by computer of the developers own intelligence in a timely manner.

4.2 Active Intelligence

Active Intelligence from a dictionary system is when the computer can act upon existing data and carry out complex, repetitive or time consuming tasks on behalf of the developer. These tasks might be impossible or impractical to do by other means or ones which, given a knowledge base, can exhibit some aspects of the skill of an expert.

Examples of active intelligence are:-

- Automated tasks

    Using fourth generation tools and relational database management systems, automated database design, performance and size prediction, program generation and production of both system and "first cut" user documentation is now demonstrable.

- Pattern Recognition

    Dictionary software can analyse text, properties and characteristics of dictionary elements and suggest where commonality exists. A future potential is the commonality of ideas, approach and direction at the business level, which will require a new level of sophistication. Finding data commonality is currently viable, but automated functional pattern recognition is more difficult to detect by computers.

- ### Standard Patterns

  A recent concept has been the introduction of a set of generic business patterns which have proven to be applicable as recurring concepts in many companies. These business models and their corresponding implementation concepts (eg programs, tables, indexes etc) can be pre-loaded into a dictionary to provide an intelligent or knowledge base from which to start. In this case the formatted and focussed intelligence of top analysts and designers can be made available through a dictionary to many different companies. One or two companies, including ORACLE Corporation, have created such dictionary based products in areas such as personnel, accountancy, assets etc.

- ### Help

  What do I do next?
  Where am I?
  What will be affected if I change this?
  These are some of the questions which an active dictionary containing project status knowledge can help to answer.

- ### Heuristic

  A heuristic dictionary is one which can ˋlearnˊ from previous experience. In practical terms, this might be exemplified by improved estimating, identification of previous successful designs, recall of alternatives discarded.

  Active Intelligence is the computer exhibiting positive help in terms of quality, timeliness and cost saving, on behalf of the developer. It is also the ability for the computer to carry out tasks at a high level of skill.

5   SQL* DESIGN DICTIONARY

The SQL* Design Dictionary (SDD) (see figure 3) was produced by ORACLE Corporation to help its consultants build systems for its clients and to support product development of the various application systems available from the company, such as its Accountancy and Personnel Systems. It is normally used to complement the SQL* Development Method, but is now used by hundreds of clients, some of whom use other methodologies.

The SQL* Design Dictionary and Graphics Utility provide an active computerised dictionary system based on an ORACLE database, which are available to document, quality check and provide active computer assistance to the analyst and designer. These portable tools take the tedium out of the work, provide up-to-date cross-referenced graphical and written documentation and encourage good design practice.

SDD is available on personal computers and in multi-user form on mini and mainframe computers on a wide range of manufacturerˊs machines.

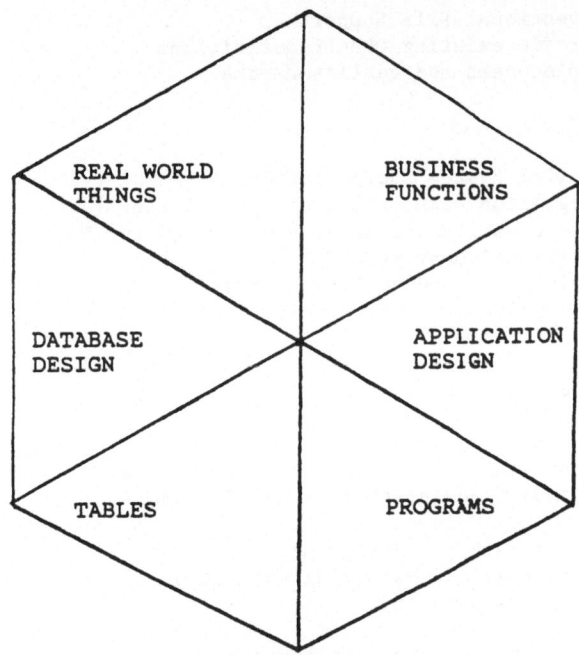

Figure 3   SQL* DESIGN DICTIONARY

SDD consists of over 90 on-line application screens, reports and programs which maintain the SDD database and provide a combination of working documents and management information.

Input and query screens, which have comprehensive validity and credibility checks, include:-

Strategy

- Multiple Application/Data Subject Area Support
- Function Hierarchy
- High Level Data Flow Definition
- Entity Definition outline
- Business Relationships
- Attributes, including domain validation
- System and Corporate Terminology (Thesaurus and Dictionary)
- Completeness and quality checks

Analysis

- Detailed Function Definition
- Dataflow, Datastore, External Entity and Process
- Detailed Entity, Attribute and Relationship Definition
- Volume and Frequencies
- Completeness and quality checks

Design

- Application, Screen, Report and Program Structure
- Default Database and Index Design
- Table and Column Definition
- Performance Indexes
- Views

- Conventional File Support
- Retrofit existing ORACLE definitions
- Completeness and quality checks

Implementation

- Detailed System Documentation
- Integration with ORACLE on-line dictionary
- Project estimation using Program Gearing Factors
- `First-cut´ user guide
- Completeness and quality checks

Production

- Impact
- Powerful Query Capability

SDD has some powerful utilities which are made available to aid the function of Database Administration and include:-

- Default database design utility
- Database and Index sizing prediction
- Dictionary security

The above list describes the main functionality provided by SDD. The following examples describe how it has been used to actively support the implementation process.

5   CASE STUDY

The company is a multi-national organisation, where the same basic business is replicated in each country. At the end of a strategy study a business model comprising business objectives, performance indicators, around 150 entities and 200 functions was loaded into SDD. The dictionary was used to cross check the completeness and to record `first cut´ ideas of attributes.

A designer then formulated an overall database design which was then fed into SDD (a one hour task). The dictionary default database designer was then used to create a fully normalised physical design, including primary keys, foreign keys, column definitions and first-cut index design. This design included rough volumes and maximum sizes for the data.

The designer was then able to invoke the database sizing utility to predict the size of the database for both data and indexes. This was obviously inaccurate, being prior to detailed analysis, but the designer could then work on the query screens to determine the most critical aspects and iterate around this process to produce a more definitive picture very quickly.

The predictions were later found to be within 10% of the production size.

On completion of the analysis stage, the above procedure was carried out again to give a highly definitive database design and sizing. The process was repeated several times in this case, to reflect each of the many instances of databases which were to be implemented; one database per country each with different sizings.

The program design was then split into two major areas. "Core" design, for programs common to each country and "country specific" for local

differences. SDD then helped to predict the effort involved in building
the system. With the online dictionary driven application generators,
screen painters and report writers available with the ORACLE Relational
Database Management System the applications were prototyped, checked with
users and implemented. The final system documentation and cross
references were held in SDD, to form the framework for future
developments and maintenance. First cut user documentation was produced
from the dictionary, pulling together definitions of terms, procedural
steps, messages etc.

Products mentioned are the:-

    SQL* DEVELOPMENT METHOD
    SQL* DESIGN DICTIONARY
    ORACLE Relational Database Management System

AUTOMATED SUPPORT USING A MAINFRAME DATA DICTIONARY FOR

ANALYSIS AND DATA MODELLING AT A MAJOR INTERNATIONAL BANK

Simon Tyrrell-Lewis

Database Consultants Europe

Woking, UK

1   INTRODUCTION

Many organisations have used data dictionaries on mainframe computers for
a number of years to support DBMS's such as IMS and IDMS, and the application systems using them. However, far fewer have used such tools
for a long period to support the analysis phase of Information Systems
development. In describing the experiences of a major international
bank, (which will be referred to as X-Bank) I wish to illustrate some of
the issues that may be faced when selecting an analysis methodology and
when preparing standards for the data dictionary.

2   PLANNING FOR IS DEVELOPMENT

At X-Bank, the past six years have been spent developing a complete new
corporate database and its associated application systems. DATAMANAGER
has been used as the documentation tool in this major project.

As these major new developments were being planned, it was decided that
an essential aspect of the procedures and techniques to be employed was
an analysis methodology, a standard way of researching what the computer
systems would have to support. Two requirements were identified for
this methodology. Firstly, it should process an approach to analysis
that would help the application teams define and understand the business
activities of the users. Secondly, it contained a method of ensuring
that the designed databases and data structures would support those
requirements efficiently and effectively.

In selecting a methodology, it is important to recognise that there have
been no fundamentally new ideas in this area for many years. Therefore,
the issue for any organisation is to select the ideas which work and
which fit together. Firstly, any methodology must address the definition
of the static data structures of an organisation - their content and
relationships. Techniques for this include the use of entity models and
entity life cycle diagrams. Secondly, techniques are needed for analysing the activities of the organisation and the dynamic element of data;
how it is created, amended, manipulated, deleted etc, and how the data is
used to 'drive' the activities. Examples of such modelling techniques
are dataflow diagrams, activity decomposition diagrams, and component

interface diagrams. The final issue is a composite of the first and second; how to analyse and describe the way in which data is utilised within a process, and how data is used by different processes.

It had been a world-wide standard within X-Bank that the Yourdon/De Marco type of activity analysis was to be used. However at the time, it was felt that the big weakness of this methodology was that it was designed to help in predominantly batch systems work where the amount of shared data was minimal. It was expected that the X-Bank systems would include a large number of transactions running on-line because of the nature of the Bank's business and the fact that large corporate databases would be involved. It was therefore agreed that data modelling techniques were also necessary to cut right across the various business functions.

A specialist group was set up and most of its members attended week-long Yourdon workshops. Application team members had experience either in the more traditional requirements driven analysis techniques or in data driven structured analysis. Staff in the new Database Administration (DBA) group within the systems department were familiar with data modelling.

3   THE METHODOLOGY AND ITS APPLICATION

It was made a requirement that the data analysts within the DBA group should work closely with the application teams to produce data models for the new systems. The application team would begin, as they consulted with the users, by drawing up dataflow diagrams and identifying the data needed to support business activities. The DBA staff would then use normalisation techniques, together with top-down methods, to prepare a data model. Finally, the database designers within DBA would take the data model and all the transactions which the team had identified as being needed, and ensure that the entity model would support them.

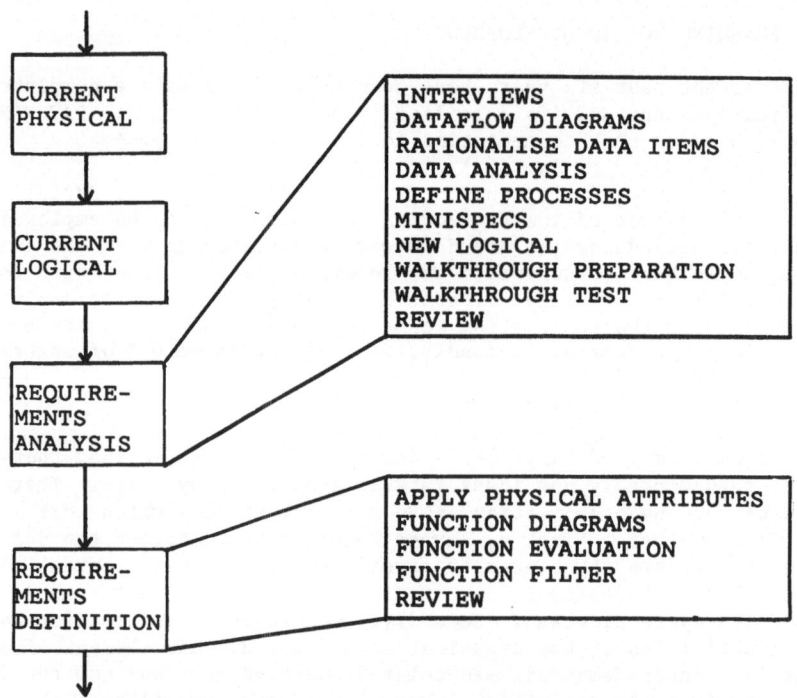

Figure 1   Data and function analysis in the ADS

However, although iterations occurred within each of the three stages as more information was collected, changes were not passed back to previous steps. In addition, it became evident that the link between the activity analysis and data modelling stages was weak. As a result, the application team analysts felt that they were doing activity analysis as part of the definition of DFDs, and again as they helped to validate the data model. In addition, there was a need to extend the methodology beyond the analysis phase to encompass the designing, writing and installation of programs, and so on.

Consequently, it was decided to develop a methodology to cover the whole Systems Life Cycle, which married together DFD techniques, data modelling and functional analysis much more closely. The standards for this methodology became one element within what became known as the Application Development Standards (ADS). These are standards covering the full Systems Life Cycle, from the initiation of a project, through analysis, design and construction, and eventually maintenance. (See Figure 1 for part of the structure of the ADS.)

4   DATAMANAGER AS A DOCUMENTATION TOOL

When tailoring methodological techniques to suit the expertise and attitudes of those within an organisation it is essential to decide what tools are to be made available. Although this may seem to be putting the cart before the horse, there is no value in collecting information that will not be maintainable or easily accessible. Once the content of a dictionary becomes out-of-date, it loses its credibility and use of the dictionary rapidly declines. At X-Bank it was decided that DATAMANAGER was the most tailorable and user friendly documentation tool available. DATAMANAGER had been installed since the early stages of the new development work and a fair quantity of DFD analysis work had been documented but unfortunately without department-wide standards and significant central monitoring, advice and control. The decision was therefore taken by DBA to develop a set of standards for DATAMANAGER use, covering DFDs and data models, and to use these in a new dictionary. The DBA group retrospectively documented the data modelling work that had been performed during the previous months.

The procedure for preparing standards to support the analysis activities using a data dictionary involves establishing the entities that the methodology uses - the meta-entities - (eg entity, relationship, activity, dataflow), their attributes (eg names, description, format, number of occurrences) and the relationships between the meta-entities. One version of the meta-entity model is given in Figure 2. The attributes needed were then identified.

DATAMANAGER permits the definition of ´aliases´, or alternative names, for each meta-entity held on the dictionary. Examples might be a full, non-abbreviated name, or special programming language aliases. The attributes are called ´clauses´ on DATAMANAGER. A number of these come as standard - such as DESCRIPTION and NOTE (which are text clauses), and CATALOGUE and CONTAINS (which document relationships between meta-entities). (For an example of clauses used for documenting an ´entity´, see Figure 3).

5   USING DATAMANAGER

As in so many companies, there was then a two part problem - how to get the project teams to use the standards devised, and how to improve the amount of documentation prepared at each stage. A word of warning is necessary at this point; the title of this conference focuses on ˝computer-based tools˝. We must not forget the people issues raised by the use of these tools. Perhaps the hardest part of any data dictionary/Analyst Workbench/Integrated Project Support Environment project is not the software - problems here will be solved in time - but the task of selling the need for methodologies and tools to management and development staff. Without their active commitment, all our efforts in the area of tools will be wasted. At X-Bank, consideration was given to the way in which the use and contents of the dictionary was controlled, the promotion of the dictionary as a tool, the training of the users, and lastly the altitudes and ˝style˝ of those involved in

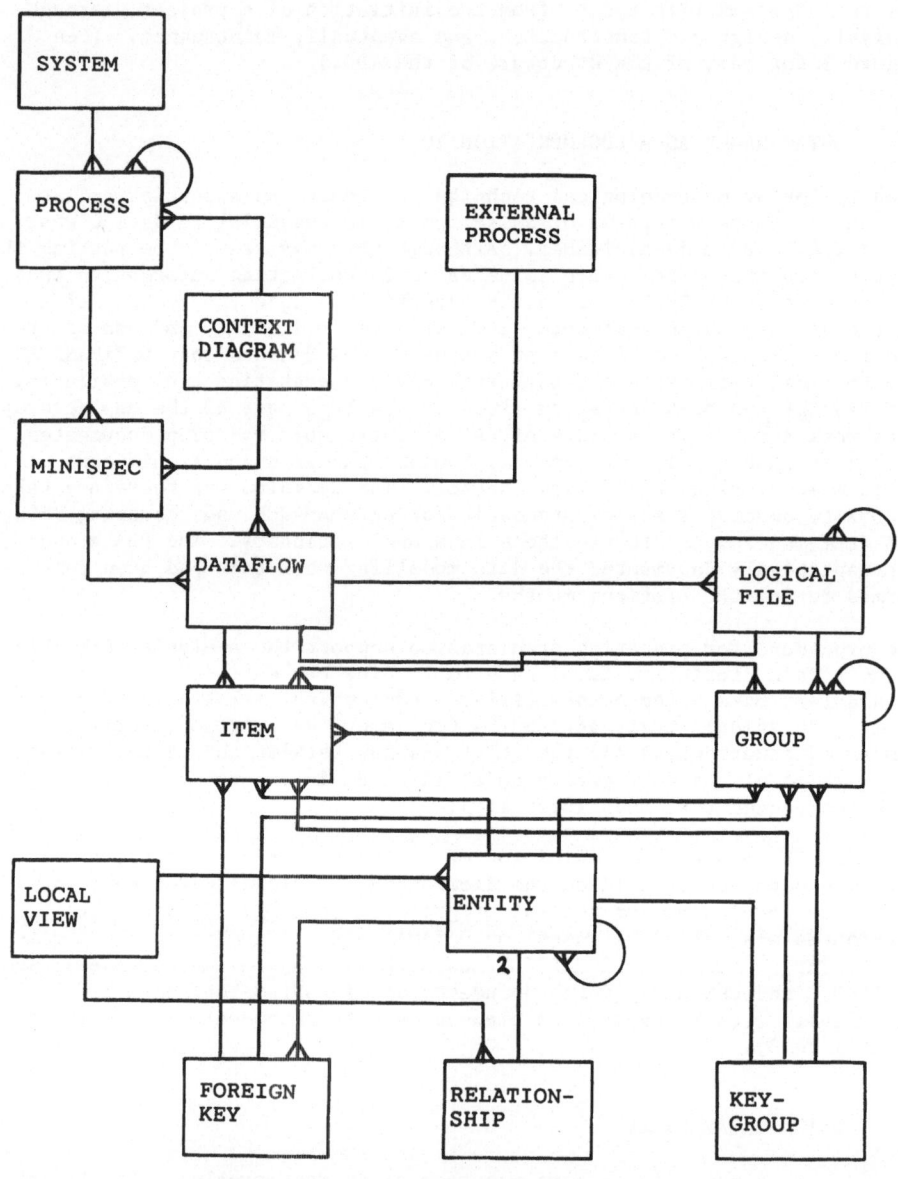

Figure 2 X-Bank Meta-Entity Model

```
200        ALIAS
201                   FULL-NAME 'NO FULL-NAME GIVEN'
  .
  .
  .

300        DESCRIPTION
305        "++++ DESCRIPTION MISSING ++++           "
1600       NOTE
1630       "INDEPENDENT/DEPENDENT                    "
1635       "        --------------                   "
  .
  .
  .

5500       CONTAINS
5505       "++++ KEY-GROUP MISSING ++++"
5510       "ENTITIES/GROUPS/ITEMS MISSING"
  .
  .
  .
```

Figure 3 Entity Skeleton

supporting the dictionary. Thus a heavy emphasis was laid on ´carrot´
approaches - encouraging the use of the dictionary, making it easy and
valuable to use, but with ´stick´ methods of control available if necessary and appropriate.

Completing a corporate data model - starting from a high level model and
connecting in ´local views´ ie business function-oriented models, was
deemed to be a high priority, along with collecting business definitions
for all the data items and groups which did not already have them. This
project has been worked on since, as well as adding new models and data
items for new applications.

About two years ago, support began to be given to application teams for
documenting their DFDs on DATAMANAGER. Pilot projects were selected,
ensuring that they were relatively independent of the existing systems
and that the staff involved were particularly keen to use the new
techniques. These characteristics made it easier for the DBA staff to
get changes to the standards accepted. It was ensured that adequate
support could be provided for each of these projects, for example to
change the team´s documentation on the dictionary if standards were being
changed, and to give additional training and guidance immediately it was
requested. More recently it was possible to insist on the use of
DATAMANAGER as a documentation tool for DFDs. Support for this measure
has been reinforced by the decision taken to export the systems developed
originally for one division into other parts of the X-Bank organisation,
and also due to pressure from auditors. Clearly the speed with which the
systems could be installed depended heavily on the amount and quality of
the documentation available.

6   CONCLUSION

Those organisations using DATAMANGER in the way that has been described,
ie to support and document the logical environment, have had great power
available to them in terms of the command syntax used and the flexibility
of the system. However, this has brought problems of its own; the very

strengths of the software have meant that it can be seen as user-unfriendly – there is a need to guide the user via panels and simple commands. This is now possible, but the standards expected by a user community increasingly familiar with tools such as ISPF, on-line documentation and PCs with their graphics, colour and element of fun have made the task of those responsible for mainframe dictionaries still harder. Building up a dictionary tends to be for the Dr Johnsons of this world; it is a fascinating and painstaking exercise. However, most of the people involved with the development of Information System are motivated more by what Rosemary Rock-Evans [ROCK86] of DCE has called an `arcade game mentality`; the preparation of documentation needs to be perceived as fun. Further complexities relating to the need to interface different dictionary and directory software to each other and to the new Analyst Workbenches and integrated IPSE tools are now evident.

There is therefore a need to develop new facilities around the mainframe data dictionary to meet urgent requirements, without investing vast amounts of effort, but at the same time positioning the organisation so that it is ready to take maximum advantage of Analyst Workbenches as they meet more of the known requirements.

At X-Bank, this is now achieved. A considerable amount of information is recorded on the dictionary in a clear structure, users have high expectations which have been met – sometimes by clear but not impossible promises, and a climate of patient enthusiasm. The standards adopted have been carefully designed to take account of existing skills within the organisation, parent company standards, the tools available, and the experiences of other organisations.

REFERENCES

[ROCK86] Rock-Evans R "Analysis: Workbench Revolution" Datalink August 4th 1986.

AN APPLICATION ENVIRONMENT

Frank Jones

bit Business Information Techniques Ltd

Bradford, UK

1   CONCEPT OF AN APPLICATION ENVIRONMENT

The use of Fourth Generation Languages (4GL) by software application
developers, is increasing. This end is brought about because of the high
productivity obtained by their use and the flexibility they offer in
system development following implementation of the first version.
Running parallel with this trend is the use of expert system shells by
non-computer specialists in prototyping small or experimental systems for
intelligent knowledge based systems (IKBS).

Both approaches suffer from a number of drawbacks. The very flexibility
the 4GL offers the software designer makes the package unusable by an end
user and therefore bars the group most likely to understand the application from its use. Similarly, with expert system shells, the lack of
standard utilities in the shell means an end user's application is often
incomplete, lacking conventional requirements like report generation or
word processing. One approach to overcome the barriers to providing a
set of software engineering tools for an end user is to provide an
'Application Environment', like **parys**, which models the characteristics
of an application set.

The approach means that the product is restrictive in the types of application it can address, but that the application can be more fully
developed, more quickly and by a less skilled designer than through the
use of a 4GL or an expert system shell. The **parys** shell is aimed at
providing a design environment for users wishing to incorporate IKBS
techniques with conventional computing for applications using analysis,
deduction and estimation as a primary requirement.

The system is designed for experts who in normal practice analyse
projects to produce recommendations on solutions and/or estimates of
costs and time scales. A typical expert user would thus:

* Analyse projects, situations or problems.

* Define requirements.

* Examine schemes, systems, products or services as possible solutions
  in the light of requirements.

*   Decide on the best solution.

*   Provide cost or time estimates for alternative schemes and proposed
        solutions.

Some example applications are given later. In each case, having built in
your own criteria for analysis, decision making and costing, you may pass
the system on to others, either for routine use "on-line", for input of a
second opinion or for training purposes.

In order to provide the type of flexible system necessary for an end user
application designer the ´Application Environment´ concept offers a
module approach which allows the user to mix and match the software
required for each application. For example a prototype environment in
parys called ´Analyser Plus´ may be integrated into the ´Generic
Application Environment´ at a later stage when more conventional
utilities need to be incorporated into the system design.

2   SOME EXAMPLE SYSTEMS

bit launched their application environment with a model system for
Personnel last year and have since developed a Tender Management system
and other applications.

An example of another user who has developed their own product using the
´**parys** Application Environment´ is Inbucon the management consultancy
practice. Inbucon purchased the **parys** Application Environment late last
year and after four months part time effort by one of their experienced
personnel experts produced their own product "HR2" which is supplied to
clients as part of their consultancy programme.

"Expert systems can fill a major gap in our kind of top-level human
resources consultancy" says Inbucon Director, Richard Alston. "The
present rapid changes in markets and technologies have created a very
high demand for help in identifying the top management ·skills and com-
petencies a business needs to survive and prosper – and how these skills
should be organised and used. There is a severe shortage of people with
the necessary training, personality and breadth of experience to provide
this advice".

Personnel specialists use the system without learning new computer skills

"Using the **parys** Applications Environment, we have provided our
Consultants with the means to incorporate what they learn on an assignment into an expert system that can be left with the client. Our
specialist works with top management to profile their environment and
needs, and the software can subsequently be used by in-house personnel
people to ´cascade´ the process down into the middle management and
staff. Our consultants are not computer people, but we have found the
system remarkably easy-to-handle".

3   COMPONENTS OF THE **parys** ´APPLICATION ENVIRONMENT´

The major components of the **parys** Application Environment are:-

–   a networked database

- a relational query language
- a series of expectation driven expert system shells
- a set of graphical packages
- an integrated word processing package
- a diary management system
- a report generator
- a library of mathematical and statistical algorithms
- a series of screen generators
- a unique knowledge base and menu editor which allows new systems to be quickly prototyped

3.1 A Networked Database and Relational Query Language

The term database has a range of meanings. Broadly it is any collection of data. More specifically it is a collection of related data. A Data Base Management System is a system for storing data and relationships and enabling the retrieval of data using the relationships as access paths to navigate the database.

Different DBMSs use different mechanisms for storing data and, more importantly, the relationships. In each case data items are grouped into records, with further data relationships being held by links between records. In hierarchical and network databases these links are generally pointers maintained by the DBMS, though in some cases programs may manipulate these pointers directly. (In a hierarchical DBMS the pointers arrange related records in a hierarchy rather than a cross-connected network). In a relational database pointers are not generated, instead the link is the duplication of a data item in the corresponding records. The relational form offers much more flexibility than the other data models but has been characterised by significant run-time overheads in index management and record searching.

DBMSs comprise a number of elements: a record access system, a data dictionary and a scheme for mapping items from physical records to logical program structures. This mapping imposes a run-time overhead on data access which may not be recognised by the programmer.

The content of the data dictionary varies but always details the layout of physical records and often describes logical views or schema. In addition data validation constraints, and screen and report formats are often set out. The data dictionary may support any ´fourth´ generation tools available with the DBMS. These include user interfaces for setting up and requesting reports, ´painting´ data entry and enquiry screens, and implementing new applications.

The efficiency of the system in terms of data storage and run-time access to the data is dictated by the record management system and the design of the database, i.e. the selection of which items are stored in which records.

The flexibility of the system depends on the degree of program dependancy on physical data formats as well as any constraints that may be imposed on the physical implementation of logical relationships.

Most DBMSs offer features designed to ensure data reliability and security. Backup and journalling systems allow recovery after system

failures with minimum data loss while password protection may be applied
to applications or even individual data items.

Distributed databases offer improvements in convenience and efficiency in
some respects but are difficult to manage and if poorly designed, or
specified without reference to future requirements, can generate huge
problems.

Classical hierarchical and network DBMSs such as IMS and IDMS tend to
impose rigidity on data structures as well as causing run-time processing
overheads. Relational systems, such as Oracle, are more flexible but
even less efficient. bit therefore have designed an indexed record
management system with a data dictionary and a (relational) query
facility. This combination provides the flexibility of access of a
relational system while enabling the implementation of frequently-used
transactions providing optimal runtime efficiency.

3.2   An Expectation Driven Shell

3.2.1   Shell Design

Diagnostic expert systems have to cope with very open-ended problems.
They are used in areas such as medical diagnosis, job analysis, fault
finding and so on. In this kind of situation the person consulting the
system has a list of facts. The question they want to ask is something
like "what do you make of this?" or "what's happening here?".

Ideally the system should begin by asking a few general questions to
determine the overall nature of the problem. Later on more specific
questions should be asked to acquire more information about the symptoms
described by the user. The system should then analyse what it has been
told, deduce what the most likely hypotheses are and then start to ask
very specific questions in order to establish some of these hypotheses as
facts.

At the later stages the user should be able to demand an explanation as
to why a question is being asked. More general information about what
the system is 'thinking' should also be available.

3.2.2   Commercial Shells

3.2.2.1 Goal Driven Systems

Most commercially available expert system shells (e.g. APES, ES/P
Advisor) use goal-directed mechanisms. This kind of system investigates
the hypotheses one by one, trying to establish them by asking questions.
The user is often frustrated by a large number of obscure and off the
point questions, the answers to many of which are unknown. As the number
of possible conclusions grows larger the situation worsens.

3.2.2.2 Data Driven Systems

Data driven systems solve some of these problems, but sometimes omit to
investigate significant hypotheses.

In this kind of system questioning proceeds in a structured manner.
Certain replies lead to further questions being asked. The user is lead
through a fairly concise and thorough interrogation. Unfortunately these
systems fail to take account of accumulating evidence for a hypothesis

and investigate further likely possibilities. This is because, essentially, the system is driven only by the user's input; it does not form
and investigate its own goals.

3.2.2.3 Expectation-Driven Approach

The ideal diagnostic shell should combine data-directed and goal-directed
search strategies. This can be done by using expectation-driven search.

The key feature of expectation-driven systems is the concept of an
'expectation'. In most expert systems a hypothesis may be true, false
(with a possible certainty factor) or unknown. In an expectation-driven
system a hypothesis may also be 'expected' or 'unexpected'. Roughly, an
'expected' hypothesis is one that is worthy of further investigation.
Any 'unexpected' hypothesis is no longer to be considered, it may later
become true, but never 'expected'.

Once it has been established that a hypothesis is 'expected' the system
attempts to establish it as true or false using a type of goal directed
search. In this search, the system assumes that all unexpected hypotheses are unknown and does not ask the host system questions relating to
them. If, later on, one of the subgoals of the hypothesis becomes true,
or expected then the hypothesis is examined again.

This scheme fits in with the data directed approach as follows:

Each hypothesis has a corresponding set of up to three rules. The rules
specify the circumstances under which the hypothesis is true, expected
and unexpected. When a hypothesis becomes expected, or when it is already expected, and one of its subgoals becomes true or false, the system
attempts to ascertain whether that hypothesis can be shown to be true or
false from its subgoals. If this can be done, the hypothesis then becomes true, otherwise the system investigates the hypothesis further by
making all of its unknown subgoals expected. If a subgoal of the hypothesis represents an unknown but askable fact then the host system is
asked a question in order to establish the hypothesis as true or false.
The system may answer 'unknown' in which case the goal becomes
unexpected. Rules for a hypothesis take the form of a logical expression
involving other hypotheses and facts. The expression may involve the
operators 'and', 'or' and 'not'.

At the start of the consultation all hypotheses are assumed to be unknown
(although certain facts may be known to the system) except for the <u>key
hypothesis</u>, which is 'expected'. Other hypotheses will become expected,
and subsequently investigated as a result of the investigation of the key
hypothesis. As a convenience, it may be specified that the key hypothesis is 'true', and that any number of other hypotheses are
'expected' if the key hypothesis is true. This enables the simulation of
a number of key hypotheses.

The system works by repeatedly investigating 'expected' hypotheses until
none remain.

3.2.3 A set of graphical packages

The provision of a graphical package for providing, say for example, an
organisational chart or a PERT chart is in itself a useful facility.
However, if the end user is required to create the chart by data input or
using drawing techniques then the package loses part of is attraction.

In **parys** graphical images are created as by-products of stored records and graphical tools are offered only as amendments to the outcomes processed by the system.

For example an organisational chart is produced from existing records as the system has the intelligence built into the graphical package of the personnel expert who would construct an organoplan in, for example, a Personnel environment.

3.2.4 An Integrated Word Processor

In conventional word processors the components mainly consist of the following:-

- a text editor for creating strings of text in a format
- a place for storing standard text
- a methodology for merging standard text with other text whether original or stored elsewhere
- format methodologies for such things as letter layout, repagination or reports etc.
- checking mechanisms such as a spelling checker etc.

The interface to the application is via a third party ´a word processing operator´ who constructs the merge command selecting manually the correct letter with the name and address list and any special format instructions.

Effectively word processing becomes a specialised separate process from the application focussing upon the specialist skills of the operator rather than the application.

In **parys** this aspect is overcome by the letter being automatically generated by the system as a by-product of the application process, with any special format or original text being generated by the originator.

3.2.5 A Diary Manager

In conventional diary management systems the user of the system constructs entries in relation to activities and tells the system what the outcome of appointments registrations were. This effectively means reliance on the diary management process is handed back to the author and diary management becomes an additional task.

In **parys** procedural steps are declared to the system and post holders impacted declared and the time span estimated. From then onwards the system prompts incomplete steps and the diary manages the individuals as a by product of the activities which happen within the application environment.

3.2.6 A Report Generator

parys offers a set of conventional spread-sheet utilities for declaring reports for either screen display or output.

3.2.7 Library of Mathematical and Statistical Algorithms

For each application environment **parys** will offer the facility to build appropriate mathematical and statistical models suitable to the application.

3.2.8 Screen Generators

To allow users to customise screens and layouts a series of screen based generating tools will be offered under **parys**.

3.2.9 Knowledge Base and Menu Editing

parys has a unique knowledge based editor which allows users to build new knowledge bases and edit the data represented by screens via a menu driven process.

This unique editor is described in more detail in **parys** sales literature. The important aspect related to the editor is that it is designed as an end user tool rather than a software engineering tool with the major problems of managing the data and representing the rules correctly being removed.

4 RATIONALE FOR AN APPLICATION ENVIRONMENT

In conclusion the rationale for using an Application Environment may be summarised as follows:-

- it overcomes the problems of poor design by offering a model system

- it is user orientated with dynamic menuing and contextual support so solving the learning problems.

- development costs of producing systems are reduced because of the available software engineering tools.

- methodologies embodied within expert systems shells normally un-usable as commercial products are overcome by their inclusion in an Application Environment.

- feedback required by the end user to the designer to adapt the system may be misinterpreted. This is solved by providing editing tools for end users.

HIGH–LEVEL DESIGN FOR OFFICE AUTOMATION WITH SUPPORTING

GRAPHICS FACILITIES

L.M.S. Lau and T.G. Gough

Department of Computer Studies, University of Leeds

Leeds, UK

ABSTRACT

This paper begins with an outline of a proposed high–level design
methodology for office automation which consists of three levels - the
first level being organisation analysis, the second office system
analysis and the third high–level design. It is based on a model of the
office in which the degree of structure of office work can be classified.
This methodology is directed at strategic planning for office automation
and an `Automatability-Index´ is calculated to provide an early indica-
tion of the suitability of an office for automation. The methodology is
heavily reliant on the use of visual presentation in analysing and
specifying the requirements of the prospective automated system and the
second part of this paper describes a demonstration package to automate
the `drawing´ of the second-level function and process charts, as one
approach to the provision of a fast, flexible and inexpensive design aid.

The paper concludes with an evaluation of the performance of the
demonstration package when the methodology was applied to a `real life´
systems study.

1   INTRODUCTION

Since the late 1970´s `Office Automation´ has become a fashionable term
to denote any application to technology in the office. Initially, the
term was usually used as a synonym for Word Processing. The availability
of increasingly sophisticated technology and increasing demands for
improved office performance have encouraged the adoption of a more wide-
ranging view of Office Automation.

In the final evaluation reports by KMG Thomson McLintock on the Office
Automation Pilots Project sponsored by the Department of Trade and
Industry is defined as "the use of electronic technology to serve business goals by raising the productivity of office staff, particularly
those who are not specialists in information technology" [MCLI86]. This
definition, however, addresses the objectives of Office Automation rather
than Office Automation itself.

Our definition of Office Automation is concerned with what Office
Automation means in terms of its effects. It is defined as "the use of

automatic tools to realise a sequence of office functions, or an office process, without the need of human control between functions." Nevertheless integration is a common thread between these two definitions. They both highlight the following points:

1   there may be a need to integrate different types and styles of technology (electronic or automatic), and

2   there will be a need to integrate the technology into the normal work pattern of the office staff (as full automation is very un-likely to be achievable in the near future).

In order to achieve the above, prior planning is essential. The purpose of this High Level Design Methodology is to assist an organisation in formulating its long-term strategy for office automation and the follow-ing issues are addressed at the outset:-

1   whether automation is an appropriate solution for the office;

2   the extent to which the office should be automated in order the match the business strategy;

3   the likely effects on existing staff;

4   the need to re-design existing jobs and provide re-training for the staff; and

5   the integration of the automated system into the existing office systems.

Since this methodology makes extensive use of graphical charts, it could share a common problem with the other techniques such as those discussed by Yourdon [YOUR86]. The considerable amount of manual effort required to create and maintain charts can deter their effective use. An initial graphics package has been developed to demonstrate the usefulness of providing an interactive tool for the analyst to solve this particular problem.

This paper begins with a brief review of the main concepts of the Methodology. It then describes the facilities provided by the graphics package. A brief evaluation of the package in use is provided at the end of the paper.

2   AN OUTLINE OF THE METHODOLOGY

The High Level Design Methodology consists of three levels. It provides a set of guidelines and tools for the analyst to specify the requirements of an automated system. It is designed to encourage effective participa-tion by management and staff in the design process so that planned development is matched to the organisation's long-term business goals.

Not all offices can benefit to the same degree from office automation and the first level of the Methodology sets out to identify the most suitable office unit for further study. The second level analyses the chosen unit in terms of the structure of the business functions involved and the distribution of these functions within the office processes. The third level produces a high-level design based on a model of a proposed automated office. Redistribution of functions may be required to achieve the most effective system.

2.1 Level One: Organisation Analysis

To plan for effective automation, it is first necessary to determine whether automation is feasible and likely to be beneficial. This may not be as straight-forward as it seems due to the `dynamic´ nature of the office environment. Moreover, what seems to be repetitive and simple may not necessarily be suitable for effective automation although some form of computer support may be useful. A questionnaire is designed to collect the relevant information to provide an early indication of the likely success of automation (using the `Automatability-Index´).

There are four major steps at Level One:-

1   The structure of the organisation is analysed and the office units identified (which may be functional groups or departments). An organisation chart is then constructed.

2   The results are validated with the office staff;

3   A questionnaire is designed to cover the following aspects:
   (a) the size of the office unit,
   (b) the number of identical or similar working units,
   (c) the span of control,
   (d) the nature and volume of work,
   (e) the mode of communication,
   (f) the degree of dispersion of units within the office,
   (g) the nature of any current problems,
   (h) the level of experience of existing personnel with computer-related technology, and
   (i) the `climate´ of the office environment towards new technology.

   The questionnaires are distributed to and completed by the managers and clerical staff working in the office units of interest. The analyst also completes one for each office unit based on observation of the office activities.

4   The completed questionnaires are then collected and an `Automatability-Index´ is calculated for each office unit. A scoring system is devised according to the following rules:-

   (a) For each question, a score is assigned for each answer. A positive score for an answer `in favour´ of automation and a negative score for `against´. A `weight´ is assigned to each group of participants (i.e. management, clerical staff and analysts) for every question. A higher number is assigned if the opinion of a particular group is considered to be more important or relevant to that particular question.

   (b) The `Automatability-Index´ for each office unit is calculated in the following way:-

   Let
   NA, NM and NC be the number of analysts, managers and clerical staff participating in answering the questionnaire respectively,
   n be the number of questions in the questionnaire,
   T_i be the subtotal score for question i,
   S_{ij} be the score for answer j to question i,
   NA_{ij}, NM_{ij} and NC_{ij} be the number of analysts, management and clerical staff giving answer j to question i respectively,
   WA_i, WM_i and WC_i be the weight given to analysts, management and clerical staff respectively for question i.

Then, the Automatability-Index (A-Index) for an office unit is given by:-

$$\text{A-Index} = \frac{\sum_{i=1}^{n} T_i}{\underline{NA} + \underline{NM} + \underline{NC}}$$

where

$$\underline{T_i} = \underline{WA_i}^* \sum_j (\underline{NA_{ij}}^* \underline{S_{ij}}) + \underline{WM_i}^* \sum_j (\underline{NM_{ij}}^* \underline{S_{ij}}) + \underline{WC_i}^* \sum_j (\underline{NC_{ij}}^* \underline{S_{ij}})$$

(c) The unit with the highest positive Automatability-Index will be chosen for the next level analysis.

2.2 Level Two: Office System Analysis

At this level, the office functions performed within the chosen unit will be analysed and classified. The flow and distribution of the different classes of functions together with their mode of communication will be charted to give a fuller picture of the possible extent of automation.

There are six main steps at Level Two:-

1   A more detailed organisation chart is constructed for the office unit under study (if the previous charts are not detailed enough).

2   The following are noted for each member of staff in the unit during fact-finding exercise :
(a) the functions and subfunctions performed by that member of staff,
(b) the work content of the functions.
(c) the role of each function (i.e. co-ordination of buffering),
(d) the frequency of occurrence for each function (e.g. daily, weekly, monthly, yearly, seasonal, adhoc),
(e) the source(s) of input and destination(s) of output for each function.

3   A set of 'Function Charts' is constructed. The notations used are depicted in figure 1. After the charts are completed, each function will be classified into one of the four classes of office functions. The classification starts from the lowest level of subfunction and moves upwards. Each function can be classified as:

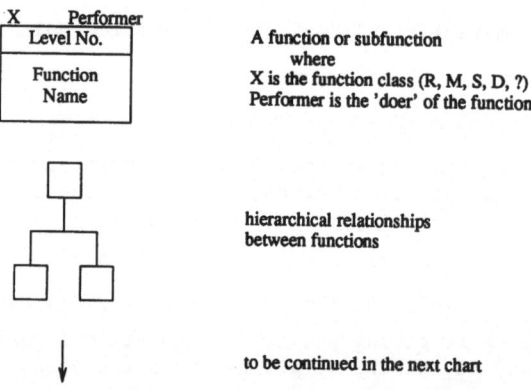

Figure 1   Notations used in function charts

- Routine work (R) when it consists of co-ordination activities only
  and occurs frequently;
- Supervision (S) when it consists of co-ordination activities but
  occurs infrequently;
- Mediation (M) when it consists of buffering activities and occurs
  frequently; or
- Decision-making (D) when is consists of buffering activities but
  occurs infrequently.
- `?´ can be used to denote a function which is not yet classified.
The degree of structure decreases in the above order. An example of
a function chart is given in figure 2.

4   The next step is to construct a set of `Process Charts´. The flow
      of the office functions and the type of communication involved
      within a process is displayed.

      The first step in constructing the process charts is to find out all
      the processes within the unit. By identifying the triggers first,
      the rest of the processes can be traced out until a final output is
      obtained or the termination of the process is reached. The nota-
      tions used in the process chart are given in figure 3. See figure 4
      for an example of Process Chart.

5   The process charts are then validated with the office staff.
      Process charts are chosen for validation instead of function
      charts

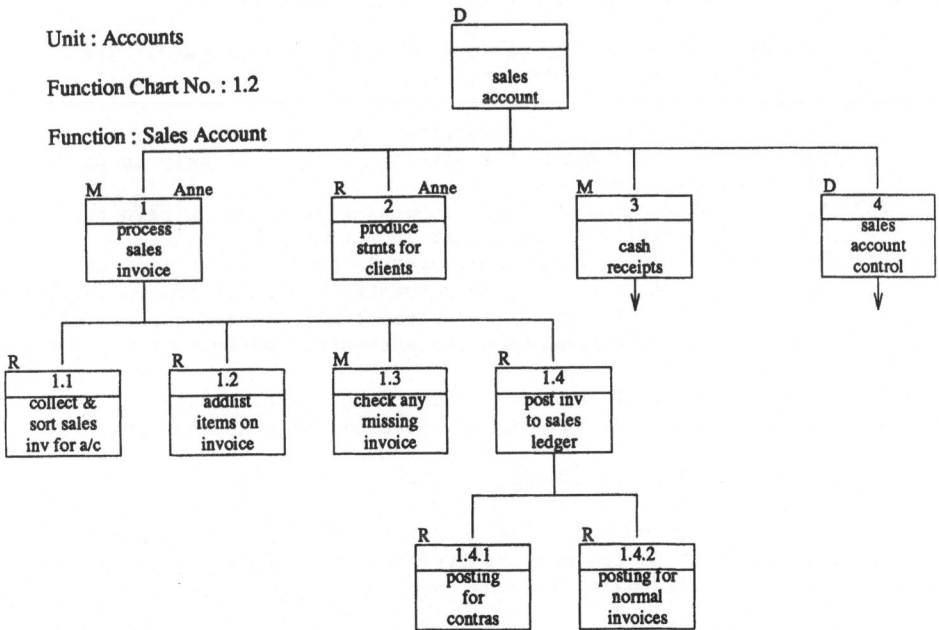

Figure 2   An example of a function chart

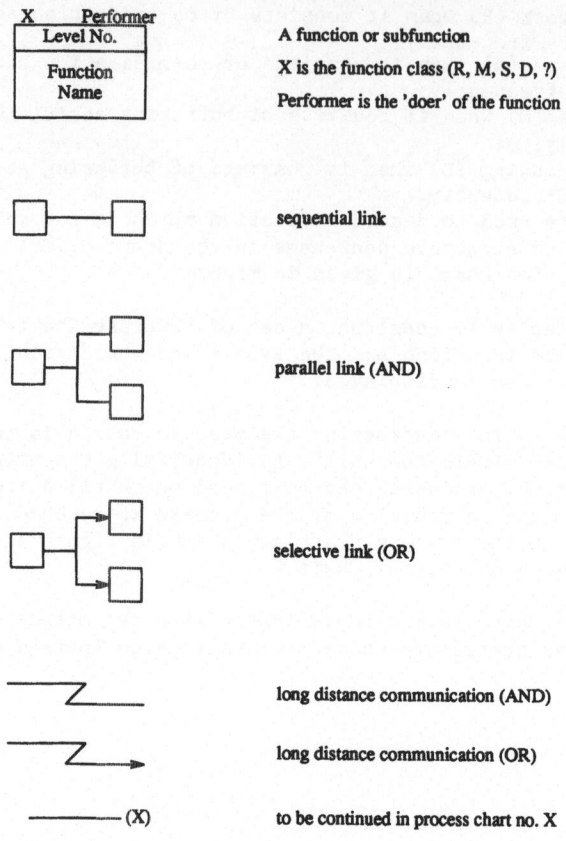

Figure 3   Notations for Process Charts

because they resemble the daily work procedure more closely.

6   The `automatability´ of the various processes in analysed. The
       following guidelines provide an indication of the `automatability´
       of processes:-
       (a) The longer the sequence of routine functions the higher the
           automatability and hence the better the return likely to be
           obtained from automation.
       (b) The fewer the number of decision-making functions within the
           process, the better candidate it is for automation.
       (c) The presence of mediation and supervision functions indicates a
           potential growth area for the automated system if the well-
           structured elements can be separated from the semi-structured
           elements and integrated into the automated system.

The office under study will then be subjected to the next stage of the
Methodology if it is seen to have a high potential for automation.

2.3 Level Three: High Level Design

At this level, a strategy for office automation will be established.
This includes a set of design and requirement specifications, the scope
of automation, possible phases for the development and a framework for

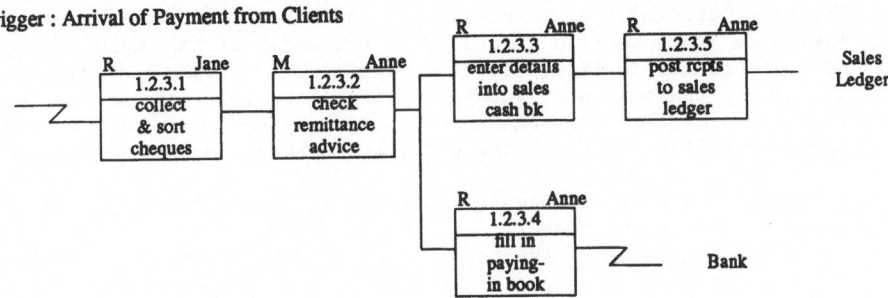

Process : Handling Cash Receipts for Sales Invoices

Trigger : Arrival of Payment from Clients

Figure 4   An example of a process chart

the management to evaluate the acceptability of the design and the proposed hardware and software.

There are five main steps at this level:

1   An initial set of `Process-Design Charts´ is drawn to show the allocation of functions between the human and the automated subsystems within each process. The notations used are similar to those in the process charts apart from the introduction of a partition line between the two subsystems (see figure 5 for an example).

2   The processes are then `streamlined´ and refined by:-
   (a) removing any redundant or obsolete functions or subfunctions,
   (b) appending any agreed additional functions and decision support facilities, and
   (c) keeping the traffic (in terms of frequency and volume) between the human and automated subsystems to a minimum. This may be achieved by re-ordering the functions so that the routine functions can be grouped together or by `automating´ the routine part of a `mediation´ or `supervision´ function.

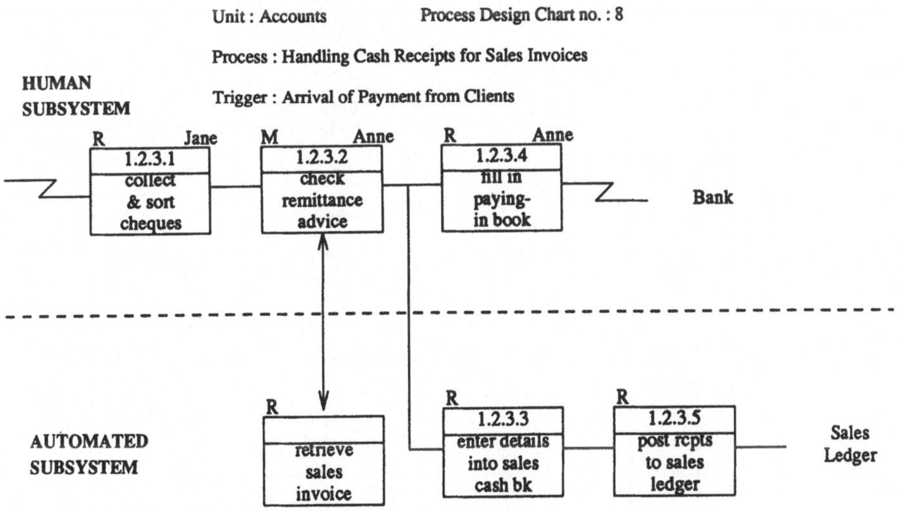

Unit : Accounts   Process Design Chart no. : 8

Process : Handling Cash Receipts for Sales Invoices

HUMAN SUBSYSTEM   Trigger : Arrival of Payment from Clients

AUTOMATED SUBSYSTEM

Figure 5   An example of a process-design chart

Contributions from management and staff will be invaluable at this stage because the effects of the proposed changes to their routines are likely to be more easily seen by them.

3 For each `streamlined` process, the requirements of the automated subsystem are specified according to the model of the automated office depicted in figure 6. The requirements of the various components of the automated subsystem (i.e. interface, checker, router, task performer and data-bank) are laid down. An interface is needed whenever a line `crosses` the partition between the two subsystems,

4 A proposal is then produced for automating the office unit. It will cover the following aspects:
   (a) a brief summary of the requirements of the automated system;
   (b) the effect on the existing human system of implementing the proposed system;

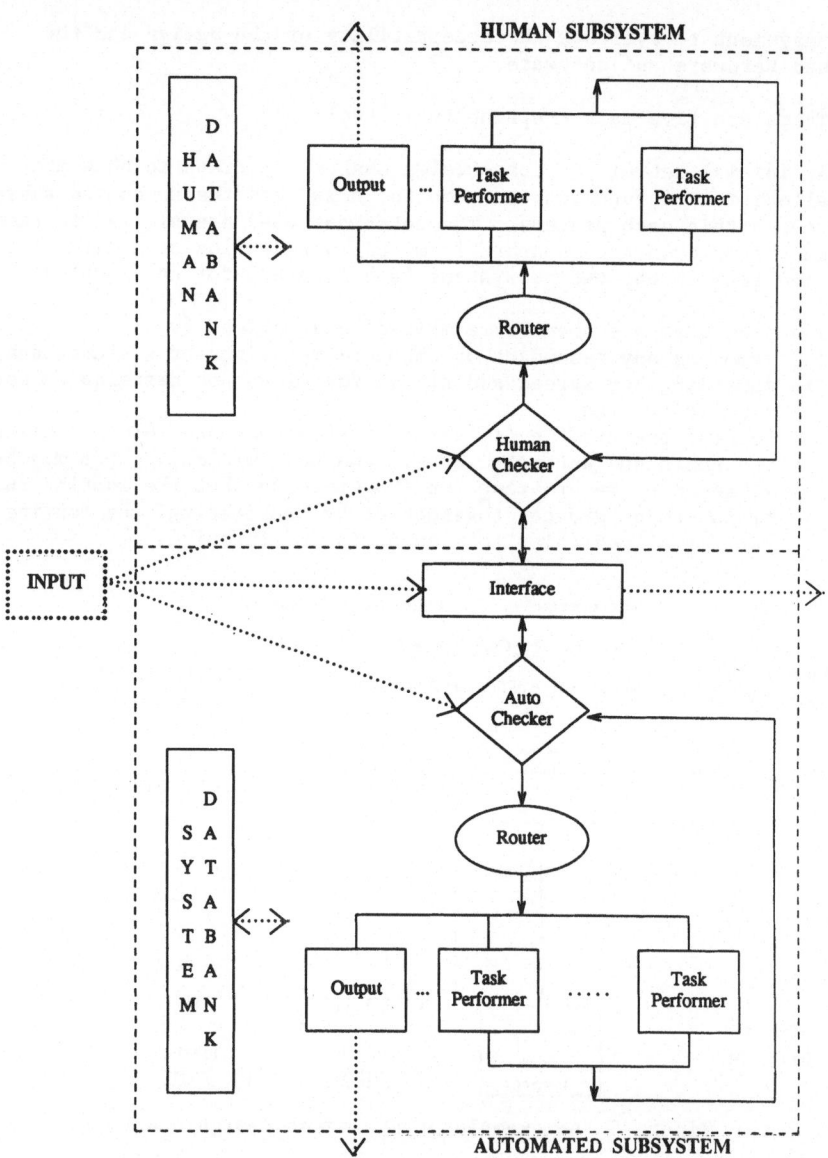

Figure 6 Basic components of an automated office

(c) a skeleton schedule for the development phases;

(d) the technology likely to be needed.

5   Management approval for the proposal and user agreement to it are
     then to be obtained. Modifications will be made if any additional
     constraints are imposed on the design at this stage.

3   COMPUTER-AIDED FACILITIES

As seen from the previous sections, this High Level Design Methodology
makes use of a lot of charts. The charts serve two main purposes.
Firstly, they enable the analyst/designer to visualise the logical
`structure´ of the existing system and the proposed system. Secondly,
they serve as a communication tool for the analyst/designer to exchange
ideas with the management and the end users. Nevertheless, the amount of
chart-drawing required by the Methodology will take up a lot of analysis
design time. Therefore, ways of reducing the effort required have to be
found to allow the analyst/designer to concentrate on the more important
aspects of analysing the data, defining the real problems(s) and then
deriving solution(s) to the problem(s) defined.

Computers have been employed to support system analysis and design since
the 1960´s. Their use varies with different techniques or methodologies
[COUG82, NUNA81], ranging from offering minimal support with documenta-
tion or report generation to playing an active role in analysis [TEIC77,
KONS82], code generation [WIGA84], prototyping [WASS82] or simulation
[ELLI82].

The use of interactive graphics for chart-drawing was seen by the authors
as an interesting area to explore in addressing the requirement to
provide the necessary charts at minimum cost in analysis/design time.

3.1 Implementation

The resulting demonstration package is implemented on the ICL PERQ
workstation (which was the best choice available at the time). The
workstation consists of a 768*1024 bit-mapped high resolution screen, a
keyboard with graphics tablet and cursor, a 16-bit processor, Winchester
disc and floppy disc drive. The language used is PASCAL under the
operating system POS. The size of the resulting executable code is
reasonably small at about 98K bytes.

While developing the facilities, the following criteria were used for
determining what features were to be implemented and how.

1   The `package´ must be easy to use.

2   Minimal learning is a requirement as the package is intended to
     speed up the analysis process.

3   It is to be at least as flexible as pen and paper which are the
     usual tools employed.

4   The package is to be robust so that any entered data will not be
     lost accidentally.

5   Finally, the computer-aided facilities to be offered are to play a
     supporting role only to free the analyst/designer from tedious
     clerical work to concentrate on the more important aspects of their
     work.

It was also decided to use Level Two of the Methodology, `Office System Analysis´, as the focus for the demonstration package because the type of interaction required here is representative of the general chart-drawing requirements.

At this Level, the analyst collects information from the interviews which will then be used in structuring the function and process charts. Hence, as a first step, the package generates forms for logging the results of the interviews. From the entered data, a set of function charts will be drawn automatically. Process charts are created interactively by the analyst from the details already captured for the function charts.

Viewing is another operation required. The package provides facilities to display both function and process charts. To overcome the small screen size (A4 vertical) two screen buffers are created to hold each page of the charts. A horizontal scrolling command is provided to move the chart sideways by pressing the buttons on the cursor.

Mistakes can be easily made while drafting charts, so editing facilities enable the analyst to restructure the charts already entered or to cor- rect any errors. An edit panel is provided which contains the appropriate commands for editing that type of chart. All commands are activated by pressing the cursor over the area of the selected command. Sometimes multiple windows are used if more than one operation is involved.

Finally, the system is capable of producing hardcopies of all the charts created and to permit enquiries. The major functions implemented are discussed in greater detail in the following sections.

3.2 The Main Menu

This is the first page presented to the user when the package is run. An example of this menu is illustrated in Appendix 1. There are altogether nine options available. After the chosen option is executed, this main menu will be returned unless the ninth option `Exit´ is chosen.

3.3 Option 1: Create Function Charts

Once the data collection forms have been completed after the interviews at level two, the `Create Function Chart´ routine is used to enter the initial draft of the function charts. A unique system code has to be assigned by the user to identify the system or office unit under investigation. Form filling technique is used to capture the function names, their class, their performers and the number of subfunctions for each function. A level number is then automatically assigned to each of the functions. An example of these forms can be found in Appendix 2.

At the top of each form, the parent function is printed to prompt for the subfunction entries. After a form is completed, there is a choice of editing the entries on the current form, quitting or saving the form and continuing. If the current form is saved, a new form will then be gener- ated automatically for a further parent function until no new subfunctions are registered.

3.4 Option 2: View Function Charts

This option allows the user to look at the function charts already created. The screen is split into two windows. The top window, which is the larger one, is used to display the charts. The lower on is a text window which is used to send messages to the user. The dimension of each function chart is extended to span across two screens and a horizontal scroll command is provided on the panel (i.e. `Movechart´). The movement of the chart is controlled by the buttons on the cursor. To leave the option, the cursor is clicked over the `stop´ area on the panel and the main menu is returned.

A chart will be split up into smaller charts if it exceeds the predefined physical dimension (i.e. ten functions in width and five functions in length at present). A downward arrow below a function indicates that there is further decomposition in another chart. The analyst can turn to that chart by clicking the cursor over that particular function. To return to the previous chart, the analyst just has to click the cursor over the top function of the current page. An example of the user inter-face can be found in Appendix 3.

3.5 Edit Function Charts

Under this option, the function charts are drawn using the same principle as that in viewing. Nine edit commands are available in addition to those provided in viewing. An example of the `edit´ panel is shown in appendix 4.

(1) Append
    To append a tree of functions to the chosen function. An example
of the interface is shown in Appendix 5.

(2) Change
    To change the content of a function (i.e. name, class or
    performer). An example is shown in Appendix 6.

(3) Delete
    To delete a single function. The system does not allow deletion of
    any function with subfunctions already attached to it. This is a
    safety precaution to prevent accidental deletion of a tree of
    subfunctions.

(4) Display
    To display the details of the chosen function (i.e. its name, level
    number, class, performer, number of subfunctions).

(5) Insert
    To insert a tree of functions to the right of the chosen function.

(6) MoveFn
    To move an existing tree of functions led by the chosen function to
    a chosen destination (using either insert or append).

(7) Quit
    To leave `edit´ and abandon all the current changes.

(8) Save
    To leave `edit´ and save all the current changes.

(9) Print
    To print the screen.

After each successful edit command, a symbol will be shown on the screen immediately at the appropriate place to indicate the type of alteration that has been made.

When the cursor is clicked over the `stop` area (i.e. to leave the option) after some changes are made, the analyst has the choice of either saving the changed version or abandoning all the changes previously saved during the edit session. If the `save` option is chosen, the changed version can be named under a different system code or under the same system code. That is, more than one version of function charts can be saved for one office unit if required.

3.6 Option 4: Create Process Identity for a New System

The fist step in drafting the process charts is to identify all the business processes involved in a particular office unit. This option is used to register all process names and their triggers. An example can be found in Appendix 7. Each process is numbered automatically by the system and a new form will be generated for further entries until the user chooses to stop.

3.7 Option 5: Edit Process Identity

This option allows the user to amend the entries saved by the previous option. All processes will be listed in the upper window. The lower window is used to enter the edit entries and to send messages to the user. An example of the interface is shown in Appendix 8. Five edit commands are provided on the panel:-

(1) Change
    To change the name of the process or its trigger.

(2) Delete
    To delete a process. As a safety precaution, the analyst is asked to confirm the deletion before it is implemented.

(3) Insert
    To insert a new process before or after a chosen process. An example can be found in Appendix 9.

(4) Save
    To save all the changes and leave the option.

(5) Quit
    To quit without saving the changes.

3.8 Option 6: Construct Process Charts

Under this option, the processes can be constructed from the created function charts. The upper window is reserved for displaying the relevant set of function charts. An edit panel is provided which enables an individual process chart to be assembled interactively. The basic mechanism in entering a connecting function is, firstly, to enter the type of linkage on the edit panel and secondly, to choose the relevant function by clicking the cursor over it in the function chart on display. An example of the interface is shown is Appendix 10.

The user is prompted automatically on which process is to be constructed in the lower window. The current status of the process chart under construction is shown immediately in the lower window and the current function awaiting connection is highlighted by reverse video.

To enter a linkage, the cursor has to be clicked over one of the four boxes - `Or´ for selective link , `And´ for sequential or parallel link, `LDOr" for selective long distance communication and `LDAnd´ for sequential or parallel long distance communication. After a linkage is entered, a function (from one of the function charts) has to be chosen. `Select Pg´ can be used to flip through the charts when looking for the connecting function. `Next Fn´ should be pressed when all the linking functions have been entered for the current highlighted function.

To enter an `output´ entry (i.e. the final output for a process), the cursor has to be clicked over the `Output´ command in the edit panel. One of the linkages is to chosen and then the system will prompt the user to enter the description of the output.

In the edit panel, apart from the usual commands like `Movechart´ for horizontal scrolling and `stop´ for leaving the option, other major commands include:-

(1) Erase
    To erase the current entry made on the edit panel.

(2) Detail
    To display the details of the current highlighted function.

(3) Select Pg
    To select a previous page or a continuing page of the current function chart. After `Select Pg´ is pressed, the cursor has to be clicked over a chosen function, as in viewing, to select the next page to be displayed. If the top level function is chosen, the previous page will be displayed. Otherwise, if one of the lowest level functions on the current page is chosen, its continuing page (if any) will be displayed.

(4) Quit
    To quit the construction process.

(5) Save
    To save the new entries.

(6) Print
    To print the current screen.

3.9   Option 7: View Process Charts

Under this option, the complete set of process charts created under a particular system code will be displayed. The usual horizontal scrolling function is provided since a process chart can span across two screens. An example of the screen is shown in Appendix 11.

    The main commands provided on the panel are as follows:-

(1) Next
    To show the next process in sequence.

(2) Select Process
    To enable the user to choose a specific process to display. A new window will appear which displays all the process numbers and names. The user is then asked to choose the required process for display. An example of the interface is shown in Appendix 12.

(3) Display FnName

This is the default mode. Each box of the process chart will show the name of a function.

(4) Display Level No.

If this is chosen, each box of the process chart will show the level number instead of the default function name.

(5) Display Class

The class of each function will be displayed on the top left hand corner of the box.

(6) Display Performer

When this is chosen, the box will show the performer of each function. This enables the user to view the flow of work in relation to the performer of the function.

(7) Print

To print the current screen.

3.10 Option 8: System Code Enquiry

This is for the user to check the system codes created or to check the meaning of a particular code. This option is especially useful if more that one system code has been created. An example is shown in Appendix 13.

4   EVALUATION AND CONCLUSION

Tests have been done using data from a real systems study and the graphics package evaluated in use against the criteria in section 3.1 above.

Firstly, the package proved very easy to use. The user-interface was designed so that most operations only require the use of the cursor for selection. Meaningful error messages or prompts advised the user on what was happening. Response time was fast (which avoided testing the patience of the user). The physical limitation of the screen size was reduced by using multiple windows and screen buffers.

Minimal learning was required to use the package. Experience in use demonstrated a considerable saving of time and drafting a set of function charts took a matter of minutes rather than hours. The complete sets of charts (including editing) took hours instead of days.

Flexibility was retained by allowing the user to start putting the initial ideas down quickly and to refine them later by using the editing facilities. The user was able to stop at any time without the feeling of being locked into the system. The option of saving various versions of the chart was also helpful and enabled the user to trace the development of the design.

The package maintained some degree of robustness by checking the validity of the input. If `illegal´ entries were encountered, the system either ignored them or returned a warning message. To prevent accidental loss of data, the system required confirmation for deletion and provided an immediate saving mechanism.

Further development is also possible. To extend the level of computer support, provision of aids for the analyst in designing the questionnaire used in Level One and in specifying all the weightings and rules for the calculation of the Automatability-Indices could be included. The package could be extended to generate the initial draft of process design charts for Level Three from the existing process charts. The designer could then use the editing tools to modify the initial draft according to the guidelines given in the Methodology. A more active role could be developed for the package in checking the completeness of the resulting charts.

The test runs showed the interactive graphical support offered by the demonstration package to be a time-saving tool for the analyst/designer following the High Level Design Methodology. Given the falling cost of appropriate hardware a commercial version of such a tool could prove relatively inexpensive.

REFERENCES

[COUG82] Cougar J.D., Colter M.A. and Knapp R.W., "Advanced System Development/Feasibility Techniques", John Wiley & Sons, 1982.

[ELLI82] Ellis C.A. and Bernal M., "Office Talk-D: an Experimental Office Information System", Proceedings of ACM SIGOA Conference on Office Systems, Philadelphia, USA, June, 1982.

[KONS82] Konsynski B.R. and Bracker L.C., "Computer Aided Analysis of Office Systems:", MIS Quarterly, March, 1982.

[MCLI86] KMG Thomson McLintock, "Profiting from Office Automation - Office Automation Pilots", Department of Trade and Industry, Vols. A and B, 1986.

[NUNA81] Nunamaker J.F. and Konsynski B., "Formal and Automated Techniques of Systems Analysis and Design - a Foundation for the 80´s, Cotterman W.W. et al (ed.), North-Holland, 1981.

[TEIC77] Teichroew D. and Hershey E.A., "PSL/PSA: a Computer-Aided Technique for Structured Documentation and Analysis of Information Processing Systems", IEEE Transactions of Software Engineering, SE-3, No. 1, 1977.

[WASS82] Wasserman A.I., "The User Software Engineering Methodology: an Overview", Information Systems Design Methodologies: a Comparative Review; IFIP W.G.8.1 Working Conference Netherlands (May 1982), Olle T.W., Sol H.G. and Verrijn-Stuart A. A. (ed.), North-Holland, 1982.

[WIGA84] Wigander K., Bvensson A., Schoug L., Rydin A. and Dahlgren "Structured Analysis and Design of Information Systems", McGraw-Hill, 1984.

[YOUR86] YOURDON E., "What Ever Happened to Structured Analysis?", Datamation, June 1986.

Appendix 1

```
****************************************************************

                    High Level Design System for
                         Office Automation

****************************************************************


    Choice       Command

      1 :   Construct Function Charts for New System

      2 :   Edit Function Charts

      3 :   Enter Process Identity for New System

      4 :   Edit Process Identity

      5 :   Construct Process Charts

      6 :   System Code Enquiry

      7 :   View Function Charts

      8 :   View Process Charts

      9 :   Exit



Please enter choice : 9
```

Parent Function is accounts

No.of Subfunctions : 4

Level No. :1

Function Name	Class	No of Subfn	Performer
purchase accounts	M	4	Pat,Jane,James
sales accounts	D	4	Anne,Jane,James
balance bank account	M	5	Jane
petty cash	M	4	Jane

Type Q-Quit, S-Save, or Press Return to carry on editing

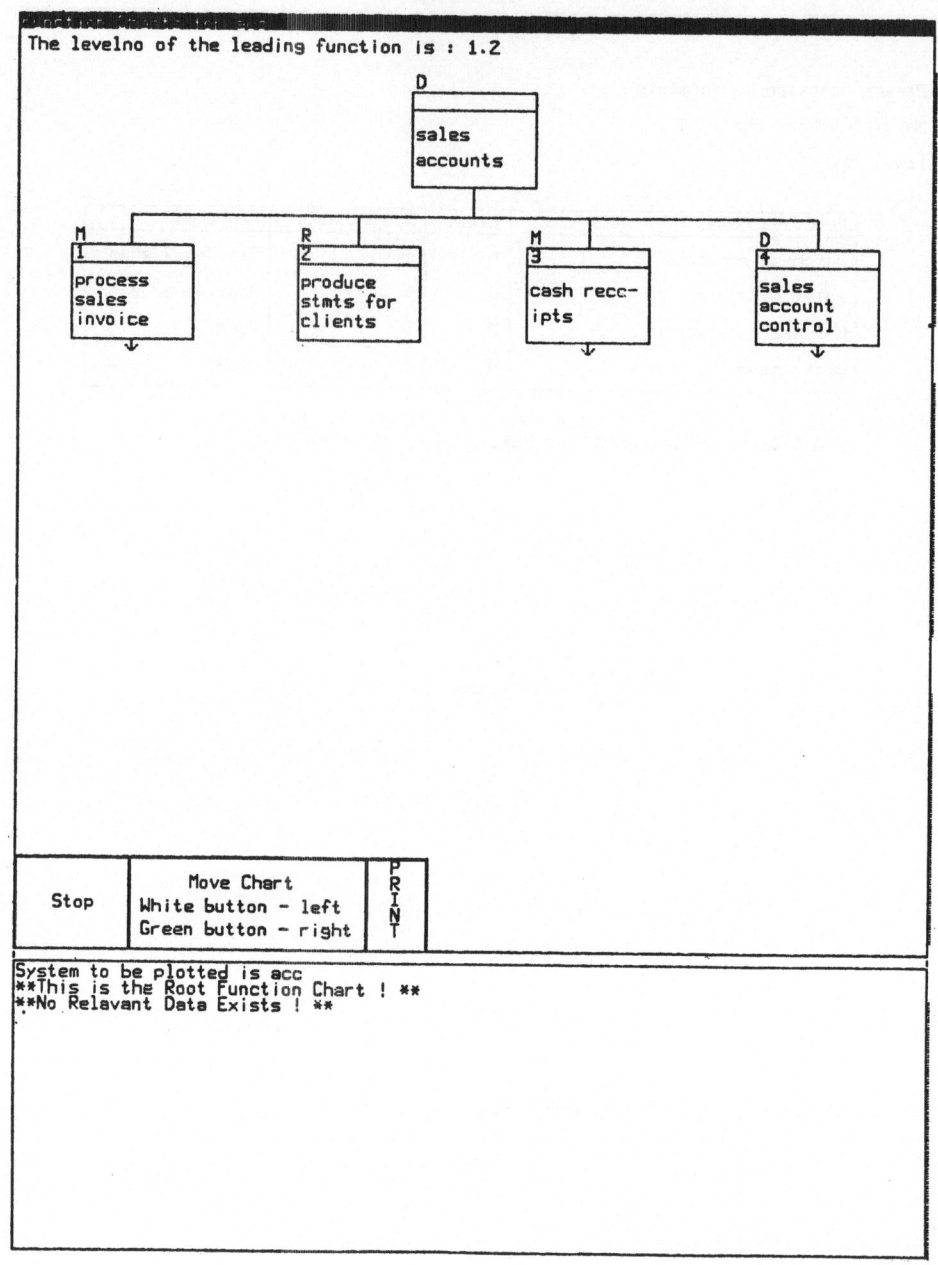

The levelno of the leading function is : 1.2

```
                              D
                          ┌─────────┐
                          │sales    │
                          │accounts │
                          └────┬────┘
          ┌────────────────┬───┴────────────┬────────────────┐
      M   │            R   │            M   │            D   │
    ┌─────┴───┐      ┌─────┴───┐      ┌─────┴───┐      ┌─────┴───┐
    │1        │      │2        │      │3        │      │4        │
    │process  │      │produce  │      │cash recc│      │sales    │
    │sales    │      │stmts for│      │-ipts    │      │account  │
    │invoice  │      │clients  │      │         │      │control  │
    └────┬────┘      └─────────┘      └────┬────┘      └────┬────┘
         ↓                                 ↓                ↓
```

Stop	Move Chart White button - left Green button - right	P R I N T

System to be plotted is acc
**This is the Root Function Chart ! **
**No Relavant Data Exists ! **

Appendix 4

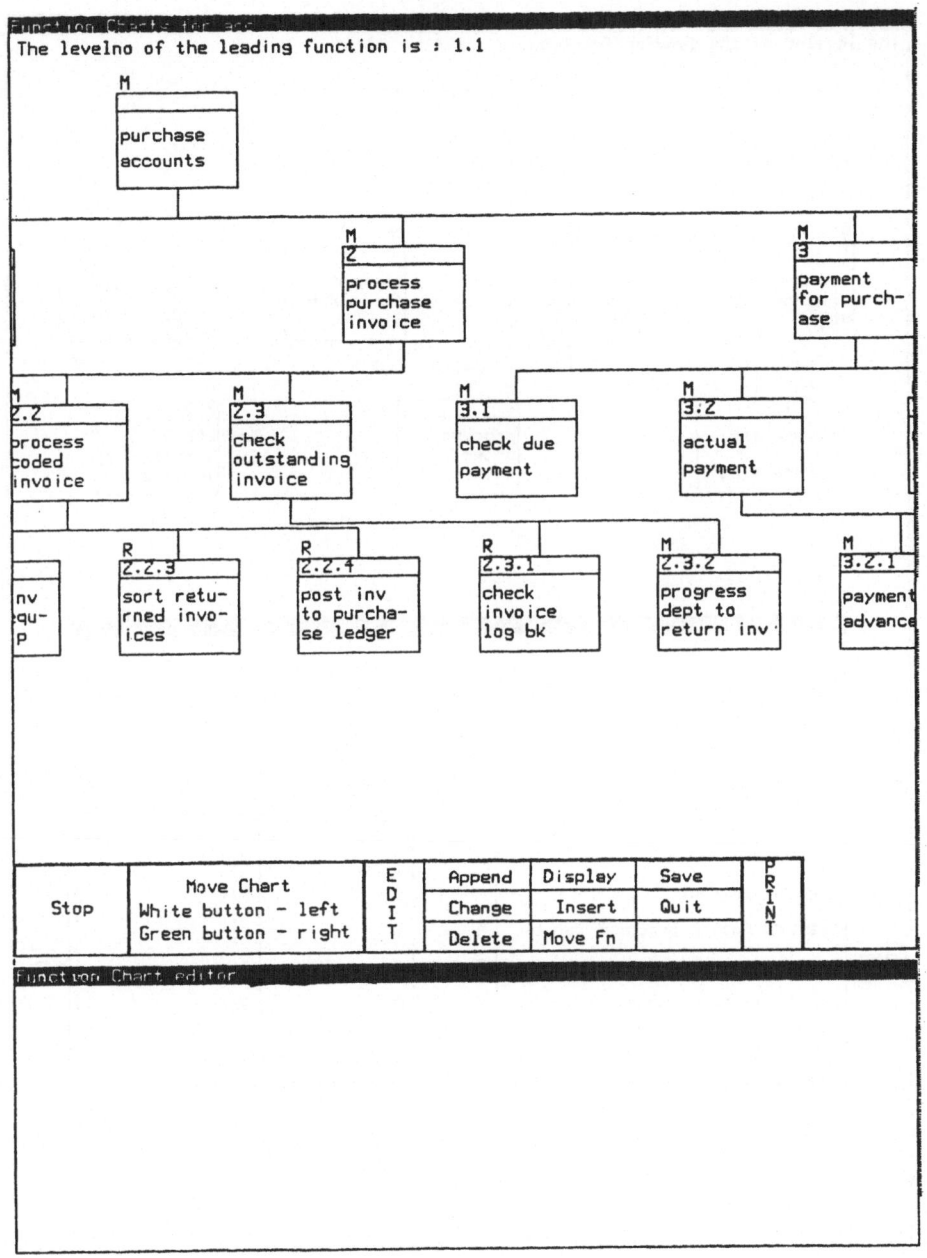

The levelno of the leading function is : 1.1

M
purchase
accounts

M
2
process
purchase
invoice

M
3
payment
for purch-
ase

M
2.2
process
coded
invoice

M
2.3
check
outstanding
invoice

M
3.1
check due
payment

M
3.2
actual
payment

inv
requ-
p

R
2.2.3
sort retu-
rned invo-
ices

R
2.2.4
post inv
to purcha-
se ledger

R
2.3.1
check
invoice
log bk

M
2.3.2
progress
dept to
return inv

M
3.2.1
payment
advance

	Move Chart	E	Append	Display	Save	P
Stop	White button — left	D	Change	Insert	Quit	R I N
	Green button — right	T	Delete	Move Fn		T

Function Chart editor

379

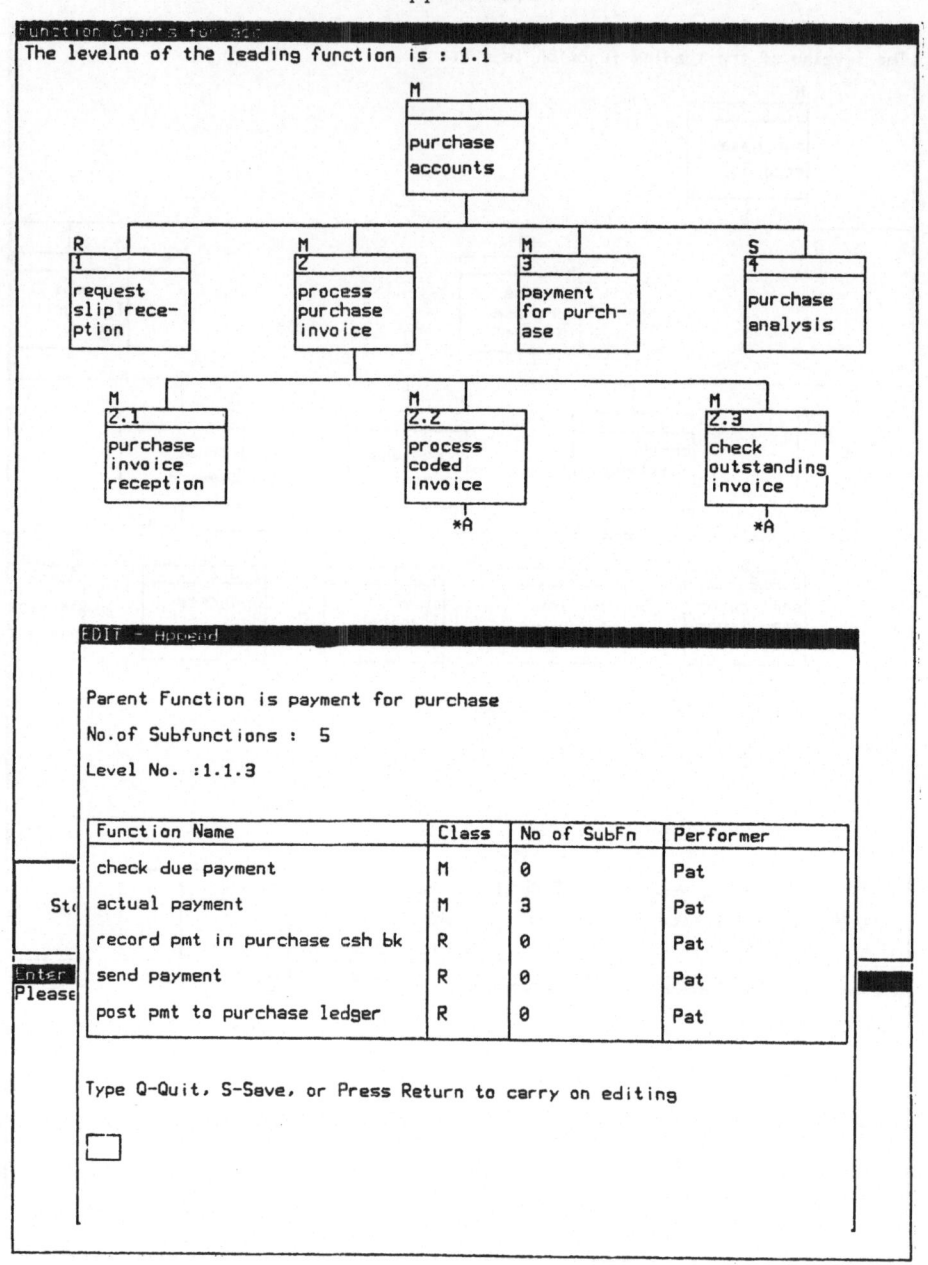

Function Charts for add

The levelno of the leading function is : 1.1

```
                              M
                        ┌──────────┐
                        │purchase  │
                        │accounts  │
                        └──────────┘
        ┌──────────────────┼──────────────────┬──────────────┐
        R                  M                   M              S
   ┌──────────┐      ┌──────────┐       ┌──────────┐   ┌──────────┐
   │1         │      │2         │       │3         │   │4         │
   │request   │      │process   │       │payment   │   │purchase  │
   │slip rece-│      │purchase  │       │for purch-│   │analysis  │
   │ption     │      │invoice   │       │ase       │   │          │
   └──────────┘      └──────────┘       └──────────┘   └──────────┘
              ┌──────────┼──────────────────┐
              M          M                  M
         ┌──────────┐ ┌──────────┐     ┌──────────┐
         │2.1       │ │2.2       │     │2.3       │
         │purchase  │ │process   │     │check     │
         │invoice   │ │coded     │     │outstanding│
         │reception │ │invoice   │     │invoice   │
         └──────────┘ └──────────┘     └──────────┘
                          *A                *A
```

EDIT - Append

Parent Function is payment for purchase

No.of Subfunctions : 5

Level No. :1.1.3

Function Name	Class	No of SubFn	Performer
check due payment	M	0	Pat
actual payment	M	3	Pat
record pmt in purchase csh bk	R	0	Pat
send payment	R	0	Pat
post pmt to purchase ledger	R	0	Pat

Type Q-Quit, S-Save, or Press Return to carry on editing

St

Enter
Please

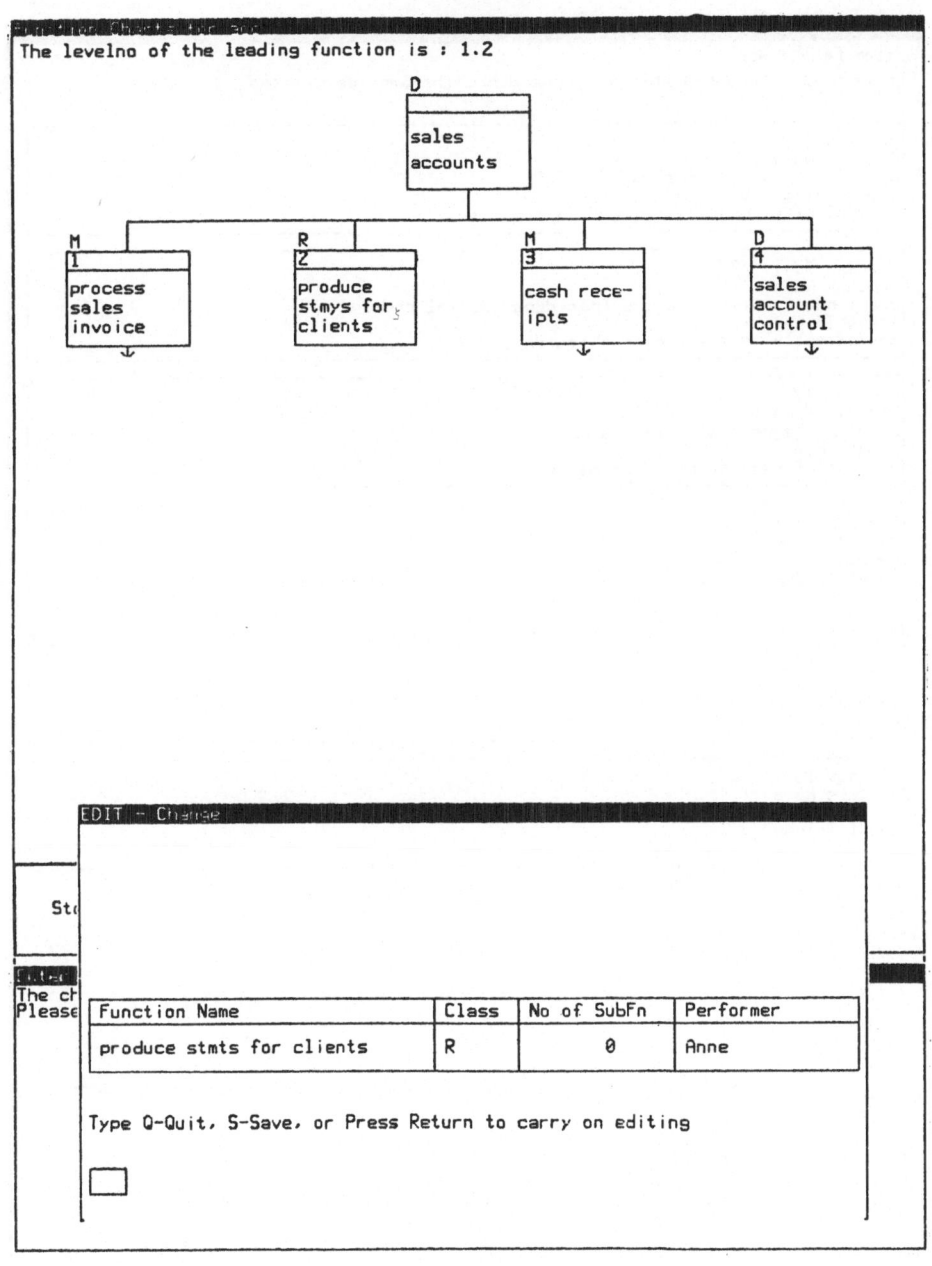

The levelno of the leading function is : 1.2

```
                              D
                          ┌─────────┐
                          │ sales   │
                          │ accounts│
                          └─────────┘
```

M	R	M	D

```
┌─────────┐   ┌─────────┐   ┌─────────┐   ┌─────────┐
│1        │   │2        │   │3        │   │4        │
│process  │   │produce  │   │cash rece-│  │sales    │
│sales    │   │stmys for│   │ipts     │   │account  │
│invoice  │   │clients  │   │         │   │control  │
└─────────┘   └─────────┘   └─────────┘   └─────────┘
```

EDIT - Change

St

The ch
Please

Function Name	Class	No of SubFn	Performer
produce stmts for clients	R	0	Anne

Type Q-Quit, S-Save, or Press Return to carry on editing

Identification of Processes

System Code : acc
System name : Accounts unit of Forward Freight Service Limited

```
Process Id :   1                                                    ^P
Process Name :
purchase invoice handling
Input Trigger :
arrival of purchase invoice from supplier
```

```
Process Id :   2                                                    ^P
Process Name :
check outstanding invoices from departmental coding
Input Trigger :
periodically, every two or three days
```

```
Process Id :   3                                                    ^P
Process Name :
handling request slip for payment
Input Trigger :
arrival of request slip for payment
```

```
Process Id :   4                                                    ^P
Process Name :
payment for airlines
Input Trigger :
month-end
```

```
Process Id :   5                                                    ^P
Process Name :
payment for ordinary purchase
Input Trigger :
periodically, daily
```

```
Process Id :.   6                                                   
Process Name :

Input Trigger :
```

While in the corner box –
        press return for editing the current entry
        press cntl-p to save current entry and continue the entry process
        press cntl-z to save current entry and terminate the entry process

Appendix 8

Process Identification for all

Id No.   Process Name
    1   purchase invoice handling
    2   check outstanding invoices from departmental coding
    3   handling request slip for payment
    4   payment for airlines
    5   payment for ordinary purchase
    6   purchase analysis
    7   handling sales invoices
    8   handling cash receipts for sales invoices
    9   sales account control
   10   balance the bank account
   11   petty cash handling
   12   petty cash control
```

| Save | E D I T | Change | Quit | P R I N T |
|------|---------|--------|------|-----------|
|      |         | Delete |      |           |
|      |         | Insert |      |           |

Edit Process Identification
```

```
Process Identification for acc

Id No.   Process Name
    1    purchase invoice handling
    2    check outstanding invoices from departmental coding
    3    handling request slip for payment
    4    payment for airlines
    5    payment for ordinary purchase
    6    purchase analysis
```

Save	E D I T	Change	Quit	P R I N T
		Delete		
		Insert		

```
Insert

Process Id :   7
Process Name :
handling sales invoices
Input Trigger :
arrival of sales invoice from operating departments

While in the Box -

Press cntl-z to quit; cntl-p to save; return to edit
```

Appendix 10

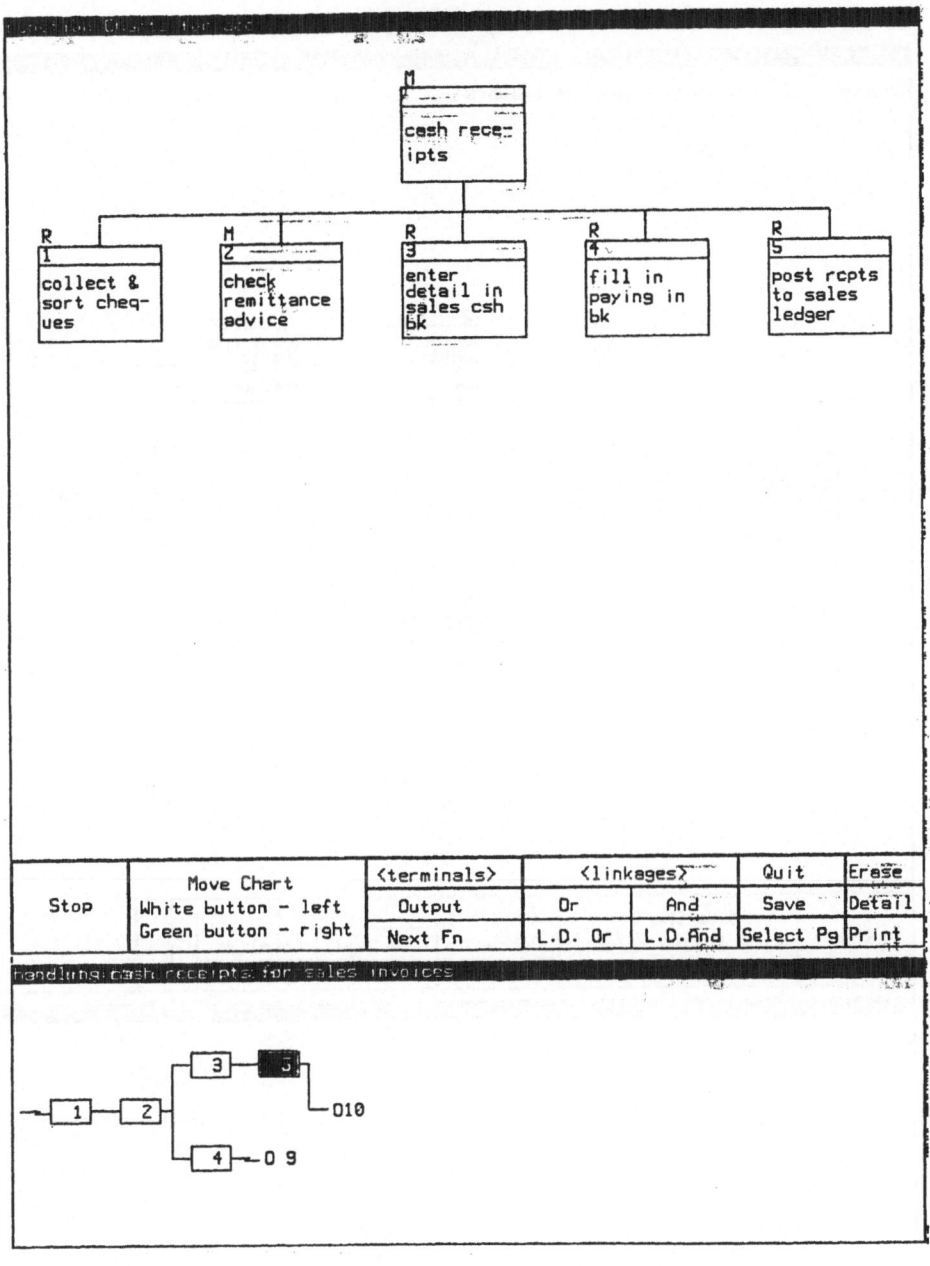

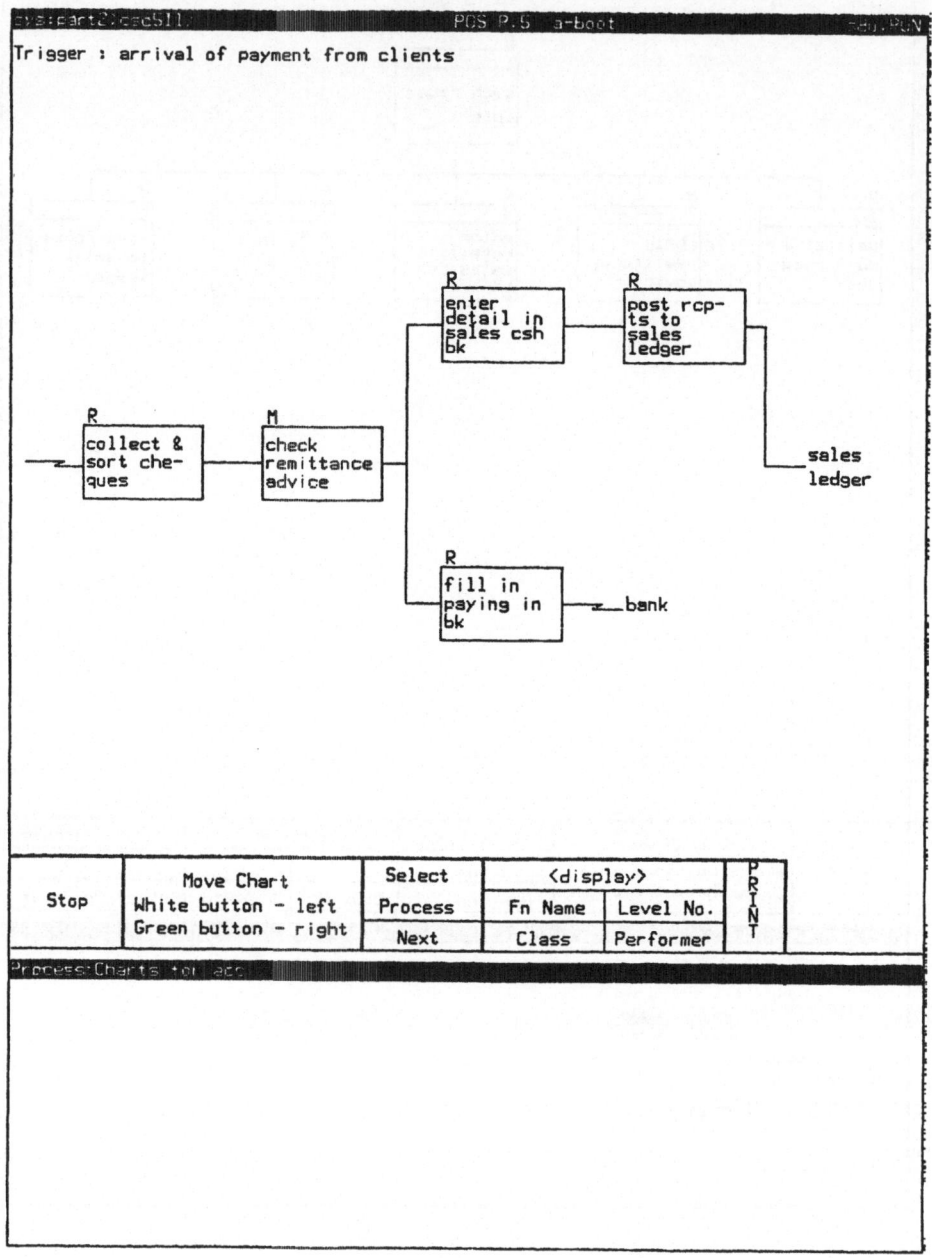

```
Version:        POS P.S  U bust           SOL.PUN
Trigger : arrival of purchase invoice from supplier




Select Process

Process No :         1
Name : purchase invoice handling

Process No :         2
Name : check outstanding invoices from departmental coding

Process No :         4
Name : payment for airlines

Process No :         5
Name : payment for ordinary purchase

Process No :         6
Name : purchase analysis

Process No :         7
Name : handling sales invoices

Process No :         8
Name : handling cash receipts for sales invoices

Process No :         9
Name : sales account control

Process No :        10
Name : balance the bank account

Process No :        11
Name : petty cash handling


Process No chosen :   P
Press return to forward to next page of this screen (if any)
Enter E to exit
```

Appendix 13

```
Code        Description Name
----        ----------------
 acc   Accounts unit of Forward Freight Service Limited
stuadm  student admission in Combined Studies
```

ARE THERE NON REAL-TIME SYSTEMS?

G. Topping

North Staffordshire Polytechnic

Beaconside, Stafford

ABSTRACT

Development methods for industrial real-time and business information
systems are compared and a contrast drawn between data and
process oriented system modelling techniques. A case is made for
adopting a more process oriented view and reasons suggested for its
comparative neglect. Jackson System Development and IRTB, an environment
for building systems from collections of collaborating processes, are
described as examples of methods and tools for encouraging a more
balanced approach to system design.

1   INTRODUCTION

The purpose of this paper is, quite simply, to advocate a more process
oriented view of system development. We shall take it as an axiom that
the answer to the question posed in the paper's title is in the negative.
A few moments reflection suggests that attempts to distinguish "real-
time" or "embedded" systems from other types of data processing or
information systems are qualitatively void. Definitions of the term
"real-time" customarily hang upon the need for such systems to respond to
unpredictable events in their environments within some fixed time
constraint. "Embedded" systems are thought of as embedded within some
wider system which they must monitor, service or control in real-time.
Examples of information systems conforming to both these definitions
abound. It might be argued that real-time systems must regard failure to
meet time constraints as a hard error rather than as a mere impairment of
performance. On the other hand information systems, being embedded
within human activity systems, must operate in a much less stable and
predictable environment than most real-time systems. However, we regard
such distinctions as secondary and relatively minor in nature.

If one accepts the essential similarity of what, for want of better
terms, we may call industrial and commercial computer applications, it is
all the more surprising to find that the practice of system design in the
two fields shows some fairly sharp and important distinctions. The
distinctions are evident at many levels. Their origins might perhaps be
traced to the education of students who are often constrained by course
structures to regard themselves as budding practioners in one field or

the other. These same students will often find the distinction confirmed
by the job descriptions and career paths offered to them by their
industrial employers. It is however the distinction at the level of
methods and techniques which concerns us here.

2   DATA AND PROCESS IN SYSTEM DEVELOPMENT

The need to capture transient and unpredictable events under exacting
time contraints tends to dominate the design of real-time systems.
Whatever their implementational mehtods, designers recognise that their
problems seem to yield best to a view of systems as collections of
collaborating, but largely autonomous, processing elements. In short,
they tend to adopt a process oriented view of system architecture. With
increasing explicitness, their software expresses this view in the
creation of concurrent processes, control over their scheduling and means
for allowing processes to interact safely. By contrast, information
systems design tends to adopt a much more data oriented architectural
view. Dominated by the end user's demand for information, design tends
to centre upon structures for recording this information, especially the
database.

This duality between data and process is one which recurs frequently in
computing science. It can be traced in the evolution of programming
technique and programming languages where advocacy of and support for
techniques such as data abstraction and functional decomposition provides
evidence. It was echoed very directly in the controversy between the
"declaratavists" and the "proceduralists" of the machine intellegence
fraternity [WINS77]. Perhaps more faintly, we may discern the same
distinction in the "database" and "spreadsheet" packages aimed at the
non-professional computer user. Scrutiny of these parallels suggests
that it is a mistake to let either the data or the process oriented
approach dominate. The lesson appears to be: not one or the other but
both, perhaps in a closer synergy than has yet been achieved.

One matter on which designers increasingly agree, whatever the sphere of
their application, is that system design has much to do with model
building [WOOD82] [FITZ85]. There is a sense in which any piece of
application software embodies a model of its problem environment and
system designers seem now widely to accept that the explicit construction
of this model is an important part of their activities. To base system
design upon an abstract description of the real world yields important
advantages. A large range of functional needs may be expressed within
the framework provided by a single object system description. Whilst
functional requirements can and do change, often abruptly and
discontinuously, the underlying model is more stable, tending to change
slowly and in an evolutionary manner. System design based on the
decomposition of functional requirements is always at the mercy of time.
Model based methods provide a more permanent background onto which
required functionality can be overlayed in modular fashion. Unlike
functionally based designs, this modularity is natural and inherent
because functions now rely upon the model but not generally upon each
other.

The model building approach is not however free from a data/process
duality which appears this time in terms of the medium in which modelling
is carried out. Models constructed in terms of facts and relationships
are favoured in data processing circles as in the entity-relationship
method of conceptual database design [CHEN76]. Real-time system
designers on the other hand tend to model their object system in terms of
processes which mimic its behaviour. At this level the alternatives are

static descriptions of reality in terms of facts and system state and dynamic descriptions in terms of activities, events and changes of state.

These relationships are summarised diagramatically in Figure 1. The vertical axis of this diagram shows the application system, with its data and procedural elements, as the image of its real world counterpart. It traces these same data and procedural elements back to a systemic method of description in terms of system structure and state on the one hand and system behaviour and the locus of state change on the other. The very symmetry of this diagram perhaps suggests that to model exclusively in terms of either data or process will lead to avoidable difficulties which we now attempt to identify.

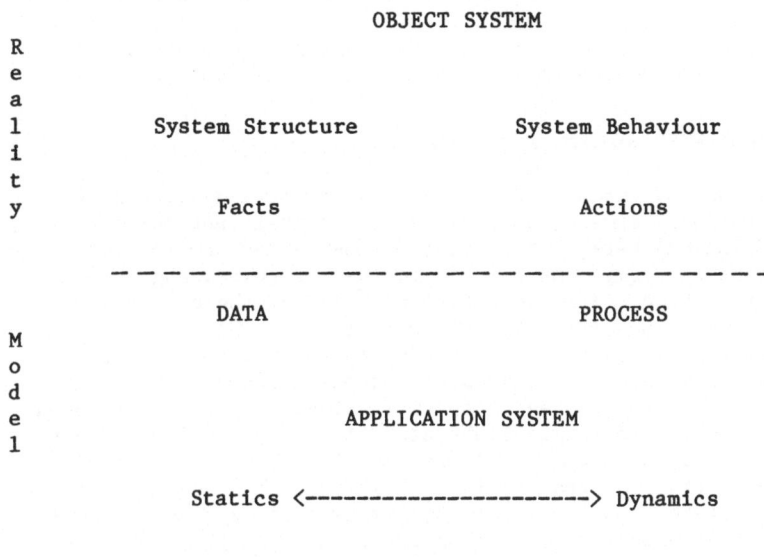

Figure 1.   System Modelling Relationships

3   DATA AND PROCESS MODELS COMPARED

Data modelling has become a widely used technique in system development [MADD78]. By its use, designers analyse and abstract the real world environment of an application in terms of the entities, their properties and relationships which they find there. These are refined into a carefully organised set of data objects which comprise the model. Application processing elements operate on this data domain either to update elements, thus tracking changes in the world modelled, or to add functionality by drawing inferences which cause activities to be promted or performed in the real world.

Process modelling, a much less widely used technique, captures the events which real world entities perform or undergo and accounts for their sequential time orderings. Observing that both the event sequences of the real world and the process descriptions of the application system may both be expressed in the language of regular expressions, the process modeller builds a model in terms of programs which describe and mimic object system behaviour.

Comparing the two types of model, we see that the data modeller, stuck with a static medium of facts in the database, cannot directly model the dynamic flow of events. Instead the modeller must resort to the use of changing patterns of entity relationships to provide snapshots of the effects of these events. The process modeller on the otherhand is possibly slighly better placed. His/her medium directly captures system dynamics whilst state information is retained in the form of the local data of mimic processes. His/her "database" is therefore present, but takes a disseminated form spread across possibly large numbers of process descriptions. This gives the process modeller some problems of data management which the data modeller has already solved by the greater centralisation and more careful organisation of data structures. In our opinion however the balance of advantage still lies with the process modeller because the problem is of a technical nature and its solution can be provided by appropriate choice of techniques and tools. The failure of data modelling to fully capture system dynamics is more fundamental. It represents a conceptual weakness which tends to hinder the effective abstraction of reality. If such an analysis is correct, we are left to account for the infrequent use of process modelling and to suggest how its virtues can be incorporated into the designers armoury.

4   PROCESS ORIENTED SYSTEM DEVELOPMENT

The best known method which leads to process oriented designs is probably Jackson's System Development, JSD [JACK83]. We shall not dwell on details of the method here, but a brief discussion of some of its features will be helpful. JSD can be regarded as comprising two main stages - specification and implementation. Linking these is a key document, the System Specification Diagram or SSD. The SSD is a complete summary of the system architecture resulting from the specification phase. It basically shows processes or process classes linked to form a process network. In the course of specification, processes are added to this network from two sources. Elaborated first are model processes. These are explicitly designed to express and track the ordering of events as they affect particular real world entities. Each modelled entity or entity type generates its own model process or process class. Model processes are connected to the environment from which they take their input. They are therefore responsible for data collection and validation. Other processes are called function processes. These address particular aspects of functionality as dictated by the statement of requirements. Function processes, generally speaking, read inputs generated by model processes and provide outputs to the environment in the form of actuations and responses, messages and reports.

Processes, model and function alike, communicate and hence synchronise and collaborate via network interconnections which are of two kinds. Much process interaction occurs via serial data streams of typed messages sent by one process and received by another. Process synchronisation is provided since a process attempting to read an empty stream is forced to wait. A receiving process often needs to merge two or more data streams into a single input on some fair basis. From the point of view of a process, serial data streams appear very much like the standard I/O streams of elementary programming. Since they convey well defined logical data sequences, Jacksons own programming methods are ideal for designing and documenting the processes which read and write to them. In addition to serial data strems the SSD typically requires another type of process interaction called a "state inspection". Here one process may asynchronously access the local data of another on a strictly read-only basis. It must be guaranteed that such inspections yield only consistent views of this state information.

From this very brief survey of one type of process oriented system model, one may discern some of the difficulties which face those who would

implement the resulting architecture on commonly used computing
machinery. The processes of the model must run concurrently either on
separate physical processors or, much more likely, by interleaved
execution on a single processor. Means must also be found for
implementing the message streams with semantics acceptably close to those
of the SSD. Finally some means of allowing state inspections must be
found which provides the necessary consistency guarantees.

Solving these implementational problems on conventional computer systems
is, of course, perfectly possible. Many operating systems have the
necessary multitasking and interprocess message capabilities. Use of
these facilities however has a systems programming feel to it which is
likely to discourage their widespread use. A better alternative is to
use a language with so-called real-time features which allow concurrency
to be expressed directly. Modula-2, ADA and Occam are better known
vehicles of the right type. All offer possibilities but all have their
snags and difficulties, not the least of which is the lack of familiarity
amongst implementors of information systems. Jackson's own prefered
means, expounded at length in his book, is to simulate the required
facilities in one of the standard data processing languages. His
approach is to use techniques of program transformation such as inversion
which he introduced into JSP as a solution to the problem of structure
clash. The idea is to implement the notion of the coroutine by
supplementing the text of a subprogram with explicit state saving
mechanisms which allow resumption at arbitrary points in its text.
Processes then become, generally speaking, coroutines and message passing
is done via the parameters of the coroutine calls. Where coroutines
alone are insufficiently powerful to handle the needs of a particular
SSD, Jackson resorts to the direct implementation of process scheduling
in Cobol or some similar language. This overstretching of a language to
convey ideas it was never designed to express seems, at least to the
author, to be deeply unconvincing. We are led to suggest therefore that
what is required is an environment within which the SSD and supporting
design decisions can be implemented directly and naturally. A
description of one such environment is the subject of the final section
of this paper.

5   IRTB - A PROCESS ORIENTED DEVELOPMENT TOOL

Industrial Real-Time BASIC (IRTB) originated from a standardisation
initiative of the ECC [IRTB81]. It provides a development system for
distributed real-time applications. It has since been enhanced and
applied in the I & AP Division of Harwell Laboratory, under the guidance
of Alan Lewis [LEWI86]. The author and collegues at North Staffordshire
Polytechnic are collaborators with the Harwell team in its further
development. There are plans by this later group to provide a fresh
implementation emphasising the IPSE aspects of IRTB whilst eliminating
its relationship to the BASIC language.

IRTB aims to provide its users with a structured and highly modular
development path for applications designed using the principles described
earlier in this paper. Separate aspects of IRTB handle the logical
description of application architecture, the creation of code for
concurrent activities, the description and management of system data and
the mapping between these elements and the hardware configuration on
which the application will ultimately run.

The Architectural Description is given in terms of a set of concurrent
activities which synchronise and communicate via paths which interconect
them. Activities may also communicate with the environment via
input/output ports and with an application database via views described

as sub-schema to a global DBMS. These facilities too are specified in the architectural description.

Code Descriptions are written in an enhanced and compiled version of BASIC. In addition to normal sequential programming facilities, the language provides the ability to read and write inter-process messages, to perform input/output via ports and to update and interrogate customised views of the database. Although syntactically distinct, these added facilities are implemented by IRTB in terms of a uniform synchronous message passing protocol which is equally suited to centralised or distributed use. The code for each activity always represents a single thread of control with no explicit or implicit parallelism. All concurrency is specified as part of the architectiral description.

Data Descriptions provide access to a DBMS which is an integral part of IRTB. Data objects may be named and typed and the resulting element descriptions bound into a data dictionary. IRTB uses this dictionary to refer to and check the consistent use of data throughout the system building process. It is also the means for contructing the run time database and regulating its use by providing to processes customised views of its contents. The system database and its sub-schema provide the mechanism whereby one process may inspect the state information of another with appropriate guarantees of its consistency. The presence of a DBMS moreover provides facilities for data management and manipulation which can replace significant amounts of procedural coding.

The Architectural Description of an application in IRTB exists at a purely logical level. It is summarised in a SPADE diagram, similar to the Jackson SSD described earlier. SPADE is an acronym of System, Paths, Activities, Database and External interfaces, and the diagram is constructed in terms of icons representing these elements. The mapping of elements onto hardware is the subject of the Configuration Description. At this stage, the number and type of processors is determined, the mapping between activities and processors is specified and details given of I/O interfaces, message paths and the physical distribution of data. IRTB then provides an implementation of this mapping by binding run time support routines appropriate to the services required on each processor. These services amount to a customised operating system tailored to the exact requirements of a particular configuration. In this way a single logical design can be mapped onto different hardware configurations ranging from a single centralised computer system to highly distributed versions involving a network of procesing units.

In its present form, IRTB offers a system development environment within which process oriented design methods can be expressed directly and simply. The developer can capitalise upon its ability to separate the different facets of system description and can call upon its system building facilities to automatically compile and configure their software implementation. It appears to provide a sound conceptual basis for further interesting development.

Two such developments are currently being undertaken. One seeks to provide additional facilities to support software quality management and control measured in terms of fitness for purpose, adequate durability and economic maintainability. As a first step, IRTB development has been moved to a UNIX environment and allows IRTB software to be targetted onto processors other than the PDP11 for which it was originally designed. Within this richer environment current work aims to interface IRTB with methods of system specification which include propositional and quantitative elements which can be related to measurable parameters of the end product and which facilitate proof of deterministic and temporal performance. At the same time opportunity will be taken to provide tighter management of different variants and versions of the same generic application product by regulating access to their descriptions.

A second objective, still in the planning stage, will provide for a new implementation of the ideas behind IRTB free from the associations implied by its development and application over several years. Amongst the objectives of this re-implementation will be to allow process descriptions to be provided in a variety of common sequential programming languages; to provide asynchronous inter-process message protocols in a form which does not compromise the ability to apply recently developed proof methods for concurrent systems [HOAR85][NGUY86] and to enhance the database facilities provided, possibly by embedding a proprietary database management facility within it. An interesting observation stemming from this work is the fruitful way in which the redesign can be performed as an application of IRTB and process oriented design methods themselves. By analogy with the way a programming language must, to be complete, be capable of programming its own interpreter, perhaps a good test for a system development tool would be its ability to desbcribe and guide its own design and implementation.

6   REFERENCES

[CHEN76] Chen P.P.S. "The Entity-Relationship model - Toward a Unified View of Data" ACM TODS 1(1)March 1976.

[FITZ85] FITZGERALD G., STOKES N. and WOOD J.R.G., "Feature Analysis of Contemporary Information Systems Methodologies" Computer Journal vol 28 no. 3 1985 pp 223 - 230.

[HOAR85] HOARE C.A.R. "Communicating Sequential Processes" Prentice-Hall Int. London 1985.

[IRTB86] "IRTB - Industrial Real-time BASIC Draft Standard" E.C.C. European Workshop on Industrial Computer Systems TC2 81/8 Sept. 1981.

[JACK83] JACKSON M. "System Development" Prentice-Hall Int. London 1983.

[LEWI86] LEWIS A. Private Communication.

[MADD78] MADDISON R.N. (ed.) "Data Analysis for Information Systems Design" Conference Papers, B.C.S. June 1978.

[NGUY86] NGUYEN V., DERMERS A., GRIES D. and OWICKI S. "A Model and Temporal Proof System for Networks of Processes" Distributed Computing vol 1 no.1 1986 pp 7 - 25.

[WINS77] WINSTON P.H., "Artificial Intellegence" Addison-Wesley, 1st Ed. 1977 p 390.

[WOOD82] Wood-Harper A.T. and Fitzgerald G. "A Taxonomy of Current Approaches to Systems Analysis" Computer Journal vol 25 no. 1 1982 pp 12 - 16.

THE USE OF FRAME-BASED KNOWLEDGE REPRESENTATION

TECHNIQUES IN PROTOTYPING

I. Potts

Sunderland Polytechnic

Sunderland, U.K.

1   INTRODUCTION

The prototyping approach to systems development involves using 4th Generation Languages (4GLs) to enable applications to be built quickly. Speed of development and change is the key issue.

Although the use of prototyping for systems development has been compared with the prototyping concepts of other disciplines, there are major differences. Few people would fly in a prototype aircraft, yet many people argue that a prototype computer application should be adopted as the target system. This reflects not necessarily wrong thinking, but that better prototyping tools are required. When these tools become available prototyping will be seen to be an essential but complementary part of formal structured systems design.

Over the last two to three years there have been a number of publications on the topic of prototyping (e.g. [BOAR84, INFO86]). A good overview of the topic is given by the National Computing Centre Report [LAW83], and the Workshop proceedings edited by Budde [BUDD83] highlights the wide range of tools and techniques appropriate for prototyping.

2   CURRENT PROTOTYPING SYSTEMS AND LANGUAGES

There are many prototyping languages and approaches currently available, each with its own strengths and weaknesses. For example, dialogue languages are most appropriate for screen and I/O handling, 4GL's and Relational Databases for database access, Prolog for tree structure processing, LISP for list processing and APL for array processing.

A language is chosen if the strengths of that language map as closely as possible to the needs of the application being prototyped. However, because only one language is chosen, the elements of the language that are weak are always present to some extent. These weaknesses may degrade the prototype or require extreme circumvention to overcome them.

For example, dialogue languages are strong in input/output handling, screen painting and transition handling but weak in database access and data processing. 4GL's and Database Systems tend to complement dialogue languages because of their superior data handling facilities.

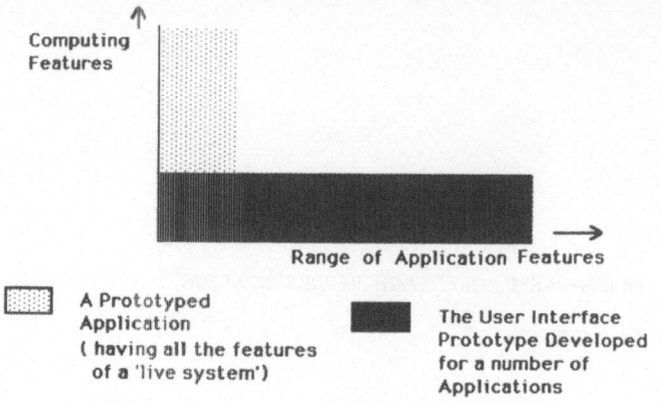

Figure 1 Current prototyping practice

The computer system and application features that are required to be prototyped can be viewed as a two-dimensional space. The graphical representation of current prototyping practice might look something like figure 1. Instead what should be available, and is available in other disciplines, is something similar to figure 2, a much more ´fine-grained´ view of prototyping. There is an inability with current prototyping systems to examine microscopic aspects of design.

In computer systems prototyping we do not have the capability to prototype ´small and quick´. Small requires a redefinition in software terms of the word MODULARITY. No longer PROGRAM MODULARITY but OBJECT MODULARITY. We are some way down the road to "quick" with declarative styles of programming and testing using interpreters.

What this paper proposes is:

a) a higher level of definition using visual programming;

b) improvements in software re-usability;

c) using an object-oriented architecture to prototype systems.

The remainder of this paper expands upon these issues in greater detail. Section 3 introduces the basic concepts of objects, messages and frames. Section 4 illustrates these concepts with a low level example of drawing a window. The proposed environment is described in section 5 and illustrated with a detailed example in section 6.

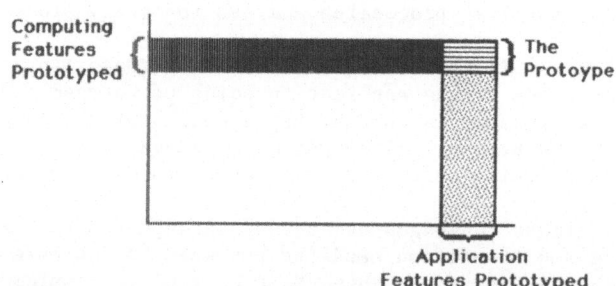

Figure 2 More fine-grained view of prototyping

The two central concepts of most object-oriented designs are:

- the objects themselves;

- the messages that are exchanged between objects;

3.1 Objects

An object can be loosely described as something that exists in the software component domain (either temporarily or permanently) ie. something that is created and can be destroyed.

Most of the early literature on objects and messages centred upon language implementation using SIMULA, SMALLTALK-80 and ADA [BYTE81, GOLD83]. B J Cox gives one of the most detailed explanations of objects and messages without a predominant reference to language implementation [COX86], and an increasing number of publications give details of object implementation in PROLOG [e.g.ZANI84].

Objects belong to two main areas:

a) visual objects eg. the screen, windows, formats, menus, keyboard characters, function keys, graphs, lines, messages.

b) data objects eg. files, records, tables, lists, arrays, relations, indexes, disk areas, multi-list structures.

The power of objects is the descriptive power that can be achieved through the natural associations between them. These associations have been identified by a number of authors, particularly Mylopoulos and Levesque [MYLO84]. They identify:

Classification

The association of an object with its generic type (CLASS) eg. a STUDENT named GREEN is an object of the class STUDENT. This is the standard 'instance-of' relationship.

The remaining types of relationships relate different classes together and thereby different objects together.

Generalisation

In generalisation a class is related directly to a more generic type. This is the 'is-a' relationship. For example STUDENT is-a PERSON, ie. the STUDENT Class 'is-a' sub-class of the PERSON class. Often the inverse relationship of specialisation is more obvious: an INDEX is a specialisation of TABLE, ie. a TABLE is a generalisation of an INDEX.

Aggregation

A collection of different classes to form a new class eg. the class INDEXED SEQUENTIAL FILE is made-up-of (aggregation of) INDEX class and RECORD class.

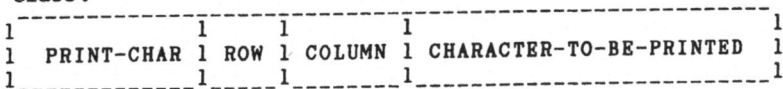

Figure 3 A Message

3.2 Messages

In a way the whole concept of OBJECTS and MESSAGES is analogous to NODES and MESSAGES in a Data Communication System. All messages communicate from a SENDING OBJECT to a RECEIVING OBJECT.

The message identifies a METHOD (FUNCTION) in the receiving object that is to be executed. The message not only carries an identification of the METHOD but also parameters that are to be used in the execution of the method. A 'triggered' method may then send a further message to a different object or objects.

For example one of the methods associated with the SCREEN object is PRINT-CHAR. The message identifies method PRINT-CHAR together with the necessary parameters - ROW, COLUMN and CHARACTER-TO-BE- PRINTED (figure 3).

Messages can be formed into message structures. A collection of different messages can be aggregated into a larger named MESSAGE-GROUP. Each message or message-group can be sent iteratively using a variety of control mechanisms but each message iteration replies to the sender. Furthermore, messages can be recursive when a sending method sends a message to itself. This is illustrated in section 6 where a tree-structured index is defined as an INDEX which sends a message to itself to access the next lower level of the INDEX.

3.3 Frames

A CLASS structure is a means by which OBJECTs are categorised. Classes describe objects. A FRAME is a data structure that describes the objects of a class and the procedures (METHODS) that operate upon the object.

A frame together with data and method definition can be visually portrayed as a rectangular box on the screen. This is described in more detail in section 4.1.

It was Minsky's paper in 1975 [MINS75] which introduced the concept of frame and the concept of slot attachment for data and functions. One of the most extensive explanations of the use of the frame is in Bobrows exposition of KRL (Knowledge Representation Language) [BOBR77].

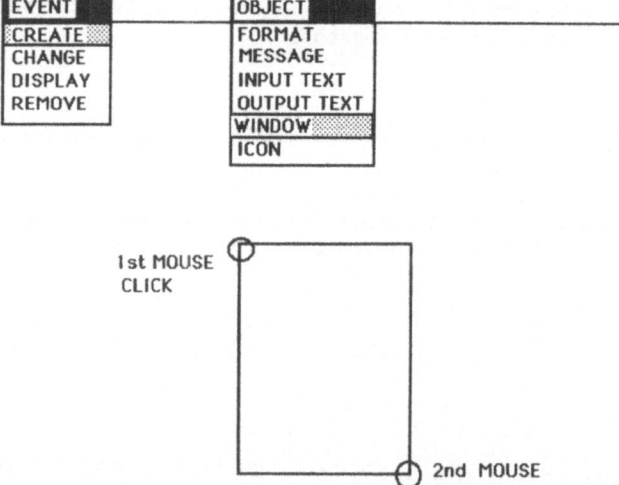

Figure 4 The window positioning

Figure 5 Naming a window

The use of frames and messages is illustrated in the next section through the example; CREATING A WINDOW.

4   AN EXAMPLE - CREATING A WINDOW

As a first step it is worthwhile identifying the input and output activities associated with creating a window.

There are two main input activities:

- naming the window

- identifying the window's location on the screen

and the single output activity:

- draw the window upon the screen

Terminal Input

    Naming the window -

This would be achived by a single line input:

    e.g. NAME:DIARY

    Positioning the window -

This is achieved by locating the top left hand corner and bottom right hand corner of the window area using a mouse (Figs. 4 and 5).

4.1 Visual Programming for Object-Oriented Software

Most of the recent developments in visual presentation using visual objects have their origin with the work carried out at XEROX [LIPK82]. There have been some developments in the pictorial presentation of procedural [GLIN84] and non-procedural languages such as QUERY-BY-EXAMPLE [ZLOO77].

There are two major difficulties with current techniques used to develop object-oriented systems:

1   Although object systems can provide visual environments they
     don't use visual techniques for object programming. These   sys-
     tems are still locked into standard line-by-line syntax.

2   The presentation of details about available software (objects and
     methods) is cumbersome.

The remainder of this paper describes a possible solution to overcoming
this problem. The illustration is of a WINDOW definition on a screen.
But before detailing the programming steps, a little about the visual
techniques used.

'Pull-Down' Menu's:

One of the critical problems of visual programming is the restricted
space available. There are two rules that can be applied to ease this
problem:

1   Restrict the viewing to the three elements of the system   cur-
     rently being programmed, ie. the only view required is:

     - the sending object

     - the receiving object

     - the message

2   To compress details of the three elements by using pull-down menu's
     wherever possible. The visual appearance of a frame when collapsed
     and when expanded is illustrated in figure 6.

The visual description of two objects linked by a message is shown in
figure 7.

4.2 Visual Definition of a Rectangle

This section describes the drawing of a rectangle for the window. This
requires the definition of HORIZONTAL-LINE and VERTICAL-LINE upon the
screen.

'SCREEN CLASS' is an existing class selected from the 'CLASS' menu and
displayed on the screen as a 'Frame header' (Fig.8). The frame header
consists of two pull-down menu windows as follows (Fig.9):

1   A pull-down menu for data that describes an object of the class ie.
     FRAME DATA SLOTS.

A FRAME HEADER

A 'PULLED-DOWN' FRAME

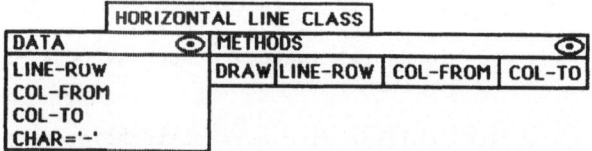

Figure 6 "Collapsed" and expanded frame

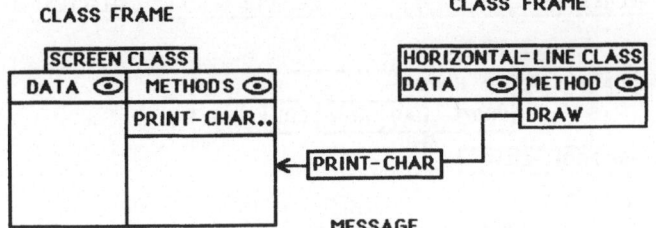

Figure 7 Linking frames by a message

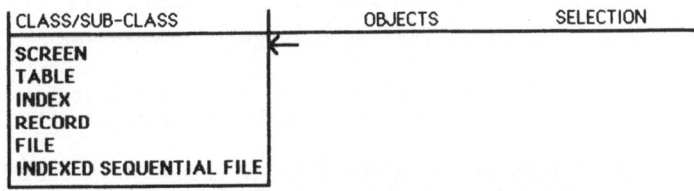

Figure 8 displaying the frame header

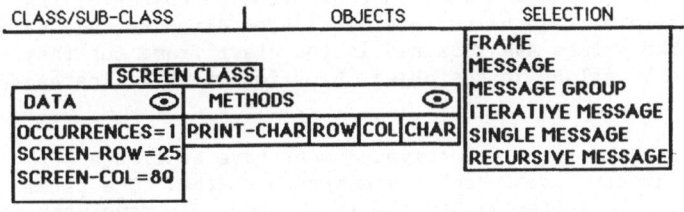

Figure 9 Data and Methods pull-down menus

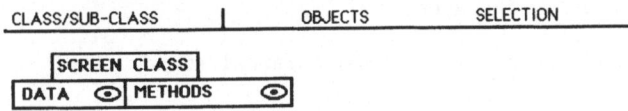

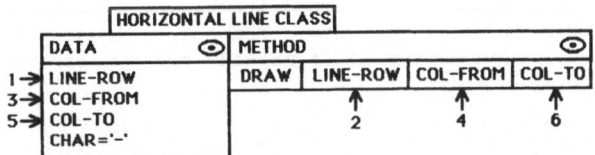

Figure 10 Prompting for parameter names

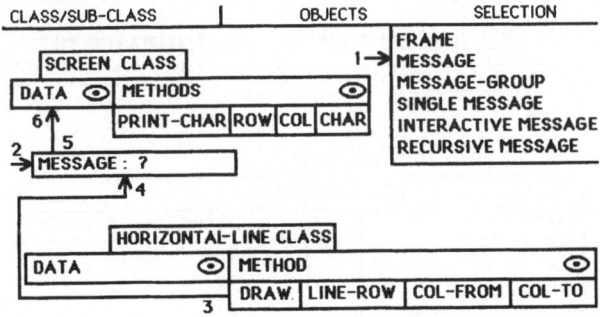

Figure 11 Defining the message, sender and receiver

```
        SCREEN CLASS
   DATA  ⊙  METHODS                    ⊙
              PRINT-CHAR  ROW  COL  CHAR

 →  PRINT-CHAR          ↑
 2                      1

            HORIZONTAL-LINE CLASS
     DATA         ⊙  METHOD                      ⊙
                      DRAW  LINE-ROW  COL-FROM  COL-TO
```

Figure 12 Directing the message to a receiver

2   A pull-down menu for each METHOD (function) that operates upon objects of the class together with each method's parameter list.

Each menu can be pulled down independently and stays down until either release button is pressed.

The data slots define the data that describe an object of the class. However, where certain values are considered defaults, eg. screen size (Fig.9), then values are retained in the class frame but they can be over-ridden by values in the object (ie. for specific instances of a SCREEN).

All methods that are to be activated must have available zero, one or several parameters upon which the method operates. The parameters are usually data slots from within the same frame. The developer is prompted for the parameter names (Fig.10), which are then selected by pointing to the named data using the mouse.

Data and methods can be deleted and inserted at any time.

3   To draw HORIZONTAL-LINE requires the screen's primitive method 'PRINT-CHAR' to be called 'n' times; 'n' is the character length of the line; ie. a method (DRAW) is described in terms of another method (PRINT_CHAR). The first step in the method DRAW definition is to link the two methods. This is achieved by selecting MESSAGE (arrow 1) (Fig.11) from the menu, then pointing using the mouse to identify the sender (arrow 3) (a method) and the receiver (arrow 6) (a frame) in that order.

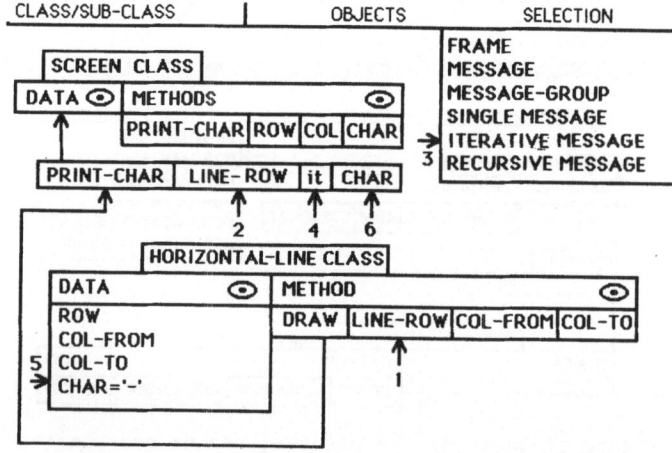

Figure 13 Prompting for required parameters

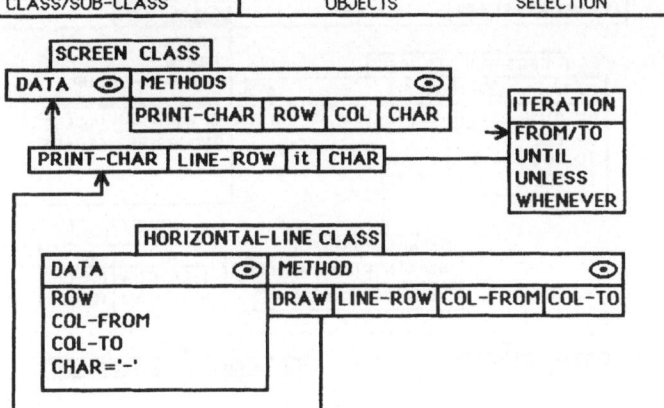

Figure 14 Pull-down menu of iterative constructs

Similarly methods that operate on objects are defined at the class level
if a method applies to all or most objects under that class. Again overriding can take place by assigning methods to specific objects. If this
allocation method at the object level occurs frequently for any one
object this probably suggests that the object belongs to an as yet un-
defined (and unrecognised) sub-class of the original class.

Defining the ˊPRINT_CHARˊ Message

Having defined the message name and linked sending and receiving frames
(Fig.11) then the message is defined as follows:

1   The message box requests the identification of the method in the
     receiver to which this message is directed (Fig.12).

2   The identified method (PRINT_CHAR) then prompts for the message
     parameters required (Fig.13), ie. what data represents the row,
     column and character to be printed. The row and character are
     mapped directly from the sending frame ˊItˊ indicates the ˊCOLˊ

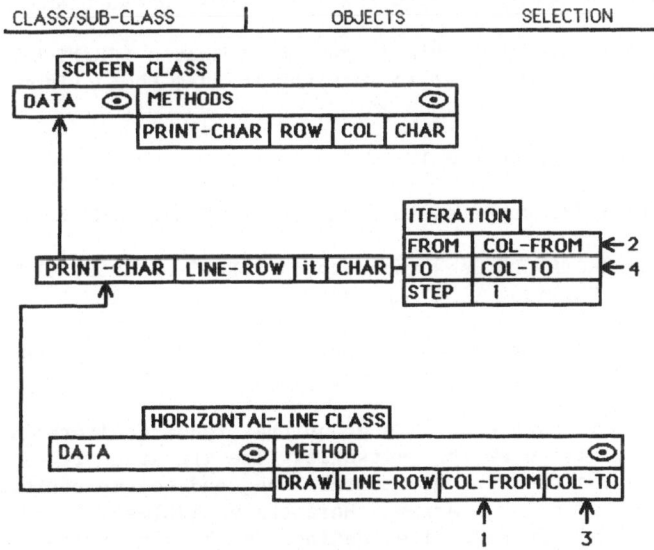

Figure 15 selecting start and end columns

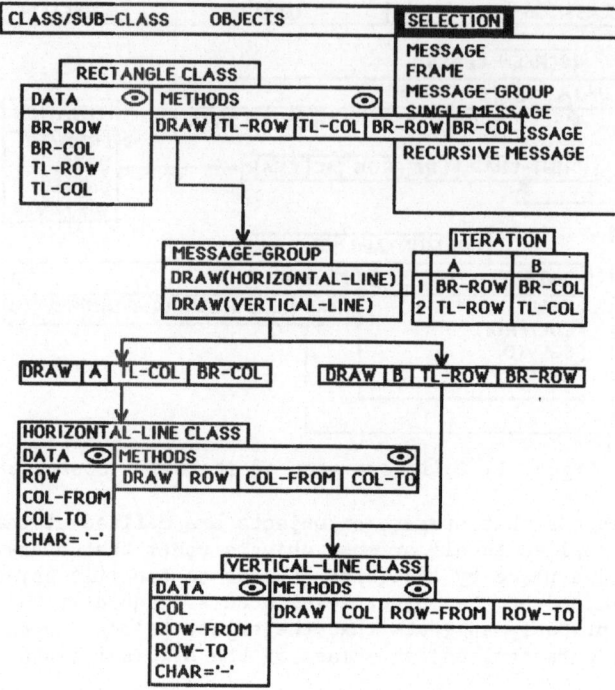

Figure 16 Grouping messages into a larger structure

parameter is under the iterative control imposed upon the transmission of the message. The ´it´ is generated not by typing ´it´ but by selecting ´ITERATION´ from the selected menu, (arrow 3).

3   The box containing ´ITERATION´ is a pull-down menu which identifies the different possible iterative constructs (Fig.14). The selection of ´FROM-TO´ replaces the menu with a ´FROM-TO template´ that defines the iterative controls. ´STEP´ defaults to ´1´ but can be changed. The ´COL-FROM´ and ´COL-TO´ are selected by pointing to these data names in the sending frame (HORIZONTAL-LINE) (Fig.15).

The logical intent of this iteration is that n (PRINT-CHAR) messages will be sent from sender to receiver to draw the horizontal line where:

n = COL_TO - COL_FROM + 1

4   These steps are repeated to ´DRAW´ a ´VERTICAL-LINE´.

5   The frame RECTANGLE uses the methods ´DRAW´ of ´HORIZONTAL LINE´ and ´DRAW´ of ´VERTICAL LINE´ to construct a rectangle.

6   There is a new requirement the ability to define a group of messages to form a larger message structure (Fig.16).

In this example it is the message group that requires iteration. Iterating twice will draw the rectangle. The iteration requires the definition row position for horizontal line, and column position for vertical lines, as a 2 x 2 array. Here the variables ´A´ and ´B´ denote working variables which are first defined in the definition of the individual messages HORIZONTAL-LINE and VERTICAL-LINE. The system knows that values must be given for ´A´ and ´B´ at the point of iteration.

There are alternative methods for defining a rectangle, eg:

- draw lines

- describe 90 angle

- iterate until the end-of-line co-ordinates equal the   rectangle top-left-corner co-ordinates.

4.3 Transient and Named Objects

Object definition is achieved by executing methods associated with object
classes. The creation of an object such as a window, requires that the
object be named to differentiate a window OBJECT from any other window
OBJECT. For example, if the window is to contain a menu of medical
symptoms, the developer may name the window SYMPTOMS. The full name
definition of an object is the object name prefixed by the class name,
eg:

WINDOW:SYMPTOMS

Usually objects that have no explicit name associated with them are
considered to be an object in the system that is of interest as a logical
object of processing.

However, certain classes need only have transient objects. The RECTANGLE
and LINE classes are examples of classes having transient objects. These
objects do not exist in their own right (ie. individually named) but as
components of a larger name object, the WINDOW.

5   BUILDING A PROTOTYPE

How does ´drawing a rectangle´ to define a WINDOW help in generating a
prototype system? After all ´drawing a rectangle´ is a very low level
task.

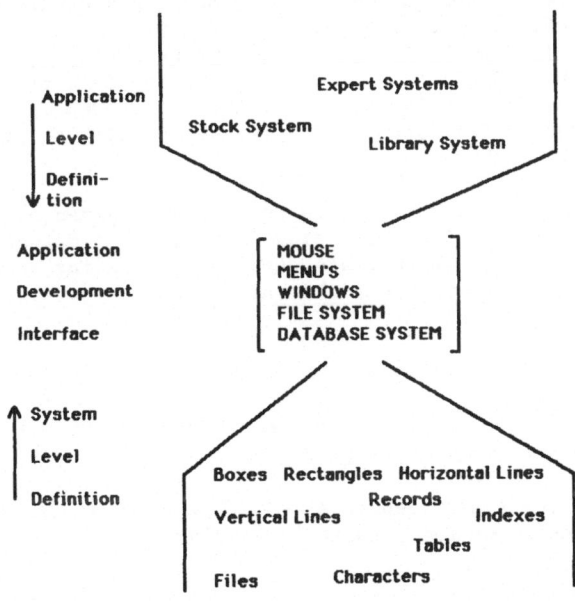

Figure 17 "Egg-timer" view of software development

The concept of objects enables the generation of software prototypes to be developed at two levels:

- the systems level

- the application level

Figure 17 describes the "egg-timer" view of software development using these two levels.

It is "egg-timer" in concept because, at the system level, development is bottom-up using a number of component object classes to form a smaller number of object classes that can be used to build applications. The system level provides ´pre-fabrication´ of classes that can be used to build complex applications.

It is top-down from the application prototype level. Only a restricted set of object classes are available and visible to the application builder in developing a prototype.

The prototyping environment uses an interpreter to analyse a message and invoke a method which will perform some frame processing. The modularity of definition and processing execution (ie. two frames and a message passed between frames) enables very small tests to be performed under the control of the interpreting environment.

There are two forms of testing proposed:

i) Data slot values are defined in a frame and the action of a message on the receiving frame shows the effect of the message upon the frame.

ii) A number of frames can be linked and tested in a full test eg. to draw a rectangle on the screen.

Compilation:

At an ´appropriate level´ a number of frames and messages can be compiled to produce an efficient processing environment. An ´appropriate level´ of processing might be a collection of messages that operate upon a named object eg. DRAW A WINDOW. Inefficiencies in the interpreted version exist because of ´cascade´ message calling. Performance through compilation is achieved by ´collapsing´ the message passing to permit efficient execution of the task.

Of course the nature of compilation would change given a different target machine architecture. The definition of frames and messages could be easily mapped on to an appropriate parallel processing architecture because message processing could be carried out in parallel for a particular processing task.

6   PROTOTYPING AN APPLICATION

There are three major software components involved in the processing of a screen-to-screen transition (Fig.18).

Once the input event has been received, flow between the components is under the direction of the Transition Handler.

408

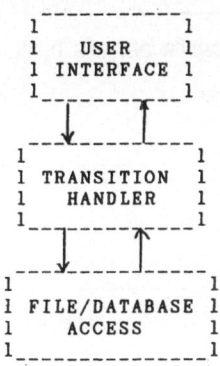

Figure 18   Screen-to-Screen Transition

Already we have seen how a basic function can be defined to support a
visual object (ie. drawing a window). The application builder uses these
visual objects and associated functions to build complex application
interfaces. The presentation of the use of objects such as a window is
in a form suitable for use by a systems analyst. It is not in the form
of frames and messages. This object architecture, although under-pinning
the software, is hidden from systems analysts and application users.

The example below is of a read access to an indexed sequential file. The
issues that this example raises are:

1   The different levels of definition that are required in building a
     file prototype.

2   How object modularity can allow fundamental changes in file
     design to be incorporated.

3   Message interfacing between transition handler and data handler and
     access using a relational SQL interface.

6.1   The File Access Example

Figure 19 illustrates the input screen to a ´read ORDERS record´
application. The reply is the display of the record´s contents on the
screen (Fig.20).

There are two major processing requirments in this transaction:

     i) The input/output handling at the interface

     ii) The file access

The transition handling simply acts as a communication interface between
the User Interface and the File Handler.

The purpose of this section is to look at the structure of the message
that the transition handler generates and passes to the file handler.
The processing of the message is explained in the next section. This
section also describes the structure of message, if the ORDERs data is
stored on a relational database.

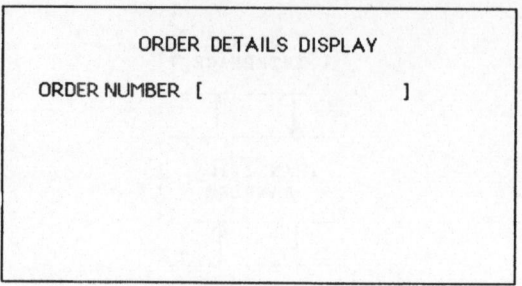

Figure 19 "Read orders record" input

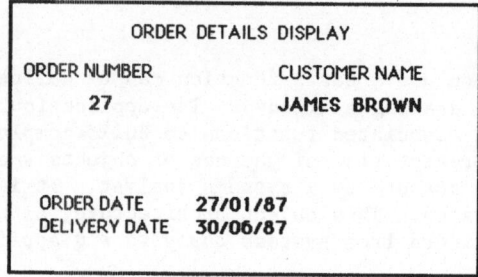

Figure 20 Reply to read orders

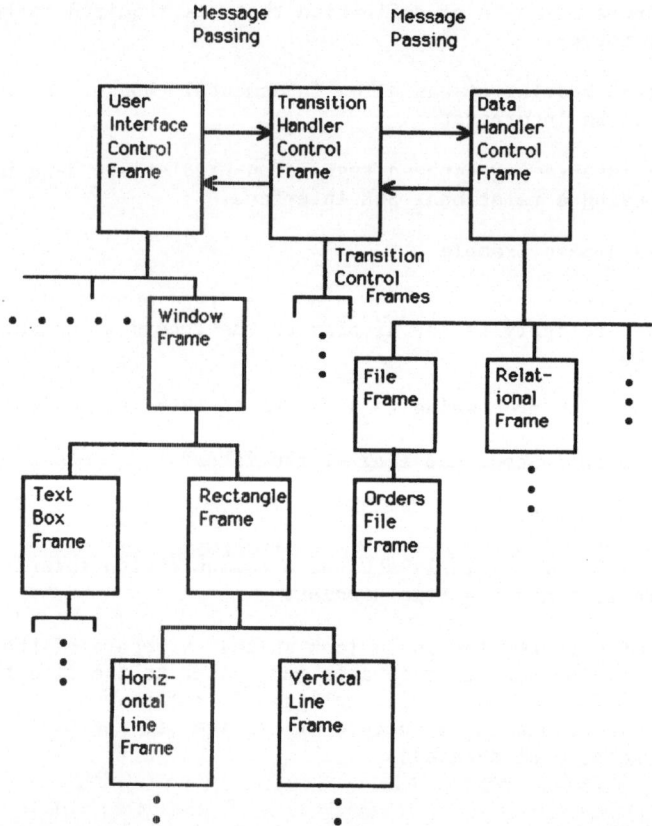

Figure 21 Communication between file handler and transition handler

```
1-----------------1---------------1---------------1
1                 1               1               1
1  ISFILE_READ    1  FILENAME     1  PKEY_VALUE   1
1_____1_____1_____1
```

Figure 22 structure of IS file read message

6.2 Structure of an Indexed Sequential (I.S.) File Read Message

Communication between Transition Handler and File Handler is depicted in
Figure 21. The handlers are formed into a frame structure with each
handler only communicating at the highest level. Figure 22 describes the
structure of the I.S. File Read Message. This message is generated as a
result of the screen input by the transition handler.

ISFILE_READ is a method in the DATA HANDLER CONTROL FRAME. The method
directs processing to the particular ISFILE and ORDERS_FILE frames using
the PKEY_VALUE to locate the appropriate record occurrence. If there is
secondary key access then the message will need to carry key-type as well
as key-value.

6.3 Relational Database Message Structure

If the orders were stored in a relational database then the structure of
the relational database message would be a message group as follows
(Fig.23).

This is an example message occurrence. The message group ´RDB_ READ´ is
made up of:

- A ´WHERE´ message which defines the ´SELECTION´, ´JOINS´ etc.
  required to identify the tuples to be retrieved in the specific
  order required.

- TARGET messages identify the items of data to be retrieved.

6.4 Prototyping Definition Levels

The transaction definition, of which the ´ORDERS read´ is an example, is
generated at a high level by the analyst for the benefit of the user to
which the prototype is aimed. There are two other definition levels that
are required before the application definition can be defined.

i) Definition of Basic File Types

This is the base level definition which enables different file or
database types to be defined, eg. IS files, Random File, Relational
Databases.

At the same definition level different indexed sequential file types can
be defined. The indexed sequential file type in this example uses
multiple levels of index and no overflow but there can be a large number
of variants:

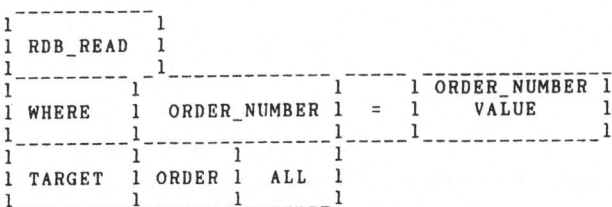

```
1-----------1
1           1
1 RDB_READ  1
1_____ _1_____ _____ _____
1         1                1      1 ORDER_NUMBER 1
1 WHERE    1  ORDER_NUMBER 1 = 1      VALUE       1
1_____1_____1____1_____1
1         1        1       1
1 TARGET  1 ORDER  1  ALL  1
1_____1_____1_____1
```

Figure 23 Message to Read a relational database

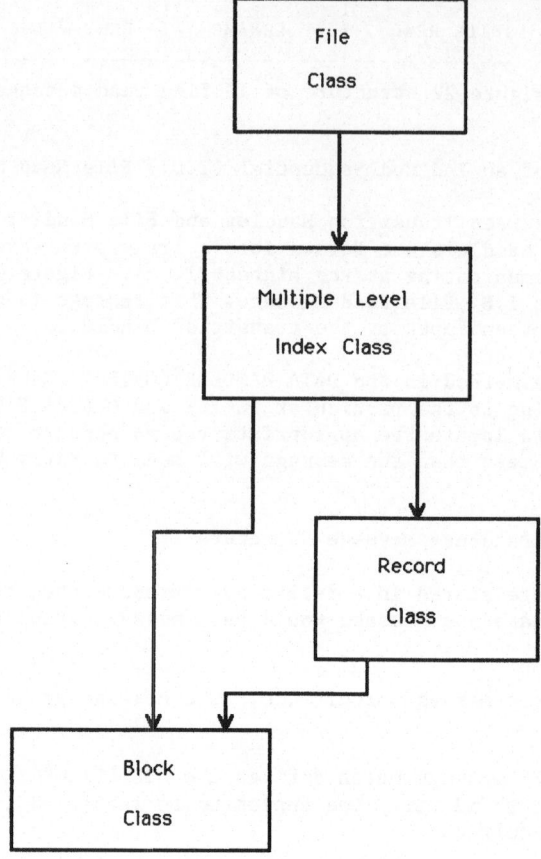

Figure 24 Frame structure of IS file

- files with record overflow

- files with block overflow

- overflow records placed in prime area

- single level indexes

- B-tree indexes

```
                    ORDERS  FILE
                 DATA ELEMENT DEFINITION

        ATTRIBUTE         TYPE        LENGTH(BYTES)
        Order_Number       X               8
        Customer_Name      X              30
        Order_Date         9               4
        Delivery_Date      9               4
```

Figure 25 Define record contents screen definition

```
                 ORDERS  FILE
                 KEY  DEFINITION

    KEY ATTRIBUTES        BYTE FROM      BYTE TO

    Order_Number              1             8
```

Figure 26 Define the file key screen definition

defined by the prototyping package programmer or by some technical support function at the user site.

The frame structure of the indexed sequential file described in this
example is illustrated in Figure 24.

This is the basic class structure of the indexed sequential file used in
this example. The file maps onto a structured index and records. This
logical representation then maps onto physical storage blocks.

ii) Definition of Specific Files

The generation of a file occurrence using one of the base file types is
the next level of definition eg. the generation of the ORDERS file. The
definition of the ORDERS file is performed by the analyst using an interface supplied by the prototyping system.

Two such definition screens might be:

   - to define the record contents (Fig.25)

   - to define the file key (Fig.26)

This definition of the specific characteristics of a file causes the
class structure to be extended automatically. The frame and message
structures are generated automatically from the screen dialogue above
(figs. 25 and 26) without the need to drop down into the visual programming level. This definition of a specific file instance from a file type
illustrates the inheritance capabilities of the prototyping system.

Figure 27 gives the class relationships for the ORDERS file. It is an
extension of the structure in Figure 24.

If a secondary key access method is required then all that is required is
to add a secondary key class.

6.5 The Order Record Reading Transaction

The read indexed sequential record is specified once for any indexed
sequential file. The characteristics of the specific file (eg. ORDERS)
enables the ´read ORDERS record´ to be automatically generated by in-
heriting the generic read operation.

To illustrate how this generic indexed sequential read is executed for
the ORDERS file, Figure 28 shows how the class frames are linked by
messages.

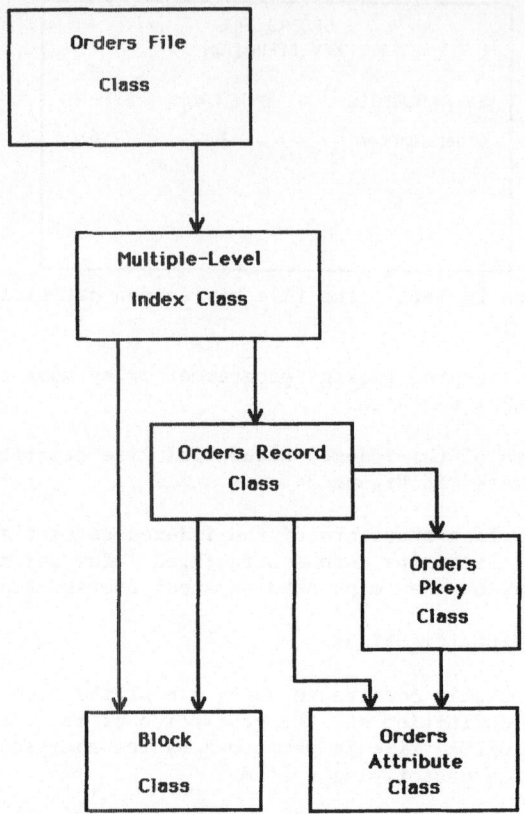

Figure 27 Extensions to figure 24

The execution of the above frames is best illustrated by looking at an example orders file (fig.29). The action of the messages in Figure 28 is briefly illustrated.

INITIAL_READ   This message group causes the top level index block to be read (READ_BLOCK) then searched (LOCATED_ENTRY).

READ_INDEX   After locating the appropriate index entry the block at the next index level is read (READ_BLOCK) and searched (LOCATE_ENTRY).

READ_DATA   At the bottom level of the index the next block read is the data block (READ_BLOCK) and the LOCATE_RECORD message locates the record in the block.

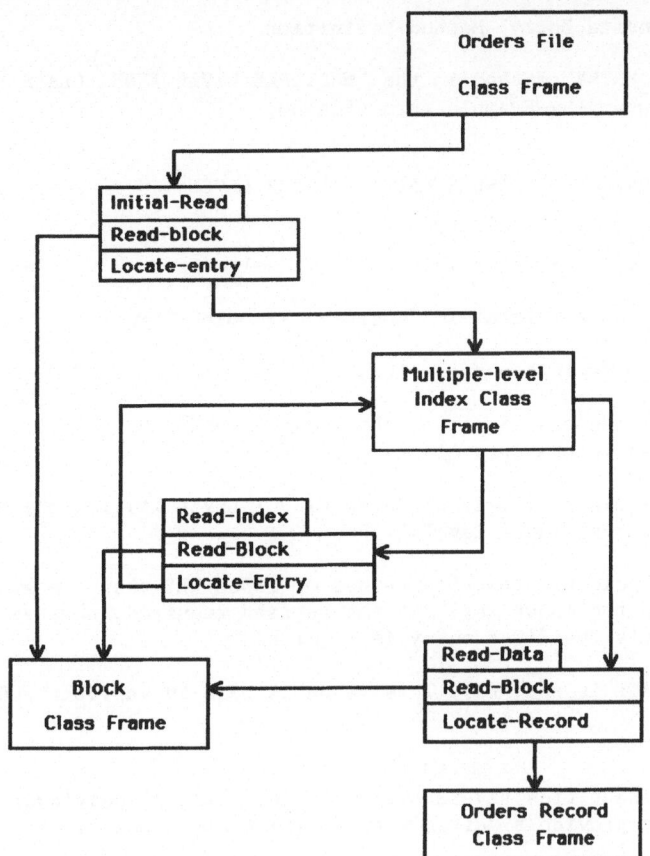

Figure 28 Linking class frames by messages

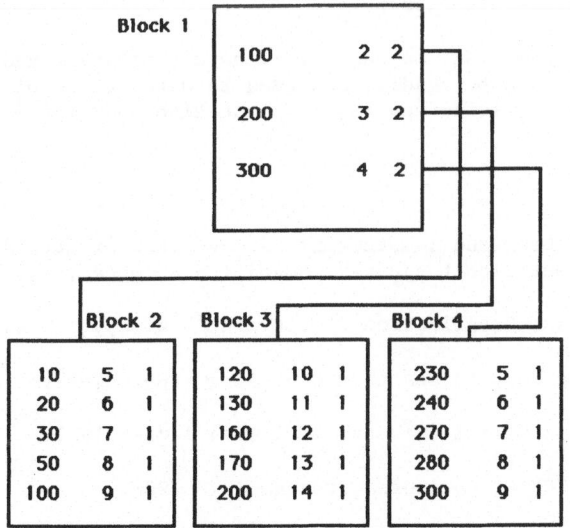

Figure 29 execution of frames in fig. 28

6.6 The 'Locate Entry' Method Definition

The 'LOCATE_ENTRY' method in the 'MULTIPLE_LEVEL INDEX CLASS' frame is
defined in Query-by-Example form (Fig.30).

	INDEX_KEY	INDEX_PAGE	INDEX_LEVEL
F	>VAL	R.IND	>1
F	>VAL	R.IND	=1

Fig.30 Method Definition in 'Query-by-Example' Form

There are two definitions required:

    i) For the base level of the index (INDEX_LEVEL = 1) ie. next
       read is the data block.

    ii) For higher levels of index (INDEX_LEVEL >1) ie. the next read is
       the next index level.

The '>VAL' indicates that the values of INDEX_KEY that are >VAL (ie.
greater than the input key) are the entries required, however, 'F' indicate that only the first entry is required.

The INDEX_PAGE is read (R). This value is held in variable IND.

7 CONCLUSION

This paper identifies several major features which individually and
collectively provide a suitable prototyping environment. The approach
provides:

Modularity and extensive inheritance capability and thus re-usability of
software.

A visual form of programming at the lowest systems level.

Multiple levels of definition and description providing maximum flexibility in prototype development.

The concepts of frames and messages provide a consistent and coherent
architecture that can be readily extended to support not only interactive
commercial data processing applications but also knowledge-based expert
systems.

References

[BOBR77]   D.G. Bobrow and T. Winograd "An Overview of KRL, A Knoiwledge
        Representation Language" Cognitive Science Vol.1 No.1, 1977.

[BOAR84]   B.H. Boar "Application Prototyping" (Wiley), 1984.

[BUDD83]   R Budde "Approaches to Prototyping" (Springer Verlag), 1983.

[BYTE81]   'Byte' MAGAZINE (Several Articles) August 1981.

[COX86]   B Cox "Object-Oriented Programming" 1986.

[GLIN84]   E.P. Glinert and S.L. Tanimoto "PICT: An Interactive Graphical
        Programming Environment" Computer Nov. 1984 pp 7-25.

[GOLD83]   A. Goldberg and D. Robson "SMALLTALK-80 The Language and Its
           Implementation" 1983.

[INFO86]   Pergamon Infotech "State of the Art" Report on Prototyping
           1986.

[LAW83]   D Law "N.C.C. Report on Prototyping" (National Computing
           Centre) 1983.

[LIPK82]   D.E. Lipkie et al "Star Graphics: An Object-Oriented
           Implementation" Computer Graphics Vol. 16, No. 3, July 82, pp.
           115-227.

[MINS75]   M. Minsky "A Framework for Representing Knowledge in The
           Psychology of Computer Vision" Ed. P.H. Winston (McGraw Hill),
           1975, pp. 211-277.

[MYLO84]   J. Mylopoulos and H.J. Levesque "An Overview of Knowledge
           Representation" in "On Conceptual Modelling" (Springer Verlag),
           1984.

[ZANI84]   C. Zaniolo "Object-Oriented Programming in PROLOG" 1984.

[ZLOO77]   M.M. Zloof "Query-by-Example: A Data Base Language" IBM Systems
           Journal Vol.16, 1977, pp. 324-343.

SECTION SIX — FUTURE TRENDS

In this final section are five papers which reflect on the possible
developments of the next decade. Previous sections have dealt with many
products which are not yet completed and which, therefore, represent the
future to some extent. This section differs from those because the papers
advocate radical changes in the approach to the design and development of
information systems.

The first paper reflects the keynote address of the conference given by
Russel Jones, a leading U.K. writer on information systems. He argues that
the whole culture of systems development must change. "Information systems
still does not understand business and business certainly does not
understand information systems." He emphasises the need for system
developers to understand business needs and argues the necessity for more
education of business analysts. In many respects, his views echo and extend
the ideas of James Martin [MART85]. He also perceives the need to automate
the systems development process with the ultimate aim of eradicating
programming altogether. This view has been touched upon many times in the
papers in this volume.

Venken et al. build on these ideas in their paper which proclaims that the
time is right to adopt a new paradigm for systems development. The
traditional life-cycle, applications-centered approach which has dominated
systems development for 20 years is no longer adequate. Instead we need to
build a "knowledge-rich environment" which bridges the gap between the ill-
defined requirements specification and the rigorous nature of software
engineering. This paper describes the RUBRIC Esprit project which views
information systems development as "developing an organisation's knowledgebase" and takes as central the need to have a separate business policy model
in addition to the more usual functional (behavioural) and data model.

The next two papers are concerned with "meta-systems". These are systems
for "..the automatic generation of the major portions of a particular
software development environment" (DeDourek et al.). They argue that no one
methodology and no set of tools can be ideal for all the systems development
which takes place in an organisation. Instead we should be looking towards
the development of meta-systems so that suitable environments can be
generated as required by different projects. DeDourek et al.'s paper
elaborates this argument before looking in detail at an implementation of
the meta-system paradigm through the language EMDL (Environment Model

Definition Language). Redmond and Ryan pursue a similar line in their discussion of software engineering environments. There is a need to support a variety of methods and to provide active guidance in their use. Methods are objects within the environment just as tools are and can be manipulated as other objects. They describe an Esprit project which is investigating these ideas and detail their findings and future work.

The final paper by Witten et al. addresses the problem of defining procedures. They accept the view that programming will continue as an important activity, but recognise that it will performed increasingly by non-programmers. They present a view that the computer is in a good position to write its own programs if it is given some example procedures to work from. This leads to the notion of "programming by example". This method works well in situations such as teaching industrial robots, the question arises as to whether it is suitable for inferring office procedures.

The discipline of information systems is still very young and we can expect to see many radical developments over the next few years. The papers in this section offer some pointers as to where those developments may come and where research is most urgently required.

References

[MART86] Martin J. "The Information Systems Manifesto" Prentice-Hall 1986.

TIME TO CHANGE THE CULTURE OF INFORMATION SYSTEMS

DEPARTMENTS

Russel   Jones

Freelance Journalist, Cambridge, U.K.

1   INTRODUCTION

A revolution is about to take place in the working practices of
information systems (IS) staff. That revolution will usher in a totally
changed IS culture.

The philosophy that forms the underlying rationale for this revolution is
to be found within new business-oriented systems development
methodologies such as information engineering. The agents of the
revolution are analyst workbenches, a new generation of software
development tools which is already inaugurating the era of Computer Aided
Design and Manufacture (CAD/CAM) for many IS departments.

Prior to the revolution, computer systems were designed using pencil and
templates, analysis and design methods were esoterically technical in
nature, and programs were hand coded in third generation languages such
as Cobol.

Following the revolution, IS staff will use business-oriented methods of
systems analysis – methods capable of involving users fully in the
software development process – and computer systems will be designed at
powerful graphics-based workbenches. Programmers will be bypassed
altogether, with computer programs generated directly from system
designs.

Computing will never be the same again

To cope with the new software development environment ushered in by the
upcoming revolution, IS staff will not only need to alter their working
methods: they will need to change dramatically the basic culture within
which those working methods are practised.

This article explains why IS culture needs to change fundamentally, and
why implementing this change offers IS staff a golden opportunity to
boost their influence at the highest corporate levels.

2 CURRENT IS PROBLEMS

To set the scene for the new IS culture, it is first necessary to look briefly at the problems that currently beset IS departments. It must be hammered home time and time again that these problems are, by and large, not technical in nature. Rather they relate to the technically-oriented environment within which IS staff currently operate.

At the moment, many IS staff who religiously exploit the best of structured design techniques, and who follow software engineering principles to the letter, still end up writing lousy software. Not because they are idle or incompetent, but because the basic <u>business</u> designs they are working from are often just plain wrong.

In fact, IS staff within many organisations now spend upwards of 80% of their time maintaining old computer systems. In some organisations, that figure is closer to 100%. And that, in a nutshell, is why IS staff can't meet the demand from users for new systems, and why many of their business colleagues look elsewhere for information technology (IT) solutions.

But, for the most part, the burdensome work that takes up so much of the time of IS staff isn't maintenance at all. Rather, it is the "correction" of often gross errors perpetrated during the initial stages of system analysis. The earlier a mistake is made whilst designing a computer system - and missed - the more expensive it is to correct following system implementation.

The result of poor systems analysis is that many IS departments are stuck in a low productivity loop. Unsatisfactory systems analysis produces computer systems that need continual, highly geared, correction. Continually correcting badly designed systems leaves IS staff with little time for writing new ones. Poor systems analysis derives, at root, from the lack of real communication between users and IS staff. That's a cultural problem, not a technical one.

Poor systems analysis emanates from a basic lack of understanding on IS staff's part of business issues and needs. There is still an alarming fear on the part of IS staff of becoming closely involved with users.

The result is that IS still does not understand business, and business certainly does not yet understand IS. Is is surprising that so few systems meet real business needs?

3 THE NEW IS CULTURE - THE BUSINESS ORIENTATION

But business's view of the importance of IT is changing rapidly. James Martin, in his seminal book, "The Information Systems Manifesto" [MART86], advises business managers to "understand how your organisation ought to change as it becomes a fully electronic enterprise. Electronics are changing products, services, fabrication techniques, selling techniques, decision making, flows of information, mechanisms of control, and management structures".

And a recent UK report on the exploitation of IT had this to say: "companies lagging in the use of IT are six times more likely to have a poor financial performance within their sector than the companies leading in the use of IT."

The implications of those sentiments are clear. To survive in the future, all organisations must make ever greater use of IT. That means that the orientation of IS now needs to change radically.

IS staff typically have a natural tendency to focus on technology matters – networks, databases, 4GLs – rather than on business issues. Many don't realise that the emphasis in computer systems needs to shift away from an efficiency orientation – how do we cut cost? – towards an effectiveness orientation – how do we best meet the wider business objectives of our organisation?

That new orientation won't be achieved simply by refining current IS working practices. Nothing less than the adoption of a wholly new, totally business-oriented, culture will suffice.

The new IS culture needs to be a primarily outwards looking, based on an understanding of business and its needs. That's a dramatic change from existing IS culture, which tends to be based almost exclusively on a detailed knowledge of technology.

Creative business thinking needs to become the new watchword is IS – how can technology best help the business? The current technology-only culture of IS should be swept away. Lateral and proactive thinking, based on an awareness of wider business needs, should replace the reactive thinking typical of all too many IS departments.

This is no trivial matter. Many trends indicate that any organisation that is not an electronic organisation in five to ten years simply will not survive. The successful exploitation of IT is already the key to corporate success. In five years time, the unsuccessful exploitation of IT will just as certainly lead to corporate decline, or even death.

If internal IS departments cannot deliver the systems necessary to turn their organisation into an electronic organisation, senior management will simply look elsewhere for their IT support.

And, thus far in the history of computing, one thing is for certain – a technically oriented data processing (DP) culture has totally failed to deliver systems that business users require at the time they require them.

4   BUSINESS-ORIENTED DEVELOPMENT METHODS

The adoption of business-oriented methods of systems analysis is a crucial element of the new IS culture. IS staff simply must start to raise their horizons – away from the merely technical, towards the business that employs them. Let's look at just one example of how technically-oriented methods are currently failing IS staff.

One of the current fashions in IS is database. A large number of installations are re-writing their old systems using database methods. To be honest, most don't really know why they're doing it. They couldn't, for example, put their hand on their heart and tell you the wider business improvements likely to follow from implementing database technology.

The reality is that, for the most part, the move to database systems merely normalises a snapshot of the data needed to support business objectives from a random to a more structured format. But many hours are spent performing this task, simply because normalisation is seen as the next great technical touchstone for IS staff.

But such an approach completely misses the point. Let's ask the basic question — how does one decide the sort of data that should be stored within a database? Certainly not by normalising 15 year old data structures. The only realistic way of deciding what data is needed is by looking at the information that businessmen need to run their business.

But that approach needs a whole different attitude from DP staff. They need to start "growing" computer systems from the business inwards rather than from the computer room outwards.

New business-oriented development methodologies, such as information engineering, implement such a business-oriented approach. In our database example, for instance, analysis of existing data files is replaced by business-oriented entity modelling - a technique that is wholly non-technical in nature aimed at building data models based on real business information needs.

The new methodologies emphasise the need for computer systems to model the whole business and to support its overall objectives. They concentrate primarily on gaining an understanding of any business - by analysing inherent business processes and those basic data/information elements with which they are involved.

A key feature of the new methodologies is their advocacy of business analysis. At the moment most IS staff simply don't understand the significance of business analysis. They typically employ the discipline called systems analysis. This sits, as it always has, uneasily between worlds of business and computing. Its use effectively precludes users from checking the quality of the basic analysis work carried out by dp staff.

The result is that business people do not understand whether DP staff understand the business they are attempting to computerise!

The proper use of business analysis alters all that. Business analysis uses non-technical, business-oriented, techniques that are easily understood by users. Users understand the techniques inherent in business analysis simply because those techniques use the language of business, not of computing.

By implementing business analysis techniques, organisations can, often for the first time, bring effective quality control procedures to the task of building IT systems. Business analysis does this by introducing to the systems development process the only people able to comment realistically on the appropriateness of any proposed computer system's design - that systems's ultimate users.

5   AUTOMATING THE NEW IS CULTURE

But the adoption of new business-oriented methods of working represents just one half of the new IS culture. Business analysis provides a correct and rigorous backcloth for IS staff. But automated tools must be used to automate its use. The other half of the new IS culture revolves around automating business analysis and all subsequent phases of systems development.

There are also more fundamental reasons why IS staff should embrace the use of automated tools. Many of the tasks which IS professionals have traditionally performed - system design, computer programming, system testing - are tasks which are unsuited to what James Martin terms our "meat-machine brain". Humans create program designs which are full of inconsistencies and vagueness. A computer can help the human to create specifications because he - or she - cannot do that well.

A computer should also generate the code needed. Indeed, one of the aims of business-oriented methodologies such as information engineering is that of populating advanced data dictionaries - called encyclopedias - with sufficient information to enable computer systems to be generated automatically. Programming as we currently understand it disappears completely within the new IS culture.

Thankfully, power tools, such as 4GLs, IPSEs and analyst workbenches are starting to free IS staff from the tyranny of the template and the coding pad, and from the limitations of the meat machine.

That's a trend which will continue. To stay competitive in the future, organisations will be dependent absolutely upon power tools for the engineering of information systems.

6   THE NEW IS CULTURE - KEY TO IS SUCCESS

The new generation of IS power tools will free IS staff from all the old, repetitive tasks that have been the bane of their life for twenty years. That will effectively destroy the old-style IS.

We may then wonder how we ever managed with manual techniques. After all, we may say to ourselves, programming always was an essentially boring, highly error-prone, task; programming wheels were re-invented within the average IS department with alarming regularity; so were designs for wheels.

Within the new IS culture, the boring, the repetitive and the error-prone will be swept away. Computers themselves will help with as many of those old style tasks as possible. IS Staff will be left to perform the much more interesting - and fundamentally more important - task of supporting real business objectives with the effective and innovative use of new technology.

Technical enclaves will of course remain within every IS department - systems programming, for example, also networking support, and staff who understand the minutiae of databases or performance management. But the clear orientation of the IS department will be outward looking, tuned absolutely to the needs of the business.

At the moment many IS managers just don't understand the potential that exists for making IS a key element of their organisations. All of them think they ought to be on The Board, but they can't find a way of getting there.

But, if commentators such as James Martin are right, the rules of the corporate hierarchy game may be altering in IS's favour. After all, if the successful exploitation of IT is now the key to corporate success, who within most organisations, are the only people currently capable of producing computer software?

To earn their place on The Board however, the monopoly supplier of computer systems must exploit that situation. But they won't do that using current methods, within an old style IS culture. Old style IS simply does not produce systems that users want within a timescale that is any longer acceptable.

And it's no good IS trying to solve its current short term problems by simply throwing more and more technology – whether hardware or software – at them. IS must face up to the fact that, at the moment, it simply has the wrong culture. An IS department can't hope to build the sort of infrastructure computer systems needed to support the electronic organisation of the future unless it understand implicitly the business culture within which that organisation operates.

So, IS needs to change its culture rapidly – rapidly because time is running out. Market forces will dictate that those organisations that best exploit IT will be successful. Those that don't will simply die. The use of the new business-oriented methodologies within an automated, culturally altered environment offers IS staff the chance to ensure that their organisation is a survivor. By the same token, the promotion of a radically new culture is the best long term strategy for any IS department hoping to increase its profile within the corporate hierarchy.

Make no mistake, IS is currently faced with a major opportunity. But, if internal IS departments, whilst they remain monopoly suppliers of computer systems, cannot grasp the nettle of becoming fully involved in the day to life of the rest of their organisation, senior management will eventually go elsewhere for their IT advice.

If that means bypassing current IS departments completely, then so be it.

1   "information engineering" in this paper is used in a generic sense and does not refer solely to Martin's Information Engineering [MART81].

[MART81] Martin J. and Finkelstein C. "Information Engineering" SAVANT 1981.

[MART86] Martin J. "The Information Systems Manifesto" Prentice-Hall 1986.

THE RUBRIC PROJECT: A NEW PARADIGM FOR INFORMATION SYSTEMS

DEVELOPMENT

R. Venken[1], F. Van Assche[2], P. Loucopoulos,
and P.J. Layzell[3]
[1]BIM, [2]James Martin Associates, [3]UMIST
Everberg, Belgium — Brussels, Belgium — Manchester, U.K.

ABSTRACT

The purpose of the RUBRIC project is to investigate a rule based approach
to the description of business systems and the subsequent use of rules to
directly implement major parts of data processing applications. The aim
is to bridge the gap between the fuzziness and uncertainty in the
acquisition of user requirements and the remaining stages of the
development life cycle for transaction processing systems. This paper
describes the rationale and architecture of the RUBRIC system, the
workplan adopted in meeting the objectives of the RUBRIC project and the
systems's exploitation potential.

Keywords: Information Systems, Business Policy, Knowledge Engineering,
Systems Development Methods.

1   INTRODUCTION

The growing complexity of information systems and the ensuing problems of
their development, maintenance and management, have highlighted the
inadequacy of the informal way of constructing such systems. These
problems manifest themselves in computer systems which are often
unmanageable, unreliable, inflexible and hence difficult to maintain.

The response to these problems has been the emergence of a number of
software development environments, consisting of an underlying
representation model, a method by which a model is constructed and a set
of computer-assisted tools to aid model development. Despite the use of
such environments, users continue to report that lead times are long,
estimates are inadequate, development is expensive and performance is
imperfect [MORR85].

The aim of the RUBRIC project therefore is to improve the practice of
constructing large, complex information systems by developing tools to
build a knowledge-rich environment to support software engineering
practices with the objective of bridging the gap between the fuzziness
and uncertainty in the acquisition of business requirements and the rest
of the development life cycle. In particular, RUBRIC seeks to avoid the
present practice of embedding business policy and constraints within
program logic. This practice leads to inflexible systems and subsequent
difficulty in maintaining them. Instead, it is proposed to replace this

427

traditional practice with a more explicit representation of policy and constraints in all the development deliverables (specifications, designs and code). This independence of policy and constraints is thus analogous to the way a data dictionary or data base externalises data.

The RUBRIC project is funded by the European Commission for 3.5 years, under the ESPRIT Research and Development programme and is a collaborative venture between leading software houses and academia . The prime contractors are James Martin Associates (Netherlands), in collaboration with Micro Focus (UK), UMIST (UK) and BIM (Belgium). The Irish Electricity Supply Board act as evaluation partners.

The remainder of this paper describes the philosophy behind the RUBRIC project in more detail and outlines the main work to date.

2   INFORMATION SYSTEM DEVELOPMENT

2.1 The Problems

User demand for reliable computer systems, coupled with the realisation that most failures are due to poor specification and design, have resulted in the emergence of a number of software development methods. There are currently many system development methods [OLLE82; OLLE86; MADD83], each of which seek to provide a coherent development path by providing a mechanism by which the desired aspects of a system can be modelled. In addition they embody an underlying philosophy and approach by which models can be developed and a set of development steps by which resources can be organised and allocated. Furthermore, many methods now have associated computer-based tools aimed at improving productivity.

These methods may be classified at least according to one dimension of their underlying philosophy as: process oriented, e.g. SASD [DeMa78], STRADIS [Gane79], SADT [Ross77], JSD [Jack83]; or data oriented, e.g. Information Engineering [MacD86], NIAM [Verh82].

Within the life cycle approach these methods enable the systems designer to develop models starting with representations of the ˜real-world´ problem space which are closer to human perception and then gradually deriving models successively closer to the machine level. However, the effectiveness of these methods is compromised for a number of reasons. Firstly, there is a shortage of the highly skilled personnel required to build system models according to the philosophy and approach of any single method. Secondly, once these models are built they represent aggregations and abstractions of many user views. A model representation is such that it is often alien to the way users perceive a business system thus making verification of the model difficult. Thirdly, system models are rigid to the extent that they do not explicitly state the policy, uncertainty, redundancy and view multiplicity that is inherent in the real world. Fourthly, computer-based tools have their biggest impact only in the implementation and testing phases of the project life cycle. Existing tools, which can be applied at the earlier development stages, such as PSL/PSA [Teic79], various diagrammers, data dictionaries and specification encyclopedias only play a passive rather than an active role. Such tools are primarily concerned with handling some of the clerical procedures such as documentation of a system specification rather than in providing actual help during systems analysis and specification.

A major shortcoming of these methods is that the modelling of the real-world is achieved only in information systems terms, i.e. processes and data, rather than in terms more appropriate to the problem space environment. The result is that whereas end users perceive and often define a business system in terms of rules and exceptions applying to these rules, such a view is not directly visible in the derived system specification, using contemporary methods.

An information system is directly related to the business system within which it operates and is thus a manifestation of some business requirements for operational control and support of decision making. Current approaches, by concentrating solely on the information system aspects, fail to represent the effects of the business environment on the information system itself. In other words the rules which govern the behaviour of an information system (the business rules) are not explicitly represented but instead are hard-coded into program sources. This low level representation of business rules results in computer systems which are difficult to maintain as maintenance staff, who receive requirement changes in terms of the business environment, must first translate the requirement into the same terms in which the information system is described and represented. This therefore provides a wide scope for poor translation and misunderstanding, leading to systems which fail to meet their requirements.

2.2 An Example

To demonstrate the shortcoming of contemporary approaches to developing information systems, some members of the RUBRIC project team considered a relatively simple payroll system. The system takes as input a set of clock timings for each employee and produces a set of pairs

<no-of-hours, rate-of-pay>

Rates applicable to an individual are determined by information relating to the individual, the department and the company. Whilst this is relatively simple, substantial complexity is introduced in the associated payroll programs because of the interaction of a number of rules which govern the rates paid.

The way such a system would normally be developed is to first establish and document the requirements. Following any of the methods mentioned above, the requirements specification will show the flow of data in the system and the interactions between the major system components. The details regarding each component, i.e. the policy, would be defined in terms of techniques such as structured english, decision tables and decision trees and it is at this level that business policy is determined in any detail. Unfortunately, it also remains as the only policy specification. Whereas a data model for this application will be successively transformed to a database schema, thus establishing a direct link between data model specification and data base operation, business policy is embedded directly into program code. This approach results in a number of problems.

Firstly, programs become complex simply because the order of the procedure determines much of the logic of the program. Many of the rate determination rules in the above example are implemented by the order of the program statements. Secondly, it is difficult to check the correctness of a program. Few people with the knowledge of the rate calculation system will be able to understand the implementation. Finally, maintenance of programs is a time consuming activity and one frought with pitfalls, since the programs describe a procedure to determine rates of pay, rather than containing information about the method of calculation. Any changes to the business policy would require a re-ordering of the calculation.

The application was regarded by the authors as a relatively straight forward data processing application. However, examination of the implementation revealed that the program dealing with this application contained approximately three thousand lines. Yet the complexity brought about by the size of the program is not because of any complexity in the problem space, but rather in the limitations of the approach to implementing the problem. In fact the main business policy for this application is contained within the following eight rules and assertions:

1   If the company has additional premiums
            then only one rate and one premium rate may be paid
                for any worked time period
            otherwise only one rate may apply to a worked time
period.

2   A worked time period is any sub-division (in 1/100ths of an hour) between the clock-on and clock-off time.

3   Any time not attracting a higher rate is paid at the normal rate.

4   If the day is a holiday
            then if any time has been worked
            then pay at the worked holiday rate
            otherwise pay the normal day length at the holiday rate

5   If more that 8 hours are worked in a day
            then pay at the overtime rate.

6   If more than 40 normal hours are worked in a week
            then pay the overtime rate for the excess.

7   If the lunch break is outside the lunch break bounds
            then pay overtime for the lunch break period.

8   If any time worked falls within a premium time period
            then if the company has additional premiums
                then include premium rate for the time worked
                otherwise pay premium rate rather than any other
rate.

2.3 A New Paradigm

Obviously, improvements to current practices in the short term can be made by the evolutionary development of better methods, techniques and tools, thus gradually enhancing existing practices by expanding their range and effectiveness.

However, the RUBRIC project, whilst recognising the importance of the evolutionary approach, proposes a new direction in the development of information systems. This direction is a response to the premise that there is a need for a new information systems paradigm. [For example, Bube86].

This paradigm states that development of an information system should be viewed as the task of developing or augmenting an organisation's knowledge base. Within RUBRIC this knowledge base consists of data models, behavioural models, system interfaces and business policy and constraints, together with the necessary mappings to meet the objectives of the required system. In particular, RUBRIC recognises the need for explicit policy to be identifiable throughout the development of a system and to remain distinct from the procedures and elementary data operations necessary to implement the policy.

It is therefore the belief of the RUBRIC project that a new paradigm for the development of large, complex information systems, is required. In particular, it is believed that there should be a clear distinction between the structural components of a system specification and the constraints that are imposed upon the structure and so allow the easier maintenance of a system which is subjected to an evolving business environment.

Figure 1 summarises the basic buildings blocks of RUBRIC: a data model, describing the objects of interest within the system; upon which a behavioural model can be built, describing the way in which the objects are manipulated and a policy and constraints model which imposes further organisation and refinement on the system.

The remainder of this paper describes the architecture that will realise the objectives of RUBRIC, together with a description of the work to date.

3   THE RUBRIC ARCHITECTURE

Figure 2 shows the basic RUBRIC system architecture. At its heart lies four main components that form the RUBRIC system: fact and rule acquisition, analysis and integration, transformation and the unified rule base and its manager.

The following sections describe each of the modules in turn, together with how they interface with the information systems engineer, user and application.

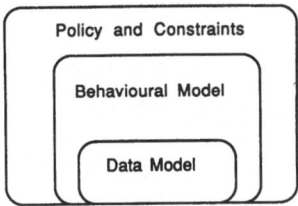

Figure 1. The RUBRIC Building Blocks

The Unified Rule Base

The Unified Rule Base (URB) is central to the RUBRIC system archiecture
and will contain, using an integrated formalism, models to describe the
structural aspects of a system and the constraints imposed upon the
structure. The structural aspects of the system will in turn be
described in two parts: the static aspects, which describes the objects
of the system that will be manipulated (i.e. the data orientation of the
system) and the dynamic aspects, which describe the behaviour of the
system and how the objects within the system will be manipulated.

The URB Manager

The URB manager performs the necessary function of updating and
retrieving the contents of the unified rule base, ensuring that the
integrity of the system is maintained and that other parts of the system
architecture do not violate the rules.

The Acquisition Module

The acquisition module is concerned with the capture, updating and
presentation to the user of the data model, event model and rules, in an
integrated and coherent fashion. It will allow for different types of
input and output, e.g. graphics, tabular reports etc. as appropriate to
the knowledge being captured or presented.

The Analysis and Integration Module

The analysis and integration module performs the integration of different

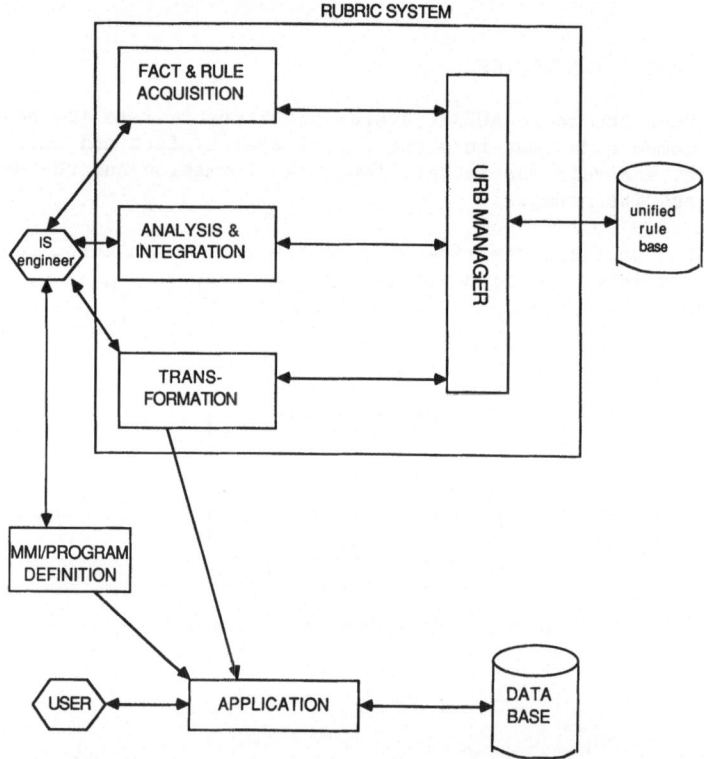

Figure 2. The RUBRIC System Architecture

user views of the system. It is likely that even for the smallest of systems, several users will input knowledge about the proposed system. This knowledge will inevitably contain redundancy, inconsistency and contradiction, as well as being incomplete. An analysis and integration module is therefore necessary in order to factorise this knowledge and highlight incompleteness and inconsistency to the information systems engineer.

The Transformation Module

Once the URB is specified, analysed and integrated, it can be translated into a form that can be used at run-time. Ideally, only those parts of the system that will remain static would need generation, with the remaining parts interpreted at run-time. This would therefore provide the user with the maximum flexibility with the system responding immediately to changes in the URB. However, it is likely that for efficiency reasons it will be desirable to generate more that the minimum necessary.

The MMI-Program Definition

It is envisaged that in order to create an application, the information systems engineer will have to go through a short design process. Within the RUBRIC project it is intended that this process imply involves MMI definition (screen layout, painting etc.) and program definition. In a more commercially-oriented system however, this process would probably also include the optimisation of a database schema, access paths etc.

4   RESEARCH ISSUES

In developing the RUBRIC paradigm, a number of key areas have been identified as requiring major research effort. These are as follows.

4.1 The Design of the Unified Rule Base

The role of the URB is central to RUBRIC as the architecture of the URB will guide not only the way in which a system description is stored, but will also have an effect upon the user's perception of how such a description is constructed and maintained. With this in mind, a number of observations can be made about the nature of the URB.

Firstly, the three models within the URB (data, behavioural and policy and constraints) whilst requiring their own formalisms for the representation of the respective elements of a system, must also be capable of being integrated into a single, overall structure.

Secondly, as the number of rules in a system grows, it will become more difficult to understand the relationships between them and other parts of the specification (Roycroft & Loucopoulos, 1985). Therefore rules will need to be organised into manageable units according to their intended use.

Thirdly, the organisation of the rules should allow for the multiplicity of views in the requirements specification. Although, a system developer would always need to reconcile differences of views, it may be quite appropriate to maintain this relativism and the URB should allow for this.

4.2 Fact Gathering and Presentation

Provided that suitable data and behavioural models are selected, fact gathering, model building and presentation may proceed along conventional development lines. However, research needs to be conducted into how the capture and presentation of rules will be conducted and how their effect can be shown upon system data and behaviour.

4.3 Using Rules in Applications

Research will need to be carried out in how applications are to be realised using the URB. Two alternatives exist: application systems can either be directly generated for the URB, data models and MMI descriptions, or partial systems can be generated using the data models and MMI descriptions, with policy being interpreted using the URB. Typically, the trade-off between execution speed and system flexibility will have to be considered and an optimal solution identified.

5   WORK TO DATE

In this section, we describe the main findings of the work to date. This can be divided into two parts: a description of the structural concepts in the underlying model (data and behaviour) to be adopted and a description of the rule types that will support the policy and constraint model.

5.1 The URB Meta-Model: Structural Concepts

In order to describe the full URB model, it is first necessary to understand the basic concepts of the model and the role they play within the modelling framework. A consistent theme of modelling formalisms is their concern about the <u>natural</u> representation of the universe of discourse in terms of things that the universe of discourse deals with and in terms of the happenings in the universe of discourse. This theme is found in a variety of research projects, including, for example, the ESPRIT METEOR project [Dubo86], the CIAM approach [Gust82] and many others.

The basic structural concepts that should be supported in RUBRIC are as follows:

*   an **entity**, which is any concrete or abstract thing and has an existence within the universe of discourse during a time period of interest

*   a **relationship**, which is an association between two entities

*   an **event**, which is an instantaneous happening which alters the state of the information system

*   a **value**, which exists only within the context of its association with an entity or event; it is drawn from a domain also associated with the entity or event type

The concepts of entity and relationship have been widely accepted and are generally well understood. The entity-relationship approach to the design of static system aspects has been used successfully in the development of information systems, either in its original form [Chen76] or in its many variations e.g. [Verh82]. For example, in a library system, **book** and **library member** may be considered entities–objects of interest which we wish to describe and model. Furthermore, there may exist a relationship between these entities called **borrows**, i.e. a library member borrows a book. Traditionally, these statements about the universe of discourse have been described in an entity–relationship diagram, as shown in figure 3:

It shows that a library member may borrow zero or more books and that a book may be borrowed by zero or one library members.

However, entities can also be thought of as having a `birth time´, a `dead time´ and a `lifetime´. In our example a book will come into an existence in the library system as soon as it has been purchased by the library and catalogued. The book will cease to exist when, at some future time, it is removed from the shelves and archived or destroyed. In between these two states of birth and death, the book will be subject to a series of lends and returns.

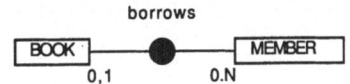

Figure 3. An E-R model for a simple library system

In modelling any information system it is important to be able to represent these events within the universe of discourse. For example, in the library system we will want to model the conditions under which a library member <u>actually</u> borrows a book.

This modelling requirement is widely supported by a number of design methodologies (e.g. JSD, SSADM etc.). In RUBRIC we introduce the concept of event which enables us to model happenings in the universe of discourse. Events thus introduce the behavioural aspect of a system and like entities and relationships may be described and constrained. Furthermore, they establish the existence of instances of entities and relate entities through the pre-defined relationship structures. Thus without events, a model could not be populated or relationships established.

Instances of events are created through the triggering of an event type. This triggering may come from outside the information system, thus representing some change within the universe of discourse, or from internal signals, which may either result from a data change or the start or termination of another event.

The concept of value, like entity and relationship is generally well understood. As noted above, value exist only in association with an entity instance and are drawn from a domain that is associated with the entity type which the entity instances belongs.

Thus the basic structural concepts of the URB are entity, relationship, event and value. For the purposes of the RUBRIC, we propose to use an entity-relationship model for the modelling of static structural aspects of systems and augmented Petri-Nets [Zism77] or Predicate Transition nets [Genr81] for the modelling of dynamic structural aspects.

In addition to these basic structures of the URB are a number of other important concepts. The first of these is the concept of **membership** of entities and events. An entity or an event is a member of an entity class or an event class respectively and thus individuals are regarded as members of these classes.

Entities and relationships are also **time dependent**. In the diagram in figure 3, the relation BORROWS is declared as being possible but need not be true at all times. In fact, it is the events **lend** and **return** that define the existence of the relationship in this particular case. Events also have a temporal dimension in the sense that they occur at a given time.

5.2   The URB Meta-Model: Constraints

In addition to the basic structural concepts within the URB, the RUBRIC philosophy envisages the use of constraints. These constraints are expressed as rules which are used to modify and limit the permitted structural relationships and place constraints on the behaviour of a system.

Thus we introduce the concept of rule:

*   a **rule** constrains entities, relationships, events, values and their interaction.

Rules are introduced in order to enhance the semantic richness of the underlying model and allow the explicit declaration of knowledge about a system. Eight rule types are identified:

436

* uniqueness rules

* membership cardinality rules

* entity population rule

* existence rules

* relationship cardinality rules

* event rules

* referential rules

* derivation rules

and these eight rule types are now briefly described.

Uniqueness Rules

Uniqueness rules are used to specify constraints upon the uniqueness or otherwise of members of an entity class. For example, all library books in a library reservation system must have a unique number. It is intended that uniqueness should apply in a wider context where more than one entity and associated class is involved. For example, in a hotel reservation system, the constraint that within a given resort hotels must have unique names, may be expressed using a uniqueness rule.

Membership Cardinality Rules

Membership cardinality rules are used to specify constraints on the minimum and maximum members of an entity class or an event class. For example, in a library lending system you might wish to impose a limit of 500 library members. This would be expressed as a membership cardinality rule.

Entity Population Rules

Entity population rules are used to constrain the entity sub-types that a member may participate in and specifies the type of membership that an entity can have at any point in time. For example, in a hotel reservation system you might wish to distinguish between different types of person known to the system: an inquirer - who is somebody who has made a request for a hotel reservation; a client - who is somebody who has accepted an offer and has made a reservation and a guest - who is somebody who has checked into a reserved room. An entity population rule might be that a member of the entity class PERSON may only be a member of one and only one of the sub-types INQUIRER, CLIENT and GUEST.

Existence Rules

Actual entity occurrences and relationships between them only exist within a timeframe. Prior to their existence some event must occur to create them and similarly an event must also destroy them. A central point of interest is to know at what point in time and under what conditions an entity or relationship exists. An existence rule therefore specifies which events define the lifetime of an entity or relationship occurrence. An existence rule may also declare that the existence of an entity (or relationship) implies that another entity (or relationship) must exist.

Consider, for example, the concept of a book being borrowed by a library member. The relationship BORROWS, which relates a book with a library member may occur several times, thus:

An existence rule will define the existence of a BORROWS relationship in terms of lend and return events for given books and library members. However, a close analysis of the BORROWS relationship will soon show that a time dimension is also required in this rule. It is not sufficient to simply say that for a given book and library member, a BORROWS relationship exists if there has been a lend event, but no return. In the above example, a return has occurred, but the book (assuming the same book) is actually out on loan. The definition of BORROWS must be further constrained by stating that for the latest lend, there must be no associated return.

Relationship Cardinality Rules

Relationship cardinality rules are used to define the number of occurrences in relationships between one member of an entity class and another. For example, in the library system you may wish to restrict the number of books that a library member may borrow to no more than 6. Note that this rule is similar to membership cardinality, but instead applies to the number of relationships that exist between entity classes, rather that the number of members.

Event Rules

Event rules are used to define the conditions under which a change to the system's data may take place (i.e. a state change). A new state is determined by the preceding state and by the events which may take place. This type of rule therefore constrains the ordering of events. An event of course will effect, through existence rules, the creation and removal of entity and relationship occurrences. For example, in the library system you might want to state that the return of a book must occur only after it has been lent.

Referential Rules

Referential Rules are used to define the constraints on the values of an entity in relation to the value of another entity. As an example of this type of rule consider the case of an entity called product with associated entities, cost price and sale price. You may wish to express the constraint that for a given entity, the cost price of any product must be less than the sale price. A referential rule would be used to describe this.

Derivation Rules

Derivation rules are used to specify the dependency of an entity in relation to other entities (functional dependency or value dependency) or the derivation of a relationship subject to the existence of other relationships (composition function). As an example consider the case where we wish to state that the sales value of any item must be the product of the quantity ordered multiplied by the price of the item.

7   CONCLUSIONS

There are currently a number of development methods and computer-based tools which assist information system developers in their task of constructing systems. However, these methods and their underlying models fail to address the clear and explicit representation of policy and constraints throughout the deliverables of the development lifecycle. The result is inflexible systems which are difficult to maintain.

It is the belief of the RUBRIC project that this situation can be improved by explicitly accommodating policy and constraints within specifications, design and coding. This will lead to more flexible and easier to maintain systems and that the completion of the RUBRIC project will demonstrate this hypothesis.

REFERENCES

[BUBE86]   Bubenko, J.A. jnr., Information System Methodologies, in [OLLE86] 3, pp.289-318

[CHEN76]   Chen, P.P., The Entity-Relationship Model: Towards a Unified View, ACM TOPS, PP. 9-36, 1976

[DEMA78]   DeMarco, T., Structured Analysis and System Specification, Yourdon Press, 1978

[DUBO86]   Dubois, E. et al, The ERAE Model: A Case Study, in [OLLE86] 3, pp87-105

[GANE79]   Gane, C. and Sarson, T., Structured Systems Analysis: Tools and Techniques, Prentice-Hall, 1979

[GENR81]   Genrich , H.J. and Lautenbach, K., System modelling with high-level Petri-Nets, Theoretical Computer Science 13, pp109-136,1981

[GUST82]   Gustafsson, M.R. et al, A Declarative Approach to Conceptual Information Modelling, in [OLLE82], pp93-141

[JACK83]   Jackson, M., System Development, Prentice-Hall, 1983

[MACD86]   MacDonald, I., Information Engineering - An approved, automatable methodology for designing data sharing systems, in [OLLE86], pp.173-224

[MADD83]   MADDISON, R., Information System Methodologies, Wiley-Heyden, 1983

[MORR85]   Morris, E.P., Strengths and weaknesses in current large scale DP, Alvey/BCS SGES workshop, January 1985

[OLLE82]   Olle, T.W. et al, CRIS 1, Information Systems Design Methodologies: A comparative Review, North-Holland, 1982

[OLLE86]   Olle, T.W. and Verrijn-Stuart, A.A., CRIS 3, Improving the Practice, North-Holland, 1986

[ROSS82]   Ross, D.T., Structured Analysis: A Language for Communicating Ideas, IEEE Transactionson Software Engineering, Vol SE-3, No.1 1982

[ROYC85]   Roycroft, A. and Loucopoulos, P., The Development of an Expert Tax System and their Applications, 5th International Workshop on Expert Systems, Avignon, May 1985

[TEIC82]   Teichroew, D. et al, The PSL/PSA Approach to Computer-Aided Analysis and documentation, in Advanced System development and Feasibility Techniques, J. Wiley, 1982

[VERH82]   Verheijen, G. and van Bekkum, J., NIAM: An Information Analysis Method, in [OLLE82]

[ZISM77]   Zisman, M.D., Representation, Specification and Automation of Office Procedures, Ph.D. Wharton School, University of Pennsylvannia, 1977

DESIGNING A METHOD DRIVEN SOFTWARE DEVELOPMENT ENVIRONMENT

James A. Redmond and Kevin T. Ryan

Dept. of Computer Science
Trinity College
Dublin 2, Ireland

ABSTRACT

A promising approach to the automation of the software production process
is the support of multiple methods. A project to produce a method-driven
environment is described. The requirements to be met by the environment
are outlined and a number of existing environments are evaluated from
this viewpoint. Some approaches to meeting their shortcomings are given
and the continuing work of the project is mentioned.

1   INTRODUCTION

The work described here forms part of a multi-national project (+) to
produce an "Advanced Support Environment for Method-driven Development
and Evolution of Packaged Software" [HORG86] [REDM85a]. The environment
is to provide **active** assistance in the design, implementation and
evolution of software. The project is unusual both in its participants,
its objectives and its approach. This paper outlines the project's main
distinguishing features, describes some of the work done so far, and
attempts to identify some of the main difficulties in building a method-
driven environment.

2   THE PROJECT TEAM

A recent survey of research efforts in the area of software engineering
environments [RIDD86] stressed the need for "eclectic" teams, ideally
drawn from "researchers, developers and practitioners". The conditions
of the ESPRIT programme require that the project teams should have
industrial participants and be drawn from at least two different
countries. Our current project involves eight groups, from four
countries. Two groups are at Universities, two are research centres, and
four are commercial software houses.

(+) Partly supported (50%) by the Commission of the European Communities
under ESPRIT Project 510 (ToolUse)

Our experience to date has been that this mix of participants provides a useful and natural tension between the inclinations of researchers and the demands of practitioners. The software houses specialise variously in commercial packages, aerospace applications, control systems, hospital systems and formal development methods. These backgrounds are reflected in the objectives of the project and in the unusual importance attached to three factors:

* usefulness within current industry practice,

* consideration of non-functional requirements and

* the support of different methods.

The major involvement of the software houses is in carrying out designs as controlled experiments. At present they use conventional support but later will use the prototype environment as it evolves. Experimentation is also being used to attempt to identify the different factors influencing the design process. In particular, we wish to "factor out" the affects of: method guidance, application domain knowledge, and non-functional requirements including target system requirements. Detailed guidelines for conducting these experiments have been produced [KEAR86]. They have been used and refined through a number of substantial case studies. Not surprisingly it has proven difficult to isolate individual factors from among the myriad of (frequently implicit) decisions that constitute a development. For example, when the JSD method was used to solve the well known "lift" (elevator) control problem it was possible to identify some of the influences of the method (guidance provided in choosing or ordering steps). It was much more difficult to identify precisely where the assumed characteristics of the "target system" came into play.

3   THE PROJECT APPROACH

In common with many others we view the entire software development process as a series of successive transformations (see e.g. [PART83], [BALZ85a]). User requirements form an initial "specification" which is usually imprecise, incomplete and contradictory. This specification is then successively transformed by the developer through the addition of detail and the elimination, in consultation with the user, of conflicts and ambiguities. The transformations continue until an acceptable implementation is achieved. Formalisation of the development process in terms of its constituent transformations is necessary before it can be automated. Balzer et al [BALZ85a] have identified the following difficult issues (amongst others) which a transformation-oriented environment must address: algorithm choice, control structure, direction of the development, representation selection, handling of intermediate results and the tradeoff between alternative implementations.

The main **automatic** support given by a transformation-oriented environment will be recording the development activities, carrying out the developer's decisions by applying transformations, and producing, accessing and formatting the information needed to make these decisions. Although some of these may be fully automated using heuristic or other means, we believe that human judgement and interaction will still be required.

The transformational approach has been characterised as "exploratory", in contrast to the more disciplined "strict" approach likely to find favour with industry [LENN86]. Many transformational systems (e.g. Affirm [GERH80], CHI [GREE83]) have been based on Interlisp, an environment that fosters an approach to development that has been characterised as "structured growth" [SAND78]. We believe that the transformational approach is the approach of the future with maintenance being effected by changes to the specification and (semi-automatic) reimplementation [WILE83] [BALZ85b]. However we also feel there are advantages to fitting the traditional Waterfall Software Lifecycle (WSLC) approach on top of the transformational approach as a special case. We are thinking particularly of initial industry acceptability, the present investment in the WSLC approach and the prospects of the gradual acceptance of a fully transformational approach.

It is a remarkable fact that even though many, if not most, software disasters are caused by failure to meet **non-functional** requirements, these are scarcely mentioned in existing methods and are unsupported in existing SEEs. The impact of non-functional requirements can best be seen in the rationale for the design history. For example, the need to meet a portability requirement will be reflected in the choice of module structure and functionality. It is unlikely that such requirements will be formalised in the near future so a more promising approach would be to incorporate them as rules in a rule-based system, where they can constrain the development of the final system. These constraints are likely to be heuristic in nature, with a degree of precision that is dependent on many factors (narrowness of the application domain, number of previous, similar projects developed and degree of expert knowledge stored in the knowledge base).

Perhaps the most important activity in the development process is that of requirements acquisition and analysis. A method-driven environment can learn from the techniques of knowledge engineering so that an intelligent front-end would help extract and formalise the requirements of the end-user. It is usually necessary to capture information, that while seemingly insignificant at the time, is critical to supporting design. We believe that requirements **acquisition** is a better phrase than requirements **definition** as usually a considerable number of the user's demands for the system are vague, if articulated at all.

4   METHOD-DRIVEN ENVIRONMENTS

A **method** can be defined as a body of knowledge that is used to guide a software development from one node of its development tree to the next. More formally, a method is knowledge which guides a series of transformations from one model to the next, where a model is defined to be a representation of a given software development at some particular node of the development from one node of its development tree to the next. The model is a set of documents which defines the current state of the problem solution, and a set of links between these documents. A **tool** is any object which can be used to support a method.

By "**method-driven**" we mean that the environment will attempt to generalise and abstract from a number of software development methods in such a way that the environment can treat methods as objects. The proposed ToolUse environment would eventually encompass a range of design methods (e.g. VDM [BJOR82], JSD [CAME86]) and be able to develop software using, for example, the JSD approach in a semi-automatic fashion. Because no universal method is likely in the foreseeable future and because different methods may be useful at different stages of a given development, we believe it is essential that the environment should support many different methods.

It has been argued [KANT85] that the ability to try multiple methods is one of the important assets of a human designer, while the insights of different methods may contribute to the burst of inspiration which is sometimes called the "Eureka" effect [BURS77]. Mostow has a similar conclusion [MOST85]. Furthermore Fickas [FICK85] states that a transformational development is no more static than a normal software development so changes will need to be made to it. For this reason the process itself becomes an object of study.

5   REQUIREMENTS FOR A METHOD-DRIVEN ENVIRONMENT

We postulate four distinguishing characteristics of a method-driven environment:

- Methods must be explicitly supported so that the user is given **active** guidance. For example, in using the JSD method, the developer should be told of the heuristics for resolving clashes or for selecting entities.

- Methods must be treated as objects which can be manipulated by the system. For example it should be possible to add to or modify applicability conditions.

- Design decisions must be explicit and must be recorded by the system. It is as important to know why some paths were not followed as it is to know why some path was followed.

- Knowledge must be incrementally accumulated over time so that the system builds up expertise. An important effect is that the system should incrementally improve itself as developments are successfully completed. For the present this improvement will be inlimited domains so that, for example, a developer producing a series of device-controllers, all written in ´C´ and all developed using VDM, will receive more support on the fifth development than on the first.

6   EXAMINATION OF SOME ENVIRONMENTS FROM A METHOD VIEWPOINT

We have studied a number of environments, proposals and papers to see how method-driven they were.

6.1. Affirm and Sprac

Both Affirm [GERH80] and SPRAC [LEMA81] are experimental SEEs designed to support the Abstract Data Type approach to program development. If it is true, as argued by Wile [WILE83], that a method-driven environment must incorporate a model of the software development process, then Sprac makes some effort towards this requirement. Sprac provides:

- Prolog-type querying of the current state and past history of the development.

- An Agenda mechanism that generates a list of tasks remaining.

- The ability to prohibit certain kinds of development steps. We consider this to be a first step towards parameterisation by method.

444

Sprac's approach is essentially a constraining one, in that it may be set up to prevent the user taking certain development steps. It can thus be said to provide a **basis** for the incorporation of a method-driven component. Affirm's only facility in this area is to allow interrogation of the current state of the development, and to provide a few elementary guidance facilities. Neither Sprac nor Affirm provide any **active** assistance to the user.

Sprac records design decisions in a database. Affirm uses the Interlisp history mechanism to record decisions command by command. Neither system records the **reason** for a design decision. We also note that in Affirm no knowledge is carried over from one session to the next.

6.2. CIP and CHI

The CIP (Computer-aided, Intuition-guided Programming) project illustrates the transformational approach [PART84]. Source schemata are transformed into target schemata according to (possibly) compound rules. However the prototype system gives no guidance in selecting the applicable transformations nor does it support the verification of applicability conditions. The system does not record the derivation history of a program or of a rule. It seems therefore that the current system is incapable of representing general development methods and so cannot form the basis for a method-driven environment.

The CHI system, on the other hand, originally set out to allow the user to store and manipulate the design history. The fact that it does not yet do so reflects the difficulty of storing these histories in a useful way. The CHI system at present is essentially method independent, although since it accumulates knowledge (in transformation rules) this may mean that it can learn any actual method from experience. However it appears to presuppose the existence of a formal and consistent specification and it provides very little support for the formal verification of designs. In fact a set of small scale methods has been formalised and partly implemented in CHI. In these methods, algorithm design principles are expressed in the form of synthesis plans (paradigm algorithms). Typical of these principles are generator incorporation (filter promotion), divide-and-conquer, and store versus recompute (dynamic programming). It is less clear how CHI could be used to support a more prescriptive method such as JSD. (Chi is now the only transformational system available commercially (as REFINE)).

6.3. Unix & Interlisp

For completeness and to provide some historical perspective we reviewed the method support given by these two environments, arguably the most widely used SEEs.

Although both of these environments support an incremental, evolutionary and exploratory approach to software development, neither provides much **active** guidance to the developer. They also differ significantly in the support they do provide. Whereas Unix [KERN81] requires the user to choose what tools to activate at any time, the tools of Interlisp [TEIT81] are tightly integrated in the environment so as to be always present and actively "eavesdropping", ready to react immediately to an explicit or implicit request.

The history mechanism in Interlisp is of particular interest. By recording each action taken by the system it allows the storage and replay of (some part of) a development history. It can then be seen as a first step towards saving and analysing design decisions so that a method

may be supported and a design knowledge base built up over time. Any
analogous Unix facility requires the user to control one more level of
detail. For example, SCCS and Make can generate a previous situation in
the development of a piece of software, but only insofar as the user
remembers and records the design decisions and dependencies.

Both Unix and Interlisp have been used as foundations for the
construction of more advanced environments e.g. PCTE and Affirm.

6.4 Method Influence In Some Other Environments

A brief search of the literature for other method influence in other
environments not directly available yielded some interesting approaches.
In general, the definition of method in these environments was at a low,
transformational level.

Glitter [FICK82], [PART83] within the TI environment maintains an
(extensible) methods (i.e. transformations) catalogue. This catalogue of
methods for achieving goals contains both source to source
transformations (tactical knowledge) and planning techniques (strategic
knowledge). If there are several applicable methods, Glitter uses a
Selection Rule Catalog to decide which to use. The basic methods to be
applied are methods for mapping specification freedoms, checking
applicability conditions or asking the developer to modify the program so
that the activation pattern will match that of a transformation which
previously failed. In a restricted domain, Glitter was able to achieve
an order of magnitude decrease in the need for interactive input.

The ZAP [FEAT82], [PART83] system supports the developer with advanced
means for concisely expressing guidance. It allows the user to write
metaprograms to be applied to NPL programs, and thus to direct the
transformation of these programs in a high-level, hierarchical fashion.
The user can also restrict ZAP's search for an applicable rule.

In HOPE [DARL81], based to some extent on ZAP, research is being pursued
on ways to express paradigm algorithms such as the general divide-and-
conquer paradigm and other general strategies.

It appears that one should distinguish between macro-methods and micro-
methods. A macro-method would be something like JSP/JSD, SADT, SREM etc.
That is, a general design framework within which a particular problem can
be solved. While not all the problem-solving process can be
unambiguously and clearly specified, the macro-method provides a basis
for solving the problem. The difficulty seems to lie in getting the
structure right. Once the overall structure of the problem formulation
is right, other more detailed problems become easier and micro-methods
can be applied. A micro-method would be, for example, divide-and-conquer,
dynamic programming, fold-unfold etc.

7   WHAT IS NEEDED?

From our survey of contemporary environments it is possible to identify a
number of features that would be essential in an environment which would
meet the criteria listed in section 5 above.

1. A wide spectrum language

This is one way to avoid the inflexibility of multi-language systems
(e.g.CIP). Other members of the ToolUse project are currently refining a
"design calculus" which will be the formal basis for a wide spectrum

development language ("DEVA") in which programs, specifications and
development can all be represented [SINT86]. The operation of the
calculus is illustrated in [JAEH86].

2. A Unified Project Knowledge Base

Our studies (reported in [REDM85b], [LEMO85], [RYAN86]), confirmed the
need for a unifying knowledge management system, and therefore the
Project Data Base and the Knowledge Base should have integrated
structures. The developers of both the TRW [BOEH84] and the CHI
environments have drawn a similar conclusion. A database alone will not
be enough. A knowledge engineering approach is needed if the system is
to accumulate and unify development histories.

3. A Model of the Development Process

It has frequently been stated that a knowledge-based environment must
embody some model of the development process, e.g. [MOST85]. Any such
model will be quite complex if design histories are to be stored,
replayed and manipulated by an "intelligent" method driven environment as
envisaged by Wile [WILE83]. Furthermore, the volume of information to be
stored from any substantial software project would be such as to pose a
data representation problem in itself. One possible approach is to
"idealise" the design history by, for example, removing unproductive dead
ends and "agglommerating" many small steps into a single more
intelligible step. To do this will require a knowledge base integrated
with a large database. Some initial work in this area has been described
by Grimson and Al-Zobaidie [ALZO86].

The ToolUse project has looked at several methods from a "Method Support"
viewpoint including VDM and JSD. Draft rule sets that express these (and
other) methods have been formulated and are being installed on a number
of expert system builders to facilitate experimentation and refinement.
It is expected that these methods will be described using the Deva design
calculus.

4. The Inclusion of Design Reasoning

The reasons for taking a particular design decision must be recorded
[SINT80]. At present, while there is considerable discussion in the
literature of design histories, it would appear the most successful
implementation of a design history is that of the Glitter system. A
design history facility was proposed for Chi but not implemented in any
signicant way. In the Glitter approach, recording a formal, machine-
usable history of the design process plays an important role. This
history includes design goals and subgoals, competing methods (i.e.
transformations) and selection criteria used to reach an implementation.

Furthermore it is our belief that the reasons for **rejecting** a particular
course of action should be recorded in the knowledge base. Not only are
both of these types of information essential if an environment is to
accumulate knowledge for later reuse, but a well-explained design history
would be very useful during subsequent maintenance.

The system must be designed to learn from experience even though its
initial range of applicability may be small and if it is then used by
experienced software engineers for a number of projects, we can
anticipate that its range, and its array of available tools, will expand
over time so that even inexperienced users can design a wide range of
software. The process of learning from actual developments can be

speeded up by observing and learning from the activities of actual
designers.

8   CURRENT TRENDS AND OPEN QUESTIONS

Shaw [SHAW85] has argued that there is a change in the character of the
problems being solved by computer systems as well as a change in the
character of the software being used to solve them. The problems now
being posed for computational solution involve selecting among competing
non-absolute preferences and other judgemental decisions; they are so
complex that solutions cannot be specified a priori but must be evolved
through experience and they involve integration of a heterogeneous set of
system components including hardware as well as software. We would argue
that this more clearly represents the problems of programming in the
large where it is much more difficult to come up with a complete,
consistent and formal specification than in the typical programming in
the small examples given in the literature.

Looking to the future there are two reasons for caution. Firstly the
participants of the Rocky Mountain workshop on software environments
[RIDD86] felt that abstraction support, transformation tools and
methodology drivers require significant advances in other areas before
they can be addressed, and do not expect them to be given concentrated
attention for eight to ten years from now (circa 1995). Their definition
of methodology drivers was automated tools that actively encourage or
enforce the use of specific software process paradigms, which is just
what was envisaged in ToolUse.

Secondly there is some evidence of premature optimism in the past for the
transformational approach. Partsch et al [PART84] quote Knuth as saying
in 1976 that the time is ripe for transformational systems.

It is envisaged that the support environment for the design calculus in
ToolUse will evolve incrementally [REDM85]. The incremental,
evolutionary approach has a good track record [KERN81], [BOEH84]. Some
exploratory studies are continuing into a toolset for the support
environment including studies of Abrial's "B" [ABRI85], ML-LCF, a
requirements acquisition tool and knowledge-oriented support for Deva.
Work continues into trying to derive further knowledge on methods,
application systems and target systems by way of medium-sized case
studies. We have begun constructing a rule set for VDM, while the JSD
rule set will be translated into Deva notation. Later in the project it
is planned to examine sample large system developments so as to further
gather knowledge on method, application and target system influence.

Many open questions remain however. Notable among those that we currently
identify are the following:

*   How to learn from experiments?

Some of the experiments performed have proved to yield little information
for example those on the Lift problem, the Package Router, and the
Message Passer. These difficulties arise from many factors. Principal
among these are the absence of a **real** user who can resolve ambiguities in
the specification in the light of his goals; the inherent "toy" nature of
these problems which contain implicit assumptions that may make the
application of the chosen method trivial (e.g. JSD applied to the Lift
problem); and the underlying assumption of these problems that they can
be stated unambiguously. In particular, it was discovered that Target

System influence often believed to be pervasive, was absent from the recorded development history because the crucial decisions were made before the history began. By the time the developers started to use a particular method, a considerable number of implicit decisions had already been made about Target Systems.

* Can we define real methods?

The question is whether a significant body of higher level program design knowledge exists. Our investigations have shown that there is a paucity of methods which can be considered to be wide and powerful enough to cover most of the software development process. A possible exception is JSD, and even this offers little support in some major areas.

* Where and how the Sintzoff [SINT86] Design Calculus should be used?

The question is whether the design calculus will underly the development process or whether it will actually be used directly by the developer. Our current view is that a range of possibilities will exist, dependent on the skill level of the developer. We consider that it should be available on call if necessary, somewhat similar to Lisp in some AI environments e.g. Kee.

* Can the macroscopic level and the microscopic levels be moved together?

The project can be seen to operate at two levels: the macroscopic, method (or metamethod?) level e.g. JSD, VDM and the microscopic level (essentially the level of single transformations) for example divide and conquer. The trick is for the project to evolve so that these two levels can meet. This means for instance that the JSD rule set should be describable using DEVA, and that the Deva notation should be able to grow so as to handle transformations useful for JSD e.g. entity selection and elimination, resolving structure clashes.

* How then can we reconcile different specifications?

Macro specifications are often ambiguous and inconsistent whereas micro specifications tend to be consistent and correct. There is a tension between the industrial partners with "real" world specifications and the desire of the formalists at the lowest DEVA level for rigorous, consistent specifications. This problem has also appeared in the work of Fickas [FICK85] and Balzer [BALZ85].

Notwithstanding these problems, and the many others that will no doubt arise in the future, we believe that with a good underlying formal notation, and with feedback on methods, applications and target systems it should be possible to make significant progress in the next three years.

ACKNOWLEDGEMENTS

Many other members of the ToolUse project team have contributed to the ideas in this paper. However, the opinions contained in it are solely those of the authors and are not those of the project team nor of the Commission of the European Community. Part of this work was completed while one of the authors (KTR) was on sabbatical leave at the Department of Computer and Information Science, Linkoping University, S-58183 Linkoping SWEDEN.

REFERENCES

[ABRI85] J R Abrial & A Guillon "Un outil de conception de logiciels", 26 Rue des Plantes Paris France 1985.

[ALZO86] A Al-Zobaidie & J B Grimson "Expert Systems & Database Systems - how can they serve each other?" Second Intl Conference on Expert Systems London Sept 1986 (to·be published).

[BALZ85a] R Balzer, T E Cheatham Jr. & C Green, "Software Technology in the 1990´s: Using a New Paradigm", Computer pp 39-45 November 1985.

[BALZ85b] R Balzer "A 15 year perspective on automatic programming" IEEE Trans Soft Eng V SE-11 No11 pp1257-1277 Nov 1985.

[BJOR82] D Bjorner and C B Jones "Formal specification and software development" Prentice Hall 1982.

[BOEH84] B W Boehm, M H Penedo, E D Stuckle, R D Williams & A B Pyster, "A Software Development Environment for Improving Productivity", Computer V17 No6, June 1984.

[BURS77] R M Burstall & J D Darlington "A Transformation System for Developing Recursive Programs", Journal ACM V24 No 1 Jan 1977 pp44-67.

[CAME86] J R Cameron "An overview of JSD", IEEE Trans. on Software Eng. V SE-12 No 2 Feb 1986 pp 222-241.

[DARL81] J Darlington "The structured description of algorithm derivations" in Algorithmic Languages, J W de Bakker & H van Vliet, editors, Elsevier North-Holland, New York pp 221-250 New York USA 1981.

[FEAT82] M S Feather " A system for assisting program transformation" ACM Trans Prog Lang Syst V4 No 1 pp 1-20 Jan 1982.

[FICK82] S F Fickas "Automating the transformational development of software" Ph.D. dissertation, Univ. of California, Irvine.

[FICK85] S F Fickas "Automating the transformational development of software" IEEE Trans on Soft Eng V SE-11 No 11 Nov 1985 pp1268-1278.

[GERH80] S Gerhart, D R Musser, D H Thompson, D A Baker, R L Bates, R W Erickson, R L London, D G Taylor & D S Wile, "An Overview of AFFIRM: a specification and verification system", in Proc. IFIP ´80, New York 1980.

[GREE83] C Green, D Luckham, R Balzer, T Cheatham & C Rich, "Report on a Knowledge-based Software Assistant", Kestrel Institute, Palo Alto 1983.

[HORG86] H Horgen "ToolUse: An advanced support environment for method-driven development and evolution of packaged software", in ESPRIT ´85 North Holland April 1986.

[JAEH86] S Jaehnichen, F Ali Hussain, M Weber, "Program Development by Transformation and Refinement" Programming Environments Workshop, Trondheim Norway June 1986.

450

[KANT85]   E Kant, "Understanding and Automating Algorithm Design" IEEE
            Trans Soft Eng V SE-11 No11 Nov 1985.

[KEAR86]   S Kearney "Guidelines for conducting experiments - second
            version" Internal ToolUse document Gen.T5.SK86c.1 Generics May
            1986.

[KERN81]   B W Kernighan & J R Mashey, "The Unix Programming
            Environment",Computer April 1981.

[LEMA81]   M Lemaitre, M Lemoine & G Zanon,"SPRAC: A Computer Assisted
            Software Software Development", in Tools and Notions for
            Program Construction, (Ed. D Neel), Cambridge UK 1981.

[LEMO85]   M Lemoine (Ed.) "Final Report of Task 4.1 - Evaluation of
            Environments", ToolUse Project, ESPRIT project 510 - CEC
            Brussels December 1985.

[LENN86]   B Lennartsson "Linnkoping University Department of Computing
            and Information Sciences Annual Report" 1986.

[MOST85]   J Mostow, "Towards Better Models of the Design Process", AI
            Magazine, Spring 1985.

[PART83]   H Partsch & R Steinbruggen, "Program Transformation Systems",
            ACM Computing Surveys V15 No 3, Sept 1983.

[PART84]   H Partsch "The CIP transformation system" in Program
            Transformation and Programming Environments, ed P Pepper
            Lecture Notes in Computer Science Springer-Verlag New York
            1984.

[REDM85a]   J A Redmond " ESPRIT Project 510 ´ToolUse´ - Description,
            Progress to date and future directions: a view from the
            trenches", Proceedings of Informatica ´85, 18´th international
            conference on computer technology & usage, Nova Gorica,
            Yugoslavia, Sept 1985 pp 36-45.

[REDM85b]   J A Redmond (Ed.) "Final Report of Task 1.1 - Evaluation of
            Tools", ToolUse Project, ESPRIT project 510 - CEC Brussels
            November 1985.

[RIDD86]   W G Riddle & L G Williams, "Software Environments Workshop
            Report", ACM Sigsoft Software Engineering Notes V11 No1 pp73-
            102 January 1986

[RYAN86]   K T Ryan, J A Redmond, B Mathews, D J O´Neill, A Hunot, M
            Lemoine, M Dausmann & K Wachsmuth, "Tools for a Method Driven
            Environment" IFIP ´86 Dublin Ireland pp895-901.

[SAND78]   E Sandewall "Programming in an interactive environment - the
            Lisp experience" Computer Surveys V10 No 1 Mar 1978.

[SHAW85]   M Shaw, "Scope ans scale: the next challenges for software
            engineering" IBM - SISU Symposium, Stokholm, Sweden Sept 16-18,
            1985.

[SINT80]   M Sintzoff "Suggestions for composing and specifying program
            design decisions" 4th Int Sym Prog Paris April 1980 Lecture
            notes in computer science vol 83 Springer Verlag.

[SINT86]   M Sintzoff, M Weber, F Ali Hussain, P de Groote, R Jacquart, S
           Jahnichen and T T Nguyen "Requirements and feasibility studies
           for a development language" Esprit Project 510 ToolUse Task 3.2
           Final Report, Unite d'Informatique, Universite Catholique de
           Louvain, Louvain-la-Neuve, Belgium May 1986.

[TEIT81]   W Teitelman & L Masinter, "The Interlisp Programming
           Environment", Computer V14 No 4, April 1981.

[WILE83]   D Wile, "Program Developments: formal explanations of
           implementations", Comm ACM V26 No 11, November 1983.

AN ENVIRONMENT DEFINITION MODEL FOR METASYSTEM SUPPORT

J.M. DeDourek, A.J. McAllister, P.G. Sorenson,
J.P. Tremblay, and L.B. Protsko

University of Saskatchewan
Saskatchewan, Canada

ABSTRACT

In the context of this paper, a metasystem is a system used to create
information system development environments. The paper reviews previous
research in the area of metasystems and specifies a number of key factors
that should be considered in metasystem development. A metamodel for
representing environment definitions is then presented. A unique feature
of this model is its support of component aggregation. Using the
metamodel as a basis, an environment model definition language, EMDL, is
derived for expressing environment definitions. An example that
illustrates the definition of a simple data flow model (DFM) in EMDL is
given, and a small example specification that is based on DFM is
described. Finally, some interesting database and tool design problems
that are being addressed in the Metaview metasystem are outlined.

1   INTRODUCTION

The importance of providing adequate support environments for the
development of software has been recognized for a number of years.
Unfortunately, it is only recently that a number of support environments
have emerged that seriously assist in the development of large software
systems. Perhaps the most well-known support environment effort is the
Ada programming support environment [COMP83, STEN81, WOLF81]. It is
proposed to facilitate the handling of software throughout its life
cycle; however, it primarily addresses the implementation stage with
facilities to improve program reliability and to promote the development
of portable software development tools.

A number of support environments are being developed to assist in the
requirements analysis and design stages. For example, PSL/PSA {TEIC77],
RSL/REVS [ALFO77], RML [BORG85], [GREE84], and SAMMDF [STEP78] support
requirements specifications and analysis, and several other methodologies
[OLLE82] support both requirements specifications and design. Some of
these systems assume or are based on an underlying analysis and/or design
methodology and therefore attempt to ensure, often through completeness
and consistency rules, that a particular methodology is adhered to by the
analyst/designer. Other systems, such as USE [WASS82] extend system
analysis and design support with the aid of prototyping facilities.

The effort to develop such support environments is very considerable. In addition, further enhancements or changes to an existing support environment to address special requirements of a particular application are nontrivial to make. In an effort to reduce significantly the implementation effort associated with producing a support environment, metasystems have been proposed [DEME82].

The primary purpose of a metasystem is the automatic generation of the major portions of a particular software development environment. In other words, metasystems are systems used to develop system development environments in an analogous manner as compiler writing systems are systems used to develop compilers. To assist in understanding the notion of a metasystem more fully, a simple architectural overview is illustrated in Figures 1 and 2. Figure 1 shows the components of an environment that could be used in the specification of some of the aspects of a system description. The one that we have chosen and the one that will be used as an example throughout the paper captures data flow aspects of a system similar to those aspects recommended in [GANE79]. It should be pointed out that a wide variety of additional environment support facilities such as graphics interfaces, graphics layout, and query languages are not shown in the diagram to keep the discussion simple. The development support for these tools will be described in Section 6 of the paper.

Figure 2 depicts the generalized metasystem approach to the development of an environment support facility. In particular, an Environment Model Analyzer and an Environment Model Processor are defined as part of the metasystem. A particular environment, that is environment "X" where X might be a data flow specification environment, can be generated at environment generation time by first defining that environment in a special language called the Environment Model Definition Language. An example model definition language called EMDL will be defined and exemplified later in Sections 4 and 5 of the paper. The specific environment model description is compiled by the Environment Model Processor to create a set of tables that are used by the Environment Model Analyzer to assist in the compilation of a specification database for "X". The subsequent completeness and consistency checking and reporting functions for a specification in "X" are also handled by the generalized Environment Model Analyzer working in conjunction with the Environment Definition tables.

The general goal of this paper is to introduce one approach to the creation of environment support facilities that is provided by the Metaview metasystem being developed as part of the DEVIEW Project [SORE86] at the University of Saskatchewan. An overview of previous metasystem research efforts and the types of features and facilities that should be provided in a specification environment is given in Section 2 of the paper. An Environment Definition Model, a metamodel for defining models of specification environments, is described in Section 3. The Environment Definition Model Language, EMDL, is presented in Section 4. It is based on the metasystem requirements described in Section 2 and the metamodel defined in Section 3. An extended example of how EMDL can be used to define a specific environment, DFL (meaning Data Flow Language), is provided in Section 5. Finally, some design considerations that must be considered when implementing a metasystem are described in Section 6, and a summary and discussion of future work is given in the final section.

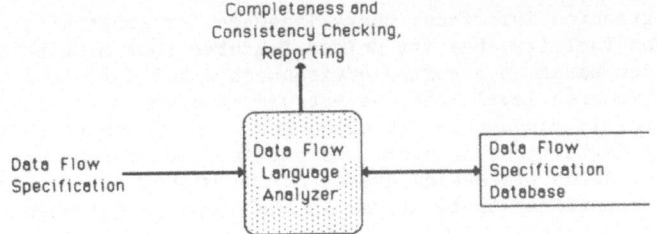

Figure 1   Typical Specification Support Environment

2   METASYSTEMS

As illustrated in Figure 2, there are three levels of specification
associated with a metasystem. At the meta level, the meta definer
defines the specification data model for the system, called the
metamodel. The meta definer should also oversee the development of
software to support the definition of specification environments. At the
environment level, the environment definer uses the environment model
processor software provided by the meta level to process an environment
definition. The environment definition includes an environment model
definition, expressed in EMDL, plus definitions for one or more support
tools generated as part of the defined specification environment. The
environment model defines the elements that are used in all tools
generated for the specification environment in support of a particular
development methodology. Each support tool, whether it be a report

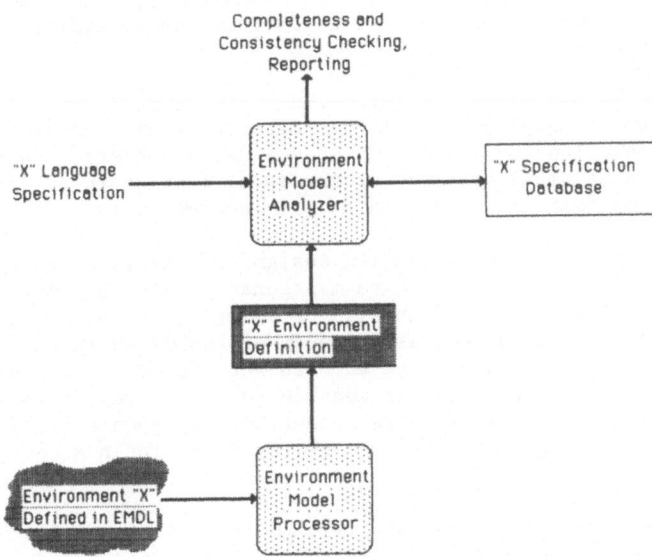

Figure 2   A Specification Environment

generator, graphics interface, query language, or constraint specification facility, has its unique features that must be defined separately yet based on a common environment model definition. Finally, at the requirements level, the analyst uses the generalized environment model analyzer in conjunction with the stored environment definition and tool support definitions to store and analyze requirement specifications for any information processing system he/she wishes to define. Each requirement specification is stored in the common requirements specification database.

The Metaview specification database is intended to maintain a variety of specifications from a variety of different specification environments. Therefore, there are several factors that should be taken into account when formulating a metamodel and developing a metasystem. Some of the important factors include:

1. The metasystem is intended to be used by both environment definers and analysts, yet neither group can be assumed to be database experts. Thus, the simplicity of the metamodel in terms of learning and use is important.

2. The expressive power of the metamodel should be maximized (keeping in mind simplicity) so as to place as few restrictions as possible on the manner in which one can represent a given type of information. As an example, it would not be desirable if all relationships among elements in a database were restricted to be binary, if some relationships are more naturally stated as ternary (or more generally n-ary).

3. Automatic checking for consistency and completeness is one of the major advantages of providing computer-aided support for specifications; therefore, the metasystem should provide support for stating constraint conditions that specify the type of information that is considered valid.

4. Specifications tend to be created incrementally, hence the metasystem should be able to represent partially complete information in a simple fashion.

5. Requirements and design specifications are created and maintained over a long time period. A large number of small revisions are made as the specification evolves towards a desired state. The metamodel should enable small portions of the specification to be identified uniquely so that revisions can be made conveniently.

6. The ability to represent complex design objects is a recognized problem in current CAD database management research [HART85], [BATO85]. The relational model, for example, forces the user to represent a design object as a number of tuples in relations. A command to delete a design object can not typically be issued as a single operation, but must be considered as several "delete Tuple" operations. The ability to represent and manipulate design objects in a convenient manner is viewed as important for a Metaview metamodel.

In the next section, these factors will be taken into consideration in the formulation of an appropriate metamodel. Prior to the presentation of the metamodel, a brief review of previous research efforts in metasystems for information systems specification environments is given.

One of the earliest systems that provided some generalization in the development of specification environments was RSL/REVS (meaning Requirements Statement Language/Requirements Engineering and Validation System) [BELL77]. RSL is a language for stating requirements specification based on the SREM methodology [ALFO85], and REVS includes a translator for RSL, a specification database manager, and a collection of analysis tools. Although RSL/REVS has a built-in language and methodology, it shares some of the properties of a metasystem by providing a facility for extending RSL to include new concepts associated with an updated or modified specification methodology. The data model for the extensible REVS database is essentially an entity-relationship model [CHEN76] in which relationships are restricted to be binary. Relationships can be expressed and are stored in complementary forms, e.g., "A CREATES B" is also stored as "B IS CREATED BY A".

The work of the ISDOS Project at the University of Michigan in metasystems is well-known. Two major projects, Meta/GA [YAMA81] and MDS/MSS [KANG82], are pioneer efforts in metasystem research. The metamodel used in both systems was based on the entity-relationship data model. Differences from the ER model as proposed in the Meta/GA system include: the introduction of intrinsic attributes (i.e., attributes such as basic name and synonym that apply to all entities), the restriction that relationships could not have attributes, and the introduction of "constants" in roles of a relationship. Two types of environment definition level constraints were supported. The combination constraint ensured the correctness of the types of entities and constants that were allowed to occupy the various roles of a particular relationship. This implied that more than one entity type can be associated with a particular role of a relationship, which is not allowed in the ER model. The connectivity constraint defined the maximum number (either "one" or "many") of relationship instances that can exist in the database with a particular entity in a given role.

The MDS/MSS (Methodology Development System/Methodology Support tool System) extended the Meta/GA system in the following respects: the concept of relationship was extended so that relationships could occupy roles in other relationships (i.e., tiered relationships were supported), and roles in relationships could be occupied by sets of entities or constants and not just singleton entities or constants. The connectivity constraint was extended to include an integer occurrence value as opposed to either "one or "many". A major constraint specification subsystem was also added to MSS to allow the environment definer to supply additional environment constraints in a predicate notation.

The SDS metasystem described in [LEVE82] also used an entity-relationship type of metamodel (the terms entity and attribute are replaced by component and property). Only binary relationships are allowed and inverse relationships are used but are not considered as distinct relationships from their inverse counterparts. A unique feature of the SDS metamodel is that relationship types were classified according to the "meaning" of the relationship. That is, relationships can be interpreted as used/used-by, part/part-of or before/after kinds of relationships. The classification assisted in the enforcement of certain types of relationship constraints.

The SDLA (System Descriptor and Logical Analyzer) metasystem and associate concept metamodel [DEME82] were developed at the Hungarian Academy of Sciences in collaboration with the ISDOS Project. Information in a concept database is organized as a set of reference relations. These relations differ from those of the relational model by allowing the domain for an attribute to be defined as abstract types that refer to entries in other relations. A simple example of a concept definition is as follows:

```
CONCEPT process (mode:text);
CONCEPT data_flow;
CONCEPT data_store (form: text, owner:text);
CONCEPT accesses (process, data_flow, data_store, frequency:text);
```

Note that both entity types (e.g., process) and relationship types (e.g., accesses) are treated as concepts, and that entities and attributes (e.g., frequency) are intermixed in roles in concept definitions. One of the more powerful features available in the concept model is the use of subtypes (or generalization) to form is-a concept hierarchies.

The final metasystem that will be discussed is the Plexsys metasystem [KOTT84] developed at the University of Arizona. The Plexsys database is, once again based on the ER model. A unique feature of the Plexsys system is, however, that some concepts of the metamodel and all of the environment definition and specification information are stored in the same database. The main reason for this "dynamism" (their word) is the desire to modify an environment definition over time with minimum interface with on going specification activities. Therefore, changes to an environment definition should cause immediate changes to the specification information in a manner that is consistent with the updated environment definition. Another proposed addition to the ER-based metamodel was the introduction of a number of role types called cases. These cases described different meanings that are associated with the roles defined for various relationship types. Some examples of role types include: actors (a performer of an action), instrument (an object used but not changed, and material (an object used and changed by some action). The introduction of role types allowed for more extensive constraint checking in the metasystem.

Using many of the factors described earlier in this section and some of the results of previous research as a basis, let us develop a metamodel suitable for the Metaview metasystem.

3   AN ENVIRONMENT DEFINITION MODEL

In this section, a model is presented of the information required to support a general specification environment definition and particular specification databases conforming to this definition. Using this model as a basis, the Environment Model Definition Language (EMDL) will be formulated in Section 4.

3.1 A Basic Environment Definition Model

As pointed out in the introduction, there are many ways (or methodologies) for describing information systems specifications. A metasystem model, therefore, must be general enough to permit multiple environments to be defined (or modelled), and, as such, behaves as a metamodel.

The types of information contained in a particular kind of specification are defined by a schema, henceforth called the specification schema. As an example, the specification schema for the entity-relationship model [CHEN76] defines the notions of entity set, relationship set, attributes, and how these concepts are related.

The metamodel proposed must support a specification schema, SS, that contains a certain set of descriptive elements. Using Chen's ER model only as a basis, the following minimum set of elements is proposed. Note that several significant changes to the definitions of Chen have been made.

SS = (ET, RT, RN, r, A, a)

where   ET: is a finite set of entity types;

RT: is a finite set of relationship types in which a given relationship type contains a finite set of entity type participants {ET1, ..., ETn};

RN: is a finite set of roles;

r: is a mapping [RT -> Powerset*(RN)] where Powerset*(RN) is the set of all subsets of RN that includes two or more members of RN;

A: is a finite set of attributes;

a: is a mapping from the set of entity types, ET, and relationship types, RT, to the set of attributes A.

As a simple example, consider the definition of a specification schema for a data flow model based on the concepts used in data flow diagrams as proposed in Gane and Sarson's Structured Systems Analysis Methodology [GANE79]. The data flow specification schema, SS(DF), would have the following elements:

ET = {Process, Data_Flow, Data_Store, Interface}

RT = {Sends = {Process, Data_Flow, Interface, Data_Store}
        Receives = {Inteface, Data_Flow, Process, Data_Store}}

RN = {Message, Sender, Receiver}

r = {Sends ->
(Process:Sender, Data_Flow:Message, Data_Store:Receiver),
(Process:Sender, Data_Flow:Message, Process:Receiver),
(Process:Sender, Data_Flow:Message, Interface:Receiver);

        Receives ->
(Data_Store:Sender, Data_Flow:Message, Process:Receiver),
(Interface:Sender, Data_Flow:Message, Process:Receiver)}

A = {problem_definer, defn_date, frequency, description, size}

a = {Process -> problem_definer, defn_date, description;
        Data-Flow -> problem_definer, defn_date;
        Data-Store -> problem_definer, defn_date, size;
        Interface -> problem_definer, defn_date;
        Sends -> problem_definer, defn_date, frequency;
        Receives -> problem_definer, defn_date, frequency}

A complete specification schema should also include the notion of value set and a mapping of attributes to value sets.

To aid in the understanding of how the different elements of the metamodel inter-relate, an ER type of diagram is presented in Figure 3. In the diagram, N, P, M, and 1 are currency specifications of the relationship participants. Observe that the relationship <participates>

corresponds to the role mapping function r described earlier. The <r_contains> and <e_contains> relationships correspond to the attribute mapping function a, and the <has> relationship maps attributes to value sets.

3.2 Advanced Modelling Feature

The metamodel just outlined is deficient in a number of the more advanced semantic-based data modelling features that are found in semantic data models today and that should be present in a metasystem for specification environments. Some of the features that should be considered are the abstraction mechanisms of aggregation, generalization, and classification.

Aggregation is used to combine a set of entities and their relationships to form a simple higher level aggregate object. Of course, the notion of aggregation applies recursively — an aggregate object can be used as part of the definition of a still higher-level object. As will be shown later in this section, aggregation is a fundamental abstraction mechanism in the development of an extended component-based metamodel.

Generalization is used to form a higher-level generic entity from its categories. It establishes the well-known "is-a" relationship between entities. Generalization can be used in developing specification environments. For example, it is helpful to be able to generalize (or inversely categorize) the notion of INTERFACE from the subcategories HUMAN_INTERFACE and MECHANICAL_INTERFACE. That is, a HUMAN_INTERFACE "is-a" INTERFACE and a MECHANICAL_INTERFACE "is-a" INTERFACE.

The final abstraction technique, classification, is a simple form of

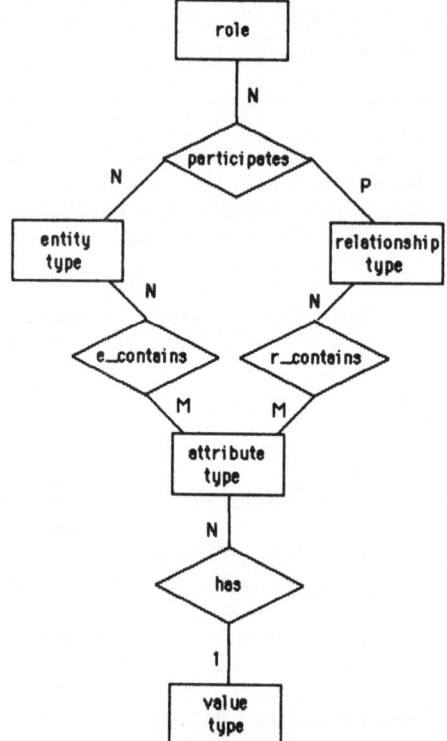

Figure 3   Metamodel for Defining Specification Environments

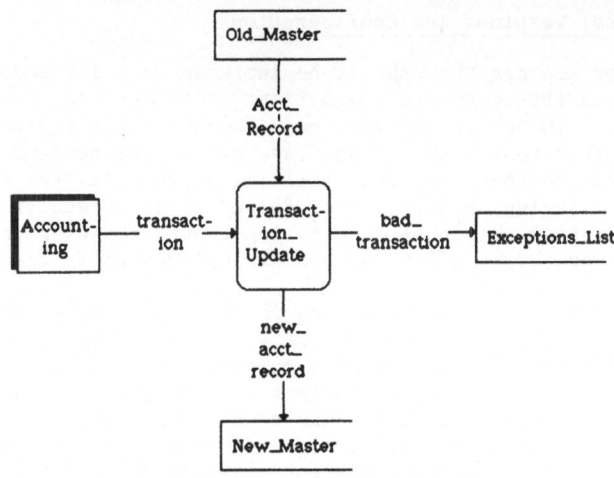

Figure 4   Small example of data flow diagram

abstraction in which an object (in this case entity or relationship) is
defined as a set of instances. It establishes an "instance-of"
relationship between a type and its instances. As an example, consider
the small data flow diagram given in Figure 4.

In the example the following classifications hold ("==>" reads "are
instances of"):

{Old_Master, New_Master, Exceptions_List} ==> DATA_STORE

{Accounting} ==> INTERFACE

{Transaction_Update} ==> PROCESS

{transaction, acct_record, new_acct_rec, bad_transaction} ==> DATAFLOW

RECEIVES(Accounting:Sender, transaction:Message,
        Transaction_Update:Receiver)
RECEIVES(Old_Master:Sender, Acct_Record:Message,
        Transaction_Update:Receiver)

==>   RECEIVES relationship, and

SENDS(Transaction_Update:Sender, new_acct_rec:Message,
        New_Master:Receiver)
SENDS(Transaction_Update:Sender, bad_transaction:Message,
        Exceptions_List:Receiver)

==>   SENDS relationship.

Similarly, "Sorenson" and "January 15, 1987" are instances of values for
the attributes problem_definer and defn_date, respectively.

An extension of our metamodel that shows the incorporation of
classification is provided in Figure 5. Note that the relationship
"type_of" has been used to show classification in the diagram.

3.3 Components, Versions and Configurations

The final major aspects that should be included in a metamodel for
specification environments are the notions of components, versions, and
configurations. These notions have been recently investigated in
conjunction with research on CAD database management systems [BAT085],
[KATZ86]. Basic to the component modelling approach is the notion of a
component-based design object (also referred to as molecular object
[HART85]). A design object is a modelling construct which has an
interface (or boundary) definition and an implementation description.

The interface definition specifies the inputs to, outputs from, and high-
level functional description of the design object. The implementation is
defined by lower-level design objects or components and their
interconnections. Each component object may, in turn, be assigned its
own interface and implementation. The concept of abstracting a set of
design objects (or entities) and their relationships into a single,
higher-level entity is called component aggregation. To illustrate these
concepts consider the data flow diagram in Figure 6. This diagram
illustrates the expansion of the Transaction_Update PROCESS to a more
detailed data flow diagram description.

In this example the interface definition for the design object,
Transaction_Update, is defined by the four relationships:

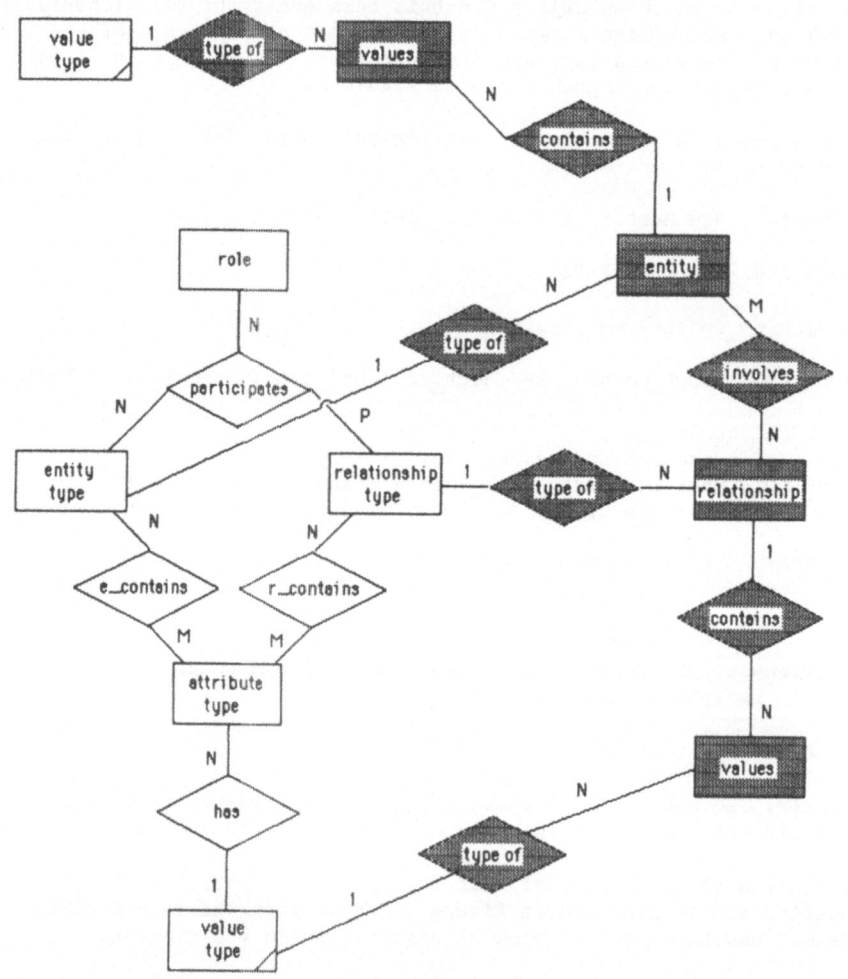

Figure 5   Extension of Metamodel to Include Classification

- RECEIVES(Accounting, transaction, Transaction_Update)
- RECEIVES(Old-Master, acct_record, Transaction_Update)
- SENDS(Transaction_Update, new_acct_rec, New_Master)
- SENDS(Transaction_Update, bad_transaction, Exceptions_List)

Observe that the roles of the relationship participants have been left out of the above, abbreviated definitions.

The implementation of design object, Transaction Update PROCESS, can be defined formally in terms of the sets and mappings (ET, RT, RN, r, A, a) as was done for the data flow diagram given in Figure 4.

Of special note is the interface consistency problem, which is illustrated in this example by the three data flows directed towards Exceptions_List. For the model to remain consistent with respect to the interface definitions of the various component objects, the correspondence between the DATA_FLOW bad_transaction at the first level and the set of three DATA_FLOWs {illegal_trans, rec_not_matched, bad_trans_data} in the implementation description of Transaction_Update must be formally defined. One method of formal definition is to define a special relationship between data flow elements. Let us call this relationship CONSISTS_OF. Then, the mapping r for CONSISTS_OF might be:

CONSISTS_OF -> (DATA_FLOW:superordinate, DATA_FLOW:subordinate).

Instances of CONSIST_OF in this small example would be:

CONSISTS_OF(bad_transaction, illegal_trans),
CONSISTS_OF(bad_transaction, rec_not_matched),
CONSISTS_OF(bad_transaction, bad_trans_data).

Mechanisms for checking consistency and completeness in a specification

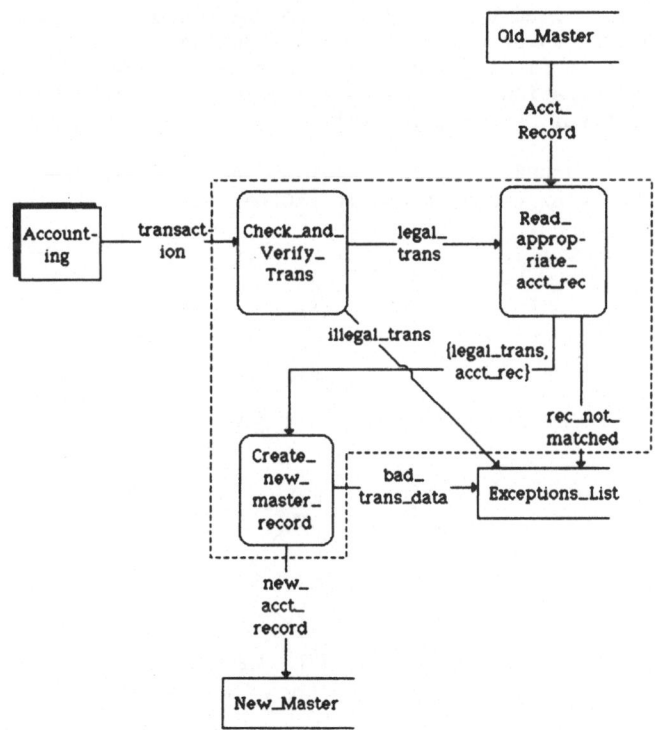

Figure 6   Detailed definition of Transaction_Update PROCESS

defined using a metasystem approach is outside the scope of this paper.
Some preliminary ideas about how and when to perform constraint checking
in metasystems are given in [MCAL87]. Similarly, the details about a
formal approach to interface definition in a component model approach are
not included in this paper, but are being defined in [MCAL87a].

Before leaving a discussion of our formal model, it is important to
consider the support of different versions of specifications of a
system.Version support is important if a variety of analysts are allowed
to work on essentially the same specification at one time. Figure 7
gives a conceptual overview of how versions are encompassed in a
component-based metamodel. We will refer to this type of graph as a
component/version graph. The circular icons represent component entities
in a specification, while the rectangular icons represent the aggregation
of components into a single version. Therefore, in the diagram, version
V2 of C2 is composed of components {C3, C4, C5}. A second version of C2
also exists, namely V3, which is composed of components {C6, C5}. C6 is
shown, in turn, to have three of its own versions V3, V4, V5 (note that
none of the components of the versions for C6 are depicted in the
diagram). It may also be important to track the derivation of a version,
i.e., version V5 may be derived from V3. If changes are made to V3, it
may be important that these same changes be reflected in V5. The broken
arrow in Figure 7 indicates that V5 is a derivative of V3, while V4 was a
version of C6 that was developed independent of the other two.

A component/version graph can be viewed as an AND/OR graph as introduced
in [TICH82]. The grouping of components to form a higher-level aggregate
object indicates the "ANDing" of components; whereas, the selection of
one of many versions to represent a particular object constitute an
"ORing" of sets of components. A configuration is simply a selected set
of versions from the OR part of the component/version graph. In the
component/version graph, every component except the ultimate ancester,
which is C1 in Figure 7, must belong to at least one version. A system
configuration is formed by traversing the OR-part of the graph beginning
at the ultimate ancestor component and proceeding, using OR selection, to
a leaf version node (i.e., a version node with no versions of its own).
An example configuration from the component/version graph in Figure 7
would be the set {C1, V1, V3, V4, V6}.

A more detailed discussion of how versions and configurations are to be
supported in Metaview can be found in [MCAL87a].

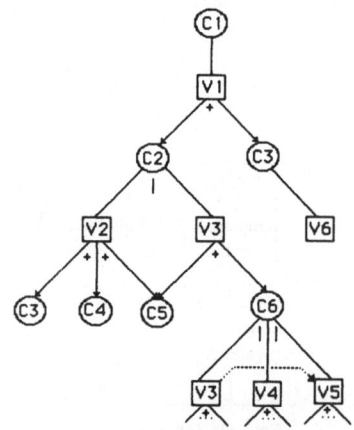

Figure 7   A component/Version Graph

The EMDL is used by the environment definer to specify a specification schema. While an interactive interface has been developed for defining schemas, the batch language version is presented here to keep the discussion simple.

The EMDL is designed with the premise that all information in a schema is related either to an entity type, a relationship type, or an attribute. Hence there are three basic statement types each of which is now described. The ENTITY_TYPE statement has the following syntax:

     <entity_stat> ::= ENTITY_TYPE <entity_type> {, <entity_type>} ;

     <entity_type> ::= identifier
                    | identifier IS AGGREGATE <component_list>
                    | identifier IS GENERIC [RESTRICTED]
                                               <category_list>

     <component_list> ::= WITH COMPONENT_TYPES <id_list>

     <category_list> ::= WITH CATEGORY_TYPES <id_list>

     <id_list> ::= identifier {, identifier}

In the above BNF-style grammar description, {...} means the syntactic unit can appear 0 or more times, and [...] means the syntactic unit is optional. The following example illustrates the ENTITY_TYPE statement:

     ENTITY_TYPE PROCESS IS AGGREGATE WITH COMPONENT_TYPES
             PROCESS, INTERFACE, DATA_OBJECT, DATA_STORE;

     ENTITY_TYPE DATA_OBJECT IS GENERIC RESTRICTED WITH
             CATEGORY_TYPES DATA_FLOW, INPUT, OUTPUT;

     ENTITY_TYPE DATA_STORE IS GENERIC WITH CATEGORY_TYPES
             MANUAL_FILE, DISK_FILE;

     ENTITY_TYPE INTERFACE, DATA_FLOW, INPUT, OUTPUT,
             MANUAL_FILE, DISK_FILE;

The first definition indicates that PROCESS is an aggregate type of entity that is composed of other PROCESSes, INTERFACEs, DATA_OBJECTs, and DATA_STOREs. This implies that a process defined at one level can be redefined in greater detail at another level of abstraction in terms of PROCESS, INTERFACE, DATA_OBJECT, and DATA_STORE entity types. DATA_OBJECT is defined to be a GENERIC type, meaning that it has subcategories of ENTITY_TYPES. In this case, a DATA_FLOW "is-a" DATA_OBJECT, as are INPUTs and OUTPUTs. DATA_OBJECT is also defined to be RESTRICTED, meaning that it exists as a generic type in the environment definition but does not appear in the database and is not visible to the analyst. It is a type that is used for definitional purposes only, such as for defining environment definition constraints. DATA_STORE is also defined to be GENERIC with two subtypes. In this case DATA_STORE is a visible (i.e., unrestricted) entity type. Finally, the last ENTITY_TYPE definition contains a list of several unrestricted, non-generic, non-aggregate entity types.

The form of the relationship type statement is as follows:

```
<relationship_stat> ::= RELATIONSHIP_TYPE identifier "(" <role>
         {, <role>} ")"
         [PARTICIPANTS ARE <combination> {, <combination> ]
         [DEPENDENCY identifier "->" identifier]

<role> ::= identifier [ "[" <role_characteristics> {,
              <role_characteristics>} "]" ]

<role_characteristics> ::= SINGLE | UNORDERED | ORDERED
         | INDEPENDENT | DEPENDENT

<combination> ::= "<" <comb_list> ">"

<comb_list> ::= <participant_list> {, <participant_list> }

<participant_list> ::= <or_list> | NOT <or_list> | <not_ident>

<or_list> ::= "(" <not_indent> OR <not_ident> {OR <not_indent>} ")"

<not_indent> ::= identifier | NOT identifier
```

An example relationship type definition is:

```
RELATIONSHIP_TYPE SENDS (sender, message [UNORDERED],
     receiver)
     PARTICIPANTS ARE <PROCESS, DATA_FLOW, (PROCESS OR
     INTERFACE OR DATA_STORE)>

RELATIONSHIP_TYPE STORES
     (store_name [SINGLE, INDEPENDENT],
      data_name [ORDERED, DEPENDENT])
     PARTICIPANTS ARE <DATA_STORE, DATA_FLOW>
     DEPENDENCY data_name -> store_name
```

The RELATIONSHIP_TYPE statement is used to define a relationship type, a
set of role names and their characteristics, and a participant type
constraint. The list of role names and associated participant's list
define the role mapping (r) in the specification schema. The role
characteristics are of two types. In the first type, a role may have a
"single" entity or relationship type, an "unordered" set of entity or
relationship types, or an "ordered" set of entity or relationship types.
A "dependent" role corresponds to the concept of a "weak entity" proposed
in [CHEN76]. A relationship type that has one or more dependent roles
must have one "independent" role. If an entity type that occupies the
independent role is deleted from the database, the relationship instance
and all of the entity or relationship types occupying the dependent roles
are deleted. The final part of the relationship type definition is the
optional DEPENDENCY clause. This clause defines the functional
dependencies between roles.

The first example definition of the relationship type SENDS describes how
various entity types are combined to specify the flow of information in a
system. An example SENDS statement in a specification language for this
portion of the schema might be:

SENDS(procA, {employee_rec, job_request}, personnel_office)

Note that the PROCESS procA appears in the sender role, an unordered list
of two DATA_FLOWs appear in the message role, and the INTERFACE
personnel_office appears in the receiver role.

The second example illustrates the DEPENDENCY clause. The binary relationship STORES is defined and it records the fact that stored data can not exist without a data store. The DEPENDENCY data_name -> store_name indicates that if a participant in the first role of STORE is deleted, the second participant (i.e., the data store) is also deleted.

The final major statement type, the ATTRIBUTE statement, defines a single attribute name and its characteristics. The general form of the statement is as follows:

```
<attribute_stat> ::= ATTRIBUTE identifier : <domain_defn>;
                     APPLIES "(" <id_list> ")"
                     [NECESSITY "(" (YES | NO) ")"]
                     [CARDINALITY "(" (ONE | MANY) ")"]

<domain_defn> ::= INTEGER | REAL | TEXT
```

An example definition of the attribute form follow:

```
ATTRIBUTE form: TEXT;
     APPLIES (DATA_STORE, INTERFACE)
     NECESSITY (NO) CARDINALITY (ONE).
```

The statement contains a list of entity and relationship types to which the attribute applies. The description may optionally be followed by a NECESSITY clause, which specifies whether the attribute must be present at all times in the APPLIES entity and relationship types. A CARDINALITY clause, if present, indicates whether ONE only or MANY values of the given attribute may be present in the entity and relationship types.

The ATTRIBUTE statement that is described in this paper is a somewhat simplified version of the statement proposed in [MCAL87a]. The full definition includes provisions for defining new domain types (in addition to the standard domains of INTEGER, REAL, and TEXT) as well as domain restrictions such as subranges and enumerated subsets on the standard domains.

To summarize our brief introduction to EMDL, the following features have been considered and incorporated in the language.

1. An entity-relationship based underlying metamodel;

2. N-ary relationships;

3. Attributes for both entity and relationship types;

4. Intrinsic attributes like date and time of last modification (supported by the language translator but not in the language per se);

5. Relationship instances participating in other relationship instances;

6. Sets as relationship participants;

7. A variety of constraints (explicit and implicit);

8. Support of generic and aggregate entity types.

In addition, an explicit interface description called a boundary is as an implicit extension to the language in support of component modelling. As

well, version control and configurations should be supported. These
latter two features have not been discussed in the context of EMDL. More
details will be given in Section 5 can can be found in [MCAL87a].

5   AN EMDL EXAMPLE

This section introduces a simple specification environment schema
definition in EMDL for a data flow environment based on a Structured
Systems Analysis (SSA) methodology [GANE79]. In SSA, a system is
represented as a collection of processes, data stores and interfaces with
data flows transmitted between these system entities. A rather complete
specification schema for the DFM, Data Flow Model is now given (parts of
this schema definition were introduced in Sections 3 and 4).

-- Comments are prefixed with "--".

-- Entity type definitions.

ENTITY_TYPE PROCESS IS AGGREGATE WITH COMPONENT TYPES
     PROCESS, INTERFACE, DATA_OBJECT, DATA_STORE.

ENTITY_TYPE DATA_OBJECT IS GENERIC RESTRICTED WITH CATEGORY_TYPES
     DATA_FLOW, INPUT, OUTPUT.

ENTITY_TYPE INTERFACE, DATA_FLOW, DATA_STORE, INPUT, OUTPUT,
     GROUP, ELEMENT.

-- Relationship type definitions.

RELATIONSHIP_TYPE SENDS (sender, message [UNORDERED], receiver)
     PARTICIPANTS ARE <PROCESS, DATA_FLOW, (PROCESS OR
                    DATA_STORE)>,
                 <PROCESS, OUTPUT, INTERFACE>.

RELATIONSHIP_TYPE RECEIVES (sender, message[UNORDERED], receiver)
     PARTICIPANTS ARE <INTERFACE, INPUT PROCESS>
                 <DATA_STORE, DATA_FLOW, PROCESS>.

RELATIONSHIP_TYPE CONTAINS (super, subordinate[UNORDERED])
     PARTICIPANTS ARE <DATA_OBJECT, (ELEMENT OR GROUP)>,
                 <GROUP, (ELEMENT OR GROUP)>.

--Attribute definitions.

ATTRIBUTE DESCRIPTION: TEXT; APPLIES TO ALL
     NECESSITY (NO) CARDINALITY (ONE).

ATTRIBUTE FREQUENCY: times_per_month;
     APPLIES TO (SENDS, RECEIVES) CARDINALITY (ONE).

ATTRIBUTE OWNER: TEXT;
     APPLIES TO (DATA_STORE).

ATTRIBUTE MODE: TEXT;
     APPLIES TO (PROCESS).

-- Domain definitions.

DOMAIN times_per_month: INTEGER (1..50000).

Figure 8 shows a simple example of a system that maintains information on the holdings of a library and allows patrons to query that information. Updates to the holdings information are shown as being performed by the librarian once a week. Librarian and patron are interfaces. Three processes and one data store are also included in the data flow diagram.

Let us examine a specification of this data flow assuming the DFM defined in the specification schema just expressed in EMDL. To provide a specification, it must be expressed in some language form. We will assume that the DFM schema can be transformed into a language translator processable form in which the major elements of the model (i.e., the entities, and relationships) appear in their own definition sections that begin with the keyword DEFINE. We will refer to this form as DFL (for Data Flow Language). The DFL expression of the requirements laid out in Figure 8 is:

```
DEFINE PROCESS Provide_Query_Access,
               Provide_Update_Access,
               Database_Access;
     MODE = "input driven".

DEFINE INTERFACE Library_Patron;
     DESCRIPTION = "A Patron is a person who uses the library and owns
     a legitimate library card".

DEFINE INTERFACE Librarian;
     DESCRIPTION = "A person who works in the library, cataloging and
     ordering books"

DEFINE DATA_STONE Library_Holdings;
     OWNER = "Library".

DEFINE SENDS (Library_Patron, Query, Provide_Query_Access);
     FREQUENCY = 3000 times_per_month.

DEFINE RECEIVES (Provide_Query_Access, Query_Reply, Library_Patron);
     FREQUENCY = 5000 times_per_month
     DESCRIPTION = "More than one reply is often required to answer a
     patron's query".
```

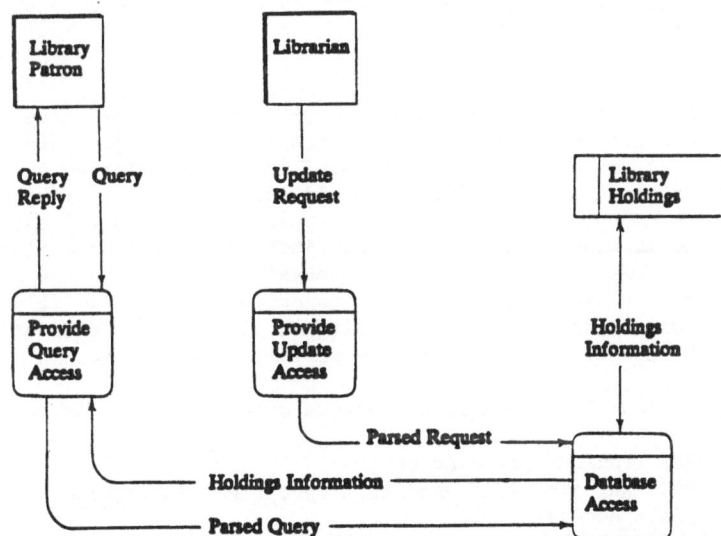

Figure 8   DFD for simple library information system.

469

```
DEFINE RECEIVES (Librarian, Update_Request, Provide_Query_Update)
    FREQUENCY = 5 times_per_month;

DEFINE SENDS (Provide_Update_Access, Parsed_Request,
        Database_Access)
    FREQUENCY = 5;
DEFINE ACCESSES (Database_Access, Holdings_Information,
        Library Holdings)
    FREQUENCY = 5000 times_per_month;

DEFINE SENDS(Provide_Query_Access, Parsed_Query, Database_Access)
    FREQUENCY = 5000 times_per_month;

DEFINE SENDS(Database_Access, Holdings_Information,
        Provide_Query_Access)
    FREQUENCY = 5000 times_per_month;

-- Data Objects

DEFINE DATA_FLOW Holdings_Info, Parsed_Query, Parsed_Request;

DEFINE INPUT Query, Update_Request;

DEFINE OUTPUT Query_Reply;

DEFINE ELEMENT LofC_No, Author, Title, Publisher, Publ_Date,
        Return_Date;

DEFINE GROUP Book_Info;
    DESCRIPTION = "Contains information about a book".

DEFINE CONTAINS (Book_Info, {LofC_No, Author, Title, Publisher,
        Publ_Date}).

DEFINE CONTAINS (Holdings_Information, {Status, Book_Info, Return_Date})

DEFINE ELEMENT Status;
    DESCRIPTION = "Possible values include --
    1) Out with a patron,
    2) Out with a pending request,
    3) Available on shelf,
    4) Out for binding or repair".
```

It is very important to realize that the DFM schema and DFL have
purposely been kept very simple in order to illustrate the basic features
of a metasystem approach to defining specification environments. A
typical environment model definition would contain three or four times
the modelling concepts given in DFM. A typical system specification
would provide much more information than just the simple data flows
expressible in DFL. To complete our discussion on the Metaview approach
to metasystems, a simple example of component aggregation is illustrated.
Figure 9 shows an exploded data flow diagram of the Provide_Update_Access
PROCESS. The associated DFL aggregate definition would be:

```
-- The definition of Provide_Update_Access must be changed as follows.

DEFINE PROCESS Provide_Update_Access;
    COMPONENTS ARE {Terminal_Handler, Input_Line, Error_Code,
        Update_Access}
    BOUNDARIES ARE {Rec_Req, DB_Req, DB_Feedback,
        Term_Feedback}.
```

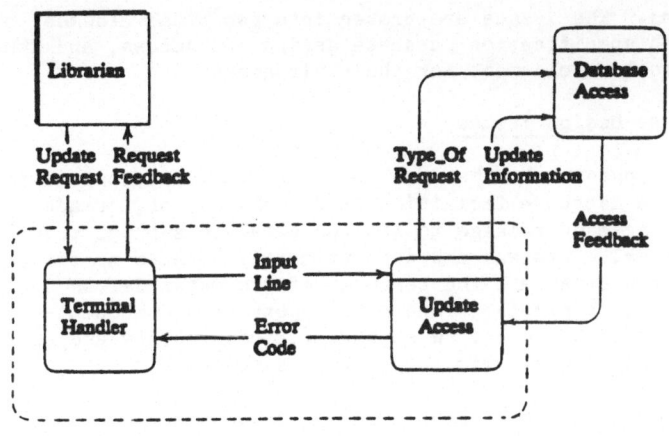

Figure 9   Exploded DFD of Provide_Update_Access

-- Components and boundary relationships defined below.

DEFINE PROCESS Terminal_Handler, Update_Access.

DEFINE DATA_FLOW Input_Line, Error_Code.

DEFINE RECEIVES (Librarian, Update_Request, Terminal_Handler)
     SYNONYM (Rec_Req).

DEFINE SENDS
     (Update_Access, {Type_of_Request, Update_Information},
         Database_Access) SYNONYM (DB_Req),
     (Database_Access, Access_Feedback, Update_Access) SYNONYM
         (DB Feedback),
     (Terminal_Handler, Request_Feedback, Librarian) SYNONYM
         (Term_Feedback);

-- Internal relationship definitions.

DEFINE SENDS
     (Terminal_Handler, Input_Line, Update_Access),
     (Update_Access, Error_Code, Terminal_Handler)

The important aspect of this example is the redefinition of the exploded
(or aggregate) process Provide_Update_Access to include a list of the
component entities and the boundary relationships. These entities and
relationships, along with the internal entities and relationships, must
then be fully defined in the detailed specification of the exploded
process. Note that references to internal relationships in the
BOUNDARIES ARE clause of Provide_Update_Access are done by SYNONYM
definitions which are assumed to be definable, when desired, for all
entity and relationship descriptions.

Our brief example provides a somewhat simplified view of component
aggregation which must be supported in Metaview. A more detailed
discussion, with more detailed examples can be found in [MCAL87a].

6   THE METAVIEW METASYSTEM

This section contains a brief overview of some of the design issues faced
in the development of a metasystem given that an underlying metamodel has

been derived. The issues are broken into two broad classes: those dealing with specification database design and access, and those involving tool development for the environment.

6.1 Database Design Issues

One obvious approach to the development of database support for the specification database facilities is to make use of, or adapt an existing database management package to fit the database support requirements of the metasystem. This was not done primarily because no existing DBMS adequately supported all the features of the metamodel as outlined in Section 3. In particular, inherent support of a component-based data modelling approach and strong support for consistency and completeness constraint checking was missing in most systems.

The choice was made to develop our own database support facilities in Prolog. Prolog provides quite naturally the constraint checking environment that is required. The task of developing the component-based database access support has been undertaken. With a component-based approach, it is possible to factor the specification database by component and to only bring into main memory the current component that the analyst is working on. Therefore, for example, when moving from the main level component description for the library system example to the exploded process specification for process Provide_Update_Access, we need only store the main level component (if changes have occurred), and then retrieve a copy (version) of the Provide_Update_Access component.

Another advantage of adopting the component-based approach to database support is that concurrency control can take place while being cognizant that a "component-at-a-time" access model is being used. Even using locking at the component level (large grain locking) can be relatively effective. More importantly, locking implemented at the record level can be made very efficient, since it is possible to lock the database a "record-at-a-time" as the analyst moves up and down the component hierarchy. Multiple record locking within a component should only be required on the currently active component. While out initial prototype implementation is supporting component-level locking only, we plan to investigate further and then implement a record-level locking system.

6.2 Tool Development Support

In the past, the DEVIEW Project has developed a number of specification environment tools in support of a particular problem specification language, SPSL/SPSA (Simple Problem Statement Language/Simple Problem Statement Analyzer) [SORE81]. The tool set includes an SPSL batch translator ; Depict [PROT85], a graphics-oriented interface to SPSL/SPSA; Mondrian [PROT84], an automatic data flow diagram layout facility from an SPSA database; and CUBUS [LEIG86], a structure chart design and automatic layout facility. Based on these experiences, a set of generalized database access routines are being developed that allow a wide variety of tools to interact efficiently with a common specification database. A set of thirty nine routines have been designed and implemented. At present, a generalized template-based editor is being developed [CHEW87] that allows for the automatic production of a template-based editor based primarily on the EMDL description of the specification environment. Future developments include the development of a generalized, iconic-based graphics interface tool generator (i.e., a generalized version of Depict), a query/constraint specification language and translator, and a generalized report writing facility.

This paper has documented the DEVIEW Project's attempt at developing a metamodel for specification environment development. The model is based on several years of experience in developing specification environment tool support and the research of several other projects dealing with specification environment metasystems as outlined in Section 2. We feel the meta model approach that has been described in Sections 3 and 4 provides a reasonable compromise between the development of a specific specification support environment that supposedly supports any system specification and a completely flexible metasystem environment, such as Plexsys [KOTT84], in which the specification environment definition is stored with and can be modified as easily as the specifications themselves. Metaview will allow an environment definer to define the environment model and associate tool support for the specification methodology that is desired. Once defined, the metasystem developed environment should ensure that analysts adhere to the chosen methodology in a strict manner. Once an environment is in use, Metaview will allow some adjustments to be made to the environment definition; however, these must be of a minor nature.

In the immediate future, a more detailed definition of the component model will be developed. A constraint processor must be defined and our approach to a graphics-oriented interface must be re-examined and generalized. The development of generalized template-based editor must take place and this can be used to verify the current implementation of our database support facility. In addition, a well-defined concurrency control technique with record-level locking must be developed and added to the database support facility. Finally, and perhaps most importantly, the metasystem must be tested by defining a wide class of different specification environments and having analysts use the different environments to provide constructive feedback that will result in improvements to the metasystem.

REFERENCES

[ALFO77}   Alford, M.W. "A Requirements Engineering Methodology for Real-Time Processing Requirements ", IEEE Trans. on Software Engineering, vol. 8 no. 1, 1977, pp. 60-69.

[ALFO85]   Alford, M. "SREM at the Age of Eight: The Distributed Computing Design System", IEEE Computer, vol. 18, no. 4, 1985, pp. 36-46.

[BATO85]   Batory, D.S. and Kim, W. "Modelling Concepts for VLSI CAD Objects", ACM Trans. on Database Systems, vol. 10, no. 3, 1985, pp. 18-32.

[BELL77]   Bell, T.E., Bixler, D.C. and Dyer, M.E. "An Extendable Approach to Computer-Aided Software Requirements Engineering", IEEE Trans. on Software Engineering, vol. 3, no. 1, 1977, pp. 49-60.

[BORG85]   Borgida, A., Greenspan, S. and Mylopolous, J. "Knowledge Representation Approach to Software Requirements Definition", IEEE Computer , vol. 18, no. 4, 1985, pp. 82-91.

[CHEN76]   Chen, P. "The Entity-Relationship Model: Towards a Unified View of Data", ACM Trans. on Database Systems, vol. 1, 1976, pp. 9-36.

[CHEW87]   Chew, T.H. "Automated Template Generation for Requirements
            Specification Languages", M.Sc. Thesis, Univ. of Saskatchewan,
            1987 (in preparation).

[COMP83]   IEEE Computer, vol. 16, no. 11, 1983, pp. 9-104.

[DEME82]   Demetrovics, J., Knuth, E., and Rado, P. "Specification
            MetaSystems", IEEE Computer, vol. 15, no. 4, 1982, pp. 20-35.

[GANE79]   Gane, C., and Sarson, T. Structured Systems Analysis: Tools
            and Techniques, Prentice_Hall, Englewood-Cliffs, N.J., 1979.

[GREE84]   Greenspan, S. "Requirements Modelling: A Knowledge
            Representation Approach to Software Requirements Definition",
            Tech. Report CSRG-155, Computer Systems Research Group, Univ.
            of Toronto, March, 1984.

[HART85]   Hartzband, D.J. and Maryanski, F.J. "Enhancing Knowledge
            Representation in Engineering Databases", IEEE Computer, vol.
            18, no. 9, 1985, pp. 39-48.

[KANG82]   Kang, K.C. "An Approach for Supporting System Development
            Methodologies for Developing a Complete and Consistent System
            Specification", Ph.D Thesis, Univ. of Michigan, Ann Arbor,
            1982.

[KATZ86]   Katz, R.H., Chang, E. and Bhateja, R. "Version Modelling
            Concepts for Computer-Aided Design Databases", Proc. of ACM
            SIGMOD'86 Int'1 Conf. on Management of Data, vol. 15, no. 2,
            1986, pp. 379-386.

[KOTT84]   Kotteman, J.E. and Konsynski, B.R. "Dynamic Metasystems for
            Information Systems Development", Proc. of the Fifth Int'1
            Conf. on Information Systems, Tucson, Arizona, 1984, pp. 187-
            204.

[LEIG86]   Leighton, H., Sorenson, P.G. and Tremblay, J.P. "CUBUS: An
            Automated System for the Generation of Structure Charts",
            Canadian Information Processing Society's Congress 86,
            Vancouver, May 1986, pp. 181-190.

[LEVE82]   Levene, T. and Mullery, G. "An Investigation of Requirements
            Specification Languages: Theory and Practice", IEEE Computer,
            vol. 15, no. 4, 1982, pp. 50-59.

[MCAL87]   McAllister, A.J., Sorenson, P.G., Tremblay, J.P. and Dedourek,
            J. "Constraints for Automatically Generated Requirements
            Specification Environments", Twentieth Annual Hawaii Int'1
            Conference on System Science, Jan, 1987, (to appear).

[MCAL87a]   McAllister, A.J. "Metasystem Support for Specification
            Environments", Ph.D. Thesis, Univ. of Saskatchewan, 1987 (in
            preparation).

[OLLE82]   Olle, E.W., Sol, H.G. and Verrijn-Stuart, A.A. (ed) Information
            Systems Design Methodologies: A Comparative Review, North-
            Holland, 1982.

[PROT84]   Protsko, L.B., Sorenson, P.G. and Tremlay, J.P. "Automatic
            Generation of Data Flow Diagrams from a Requirements
            Specification Language", Proc. of the Fifth Int.1 Conf. on

Information Systems, Tucson, Arizona, Nov. 28-30, 1984, pp. 157-171.

[PROT85}   Protsko, L.B., Kurtenbach, G., Sorenson, P.G. and Tremblay, J.P. "DEPICT: A Graphical Interface for Systems Analysis and Design", Eighteenth Annual Hawaii Conf. on Systems Sciences, Honolulu, Jan. 1985, pp. 128-139.

[SORE81]   Sorenson, P.G., Tremblay, J.P. and Friesen, A.W. "SPSL/SPSA: A Minicomputer Database System for Structured Systems Analysis and Design", Proc. of the ACM SIGSMALL and SIGMOD Workshop on Small Database Systems, Orlando, 1981, pp. 109-118.

[SORE86]   Sorenson, P.G. and Tremblay, J.P. "The DEVIEW Project Update", Tech. Report No. 86-3, Dept. of Computational Science, Univ. of Sasskatchewan, March 1986.

[STEN81]   Stenning, V., et al. "The Ada Environment: A Perspective", IEEE Computer, Vol. 14, no. 6, 1981, pp. 26-36.

[STEP78]   Stephens, S.A. and Tripp, L.L. "Requirements Expression and Verification Aid", Proc. of the Third IEEE Conf. on Software Engineering, Atlanta, Georgia, May 1978, pp. 101-108.

[TEIC77]   Teichroew, D. and Hershey, E. "PSL/PSA: A Computer Aided Technique for Structured Documentation and Analysis of Information Processing Systems", IEEE Trans. on Software Engineering, vol. 8, no. 1, 1977, pp. 48-58.

[TICH82]   Tichy, W.F. "A Data Model for Programming Support Environments and its Application, in Automated Tools for Information Systems Design, Schneider and Wasserman (eds.), North-Holland, 1982, pp. 31-48.

[WASS82]   Wasserman, A.I. "The User Software Engineering Methodology: An Overview", Proc. of the IFIP WG 8.1 Working Conf. on Comparative Reviews of Information Systems Design Methodologies, Noordwijkerhout, Netherlands, May 10-14, 1982, pp. 591-628.

[WOLF81]   Wolfe, M.L., et al. "The Ada Language System", IEEE Computer, vol. 14, no. 6, 1981, pp. 37-45.

[YAMA81]   Yamamoto, Y. "An Approach to the Generation of Software Life Cycle Support Systems", Ph.D. Thesis, Univ. of Michigan, Ann Arbor, 1981.

SPECIFYING PROCEDURES TO OFFICE SYSTEMS

Ian H. Witten, Bruce A. MacDonald and Saul Greenberg

Department of Computer Science, The University of Calgary

Canada

KEYWORDS

Office systems, machine learning, programming by example, generalization, inductive inference, knowledge acquisition.

ABSTRACT

This paper surveys current practice, research, and future prospects for communicating procedures to office computer systems, placing special emphasis on robustness and suitability for the casual user. Users of existing systems who have to specify procedures must generally resort to some kind of command language. Explicit forms programming languages, perhaps based on ideas of logic programming which suppress control structure, offer better prospects. In the more distant future, knowledge-based techniques utilizing models of office semantics may address the more general issues of problem-solving in the office. Programming by example is a promising method for specifying procedures but presents difficulties with editing, conditionals, iteration, variables and data structures. These can be partially overcome by using several example sequences or having users provide control information explicitly through a well-engineered interactive interface.

1   INTRODUCTION

How can end users - especially casual users without knowledge of or aptitude for conventional programming - be given the ability to specify and communicate procedures to a computer system? To the extent that they can, opportunities for system design and implementation are placed where they belong, directly in users' hands. A good domain for examining this question is office computing, where the notion of "casual user" is more palpable and there is evident need to automate procedures that would otherwise have to be executed manually [RAED85]. This paper surveys current practice, research, and future prospects for communicating procedures to office computer systems, placing special emphasis on robustness and suitability for the casual user.

In practice, users of existing systems who have to specify procedures are commonly forced to work through an intermediary who is an experienced programmer. Failing this, they generally resort to learning some kind of command language. Explicit forms programming languages, perhaps based on ideas of logic programming which suppress control structure, offer better prospects, while knowledge-based techniques which utilize a model of office semantics may provide a solution in the more distant future. Programming by example is a promising method for specifying procedures but presents difficulties with editing, conditionals, iteration, nesting, data structures and variables. These can be alleviated by using several example sequences or, possibly specifying goals, perhaps with the help of an automated assistant. Alternatively, control information may be provided explicitly by the user through a well-engineered interactive interface.

A neglected aspect of the problem of specifying procedures is the need for <u>robustness</u>. This concerns the ability of the system to deal with the vagaries of the real world by incorporating methods for handling errors, inconsistencies, environmental changes, and extraneous information; and by accommodating changes in user requirements and expectations. In examining casual-user programming systems, it is expedient to draw a distinction between

* the inherent ability of the <u>conceptual</u> system, and
* the ability of an <u>implemented</u> system,

to deal with variability. The first concerns the idea and the second the way it is implemented. The difference is important because much of the work we discuss is experimental, and implementations often lack robustness while the ideas underlying them may not.

The next section first introduces office procedures, showing how they pervade routine office work. It then describes two different user interface paradigms, direct manipulation and command languages, highlighting the shortcomings of each for casual-user procedure specification. The second section considers the possibility of grafting procedure specification ability on to other interfaces. It describes four possibilities: the use of a command language in conjunction with a direct-manipulation interface, forms-based programming, specifying procedures using logic, and knowledge-based systems. Thirdly, we introduce the idea of programming by example, and explain four different methods for accomplishing it. In each section we discuss the power of the procedure specification paradigm, as well as its robustness and suitability for the casual user.

2   OFFICE SYSTEMS AND PROCEDURE PROBLEM

2.1 Office Procedures

Routine tasks such as clearing one's desk, opening and filing mail, and sorting lists of names constitute simple office procedures. More complex jobs such as processing a purchase order are standard institutional procedures often controlled by a specially-designed form. The fields on the form show the information needed to perform the procedure, and the principal actions required. For example, a purchase order may involve financial authorization, tendering, ordering, shipping, customs and duty, consideration of import regulations, and so on. Each participating department will have its own detailed procedure for dealing with the form. For example, expected delivery date may be recorded so the appropriate action can be initiated in the event of non-arrival. Training new employees in the <u>modus operandi</u> is a recognized cost of staff turnover. Much of a newly-hired clerk's time and effort is expended in learning the vital office procedures. Specifying <u>new</u> tasks will always be important, even to fully trained office workers or sophisticated office computer systems. Whenever regulations, policies, or superiors change, new or modified procedures will arise.

If office procedures could be automated, much of the cost for teaching and executing them could be avoided. Of course, some will be just too complex. There is even controversy about the extent to which office work really does involve executing procedures. In a study of two office tasks, dealing with a missing invoice and using an unfamiliar copying machine, Suchman [SUCH85, SUCH83] found the subjects to be problem-solving. Once they discovered the solution, subjects rationalized their activity as procedures that "went wrong" in some respects. Much office work is concerned with handling exceptions to the usual routine; so much so that Suchman considers the exceptions normal and the procedures mythical! This paper is not about automating problem-solving in the office, but rather about automating the simple and standard procedures that do occur. Despite the predominance of problem-solving activity, establishing and performing routine tasks is important in offices, as the above examples show.

The simplest office procedures are fixed sequences of actions; the task is performed exactly the same on every occasion. For example, an office user might want to specify a complex sequence for logging on to a large computer from a personal computer [POUN87]. However, many office tasks will be more complex than this. For example, the procedure for admitting students to a University may revolve around several main events, such as receiving preliminary and final applications, reviewing stages, and admittance or rejection. Each individual event can trigger a complex procedure. Late applications must be dealt with; foreign students may be treated differently; notification of missing documents must be mailed, and so on [KUNI82]. Although specification of such an elaborate system is beyond the ken of the average office worker, adding or modifying smaller sub-procedures is not.

Table 1 shows the major constructs required in a system for specifying tasks. Conditionals allow different actions for different situations. Iteration permits part of a task to be repeated until a specified condition is met. Nesting embeds one control structure inside another, to many levels. For example, the Table shows one loop which is inside another. Data structures are needed for conveniently storing and accessing structured information, and might also be nested. Variables allow different items to be processed by the same procedure. Table 1 also shows a simple example procedure which employs all of these constructs. The procedure opens the electronic mail of the user and sorts items into folders by sender name. A new folder is created for each new sender. The variables used are New-Mail-Item and Sender. An if ... then construct is nested inside a for loop.

2.2 Direct Manipulation Interfaces

The most effective user interfaces to office systems allow pictorial representations of real office objects (files, folders, documents, text, diagrams, and the like) to be manipulated directly on the screen [SHNE83]. This leads naturally to learnability, robustness, and general ease of use [LEE83, WITT85]. The computer system provides a metaphor of the office environment. This makes it easy for users to execute procedures manually, step by step [SHNE83, LEE83]. Briefly, direct manipulation provides a robust interface suited to the casual user, with these advantages:

Table 1 major Constructs for specifying tasks

construct	form	example	

conditionals	if...
	then...
	else...
		if Name is "John Doe"
		   then alert manager
		   else (no action)	

iterations are loops	for, while, repeat	for all files in folder "New Reports" print the file	

nested control structure	structures within structures	for all folders
		   for all files in folder
		      print file	

data structures	structured information	*Name* *Phone* *Address* *Postal*	John Doe (403) 234-3467 4432 69 St NW E4A-1S4
variables	set of objects	let file be "letter1" let printer be "laser" (then later) print file on printer	

Example Procedure

open "Mail"
for each new mail item (New-Mail-Item)
    open New-Mail-Item
    let Sender be sender part of data structure New-Mail-Item
    if there is no folder called Sender
        then create a new folder called Sender
    copy New-Mail-Item into Sender folder
end for loop

*   users are enthusiastic
*   learning effort is reduced
*   the system is predictable
*   the interface is concrete, not abstract

and [WITT85]

*   you can always see what you are working on
*   you see the final form of your work, for example text to be printed out
*   you see all options available to you

However, current systems do not help when it comes to communicating sequences of actions [MYER86]; indeed, their very nature makes it difficult for users to specify procedures [ZLOO81]. Certainly a fixed string of operations could be recorded for playback later. However, for any procedure which involves generalizations, conditionals, controlled iteration, complex data structures, editing and debugging, direct manipulation falls apart. These are not simple operations on concrete objects. They are abstractions, which are specified to real office workers using complex natural language constructions. The manipulation is no longer <u>direct</u>.

2.3   <u>Command Language Interfaces</u>

The traditional way of specifying procedures to computer systems is by using an imperative language. Standard interactive computers implement an operating system command language in which procedures can be specified, saved in files and executed on demand. These are often clumsily defined and implemented; for example IBM JCL is renowned for its opacity. The UNIX <u>sh</u> command interface contains better facilities for procedure definition, but is still far from suitable for a casual office

user. In some ways such command languages are <u>more</u> difficult for a
casual user than modern programming languages, such as PASCAL, C and ADA,
because the details of syntax and semantics are tricky and opaque. For
example, this statement in UNIX <u>sh</u>

> cat <u>filename</u> | expand | awk `{ printf "%4d %s\n", NR, $0 }`

puts line numbers on the file <u>filename</u>.

Monolingual programming environments, which give a user the facility of
specifying command procedures in a programming language such as LISP (or
even BASIC) are more suitable, but presuppose the ability to write
programs in the conventional way. There is some debate on whether this
will ever become acceptable to the casual users (see [CUFF80] and ANDE80]
for opposing views). To program in a conventional language one needs to
be able to translate one's own knowledge of the task into a procedural
specification suitable for expression in the language. One also needs to
be able to construct, test, and debug the implementation.

Command languages provide a powerful ability to specify procedures, since
they are general purpose programming languages. However, they are
unsuitable for the casual user because of the need to learn tricky
details of computer syntax and semantics, and the difficulty of
articulating procedures explicitly. Moreover, they lack robustness in
that programs depend of technical and system characteristics.

3   ADDING PROCEDURE SPECIFICATION

3.1 <u>Adding a Command Language to Direct Manipulation</u>

Some office systems have added the ability to create procedures by
grafting linguistic commands on to a direct-manipulation interface.
However, there are clear contradictions between the two paradigms
involved. Not only do these systems fail to escape the above-noted
drawbacks to command languages, but they conflict with the basic metaphor
of direct manipulation too.

These problems will be briefly illustrated using the Xerox Star's CUSP
user programming language. This is an excellent example of a command
language designed to be used for office work in conjunction with a
direct-manipulation interface. Programs can be operated on text, icons,
table and form fields, record files, and other objects available in the
interface [HALB84]. For example, CUSP enables users to express programs
such as: [HALB84]

> If <u>Credit</u>Balance < 0 Then
>   Move The <u>Document</u> Whose Name Is "PleasePay" To The <u>Printer</u> Whose
>   Name is "Gutenburg";

Unfortunately, it departs sharply from the desktop metaphor. The user
has to learn a <u>different</u> method of operating the Star in order to specify
procedures. This is amply illustrated by the program (which, its
appearance notwithstanding, does <u>not</u> contain typographical errors)

> Store Mean[<u>Families</u>[<u>Row</u> Call It <u>Parent</u>
>   With <u>Parent</u>.LastName = "Smith"].<u>Children.Age</u> Into
> AverageSmithChild;

for computing and storing the mean age of the Smith children listed in the Families table [HALB84]. The direct-manipulation user, on the other hand, would accomplish the same task using a very different sequence of actions. He would call up the appropriate part of the table on the screen, and transfer the numbers to an iconic calculator to perform the arithmetic involved.

3.2 Specifying Procedures Using Forms

Some systems have added the ability to specify procedures by significantly extending a forms metaphor (eg OBE [ZLO081], OFS [TSIC82], FORMAL [SHU85]). Again, however, the method for procedure specification conflicts with the original interactive interface. We will discuss two examples.

The QBE - "query-by-example" - database retrieval system enables a user to type examples of relations in a database [ZLO077]. Some example entries in the query are constants, while other stand for variables that are to be retrieved. For instance a query with the variable N in two name fields of a form will return entries with names matching in those two fields. OBE, an extension of QBE, is claimed to provide "two dimensional programming" for non-programmers [ZLO081]. The user can write a program to produce a form letter from database entries, using example elements to specify variables to retrieve. Procedures can be automatically triggered when set conditions occur in the database; for instance to acknowledge new information, follow up previous letters, warn of undesirable conditions in the database, replenish inventory as stocks decrease, and so on. Queries can be combined with letters, reports and graphs which the user can program to extract the required data. Automatic triggers, important in office systems, can cause action to be taken under particular circumstances like low stock numbers. TRI(DAILY) PEN < 500 causes a daily trigger to check for the stock of pens being less than 500.

However, in reality the paradigm of OBE becomes muddled. Despite its name, it is not a programming by example system. Actions are specified explicity rather than by giving examples. The syntax is procedural and resembles that of a rudimentary conventional programming language. To execute something daily one enters EXECUTE(DAILY), and to update the sum of the expenses of a manager´s staff, Update.SUM.ALL.AMounT.

A second experimental forms system, OFS [TSIC82], has procedures with two parts, a precondition and an action. Both are specified as forms. The precondition is a request to the system to "find a form that looks like this". For example, one might specify an automatically triggered procedure for processing an item order by entering only the item name on an order form. When an order arrives, this precondition is satisfied, and an action, also specified on a form, can be executed. The procedure might fill in the order form, and do follow-up actions such as copying the form to appropriate users, filing a copy, and even mailing resulting requests for parts.

Like OBE, OFS is not really a programming-by-example system. Although preconditions and actions are specified on forms, the office worker must use special directives within its field to instruct the system. For example, consider an action form with fields for price, quantity, and total. The directive mult !price ?quantity entered in the total field directs the system to calculate its value by multiplying the updated field value of price by the original field value of quantity, and to insert it into the total field.

3.3 Specifying Procedures Using Logic

Logic programming languages enable users to specify procedures for database enquiry by stating goals rather than methods. A general control strategy embedded in the language interpreter frees users from having to consider control structure. For example, programs in the PROLOG [CLOC81] language can be specified generally, and according to its proponents, naturally, by anyone who knows ordinary predicate logic [ENNA82].

PROLOG accomplishes goal-directed inference by following a set of "rules" which constitute the program, and using a collection of facts represented in a database. The user formulates his enquiry by filling in known fields of a form-like statement, and PROLOG infers the unknown fields. Any set of fields can be left unfilled, and the system will retrieve all that match the partial specification; or all could be filled and the system will simply check whether the record is in the database. As well as retrieving records given a partial specification, PROLOG permits problems to be broken down into components through statements like

Goal is true if Subgoal$_1$ and Subgoal$_2$ and ... and Subgoal$_n$ are true.

Read declaratively, this statement about the relation between goals and subgoals rather than a specification of a procedure. However, the same statement can be interpreted procedurally, as

to execute the procedure Goal, execute procedures Subgoal$_1$ and Subgoal$_2$ and ...and Subgoal$_n$

A computation of a logic program amounts to the construction of a proof of an existentially quantified goal from axioms which are in effect the statements of the program. While this may seem a rather abstract way to view a procedure, it frees the user from thinking about the control structure of his program and allows him to concentrate on how the task can be decomposed into successively simpler subgoals.

A raw textual interface to PROLOG is certainly not well suited to the needs of the casual office user. However, the fundamental idea of a goal-based specification language, with control structure supplied automatically by the interpreter, could be disguised as a forms interface. Such a scheme has several advantages. Firstly, user and system would always have an equal opportunity to fill in any slot of any form. It has been persuasively argued that the principle that "everything that can be supplied or demanded by the machine can also be supplied or demanded by the user", is a sound guide to user interface design [RUNC86]. Secondly, forms could be "active", dynamically displaying the contents of unknown fields as the user fills in and removes values from known fields. Thirdly, PROLOG'S foundation in predicate logic may provide the well-educated casual user with familiar semantics [ENNA82]. Finally, a declarative, goal-oriented language may be more natural than the procedural paradigm of conventional programming languages or the ad hoc, action-oriented paradigm of the forms languages described earlier.

There are several unresolved questions in the use of logic programming to enable users to specify procedures for database enquiry. Implementations of logic programming include some procedural constructs which undermine the clean declarative semantics. Debugging normally requires a procedural approach too. Nevertheless, logic programming does seem to offer potential for specifying certain types of procedures using goals rather than methods.

3.4 Knowledge Based Systems

Outside the office, research has shown that "knowledge bases" can sometimes effectively support inference and problem-solving [HAYE83]. Rather than having to specify a procedure in response to a new requirement, we may simply be able to consult a knowledge-based system designed for the problem area. This would allow users to accomplish procedures through informal natural-language descriptions. We anticipate the eventual emergence of knowledge-based systems which support the specification of office procedures. However, existing expert systems are confined to narrow, well-defined domains, while office work is varied, wide-ranging, and open-ended. A survey of sixty odd expert systems lists no office-related ones [GEVA83]

Systems which embody detailed semantic models of certain areas of office activity have been constructed for some highly constrained domains. For example, Barber [BARB83] proposes to support office work with a knowledge-based system. However, he views office work as problem-solving and is therefore not concerned with specifying procedures. While certainly conceding that problem-solving is an essential component of office activity, we nevertheless expect many problems to be more easily solved by specifying procedures than by having to pose then correctly to a problem-solver. Several examples were given earlier.

Much of the knowledge needed for accomplishing office procedures is also needed to understand natural language questions. For example, Kaczmarek et al [KACZ83] describe an experimental natural language interface for interactive computer services such as electronic mail, personal calendar, word processing, and so on. The interface is customized to a particular set of services, and might include knowledge that

* a meeting can have an owner, some participants, a time interval, and so on
* an individual's schedule is composed of a sequence of meetings
* forwarding is an operation valid for messages but not meetings.

A vast collection of such facts would be needed by an "intelligent assistant" which could learn, understand and use office procedures, and significant research is required before we can understand how to organize this kind of detailed knowledge.

4   PROGRAMMING BY EXAMPLE

A promising method of communicating procedures is programming "by example". The user performs an example of the required procedure, and the system remembers it for later repetition. Simple examples include text editors that remember a sequence of user keystrokes, and industrial robots that can be "programmed" by leading them manually. However, such systems are limited since they can only repeat a fixed sequence. To be more useful programming by example must also permit the sequence to be edited, conditional, iteration and recursive nested control constructs to be added, data structures to be formed, and variables to replace certain objects in the example sequence. Table 1 illustrates these constructs.

Four distinct ways have been proposed to accomplish these requirements:

* inference from several example sequences [WITT81, GAIN76, AND84a]

484

* generalization from example sequences based on specific knowledge
  of the problem domain (analogously to existing methods for
  concept learning [MITC82, SAMM83, SAMM86] and robot programming
  [AND84b, AND84C])
* inference from input and output without the intervening trace
  [NIX83, NIX84]
* explicit elaboration of the example sequence by the casual user
  [SMIT75, HALB81, HALB84].

In each case the user gives one or more examples and the system is
expected to infer a procedure for performing the task. To be useful, the
procedure must work correctly not only for the original examples but in
other situations too. In this sense the inference is inductive since a
general conclusion must be derived from individual cases. The examples
must be generalized. Like any inference, such a procedure may be
incorrect in that it fails in some situations. It is up to the user to
give suitable examples in the right way.

A skilled teacher will select illuminating examples himself and thereby
simplify the learner's task. The benefits of carefully constructed
examples were appreciated in the earliest research efforts in learning.
Winston [WINS75] showed how "near misses" - constructs that differ in
just one crucial respect from examples of a concept being taught - could
radically diminish the search required for generalization. Confident
that its teacher is selecting examples helpfully, a learning system can
assume that any difference between an example being shown and its nascent
procedure is a critical feature.

Recently, Van Lehn [LEHN83] has formalized this notion of a sympathetic
teacher in terms of what he calls "felicity conditions", constraints
imposed on or satisfied by a teacher that make learning better than from
random examples. One obvious condition is that the teacher should not
(intentionally or unintentionally) mislead the student. Another is that
the examples given should correctly represent the procedure. If the
absence of something is important, the teacher should point it out
explicitly. For example, if the absence of a particular document is
crucial to an office procedure, the user should always check for it when
performing examples of the procedure. More generally, the teacher should
show all work and avoid glossing over intermediate results. Examples
should not by coincidence include features that might mislead the
learner: one should not illustrate a procedure to change the recorded
name of newly married women, by using a woman whose original family name
happens to coincide with her husband's; one should not illustrate the
geometric concept of isosceles triangles with ones that happen to be
congruent. Finally, the teacher should introduce one essential new
feature per lesson and try not to teach multiple differences at once - a
similar condition to Winston's "near miss" approach.

But how easy it is for an office worker to provide good examples to a
learning system? Office workers are not trained teachers. When systems
expect to be taught through strict felicity conditions, the user requires
not only a deep understanding of the concept, but must be capable of
selecting effective examples. Second, in practice learning systems
requiring more than a single example demand "perfect" ones - they cannot
infer effectively from the (typically) noisy traces provided. Third,
there is a question of confidence - when does the user feel he can trust
the inferred program? Finally, the notion of "ease of use" may mislead
the user into expectations that cannot be delivered (THIM86].

The general problem of inducing procedures from examples is rather
intractable. Inference of rules from examples has long been studied, is

in general very difficult, and requires either exploration of vast search
spaces or the cooperation of the user in augmenting examples with more
general control information. Despite these difficulties, however,
programming by example fits naturally into the paradigm of direct
manipulation in office systems. Indeed, it is hard to see how the
potential benefits of direct manipulation can be fully realized in the
absence of a method for showing the system how to do routine procedures.
Following an initial introduction to the easy problem of specifying
straight sequences of actions by examples, we report four ways which have
been proposed for demonstrating more complex tasks. The systems
described are limited and experimental, but nevertheless instructive.
Although not all are confined to examples of office procedures, their
techniques could be applied to offices in the future.

4.1 Macro Operations

Programming by example has long been used for specifying procedures that
are simply sequences or "macros" of elementary operations. No inference
is required since the example is the procedure. For instance, the method
of leading industrial robots "by the hand" is a popular way of specifying
a movement sequence to a robot [ALLA79, MACD84]. Spray-painting robots
are taught by being led through the painting sequence, the operator
actually painting a sample object as he goes [VACC82, HAU74a, HAU74b,
PROD82, INDU82]. The robot can then repeat the sequence, painting
another object, which must be in the same position and orientation. Even
though the technique can capture only fixed sequences, it overcomes the
difficulty of having to specify continuous painting movements in the six
dimensions of robot hand position and orientation.

In another domain, the use of "start-remembering", "stop-remembering",
and "do-it" commands [GOSL81] enable a text editor to learn editing
sequences by example. Such sequences can be named and filed for later
use. One sequence can invoke another, allowing a complex hierarchy of
nested sequences to be specified. However, such constructs as iteration,
conditionals, variables and data structures are not accommodated. A
practical difficulty with having a special mode - remembering mode - for
recording a sequence is that one frequently has already started the
sequence before deciding to record it, and so must retrace one's steps
and begin again. Also, some mechanism should be available to the user
for 'removing errors as they occur or for editing them out afterwards.
Otherwise, the error will remain in the trace, possibly rendering it
useless.

To specify procedures more complex than a fixed sequence, it is not
enough to record just one example. There are two ways to view the
problem. On the one hand, we might consider that to create such
procedures, variables, conditional and iterative constructs, and perhaps
data structures, are required. Moreover, the resulting structure should
be editable. On the other, we might regard the given sequence as an
example of performance which is to be generalized into the desired
procedure. The procedure might still contain variables, data structures,
conditionals, iteration and nesting, since these are all themselves
generalizations of elements in the example.

4.2 Inference From Traces

Practical systems for inferring procedures from example traces of their
execution lie somewhere between two extremes. One pole involves no
knowledge of the semantic domain within which procedures are constructed,
while the other relies on domain knowledge to guide generalization of the
examples. And while one might regard the two poles as similar in

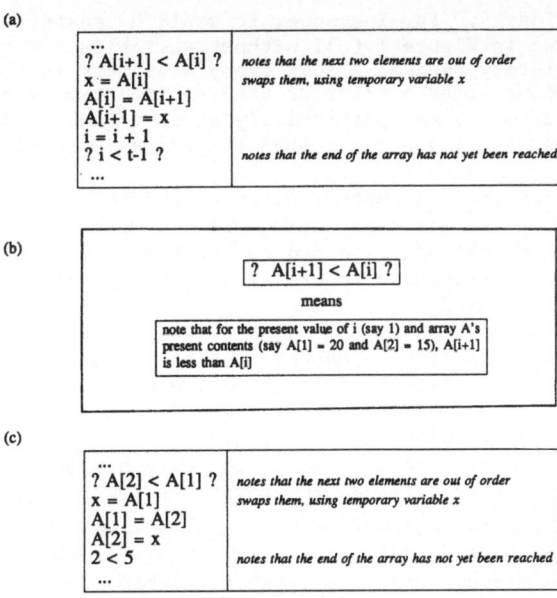

Figure 1 programming by Example . sorting

principle, differing only in the amount of domain knowledge available, in
practice different techniques are employed. This section introduces
three systems with little domain knowledge.

* inference of a sorting procedure
* a self-programming calculator
* learning to "count in the head", or internalizing numerical
  manipulation;

and contains a more extended discussion of one with substantial domain
knowledge:

* acquiring robot procedures from examples.

INFERENCE OF A SORTING PROCEDURE. Programming by example can be trivial
if the examples are presented in the right way. Gaines [GAIN76] showed
how a program to sort a list of numbers can be inferred from a trace of
execution on a single example. The trace is expressed in a programming
language notation. The fragment of Figure 1(a) shows how a particular
five element array A can be sorted using a bubble sort in 86 statements,
six of which are reproduced. Figure 1(b) explains how conditionals are
included by noting the condition that held at the time.

Due to the use of variables, many statements are repeated in the trace.
The entire 86 statements include only 15 different ones, six of which
appear in the Figure. When these 15 statements are connected into a
directed graph according to their position in the trace, a correct and
almost complete flowchart for a bubble sort appears! Only a link
necessary for sorting an empty array is missing, and an example with the
empty array completes the procedure.

While this is an impressive demonstration that programming by example is
possible, it does place a heavy burden of the user. He must choose

variables judiciously. For instance, it would be easier to give traces in the form shown in Figure 1 (c), without variables. Then the method would fail completely because almost every statement in the trace would be different. Generating a trace of the required type for a bubble sort is tedious and error-prone, particularly since variables must be incorporated and mentally updated when the trace is compiled.

The system does assimilate control constructs from examples. Still, the user must make all the tests explicit. If ... then ...else is performed by "? ... ?" statements which record the results of conditional tests in the example trace. Branching occurs naturally from this once the directed graph is formed.

SELF-PROGRAMMING CALCULATOR. Another project studied the inference of iterative computations from examples executed on an electronic calculator [WITT81]. People who use interactive computers regularly know that there are many situations in which it is difficult to decide whether to do a minor, but repetitive, task by hand or to write a program to accomplish it. Simple, repetitive, arithmetic operations frequently present this quandary. For example, one may wish to plot $y = xe^{1-x}$ for a dozen or so values of x; should it be done on a hand calculator or by writing a BASIC program? The self-programming calculator watched the keystrokes made by a person calculating $.1e^{1-.1}$ and then $.2e^{1-.2}$, and inferred the sequence by halfway through the second iteration. Figure 2 illustrates this example. Once it has inferred the sequence, the calculator behaves as though it had explicitly programmed for the job, pausing for input of x and then immediately calculating the corresponding value of y.

The generalization scheme is simple but effective. The calculator must infer that .1 typed by the user is an input variable, but that the 1 in the exponent is not. It does so by waiting for a second confirmation of a constant number before accepting it as part of the predictable sequence. Thus the user needs to enter the "1" in xe^{1-x} twice before the system will incorporate it as a constant into its stored procedure. However, the problem is not so easily solved in general. For example, if the user had entered the sequence given in Figure 2(b), the calculator would never have realized that the two occurrences of x were the same parameter.

The calculator modelled did not have conditionals, so these were not inferred. Only the outer, infinite iteration was inferred. Also the calculator does not enable the sequence to be edited, and has no facility for such things as single-stepping through the taught program. Although these appear to be implementation considerations, they may also have implications at the conceptual level.

INTERNALIZING NUMERICAL MANIPULATION. A scheme has been described which learns to count with the aid of an external counter [AND84a]. It can push buttons to clock over the digits of a three-digit counter, then when the counter is removed it can count "in its head", thus internalizing the externally supported counting. The system's teacher takes it action by action through an example sequence. As the interaction proceeds, the system gradually makes more and more decisions for itself, eventually being able to count internally. The learning sequences are too long to reproduce here. The summary of Figure 3 only shows crucial events in a trace fragment; less significant events intervene between all those shown. Actions are for counting "out loud", or for pushing buttons on the counter. The values of counter digits are inputs to the system.

Figure 3(a) shows the teaching of a few counting combinations, using the counters. Of the vast number of possible combinations, only enough are

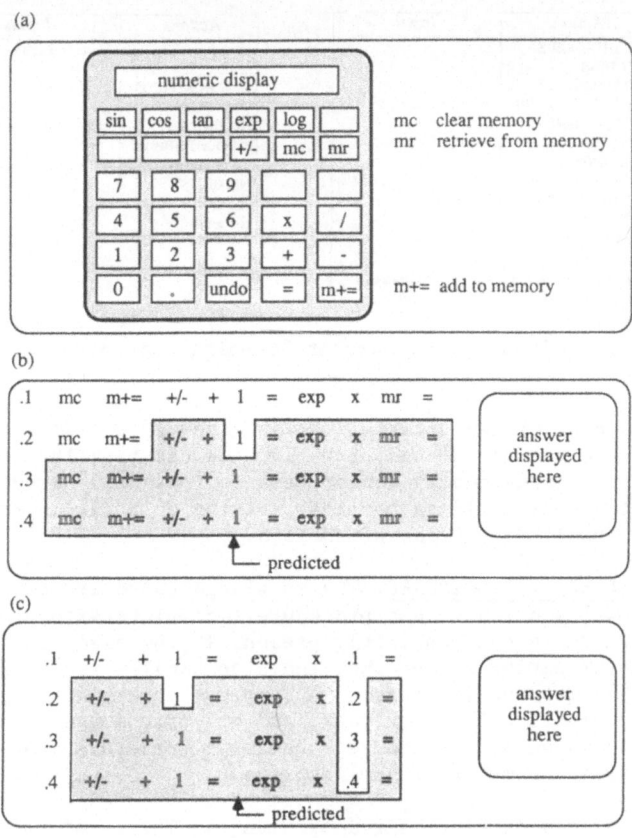

Figure 2 Self programming calculator

taught to illustrate digit incrementing, names of digits and transfer of
carries. The system is taught to count from zero using a counter with
three digits, and a button for incrementing each digit. Teaching is done
in a cycle of three main steps:

* output current count
* push an increment button on the counter
* see new count digit.

On being presented with a stimulus for hundreds, tens or units –
representing a one, ten or one hundred value monetary note – the system
is able to count without the aid of the counters, by "imagining" the
counters "in its head" (Figure 3(b)).

The system remembers multiple fixed length sequences of events - a
multiple context - from the example counting sequence. Later it uses
these remembered sequences to predict and perform actions for counting
monetary values.

We have now seen three systems which infer procedures from traces using
little domain knowledge. They vary widely in suitability for the casual
user. The self-programming calculator is easiest to use, while the
others require special knowledge of the user when specifying a procedure.
The sorting system required the user to use variables explicitly and
indicate conditional tests in trace fragments. The counting system
requires the user to give all actions in the fragment traces, including
some required for the internal operation of the learning system that are

Action	Input
NO HUNDREDS	-
NO TENS	
NO UNITS	-
push units button	see units digit "1"
NO HUNDREDS	-
NO TENS	
ONE UNIT	-
push units button	see units digit "2"
NO HUNDREDS	-
NO TENS	
TWO UNITS	-
...	

(the teaching continues on to teach other combinations, but it is not necessary to teach every one possible)

(b)

Actions	Inputs
(the count is presently at 120)	
...	
ONE HUNDREDS	-
TWO TENS	-
NO UNITS	see hundred unit note
TWO HUNDREDS	-
TWO TENS	-
NO UNITS	-
...	
(and so on)	

Figure 3 Summary of learning suquences

not obviously part of the external task. Although the implementations themselves are experimental and probably somewhat fragile, we regard all three systems as conceptually robust because they deal directly with traces from the real world rather than relying on built-in knowledge and its inherent fragility in real situations.

ACQUISITION OF ROBOT PROCEDURES. The knowledge-based system NODDY [AND84B, AND84c] acquires robot procedures, complete with control information which is not explicitly present in the examples. It copes with problems of action sequencing, and also handles real numbers representing angles and distances. It employs an explicit, pre-programmed, generalization hierarchy, and pre-programmed information on about 30 basic mathematical and set-theoretic operators that may be combined to create complex generalizations.

Examples are traces of the desired procedure. The first trace is taken to be the initial version of the procedure. As further traces are seen they are merged with the nascent procedure, generalizing it in various ways. The system cannot reconsider generalizations it has made in the current version of the procedure, and therefore adopts a conservative policy of requiring considerable evidence before generalizing. The elements that make up the traces are called "descriptors".

The principle problem is to meld two example traces of execution of a procedure into one augmented state-transition representation that encompasses them both. In the first stage of generalization, if two descriptors are identical and unique within each example trace, they are assumed to emanate from the same state. In particular each trace begins with a start descriptor which forces the initial states of the two sequences to be merged, and ends with stop which merges final states. This builds one state model from the two traces. However the parts corresponding to each still remain largely separate, since descriptors are rarely identical (apart from start and stop). The second stage of generalization examines states that are different but whose predecessor states are the same, or whose successor states are the same, and attempts to unify the descriptors associated with each. If they can be unified, then the states are coalesced. Unification is done through the generalization hierarchy, and succeeds if the two descriptors have a common generalization. Since two states may be unified only if their successors or predecessors have been unified, the process proceeds from states matched at the first stage, propagating both backward and forward. Finally, a third stage examines states that are different but whose predecessors and successors are the same, and again attempts to unify the descriptors but this time with a more liberal unification procedure. This uses the same generalization hierarchy as before, but involves synthesizing functions which unify parameters of the descriptors.

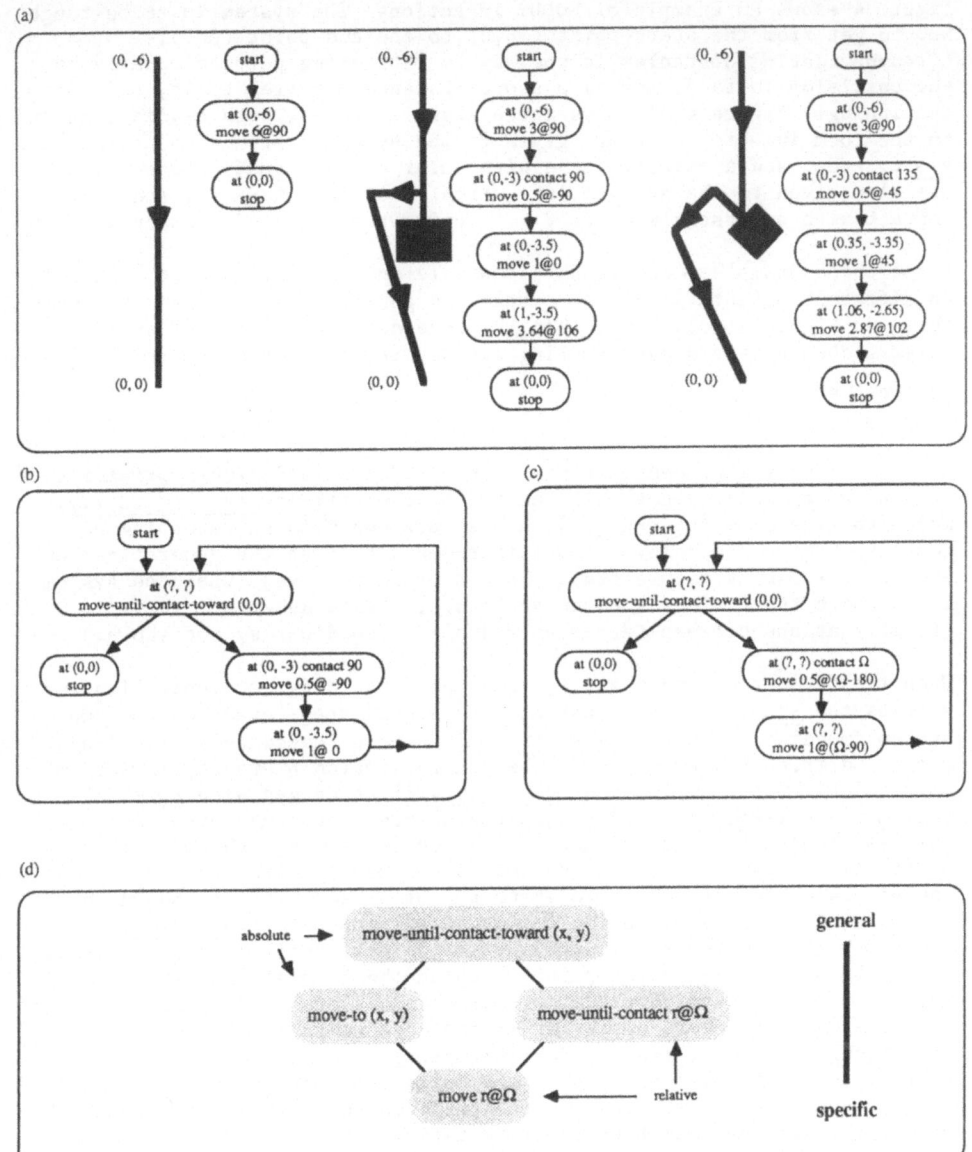

Figure 4 Example of NODDY system

Synthesis is accomplished by searching a function space, possibly using numbers which have been "mentioned" in nearby descriptors as components of the function. This introduces variables into the state-transition representation, effectively creating a form of augmented state-transition network [WOOD70]. It is a very expensive process in in terms of search time, and is only undertaken when there is strong evidence (identical predecessor and successor states) that the descriptors match[+].

[+] In fact, the procedure does not require both predecessor states to be identical, but is applied to parallel chains of states that begin and end in the same state and, if successful, merges corresponding members of the chains. Consequently the merging is only done if both predecessor and successor states end up being identical.

Figure 4 shows an example of NODDY in action. The system is to be taught how to get from the start point (-6,0) to the end point (0,0), circumnavigating obstacles in the way by retreating perpendicularly to the collision surface, moving a short distance parallel to it, and then continuing. Figure 4(a) shows three example traces, both as diagrams and in the form in which they are given to the system. Primitive actions are start, stop, and a relative move with polar coordinates. Observations are also given to the system: its current position at (x,y), and any contact with an obstacle contact (being the angle of contact). From

these three examples, one with no obstacle and two with single obstacles in different orientations, the system can generate the desired procedure shown in Figure 4 (c). Note that the procedure is capable of avoiding several obstacles and even feeling its way round a large obstacle of any

(convex) shape‡.

Inspection of the procedure shows that it uses an additional primitive not in the example traces. The action moves-until-contact-toward(x,y) moves towards a point specified in absolute coordinates, stopping on contact with an obstacle. It was introduced through the generalization hierarchy shown if Figure 4(d). This hierarchy conveys what the system knows about the various actions available. (Also known are the transformations between Cartesian and polar coordinates, not shown.)

When the first two traces are merged, the first stage of generalization unifies the start and stop states. The second stage examines the two states immediately following start, and the two immediately preceding stop, and tries to merge them. The generalization hierarchy is used at this point. For example, the move 6@90 will be merged with move 3@90 into move-until-contact 6@90 since the shorter move ends with contact. The result of this stage of generalization is to merge the middle state of the first trace with both the second and penultimate state of the second trace, forming a single state out of three. This is shown in Figure 4(b) as the state at(?,?); move-until-contact-toward(0,0), in other words, from anywhere, move toward the goal until contact is made. As can be seen, this is the point at which the loop in the procedure appears. When the third trace is considered, state merging is prevented by different parameters appearing in the move actions. However, there are strong structural reasons for attempting to merge corresponding states, and so NODDY embarks upon the third stage of generalization, namely functional induction. It rationalizes the difference between the move parameters because they are functions of the contact angle already observed. This produces the final procedure.

NODDY has an inherent robustness in requiring considerable justification for its generalizations. However, once an incorrect generalization is made the mistake cannot be corrected. Still, NODDY is yet an experimental system.

A problem closely related to programming procedures by example is "concept learning"; for example learning the concept of a royal flush poker hand. In fact the distinction between procedure and concepts is blurred, since descriptions can be executed by modern programming languages such as PROLOG [WITT87]. Established theoretical results for identifying languages show that there is no alternative to searching the space of candidate descriptions [GOLD67, ANG183, WITT87]. In general this makes acquiring procedures from examples intractable, because of the huge spaces that would need to be searched. However, practical systems

‡ NODDY can also negotiate some concave objects.

provide methods for limiting the search. Andreae's [AND84b, AND84c] system effectively uses built-in knowledge and the requirement for justification to limit this search. The version space method stores the finite upper and lower lattice edges of the plausible generalizations set, attempting to merge the two as examples are presented [MITC82]. Thus it enables a search of a finitely deep, lattice of generalizations [WITT87]. MARVIN [SAMM83, SAMM86] synthesizes general purpose computer programs from examples, requiring the teacher to give considerable guidance about what already known procedures might be used in the new one, thus drastically limiting the search. Witten and MacDonald [WITT87] investigate the practical and fundamental issues of concept learning. While holding great promise for the future, concept learning is not yet a mature technology suitable for practicing knowledge engineers or office system users.

4.3 Inference From Input and Output

All the above systems for programming by example attempt to generalize the user's action sequences into procedures. The user's actions in each case are a single sequence, a "trace" of an execution of the desired procedure. But inference need not use traces; instead it could be based solely on the initial and final states exhibited in the examples. One might say that the user shows the system what to do rather than how to do it.

The Editing by Example system of Nix [NIX83], embedded within a screen editor, allows users to exemplify a text transformation. The system then attempts to synthesize a procedure for selecting other parts of the file which contain "similar" text and performing the transformation on them too. If only one example is specified, the system will seek a literal match with the input elsewhere in the file and simply replace it. However, other examples serve to show which parts of the text are "constant" and which may vary. A template is constructed which

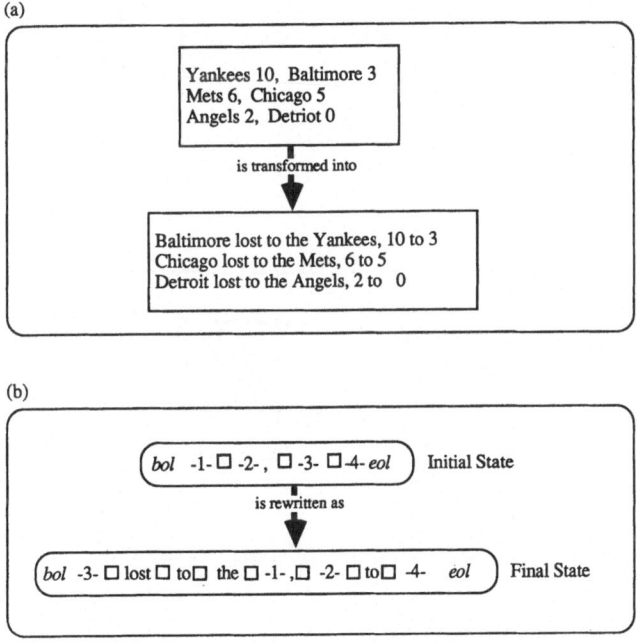

Figure 5 Example of Gap grammer

(a)

Select Report
Move Report to Reports-Folder

(b)

Action	Generalization
start recording	
select *Letters*	ask for a similar object
opent *Letters*	
select *To-Smith*	same place
movet	
set down cursor on the desktop	
closet *Letters*	
stop recording	

†These generic system actions are selected by function keys

(c)

Define A to be the icon asked for by "Select a Folder, then resume.";
Open A;
Define B to be the icon in row 1 of A;
Move B to the Desktop;
Close A;

(d)

same name
same place
ask for a similar object

Figure 6 asking users to Generalise

distinguishes constant and variable parts, and an editing transformation is built which re-arranges the variable parts appropriately. The transformation is represented as a "gap grammar", a set of grammatical rules in which both gaps and strings appear. Figure 5(a) shows sample input and output texts, while (b) gives a gap program which implements the transformation and could be inferred from the examples.

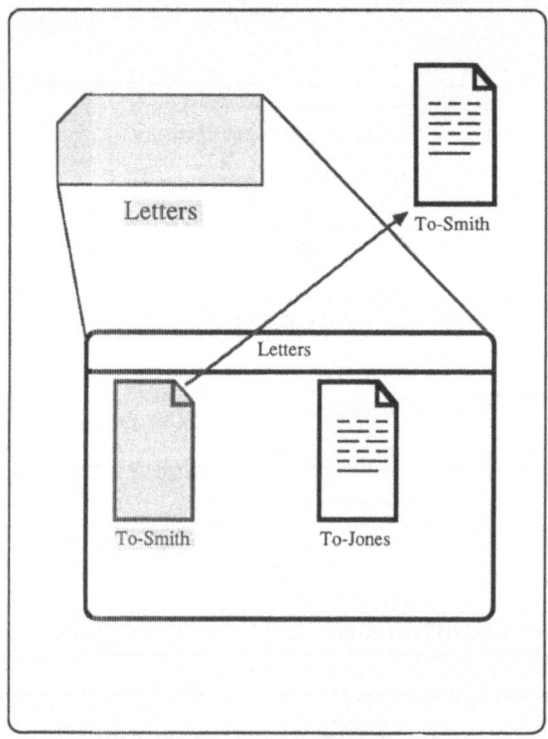

Figure 7 Screen layout for example from fig. 6

The scheme is interesting in that input/output pairs are used to exemplify a procedure. Information about <u>how</u> the user performs the transformation is discarded. While it seems rather rash to jettison potentially useful information, Nix notes that any reasonably rich editor will offer many ways for performing any given job. For example, a user might search for a string visually and move the cursor to it, or use a search command. Moreover, users make errors and repair them as they go, perhaps accidently deleting text and retyping it. Such operations should not be faithfully repeated when the procedure is executed! Analyzing traces would be virtually impossible if users were to define new commands in an extensible editor. Nix concludes that little is lost in discarding such unreliable information.

This may be so in an environment like an editor, where inputs and outputs are well defined. However, the argument is unlikely to apply in general. In ill-defined environments it may well be hopeless to attempt to infer procedures just from input and output. At the very least, traces give clues as to the sequence the procedure might follow.

4.4 Improved Explicit Methods

An experimental "programming by example" interface has been constructed for the Xerox Star office workstation which operates according to the direct manipulation paradigm [HALB81, HALB84]. First, a method for recording sequences of actions were established, with commands for:

* start-remembering
* stop-remembering
* do-it,

similar to the robot and text editor methods described above. Actions were recorded at a level of abstraction which matches the user's conceptualization, as illustrated in Figure 6. Part (a) shows a simple sequence for moving a file to another folder. Note the level of abstraction in "select Report" rather than "move the cursor to point (260,410)".

When an icon is selected on the screen, it is necessary to disambiguate the mode of reference. The significance for the user may be in the icon's name or its position; alternatively there may be no significance in that particular selection (for instance, when iterating through all icons). Which choice is made will radically affect future executions of the procedure. This is the problem of generalization: how does a system infer general descriptions given only some examples? The self-programming calculator system resolved the question by waiting until it had seen a couple of iterations and inferring that items that were changed were input. A similar but more sophisticated approach is taken by Mitchell [MITC82], who assumes a hierarchy for generalization of items, rather than the calculator's "constant-or-variable" dichotomy. However, in the office context this would require a strong semantic model.

Instead, one can ask users to indicate explicitly how to generalize example icons, an approach pioneered originally by Smith [SMIT75]. Halbert's first system [HALB81] had users select the generalization from a pop-up menu. To open a folder and extract the first item, putting it on the desktop and closing the folder, a user might perform the steps shown in Figure 6(b). After each selection he would indicate how to generalize the icon using the choices shown in (d). For example, "same place" after "select <u>To-Smith</u>" indicates that the program should choose whatever is in that position on the screen. The procedure formed is shown in CUSP notation in (c), while Figure 7 indicates what the screen might look like when the initial example has finished. Unfortunately it is all too easy to forget to generalize an item while recording, so [HALB84] had users specify this at the end of the example instead. Users manipulated the program itself, using an interface of icons, menus for generalization and iteration, and so on. For example, when recording the sequence of Figure 6(b), the user would omit the lines "ask for a similar object" and "same place". When he had finished he would be prompted to select a generalization from Figure 6(d) for each item involved (ie Letters and To-Smith). Halbert's design change reflects his belief that it is hard to denote programming constructs when tracing through an example, but easy to do so afterwards. Whereas CUSP is hard to write, he considers it easy to edit.

Both Halbet's systems represent a considerable improvement over other explicit methods such as command languages. However, they do not avoid the difficulty some users will have in articulating algorithms for complex procedures.

Two systems have recently appeared for programming by example on personal computers: the TEMPO system (Affinity Microsystems Ltd) and AUTOMATOR [POUN87]. Both have limited ability for the casual user to specify control and data structures, sacrificing power for ease of use. TEMPO works within a direct-manipulation interface. The user selects branches and loops explicitly, but conditions are restricted to simple textual comparisons; Figure 8 shows an example. AUTOMATOR is more powerful. It incorporates a general-purpose command language, and thus moves away from the programming by example paradigm. Still, it is claimed that a casual user can easily teach the system such tasks as logging on to a large computer, awaiting a response, retrieving mail, and so on.

5   CONCLUSION

Table 2 summarizes the issues raised by our study of current and future prospects for casual-user specification of office procedures. The most effective user interfaces represent real office objects iconically and allow users to manipulate them directly on the screen. However, the direct-manipulation metaphor - at least as presently conceived - does not help when it comes to communicating procedures. Command language systems and monolingual programming environments permit procedures to be specified, but are unsuited to casual users. Even custom-designed command languages such as CUSP fall far short of the ideal for a casual-user interface. Forms-based systems which revolve around a database provide an alternative to icon-oriented systems, and forms programming languages have been defined and implemented. Again, however, these seem to reduce to primitive command languages, lightly disguised. The root problem is that procedural programming in either icon or forms-based systems conflicts with the basic metaphor of the interface. There is some hope that logic programming techniques might be usable within a casual-user forms interface, enabling users to specify procedures for database enquiry by stating goals rather than methods. Another possibility is that knowledge-based systems may eventually allow users to specify some office procedures informally through natural-language descriptions.

A promising method of communicating procedures is programming "by example". To be useful programming by example must permit the specification of conditionals, iteration, nested structures, variables, data structures and editing. Four distinct ways have been proposed to

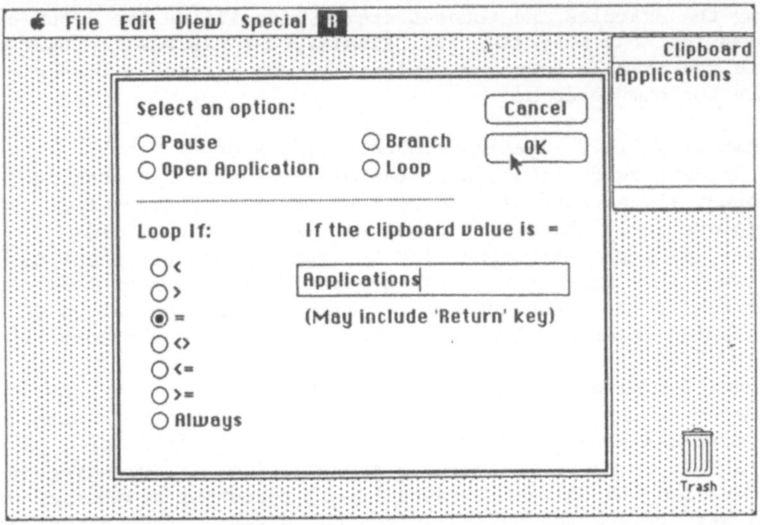

Tempo is recording user actions in the direct manipulation interface
to the Apple MacIntosh. The user has explicitly selected the option
"Loop If", and selected "=" as the test between the clipboard
contents and the text "Applications". The clipboard is shown at top
right with that same text in it. So in this case the loop would
continue.

Figure 8 Example of "Tempo"

accomplish these requirements, and each has been exemplified by a
description of one or more experimental systems. The basic problem is
that of <u>generalization</u>: an example does not by itself provide enough
information to unambiguously define the procedure. One way of
generalizing is to make inferences from several example sequences.
Another is to use specific pre-programmed knowledge of the problem
domain. A third is to discard the sequence of steps involved in

Table 2 Summary of systems

Method	Robustness	Suitability for the casual user	Procedure specification	Systems
Direct Manipulation	good	excellent	no	Macintosh, Star
Command Languages	no (idea) yes (implementation)	no	powerful	Unix sh, IBM JCL, BASIC, Lisp, Pascal, Ada, ...
Forms	good	good in limited domains	muddled	QBE, OBE, OFS, Prolog
Knowledge-based	experimental	experimental	pose problem in narrow domain	Barber, Kaczmarek
PBE† — sequences	no	good	limited	Emacs, industrial robots
PBE — traces with little domain knowledge	good (has all information recorded in traces)	experimental	good	Gaines, Witten, J.Andreae
PBE — traces with domain knowledge	experimental	experimental	limited to narrow domains	P.Andreae
PBE — from input/output	yes	yes	limited to well-defined domains such as text transformation	Nix
PBE — explicit	good	yes, so long as the procedure does not become complex	good	Halbert

† PBE stands for Programming-by-example

executing the examples and concentrate on formalizing the input-output transformation that they exhibit. Finally, one can ask the user to elaborate the example sequence explicitly, and provide a convenient interface for him to do so.

The column of Table 2 labelled "robustness" is of particular interest. Systems which provide feedback to the user directly and unambiguously are quite robust since users will seize the opportunity to correct any errors of interpretation. These include direct manipulation, forms interfaces,and explicit programming by example. In all these cases users can see what they are doing. This contrasts with command languages, which present great opportunities for misunderstanding, although in practice human interface technology has developed to the point where the dangers
can be anticipated and defused (by such techniques as alert messages and undo commands). Programming by example with only non-branching sequences lacks robustness because small changes in the definition of a problem can easily take it outside the system's capabilities. Programming by example with traces has the potential to be highly robust by dispensing with any a priori assumptions and making inferences directly from actual data. Moreover such systems typically retain almost all the information in examples they have seen, so conclusions can always be reconsidered. Knowledge-based systems, on the other hand, are likely to lack robustness at least until knowledge bases are much larger than they tend to be at present.

Although there are no easy solutions to the problem of end-user definition of office procedures, programming by example - with either explicit or implicit generalization - appears to have considerable potential in the near future.

6   ACKNOWLEDGEMENTS

This work is supported by the Natural Science and Engineering Research Council of Canada. David Pauli made some useful observations about NODDY and concave objects.

7   REFERENCES

[ALLA79] Allan, R. (1979) "Busy Robots Spur Productivity" IEEE Spectrum, 16 (9) 31-6.

[ANDE80] Anderson, B. (1980) "Programming in the home of the future" Int J Man-Machine Studies, 12 (4) 341-365, May.

[AND84a] Andreae, J.H. (1984) "Numbers in the head" 5-28, Man-Machine Studies Progress Report UC-DSE/24, Department of Electrical and Electronic Engineering, University of Canterbury, Christchurch, New Zealand.

[AND84b] Andreae, P.M. (1984) "Constraint limited generalization: acquiring procedures from examples" Proc American Association on Artificial Intelligence, Austin, TX, August.

[AND84c] Andreae, P.M. (1984) "Justified generalization: acquiring procedures from examples" PhD Thesis, Department of Electrical and Computer Science, MIT.

[ANG183] Angluin, D. and Smith, C.H. (1983) "Inductive Inference: Theory and Methods" Computing Surveys,15 (3) 237-269, September.

[BARB83] Barber, G.R. (1983) "Supporting organizational problem solving with a workstation" ACM Trans Office Information Systems, 1(1) 45-67, January.

[CLOC81] Clocksin, W.F. and Mellish, C.S. (1981) Programming in Prolog. Springer-Verlag, Berlin.

[CUFF80] Cuff, R.N. (1980) "On casual users" Int J Man-Machine Studies, 12, 163-187.

[ENNA82] ENNALS, R. (1982) "Teaching logic as a computer language in schools" February.

[GAIN76] Gaines, B.R. (1976) "Behaviour/structure transformations under uncertainty" Int J Man-Machine Studies, 8, 337-365.

[GEVA83] Gevarter, W.B. (1983) "Expert systems: limited but powerful" IEEE Spectrum, 39-45, August.

[GOLD67] Gold, E.M. (1967) "Language identification in the limit" Information and control, 10, 447-474.

[GOSL81] Gosling, J.A. (1981) Unix Emacs manual. Carnegie-Mellon University.

[HALB81] Halbert, D.C. (1981) "An example of programming by example" Technical Report, Xerox Office Products Division. Palo Alto, California.

[HALB84] Halbert, D.C. (1984) "Programming by example" Technical report, Xerox Office Products Division, Palo Alto, California, December.

[HAU74a] Haugan K.M. (1974) "Spray Painting Robots: Advanced Paint Shop Automation" The Industrial Robot, 270-2, December.

[HAU74b] Haugan, K.M. and Jarvis, D.E. (1974) "Electronically Controlled for Spray Gun Applications" The Industrial Robot, 119-21, March.

[HAYE83] Hayes-Roth, F., Waterman, D.A., and Lenat, D.B. (1983) Building expert systems. Addison-Wesley, Reading. Mass., (editors).

[INDU82] (1982) "New Products from Trallfa" Industrial Robot, The, 78, June.

[KACZ83] Kaczmarek, T., Mark, W., and Sondheimer, N. (1983) :"The Consul/CUE interface: an integrated interactive environment" Proc ACM CHI 83 Human factors in Computing Systems, 98,102, Boston, December 12-15.

[KUNI82] Kunin, J.S. (1982) "Analysis and specification of office procedures" PhD Thesis, Department of Electrical Engineering and Computer Science, MIT, February.

[LEE83] Lee, A and Lochovsky, F.H. (1983) "Enhancing the usability of an office information system through direct manipulation" Proc ACM CHI 83 Human Factors in Computing System, 130-134, Boston, December 12-15.

[LEHN83] Van Lehn, K. (1983) "Felicity conditions for human skill acquisition: validating an AI-based theory." Research Report CIS-21, Xerox PARC, Palo Alto, November.

[MACD84] MacDonald, B.A. (1984) "Designing Teachable Robots" PhD thesis, Canterbury University, Christchurch, New Zealand.

[MITC82] Mitchell, T.M. (1982) "Generalization as search" Artificial Intelligence, 18, 203-226.

[MYER86] Myers, B.A. (1986) "Visual programming, programming by example, and program visualization: a taxonomy" Proc ACM CHI 86 Human Factors in Computing Systems, 59-66, Boston, MA, April 13-17.

[NIX83] Nix, R. (1983) "Editing by example" PhD Dissertation, Computer Science Department, Yale University, New Haven, CT.

[NIX84] Nix, R. (1984) "Editing by example" Proc 11th ACM Symposium on Principles of Programming Languages, 186-195, Salt Lake City, Utah.

[POUN87] Pountain, D. (1987) "The Software Robot" Byte January, 383-390.

[PROD92] (1982) "Painting robots Halve Cycle Times for Subcontractor" Production Engineer, The, 50-51, May.

[RAED85] Raeder, G. (1985) "A survey of current graphical programming techniques" IEEE Computer, 18 (8) 11-25.

[RUNC86] Runciman, C. and Thimbleby, H. (1986) "Equal opportunity interactive systems" Report, Computer Science Department, University of York, York.

[SAMM83] Sammut, C. and Banerji, R. (1983) "Hierarchical memories: an aid to concept learning" Proc International Machine Learning Workshop, 74-80, Allerton House, Monticello, IL, June 22-24.

[SAMM86] Sammut, C. and Banerji, R. (1986) "Learning concept by asking questions" in Machine learning Volume 2, edited by R.S. Michalski, J.G. Carbonall, and T.M. Mitchell, pp 167-191. Morgan Kaufmann Inc. Los Altos, CA.

[SHEN83] Shneiderman, B. (1983) "Direct manipulation: a step beyond programming languages" IEEE Computer, 16 (8) 57-69, August.

[SHU85] Shu, C.S. (1985) "FORMAL: A forms-oriented visual-directed application development system" IEEE Computer, 18 (8) 38-49.

[SMIT75] Smith, D.C. (1975) "Pygmalion: A computer program to model and stimulate creative thought" PhD thesis, Department of Computer Science, Stanford University.

[SUCH83] Suchman, L.A. (1983) "Office procedure as practical action: models of work and system design" ACM Trans on Office Information Systems, I (4) 320-328.

[SUCH85] Suchman, L.A. (1985) "Plans and situated actions: the problem of human-machine communication" PhD Thesis, Xerox PARC, Palo Alto, CA.

[THIM86] Thimbleby, H. (1986) "Ease of use - the ultimate deception" in People and Computers: Designing for Usability (Proceeding of the Second Conference of the British Computer Society Human Computer Ineraction Specialist Group), edited by M.D. Harrison and A.F. Monk. University of York, September 23-26.

[TSIC82] Tsichritzis, D. (1982) "Form management" Communications of the Association for Computing Machinery, 25 (7) 453-478, July.

[VACC82] Vaccari, J.A. (1982) "Robots that paint create jobs" American Machinist, 131-134, January.

[WINS75] Winston, P.H. (1975) "Learning structural descriptions from examples" in The psychology of computer vision, edited by P.H. Winston. McGraw Hill, New York, NY.

[WITT81] Witten, I.H. (1981) "Programming by example for the casual user: a case study" Proc. Canadian Man-Computer Communication Conference, 105-113. Waterloo, Ontario, June.

[WITT85] Witten, I.H. and Greenberg, S. (1985) "User interfaces for office systems" Oxford Surveys in Information Technology, 2, 69-104

[WITT87] Witten, I.H. and MacDonald, B.A. (1987) "Concept Learning: A Practical Tool for Knowledge Acquisition?" submitted to Workshop on Expert Systems and Their Application, Avignon, also available as report ???? Computer Science Dept., University of Calgary.

[WOOD70] Woods, W.A. (1970) "Transition network grammars for natural language analysis" Communications of the Association for Compouting Machinery, 13 (10) 591-606, October.

[ZLOO77] Zloof, M.M. (1977) "Query-by-example: a data base language" IBM Systems J, 4, 324-343.

[ZLOO81] Zloof, M.M. (1981) "QBE/OBE" A language for office and business automation" IEEE Computer, 13-22, May.

INDEX

Abstract data types, 288, 289, 294, 202
Action diagrammer, 21
Action diagrams, 207
Activity analysis, 347, 349
Ada, 140, 288, 295, 393, 399, 453, 481
Alvey, 111, 131, 187, 226, 257, 262, 265, 268, 283, 296, 299
Analysts Workbench, 23, 30, 38, 204, 237, 245, 333, 350, 352, 421, 425
APL, 397
Application Environment, 353, 354
Application tasks, 63, 67
Aspect, 283, 289-296, 299, 311, 312
Augmented transition network (ATN), 268-278, 280
Automate+, 161, 235

BASIC, 10, 27, 393, 394, 481
BIM, 428
BIS, 245
BIT, 353
Business models, 93, 422, 423, 426, 431

C, 206, 277, 293, 444, 481
C++, 295
CAD/CAM, 136, 261, 421, 456, 462
CADME (Computer aided development and maintenance environment), 221, 226
CAP, 111, 257, 267
CASE tools, 221, 226
Change control, see Version control
COBOL, 1, 9, 19, 24, 28, 126, 190, 321, 393, 421
Communication and control, 245, 246
Context diagram, 195, 200

Data administration, 333, 335, 348
Database, 24, 94, 254-258, 285-289, 295, 300, 332, 355, 390, 423, 428, 429,
    447, 456, 482 (see also Relational database)
    distributed, 114
Database design, see Data models
Data dictionaries, 27, 37, 204, 236, 248, 307, 331-336, 338-345, 347-352,
    355, 356, 394, 425, 428
Data Flow Diagrams (DFDs), 83, 234-236, 347, 454, 455, 461-463
    data model of, 468-471
DATAMANAGER, 331, 347
Data management, see Data administration
Data models, 30, 37, 301, 302, 347, 391, 392, 428, 432, 457, 460, 472
    (see also Entity-Relationship model and RM/T)
    corporate, 350